Gregory of Nyssa
Homilies on Ecclesiastes

Gregory of Nyssa
Homilies on Ecclesiastes

An English Version with Supporting Studies

Proceedings of the Seventh International Colloquium
on Gregory of Nyssa
(St Andrews, 5—10 September 1990)

Edited by
Stuart George Hall

Walter de Gruyter · Berlin · New York
1993

Library of Congress Cataloging-in-Publication Data

International Colloquium on Gregory of Nyssa (7th : 1990 : Saint
  Andrews, Scotland)
    Gregory of Nyssa : Homilies on Ecclesiastes : an English
  version with supporting studies : proceedings of the Seventh
  International Colloquium on Gregory of Nyssa (St. Andrews.
  5 – 10 September 1990) / edited by Stuart George Hall.
        p.   cm.
    English, French, German, Italian, and Spanish, with summa-
  ries in English.
    ISBN 3-11-013586-8 (alk. paper)
    1. Bible. O. T. Ecclesiastes – Sermons – Congresses. 2. Ser-
  mons, Greek – Translations into English – Early works
  to 1800 – Congresses. 3. Sermons, Greek – History and
  criticism – Congresses. 4. Gregory, of Nyssa, Saint, ca. 335 –
  ca. 394 – Congresses. I. Hall, Stuart George. II. Gregory, of
  Nyssa, Saint, ca. 335 – ca. 394. In Ecclesiasten homiliae. English. 1993. III. Title.
  BS1475.I68   1990
  223'.807 – dc20

Die Deutsche Bibliothek — Cataloging in Publication Data

Gregory of Nyssa, Homilies on ecclesiastes : an English version
with supporting studies ; proceedings of the Seventh International
Colloquium on Gregory of Nyssa (St. Andrews, 5–10 September
1990) / ed. by Stuart George Hall. — Berlin ; New York : de
Gruyter, 1993
    ISBN 3-11-013586-8
NE: Hall, Stuart George [Hrsg.]; International Colloquium on
    Gregory of Nyssa ⟨07, 1990, Saint Andrews⟩; Gregorius ⟨Nys-
    senus⟩: Homilies on ecclesiastes

Preface

Those who took part in the happy meeting at St Andrews of the Seventh International Colloquium on Gregory of Nyssa followed their predecessors in taking material from the critical edition of *Gregorii Nysseni Opera* and studying it. Here the reader will find their achievement. We present an English version of Gregory's eight homilies, to which are added analytical chapter-headings and a bible text reconstructed from Gregory's own quotations and interpretations. The translation is preceded by an Introduction in which the translators explain their procedures, and express their debt to other members of the Colloquium in improving and correcting their work. The translation is followed by studies expounding particular homilies or themes within them. Finally we present a number of wider studies of Gregory's thought and on the interpretation of Ecclesiastes among the ancients, concluding with a bibliographical article.

We must acknowledge our debts and express thanks. First come the Colleges which sponsored the Colloquium. King's College London not only provided the base for the practical preparations and allowed me leave to make preparatory studies, but also made grants of money towards the expenses of the Colloquium and especially the costs of participants from King's College. St Mary's College at St Andrews not only gave the Colloquium an agreeable and historic environment, but through the good offices of Dr J. S. Alexander and colleagues in the Faculty of Theology took great pains to see us comfortably provided for. The Colloquium is also greatly indebted to the Bristish Academy, which provided funds to enable scholars to travel from overseas. I personally must acknowledge the help of Dr H. v. Bassi and his colleagues at Walter de Gruyter's for their kindness and patience while this book has been over-long in preparation, and to my wife Brenda Hall for constant assistance, both in preparing and organizing the meeting of the Colloquium and in the typing and editing of these Proceedings for publication.

Stuart George Hall   15 January 1993

Editor's note to the reader

I ask the tolerant indulgence of readers and contributors for inconsistencies of presentation. We made some attempt to make references consistent throughout the book, but were obliged to give up. Each contributor is, we believe, self-consistent and clear, and scholarship will not be greatly impeded if some use Roman numerals where others use Arabic.

All abbreviations, unless otherwise indicated, follow Siegfried M. Schwertner, Internationales Abkürzungsverzeichnis für Theologie und Grenzgebiete, Berlin: Walter de Gruyter ²1992 (= IATG²). Most of these abbreviations are accessible in IATG¹ (1974) as published with the *Theologische Realenzyklopädie*.

Contents

I INTRODUCTION

— 1 —

Adjustments to the text of Gregory

Stuart George Hall

The origin and circumstances of Gregory's eight Homilies on Ecclesiastes must be deduced from what he writes. Internal evidence makes it clear that they are addressed to an ecclesial congregation (see for instance 298,5-299,10), and that it was during the prevalence of heresy in the eastern Empire (382,15-18; cf 408,14-409,2); most scholars place the composition about 380, shortly before the Council of Constantinople. Other particulars of Gregory's purposes, sources and thought emerge from the studies in this book. My concern here is with the textual basis of our translation, which itself forms an important tool for understanding Gregory.

The groundwork of collating manuscripts and producing a critical text and apparatus has been well done for us. We follow *In Ecclesiasten homiliae. Edidit Paulus Alexander* in *Gregorii Nysseni opera. Auxilio aliorum virorum doctorum edenda curavit Wernerus Jaeger. Volumen V* (Leiden 1986), pp. 195-442. Throughout this volume, where other indications are not given, page and line numbers refer to this text.

Almost everywhere the text is satisfactory. But there are places where the present translators have decided to adopt a different reading or punctuation from Alexander's, and this paper is chiefly to explain the most significant of those cases.

First however we must consider Gregory's Bible text, since it figures in several of our textual comments. Alexander provides footnotes in which he refers to the text in *Septuaginta. Edidit A. Rahlfs*, Stuttgart 1935, giving chapter, verse and line. This is helpful for reference, and we shall follow it too. But Gregory's Bible plainly did not agree with the Rahlfs LXX, often differing widely. This is chiefly because of the character of Rahlfs' edition. He tried to reconstruct an 'original' text of the Greek *Ecclesiastes*, using the Hebrew to correct the Greek of the MS tradition, often on lines suggested by Lagarde. That Greek bible text appears to have been produced, if not by Aqila, then by a translator of his school, and consequently exhibits such strange phenomena as σύν representing the Hebrew accusative particle, and followed by an accusative in Greek (so in Hom. 5 at 362,6 σὺν τὴν ζωήν = Eccl. 2,17,1). Rahlfs rightly postulated that the Greek of Ecclesiastes is so strange that it probably suffered badly in transmission, as scribes tried to make sense of impossible constructions. In using Rahlfs' text therefore, one must expect to find the reading of the MSS in the *apparatus criticus*, and with it often Gregory's reading too. The other critical edition of the Greek Bible, *The Old Testament in Greek*, edited by Henry Barclay Swete (Cambridge ³1907 = 1922) is nearer Gregory, since it prints the text of the Codex Vaticanus, adding the readings of other chief uncials in the *apparatus*. But it is not convenient for our use, because the verses are subdivided differently from the Rahlfs references used by Alexander, and copies are not so readily available as Rahlfs.

In our translation we decided to offer at the head of each homily the Bible text in English. Since English Bibles are based on the Hebrew, their text is very far from Gregory's Greek; we could not therefore use an existing version. Nor could we translate from Rahlfs, since that text is so far different from Gregory's. Even Swete does not always agree. We have therefore postulated a Greek text from Gregory's own quotations and expositions. Our translation is based upon the Greek which we think Gregory saw and heard in his Bible.

Even then our troubles are not over. For one thing, Gregory does not read the Greek in its original sense: a good example is Hom. 1 287,21-288,3, where he takes ἐπιστρέφει τὸ πνεῦμα as, 'you turn your spirit round' (2nd person singular middle verb),[1] when it clearly meant (like the Hebrew original), 'the wind turns about' (3rd person singular active verb). We therefore have to read the Greek *with the meaning Gregory saw in it*. There is one further problem, as we shall shortly see. Where Gregory's quotations depart from the MSS of the LXX, his own MSS often disagree, some agreeing with the LXX, others not. Assimilation of Gregory's text to a known text of Scripture was bound to occur, especially in the MSS of the Mixed Recension (GΘP of those regularly cited) where the Bible text stood at the head of each homily, rather as in our English version. It is a delicate matter to decide at each place, first whether Gregory's original agreed with the LXX or not, and secondly, whether he was quoting strictly what his Bible read, or quoting loosely; and these two questions can come together, making a difficult judgment. In a few cases, I think Alexander got it wrong.

We now turn to the particular cases. Throughout the translation, where any departure from Alexander's text or punctuation occurs, the change is marked by an asterisk so: *. Any changes not referred to below are, we hope, self-explanatory. In a number of cases I am pleased to note that our findings agree with those made independently and earlier by Sandro Leanza in his Italian translation (*Gregorio di Nissa, Omelie sull'Ecclesiaste*, CTP 86, 1990), to whom we are in various ways indebted.

281,3-4 Eccl. 1,2 is quoted without the repetition after ἐκκλησιαστής of ματαιότης ματαιοτήτων. Here the MSS of Gregory are unanimous. What is more, the argument about the intensification of meaning by repetition (282,10-283,17) would have been strengthened if he could

---

1   Some members of the Colloquium dissent from this understanding of Gregory, and render, 'the spirit turns round.' Even if this is accepted, Gregory takes πνεῦμα in a psychological sense, and not as the Hebrew. I prefer to see ἐπιστρέφει as 2nd person middle, however, because otherwise in Gregory's preceding paraphrase the σόν is quite gratuitous: τὸ σὸν πορεύεται πνεῦμα. It was this phrase whoich led me to the favoured rendering.

have added that the Bible had the words twice. I deduce that Gregory's Bible lacked these words. Such a shortened text is not attested in Swete or Rahlfs.

285,4 τὸ διὰ τῶν φαινομένων θαυμαζόμενον. S reads τὸν, 'fortasse recte' (Alexander), which we accept.

285,13 After ἀνθρώπῳ 4 MSS and Migne add ἐν παντὶ μόχθῳ αὐτοῦ in agreement with the LXX. Alexander rejects it from his text, suspecting assimilation to the Bible, and referring to the unanimous text when the sentence appears again at 291,3. I believe he is wrong. First, the quotation at 291,3 is informal, and Gregory might have quoted more briefly there. Secondly, the exegesis which follows implies the presence of the actual noun μόχθος: 'He calls (προσηγόρευσε) life in the body μόχθος.'

285,14 Alexander has rejected μόχθον before τὴν, although the MSS are almost unanimous; I would accept it, and would punctuate again after προσηγόρευσε.

285,13-288,6 In this passage Eccles. 1,5-7 is discussed, but apart from 1,6,3-4 is never quoted, only paraphrased. There is no implied deviation from LXX. This phenomenon occurs elsewhere, as at 406,1-416,10, where Eccles. 3,7 is fully discussed but not actually quoted.

289,18 Alexander divides at 290,7, but the sentence there follows closely what immediately precedes. The earlier break is better.

291,1 Alexander follows a suggestion of Jaeger in reading λέγων against MSS λέγομεν (λέγωμεν E). He presumably interprets the long sentence thus:

> 290,15 As it seems to me, even the great Ecclesiast ..., said just what we also are likely to say one day, ... , (290,18) *when he said*, Futility of futilities, all is futility, and, What advantage is there for man, wherein he toils under the sun?

This makes sense, and the presence of a unanimous error in the next line (οὐδεὶς [οὔτις v] for τὸ Τίς) might suggest a smudge in the archetype. It is an improvement on the reading λέγομεν if we take that to mean, 'We say.' But I question whether either λέγων or λέγομεν can in this sense properly be followed by the article τό and the words of the quotation; one expects ὅτι. We have therefore kept the MS reading λέγομεν, and have taken it to express Gregory's own explanation of what it is that the Ecclesiast says and we mortals shall one day say:

..., I mean, Futility of futilities ...'

Hom. 2 306,20-23 Alexander's punctuation here makes the period unintelligible. I would treat 306,20 ἥ τε γὰρ - 306,23 ἐπικόπτοντος as a single parenthesis bounded by brackets, replacing the colon in 306,20 with a comma. See 306,19-307,4 in the translation, which begins:

306,19. Since then there was nothing to prevent him from having anything he desired — for his wealth matched his desire, and his leisure could be freely devoted to enjoyment, with nothing unintended interrupting his attention to his desires — being generally wise and particularly competent by virtue of his understanding to investigate a matter affecting pleasures, he says etc.

Hom. 3 332,21 Here Alexander has made a great mistake in marking a paragraph. It is not present in Migne, though there is a full stop. The sentence 332,17-20 is grammatically incomplete. We have therefore attached to it the next sentence, 332,21-333,3, so that ταῦτα in 332,21 resumes πάντα ταῦτα καὶ εἴ τι ἄλλο in 332,17-18. It makes and excellent conclusion to the preceding paragraph:

All these things, and whatever else in horticulture art has invented by distorting nature, which the need to maintain life did not require, but was sought by undisciplined desire, these, [p333] so the one who makes confession of his deeds says, came about in his loving attention to vegetable-plots and gardens; for the one who says, I planted every tree of fruit, by using this comprehensive expression also indicates that he has omitted nothing of this kind.

Hom. 4 342,12 It is difficult to give a satisfactory translation of δέρριν, which means something of leather to which necklaces are

attached.   Most MSS have δέρην, from the Attic form δέρη of the
Homeric δειρή, under which it is listed in Liddell and Scott, meaning
'neck' (cf. δέραια, rightly read at 342,6 and variants in MSS).

349,10–350,1 Alexander emends this passage.   The MSS are plainly
confused.   The form in the WS group, the oldest, is this (set out in
phrases for clarity):

a.   ὥσπερ οὐκ ἔστιν

b.   ἐκ τοῦ οὐραίου τῆς χ(ρ)ειᾶς (in W altered to ραχειας) τῆς
     καταδύσεως

c.   ὅ ἐστιν τοῦ φωλεοῦ (-αιου W)

d.   τὸν ὄφιν ἀνελκυσθῆναι

e.   φυσικῶς τῆς φολίδος πρὸς τὸ ἔμπαλιν τοῖς ἐφελκομένοις
     ἀντιβαινούσης, ...

This would mean something nonsensical like this:

'As it is not possible for the snake to be dragged out from
its tail by the hole (χειᾶς) of its descent, that is, its lair,
since the scales naturally pull in the opposite direction to
those tugging at it, ...'

Alexander identifies one problem: χειᾶς falsum est cum locus unde
extrahitur genitivo simplici exprimi non possit: you cannot describe the
hole from which the snake is dragged by a simple genitive. He failed
to note the converse: ἐκ τοῦ οὐραίου is also impossible in this
context, since the part by which one holds something in the case of
the verb (ἀν)έλκειν does require a simple genitive, and would not be
expressed by ἐκ.   If we assume that ἐκ was accidentally omitted
before τῆς χειᾶς, and then reinserted in the wrong place in the
archetype, the sentence makes good sense:

'As it is not possible for the snake to be dragged by its tail
from the hole (τοῦ οὐραίου ἐκ τῆς χειᾶς) into which it descends
(that is, its lair), since the scales naturally pull in the
opposite direction to those tugging at it, ...'

EΛv (the leading witnesses of the other main group) have:

a.   ὥσπερ οὐκ ἔστιν

b.   ἐκ τοῦ οὐραίου τῆς ῥαχίας

c.   —

d.   τὸν ὄφιν ἀνελκυσθῆναι

e.   φυσικῶς τῆς φολίδος πρὸς τὸ ἔμπαλιν τοῖς ἐφελκομένοις
      ἀντιβαινούσης, ...

Alexander rejects ῥαχίας: *nam quid sibi vult 'cauda spinae' vel 'spina caudae'?* But as it stands, grammar suggests the meaning, '... to drag the snake by its backbone from its tail.' The idea might be of breaking the snake in two. If the WS reading is original, a puzzled scribe must have omitted the rest of b and c.

The readings of the mixed tradition (GΘP) are selective conflations of the two primary readings. They are worthless.

In reconstructing the text, Alexander took the shorter EΛv reading, altered τῆς ῥαχίας to τῆς τραχείας, on the strength of a parallel passage in Orat. cat. 5, and moved these words to the beginning of e, suppressing τῆς before φολίδος:

'As it is not possible for the snake to be dragged out of (?)
its tail since the naturally rough scales pull in the opposite
direction to those tugging it, ...'

But this fails to relieve the fundamental problem: if you drag a snake by the tail and use the Greek verb ἀνέλκειν you would express what is held in the hand with a simple genitive, not with ἐκ.

The reading of WS seems to be the nearest to the archetype, and needs only the shift of ἐκ to make perfect sense. I also think χειᾶς looks original. The parenthesis ὅ ἐστιν τοῦ φωλεοῦ may be a gloss upon it, and its absence in the EΛv group, which evaded the difficult word in another way, confirms this. We therefore read:

ὥσπερ οὐκ ἔστιν τοῦ οὐραίου ἐκ τῆς χειᾶς τῆς καταδύσεως τὸν
ὄφιν ἀνελκυσθῆναι, φυσικῶς τῆς φολίδος πρὸς τὸ ἔμπαλιν τοῖς
ἐφελκομένοις ἀντιβαινούσης, ...

350,19 The comma after Ἰερουσαλήμ must be replaced by a full stop.
The following clause in fact introduces a new topic and text, and we
have marked a sub-paragraph in translating.

Hom. 5 355,3 It is difficult to see why Alexander (following Jaeger)
defied the MSS by altering περιφορὰν ('whirling, dizziness') to the
unattested παραφορὰν ('derangement, madness').   In the LXX
παραφορὰν is read by Codex Alexandrinus, but not by the majority of
witnesses, and we should accept that Gregory has the more regular
Bible reading.   περιφορά has to be understood in an unusual sense,
and perhaps the LXX translator intended the meaning παραφορά;
nevertheless he uses περιφορά frequently.   At 310,7.16 Alexander
allows περιφορά to stand in the quotations of Eccles. 2,2, even
against some of the MSS of Gregory.

357,1 The LXX has a redundant αὐτοῦ after ὀφθαλμοὶ, and this word
appears in one of the two prime groups of MSS, WS.   Gregory omits
the redundant αὐτοῦ in his less precise quotations at 358,11 and
360,17.   Here however he is specifically quoting, and it might be
thought that the reading should be upheld as *lectio difficilior*, in spite
of the agreement with the Bible.

360,16 A paragraph is marked here both in Alexander and in Migne.
It is true that 360,16-22 discuss a new text, ὁ ἄφρων ἐν σκοτίᾳ
πορεύεται.   But 360,22 marks a new departure in the argument, and it
is much more satisfactory to treat 360,16-22 as a tail-piece to the
discussion of the wise man's eyes.   We therefore make a major
paragraph at the later point.

363,4 The problem here is ὅς, in which the majority of Gregory's MSS
agree with Rahlfs' text, even though that is supported in the Biblical
books only by the corrector of Sinaiticus.   In the MSS of Gregory S
omits the word, agreeing with one authority of the LXX.   But most
of the biblical texts read ᾧ, as does Gregory at 369,8.   If Alexander
is right, Gregory read one text-form in his bible at 363,4, and

another at 369,9. Given the odd structure of the Homily, that is not impossible, since he could have written the two interpretations at different times, or followed a different exegetical source for his ideas on one occasion, another on another occasion. We have allowed ὅς to stand. The alternative would be to correct to ᾧ on the basis of 369,8.

363,22 The exegesis given by Gregory just above seems to require the translation:

> There is no good in a man; what he shall eat and drink and show to his soul is good in his toil.

We therefore need a colon after ἀνθρώπῳ, not a comma. The same applies to 370,19.

364,1-2 The accentuation ὅ τί τις φάγεται καί τις πίεται makes no sense in the context. The same words are accented better at 370,22: ὅτι τίς φάγεται καὶ τίς πίεται. But in both cases the punctuation is wrong: a colon or full stop is required after ἐστιν, and a question mark after αὐτοῦ. So we translate:

> This also I saw, that it is from God's hand; for who shall eat and who drink apart from him?

367,15 Both Alexander and Migne mark a paragraph here. I find this quite wrong. The argument which centres upon the text in 368,4-8 clearly begins at 367,5, and we have so set out the translation.

370,19.22 See notes on 363,22 and 364,1-2.

Hom. 6 376,22 The punctuation with a question-mark would require τοῦ χάριν. Translate: 'The reason for our preceding considerations is that ...'

384,13-15 The full stop at the end of 13 is a mistake. The immediately following clause (τοῦτο δέ ...) is a parenthesis explaining the medicine of line 13, and the ὥστε-clause must be attached syntactically to 13.

Hom. 7 400,8-10 The paragraphing of Alexander seems perverse, and the more natural division comes at 400,8.

401,21 As punctuated by Alexander, τὰ ἄλλα πάντα is accusative of respect after πενόμενοι, where a genitive (cf πλούτου 401,20) would be expected. We attach the words to the following sentence.

402,13-15 A colon is needed after ἀπιστίας, and the comma should be deleted in the next line. The sentence then matches closely what is written next about Isaiah. It also presents a more Gregorian, and less Augustinian, concept of divine grace.

414,12 Alexander adds ⟨προφῆται⟩ ('*exempli gratia*' as he says), presumably deeming οἱ μεγάλοι intolerable without a noun. But there are rare uses of μέγας to mean 'old, ancient', and one of the monks is addressed as ὁ μέγας in Palladius, *hist. laus.* 21. That might justify the absolute use here.

Hom. 8 426,13 Alexander adopts Jaeger's conjecture ὑπηλλαγμένη, suggesting that attitudes to good and evil are 'reversed'; the same verb appears in this sense in 426,21. The same meaning could be derived from ἐνηλλαγμένη of the majority of MSS. We have however assumed that ἐπηλλαγμένη of WG is correct; it is an Aristotelian word for something logically or substantially 'confused', making good sense at this point.

426,16 Alexander retains the accentuation ἢ γὰρ, as in Mat 6,24, '... for *either* he will love the one and hate the other, ...' But that quotation makes no sense without the following ἤ: '*or else* he will hold to the one and despise the other.' But Gregory's logic requires a definite statement, that he *will* hate one and love the other. He therefore understands ἦ γὰρ, '... for *surely* he will hate the one and love the other.'

429,1 Alexander, following Migne, has misplaced the paragraphing. The new argument begins with the sentence introducing πολεμήσωμεν at 428,19.

432,12 Here Alexander indicates a lacuna after ὑψικάρηνοι, and says in his notes that horses do not use words as hooves (ῥήμασιν οἷόν τισιν ὁπλαῖς κοίλαις). He thinks that a description of the activity of proud horses has fallen out, concluding with words like οὕτω καὶ οἱ ὑπερφανοῦντες, referring to those who kick with empty words. So much is not necessary. If we add one word and read ὑψικάρηνοι ⟨οἱ⟩, we can translate the whole:

> 'Those who use exaggerated words of bombast like hollow hooves to lash out at gentle people, are quite simply horses with arching neck and tossing head.'

It is impossible to get in English the pun in κατακροαίνοντες.   The verb refers literally to stamping with the hoof, but presumably could, like κροαίνω, be used metaphorically of luxuriant or wanton oratory (see PGL ⋕κατακροαίνω, LSJ κροαίνω).   There is also a pun in 'hollow', which refers both to the shape of the hoof and to the emptiness of the rhetoric.

436,18 The first sentence should be attached to what precedes, and the paragraph begins at 436,20.

437,9.12 The first clause is clearly a question, which the colon at 437,9 obscures.   What follows is still governed by οὐχ.

437,20 The first sentence is better attached to the end of the previous paragraph, a reprise of the text being expounded there.   The long quotation following begins a wholly new argument, which has nothing directly to do with what precedes.

440,2 We have divided the quotation.   The first clause concludes one argument, the second is the beginning of another.

Translating the Homilies

Rachel Moriarty

Gregory of Nazianzus once accused his friend Gregory of Nyssa of having turned to 'salty and undrinkable' writing (τὰς δὲ ἁλμυρὰς καὶ ἀπότους βίβλους), more like rhetorical than Christian prose (Letter 11). The translator of the Homilies on Ecclesiastes can feel some sympathy for him, if what he means is that one cannot gulp it down easily. Gregory is not easy to translate, because of the subtlety of both his Christian preaching and his sophisticated rhetoric, illustrated with an astonishing range of modern instances; but eventually it is far from unpalatable. We hope we have done him justice.

The translation was prepared in draft before any of the papers for the colloquium were available to us, though we have since revised it to take account of many helpful comments and suggestions. This paper is an account of some of the issues which faced us during the original process of translation, some guide-lines we laid down and some detailed decisions we made. These cover the layout of the text as well as its style and register, and our handling of particular words and ideas, from scripture, from Christian or philosophical thought, and from Gregory's everyday instances. It will immediately be clear that we have not always followed our own advice, but it may illuminate our thinking and stimulate thought on patristic translation in general.

Layout of text,[1] references and notes

The reader needs two sets of references, to Gregory's commentary and to the text of Ecclesiastes which he expounds. For Gregory, we have the text in Gregorii Nysseni Opera V (GNO), whose page- and line-numbers we use as the basis of our numbering. We have in general followed its paragraphing, and for each paragraph we have provided a heading of our own; these taken together form a summary of Gregory's argument as we understand it. This still left long unrelieved passages, and so we have divided it further into shorter sections, with page- and line-numbers but no headings, and these provide numbered references on every page. In more than one place we have added headings in mid-paragraph to make our interpretation of the complicated argument clear (e.g. 364ff). We have noted in the text in square brackets [ ] the point at which one turns to each new page in the Greek.

Quotations from Ecclesiastes must be from the text as Gregory read it, so we have set out in bold type at the head of each Homily a version of the whole of the text Gregory expounds in it, using the line-structure from Rahlfs, and we have matched this with bold type for his quotations from it in the exegesis. Reference to the verses discussed in each major paragraph is given with the heading to the paragraph.

Bold type is used in the translation only for direct quotation from Ecclesiastes. Other direct scriptural quotations appear in Italics. Gregory usually introduces them himself, *the prophet says ...*, *great Paul says ...*, and so on, but sometimes he quotes directly without acknowledgement and when this is clear we have used italics here too. In general we have considered 'direct' any reading which is supported by Mss quoted in LXX (Rahlfs or Swete) or New Testament (Nestlé-Aland) text or in the *apparatus criticus* to each of these, and we have not used italics for words which Gregory has apparently

---

1   For our texts of Ecclesiastes and Gregory see Stuart Hall's paper on Adjustments to the Text.

added or changed for grammatical purposes, or for indirect quotation or allusion. Where a direct or indirect citation is clearly being made, its biblical reference follows immediately within the text. For the Psalms we quote the Hebrew Bible numbering first, followed by the Latin.

Most of our scripture references are taken from Alexander's exhaustive notes, but we have added one or two more, notably at 325,2-3, where a chance echo of the English Psalter in our own discussion (*much fine gold ...* (Ps 19,10)) led us to a whole line of the LXX; but we have not noted Alexander's more remote allusions to scripture. Even so, we cannot claim to have picked up every one even of Gregory's direct quotations and allusions, especially from LXX (let the devout reader, in identifying further references, reflect on the depth and vitality of Gregory's use and knowledge of scripture).

Italics also appear for the quotation of well-known classical dicta (375,12-13). Where Gregory seems to be drawing on classical sources, we have in some cases indicated these, following Alexander, but our criteria are narrower than his and we do not include them all.

Lexicons and works of reference

Our most valuable source of vocabulary was Liddell and Scott, ed Jones (ninth edition, LSJ), supplemented by the eighth edition (LS 8th ed), which still includes patristic references but is elsewhere modified by its successor. These two covered the great bulk of Gregory's vocabulary, including his many specialized medical terms. Special patristic vocabulary, and a number of late non-technical words, usually compounds, are covered by Lampe's Patristic Greek Lexicon (PGL), which was invaluable but needed for a relatively small number of words. For NT quotations we consulted Arndt and Gringrich's version of Bauer's Lexicon of the NT (Bauer). Texts of the LXX and NT are discussed above and in Stuart Hall's article; in making our own biblical translation we referred to English versions, from the Authorized (King James) Version of 1611 (AV) to the Revised English Bible (REB), published while we were translating.

Gregory's use of language, though sometimes bizarre, usually falls somewhere within normal classical Greek usage and could be supported from standard grammars or examples quoted in LSJ or PGL.

One word is unattested elsewhere; ἐγκακοπαθεῖ, (437,2), which we translate *he endures the hardships of. . .,* comes from the compound ἐγκακοπαθέω, which does not appear in any lexicon, though its meaning is not in doubt.

Style

Modern English does not favour the combination of serious argument with rhetorical flourish, except in a very restrained sense, and Gregory's translator is caught between the Scylla of literary display and the Charybdis of literalism. For this scholarly purpose, we have leaned towards the literal, seeking some equivalent of Greek rhetoric in a precisely modulated use of English. We have tried to adopt a measured English style which acknowledges its rhetorical source in attention to sound, rhythm and cadence, with a wide vocabulary to match Gregory's own; in philosophical argument we have tried to be clear above all, and, however faintly, to echo the astonishing richness and variety of Gregory's imagery. We have retained his long periods and subordinate clauses, and kept the order of his words and clauses, as far as this is compatible in English with our other concerns, and with the primary need to represent his thought faithfully and clearly. The way we put this noble ideal into practice is the subject of the rest of this paper. Perhaps the result is a little old-fashioned, and reveals the age and traditional English classical education of the translators; but that may not be so far from Gregory's own.

Inclusive language

Gregory's use of the masculine gender or male words follows normal Greek practice and as such says nothing about his views about men and women; but for us to keep to masculine forms might be read as sexist.   We hope to avoid this charge, though English usage in this sensitive area is fluid and one person's sensible generality may easily be offensive sexism to another. Patristic translation brings up the problem particularly sharply.   It would be false to deny the social assumptions of the fourth century, and thus anachronistic to work too hard to include women in every reference;   on the other hand we should not translate what was intended to be general into English which now seems gratuitously patriarchal.   Some examples of our practice will show the dilemmas we faced.

The word *man*, in spite of its two senses *human* and *male*, is easily seen as sexist (especially in liturgical contexts), and we tried not to use it here, but sometimes the price of avoiding it, either for ἄνθρωπος or a masculine pronoun, has seemed too high in terms of rhythm, euphony and economy.   Where possible we have rendered the article with the participle, and τις, as *the one who ..., the person who ..., people, anyone, someone*, rather than *the man who ....* ἄνθρωπος can usually be turned by *people, mankind* or *human beings*, but not always: where the singular is important, perhaps to preserve a singular verb, 'man' used in the generic sense may be neater and more elegant, as in *the good man ... utters ...* (301,15), and need not exclude women;   and this is also true in phrases like *the sons of men* (Eccl 1,13;   301,7).   In one passage Gregory uses ἀνήρ and ἄνθρωπος indiscriminately in quotation and exegesis of the same phrase, quoting Eccl 1,8 as οὐ δυνήσεται ἀνήρ τοῦ λαλεῖν at 291,15 etc, but using ἄνθρωπος a few pages later (294,4), without apparent change of sense;   but we have varied our translation, using *man* and *human being* to match his words.

Pronouns and their adjectives are impossible to make genderless, as English pronouns refer to males, females and things even more precisely than those in languages with wider use of genders.   *He or she* is cumbersome, and we have stuck to *he* for general use.   We have been guided partly by sound and cadence, as presumably Gregory was, and in spite of our principles we have sometimes preferred this to a precise use of inclusive terms;   and in any case we want to reflect at least the flavour of Gregory's own use.   We cannot claim to have been completely consistent, as our custom emerged gradually as translation proceeded; and adjustment may already seem desirable amid the rapid changes in contemporary English usage.

Gregory has the last word on the matter of gender. In translating his images of pregnancy and childbirth we use *one*, when pregnancy is imagined figuratively for both sexes (380,1), but we could only stick to *he* for the miserly (masculine) money-lender *pregnant in the wallet*, ἐγκύμων τῷ βαλλαντίῳ (345,4), and for the male, ὁ διαμαρτών, who *labours in the pains of his own destruction, and is midwife at his soul's death* (380,20-1). Such imagery goes beyond what even the most inclusive of language can embrace.

Scripture

All our biblical translation has been done from Gregory's Greek, though we have sometimes consulted English bibles. The interest in Gregory's version of scripture lies partly in the form of the text he quotes, and partly in the way he takes it, and both factors affected our version.

Ecclesiastes.

The text is particularly hard to translate into English which conveys both the obscurity of the Greek and its potential for pregnant interpretation. Some particular issues follow.

At the start we were faced with the key word ἐκκλησιαστής. This word has a dense package of meanings, all but impossible to unite in English, but leant on by Gregory in telling passages at the beginning of Homilies 1 and 2. The root meaning, from ἐκκαλέω, is *assemble* or *gather*, and it and its cognates had a noble political past; but by the fourth century the ecclesiastical sense was predominant and the verb ἐκκλησιάζω seems to have had the double sense of belonging to a church and of preaching (PGL). Gregory uses it elsewhere to mean *Leader of the Church* (Hom 6 in Cant, PG 44,905A), and Solomon, as the author of Ecclesiastes, is said to be so called *because he* ἐξεκλησίαζε *the people* (?Ath, synops 23,

PG 28,348B);   the sense, though not quite precise, seems to be of leadership and preaching.   The English AV, based on the Hebrew, gave the book the title 'Ecclesiastes, or The Preacher', and the English *Ecclesiast* was so understood until the nineteenth century, but to a modern public *preacher* has too limited a sense.   We entertained the alternatives *Assembler*, *Gatherer*, *Convenor*, *Churchman*, but these either did not adequately reflect the meaning or had inappropriate modern overtones, especially the last.

Our choice of *Ecclesiast* signals a special sense through our failure to translate it at all (though an obsolete use quoted in the OED, *church administrator*, may suggest that we are archaizing and not innovating).   We tried to bring out the most important sense, that the word is the key to the essential link between the biblical text and the Christian *ecclesia* which is the basis of Gregory's exegesis;   the best way to echo this seemed to be to exploit the English link between the name of book and 'author', Ecclesiastes, and the cognate *ecclesiastical* and related words.   Where Gregory's argument depends explicitly on this connexion, and the English does not show it, as in his discussion of the title at 279,4 – 281,2, and with a particular instance at 299,3-4, we have transliterated the Greek to make it clear.

Another key word is ματαιότης.   Traditional English renders it *vanity*, with its adjective *vain*, but these words have lost this primary meaning of uselessness except in certain idomatic phrases.   Gregory needs a word which carries unequivocally the sense of worthlessness, but fortunately, in the best tradition of modern linguistic philosophy, he provides his own analysis of the ordinary use of the word (281,3 – 282,9).   From his examples it is clear that *futile* is a good equivalent, having for extra value appropriate overtones of the feeling being all in the mind.

The series of καιρός verses (Eccl 3,1-8) rely on consistency and rhythm, and the translation had to bear not only the biblical sense but also Gregory's exegesis in the last three Homilies: *moment* seemed to convey the sense best, since *time* was too general and the conventional *opportunity* gave the wrong meaning.   There seemed a

subtle difference between *a moment to ...* and *a moment for ...*, and
we chose *for* as appropriately emphasizing action and not simply
occasion;   but there is room for disagreement here, as in many
places.   In these verses we entertained the possibility that Gregory
understood them to mean *the moment for ... is the moment for ...*,
and so on, instead of *there is a moment ... and a moment ...* — there
is no verb and one must be supplied;   but we concluded that although
many   of   the   verses   could   be   taken   like   that,   the   general
interpretation   was   ruled   out   in   409,10-11,   where   Gregory   expounds
verse 7, *He puts first* (προτέτακται), *a moment for keeping silent, and
after the silence* (μετὰ τὴν σιγήν), *he grants a moment to speak.*

περιφορά (Eccl 2,2) offers an interesting case where the normal
Greek sense of a word was changed in patristic contexts, but still
carried the ghost of its former connotation. The word ordinarily
means various kinds of 'circulating', from its literal root (LSJ);   in
the Cappadocians it regularly also means 'accident,' 'distraction' or
'turbulence' (PGL).   Gregory makes it clear that he thinks *it is
equivalent in meaning* (ἴσον) *to 'frenzy'* (παραφορά) *or 'madness'*
(παράνοια) (310,8-9), and he is probably not the first exegete of
Ecclesiastes to explain it like this;   Lampe quotes a similar
explanation in the fragment on Ecclesiastes attributed to the third-
century Dionysius Alexandrinus.   Our problem was to find a word which
carried the same load — a normal sense of circular motion with some
connotation   of   mental   derangement.   We   chose   *dizziness*   for   its
primary sense of disorientation caused by going round in circles, and
its colloquial notion of irresponsibility;   but the alternative *whirling*
may create the effect better.

Other Septuagintal books

There is a special pleasure in the over-literal Greek of the
LXX, which produces some surprising results, as for instance *holy
stones roll about on the ground* (Zech 9,16;   396,19) for 'they are
the precious stones in a crown' of the Hebrew (in a modern English
version, REB).   That was clearly Gregory's understanding and does not
present a problem of translation, but some other cases do: for
instance, Gregory seems to take δουλεία in Ps 104/103,14 in the

concrete sense of 'a body or team of slaves', rather than the more usual *slavery* or *service*; so we have *green plants for the slaves of men* (336,3-4).

New Testament

In one case, Gregory's slight departure from the usual text apparently made a difference to his understanding of the sense. At 305,16-17 he quotes Heb 4,15, but varies the NT MSS reading πεπειρασμένος with the more regular Greek πεπειραμένος; the *apparatus criticus* does not suggest an alternative reading. The NT word comes from πειράζω, a verb hardly used outside biblical contexts, where it has the meaning *test, tempt,* and in the Hebrews passage is usually understood and translated as something like *tempted in every way as we are ...;*   Gregory's word comes from the weaker verb πειράω, commoner in general but one which does not appear in the NT; it means *attempt, try,* occasionally *test,* but in this perfect passive form regularly carries the meaning *have experience of, try out.* It seems that in this discussion Gregory wants to show that Solomon *experienced* the full range of human activity, without laying stress on the notion of temptation; but that sense is there, as the later discussion of Solomon's *confession* shows (317,14f). Gregory develops his case with frequent use of the cognate noun πεῖρα, which again has the usual sense of experience, but in certain Christian contexts meant what we understand by *temptation.* We could not find an English word with quite the same ambiguity; in spite of apparent similarities in the two senses of *test* or *try* in English, in practice usage keeps them distinct, and for this purpose we pointed up the *experience,* with *he who has had experience like us in all things, without sin,* but the solution is not ideal (see LSJ, LS 8th ed, PGL, Bauer).

Finally, although we resisted slavish following of familiar English biblical quotations, the language of the Authorized Version still penetrates the thought of English people of Christian background and we have not altogether avoided using it, sometimes deliberately and sometimes unconsciously, in some familiar phrases where individual words are now archaic. We have, for instance, kept *the son of perdition* (John 17,12;   304,19 and 380,16), and *let us make man in our own image* (Gen 1,26;   295,15 etc);   and there may be places where our version seems archaic and obscure to those unfamiliar with the AV.

Philosophy and Christianity

Gregory's argument depends on weaving Christianity with contemporary philosophy, and the vocabulary and language of both is deployed in the Homilies, though in rather different ways. Christian terminology as Gregory used it was still largely the ordinary language of his hearers and had not acquired the special connotations which *free will*, *grace* and others were later to gain, but on the other hand contemporary higher education dealt extensively in philosophical concepts and he could expect an understanding of its special language and concepts. The problem for the translator is to render philosophical ideas so as to make them seem comprehensible, even familiar, and to render Christian ideas without using words which too strongly evoke later Christian connotation.

Philosophy

These words fall into several groups: those related to the concepts of Being and Becoming, Reality, Substance and so on, already familiar in Platonic and Christian thought; those which explain Aristotelian ideas, like the Mean; and those dealing with subjects widely discussed by contemporary pagan and Christian writers, like free will, or the concerns and experience of fleshly humanity as opposed to what is spiritual.

The words for Being, which include τὸ ὄν, οὐσία, and parts of εἶναι, and the related ideas contained in ὑπάρχω, ὑπόστασις and compounds, are numerous and form part of the standard, almost technical, vocabulary of classical thought. In translating them it is tempting to look for consistency (ie a regular correspondence between individual Greek words and an English equivalent), but this proves so unsatisfactory in English that, in common with many translators of such works, we abandoned it in favour, we hope, of clarity. English *be, is* and so on have not the weight or flexibility of their Greek counterparts and must therefore be varied in a different way from the Greek, which can lean on a more varied morphology for interest and effect.   Strict consistency here would impede clarity.

This problem, and our tentative solutions, can be illustrated from two passages, one at 406,1 to 407,17, where Gregory explains *a moment to rend and a moment to mend* with an excursion into *the somewhat profound matter of the philosophy of being* (τὴν περὶ τῶν ὄντων φιλοσοφίαν), and the other the discussion of evil at 299,20 to 303,13 and beyond.   In these passages, εἶναι appears in several forms, each requiring a different version in English, sometimes using a noun, *reality* (406,4), *(has) existence* (407,10) or, as above, *being*, and sometimes a phrase, *what is* (407,13), *that which is* (407,14 and 15); and sometimes different technical terms are needed, as when τὸ ὄντως ὄν ἡ αὐτοαγαθότης (406,7) becomes *what really is, is Absolute Good.* These passages also illustrate the problems attending γίνομαι (and compounds), which within a short space are *become* (301,22 and 302,3), *come about* (300,19), *be made* (303,13) or *be put* (302,17), *happen* (309,14), or simply *be* (309,8, where it is immediately followed by *become*). For ὑπάρχω and other words which are familiar Greek variants of εἶναι we have tried to use comparable English words, *be real, exist,* and for ὑπόστασις we have been rash enough to choose *substance* (300,22-3).   Thus it would not be possible to draw conclusions about Gregory's use of particular words from this translation, but we hope to have faithfully mirrored his thinking.

When Gregory uses Aristotle as his source he seems not to borrow his language closely, and I offer two examples.   The discussion of αἰδώς and αἰσχύνη (315,8 - 317,12) owes something to Nicomachean Ethics IV, and other works, but it is not a quotation, and the substance is different;   the two words complement one another in Aristotle, but are distinguished in Gregory.   Their meanings are wide: αἰδώς covers *reverence, respect, honour* and *shame,* for 'the opinion of others or one's own conscience' (LSJ), and αἰσχύνη means *shame, dishonour* and *disgrace,* but can also overlap with αἰδώς. There are many possibilities, but the translation *shame* and *sense of disgrace* which works for Aristotle (tr Ross, Oxford 1925), does not suit Gregory's meaning. Since Gregory himself is concerned here with use and definition, we have stuck to *modesty* for αἰδώς and *shame* for αἰσχύνη, which reflects his meaning, although it does, perhaps, reduce the Aristotelian resonance. In discussing the idea usually called the *Mean* (374,15 - 378,5), Gregory uses Aristotelian ideas (Nic Eth II, 6-8), but he does so without Aristotle's key word τὸ μέσον, and constructs his argument round τὸ μέτρον, συμμετρία and the verb μετρέω instead; *measure* is our translation of this, but *lack of proportion* for ἀμετρία (378,4), while for μεσότης (375,5) we have *middle point*. The question of Gregory's source for Aristotle's ideas, and also for some of Plato's examples, for instance the beleaguered city at 428,19f, is intriguing.

The third and largest group, of other philosophical words important to Gregory's argument, presents the same problems, and again we have reflected their complex meanings with a variety of English words. Among them are πάθος, σπουδή, διάστημα and ὅρος, which will serve as examples. πάθος is *emotion* (315,12-19), *suffering* (319,10), *feeling(s)* (316,14; 317,11), *passion(s)* (430,13), (with *passionate* for ἐμπαθής, 307,11), even *disease* (439,19); and its negative ἀπαθής, which has a past in Stoicism and Origenic spirituality, echoes that in *passion-free* (340,11). σπουδή and cognates, nouns and verbs, are *concern* (363,19), *zeal* (327,16), *effort* (282,8; 362,15), *pursuit* and *pursued* (305,14-307,14 *passim*, etc), and, again as a verb, *strive for* (437,10). These various English renderings have no necessary link with one another in English, but for Gregory's hearers one word carried the whole load, and we could do no more than give the meaning in context.

Occasionally ingenuity brought rewards: διάστημα, with its adjective διαστηματικός, means an *interval* or *extent* of time or space, but except in modern physics the two uses are ordinarily distinguished; *period (of time)* (377,3), *extended (space)* (412,18), or *life-span* (372,6) usually had to do, but *extension* (412,10-19 *passim* in various forms) and, for διαστηματικός, *dimensional* (440,3), solved the problem in some instances. Gregory is fond of the notion of *boundaries* and often uses ὁρίζω, ἀόριστος, ὅρος, sometimes in metaphorical senses; fortunately English, via its Latinate forms, does the same thing, and where *boundary* (415,23) and *limit* (411,20) would not do there was *determine* (441,4), and *define* (420,3)

Christianity

Words of Christian significance, and those which are particular to Gregory's own philosophy, we have translated with their ordinary Greek meaning, and left him to explain them; again, one consistent version was impossible, and for a precise analysis of terms there can be no substitute for the original. The most obvious example is λόγος, used in all its many ordinary senses as well as its familiar patristic ones as *word* (Scripture) and *Word of God* (Christ). All of these appear in Gregory's own discussion of language at 291,15-294,17, a passage whose neatness it is impossible to reproduce.

As for actual Christian practice, there are mentions of Baptism (404,23), and the Eucharist (423,4ff), but the vocabulary is not technical, or, apparently, liturgical. In the first case we found ourselves using language more technical than Gregory's own, *baptism* for his *washing* (τοῦ λουτροῦ) in order to convey this meaning; and at times we used capitals, for instance to make clear who the *Adversary* (eg at 436,13-14 τὸν ἀντίπαλον) or the *Enemy* (425,14 τοῦ ἐναντίου) is. Our solution to ἐκκλησιαστής has been discussed above; and, in another example, the ecclesiastical overtones to ἐξαγόρευσις (317,14f) are included in *confession*, which seems in any case the best rendering.

Other special vocabulary

There are several points in the Homilies where argument turns on particular words, often in pairs or threes, like ζωή/βίος (throughout Homily 5, especially 360,20-372,19), κύριος/δεσπότης, ἀρχή/ἐξουσία/ δυναστεία (both groups at 334,5-338,22), sometimes single, like φύσις and διάθεσις (*passim*). While these are not strictly philosophical terms, they are used to illustrate or carry forward philosophical discussion. It is not always clear whether the words in these groups have a consistently different emphasis, and perhaps a special connotation, or whether they are simply elegant variations used for rhetorical effect. As often as one identifies a special sense for a particular word one can find an instance of the same word being used as a synonym for its partner. The patristic field is not as well-tilled in lexicons as the classical as far as such vocabulary is concerned, and in the end subtleties of meaning must be discovered through Gregory's own practice, instanced in his other works as well as in these Homilies. Professor Bergadá discusses Gregory's use of αὐτεξούσιος and ἐλευθέριος and their cognates in her conference paper, and so illuminates the passages in the Homilies where these words occur (αὐτεξούσιος at 301,20 and 22, 335,6 and 407,6, for instance, and ἐλευθέριος at 334,4-338,23), and other papers offer further elucidation.

Rhetoric

Translation of this kind of work raises two questions: how far did precise terminology in this kind of writing override the variety which the techniques of formal rhetoric demanded? and how can both the philosophy and the rhetoric best be represented in English?

Exact use of terms was apparently less significant to ancient philosophers than it is to us, educated as we are in scientific definition. Gregory's own distinctive ideas, like that of *epectasis*, do not rely on key words in Greek (400,8f), and we create them as scholarly shorthand. This is what one would expect, considering the importance rhetorical theory attached to the elegant use of such devices as onomatopoiea, alliteration, antithesis and so on, which rely on flexible use of language to produce effects. To an educated fourth-century public, the explanation of a philosophical concept in a rhetorical style, and varied and well-articulated Greek vocabulary, probably did more to make it memorable than the key words and phrases on which we in a more scientific society rely.

If this is so, translation into English may also depend partly on appropriate rhetorical effects, although the clarity of the ideas must be paramount. We have seen above that this is partly achieved by

well-modulated style, but there were a few opportunities for display,
notably the apt discovery that *rend* and *mend* would reproduce
admirably the ῥῆξαι/ῥάψαι contrast in Eccl 3,7, discussed by Gregory
at 406,1-409,7; he would have appreciated it as an echo of his own
παρονομασία. Most of his puns were impossible to reproduce, though
discussion and experiment were entertaining; how can one capture the
ramblings of the *fool*, ἄφρων, described as *froth*, ἀφρός (365,3)? or
the word-play on the worldly *covering*, σκέπη, of clothes which
indicate a person's worldly *end*, σκοπός (327,3-4)? or the famous
classical *double-entendre* which links the two meanings of τόκος, *child*,
and *interest*, found in more than one classical denunciation of usury
(here 344,7-345,16)? While this double meaning is present in English,
in such financial notions as *growth*, *issue*, *stock*, *generation*,
(re)produce, as well as in the biblical words *increase*, *multiply*, it
proved beyond us to make it work here, and we had to resort to
notes in brackets. How can one convey that ὅπλον means both
weapon and *armour*, when no English word covers both (433,16 –
434,21)? or reflect the political and juridical systems which change
ψῆφος from *vote* to *verdict* (437,4)? The translation will show how
successful we were.

In avoiding explicit rhetoric we may have lost some dramatic or
idiomatic effects. The rhetorical sarcasm in Gregory's argument that
speech cannot describe God is probably muted in our rendering, *What
a wonderful thing, that speech was afraid to approach the thought of
the divine nature* ... (415,2), but it remains close to Gregory's
language. The dramatic possibilities of ὦ or μέν and δέ, cannot be
fully realized in the account of the erotic banquet (347,8f) by *what a
...!, on the one hand ... on the other*; but neither would it be
appropriate to blur the Greek by an 'imaginatively equivalent'
rendering, and Gregory must speak literally to his present
congregation. Readers may picture for themselves the preaching
effects which may have been produced.

Vocabulary from other fields

A particular pleasure was the untangling of the vast vocabulary Gregory uses to illustrate his points. His imagery and examples are drawn from the pursuits of a wide and busy community, and sometimes provide glimpses of its preoccupations as telling as excavations in a Cappadocian city. A surprising number are medical, and it would not be entirely frivolous to imagine his audience as rich medical students, partly concerned to draw moral conclusions from their professional knowledge, and partly tempted to enhance their material status with ostentatious houses and indulgent life-styles. It is interesting to come upon the Greek for *tapeworm*, ἕλμινς (384,3), only once quoted in LSJ outside scientific works, and an explanation of the origin and treatment of it; to get an insight into table manners which cause a risk of damage to the eyes at dinner from a neighbour's περόνη, a spoon with a spike at the handle end (438,14ff) and elsewhere the subject of archaeological and literary comment; and to learn details of fashionable architecture. Prestigious dwellings have rooms covered with *trompe l'oeil* decoration, ...διὰ τῶν σοφισμάτων τῆς τέχνης (322,2); their pillars have capitals, γλύφοι (322,3 and 8), which more commonly means the notched head of an arrow, a chisel or a penknife, encased in gold leaf; and their grounds (331,12 - 333,3) are cultivated as (a difficult distinction) κῆποι, *vegetable-plots*, described scornfully as producing *food for the weak in health* (331,16) and παράδεισοι, *gardens*, full of exotic fruit (332,14), in contrast to the eponymous Garden of Paradise.

The problems I have described were secondary ones, only arising after we had decided what the text actually meant. This was not always easy. Gregory's Greek is forceful and elegant but not lucid, and we cannot always be sure that we have got his meaning, though we hope we can justify what we have put. There is also the error factor; even with two of us scrutinizing text and translation, we discovered slips up to the moment of copying, and continue to notice more, often in direct contradiction to the principles outlined above, and unexpunged traces of earlier ideas. We are grateful to those who have pointed out mistakes, and readily take responsibility for any which remain.

Translations are frequently done by two people, but the division of labour is not always apparent. In this case, the distinguished patristic scholarship and experience of Gregory's thought, as well as the practised ear for a felicitous phrase, were of course Stuart Hall's; making a preliminary draft and the writing up were mine, and in the detailed discussions which linked these two tasks I learned much more than I contributed. Any translation is the better for discussion, and we grateful to all who offered encouragement, comment and suggestions for improvement. In particular we must thank Professor Christopher Stead, who read through the whole text and illuminated invaluably and charitably both its thorniest problems and its avoidable blemishes, and Professor Andreas Spira and his students for early comments on Homily 1. Professor Sandro Leanza's Italian version was published between our draft and its revision, and has provided much help in solving problems of interpretation.

As we completed the translation, we could not agree with the Ecclesiast that **All words are laborious; a man** (person in our case) **will not be able to speak** (Eccl 1,8), but we are inclined to share Gregory's view that *no word will be found which exactly describes in itself the thing in question* (294,14-15).

II   TRANSLATION

— 3 —

Gregory, Bishop of Nyssa: Homilies on Ecclesiastes

Translation by Stuart George Hall and Rachel Moriarty

The First Homily

The text of Ecclesiastes 1,1-11.[1]

1, 1   Words of the Ecclesiast, the Son of David,
        the King of Israel.

2   Futility of futilities, said the Ecclesiast,
        all things are futility.

3   For what advantage is there for man,
        in all his toil, wherein he toils under the sun?

4   Generation goes and generation comes,
        and the earth stands to eternity.

5   And the sun rises and the sun sets
        and draws to its place;

6   as it rises it goes there towards the south
        and circles towards the north;
        it circles circling.   The spirit goes,
        and in its circles you turn your spirit round.

7   All the torrents go to the sea,
        and the sea will not be filled up;
        in the places where the torrents go,
        there they turn back to go.

---

1   The lines and verses of the text follow Rahlfs' Septuaginta.   The
    wording however assumes the Greek text which Gregory actually
    used, so far as it can be reconstructed from his quotations and
    explanations.   See further pp. 9-11.

8   All words are laborious;

          a man will not be able to speak.

          An eye will not have its fill of seeing,
          nor will an ear have its fill of hearing.

9   What is it that has come to be? the same as
                                              what shall be;
          and what is it that has been made? the same as
                                              shall be made;
          and there is nothing fresh under the sun,

10   he who shall speak shall also say, Behold, this is
                                                        new!

          It has already been in the ages
          which have been from before us.

11   There is no memory for the first,
          and indeed for those who come last
          there will be no memory of them
          with those who have come to be at the last.

277 - 279,3

Introduction. Higher meaning in Ecclesiastes than in Proverbs

277,3.   Before us for exposition lies Ecclesiastes, which requires
labour in spiritual interpretation quite as great as the benefit to be
obtained.   The thoughts of Proverbs having already prepared the mind
by exercise, thoughts whose obscure words and wise *sayings and
riddles* (Pr 1,6) and complicated twists of argument (Pr 1,3), as the
opening passage of that book describes, ⟨introduced us to the desire
for virtue⟩ ... then for those who have developed to the more
advanced stages of learning [p278] there comes the ascent towards
this truly sublime and God-inspired work of scripture.   If then the
exercise in proverbial expressions which prepares us for these lessons
is so painful and difficult to understand, how great an effort must
be envisaged in these lofty thoughts which now lie before us for
interpretation?

278,5.   For just as those who have trained in wrestling in the gymnasium strip for greater exertions and efforts in the athletic contests, so it seems to me that the teaching of Proverbs is an exercise, which trains our souls and makes them supple for the struggle with Ecclesiastes.   If therefore the exercise is accomplished with such great exertions and efforts, what view are we to take of the actual contests?   Indeed, one could think of every hyperbole and still not properly express in words what great struggles the contest with this scripture involves for the contestants, as they fight for a foothold for their thoughts, using their skill as athletes so that they may not find their argument overthrown, but in every intellectual encounter keep the mind on its feet to the end through the truth.

278,17.   Nevertheless, since it is also one of the Master's commands, that we must *search the scriptures* (Jn 5,39), there is an absolute necessity, even if our mind falls short of the truth, failing to match the greatness of the ideas, that we should still ensure by all the zeal for the Word of which we are capable that we do not appear to disregard the Lord's command.   Let us therefore search the [p279] scripture lying before us to the best of our ability.   For surely he who has given the command to search the scriptures will also give us the ability to do so, as it is written, *The Lord will give a word to those who preach good news with great power* (Ps 68,11/67,12).

279,4 - 281,2   Eccl 1,1

The meaning of the title 'Ecclesiastes'

279,4.   First let the title of the book be brought before us for interpretation.   In every church Moses and the Law are read;   the Prophets, the Psalms, the whole of the Histories and whatever else is included in either the Old Testament or the New, all these are proclaimed in ecclesial assemblies.   How then is this alone and in particular embellished with the title **Ecclesiastes**, 'the Churchman', or 'the Ecclesiast'?   What conclusion have we reached about this?   In all the other scriptures, whether histories or prophecies, the aim of the book also includes other things not wholly of service to the

Church. Why should the Church be concerned to learn precisely the circumstances of battles, or who became the rulers of nations and founders of cities, which settlers originated where, or what kingdoms will appear in time to come, and all the marriages and births which were diligently recorded, and all the details of this kind which can be learned from each book of scripture? Why should it help the Church so much in its struggle towards its goal of godliness?

279,20. Now the teaching of this book looks exclusively to the conduct of the Church, [p280] and gives instruction in those things by which one would achieve the life of virtue. For the object of what is said here is to raise the mind above sensation, to persuade it to abandon all that seems to be great and splendid in the world of existence, to catch a glimpse through the eyes of the soul of those things which are unattainable by sense-perception, and to conceive a desire for those things to which sense does not attain.

280,7. Perhaps the title of the book also envisages the one who leads the Church (*ecclesia*). For the true Ecclesiast, he who collects into one body what has been *scattered*, and assembles (*ecclesiazon*) *into one* whole those who have been led astray in many ways by various deceits (Jn 11,52) — who else would he be but the true King of Israel, the Son of God, to whom Nathanael said, *You are the Son of God, you are the King of Israel* (Jn 1,49)? If therefore these are words of the King of Israel, and this same one is also the Son of God, as the Gospel says, then the same one is called Ecclesiast (*Assembler*). Perhaps we may not unreasonably give this sense to the expression used in the title, so that we may learn by this that the meaning of these words has reference to him who established the Church for ever through the Gospel message. Words, it says, of the Ecclesiast, the Son of David. And [p281] Matthew so names him at the beginning of his Gospel, calling the Lord *Son of David* (Mt 1,1).

281,3 – 282,9   Eccl 1,2

The meaning of 'futility'

281,3. Futility of futilities, said the Ecclesiast, all things are futility. The insubstantial is deemed 'futile', that which has existence only in the utterance of the word. No substantial object is simultaneously indicated when the term is used, but it is a kind of idle and empty sound, expressed by syllables in the form of a word, striking the ear at random without meaning, the sort of word people make up for a joke, but which means nothing. This then is one sort of futility. Another sense of 'futility' is the pointlessness of things done earnestly to no purpose, like the sandcastles children build, and shooting arrows at stars, and chasing the winds, and racing against one's own shadow and trying to step on its head, and anything else of the same kind which we find done pointlessly. All these activites are included in the meaning of 'futility'.

281,18. It is also often called 'futile' in ordinary language, when someone does everything with some purpose in view, energetically pursuing it as contributing to his object, but then, when some obstacle presents itself, the labour turns out to be useless; then [p282] the expense of effort without achieving anything is denoted by the word 'futile'. Ordinary language says of such actions, 'My effort was futile,' or, 'My expectations were futile,' or, 'It was futile for me to go to all that trouble.' And, not to go in detail through all the things to which the term 'futility' can properly be applied, we shall briefly sum up the sense of this word. 'Futility' is either a meaningless word, or an unprofitable activity, or an unrealized plan, or unsuccessul effort, or in general what serves no useful purpose at all.

282,10 – 283,17   Eccl 1,2

The meaning of 'futility of futilities'

282,10. If therefore the idea of 'futile' has now been understood by us, we must investigate what **futility of futilities** means. The idea which is being examined might perhaps become more intelligible to us, if at the same time we were to examine the scriptural usage on what things are thought of as superior. To do what is necessary and useful is termed '*work*' in scripture, but the more exalted endeavours, concerned directly with the service of God, is called *work of works*

(Num 4,47), as the story shows, the scripture, I think, by analogy indicating to us by *the work of works* which among our goals is most worthwhile.   For the relation which active effort has to complete inaction is the same as that which activity directed towards the higher and more precious goals has to other works.   Similarly something is said to be *holy* in scripture, and something else [p283] is *holy of holies* (Ex 26,33-34), suggesting that in the same degree that the holy is superior to the profane, the holy of holies is superior to the holy, being considered supreme in holiness.

283,3.   What therefore we have learned about superior value, since scriptural usage indicates by such an idiom the intensification of the underlying thought – if we apply the lesson also to **futility of futilites, we** shall not go wrong.   It means that the visible universe is not simply futile, but that such things are an extreme form of the meaning of 'futile';   as if someone might say, 'deader than dead' or 'more lifeless than lifeless'.   Although comparative intensification does not allow such expressions, nevertheless they are put in these terms to make absolutely clear what is being stated.   So just as there are concepts of *works of works* and *holy of holies*, whereby the more exalted expression is used to indicate what is superior, so also **futility of futilities** indicates the absolute extreme of what is futile.

283,18 - 285,12   Eccl 1,2

The futility of all things does not condemn God's creation

283,18.   Let no one suppose that the words are an indictment of creation.   For surely the charge would also implicate him who has made all things, if the one who constructed all things from nothing were manifested to us as creator of things of this kind, if indeed **all things were futility.** [p284] But since man's nature is twofold, soul combining with body, the precise form of its existence has been allotted in an appropriate way to each of the elements observed in us.   Life of the soul is one thing, and that of the body another. That of the body is mortal and subject to death, while that of the soul is impassible and not affected by death;   and while the one has only the present as its prospect, the point of view of the other extends to eternity.   Since therefore there is a great difference between the mortal and the immortal, and between the temporal and the eternal, the words of the Ecclesiast point to this truth, - that one ought not to look to this life of the senses, which compared with the true life is unreal and insubstantial.

284,12.   One might nonetheless say that even this argument is not without reproach to the Creator, since he is the source both of the soul and of the body, so that if fault is found with life in the flesh, and God is creator of the flesh, the blame for this would necessarily lie with him.   But surely these will be the words of one who has not yet escaped from the flesh, nor truly glimpsed the higher life.   For anyone trained in the divine mysteries is surely aware that the life conformed to the divine nature is proper and natural to mankind, while the life of sense-perception, lived through the activity of the senses, has been granted to that nature in order [p285] that the knowledge of the visible world might become a guide to the soul for knowledge of things unseen, as Wisdom says that *by analogy from the greatness and beauty of his creatures* the originator of all things is perceived (Wisdom 13,5);   yet human misjudgment did not see *the one[2] who is revered through the physical order, but revered what it actually saw.

285,5.   Since therefore the action of the senses is temporary and shortlived, what we learn through this sublime phrase is that he who looks to these things, looks at nothing.   But the one who is being guided through these things to the perception of that which is, and by means of the transient has perceived a stable reality and has comprehended that which remains for ever the same, that person has seen the Good that really is, and has taken possession of what he has seen;   for to know this Good is to possess it.

---

2   An asterisk * indicates a departure from the text or punctuation of Alexander in GNO V. Most of these cases are explained on pp. 11-18. Here τὸν (S) is read instead of τό.

Wordly pleasures never satisfy

285,13.   For what advantage, he says, is there for man *in all his
toil, wherein he toils under the sun?   He calls the life in the body
toil, *toil pursued to no conclusion, unprofitably.   For what
advantage, he says, is there for man?   That is, what does the soul
gain by the toil of this life in the case of those who live for the
visible?   In what does life even exist, or what visible [p286] good
lasts unchanged?   The sun goes round its own course, bringing light
and darkness in turn, lighting up the air above us whenever it shows
itself above the earth, and bringing darkness in its settings.   And the
earth stands in its place and remains unmoved on its foundation, and
what stands still does not move, and what moves does not stand still,
and all things are shown to have the same cycles in every period of
time, without any variation at all by way of change into anything new.

286,8.   The sea is a receptacle for the confluence of waters from
every direction, and neither does the confluence cease, nor does the
sea increase.   What is the point of the activity as far as the waters
are concerned, always filling what is not filled?   To what end does
the sea receive the inflow of the waters, remaining unincreased by
what is added?   He says these things so that from the very elements
among which man's life is spent he might explain in advance the
unreality of the things sought after among us.

286,16.   For if this urgent cycle of the sun has no end, and the
successive changes of light and darkness never cease, and the earth,
condemned to immobility, remains unmoved in its fixed place, and the
rivers toil without effect, being swallowed up by the insatiable nature
of the sea, and in vain the sea receives the inflow of the waters,
taking to its bosom without increase what forever pours into it — if
these things are in this condition, what is likely to be the state of
the humanity which spends its life among them?   Why are we surprised
if generation goes and generation comes, and [p287] this cycle does
not leave aside its natural rhythm, as the generation of men

constantly arriving expels its predecessor, and is expelled by the one succeeding?

287,4 - 288,6   Eccl 1,5-6

The circling sun and the spirit

287,4. What then does the Word here proclaim to the Church? He says, 'You human beings, as you look upon the universe, recognize your own nature. What you see in the sky and the earth, what you observe in the sun, what you notice in the sea, let this interpret to you your own nature too.' For there is a rising and a setting of our nature corresponding to that of the sun. There is one path for all things, one cycle for the journey through life. Whenever we rise through birth, we are drawn back down to our native place. When our life sinks down, our light too goes underground, when the sense that perceives the light becomes earth. Assuredly the earth dissolves into its native element, and this is a cycle which continually rolls around in the same way.

287,16. Just as the Word says of the sun, that as it rises it travels over the upper side of the earth in the south, but when it is below the horizon it passes under the opposite part of the world to the north, and revolving for ever like this, it circles round its course and once more goes on with its circular revolution - for it circles circling, he says; and in the same way therefore your own spirit goes (part for whole, he refers to the whole human being as 'spirit'), [p288] travelling this circular course by the same route. For, he says, the spirit goes, and in its circles you turn your spirit round. One who has comprehended this might be considerably helped in his own life. What is brighter than the light? What is clearer than the sunbeam? But yet, when the sun goes under the earth, its brightness is hidden and its beam vanishes.

The advantages of stability

288,7.   Let anyone who considers these things pass his own life more
circumspectly, despising celebrity here, having learnt from what is
visible that its features do not last to eternity, but that the
succession of opposite states follows swiftly one after the other.
Nothing remains for ever in its present state, not youth, not beauty,
not the celebrity of dynastic power.   These things, too, are for
those who enjoy a degree of good fortune.   But as for those to
whom a life directed towards virtue seems burdensome, let their soul
be trained by the example of the earth so as to persevere under
hardship. **The earth stands to eternity.**   What is more laborious than
this fixed immobility?   And yet this unchanging state extends until
eternity.

288,18.   But you, whose period of struggle is short, do not become
more lifeless than the earth, do not become more unthinking than the
insensible, for you are endowed with thought and directed by reason
towards life.   Instead, as the Apostle says, *Continue in the things
you have learnt and been convinced of* (II Tim 3,14), in that
steadfast and immoveable stability, since this also is one of the
divine commands, that you [p289] *be steadfast* and *immoveable* (1 Cor
15,58).   Let your sobriety abide unshaken, your faith firm, your love
constant, your stability in every good thing unmoved, so that **the
earth** in you may **stand to eternity.**

289,3.   But if any one, yearning for greater possessions, and letting
his desire become as boundless as a sea, has an insatiable greed for
the streams of gain flowing in from every side, let him treat his
disease by looking at the real sea.   For as the sea does not exceed
its boundary with the innumerable streams of water flowing into it,
but remains at the same volume just as though it were receiving no
new water from streams, in the same way human nature too, restricted by specific limits in the enjoyment of what comes to it, cannot
enlarge its appetite to match the extent of its acquisitions;   while
the intake is endless, the capacity for enjoyment is kept within its

set limit.   If therefore enjoyment cannot exceed the amount fixed by nature, for what reason do we attract in the flood of acquisitions, never overflowing for the benefit of others from our additional income?

*289,18 – 291,14   Eccl 1,2-7

Human life as futility

*289,18.   Since, according to the idea of futility we have presented, futility is either senseless speech or purposeless action, the writer does well to begin the work with that point, so that [p290] we may not regard anything done or said as substantial if it looks to a purpose here.   Any interest which people have in worldly things is quite simply the same as children's *toys of sand* (Homer, Il. 15,363-364), in which the enjoyment of the products ends with the interest in their construction.   As soon as they cease from their toil, the sand collapses, leaving behind no trace of what the children worked at.

290,7.   This is human life: ambition is sand, power is sand, wealth is sand, and sand each of the pleasures eagerly enjoyed in the flesh.   If only childish souls pointlessly engrossed in these insubstantial things, and enduring many toils for each of them, would forsake the place of sand (I mean the life lived in the flesh), then they would recognize the futility of the life spent here;   for even the enjoyment is left behind with the physical world, while they take with them nothing but the mere recollection.   As it seems to me, even the great Ecclesiast, as though he had escaped from these things and with his soul stripped were living the immaterial life, said just what we also are likely to say one day, when we get away from this seaside place, where the sand is that thrown up by the sea of life, and when we separate ourselves from all the breakers which thunder and roar around us, [p291] taking from the sea we have contemplated only the memory of the things we pursued here;   *I mean **Futility of futilities, all is futility**, and, **What advantage is there for man, wherein he toils under the sun?**

291,3.   For truly, as I understand it, this is the thought of every soul when, divested of the things of this world, it moves to the hoped-for life.   For if the soul has successfully achieved any of the higher things in this life, it condemns this world in which it used to be, despising the past in comparison with the present possession.   But if, having been warmly disposed to the material, it sees the unexpected and by experience learns the unprofitability of the things valued by it in this life, then it will with sorrow utter these words (as we men do in repentance, when we recount with lamentation our misjudgments), Futility of futilities and so forth.

291,15 – 293,1   Eccl 1,8

The labour of words with virtue

291,15.   All words, he says, are laborious, and a man will not be able to speak.   Yet in the obvious sense nothing is thought to be easier than speaking.   What labour is it for the speaker to say what he likes?   The tongue is supple and pliable and shapes itself without effort to whatever kind of words it wishes.   There is nothing to stop air being breathed in and used to make sounds.   The service performed by the cheeks is painless and the lips [p292] cooperate in pronouncing what is said.   What labour therefore does he see in speech, when bodily effort does not make speaking laborious?   We do not make a passage for speech by digging soil, dislodging boulders or carrying them on our shoulders, or performing any other burdensome task, but thought, taking shape in us, revealed through sound, becomes speech.

292,6.   But since a word of this kind does not cause labour, we ought to consider what are the laborious words which a man will not be able to speak.   *Let the elders*, it says, *be deemed worthy of double honour, especially those who labour in the word* (I Tim 5,17). One who has left behind the unruliness of youth and has reached the settled condition of old age is in common usage called an elder;   so the sort of person who is not at peace in his thoughts and has a

disorderly way of life is not yet an elder, even if he looks grey-
haired, but he is still just an adult.   Surely then, words — words in
the true sense, words uttered for spiritual benefit and the service of
mankind — are full of sweat and effort, and cause much labour in
order to become words.   *The one who labours at cultivation must
first share the produce* (II Tim 2,6), says the expert in this kind of
words, on the grounds that the word ought not to be thought of as
speech, but that actual virtue, which is presented to those who see it
as instruction for living, should serve as the word for those being
taught.   Therefore all such words are laborious, since those who
instruct in virtue first achieve within themselves the things which they
teach.   This is the meaning of *must first share the produce*, that
produce which [p293] before others we cultivate for ourselves through
virtue.

293,2 - 294,17   Eccl 1,8

Words are too weak to express heavenly things

293,2.   Perhaps the text makes plain also the frailty of our
intellectual nature.   For whenever the mind, getting away from the
senses which have been called futility, and escaping as it were to the
contemplation of the unseen world, tries to present its thought in
speech, there is then great labour in speaking, since this expository
voice finds no device for explaining the inexpressible.   We see sky, we
have a perception of the beams of the heavenly bodies, we tread the
earth, we draw the air into the mouth, we put water to the use which
nature suggests, we accept fire to participate in life.   Should we
wish to understand, in connexion with these elements,   what each
visible thing consists of in its essential structure, or how it got its
being, a man will not be able to speak, even if he happens to be
superior to the rest, since all conceptual understanding is too weak
to explain what is beyond our reach.

293,16.   Now if speaking of these things is a labour beyond the
power and nature of humanity to utter, what would one say is the
case with words about the Word himself or the Father of the Word?

Surely every lofty expression and grandiloquence is a sort of speechlessness and silence, compared with the true meaning of the subject, so that [p294] one may properly say only this of it: although one were to deploy all powers of thought and omit no idea worthy of God, if the expression is compared with what is truly worthy of the subject matter, whatever may be said, it is not a 'word', for a human being will not be able to speak.

294,5. Sight did not not produce the interpretation of the visible world which develops in the soul through the eyes, but, although we are constantly using our eyes, we receive a visual impression as those who have seen nothing and are still in ignorance. For sight is not able to go beyond the surface, but has as a limit to its proper function what is displayed to it by the outward appearance of what is there. That is why he says, An eye will not have its fill of seeing, nor will an ear have its fill of hearing. The hearing power, which takes in the word for each particular, by its nature cannot be filled. For no word will be found which exactly describes in itself the subject in question. How therefore will the ear have its fill of hearing about those subjects, when there is nothing which can fill it?

294,18 – 296,18   Eccl 1,9

Past and future, soul and body

294,18. Next after these words he puts himself questions and answers himself. After asking, What is it that has come to be? The same, he says, as what shall be. And what is it that has been made? The same, he says, as shall be made. What is the purpose of the questioning? It is as if as a consequence of what we have been told [p295] we were to put an objection to him and say, 'If everything is futility, it is clear that not even one of these things which do not exist has come to be. For the futile is totally without reality, and one would not reckon the unreal among things that have come to be. If indeed these things do not exist, tell us, what is it that came to be and continues in existence?'

295,5. He has an immediate anwer to the question: 'Do you wish to know what it is that came to be? Think what it is that will be, and you will know what has been. That is: 'Think, you human being,' he says, 'what you will become by elevating yourself through virtue. If you shape your soul in every respect with good characteristics, if you free yourself from the defilements of evil, if you wash away from your nature all stain of the filth of matter, what will you become as you beautify yourself in such ways? What loveliness will you put on? If you carefully consider this with your mind, you have been taught what came to be in the beginning, which indeed will truly come to be, what is *in the image and likeness of God* (Gen 1,26)?' 'And where is now,' I shall say to him who teaches these things, 'that which once existed and is hoped for again hereafter, but does not now exist?' But surely [p296] he who gives lessons in the sublime answers us with exactly the same thought: 'The present condition is called **futility** precisely because in the present that thing does not exist.'

296,3. **And what is it**, he says, **that has been made? The same as shall be made.** Let none of those listening think that there is a longwinded and meaningless repetition of words in the distinction between what has come to be and what has been made. The text points out in each of the expressions the difference between the soul and the flesh. The soul has come to be and the body has been made. It is not because the words have two different meanings that the text uses this distinction of terminology for each of the things referred to, but to enable you to reckon what is advantageous in each case. The soul came to be in the beginning the same as it will again appear hereafter, when it has been purified. The body shaped by the hands of God was made what the resurrection of the dead in due time will reveal it to be. For such as you may see it after the resurrection of the dead, just such it was made at the first. The resurrection of the dead is nothing but the complete restoration of the original state.

What is new, is not

296,19.   To these arguments therefore he also adds what follows, saying that there exists nothing outside its original state. For **there is nothing fresh**, he says, **under the sun**, as if he were saying, 'Unless something exists in its original state, it does not exist at all, but is only thought to exist.' [p297] For **there is nothing fresh**, he says, **under the sun**, such that someone might speak and point out that a thing which has come about is new and has really come into existence. This is the sense of the words, but the passage itself runs like this: **And there is nothing fresh under the sun, he who shall speak shall also say, Behold this is new!** He emphasizes his point with the words immediately following: if anything has truly come to be, he says, it is that which came to be in the ages before us. The actual words of the scripture give this meaning, reading as follows: **It has already been in the ages which have been from before us.**

297,11.   If oblivion has overtaken things which were, do not be surprised; for those that now are will also be veiled in oblivion. When our nature inclined to evil we became forgetful of the good; when we are set free again for the good, evil in turn will be veiled in oblivion. For I think this is the meaning of the text, in which he says, **There is no memory for the first, and indeed for those who come last there will be no memory of them.** It is as if he were saying that the memory of events which followed our blessed state at the beginning, through which humanity has come to be among evils, will be obliterated by what again supervenes at the End. For **there will be no memory of them with those who have come to be at the last.** That means, the final restoration will make the memory of evil things utterly vanish in our nature, in Jesus Christ our Lord, to whom be the glory for ever and ever. AMEN.

The Second Homily

The text of Ecclesiastes 1,12 - 2,3

1,12   I, the Ecclesiast, have become
        king over Israel in Jerusalem.

1,13   I gave my heart to enquiring into
        and investigating by wisdom all
        that has come about under the heaven;
        because evil distress
        God gave to the sons of man,
        for them to be distressed with.

14   I saw all the doings
        that have been done under the sun,
        and behold, all is futility and choice of spirit.

15   What is crooked will not be able to be put in order,
        and a want will not be able to be counted in the
                                                total.

16   I spoke in my heart, saying,
        behold, I have become great,
        and I acquired wisdom among all
        who were before me in Jerusalem.
        My heart saw many things, wisdom and knowledge.

17   I gave my heart to learn wisdom and knowledge,
        parables and science I know,
        because this is choice of spirit,

18   that in fullness of wisdom is fullness of knowledge,
        and one who increases knowledge will increase pain.

2,1   I said in my heart,
        Come hither, I will test you in merriment, and also
                                                in good,
        and behold, this too is futility.

2   To laughter I said, Dizziness,
        and to merriment, Why are you doing this?

3   I examined my heart,

           to see if it would swallow my flesh like wine;

           and my heart led me in the way of wisdom,

           for gaining mastery over merriment,

           until I could see what is the Good for the sons of

                                                              man,

           which they will do under the sun,

           the number of days of their life.

298,4 - 299,14   Eccl 1,12

The King in Jerusalem

298,5.   I, he says, the Ecclesiast.   We have learned who the
Ecclesiast is, he who gathers into one what has gone astray and has
been scattered abroad, and makes it all one church and one flock,
that none may be deaf to the shepherd's kindly voice, which gives life
to all. For *the words which I speak*, he says, *are spirit and are life*
(John 6,63). This is the one who calls himself **Ecclesiast**, just as he
calls himself *Physician*, and *Life*, and *Resurrection*, and *Light*, and
Way, and Door and *Truth*, and all the names of his love for human
kind (Mat 9,12; John 14,6; John 11,25; John 12,46; John 10,7).

298,13.   Therefore, just as the name of Physician is appropriate for
those who are sick, and the title *Life* functions among the dead, who
hear the voice of the Son of Man (John 5,25) and no longer remain in
their former deadness;   and as those who are in the tombs [p299]
seek the voice of the *Resurrection*, and the title *Light* is fitting for
those who are in darkness, and *Way* for those who have strayed, and
likewise *Door* for those who need to enter; in the same way the
Ecclesiast speaks to those in the ecclesial assembly.   It is therefore
to us that he speaks.   Let us then hear his words, we who are the
Church.   As the chorus looks to its conductor, the rowers to the
helmsman, and an army in line to its general, so we who belong to the
ecclesial congregation (the Church) look to the Ecclesiast.

299,10.   What does the Ecclesiast say?   I have become King over
Israel in Jerusalem.   When is this?   Surely when *He was set up as*

king by him on Mount Zion, his holy mountain, proclaiming the Lord's commandment (Ps 2,6-7). To him the Lord said *You are my Son*, and *Today I have begotten you* (Ps 2,7). He says that today he has begotten the Maker of all, the Father of the ages, so that by applying a temporal term to the moment of his birth, the text might demonstrate not his existence before the ages but his fleshly birth in time, for the salvation of mankind.

299,20 - 301,2   Eccl 1,13

Searching out the earth

299,20. These are the things which the true Ecclesiast recounts as he teaches, so I believe, the great mystery of salvation, the reason why God was revealed in flesh. **I gave my heart**, he says, **to enquiring into and investigating by wisdom all that had come about under the heaven.** This is the reason for [p300] the Lord's fleshly coming to dwell with men, to give his heart to investigating in his own wisdom what has come about under the heaven. What is above the heaven had no need of investigation, just as there is no need of a medical attendant for what is not in the grip of illness (Luke 5,31). So because the evils were on earth — for the creeping animal, the serpent, which crawls *on its breast and on its belly*, makes the earth its food, eating nothing from heaven (Gen 3,14); as it crawls on trodden ground it always looks at what treads on it, *watching for the traveller's heel* (Gen 3,15) and injecting its venom into those who have lost *the power to tread upon serpents* (Luke 10,19) — for this reason he gave his **heart to enquiring into and investigating all that has come about under the heaven.**

300,13. For in what is above the heavens the prophet sees the divine significance not brought low, and says, *Your majesty is exalted above the heavens* (Ps 8,2). But because later the part of creation below heaven was brought low through evil, — as the psalmist says, *because of their sin they were brought low* (Ps 107/106,17), — what the Preacher came to consider is this: what has come about under the heaven which was not there before? how did futility enter in? how

did the unreal gain control? and what power has unreality? For evil
has no substance, since it takes its substance from what does not
exist; what comes from the non-existent does not even exist [p301]
at all in terms of its own nature, but even so futility gains control
over things which have become like itself.

301,3 - 303,11   Eccl 1,13-14

Evil caused by abuse of God's gift of freedom

301,3. He came, then, to enquire by his own wisdom what has come
about under the sun, what the confusion is of things here on earth,
how being became the slave of non-being, how the unreal dominates
being. And he saw that **evil distress God gave to the sons of man,
for them to be distressed with.** This does not mean, as one might
assume at first glance, that it is devout to think that God gave evil
distress to men himself: for then the responsibility for ills would be
laid on him. He who is good by nature is surely also the producer of
all good, because thus *Every good tree brings forth good fruit*, and
grapes do not grow on thistles, nor thistles on a vine (Mat 7,16-17).
For the one who is good by nature would not produce anything evil
from his own storehouses, any more than the good man *from the
abundance of his heart utters* bad things, but speaks in accordance
with his own nature (Luke 6,45). How much more true is it,
therefore, that the fountain of goodness would not let anything evil
flow from his own nature?

301,19. What the more devout understanding is disposed to think is
this: that the good gift of God, that is, freedom of action, became a
means to sin through the sinful use mankind made of it. For
unfettered free will is good by nature, and nobody would [p302] reckon
among good things anything which was constrained by the yoke of
necessity. But that free impulse of the mind rushing unschooled
towards the choice of evil became a source of distress for the soul,
as it was dragged down from the sublime and honourable towards the
urges of the natural passions. This is what **gave** means, not that he

made the evil in human life himself, but that man through folly used God's good gifts in the service of evil.

302,8.   It is the practice in Holy Scripture to express ideas of this kind in language of this kind.   For example, *God gave them up to shameful passions* (Rom 1,26), and *He gave them up to depraved reason* (Rom 1,28) and *He hardened Pharaoh's heart* (Ex 9,12), and *Why did you make us go astray, Lord, out of your way? You hardened our hearts, so that we did not fear you* (Is 63,17), and *He made them go astray in a pathless place out of the way* (Ps 107/106,40), and *You have deceived me and I was deceived* (Jer 20,7) – and all the other similar instances.   On the basis of these, a correct under-standing does not conclude that anything bad has been put in human nature by God, but blames our capacity to choose, which [p303] is in itself a good thing, and a gift of God granted to our nature, but through folly has become a force tipping the balance the opposite way.

303,3.   Therefore the Ecclesiast **saw all the doings that have been done** in life **under the sun**, that it was all futility.   For there was not one who *understood*, there was not one who *sought God; since all had fallen away, and become worthless altogether* (Ps 14/13,2-3). Because of this, when he says **And behold, all is futility** he is claiming as the reason for it that the cause of these things is not God, but the **choice** made by human impulse, which he calls **spirit**.   He blames this spirit, not because it was like this from the beginning – for if it had been, it would not be open to blame – but because by becoming crooked it has ceased to fit the design of the world.

303,12 – 305,13   Eccl 1,15

Putting the crooked in order and restoring the lost

303,12.   **What is crooked, he says, will not be able to be put in order;**   in other words, what is twisted could never fit the creation set in order by God.   I give an example: a carpenter who is making himself something to a design straightens with ruler and line the edges which, by their skilful adjustment to each other, join to produce the piece of furniture;   but if one of them does not [p304] lie straight along the line, the properly-made part will of course not fit the crooked part, and that has to be matched with the line too and made straight, if it is to fit the straight part.   In the same way the Ecclesiast is saying that a nature made crooked by evil cannot belong to a creation designed by the true Word.

304,6.   **A want will not be able to be counted in the total,** he says. The language used in scripture teaches us that anything lacking is a want, and this is supported by many instances: for Paul, initiated *in every way and in all things,* knew what it was both *to suffer want* and *to have abundance* (Phil 4,12).   The one who wasted his father's substance in debauchery *began to feel want* as hunger overcame him (Luke 15,14);   and Paul, in going through examples of the saints, describes their other physical sufferings, and includes this: *they suffered want* and *they were in misery* (Heb 11,37).   In our text too the word **want** has the meaning 'what is left out';   what is left out cannot be part of the total of things that exist.   In the case of the disciples, as long as they were at their full strength there were twelve of them;   but when the *son of perdition* (John 17,12) had perished the number fell short, as 'the one left out' could not be counted as one of those who were there.   After Judas, there were eleven of them, and they were called *The Eleven* (e.g. Mat 28,16). Therefore the Ecclesiast says, **a want will not be able to be counted in the total.**

304,23.   What does he mean by this sentence? He means that once our humanity too was once [p305] counted within the totality of existence;   for we too went to make up the sacred hundred sheep, the rational beings.   But when the one sheep — our nature — was led astray from the heavenly way by evil, and was dragged down to this parched salty place, the flock which had not strayed did not add up to the same number as before, but are said to be *ninety-nine* (Mat 18,12-13; Luke 15,4).   The futile is left outside the total of existing things, and thus **a want will not be able to be counted in the total.** Therefore *he came to seek and to save that which was lost* (Luke 19,10), and, laying it on his shoulders (Luke 15,5), to bring back into existence what was being lost through the futility of unreal things, so that the total of God's creation should be complete again, when the lost has been restored to those who are not lost.

305,14 - 307,14   Eccl 1,16ff.

Like Solomon, Christ experienced all things

305,14.   What is the way back for the wanderer, and the way of escape from evil, and towards good, we learn next.   For he *who has had experience like us in all things, without sin* (Heb 4,15), speaks to us from our own condition.   *He took our weaknesses upon him* (Mat 8,17), and through these very weaknesses of our nature shows us the way out of the reach of evil.   Now note, please, that Wisdom speaks to us through Solomon himself after the flesh, and speaks about those things by which we may most readily be led to despise the things which are pursued by men.

305,23.   The way the word comes from him is not the same as with most people, who do not have [p306] opportunity to match their desire, so that it is unworthy of credit for the reason that it criticizes things of which he has no experience.   For we do not learn everything from our own experience, but we know only in theory about things from whose delightfully enjoyable experience we are prevented by poverty.   If someone is faced with our advice that he should consider human pursuits as worthless, the hearer's answer is ready to hand: we only fail to value them because we have not learnt from experience the pleasure there is in them.

306,10.   In the presence of the person who discusses these things with us, the whole of this kind of objection fails.   For it is Solomon who speaks these words.   This Solomon was the third king of Israel, after King Saul and David, the chosen of the Lord.   He succeeded his father on the throne, and was proclaimed king when the power of the Israelites had already reached its height;   he did not go on wearing his people out with war and fighting, but lived in peace as far as lay

in his power, making it his task not to acquire what did not belong to
him, but to enjoy what he already had in abundance.

306,19.   Since then there was nothing to prevent him from having
anything he desired — *for his wealth matched his desire, and his
leisure could be freely devoted to enjoyment, with nothing unintended
interrupting his attention to his desires — being generally wise and
particularly competent by virtue of his intelligence to investigate any
matter connected with pleasures, [p307] having done any *you might
mention of the things pursued for enjoyment, and after doing all
those things which he subsequently lists in the text, he says that he
has learnt through actual experience that there is but one end of the
things pursued by these means, futility.

307,4.   Such is the order he adopts in his account, that first in the
early years of his life he devotes his time to education and does not
take the easy course in the face of the hard work such study involves, but uses the choice of his spirit, that is, his natural impulse,
for the accumulation of knowledge, even though his goal was achieved
by hard work;   and thus, when he has matured in wisdom, he does not
merely theoretically observe the passionate and irrational deception of
mankind in the matter of bodily enjoyments, but through the actual
experience of each of the things they pursue recognizes their futility.

307,15 - 309,17   Eccl 1,16-18

The effort of acquiring wisdom

307,15.   Such then is the general tenor of what is written after what
we have previously examined; now would be the time to set out a
word-by-word interpretation systematically, following the sequence of
the words.   I spoke in my heart, saying, behold, I have become great.
'For when I saw around me', he says, 'the majesty my dominion
brought and the might of the kingdom which came to me all at once, I
did not stand still with things as they were, nor did I think that what
was acquired effortlessly led of its own accord to prosperity in life;
instead, before these things I valued above all the acquisition of

wisdom, and this it was impossible to acquire without effort [p308] and sweat.'

308,1.   Therefore when he said, I spoke in my heart, saying, behold, I have become great, he added, and I acquired wisdom.   'For I increased the might of the power which came to me of itself, by the addition of wisdom;   and I said to myself, that in this way above all I must be shown to be superior to the kings before me, and to exceed them in wisdom.   For I acquired wisdom among all who were before me in Jerusalem, and I considered how this might come about.'

308,9.   Who does not know that for those who are diligent, wisdom depends on the knowledge of what others have laboured over before? This is why he says, my heart saw many things, wisdom and knowledge, not because the knowledge of such things came of its own accord, without effort, but because, he says, I gave my heart to learn wisdom and knowledge, in the sense that he would not have learnt them if effort and diligence had not taught the knowledge of them;   but he says   parables and science I know, that is, the grasp of the transcendent which is gained by analogy, when familiar things are set alongside for comparison.   And he claims he has learnt [p309] these things: for parables and science, he says, I know, just as in the Gospel the Lord, as he teaches those who hear him, introduces the message about the kingdom with a visual image, speaking about a pearl, or treasure, or a wedding, or a seed, or yeast, or something like that;   he is not saying that these things are the kingdom, but through the similarity of   what is signified by them he shows his listeners in a parable some glimmer or clue to things beyond comprehension (Mat,13,31-33.44-45; 22,2 par.).

309,8.   'And', he says, 'the choice of spirit has in my case been this, that I should acquire the fullness of wisdom, so that in becoming wise I should not fail to gain the knowledge of what is, nor miss any opportunity for profitable discovery.'   For knowledge is produced from wisdom, and knowledge makes easier the discernment of what is beyond us.   This does not simply happen without effort to those who pursue it, but the person who increases his knowledge exactly matches effort to learning. Because of this he says, one who increases knowledge will increase pain.

#309,17 - 311,14   Eccl 2,1-2

How the Ecclesiast tested pleasure and found it wanting

309,17. Once he has become like this, he condemns pleasures as futile. For he says, I said in my heart, Come hither, I will test you in merriment, and also in good, and this too is futility. For he did not give himself to this kind of experience straight away, nor slide into partaking of pleasures without having tasted the austere and more devout life. Rather, after training himself [p310] with these things, and achieving in his character the severity and determination through which the lessons of wisdom come most readily to those who pursue them, he then descends to things considered agreeable to the senses, not because he is drawn down to them by passion, but in order to investigate whether the sensual experience of them makes any contribution to the knowledge of true Good.

310,6. That is why he makes his own what he had originally regarded as alien, laughter, and calls the condition dizziness, in that it is equivalent in meaning to 'frenzy' or 'madness'; for what else would anyone properly call laughter? It is neither speech nor activity directed to any end, but an unseemly loss of bodily control — convulsions in the breath, paroxysms of the whole body, distention of the cheeks, exposure of the teeth, gums and palate, bending of the neck, unpredictable weakness in the voice, punctuated by gasps of breath: what else could this be, he says, but madness? That is why he says, to laughter I said, Dizziness, as if he were saying to laughter, 'you are mad, you are beside yourself, you have gone beyond the limits of sanity, deliberately behaving in an unseemly way, and distorting [p311] your appearance with passion, without accomplishing anything useful by the distortion.' (Cf Aristotle, Prob. 35,6,9b5a 14).

311,2. But I said also to merriment, Why are you doing this? This is equivalent to saying 'I set my face against pleasure, being suspicious of its approach like a thief's, who slinks in secretly past the soul's attendants;   I have never let it get control of my mind.   For if I were once to recognize pleasure, prowling round my senses like some wild animal, I would immediately fight it and challenge it.   I would say to this servile and mindless merriment, 'Why are you are doing these things?   why do you let womanly softness take over a manly nature? why do you slacken the keenly-tuned mind?   why do you cut the sinews of the spirit?   why do you let your thoughts do such damage? why, I ask you, do you turn murky the clear atmosphere of intelligent ideas murky with the pollution you bring?'

311,15 - 314,10   Eccl 2,3

The desires of flesh and spirit, and their modes of satisfaction

311,15.   After practising these and similar things, he says, I examined my heart, to see if it would swallow my flesh like wine;   that is, how concern for intelligible things might overcome the inclinations of the flesh, so that our nature might not be at war with itself, with the mind choosing some things and the body pulling it towards others, but instead might make [p312] the pride of our flesh submissive and obedient to the rational part of the soul, with the lesser part being swallowed and gulped down inside the larger part, as is the way with thirsty people.   For the wine does not stay in the cup, at least if it is raised to the thirsty man's lips, but it runs towards the drinker, and disappears as it is quickly sucked down into his inside.

312,5.   When that happened, the way it led to the knowledge of reality was unambiguous and obvious to me.   For my heart, he says, led me in the way of wisdom, through which I mastered the rebellious- ness of pleasures, and training was the reason for gaining mastery over merriment.   For this is how the argument continues: my chief object in acquiring knowledge was to devote my life to nothing futile, but to find the true Good, to obtain which is to achieve the discern- ment of what is right;   it is enduring, not transitory, and it lasts all our life long, equally good at every age, in early youth, in middle age, at the end, indeed throughout the whole number of our days — until I

could see, he says, what is the Good for the sons of men, which they
will do under the sun, the number of days of their life.

312,19.   For things pursued in the flesh, however much they entice
the sense to what is at hand, gratify only for an instant; for there
is no bodily activity which can give lasting pleasure.   The pleasure of
drinking comes to an end in sufficiency, [p313] and likewise, after
eating food, fullness quenches the appetite;   and in the same way
every other desire fades in the participation of what is desired;   and
even if it returns, it fades again;   no sensual delight lasts for ever,
nor stays the same.   And furthermore, one thing is good in youth,
another in the prime of life, another in middle age and yet another in
retirement, and another again in old age, when one is bent down
towards the earth.

313,8.   But I, he says, sought the true Good, which is equally good
at any age and every time of life, and of which satiety is not
expected, nor fullness found.   Appetite for it and partaking of it are
exactly matched, and longing flourishes together with enjoyment, and
is not limited by the attainment of what is desired;   the more it
delights in the Good, the more desire flames up with delight;   the
delight matches the desire, and at each stage of life it is always a
lovely thing to those who partake of it.   Amid the changes of age
and time the Good alters not at all;   when our eyes are closed and
when they are open, when we are happy and when we are sorrowful, by
day and by night, on land and on the sea, active and at rest, ruling
and serving – for every person alive it is equally absolutely good,
since the accidents inflicted on one by chance [p314] make it neither
worse nor better, nor smaller nor larger.

314,2.   This, as I understand it, is the Good that truly is, the thing
Solomon sought to see, which people will do under the sun throughout
all the number of the days of their life.   This seems to me to be
none other than the work of faith, the performance of which is
common to all, available on equal terms to those who wish for it,
lasting in full strength continuously throughout life.   This is the good
work, which I pray may be done in us too, in Christ Jesus our Lord,
to whom be the glory for ever and ever.   AMEN.

The Third Homily

The text of Ecclesiastes 2,4-6.

2,4	I enlarged my doing,
	I built me houses,
	I planted me vineyards,
5	I made me vegetable-plots and gardens,
	and I planted every tree of fruit;
6	I made me pools of water
	to water from them a copse producing trees.

314,11 - 315,7

Introduction. Summary of the first two homilies

314,11. Now it is time to examine what the voice of the Ecclesiast teaches us after this. We learnt first the lesson that this Ecclesiast, who calls together the whole creation, and seeks out the lost, and gathers into one what has gone astray, investigates earthly life. The subcelestial life - what the Word calls under the heaven - is earthly, for in it [p315] falsehood and futility and unreality prevail.

315,2. In the second homily we learnt that the condemnation of the attitude to life based on enjoyment and emotion comes from the mouth of Solomon, in order to make its rejection convincing to us; for he had absolute freedom to practise a life aimed at pleasure and enjoyment, and utterly repudiates all that seems to be sought after by mankind.

315,8 - 317,12

Modesty and shame as aids to virtue

315,8.   What is our third lesson, as we come to what follows in this
present homily? — one which I believe is particularly appropriate to
the members of the church;   I mean the confession of things not
rightly done, which produces a feeling of shame in the soul through
the public acknowledgement of sins. The sense of modesty which is
inherent in mankind is often a great and powerful weapon for avoiding
sin, and I believe it was placed in our nature by God for this very
purpose, that such a disposition of our soul might turn us away from
worse things.   The feeling of modesty and the feeling of shame are
closely related and belong to one another, and sin is restrained by
them both, provided one is willing to use such a disposition of the
soul for this purpose.

315,20.   Modesty is often a better tutor than fear for avoiding sins;
but at the same time the shame which follows criticisms of a fault is
enough by itself to correct [p316] the sinner, so that he does not
get into the same position again.   So as to state the difference
between them by definition: shame is modesty intensified, and modesty,
on the other hand, is shame moderated.   The difference between the
two feelings and their similarity is shown by the colour in a person's
face.   Modesty is revealed only by a blush, as the body somehow
shares the feelings of the soul through some natural sympathy
between their dispositions;   the heat round the heart surges up to
appear in the face.   But the person who feels ashamed when his fault
is exposed turns livid and reddish, as fear adds bile to his blush.
Such a feeling might be a suitable way to prevent those already
caught in some sin from continuing to be involved in those things, of
which they would get themselves convicted by shame. (Cf. Aristotle,
Nic. Eth. IV).

316,14.   If this is so, and the text is concerned with the feelings, as
it must be, in the sense [p317] that this kind of disposition is
implanted in our nature to guard against wrongdoing, it is right to
regard   as   a   proper   discipline   of   the   church   the   correction   by

confession of things done wrong;   for through this means one can make one's own soul secure with the weapon of shame.

317,5.   This is like the case of a person who through excessive greed accumulates in himself a mixture of indigestible fluids, and then, when his body develops a fever, is treated with lancing and cauterization and has the disease as a sort of tutor in discipline for the rest of his life as he sees the scar of the cauterization on his body.   In the same way the person who has branded himself by confessing his secret sins will be given lessons by the memory of his feeling of shame for the rest of his life.

317,13 - 319,10

Solomon's involvement in wordly pleasure

317,13.   This therefore is what the church learns through the present reading of what is written in Ecclesiastes.   For Solomon says this quite frankly, making a public statement, and setting up for all to see, like a written notice, the confession of the things he has done, which are such that ignorance of them and silence are more honourable than words.   He says it;   whether he really did these things, or made the story up for our benefit, so that the argument might reach its logical conclusion, I cannot say precisely;   but nevertheless he does speak of things which nobody [p318] who was aiming at virtue would willingly be associated with.   However, whether it is by benevolent design that he discusses things which had not happened as if they had, and condemns them as though he had experienced them, in order that we might turn away from desire for what is condemned before the experience, or whether he deliberately lowered himself to the enjoyment of such things, so as to train his senses rigorously by using alien things, it is for each to decide freely for himself, whichever conjecture he likes to pursue.

318,8.   If however anyone were to say that Solomon really was involved in the practical experience of pleasures, I would agree.   He is like those who dive to the depths of the sea and search in the bottom of the water, to try to find there some pearl or other thing

of the kind produced in the depths;   their exertions under the water
bring them no pleasure, but it is the hope of gain that makes them
into divers;   in the same way, if Solomon engaged in these activities,
then surely, like one of the underwater purple-fishers, he submerged
himself in luxury not so as to fill himself with the salt of the sea
(by salt I mean pleasure), but to seek for something useful to the
mind in depths of this kind.   Something useful would be achieved by
such means, on the view I have adopted: either he has blunted the
body's appetites through [p319] making freely available what he wants
(for nature always moves more eagerly towards what is forbidden), or
else the teacher engages in these things to add plausibility, to make
no longer acceptable to mankind an activity which is spurned by the
person who has learnt its futility by experience.   In fact, it is said
that doctors particularly improve their skill in that case where they
become acquainted with the symptoms of an ailment through their own
bodies.   They become more reliable in diagnosing and treating such
complaints as they have come to understand by being treated
themselves in the past, insofar as they have already learnt from their
own suffering.

319,11 - 324,2   Eccl 2,4

The lavish and precious adornment of houses

319,11.   Let us see then what the Ecclesiast says he experienced,
since he heals our life through his account of his own.   I enlarged
my doing, he says, I built me houses.   The text begins straigh away
with an indictment: he does not say 'God's doing (poiema), which is
what I am myself,' but 'I enlarged my doing.'   'My doing' is nothing
other than what brings pleasure to the senses.   And this 'doing' is in
the generic sense singular, but by division into particulars it becomes
manifold, distributively, in the practices of luxury.   For once a
person is sunk in the depths of matter he will certainly cast his eye
round in all directions for a place from which pleasure could arise.

319,21.   From one spring water is channelled in different directions
through pipes, and [p320] the water distributed from the one source is

nevertheless one, though it may flow in thousands of channels; in the same way pleasure is one by nature, but flows this way and that, seeping into various activities, and everywhere insinuates itself alongside life's necessities.

320,5.   Thus life makes housing a necessity of nature; for humanity is too weak to bear the extremes of heat and cold; to this extent a house has a use to maintain life.   But pleasure forces the person to go beyond the bounds of necessity.   For when he is not providing essentials for the body, but concerns himself with things to please and delight the eyes, he is almost disappointed that he has not brought the sky itself inside the house, and cannot build the very beams of the sun into his roof.   This is why he extends the dimensions of his projected building in all directions, marking out the frontiers of his building like some New World, and makes the walls reach up as high as possible, and embellishes them with decorations inside the buildings, one design combining with another ... providing variety for furnishing the interior of the houses.

320,19.   Then [p321] stone from Laconia and Thessaly and from Carystos is split apart with iron tools into slabs, and the quarries of the Nile and of Numidia are scoured, and maybe even the Phrygian stone is called in for these endeavours, because, having sprinkled purple dye at random on the whiteness of its marble, it becomes a luxury for greedy eyes, as it depicts the pattern of the colour in many different forms and shapes against the white.   What great pains, what great ingenuity, are spent over these things, as some saw through the materials with water and iron, while others toil day and night with human hands as they finish the work of cutting!

321,11.   This still fails to satisfy those who toil over the futile decoration, but even the clarity of glass is stained different colours with dyes, so that this may also contribute something to the feast for the eyes.   One could hardly speak [p322] of the extravagant designs of the ceilings, against which pillars of wood made from trees change back through cunning art, and are reckoned as trees again, growing branches and leaves and fruit on the capitals.   I say nothing about the gold beaten into light and airy foil and wrapped completely round them, so as to draw the lust of the eyes towards itself, or about the contribution of ivory to the unnecessary embellishment of the doorways, and the gold with which their capitals are painted, or about the silver hammered on with studs — and everything else of the same kind. Why should one speak of the floors of the houses, gleaming with many-coloured stones, so that even their feet may luxuriate in the brilliance of light from the stones? — and the ostentatiousness of such buildings in the multiplicity of their parts, in which it is not the needs of life which make the provision necessary, but desire, which extends through useless things to invent what is not opportune.

322,16.   Some of the buildings must be promenades, some cloisters, some entrance-porches, some pre-entrance-porches, and others [p323] gate-extensions;   for they do not consider gates and gateways and the space inside the gates enough to boast of, if there is not something to confront visitors such as will immediately impress the person entering with the grandeur of the spectacle.   And, besides these, there are baths, going far beyond what is necessary in ostentatiousness, gushing with floods of water in whole rivers with the abundance of their streams;   and gymnasiums set up in front, themselves also over-ornamented with coloured marble for decoration; and porticos all round the building, supported on columns from Numidia or Thessaly or Syene;   and bronze statues fashioned into a thousand shapes — into whatever the desire for extravagance moulds the metal — and images in marble, and paintings on panels, through which they fornicate even with their eyes, as art exposes [p324] in a representation things which should not be seen, and whatever there is to see of the same kind, contrived for a striking and elegant effect.

324,3 - 327,20   Eccl 2,4

The spiritual adornment of those who dwell humbly

324,3.   How is it possible to give a detailed account of matters in which earnest effort is the indictment and proof of indifference about things of greater worth?   The more someone increases his efforts at construction in terms of size and extravagant use of materials, the more he proves the unadorned bareness of his soul. For one who looks to himself, and beautifies the dwelling which is really his own, so as eventually to take God into residence, has different materials from which beauty is gathered for such a dwelling. I know as gold, glittering with such works, that which is mined from the thoughts of scripture; I know as silver the divine words, refined in the fire, whose lustre flashes out, radiant with the truth. If you reckoned the glints from many different gemstones, with which the walls of such a temple are decorated, and the foundations of the building, to be the various virtuous habits, you would not be mistaken about the decoration proper to this house.

324,18.   Let the foundation be laid with self-control, through which the dust of earthly concerns will not disturb the life one leads.   Let the hope of heavenly things adorn the roof; by looking to that with the soul's eye, [p325] you will not fix your gaze on images of beauty shaped with chisels, but will see the archetype of Beauty itself, not decked out with any gold and silver, but a thing which is *precious above much gold and much gemstone* (Ps 19,10/18,11).   If there is need to include the decoration of the floors and walls in my account, then here let incorruptibility and freedom from passion pave the room, and there let justice and good temper adorn the dwelling; let humility and patience shine on one side, and on the other reverence for what is from God.   Let Love, the good craftsman, fit all these things to each other in proper order.   If you long for baths, you have, if you wish, even a domestic bath and private watertaps, with which you may wash away the stains of the soul - one which great David used *every night*, delighting in such a washing (Ps 6,7).

325,13.   As to pillars to support the portico of your soul, do not bother with any of Phrygian stone or of porphyry, but let steadfastness in every good thing, and stability, be for you much more precious than these material embellishments.   As for images of all kinds, in paintings and sculpture, which men devise to mimic the truth with falsehood, such a [p326] dwelling does not admit them, since in it the figures of true reality are complete.   If you long for promenades and cloisters, you have the pastimes of the commandments. For thus Wisdom speaks: *I walk in the ways of justice, and I lead my life in the midst of the ways of just action* (Prov. 8,20). How good it is to stroll and exercise one's soul in those, and making one's way through the place of the commandment, to return again and again to the same spot - that is, to fulfil again the commandment one has cherished, and not to tire as the path of piety leads one back a second or a third time, or many more.

326,9. Let the entrance porches and pre-entrance porches be beautified by integrity of character and graciousness of life. The person who in this manner decks out his building for beauty will think little of earthly materials, will not make demands on quarries, will not cross the Indian oceans to acquire the tusks of elephants, will not hire craftsmen of the superfluous, whose craft is limited to their material; instead he will have in his own home the wealth which provides the materials for this kind of construction; and free choice is wealth.

326,18. As long as he lives in the flesh he will care for the physical nature of his own body just enough to prevent its being deprived of anything necessary. He will surround himself with a dwelling sufficient [p327] only to keep him warm, if there is need of that, and to shelter him in turn when human bodies are scorched by the burning heat of the sun's rays; with the same end in view he will provide the shelter of clothing, to cover the nakedness of the body, not seeking out any purple-fishers and scarlet-dyers, or those who twist golden metal into thread, nor lavishing effort on silkworms from China and making the thread from them, with weavers' excessive labours, into clothes which are a blend of gold and purple; and he will meet his immediate needs with the food that comes to hand, disregarding culinary charms.

327,11. Content with little, he will give service through what befalls him in the flesh, and will devote his life to the care of his soul [Plat Apol 29d-30b etc], enlarging the doing of God and not his own, that he may never come himself into the necessity of publicly acknowledging his futile zeal through confession, as we have now

learned from the one who said, I enlarged my doing - not God's doing,
which is what he was himself, but his own, which is what the dwelling-
place of the flesh was, not restricted to necessities, but as
extensive as his futile desires.

327,21 - 331,10   Eccl 2,4

Vineyards and drunkenness

327,21.   The text adds to these arguments a confession of another
matter, something which one would not be wrong in calling the root
cause both of mental frenzy and of abnormal wild behaviour.   This is
the damage to the reason caused by wine.   For when he says I
enlarged my doing and I built me houses he adds to this also, I
planted [p328] me vineyards.   It is clear that I enlarged applies more
or less generally to the subsequent series of ideas.   With this
argument therefore he gives us to understand that, since the planting
of vines too exceeds what is needful through being 'enlarged', I
planted me vineyards — which amounts to saying, 'I prepared wood
for the fire, with which I stoked up the flames of pleasures,' or else,
'I buried my mind deep, piling drunkenness on my intellect like a burial
mound.'

328,8.   I planted me vineyards — I was not chastened, he says, by
the tale of the derangement of Noah, in which he too was stripped of
the dignity of decency by such a planting and exposed to the
onlookers as an object at once of pity and of ridicule.   To his more
loyal sons his unseemliness was thought worthy of pity, but to the
arrogant and boorish one the spectacle of his drunkenness was an
occasion for laughter (see Gen 9,20-23).

328,15.   The confession about planting vines encompasses a great
catalogue of effects on the person.   The text includes in its meaning
the full extent and nature of the effects caused by wine.   Who in
the world does not know that once wine immoderately exceeds what is
necessary, it is tinder for licentiousness, the means to self-
indulgence, injury to youth, [p329] deformity to age, dishonour for
women, a poison inducing madness, sustenance for insanity, destruction

to the soul, death to the understanding, estrangement from virtue? From it comes unjustified mirth, lamentation without reason, senseless tears, unfounded boasting, shameless lying, craving for the unreal, expectation of the impracticable, monstrous threats, groundless fear, unawareness of what is really to be feared, unreasonable jealousy, excessive bonhomie, the promise of impossible things; — not to mention the unseemly nodding of the head, the shaky, topheavy gait, the indecency due to immoderate intake, uncontrolled movement of the limbs, the bending of the neck which can no longer support itself on the shoulders, when the flabbiness brought about by the wine relaxes the neck-muscles.

329,13.   What caused the unlawful heinous act of incest with daughters?   What distracted Lot's mind from what was happening, when he both committed the heinous act and was ignorant of what he committed (Gen 19,30-38)?   Who invented, like a riddle, the weird names of those children?   How did the mothers of the accursed progeny become the sisters of their own children?   How did the boys have the same man both as father and grandfather?   Who was it who muddled their identity by breaking the law?   Was it not wine, exceeding moderation, which caused this unbelievable tragedy?   Was it not drunkenness which shaped such a myth into history [p330], one which surpasses real myths in its monstrosity?

330,1.   *They gave their father wine to drink* (Gen. 19,33.35), it says, and thus, when his reason was expelled, he was seized by the wine as by some madness and left to history this tragic tale, being robbed of sense by drunkenness at the moment of the heinous deed.   O those women who wickedly brought out the wine with them from the Sodomite cellars!   O the wicked love-cup they poured from an evil wine-bowl for their father!   How much better it would have been if that wine too had been destroyed with everything else in Sodom, before it became the means to such a tragedy!

330,12.   Since the evils which arise in life every day from wine are of such a kind and on such a scale, the one who without compunction publicizes his own condition by confession says that he has done this too - not only that he actually used wine, but that he also planned ways of making the supply of such stuff abundant. **I planted me vineyards**, he says, which the one who himself became a *fruitful vine* would not need (Ps 128/127,3;   and see Ezek 17,6), the spiritual vine, flourishing and abundant, twining round its own kind with the branches its life produces and the tendrils of love, and adorned, in place of leaves, with beauty of conduct, [p331] nurturing the sweet and mellow grapes of virtue.

331,1.   One who plants these things in his own soul, and cultivates the wine which makes glad the heart (Ps 104/103,15 and Ecclus 40,20), and is *working his own land* according to the words of Proverbs (Prov 12,11;   28,19), as the principles of such husbandry demand;   who hoes his life, as it were, with reason and pulls out the bastard suckers from the roots of the virtues, waters his soul with learning, and with the sickle of judicious thought prunes away his mind's crop of superfluous and profitless ideas – such a one will be most blessed in his husbandry, as he presses his own grapes into the cup of wisdom.

331,11 – 333,3   Eccl 2,5

The luxury of gardens

331,11.   Such viticulture is unknown to one who looks to the earth and loves what is from it.   For he adds to these things the adornments of wealth, vegetable-plots and gardens.   What need of gardens has he who looks to the one Garden?   What use have I for a vegetable-plot which grows plants, the food of the weak in health? If I sat in the one Garden, I should not be distracted towards the desire for many gardens.   If I kept my soul healthy, so as to be able to take more substantial food,   I should not be wasting my time on plants, growing for myself the food appropriate to illness.   But when once luxury comes in alongside necessity, and desire goes beyond its limits, [p332] then, after extravagant spending inside buildings, and money lavished on indoor futilities, a man turns his attention to outdoor luxury, and uses the natural open air in the service of pleasures.

332,4.   He has trees deliberately cultivated to be evergreen and
leafy, and to act as a roof in the open, so that he can luxuriate
outside as he does in the house, and the surface of the ground is
clothed by the skill of the gardeners with various leafy plants, so
that from every side all kinds of delight strike the eye, wherever he
turns his glance;   and he is always among the things dear to his
heart, and at each season of the year sees things out of season,
leaves in winter, and flowers before their time, and the tree-climbing
vine entwining its shoots with alien ones, and the smooth coils of ivy
against the trees;   and again all the types of fruit which are
artificially produced by crossing different species with each other,
giving an ambiguous impression in appearance and taste, so as to
seem to be both kinds when they are a mixture of two different ones.
All these things, and whatever else in horticulture art has invented by
distorting nature, which the need to maintain life did not require, but
was sought by undisciplined desire, *these, [p333] so the one who
makes confession of his deeds says, came about in his loving attention to vegetable-plots and gardens;   for the one who says, I planted
every tree of fruit, by using this comprehensive expression also
indicates that he has omitted nothing of this kind.

333,4 - 334,3   Eccl 2,6

Garden pools

333,4.   Then after the luxury indoors and out he does not leave even
water free from making a contribution to the pleasures, as though he
must find luxury all the elements: in the earth through the buildings,
in the air through the trees, in the water through the artificial sea.
For, to make the sight of the water add interest to the deception of
the eyes, the ground becomes a lake as the water is walled round, so
that swimming may bring joy to those who are washing their bodies,
and the stream which flows out may make the gardens more abundant
in flowers, as it divides in all directions according to the need for
irrigation.   For he says, I made me pools of water, to water from
them a copse producing trees.

333,15.   If I had the spring of the Garden - that is, training in the virtues through which the soul's dryness is moistened, I should despise earthly waters, whose pleasure is temporary and whose nature is transient.   Surely it would be better [p334] to tap for ourselves a little stream from the divine spring, from which the virtues of the soul germinate and are watered, so that the grove of good habits may flourish in our souls, through our Lord Jesus Christ, to whom be the glory for ever and ever.   AMEN.

The Fourth Homily

The text of Ecclesiastes 2,7-11

2,7   I got me slaves and slave-girls,
and homebred slaves were born for me,
and much property in cattle and sheep became mine,
above all who had been
before me in Jerusalem.

8   I gathered for me both silver and gold,
the peculiar treasure of kings and of the countries;
I got men and women singers,
and luxuries of sons of man,
men and women wine-pourers;

9   I was enlarged and I acquired more
than all those who had been
before me in Jerusalem;
my wisdom stood in me.

10   And all that my eyes wanted,
I did not withold from them,
I did not keep my heart
from every happiness,
for my heart rejoiced in all my labour,
and this became my portion
from my labour.

11   I looked at all my doings,
which my hands did,
and on all my labour, which I laboured to do,
and behold, all is futility and choice of spirit,
and there is no advantage under the sun.

334,4 - 338,22   Eccl. 2,7

The evils of slave-owning

334,5.   We still find the occasion for confession controlling the
argument.   The one who gives an account of his doings relates one
after another almost all the things through which the futility of the
activities of this life is recognized.   But now he reaches as it were
a more serious indictment of things he has done, as a result of which
one is accused of the feeling of Pride.   For what is such a gross
example of arrogance in the matters enumerated above - an opulent
house, and an abundance of vines, and ripeness in vegetable-plots, and
collecting waters in pools and channelling them in gardens - as for a
human being to think himself the master of his own kind?   I got me
slaves and slave-girls, he says, and homebred slaves were born for
me.   Do you notice the enormity of the boast?   This kind of language
is raised up as a challenge to God.   For we hear from prophecy that
all things are the slaves of the power that transcends all [Ps
119/118,91].   So, when someone [p335] turns the property of God into
his own property and arrogates dominion to his own kind, so as to
think himself the owner of men and women, what is he doing but
overstepping his own nature through pride, regarding himself as
something different from his subordinates?

335,5.   I got me slaves and slave-girls.   What do you mean?   You
condemn man to slavery, when his nature is free and possesses free
will*, and you legislate in competition with God, overturning his law
for the human species.   The one made on the specific terms that he
should be the owner of the earth, and appointed to government by the
Creator — him you bring under the yoke of slavery, as though defying
and fighting against the divine decree.

335,11.   You have forgotten the limits of your authority, and that
your rule is confined to control over things without reason.   For it
says *Let them rule over* winged creatures and fishes and four-footed
things and creeping things (Gen, 1,26).   Why do you go beyond what is
subject to you and raise yourself up against the very species which
is free, counting your own kind on a level with four-footed things and

even footless things? *You have subjected all things* to man, declares
the word through the prophecy, and in the text it lists the things
subject, *cattle* and *oxen* and *sheep* (Ps 8,7-8). Surely [p336] human
beings have not been produced from your cattle? Surely cows have
not conceived human stock? Irrational beasts are the only slaves of
mankind. But to you these things are of small account. *Raising*
fodder for the cattle, and green plants for the slaves of men, it
says (Ps 104/103,14). But by dividing the human species in two with
'slavery' and 'ownership' you have caused it to be enslaved to itself,
and to be the owner of itself.

336,6.   **I got me slaves and slave-girls.**   For what price, tell me?
What did you find in existence worth as much as this human nature?
What price did you put on rationality?   How many obols did you
reckon the equivalent of the likeness of God?   How many staters did
you get for selling the being shaped by God?   *God said, let us make*
man in our own image and likeness (Gen 1,26). If he is in the
likeness of God, and rules the whole earth, and has been granted
authority over everything on earth from God, who is his buyer, tell
me? who is his seller? To God alone belongs this power; or rather,
not even to God himself. For *his gracious gifts*, it says, *are*
irrevocable (Rom 11,29). God would not therefore reduce the human
race to slavery, since he himself, when we had been enslaved to sin,
spontaneously recalled us to freedom. But if God does not enslave
what is free, who is he that sets his own power above God's?

336,20.   How too shall the ruler of the whole earth and all earthly
things be put up for sale? [p337] For the property of the person sold
is bound to be sold with him, too. So how much do we think the
whole earth is worth? And how much all the things on the earth (Gen
1,26)? If they are priceless, what price is the one above them
worth, tell me? Though you were to say *the whole world*, even so
you have not found the price he is worth (Mat 16,26; Mk 8,36). He
who knew the nature of mankind rightly said that the whole world was
not worth giving in exchange for a human soul. Whenever a human
being is for sale, therefore, nothing less than the owner of the earth
is led into the sale-room. Presumably, then, the property belonging to

him is up for auction too.   That means the earth, the islands, the
sea, and all that is in them.   What will the buyer pay, and what will
the vendor accept, considering how much property is entailed in the
deal?

337,13.   But has the scrap of paper, and the written contract, and
the counting out of obols deceived you into thinking yourself the
master of *the image of God*? What folly! If the contract were lost,
if the writing were eaten away by worms, if a drop of water should
somehow seep in and obliterate it, what guarantee have you of their
slavery?   what have you to sustain your title as owner?   I see no
superiority over the subordinate [p338] accruing to you from the title
other than the mere title.   What does this power contribute to you as
a person? — not longevity, nor beauty, nor good health, nor
superiority in virtue.   Your origin is from the same ancestors, your
life is of the same kind, sufferings of soul and body prevail alike
over you who own him and over the one who is subject to your
ownership — pains and pleasures, merriment and distress, sorrows and
delights, rages and terrors, sickness and death.   Is there any
difference in these things between the slave and his owner?   Do they
not draw in the same air as they breathe?   Do they not see the sun
in the same way?   Do they not alike sustain their being by
consuming food?   Is not the arrangement of their guts the same?
Are not the two one dust after death?   Is there not one judgment
for them? — a common Kingdom, and a common Gehenna?

338,14.   If you are equal in all these ways, therefore, in what
respect have you something extra, tell me, that you who are human
think yourself the master of a human being, and say, **I got me slaves
and slave-girls,** like herds of goats or pigs.   For when he said, **I got
me slaves and slave-girls,** he added that abundance in flocks of sheep
and cattle came to him.   For he says, **and much property in cattle
and sheep became mine,** as though both cattle and slaves were subject
to his authority to an equal degree.

The uselessness of gold

338,23.   On top of this [p339] the confession goes even further to
the greatest of sins.   For he denounces himself for *the root of all
evils*, which is *the love of money* (I Tim 6,10).   He says this in these
very words, **I gathered for me both silver and gold**.   Why did he
disturb the gold mingled in the earth and poured out in those places
in which it was put from the beginning by its Maker?   What more did
the Creator make the earth owe you, besides its crops?   Did he not
allot you only the fruits and the seeds for food?   Why do you
overstep the bounds of your authority?   Or else, show me that these
things too have been granted to you by your Creator, that you may
mine what lies underground, and dig it up and refine it with fire, and
gather what you have not sown (cf Mat 25,26;   Lk 19,21).

339,12.   Perhaps, however, someone will think there is no objection to
gathering these riches thus for oneself from the mines in the earth.
But when to this sentence is added **the peculiar treasure of kings and
of the countries**, the meaning of 'gathering' no longer admits of an
innocent interpretation.   For as it is possible for royal power to
gather an abundance of riches from countries — that means, to
impose tribute, to exact tithes, to compel their subjects to pay taxes
— just so, he says, he has collected silver and gold.

339,21.   But whether like this, or otherwise, I should like to know
what will be the gain for the one [p340] who gathers such stuff.   Let
us grant for argument's sake that it comes to those who love riches
not by the mna or by the drachma or by the talent, but that
everything turns to gold for them together.   Let us suppose that the
earth, the sand, the mountains, the plains, the valleys, everything, has
suddenly been changed into this stuff all at once.   What more will
life give through these things in terms of happiness?   If he sees on
every side what he now sees on a small scale, which of the soul's
goods, or of the things sought after for the body, will accrue from
an abundance of this kind?   Thus, what hope is there, that someone
who lives amidst so much gold will thereby become wise, sagacious,

reflective, learned, a friend of God, prudent, pure, passion-free, detached and aloof from all that draws him down towards evil? or, alternatively, physically strong, pleasant to look at, extending life for many centuries, free from ageing, disease and pain, and all the things sought for in the life of the flesh? But nobody is so absurd or so unobservant of our common humanity as to think that these things would come to human beings, if only money were poured out before everyone in vast quantities on demand; even now one may see many of those already better endowed with such wealth living in a pitiful state of health, so that if their servants were not at hand they would not be able to go on living. If, therefore, the abundance of gold proposed in our argument [p341] offers no benefit in body or in soul, it is far more likely that when it is available on a small scale it will prove useless to those who possess it.

341,3.   What benefit would there be to its owner in the substance itself, which is inert to taste and smell and hearing, and which feels to the touch of the same value as all its rivals? Let nobody put as an objection the food or clothing obtained by purchase with gold. For someone who buys bread or clothes with gold gets something useful in exchange for something useless, and lives because he has made bread his food, not gold. But if a person gathers this stuff for himself through such transactions as these, what joy does he have of his money? what practical advice does he get from it? what training in public affairs? what prediction of the future? what comfort for the pains of the body? He gets it, he counts it, he stows it away, he stamps it with his seal, he refuses it when asked, he even swears by it when disbelieved. That is the blessedness, that is the object of endeavour, that is the benefit, that is the extent of the happiness — to provide himself with the means of committing perjury!

341,18.   'But gold is a fine colour to look at', he says. Surely not finer even than fire? or more beautiful than the stars? or brighter than the rays of the sun? Who is to prevent you from enjoying these, that [p342] you have to provide pleasures for the eyes through the fine colour of gold? 'But fire goes out,' he says, 'and the sun sets, and the beauty of the bright display is not sustained'. Tell me, what is the difference in the dark between gold and lead?

342,5. 'But we could not get necklaces from fire or the stars,' he says, 'and bracelets and buckles and belts and collars and crowns and things like that;   but gold does make these, and everything else needed for adornment.'   His case for the substance has taken his enthusiasm to the height of futility.   This is what I would say to them: What is the purpose of the person who decorates the hair with gold, or fits earrings into the ears, or fastens an ornamental necklace round the delicate #neck or wears gold on some other part of the body?   He displays the gold wherever he happens to have put it on the body, but is not in any way changed into the gleam of the gold himself.   For anyone who looks at the gold-clad person sees the gold in the same way as if it happened to be on display in the market, but [p343] he sees the wearer just as he naturally is.

343,1.   Even if the gold is well-made and shaped, and even if you set in it stones which are green or fiery-bright, the person does not any more for that assume the appearance of what is attached to him, but if there is some blemish on his face or if he is without some feature — an eye lost, or a cheek gouged out in an ugly scar — the deformity remains in his appearance, not at all concealed by the gleam of the gold;   and if someone happens to be in some bodily pain, the stuff brings him no comfort in his distress.

343,10 - 346,14   Eccl 2,8

Against usury

343,10.   If therefore something brings no benefit to those who pursue it, whether in terms of beauty or of physical well-being or of the relief of pains, for what reason is it pursued?   and what is the affection of those who have set their heart on the stuff, when they come to be aware of such a possession?   do they congratulate themselves because they have gained something?   If someone were to ask them whether they would welcome the chance to have their nature changed into it, and themselves to become what is honoured among them with such affection, would they choose the change, so as to be transformed from humanity into gold, and be proved no longer rational, intelligent, or able to use the sense-organs for living, but yellow and heavy and speechless, lifeless and senseless, as gold is? I do not think that even those [p344] who set their desire passionately on the stuff would choose this.

344,1. If, therefore, for right-thinking people it would be a kind of curse to acquire the properties of this inanimate stuff, what is the mindless frenzy over the acquisition of things whose goal is futility, so that for this reason those who are driven mad with the desire for riches even commit murders and robbery? - and not only these things, but also the pernicious idea of interest (tokōn <literally 'children'>), which one might call another kind of robbery or bloodshed without being far from the truth. What is the difference between getting someone else's property by seizing it through covert housebreaking or taking possession of the goods of a passer-by by murdering him, and acquiring what is not one's own by exacting interest? What a misuse of words! 'Child' (tokos <= interest>) becomes a name for robbery. What a sour marriage! What an evil union, which nature knows not, but which the vice of the covetous invented between inanimate parties! What intolerable pregnancies, from which such a 'child' is produced!

344,16. Among created things, only what is living can be divided into the male and the female (Gen 1,27). It was to them that God their Creator said, Increase and multiply (Gen 1,22 and 28), so that through producing children one from another the new life might increase abundantly; but from what kind of marriage is the 'child' of gold generated? From what sort of pregnancy is it produced? I know the pains of such childbirth, as I learn from the prophet, Behold, he says, he was in labour with injustice, he conceived toil and gave birth to wickedness (Ps 7,14/15). This is that 'child' [p345] with which greed was in labour, and to which wickedness gave birth, and whose midwife is miserliness. The one who always conceals his fortune, and swears that he has nothing — when he sees someone crushed by want, then he appears pregnant in the wallet, then he is in labour with the evil 'child' of desire for profit, he holds out hope of a loan to the one

in distress, he piles money on his misfortune like someone quenching a
fire with oil.

345,7.   For he does not heal the injury with the loan, but makes it
worse;   and, as in times of drought the fields produce crops of
thistles of their own accord, so also among the calamities of those
in financial straits the 'children' of the extortioners run riot.   It is
then he reaches out his hand full of money, as the line reaches out
the hook concealed in the bait, and the victim, snapping at his
momentary prosperity, disgorges all his hidden inner parts with the
hook when it is pulled.   Such are the benefits of interest (tokōn)!

345,16.   If someone takes someone else's money by force, or steals
it secretly, he is called a violent criminal or a burglar or something
like that (Aristotle, *Eth Nic* I 5 1096a 5);   but the one who
advertises his felony in financial agreements, and who provides
evidence of his own cruelty, and who [p346] enforces his crime by
contracts, is called a philanthropist and a benefactor and a saviour
and all the worthiest of names;   and the profit from thieving is
called 'loot', but the person who strips his debtor naked by this kind
of compulsion gives his harshness the euphemism 'philanthropy'.   This
is what they call the damage done to those in distress.

346,6.   I gathered for me both silver and gold.   Yes, but the reason
why the one who trains mankind wisely includes this also in the list of
things confessed is that human beings may learn, from one who has
formed the judgment from experience, that this is one of the things
condemned as wrong, and may guard before the experience against the
onslaught of evil, just as it is possible to pass unscathed by places
infested with robbers and wild animals through the previous knowledge
of others previously imperilled there.

346,15 – 348,14   Eccl 2,8

The perils of music and wine

346,15.   The divine apostle gives an excellent description of the
passion of money-loving, when he declares it to be the *root of all*

the evils (1 Tim 6,10). For just as, if a humour accumulates in some part of the body, infected and festering, and inflammation develops in the place, it is absolutely essential for relief and elimination that the collected fluid should burst out when the pus has eaten through the surface, so, in the case of those [p347] infected by the disease of money-loving, the condition for the most part issues in intemperate behaviour. For this reason, next to the abundance of silver and gold he puts the consequent indecency which results from the disease already caught.   I got **men and women singers**, the **luxuries** at the **banquets, men and women wine-pourers**. The mention of the names is enough to expose the passion, the very thing the money-disease has prepared the way for.

347,8.   What a grotesque art-form this is!   What a massive assault the flood of pleasures makes, swamping souls by a twofold torrent, through hearing and sight, so that evil may be both seen and heard! The singing overcomes hearing, the sight prevails over sight.   On the one hand, a treble voice brings with it passions into the heart through the melting harmony of the songs;   on the other, what is seen, assaulting like a siege-engine the eyes of one already quite undone by the singing, overcomes his soul.   The wine is captain in this assault, shooting down the man with pairs of arrows like a deadly archer, aiming the points of the pleasures at hearing and sight;   for the singing becomes a weapon against the hearing, and what is seen, against the sight.

347,21.   The name 'wine-pourers' is not without significance, but the title comes precisely from the job.   When, therefore, [p348] the neat wine is poured out freely for the drinkers, and young persons perform such a service, adorned for beauty, whether they are boys dressed like women or actually of the female sex, busy at the feast and mixing the unseemly stimulant in the loving-cups, what end can such pursuits possibly have?   The one who makes pleasure the goal of each of his activities and pays attention to superfluous matters, the adornment of women musicians for singing, and what dress to put on the wine-pourers — we must be silent on such matters, rather than go deeply into these details in our speech, so that recalling them may

not by the very description aggravate the wounds of the more passionate.   The reasons for the gold, the purposes of the silver, were
this: that you might procure things of this kind as luxurious baits.

348,15 - 353,9   Eccl 2,9-11

Insinuating pleasure and the Ecclesiast's experience of it

348,15. Perhaps that is why the sense of pleasure is called in
scripture a *serpent* (Gen 3,1), which has the natural ability, if its
head slips into a chink in the wall, to pull all the rest of its coils in
behind it.   What do I mean?   Nature makes housing necessary for
humans, but [p349] pleasure, slipping by means of this need into the
chink in the soul, turns the need into an immoderate extravagance in
beautification and transfers the urge to that. Then it is to vines and
pools and gardens and the adornment of vegetable-plots that the
beast, pleasure, crawls onward.   After this she comes to a peak of
arrogance and winds pride round her, fastening under her the dominion
over her own kindred.   She drags her coil of desire for money over
these, and with that necessarily goes licence, the hindmost part and
tail of the bestiality of pleasure.

349,10.   *Just as it is impossible for the snake to be dragged out
by the end of its tail from the hole it creeps down into, since the
scales naturally [p350] pull in the opposite direction to those tugging
it, so it is not possible to begin from the end-results to expel the
insinuation of pleasure, unless one has prevented evil entering in the
first place.   Therefore the guide in virtue also bids us *watch for its
head* (Gen 3,15), calling the beginnings of evil 'head', since if this is
not allowed in the remainder is ineffectual.   The one who has entirely
set his face against pleasure will not be brought down by the individual onslaughts of passion, but the one who has let in the beginning
of passion has admitted the whole beast into himself.

350,10.   This is why, after going through everything, the one who
publicly describes such emotions brings his account to a head.   For
having said at the start, I enlarged my doing, he now adds after the
detailed exposition of what he has done, I was enlarged, showing that

knowledge of what should be resisted came to him not through small
examples, but in such a way that his experience advanced to the
greatest possible extent, so that no memory of like things among his
predecessors equalled it.   For he says I was enlarged and I acquired
more than all those who had been before me in Jerusalem.

350,19. *And now he reveals the purpose for which, when he was
already trained in all wisdom, he descended to the experience of such
things.   For, My wisdom, he says, stood in me.   By these words he
means, 'Through wisdom I explored every conceivable enjoyment, and
understanding stood in me at the highest pinnacle of what was [p351]
found there.   For sight worked alongside desire, and free choice
through the pleasure of the sights took its fill of desirable things;
so nothing was omitted of the things considered as enjoyment, but
participation in pleasurable things became to me a portion of
property.' That seems to me to mean nothing else but this: 'I
encompassed in myself every conceivable enjoyment, reaping happiness
from what happened as from a piece of property.   I did not keep my
heart, he says, from every happiness, and my heart rejoiced in all my
labour, and this became my portion from all my labour - meaning by
'portion' his property.

351,11. When, therefore, he has recounted his extravagance in detail,
running through it from beginning to end and recounting in his tale
everything from which pleasures are gathered by those who enjoy them
— the beauties of buildings, vines, vegetable-plots, pools, gardens, rule
over one's kindred, excessive riches, the provision of entertainment at
feasts — all the luxuries, as he names them himself, which his wisdom
studied, investigating and bringing to his understanding the kind of
thing which he says he enjoyed with every sense, the eyes finding
what pleased them and the soul having all it desired, without restraint
— then he interprets the first word, which was uttered in the
introduction to the work, [p352] declaring that all things are futile.
He says that when he saw these things he declared of human life, all
things are futility, all that the sense sees and whatever is pursued
for happiness by mankind.   I looked at all my doings, which my hands
did, and on all my labour, which I laboured to do, and behold, all is

futility and choice of spirit, and there is no advantage under the sun. For all power and activity of the senses has life under the sun as its limit, and the sensual nature cannot reach what is beyond it and comprehend the good things which lie above. After examining all such things, therefore, he trains mankind to be favourably inclined to nothing here, such as wealth, ambition, rule over subjects, revelry and luxury and feasts and everything else which is reckoned estimable, but to see that the only end of such things is futility, whose advantage is afterwards not to be found.

352,17.   People who write in water are engaged in drawing the shapes of the letters in the liquid by writing with the hand, but nothing remains of the shape of the letters, and the interest in the writing consists solely in the act of writing (for the surface of the water continually follows the hand, obliterating what is written);   in the same way all enjoyable interest [p353] and activity disappears with its accomplishment.   When the activity ceases the enjoyment too is wiped out, and nothing is stored up for the future, nor is any trace or remnant of happiness left to the pleasure-takers when the pleasant activity passes away.   This is what the text means when it says there is no advantage under the sun for those who labour for such things, whose end is futility;   and may we too be beyond them, by the grace of our Lord Jesus Christ, to whom be the glory for ever. AMEN.

The Fifth Homily

The text of Ecclesiastes 2,12-26

2,12   I looked myself to see wisdom,

and also dizziness and folly;

for what man is there, who will go after counsel,

the many things she has made?

13   and I saw that there is advantage for wisdom over

folly,

as advantage of light over darkness;

14   the wise man, his eyes are in his head,

but the fool walks in darkness.

15   I learned, even I,

that one fate will happen to them all.

And I said in my heart,

that the fool's fate

will happen also to me,

and for what have I become wise?

I spoke a superfluous thing in my heart,

because the fool speaks from superfluity

because this too is futility.

16   For the memory of the wise is not

with the fool for ever,

inasmuch as now are the days which are coming,

all things have been forgotten;

and how shall the wise die with the fool?

17   And I hated together life,

because the doing is wicked in me,

that is done under the sun,

because all is futility and choice of spirit.

18   And I hated all my toil,

which I toil at under the sun,

because I shall leave it to the man who comes

after me;

19   and who knows whether he will be a wise man or a

fool,

and if he will take control in all my toil,

at which I toiled and became wise under the sun?

this also is futility.

20   I myself turned to reject the thought of my heart

in all my toil, at which I toiled under the sun,

21   that there is a man, that his toil

is in wisdom and in knowledge and in courage,

and a man, to him who has not toiled in it

he will give him his portion;

this also is futility and great evil.

22   For he knows that for man in all his toil

and in choice of his heart,

in which he toils under the sun,

23   that all his days

are his distraction of pains and passion,

and in the night his heart does not rest;

this also is futility.

24   There is no good in a man;

what he shall eat and drink and show to his soul

is good in his toil.

This also I saw, that it is from God's hand;

25   for who shall eat and who shall drink apart from

him?

26   For to the man, the good one

before his face, he has given wisdom

and knowledge and joy;

and to the sinner he has given distraction,

to add and to collect,

to give to the good before the face of God;

because this too is futility and choice of spirit.

353,10 - 354,24

Turning from evil the prelude to higher wisdom

353,10.   Now there comes to us from the great guide of the church initiation into the higher kinds of learning.   After purging souls with the foregoing words, and removing the desire for futility which human beings conceive, he applies his mind to the truth, shaking off the load of futile things like a burden from his shoulders.   Let the church be trained in such matters as fundamental, learning through the teaching before us that [p354] the escape from evil is the beginning of the virtuous life.

354,2.   Even great David, who gives elementary guidance for pure conduct in the Psalms, does not begin his work with the final achievement of the things considered in his blessing.   For he does not say in his opening that the person is blessed who prospers in all things, who resembles a tree which takes root at the channels of the waters, who is constantly fruitful in good things, who in due season gathers the harvest of his own life;   instead he makes separation from evil the beginning of blessing, so that he cannot become good until after the filth of evil has been washed away (Ps 1,1-3).   So therefore this great Ecclesiast first eliminates futile things in his discussion, so that, as with a sick person, when the disease has been cured by proper treatment, the benefit of good health may come in. This is why he inveighs against futility in his work, says that sense is not a safe yardstick of the good, brings before our eyes the unreality in our pursuits, separates passionate inclination from physical enjoyment;   and so he indicates what we should really choose, what we should truly desire, whose goal is something actual and substantial, and which remains for ever for those who share in it, separated from all thought of what is futile. [p355]

355,1 - 356,19   Eccl 2,12-13

The higher wisdom in which all that is real consists

355,1.   I looked myself, he says, to see wisdom.   So that I might see precisely what I longed for, I first looked also at #dizziness and

folly. The understanding of objects desired becomes more exact when
we compare them with their opposites. He also calls wisdom counsel,
for, he says, what man is there, who will go after counsel, the many
things she has made?. He therefore teaches what human wisdom is,
that to follow the real wisdom, — which he also calls counsel, which
brings about what truly is and has substance, and is not thought of
as among futile things, — to follow that is the sum of human wisdom;
but real wisdom and counsel, on my reckoning, is none other than the
Wisdom which is conceived of as before the universe. It is that
wisdom by which God made all things, as the prophet says, *by wisdom
you made all things* (Ps 104/103,24), and *Christ is the power of God
and the wisdom of God* (I Cor 1,24), by which all things came to be
and were set in order. If, therefore, this is human wisdom, to have
pondered the true works of real Wisdom and Counsel, and if, as I
reckon, the work of that Counsel, or Wisdom, is immortality, blessedness of soul, courage, justice, prudence, and every name and idea
applied to virtue, then perhaps in consequence [p356] we are being led
on to the knowledge of good things.

356,1. When I saw these things, he says, and weighed, as in a
balance, what is, against what is not, I found that the difference
between wisdom and folly was the same as one would find if light
were measured against the dark. I think it is appropriate that he
uses the analogy of light in the discernment of the good. Since
darkness is in its own nature unreal (for if there were nothing to
obstruct the sun's rays, there would be no darkness), whereas light is
of itself, perceived in its own essence, he shows by this analogy that
evil does not exist by itself, but arises from deprivation of good,
whereas good is always as it is, stable and steadfast, and does not
arise from the deprivation of anything which is prior to it. What is
perceived as essentially opposed to good, is not; for what in itself
is not, does not exist at all; for evil is the deprivation of being,
and not something existing. Thus the difference is the same between
light and darkness and between wisdom and folly. Part for whole, he
embraces all good in the word 'wisdom' and includes the nature of evil
in his understanding of 'folly'.

356,20 - 360,22   Eccl 2,14

The eyes of the wise are spiritually in his head

356,20. What would be the use of our revering the good, if some
means of acquiring it had not also been indicated by the teacher?
Let us hear, therefore, from the teacher how we too can come to
participate in the good. The wise man, [p357] he says, *his eyes are
in his head. What does this mean? Is there any animal at all which
has its eye-organs anywhere but in its head, whether you speak of
creatures in water, or on land, or in the air? In every one, the eye
is set in the front of the body, and planted on the head of such as
have heads. Why then does he say here that only the wise man's
head is equipped with eyes?

357,7. What he means by the saying is surely this, that there is an
analogy between what is thought to belong to the soul and the parts
of the body. As in the bodily conformation the part which projects
from the rest is called a head, so too in the soul the leading and
foremost part is presumed to act as head; and in the same way as
we refer to the base of the foot as the 'heel', so there could also
be a base of the soul, through which it is in contact with the
organism of the body, and applies the force and activity of the
senses to what lies below. Whenever the soul's power of vision and
contemplation is engaged with the objects of sense, its eyes are
transferred to its heels, and through them it sees the things below,
remaining unable to see the sights above. But if it should learn the
futility of what lies below, and raise its eyes to its own Head, which
is Christ, as Paul explains (Eph 1,22; 4,15; Col 1,18; 2,19), it would
be blessed in its clarity of vision, [p358] having its eyes where the
obscuring effect of evil does not exist. Great Paul and others great
like him had eyes in the head, and so have all those who live and
move and are in Christ (cf Acts, 17,28). For as the one who is in
light cannot see darkness, so the one who has his eye in Christ
cannot fix it on anything futile. The one, therefore, who has eyes in
the head (by head we mean the Origin of everything) has his eyes in

every virtue (for Christ is perfect virtue) — in truth, in justice, in immortality, in every good thing.

358,11. **The wise man's eyes, then, are in his head, but the fool walks in darkness.** For the one who does not display his light on a lamp-stand (Mat 5,15; Mark 4,21; Luke 8,16; 11,33), but puts it underneath the bed, makes light into darkness for himself, becoming a manufacturer of the unreal — and the unreal is futile. Thus darkness is equivalent in meaning to futility. The fool's soul, which has become a body-loving and fleshlike thing, in looking at these things looks at nothing; for clarity of vision of these things is truly darkness. Do you see how those clever ones, well-versed in the world, whom we call attorneys, deliberately facilitate injustice for themselves, by means of witnesses, advocates, documents, and currying favour with the judges, both to achieve wrong and to avoid punishment? Who does not admire [p359] the shrewdness and circumspection of such people? But all the same they are blind, if they are compared with that eye which looks to things above, and which is set in the Head of what is. Utterly blind are those who lovingly adorn the heel which is torn by the fangs of the serpent; the means by which they look at things below are the means by which they wound themselves with the toothmarks of sin. *The one who loves injustice hates his own soul* (Ps 11/10,5), and their happiness among human beings is to be pitied more than any ill-fortune.

359,9. Again, on the other hand, how many people, filled with the good things on high and occupied in the contemplation of what really is, are regarded as blind and senseless in material affairs, the sort of person Paul also boasted of being, calling himself 'a fool for Christ's sake', for his understanding and wisdom were engaged in none of the things pursued here on earth; so when he says *we are fools for Christ's sake* (I Cor 4,10), it is as though he were saying, 'we are blind to the life below, because we look to what is above and have our eyes in the head'. This is why he was without shelter or food, poor, vagrant, naked, worn out with hunger and thirst (II Cor 11,27). But the one who is like this on earth, look what he is like in the places above! [p360] Lifted up *as far as the third heaven* (II Cor

12,2), where his Head was, he had eyes there, as he rejoiced in the secret mysteries of paradise, and saw the invisible things, and delighted in all those things which are beyond perception and sense.

360,4.   Who would not think him pitiable. seeing him a prisoner, smitten with blows, in the deep after shipwreck, tossed to and fro by the waves, chains and all (II Cor 11,23-26)?   Nevertheless, though his human circumstances were such as these, he did not cease to have his eyes in the head, saying, *Who shall separate us from the love of God in Christ Jesus? Shall tribulation, or oppression, or persecution, or hunger, or nakedness, or peril, or the sword* (Rom 8,35)?   This is equivalent to saying, 'Who shall gouge out the eyes from my head and move them to the trodden and earthy part of me?'   This same thing he instructs us to do in his invitation to think of the things above — which is like saying, to have eyes in the head.   *If we now understand how **the wise** man's **eyes are in his head**, let us flee from folly, which is **darkness** to those who walk in this life. **The fool**, he says, **walks in darkness**.   The fool, as the prophecy says, is the one who says in his heart that there is no God, and who is corrupt and disgusting in his habits (Ps 14/13,1).

#360,22 - 364,6   Eccl 2,15-26

Summary of objections to the life of virtue;   their refutation

360,22.   The subsequent argument, [p361] through its next words, seems to favour those who take a narrow view restricted to this life. For them death is considered an evil, and there is held to be no advantage in virtuous living for those who partake of the higher life, on the ground that in both cases life has the same end, and it is not possible to devise an escape from death by a more decent life. Making such objections as these as it were from his own person, he again deals with the wickedness of those who make these claims, on the grounds that they take no account of the nature of what really is, and he teaches the difference, that is, the way in which virtue has the advantage over evil, not because any sort of equal value is expected in them by reason of the common experience of death, but because of the difference found between the good and evil things awaiting hereafter. He expresses the contrast like this: I learned, even I, that one fate will happen to them all. And I said in my heart, that the fool's fate will happen also to me, and for what have I become wise? I spoke a superfluous thing in my heart, because the fool speaks from superfluity, because this too is futility. For the memory of the wise is not with the fool for ever, inasmuch as now are the days which are coming, all things have been forgotten; and how shall the wise die with the fool?

361,22. He goes on next to think hateful everything to [p362] which he had formerly been addicted, when he embraced the futile as if it were good; and he says that he has hated all those things he toiled over when he looked to this life, because none was for himself, but all his toil was for the one after him, and for what purpose he will use what has been toiled over it is impossible to predict, beause of uncertainty about the future. The text puts it like this: And I hated together life, because the doing is wicked in me that is done under the sun, because all is futility and choice of spirit. And I hated all my toil, which I toil at under the sun, because I shall leave it to the man who comes after me; and who knows whether he will be a wise man or a fool, and if he will take control in all my toil, at which I toiled and became wise under the sun? This also is futility.

362,13. Having said this, he says that he is opposed in his mind also to the proposition that the portion is the same for the one who has lived virtuously as for the one who has made no effort at it. For the one, he says, toil is in wisdom and knowledge and courage, but for the other in the passion and pains arising from concern with this life. To treat these as on an equal footing, he says, denotes not only futility but also wickedness. This passage runs thus: [p363] I myself turned to reject the thought of my heart in all my toil, at which I toiled under the sun, that there is a man, that his toil is in wisdom and in knowledge and in courage, and a man #who has not toiled in it, he will give him his portion; this also is futility and great evil. For he knows, for man in all his toil and in choice of his heart, in which he toils under the sun, that all his days are his

distraction of pains and passion, and in the night his heart does not
rest;   this also is futility.

363,10.   Again he puts to himself another objection from those who
judge the life of enjoyment more worthwhile than the higher life, and
overturns the proposal, recounting both sides in his own person, both
the refutation and the objection.   The objection is that one ought to
think nothing good except what one admits into oneself, that is, food
and drink;   but the reply to this is that these are not the things
through which mankind is nourished and cheered, but wisdom and
understanding, since it is good to be concerned about these things,
whereas concern for the flesh is distraction of soul and futility.
The words of the sublime teaching take this form: There is no good
in a man;   #what he shall eat and drink and show to his soul is good
in his toil.   This also [p364] I saw, that it is from God's hand;   #for
who shall eat and who shall drink apart from him?   For to the man,
the good one before his face, he has given wisdom and knowledge and
joy, and to the sinner he has given distraction, to add and to
collect, to give to the good before the face of God;   because this
too is futility and choice of spirit.

364,7 - 370,11   Eccl 2,15-18

First objection: The same fate for the wise and the fool
Eccl 2,15

364,7.   Such is the sense of the next passage, and the preliminary
interpretation of the argument, as I have just briefly stated.   But
now it is perhaps time to return to the text and fit the thoughts
exactly to the words.   And I learned, even I, that one fate will befall
them all.   And I said that the fool's fate will happen also to me, and
for what have I become wise?   This is the objection which he makes
to himself, saying, 'If the fate of death is one for both, and virtue
does not rescue from participation in death the one made wise, the
quest for wisdom has been for me in vain.'

364,18.   What is the reply of scripture to these words?   I, he says,
spoke this superfluous thing in my heart, because the fool speaks

from superfluity, because this too is futility. For a memory of the wise is not with the fool for ever. He condemns this objection as superfluously and illogically raised, and calls the argument foolish, [p365] since it is not in the store of sayings, nor is it put forward from the treasuries of wisdom, but is like some superfluous piece of thought, spat out as froth. For the fool, he says, speaks from superfluity; and to cite the words without sense is futile and unprofitable, since the words have no other purpose than to persuade people not to look at visible things.

First answer: The wise lives, the fool is forgotten Eccl 2,16-17

365,7. The objector bases his attack on what is seen: for death too is one of the visible things; so what does he say? 'Does not the distinction between the virtuous and the wicked life consist of this, that only the wicked person has to die in body, while the good remains exempt from bodily death?' — unaware what the immortality of virtue consists of, and what the death is of those who live evil lives.

365,13. For the memory of the wise, he says, lives for ever and lasts as long as eternity, but even the remembrance of the fool is extinguished with him. On such matters the prophet also says, *Their memory has perished* — conspicuously and plainly; for that is what the addition of their *sound* shows (Ps 9,6/7). He says, a memory of the wise is not with the fool for ever, but the life of the wise endures through the memory, while oblivion embraces [p366] the fool; for in the days coming all the fool's affairs are in oblivion, as he puts it in the text, inasmuch as now are the days which are coming, all things have been forgotten.

366,3. If therefore the wise lives in wisdom, but the fool has vanished in the death of oblivion, how, he says, do you say that the wise will die with the fool? This is why he is grieved and ashamed of the things he was concerned with in this life, and says he hates everything he vigorously sought after in this life, suffering the same thing as someone who has gorged himself shamelessly on drugged honey, out of greed, and then, when the delicacy turns to a foul taste for him, he catches in his vomit the flavour of the drug mixed in the honey, as he spews it out, and so because of the memory of his nausea he hates honey, since indulgence in it with the drug caused his upset.   For this reason the one who fills himself full of the pursuits of luxury, and in the vomit of his confession feels loathing and disgust at the shame of what he has done, as at the taste of something noxious, cries that he hates that life, saying in just these words, And I hated together life, because the doing is wicked in me, that is done [p367] under the sun.   Not for anyone else, he says, but for myself I have become wicked, in the things I did under the sun. For nothing I did stands, but all that I pursued is vanity and impulse of choice.   All is futility, he says, and choice of spirit.

   *Second answer: Another inherits   Eccl 2,18-19
367,5.   He goes on to say that concern for things here is hateful, because a person works not for himself but for the one after him, whatever he may achieve by his efforts in this life — docks, harbours, brilliant and ornate constructions of parapets and buildings, gateways and towers and colossal statues, and the work cherished on the ground, varied groves of trees and beautiful meadows, and vineyards wide enough to imitate the sea, and whatever else there is of that sort, which anyone who may have done the work works at, while the one who lives in the world after him enjoys it.
367,15.   *Nor is it clear that he will not make his own abundance a cause of evil.   Not everybody can for the sake of knowledge indulge his senses in the experience of such things, 'which I have done,' he says, 'at wisdom's behest.   Having for a while set the impulse of nature free, like a young colt, to gambol as it wished in the lower passions, I bridled it with the harness of reason and [p368] curbed it with the force of intellect.   Who knows,' he says, 'whether even that one who at a time after us comes among these will be in control of enjoyment, and will not instead be mastered by it himself, bowing slavishly to the force of pleasure?'   For this reason, he says, I hated all my toil, which I toil at under the sun, for I shall leave it to the one who *comes after me.   And who knows whether he will be a wise man or a fool, and if he will take control in all my toil, at which I toiled and became wise under the sun?

368,9.   I think the meaning of this saying is this, that he did not slide down passively to the life of enjoyment, but came to it by some reason of wisdom, deliberately acquiring a share in it, and not himself being mastered by this dominating power.   'Who can be sure,' he therefore says, 'that my successor will not be controlled by these things at which I toiled, not from passion, but prompted by wisdom?' He makes clear, by calling luxury toil, that he forced himself to undertake engagement with pleasure, like some difficult conflict. 'Even this, then', he says, 'must be counted among the futile things.'

Third answer: It is wicked to regard worldliness and virtuous life as the same   Eccl 2,20-23

368,18.   There is yet another of the things here which he says his soul has renounced, and in the text he makes clear what he means. He takes issue with the offence against sound judgment, when someone, seeing that the difference between two contrasting lives is obvious, because one of them works hard for virtue and [p369] directs his desire to no human end, while the other, on the contrary, endures no hard work in the virtues, but devotes himself to bodily effort alone, — when that person still gives his vote about the good to this life, disregarding the life superior in wisdom, then the Ecclesiast declares that this wrong judgment is not only futile but also evil. He expresses it in these words: **I myself turned to reject the thought of my heart besides the other toil, at which I toiled under the sun. What is it I rejected? That there is a man, that his toil is in wisdom and in knowledge and in courage**, and there is another man who has spent no labour on such things. How then will anyone give his portion of esteem to someone like this? **And a man**, he says, **to him who has not toiled in it** (that is, to the one who has not toiled in the good) **he will give him his portion** (in other words, he will deem this kind of life to be something good). But **this**, he says, **is futility and great evil.**

369,16.   How can it not be **great evil**, when he knows the purpose and choice about his toils which reside in the man? This is what is meant when he says, **For he knows, for man in all his toil and in the choice of his heart, in which he toils under the sun** — What is it that

he knows? — that all his days, he says, are his distraction of pains
and passion, and in the night his heart does not rest. Certainly for
those who [p370] devote the soul to this distraction, life is painful,
pricking the soul with desires for more, like goads, and the pursuit of
profit is agonizing, not enjoying the things it has so much as
regretting those that are missing; for them, work is allocated to
both day and night, carried on successively through each in turn, with
the day spent in toil, and the night banishing sleep from the eyes;
for thoughts of profit drive away sleep. How then can the one who
observes these things fail to give his verdict against the futility of
this quest? This is why he adds these words to his text: this also is
futility.

370,12 – 372,19   Eccl 2,24-26

   Second objection: Food and drink are God-given   Eccl 2,24

370,12. Again he deals with another objection, and the point raised
is this: 'If you count what is outside us as futile, O Teacher, what
we take up into ourselves could not reasonably be condemned as
futile. And yet food and drink get to be inside us. Surely this sort
of thing is not to be discarded, but one might reckon such a benefit
as a divine gift.' Such is the sense of the objection, but the words
of the text take this form: *There is no good in a man; what he
shall eat and drink and show to his soul is good in his toil. And this
also I saw, that it is from God's hand; for who shall eat and who
shall drink apart from him*? [p371] That is how the advocate of
gluttony makes out his case against the Teacher.

First answer: God gives to the good man wisdom, knowledge and joy
                                                        Eccl 2,24

371.2. What does the Guide in wisdom say in reply to the man, the
good one? The addition of 'the good one' surely also indicates the
contrast, so that it is clear from its opposite what is understood by
goodness. So to man — not the bullock-shaped man who is bent down
over his own belly, and has got a gullet instead of a faculty of
reason, but the man who is good and lives in the image of the one

Good — God did not ordain this food, which the bestial nature craves, but he has given him, he says, instead of food, **wisdom and knowledge and joy.**

371,11. How could anyone increase goodness through what nurtures the flesh? *Man shall not live by bread alone* (Mat 4,4) is the word of the true Word; virtue is not nourished by bread, nor does the power of the soul grow healthy and fat on steaks. It is on different dishes that the sublime life is nourished and ripens; prudence is the good one's food, wisdom his bread, justice his sauce, freedom from passion his drink, and his pleasure is not the body's pleasure, like the habit of doing as one pleases, but the one whose name and function is gladness. This is why he gives this name (*euphrosyne*), to the inclination towards the good which develops in the soul, because this kind of mental disposition arises from right thinking (*eu phronein*).

Second answer: Worldly distraction drags the sinner down

Eccl 2,26

371,22. We should therefore learn from this instance too, as [p372] we have also heard from the Apostle, that *the kingdom of God is not food and drink, but justice and* freedom from passion and blessedness (Rom 14,17). The goals pursued by humans for the sake of bodily pleasure are goals of sinners and distraction of a soul dragged down from the things above to the things below, whose whole life-span in this world is spent on the quest for adding and collecting. The one who judges this as good in the face of God does not know that he is fixing the good in what is futile. These things I have said in my own words, but the passage from the divine scriptures confirms this thought; for it says, **to the sinner he has given distraction, to add and to collect, to give to the good before the face of God; because this too is futility and choice of spirit.**

372,15. So may all that we have learned by setting the good and the bad alongside one another for comparison in our present reading be helpful to us in fleeing from what is condemned, and a support for the things which are directed to what is superior, in Christ Jesus our Lord, to whom be the glory for ever. AMEN.

The Sixth Homily

The text of Ecclesiastes 3,1-4

3,1   For all things the time,
and a moment for every activity under the heaven.

2   A moment for giving birth, and a moment for dying,
a moment for planting and a moment for weeding
out what is planted,

3   a moment for killing and a moment for healing,
a moment for demolishing and a moment for building,

4   a moment for weeping and a moment for laughing,
a moment for mourning and a moment for dancing.

372,20 - 374,14   Eccl 3,1

Material and spiritual opportunities

372,21.   For all things the time, and a moment for every activity [p373] under the heaven; this is the beginning of the passage before us for interpretation. The task of examining it is not slight, and the gain from the labour is worthy of the labour. The purpose of the matters considered in the earlier chapters of the book will perhaps appear most clearly to us in this part, as the next passage will show as it proceeds. In the previous passages, everything pursued in human life with no advantage to the soul was condemned as futility. The Good was described, to which one should look through eyes set in the head, and food for wisdom was contrasted with things that promise bodily enjoyment.

373,11.   It remains to learn how one may live virtuously, by obtaining from the text some art and method. so to speak, of successful living. These then are the things which the present examination of the oracles announces to us in its opening, when it declares, for all things the time, and a moment for every activity under the heaven. If one looked into the depths of the meaning, one would find much philosophy in the words, both theoretical and providing practical advice about duty. So that we may have some succinct means of interpreting the scripture, we shall consider the text in the following way: of things that are, one part is material [p374] and sensory, and one part intellectual and immaterial. Of these, the non-bodily part is superior to the sensory perception, as we shall discover when we strip off our senses; but sense, which has the capacity to apprehend the material nature, cannot naturally pass beyond the heavenly sphere, and penetrate to what is beyond the visible. For this reason the text deals with things on earth and under heaven, so that we may go through life on earth without stumbling.

374,8. This world is material, life is in the flesh, but contemplation of the good is somehow obscured through the things manifest to sense. We therefore need some training in the discernment of the good, so that, as in construction-work, there may be a standard which sets everything done against a measured rule. It is made clear to us by the text, through which our life is directed towards what is right.

374,15 - 376,11   Eccl 3,1

Time and measure

374,15. He says that there are two tests for good in the world, for each of the things pursued in this life — measure and timeliness. He states this principle here, saying, **for all things time, and a moment for every activity;** for time we should understand 'measure', since time stretches alongside all that happens. These, then, are the criteria of the good. Whether [p375] they apply appropriately and absolutely for establishing every virtue, I shall not yet decide, until the text as it proceeds makes it clear. But that the greater part of our appointed life is kept right by such observance, is clear for anyone to see. For who does not know that virtue is a measurement, determined by the middle point between contrasting things? It would not be virtue if it either fell short of proper measure, or went beyond it, as for example in the case of courage, where what falls short is cowardice, and what goes too far is rashness (cf Arist Nic Eth II,6-8). This is why certain secular philosophers, becoming thieves, no doubt, of what is ours, have divided between them the thought presented in this saying, one recommending in his dictum that nothing fall short, and the other advising against going too far; for one declared, 'Measure is best', and the other advocated, 'Nothing too much'. It is shown by these two both that not achieving the required mean for virtue is to be condemned, and also that to exceed it is unacceptable.

375,16. In the part which concerns timeliness, too, we might give the same explanation, that neither anticipating the proper time nor being late is judged a good thing. What use is it for the farmer if he rushes to cut the corn before the [p376] crops are in due season ripe, or if he puts off his effort at the harvest until the grains fall off the stalk? In neither case is his effort productive, since in each one timing destroys the profit because the reaping is done at the wrong moment. What has been said of one case can be applied to all. For navigation too knows about timing, whether one is acting prematurely, or waiting too long. And what about medical matters, how much damage too much or too little can do, in terms of the right moment and measure of treatment? But we must leave these things, since the following text, in the Ecclesiast's own words, shows it more clearly with examples.

376,12 - 378,5   Eccl 3,1

Time measures all things

376,12. *The reason for our preceding consideration of these things is that neither the immoderate nor the untimely is good, but the good and right is perfect in both respects. If only one of them is pursued and the other one left out, even what is satisfactory will be useless because of what is missing. Just as we move along on two feet, and if something happens to one foot the unaffected one is no use for running because of the weakness of its partner, so, if measure lacks timeliness or timeliness lacks measure, even what is there is surely disabled, as well as what is missing. On the other hand, measure at the right moment and timeliness with measure produces results.

376,23. 'Time', therefore, is understood by us to mean 'measure', because [p377] time is the measure of every particular thing that is measured. What takes place certainly takes place in time, and the period of time lasts just as long as each event lasts, short if it is shorter and longer if it is longer. Time is the measure of pregnancy, the measure of the growth of crops, the measure of the ripening of fruits, the measure of navigation, the measure of a journey, the measure of the age of each person — baby, toddler, infant, child, adolescent, adult, maturing, at the height of his powers, senior, elderly, old. Inasmuch, then, as the measure of time is not the same for everything that comes to be (for it is not possible for everything to be of the same extent because of the difference between subjects), but time, as has been said, is the standard of measurement common to all measured things, as it embraces everything within itself, the reason that he does not say there is a measure for all things is the great disparity between the larger and the smaller among the things measured; but he calls time the universal measure for everything, by which all that comes to be is measured.

377,17. As in the course of human life advanced age is weak, while immaturity is undisciplined, and the mean between the two is the best, precisely because it avoids the undesirable features of both sides, and in it the strength of youth is displayed separated from its indiscipline, and the wisdom of age detached from its feebleness, so that [p378] strength is combined with wisdom, equally avoiding the weakness of age and the rashness of youth — in the same way the one who decrees a time for all things by his words excludes on each side the evil resulting from lack of proportion, repudiating what is beyond its time and rejecting what falls short of it.

378,6 - 379,13   Eccl 3,2

Birth and death belong together

378,6. Now perhaps it is time for us to proceed to the interpretation of the divinely-inspired oracles. A moment, he says, for giving birth, and a moment for dying. It is right that at the start he makes this tight bond linking death to birth; for death inevitably follows birth, and everything born dissolves in decay; he intends, through the demonstration that death and birth are connected, by using the reference to death as a goad, to wake from sleep those who are sunk deep in fleshly existence and love the present life, and to rouse them to awareness of the future.

378,16. This insight Moses, the friend of God, used secretly in the first books of scripture, writing Exodus immediately after Genesis, so that those who read what has been written may learn what affects them even through the very arrangement of the books; for it is impossible to hear of a birth (genesis) without also envisaging a departure (exodus). Here also the great Ecclesiast, having noticed this, points it out, classing death with birth. He says a moment for giving birth and a moment for dying. 'The moment came and I was born, [p379] the moment will come and I shall die.'

379,1. If we all looked to this, we should not forsake the direct path of life and move in the circles of the ungodly (Ps 12/11,9), deliberately wandering circuitously through life among power and ostentation and wealth, by means of which, perplexed by the many tracks in this world, we can no longer find the way out of the labyrinth of this life; the very things which command our attention confuse for us the pointers to a route free from error. How blessed are those persons who leave the circuitous deceits of this life and put themselves on the direct path of virtue! Virtue means to turn one's soul to nothing here on earth, but to have one's effort directed towards what through faith lies in our hopes before us.

379,14 – 381,18   Eccl 3,2

Giving birth and dying

379,14. Let us address ourselves again to the text. A moment, he says, for giving birth and a moment for dying. May I too enjoy birth in due season and timely death! For one would not say that physical childbirth, which is uncontrollable, and death which comes when it chooses are pointed out by the Ecclesiast as contributing to the achievement of virtue; labour pains are not a matter of will for the woman, nor is death a matter of choice for the dying. What is not within our control cannot be described as either virtue or vice.

379,22. We ought therefore to consider the timely birth, and the death which happens at a good moment. It seems to me that a birth is seasonable, and not premature, when, [p380] as Isaiah says, one is pregnant by the fear of God and gives birth to one's own salvation through the soul's labour-pains (Is 26,17-18); for we become in a way our own parents when through good choice we shape ourselves and bear ourselves and bring ourselves forth to the light. We do this through taking God into ourselves, when we become *children of God* (Rom 8,16), and children of power (Judges 18,2; Lk 32,35), and *sons of the highest* (Luke 6,35). Again, we miscarry and produce premature births or mere wind, when the shape of Christ, as the apostle says, has not been formed in us (Gal 4,19). The man of God, he says, must be fully grown (II Tim 3,17). He, surely, is fully grown in whom the natural design is fully realized.

380,12. Surely then, if someone makes himself a child of God through virtue, having taken command of this nobility, that person knows the moment of the good birth, and aptly rejoices according to the Gospel, *because a human being is born into the world* (John 16,21). But the one who has been born a child of *wrath* (Eph 2,3), and *a son of perdition* (John 17,12), and offspring *of darkness* (I Thess 5,5), viper's progeny (Mat 3,7), evil offspring (Prov 30,11-14/24,34-37) and all the other names by which the wicked birth is discredited, does not know the moment for living things to be born; for there is one moment, and not many, which produces live offspring. The one who misses this by giving birth at the wrong moment labours in the pains of his own destruction, and is midwife at his soul's death. [p381]

381,1. If it is clear how we give birth at a proper moment, it should be clear how we also die at a proper moment, as for holy Paul every moment was timely for the good death. He declares it in his own words, using a kind of oath, when he says, *I die every day, by my pride in you* (I Cor 15,31), and also, *For your sake we are put to death all day* (Rom 8,36) and, *we have had passed on us the sentence of death* (II Cor 1,9). It is surely quite clear how Paul dies every day, since he never lived to sin (Rom 6,6), but continually mortified his fleshly members (Col 3,5), carried about in himself the dying of the body of Christ (II Cor 4,10), was always crucified with Christ, never lived for himself (Gal 2,19-20), but had Christ living in him.

381,12. This would in my judgment be the timely death, the one which becomes the agent of the true life. *I*, it says, *shall kill, and I shall make alive* (Deut 32,39), so that it may be believed that dying to sin and coming alive in the spirit is truly God's gift (I Pet 3,18); for the divine voice assures us that life comes through killing (I Cor 15,36).

381,19 - 383,12   Eccl 3,2

Planting and weeding

381,19. Similar to these sayings is what follows: **A moment,** he says, **for planting and a moment for weeding out what is planted** . We know [p382] who is our *gardener* and whose *garden* we are. We have learnt one from Christ, the other from Christ's servant Paul. For the Lord says, *my Father is the gardener* (Jn 15,1), and the Apostle says to us, *you are God's garden* (I Cor 3,9). The great gardener, therefore, can only plant good things (for *God planted a Paradise in Eden to the East* (Gen 2,8)), but he weeds out things that are the opposite of good; for *every plant which my heavenly Father has not planted will be rooted out* (Mat 15,13). Surely, then, the Pharisees' wickedness and unbelief, and insensitivity to the miracles done by God — these are the plants which are weeded out. The proclamation of salvation must prevail, *the Gospel* must be proclaimed *in the whole world* (Mat 26,13), *every tongue* must confess *that Jesus Christ is Lord, to the glory of God the Father* (Phil 2,11).

382,15. Since, therefore, these things must certainly happen, the unbelief of certain persons which presently prevails is not of the Father's planting, but is of the one who sows *weeds* alongside (Mat

13,25f), or of the one who plants cuttings of Sodomite vine beside
the master's grapevine (Deut 32,32 [LXX]).   What we were taught
there in the Gospel by the Lord's voice, we are now taught in the
Ecclesiast's riddle, that there is the same moment for both [p383]
receiving the saving plant of faith and pulling up the weeds of
unbelief.

383,2.   What has been said about success with faith in particular one
may also understand correspondingly for every virtue.   There is a
moment for planting self-control and for weeding out the shoot of
licence.   So too when justice has been planted in, the iniquitous
growth is rooted out, and the plant of humility overturns pride, while
love as it grows dries up the evil tree of hatred.   The same thing
happens the other way about: injustice increasing makes love grow
cold (Mat 24,12), and if we regard all the others in the same way —
so as not to waste time mentioning each one — we shall not be
mistaken.

383,13 - 384,15   Eccl 3,3

Killing and healing

383,13.   Again, the following text agrees with what has just been
discussed.   A moment, he says, for killing and a moment for healing.
This has been clearly explained before in the saying of the prophet,
which he spoke in the character of God, *I shall kill, and I shall make
alive* (Deut 32,39).   If we do not kill *hostility* (Eph 2,16), we shall not
heal the loving inclination in us which has become ill through hatred.
So with all the other things which live in us for evil, I mean the evil
array of the passions, and that internecine war which campaigns
within us through pleasures (Plato *Resp* VIII 560a-c), and makes us
captive to [p384] the *law of sin* (Rom 7,23) — it is the moment for
killing them.   The slaughter of such things becomes the healing of the
person who is incapacitated through sin.

384,3.   Doctors say that tapeworms and some other similar parasites,
whose life is a disease in the body, are engendered in our intestines
by some faulty humour;   if they are destroyed by some medicine the

patient will be restored to health again.   There is an analogy between such physical conditions and diseases of the soul.   When anger, sucking within, or enervating by resentment the vigour of the soul and the rational powers, generates the parasite of envy, or malice generates some other such evil, the one who perceives that his soul is nourishing a parasite inside him will use in good time the medicine which eliminates diseases *(that is, the teaching of the Gospel), so that, when they have been killed, healing may be implanted in the one who was ill.

384,16 – 385,19   Eccl 3,3

Demolition and building

384,16.   **A moment for demolishing and a moment for building.**   One can learn these things also from the words of God to the prophet Jeremiah, in which power is given from God first to demolish and *uproot and raze to the ground,* and then to restore and *build up and plant* (Jer 1,10).   We must [p385] first tear down the buildings of evil in us and then find a moment and a clear space for the construction of the temple of God which is built in our souls, whose fabric is virtue.   *If one builds on this foundation in gold, silver and precious stones* (I Cor 3,12) that is called virtue;   but the nature of evil is described as wood, straw and reeds, which is prepared only to be consumed in fire.   When the buildings are made of straw and reeds, that is, of injustice and arrogance and the rest of the world's evil, the Word orders us first to get rid of these things, and so afterwards make the gold of virtue our material for building the spiritual house.   It is not possible to combine silver with reeds, nor to enrich gold with straw, or pearl with wood, but if the one is to be there, the other must be completely done away with.   For *what do light and dark have in common* (II Cor 6,14)?   Therefore let *the works of darkness* (Rom 13,12) be destroyed, and then will be constructed the resplendent buildings of life.

Weeping and laughing

385,20. **A moment for weeping and a moment for laughing.** This
sentence is explained by the words in the Gospel which come personally [p386] from the Lord, *Blessed are those who mourn, for they will
be comforted* (Mat 5,4). Now, therefore, is the moment for weeping,
but the moment for laughing is in store for us through hope; for the
present sorrow will become mother of the joy that is hoped for. Who
would not spend all his life in lamentation and sadness, if he actually
becomes acquainted with himself, and knows his condition, what he
once had and what he has lost, and the state his nature was in at
the beginning and the state it is in at present? Then there was no
death, disease was absent, 'mine' and 'yours', those wicked words,
were far away from the life of the first humans. As the sun was
shared, and the air was shared, and above all the grace and praise
of God were shared, so too participation in everything good was
freely available on equal terms, and the disease of acquisitiveness
was unknown, and there was no resentment over inferiority against
superiors (for there was no such thing as superiority), and there were
thousands of other things besides these, which no one could describe
in words, since they utterly exceed in magnificence those mentioned −
I mean equality in honour with the angels, freedom to speak before
God, the contemplation of the good things in the realms above, our
own adornment with the unspeakable beauty of the blessed nature,
when we show in ourselves the divine image, [p387] glistening with
beauty of soul.

387,1. As to what we have instead, such as the malignant swarm of
passions, and the evil hornets' nest of painful things, what would one
say was the chief of life's evils? They are all as bad as each
other, all claim precedence in evil, all give rise to equal lamentations.
Which misery will one most lament? What is most to be deplored
about our existence? − the shortness of life, its painfulness, its
beginning with tears and its end in tears, pitiable childhood, dementia
in age, unsettled youth, the constant toil of adult life, burdensome

marriage, lonely celibacy, the troublesome multitude of children, sterile childlessness, miserliness over wealth, the anguish of poverty?

387,13.   I do not mention the many different forms of illness, mutilations, amputations, putrefying diseases, impairment of sense-organs, derangement due to demons, and all such things as our nature is prone to, which potentially every human being always has in his nature as afflictions.   The frenzy of sexual lusts, and the stinking filth in which this kind of passion results, I pass over;   and the unpleasantness associated with food through defecation, I do not mention, so as not to seem to inveigh in my homily against life in all its aspects, [p388] by showing how our nature is a dung-heap.

388,1.   Setting all these things aside, and those like them, I say that what is particularly deplorable to those with sense is this: we all know that, when this shadowy life has gone by, there awaits us *a terrible prospect of judgment, and a burning fire ready to consume the enemies* (Heb 10,27).   Would not one who considers these things and those like them live in constant lamentation?   This would therefore be the moment to take account of these things.   A pessimistic attitude to the present life may well produce faultless conduct in it.   When that is achieved the promised grace of joy will await us through hope.   *And hope does not make us ashamed* (Rom 5,5), as the Apostle says.

388,13 - 389,22   Eccl 3,4

Mourning and dancing

388,13.   The next passage is a sort of repetition of the one before. After speaking of timely weeping and laughter he goes on, **A moment for mourning and a moment for dancing,** which is nothing but emphasizing the two items already mentioned.   Passionate and profound lamentation is called 'mourning' in Scripture.   Similarly, dancing also indicates the strength of joy, as we learn in the Gospel, where it says *we played to you and you did not dance, we lamented and you did not mourn* (Mat 11,17).   In the same way [p389] history relates that the Israelites mourned at Moses' death (see Deut 34,8), and that

David danced as he went at the front of the procession of the Ark, when he carried it away from the foreigners, not appearing in his usual clothes. It says that he sang, playing an accompaniment on his musical instrument, and moved to the rhythm with his feet, and by the rhythmic movement of the body made public his devotion (II Sam 6,14-17).

389,8.   Since, then, a human being is twofold, I mean made of soul and of body, and correspondingly twofold also the life operating in each of them within us, it would be a good thing to mourn in our bodily life — and there are many occasions for lamentation in this life — and prepare for our soul the harmonious dance. For the more life is made miserable with sadness, the more occasions for joy accumulate in the soul. Self-control is gloomy, humility is dreary, being punished is a grief, not being equal with the powerful is a reason for sorrow, but *the one who humbles himself will be lifted up* (Luke 14,11), and the one who struggles in poverty will be crowned, and the one covered with sores, who exhibits his lifs as thoroughly lamentable will rest in the bosom of the patriarch (Luke 16,22);   may we too rest in it, through the mercy of our Saviour Jesus Christ, to whom be the glory for ever.   AMEN.

The Seventh Homily

The text ofEcclesiastes 3,5-7.

3,5   A moment for throwing stones and a moment for
collecting stones,

a moment for embracing and a moment for avoiding
an embrace,

6   a moment for seeking and a moment for losing,

a moment for keeping and a moment for discarding,

7   a moment for rending and a moment for mending,

a moment for keeping silent and a moment for
speaking.

390,1 – 391, 14   Eccl 3,5

Throwing and collecting stones

390,2.   A moment for throwing stones and a moment for collecting stones. Through what he has taught the one who commands the ecclesiastical force has already increased the fighting power of his hearers, so that they can both pelt their adversaries and gather missiles to throw. What we have already been taught, through which we have learnt to apply the measurement of time to everything and to make timeliness in all respects our standard of goodness, brings us to a pitch of strength where the arm of our soul is braced accurately to discharge stones to destroy the enemy, and to recover those with which we have struck the adversary, so as to be able to pelt our opponent continually with the same missiles.

390,13.   Those, therefore, who look only to the literal meaning and support the superficial interpretation of the words perhaps fit the law of Moses to the text before us, in cases where the law enjoins [p391] the pelting with stones of persons convicted of a felony (see

Ex 19,13; Lev 20,2 etc; Deut 17,5 etc); we have learned examples from the scriptural account itself in the case of sabbath-breakers (Num 15,32-36), and the one who had stolen sacred things (Josh 7,10-25?), and other offences, for which the law imposed a penalty of stoning (see Lev 24,10-23). For my part, if the Ecclesiast had not claimed that collecting stones was also something timely, about which no law directs and no event in biblical history suggests a comparable precept, I might agree with those who interpret the passage through the law, that the moment for throwing stones is when someone has broken the Sabbath or stolen something dedicated. But as it is, the addition of the requirement to collect stones again, which is prescribed by no law, leads us to a different interpretation, so that we may learn what kind of stones it is which after being thrown must again become the property of the thrower.

391,15 - 395,17   Eccl 3,5

Stoning for Sabbath-breaking

391,15. Once we have thrown stones at the right moment, we are taught to collect them again at the right moment. I think, therefore, that it is not right to take the law literally in that way, according to the immediate sense. What divine and great meaning [p392] is indicated by the bare sense of the words? If someone is caught gathering sticks on the Sabbath (Num 15,32), is it right for the person to be stoned to death for this, when no moral fault is evident in the offence? What wrong has the person committed in collecting a few twigs scattered at random in the wilderness, because of his need for a fire? It is not taking something belonging to someone else that he is accused of, making it seem reasonable for the offence to be punished, but something available to all becomes the reason for his being stoned.

392,8.   Just because he did it on the Sabbath, is he condemned as a criminal*? Who does not know that every deed is judged according to its own nature, as evil or not, but that the time at which the action was performed is regarded as irrelevant to the nature of the deed? What has the period of time to do with what is accomplished of our own free will? If someone asks us what 'day' is, we shall surely answer that it is the sun being above the earth, and we make its limits daybreak and evening. Such a definition of 'day' will not be applied to only one of those which go round in the weekly cycle, but for the first and the second and so on to the seventh day the definition is the same, and the Sabbath day is no different from the others as far as being a day is concerned. [p393]

393,1. If someone is investigating the meaning of sin, we shall surely say that one should not do anything against one's neighbour, for instance, *You, shall not commit adultery, you shall not commit murder, you shall not steal* and the other things (Ex 20,13-15), about which there is a general and comprehensive law, which includes within it each particular law — the one about loving *one's neighbour as oneself* (Lev 19,18; Mat 22,39 etc). Every day alike, surely, these actions, as they comply with the law or break it, are deemed either right or wrong. If something had been judged evil on one day, whether the offence were murder or something else forbidden, no one would judge the same thing to be good on the next day. If, therefore, evil is always evil, at whatever time it may be committed, neither surely would anything innocent ever become criminal by virtue of its time. Therefore. if gathering sticks and lighting a fire before the Sabbath does not involve crime and punishment, how does the same thing become an offence on the following day?

393,15. I know the Sabbath of rest, I know the law of inactivity; it does not shackle a man, nor bid him refrain from his natural activity. Indeed, it would be giving impossible orders, commanding us to be idle, when, apart from other works, for us life itself is in its essence a work. Everybody knows that sight is the work of eyes, that of hearing is its own natural [p394] action, that of the nostrils is smelling, that of the mouth breathing, that of the tongue is speech; to teeth belongs the management of food, to intestines digestion, to feet belongs movement, and to hands the tasks which these limbs exist to perform for us. How then is it possible for the law of stopping work to be sustained, when nature does not allow idleness? How shall I persuade the eye not to see on the Sabbath, when its nature is always to be looking at something? How do I restrain the hearing process? How will my nostril ever be persuaded to abstain from the sense which recognises smells on the Sabbath? How will the intestines not perform their own function in obedience to the law, so that the food stays undigested in the body, to show that nature is idle on the Sabbath? If the rest of our body cannot accept the law of idleness (for it will not be alive at all if it is not active), it is surely impossible not to break the law on the Sabbath, even if the hand or the foot stays motionless in the same attitude and position. Since, then, the law applies not to a particular part but to the whole of a person, we shall no more observe the law by keeping one part of the body idle than we shall break it by using the remaining senses in their natural way.

394,21. Nevertheless the law is from God, but none of the [p395] things commanded by God is such that it is either contrary to nature or demonstrably outside the definition of virtue; but irrational idleness is not virtue. It is proper to find out what the imposition of Sabbath idleness means. I myself maintain that since all law-making comes from God its only object is to keep those who have accepted the law pure from the deeds of evil, and every law which bans forbidden things gives orders to 'keep the Sabbath' from wicked deeds. This is what the tablets were for, the levitical observances, the precise rules in Deuteronomy, that we should be idle and inactive in the things whose performance is evil.

395,11. So, if one may take the law in the sense that a person is to be idle about vice, I too agree that the wise Ecclesiast sets a moment for throwing stones at the person gathering wood for himself, whereby is prevented the collecting of the sticks of vice, gathered as fuel for the fire; but if someone stands by the mere letter, I do not know how what is worthy of God may be understood in the law.

Collecting spiritual stones

395,18. We must consider, then, what the spiritual stones are which
are thrown at such a person, so that his zeal for gathering sticks
does not achieve its purpose. What is the wood with which the fire
is [p396] kindled by the person who has gathered it? These things
are surely not obscure to one who is in any way skilled in texts with
mystic meaning. If the apostle rightly describes wicked construction
as wood and reed and straw (I Cor 3,12), since such buildings as
these at the moment of judgment go up in flames, and the voice of
the Gospel says that the chaff is made ready for fire (Mat 3,12;
Luke 3,17), and shows that the unfruitful vine is fit only for the fire
(John 15,5-6), it should be clear that the futile habits of the world
are the wood collected as fuel for a fire, and the person stoned at
the right moment we can interpret as the mind creeping towards evil
thoughts, without being far from the truth. We certainly ought to
consider that thoughts destructive of evil are the very stones
accurately aimed by the Ecclesiast, which must be continually cast
and collected; cast, to put an end to the one who rises in pride
against our life, and collected, to keep the soul's lap always full of
such missiles, ready to be thrown at the enemy, whenever he may plan
some fresh assault on us.

396,19.   Where, then, are we to collect stones, with which we shall
stone the enemy to death? I have heard the prophecy which said,
holy stones roll about on the ground (Zech 9,16 [LXX]). These might
be the [p397] words which come down to us from the divinely inspired
writings, which we should collect in our soul's lap, to use at the right
moment against those who vex us, and which when they are thrown
destroy the enemy and yet do not leave the hand of the thrower.
The one who pelts with the stone of self-control the unbridled
thought which gathers fuel for the fire through the pleasures, both
defeats it with his attack and always keeps his weapons in his hand.
Thus justice both becomes the stone against injustice and defeats it,
and is kept in the lap of the one who throws it. In the same way all
thoughts directed to better things are destructive of worse things,

and do not leave the one who lives rightly in virtue. This, in my opinion, is 'throwing stones at the right moment' and 'collecting them at the right moment', so that we always cast good volleys of stones for the destruction of what is bad, and the supply of such weapons never runs out.

397,16 — 400,9   Eccl 3,5

Embracing and avoiding an embrace

397,16. The next phrase before us in the passage prescribes a right and wrong moment for some kind of embrace; the text goes thus: A moment for embracing and a moment for avoiding an embrace. These ideas cannot possibly become clear to us unless the passage has first been interpreted through the scripture, [p398] so that it has become clear to us in what connexion the divinely-inspired word consciously uses the word 'embrace'. Great David exhorts us in the words of the Psalm, *Circle Sion and embrace her* (Ps 48,12/47,13) and even Solomon himself, when he was describing poetically the spiritual marriage of the one in love with Wisdom, mentions a number of ways in which union with virtue becomes ours and adds this: *Honour her, so that she may embrace you* (Pr 4,8). If, then, David tells us to embrace Sion, and Solomon says that those who honour Wisdom are embraced by her, perhaps we have not missed the correct interpretation if we have identified the object which it is timely to embrace. For Mount Sion rises above the Upper City of Jerusalem; thus the one who urges you to embrace her is bidding you to attach yourself to high principles, so that you hasten to reach the very citadel of the virtues, which he indicates allegorically by the name Sion; and the one who makes you live with wisdom [p399] announces the good news of the embrace she will give you in the future. Therefore there is a moment for embracing Sion and for being embraced by Wisdom, since the name Sion denotes the pinnacle of conduct and Wisdom in herself means every instance of virtue.

399,5. If we have learned through these words the right moment for embracing, we have been taught through the same words in what cases separation is more beneficial than union. For he says, **A moment for avoiding an embrace.** The one who has become familiar with virtue is a stranger to the state of evil. *What has light in common with darkness,* or *Christ with Beliar* (II Cor 6,14-15)? Or how is it possible for one serving two masters to be loyal to both (Mat 6,24)? The love of one produces hatred of the other. So when the loving disposition clings to the good — that is the 'right moment' — the result is surely estrangement from its opposite. If you really love self-control then of course you hate its opposite. If you look with love at purity, you obviously loathe the stink of filth. If you have become attached to the good, you surely avoid attachment to evil.

399,20. If someone applies the sense of 'embrace' also to the grip of wealth, this text also shows what sort of wealth it is good to grasp firmly, [p400] and what possessions' grip to avoid. I know as longed-for treasure the one which is *hidden in the field,* not the one visible to all (Mat 13,44). Again, I know as despised riches not those yet awaited but those set before our eyes. This is what the apostle's voice teaches when it says, *As we look not at what is seen, but at what is unseen; for what is seen is transient, but what is seen is eternal* (II Cor 4,18).

#400,8 - 403,20   Eccl 3,6

Seeking and losing

400,8. If we understand these things, we shall already understand through them the text which follows. **A moment,** he says, **for seeking, and a moment for losing.** The one who has understood from the preceding study whose clasp it is right to avoid and whose to join, would know what it is proper to seek, and what are the things whose loss is a gain. **A moment,** he says, **for seeking and a moment for losing.** What is it that I should seek, in order to catch the right moment? What must be sought the prophecy shows when it says, *Seek the Lord and be strong* (Ps 105/104,4); and again, *Seek the Lord and call on him when you find him* (Is 55,6), and, *Let the heart of those who seek the Lord rejoice* (Ps 105/104,3). From the words quoted I know something which must be sought, yet to find it is to seek it for ever. For it is not [p401] one thing to seek, and another to find, but the reward of seeking is the actual seeking.

401,2.   Do you want to learn, too, the right moment to seek the Lord? To put it briefly — all your life. In this case alone the one moment to pursue it is the whole of life. For it is not at a fixed moment and an appointed time that it is good to seek the Lord, but never to cease from continual search — that is real timeliness. *My eyes*, it says, *are always towards the Lord* (Ps 25/24,15). Do you notice how the eye searches diligently for its object, giving itself no rest nor pause in looking for its object? By the addition of 'always' is indicated the continuous and incessant nature of the pursuit.

401,13.   In the same way let us consider also the **moment for losing**, judging it as a gain to lose that, to own which damages the owner. Love of money is a bad possession; so let us get rid of it. Grudges are a wicked thing to store up; so let us discard them. Unbridled desire is a destructive possession; let us be paupers in that above all else, so that by such poverty we may gain the kingdom. *Blessed are the poor in spirit* (Mat 5,3) — obviously those who are poor in this kind of riches*. As to all the rest of the devil's evil treasures, it is more blessed not even to acquire any in the first place, so that [p402] we may be completely devoid of things which defile; nevertheless, it is good for the one caught already in evil possession to get rid of such goods and make them vanish.

402,3.   Never to have any part at all in such things is more than human nature can manage, but to dispose of what one has acquired, that is something even human capacity has the strength for. To have had no part therefore in the posssessions of the Adversary belongs to the Lord alone, who shared in the same experiences as ourselves, but *without sin* (Heb 4,15). *For the prince of* this *world is coming*, he says, *and in me* he finds *nothing* that is his (John 14,30).

402,11.   Self-purifying through meticuluous repentance, that one can see in the case of people who make themselves shine with virtue. Paul got rid of the evil possession of faithlessness;* through the one who effected in him the grace of prophecy, he became full of the treasure which he sought.   Isaiah, by his cleansing with the divine coal, lost every unclean word and thought (Is 6,6-7);   for this reason he was filled with the Holy Spirit.   Every one by participation in what is superior loses all trace of its contrary.   Thus the self-controlled person loses intemperance, the just person injustice, the modest person pride, the generous-hearted person envy, the loving person hatred.

402,22.   Just as the blind man in the Gospel found what he had not, in losing what he had, for in place of the blindness which was taken away the [p403] beam of the light entered him;   and just as in the case of the leper, when his disease was removed, the gift of health returned (Mat 8,1-4 etc);   and just as with those who rose from death, deadness gave place to the arrival of life — in just the same way, in the philosophy offered to us, it is impossible for us to gain any of the higher things without losing interest in what is earthly and low.   For in finding these, things more valuable are lost to us, and conversely the loss of them procures valuable things.

403,9.   We have learnt this from the voice of the Lord: *The one who finds his soul will lose it, and the one who loses his soul for my sake will find it* (Mat 10,39).   For the soul to be found among the commitments of the material order becomes the cause of its not being found in what is truly good, and conversely the deprivation and loss of these things becomes the possession of things hoped for.   *For what does a person gain if he wins the whole world, but pays for it with his soul* (Mat 16,26)?   **A moment, he says, for seeking, and a moment for losing.**   If therefore we know what is the gain we seek, which is found by losing ill-gotten gains, let us seek the one and lose the other;   let us seek good things and lose evil things.

403,21 - 405,24   **Eccl 3,6**

Keeping and discarding

403,21.   The next passage of the text follows neatly and appropriately from what precedes it. He says, **A moment** [p404] **for** keeping and a moment for discarding. For keeping what? obviously, what we have found by seeking. For discarding what? — surely that thing whose loss was reckoned a gain. You have a propitious thought, a desire has come upon you to see God, your *soul has thirsted for the strong and living God* (Ps 42/41,3), a longing has come over you to be *in the courts of the Lord* (Ps 84/83,3) (the courts of the Lord, in my view, would be the virtues, in which the Word dwells, and every one who follows the Word). These are what you must keep so that the riches which are the mind's pure possession are not dispersed. Some thought of the opposite kind slips in, like a burglar, causing the disappearance of pure thoughts; this must be discarded and dismissed from the mind. By its banishment our treasury of good things will be kept safe.

404,14. If the spoiler is not thrown out there will be no gain in acquiring possessions, as the stock is gradually lost by the machinations of housebreakers. Since, then, we have been taught the moment for seeking, and *Everyone who seeks, finds* (Mat 7,8), let us set a secure watch on our treasure so that what has been found may be preserved. *Watch your heart*, it says, *with all vigilance* (Prov 4,23) after you have found what you sought; for a greater task than finding is keeping the grace that is found; for instance, the one who comes forward in faith finds purification by baptism, [p405] but there is greater labour in keeping what he has received than in finding what he did not possess.

405,2. Just as we said that the right moment for seeking was not confined to a particular time, but that life was all one moment for that good search, so we declare that the moment for keeping is measured by the whole of life, setting before ourselves again the same words of the prophecy which read, *My eyes are always towards the Lord, for he shall draw my feet from the snare* (Ps 25/24,15). The means whereby we keep safe our good possession is in making God the keeper of what is ours. When my eyes are always towards the Lord, then the snares of the Enemy, through which he devises his plot against what is precious in the soul, become ineffectual. *Do not*, it says, *let your foot be unsteady*, and *the one who keeps you will not fall asleep* (Ps 121/120,3).

405,15.   Therefore the text before us follows the sense of the preceding passage.   That told us to seek so that we might find, and this one advises us to keep so that we may not lose.   But the way to keep the good is to discard the thoughts contrary to it, just as in a city under attack the guard is more secure when the traitors have been driven out, but as long as they are inside, the secret enemies plot more dangerously in hiding than the open ones. A moment, he says, for keeping, and a moment for discarding. [p406]

406,1 - 409,7   Eccl 3,7

Rending and mending

406,1.   The next passage in the text leads the soul to the somewhat profound matter of the philosophy of being.   It shows that the universe is a continuous whole and that the bond of reality admits no break;   there is a sympathy of all things with each other.   The whole is not released from connexion with itself, but all things stay in being because they are held fast by the power of what really is.   What really is, is Absolute Good, or whatever name beyond this one conceives to denote the indescribable Being.   How could anyone find a name for that which the divine voice of the Apostle says is *above every name* (Phil 2,9)?   However, whatever word is actually found to explain the inexpressible Power and Nature, what is denoted is certainly good.   This good, then, or more than good, both itself really is, and through itself has given and still gives power to existing things to come into being, and continuance in being;   but everything which is thought of as outside it, is unreality;   for what is outside what is, is not in being.

406,17.   So, since [p407] evil is regarded as the opposite of good, and absolute virtue is God, evil must be outside God, because its nature is not apprehended in its being something, but in its not being good;   for we give the name of evil to what is perceived as outside the good.   Thus evil is regarded as the opposite of good, in the same way as non-being is distinguished from being. So, when in the freedom of our impulse we fell away from the good, as those who close their eyes in daylight are said to 'see darkness' — for to see darkness is a way of seeing nothing — then the unreal nature of evil took substance in those who had fallen away from the good, and it has existence just as long as we are outside the good.

407,11. If the free movement of our will is again wrenched away from its attitude to unreality and becomes united with what is, that nature, no longer able to exist in me, will not be able to exist at all — for an evil resting by itself apart from our free choice does not exist — but I, if I have clung and attached myself to that which really is, shall remain in that which is; and he forever was, and forever will be, and now is (Exodus 3,14).

407,17. These seem to me the ideas which a **moment for rending** and a **moment for mending** suggest, so that [p408] we may be torn from that with which we were wickedly united, and cling to that which it is good to cling to. *It is good for me to cling to God, and to put my hope in the Lord* (Ps 73/72,28).

408,4. It could be said in many other cases too that this is good advice, as in *Remove the evil one from among you* (I Cor 5,13). These are the orders of the divine Apostle when he orders the one convicted of unlawful intercourse to be torn out from the total body of the Church, so that a *little leaven*, as he says, of the evil of the one convicted does not spoil the whole *lump* of the Church's prayer (I Cor 5,6). The one torn away through sin he joins on again through repentance, saying, *Do not let such a person be overwhelmed by excessive remorse* (II Cor 2,7). Thus he knows the moment to tear out the stained part from the garment of the Church (Jude 23), and the moment to sew it on again, when the dirt has been thoroughly washed out by repentance.

408,15. Many similar examples can be seen, both in the more ancient accounts and in our own lifetime, measures taken in the light of circumstances in the churches. For you know what things we are torn away from and to what we are always being joined; for when we are split off from heresy, then [p409] we are continually being attached to true belief, seeing the garment of the Church, untorn when once it has been torn away from its links with heresy.   But whether the text is philosophizing about things that are, along the lines of the interpretation we first set out, or whether by the advice given it is teaching things of this other kind, in every way the expression contains something helpful and useful when it speaks of timely tearing away of the things with which connexion is wicked, and timely attachment again to the things with which union is helpful.

409,8 — 416,10   Eccl 3,7

Silence and speaking

409,8.   Let us go on to the next passage, where the thought which is applied to the higher philosophy seems to me to be closely related to what is said.   He puts first, A moment for keeping silent, and after the silence he grants a moment for speaking.   At what time, then, and on what subjects, is it better to keep silent?   Someone with an eye to conduct might say that in many circumstances silence is more becoming than speech, as, for instance, Paul distinguishes the right moment for silence and speech, now enjoining silence and now recommending speech.   *Let no filthy word come out of your mouth* — this is the rule of silence;   *but one that is good for building up faith, so that it may give grace to those who hear it* (Eph 4,29) — this is the moment for speaking.   *Wives should keep silent in the churches* — again, he sets the moment for silence;   *but if* [p410] *they want to learn something* of which they are ignorant, *they should ask their own husbands at home* (I Cor 14,35) — again he indicates the right moment for speech.   *Do not lie to one another* (Col 3,9) — this too is a timely moment for silence;   *Speak the truth, each one to his neighbour* (Eph 4,25) — again the chance for speech.

410,5.   Many similar instances could be given from the more ancient scriptures also: *When the sinner confronted me I was dumb and I humbled myself and I kept silent from good things* (Ps 39/38,2-3), and, *Like a deaf person I did not hear, and like a dumb person not opening his mouth* (Ps 38,13/37,14).   Even when the sinner confronts him, the one who is not moved to retaliate with evil becomes dumb, but when it is fitting to use words he opens his mouth in parables, he poses riddles (Ps 78/77,2), he fills his mouth with praise (Ps 71/70,8), he makes his tongue a pen (Ps 45/44,2).

410,13.   What need is there, however, when there are thousands of examples in scripture, to go into detail over acknowledged facts? But what previously occurred to my mind, namely that the right moment for silence and speech harmonizes with the explanation given of rending and mending — this is what I want to take up again and discuss briefly.   For the argument there, in tearing the soul away when it was wrongly attached to what is opposed to it, led it [p411] to the knowledge of what really is, by making it cling to it, something which the previous passage explained as being beyond words;   and here silence seems to me to be placed first, for this reason, that that which is above every concept and name (Phil 2,9), which the soul torn away from evil both seeks continually and aims to be attached to once it has been found — that transcends any word of explanation; one who strives to reduce it to verbal expression unknowingly errs about the divine;   for what faith holds to be above everything must surely also be above language.   The one who tries to deal in words with the infinite no longer allows that to which he matches his argument to be above everything, because he thinks it is of such a kind and such a magnitude as his argument has been able to describe, and does not realize that, in the very conviction that the divine is beyond knowledge, the godly understanding of what really is, is protected.

411,14.   Why is this?   Because everything that is in creation looks towards what is naturally akin to it, and nothing that is, if it gets outside itself, remains in being, not fire in water nor water in fire, not the terrestrial in the deep nor the aquatic on dry land, not the earth-bound in the air nor again the aerial on the ground;   but each thing, staying within the limits of its nature, exists just so long as it remains within its own limits.   But if it gets outside itself it will also get outside being.   [p412] Just as with the sense-organs the sense remains in its natural functions and cannot change into its neighbour — for the eye does not act for the ear, nor does the sense of touch practise argument, nor does the hearing taste, nor the tongue perform the task of sight or hearing, but each has its natural activity as the limit of its own power — in the same way the whole creation also cannot get outside itself by the comprehending power of thought, but always stays within itself, and sees itself, whatever it looks at; even if it thinks it sees something beyond itself, it has not the capacity to see what is outside itself.

412,10. For example, in the contemplation of what is, creation is compelled to go beyond the concept of extension, yet it does not get beyond it. Together with every concept it thinks of, it surely envisages, comprehended at the same time as the being of what is conceived, its extension; but extension is nothing but a creature. Yet that Good which we have learned to seek and to guard, and which we are advised to grasp and cling to, being above creation, is above comprehension. How could our understanding, which moves about within extended space, comprehend what has no extension? It goes back through time, continually searching out by logical analysis [p413] things further back than those it has reached. In its inquisitiveness it speeds past all that may be learnt, but finds no method of speeding past the concept of temporality, so as to stand outside itself and transcend the temporality envisaged as prior to existing things.

413,5. It is like a person who finds himself on a mountain — suppose it is a sheer precipitous rockface, which in its lower part stretches up with a vertical smooth surface for a vast distance, and high above raises that peak, which from its beetling crag plunges down to an immense depth — what he is likely to experience when with his toe he feels the ridge overhanging the drop and finds neither foothold nor handhold — that, I believe, is [p414] the experience of the soul when it goes beyond what is accessible to time-bound thoughts in search of what is before time and has no extension. Having nothing to catch hold of, neither place, nor time, nor space, nor anything else of the kind which offers a foothold to our intellect, but slipping in all directions from what it cannot grasp, it becomes giddy and perplexed, and turns back again to what is akin to it, content to know only enough about the transcendent to be sure that it is something other than what can be known.

414,9.   That is why, when speech reaches what is beyond speech, then is a moment for keeping silent, and to keep the wonder of that ineffable Power unexpressed in the secrecy of inward knowledge, since it knows that even the *ancients spoke of the works of God, and not of God, when they said, *Who will speak of the mighty acts of the Lord* (Ps 106/105,2)? and, *I shall relate all your* works (Ps 74,3 [LXX];   Ps 118/117,17) and, *Generation upon generation shall praise your works* (Ps 145/144,4).   These things they tell, and they recount them fully and commit to speech the story of what has been done. But once their speech is about what transcends all thought, they immediately enjoin silence by the things they say. [p415]

415,1.   They say, *Of the splendour of the glory of his holiness there is no end* (Ps 145/144,3&5).   What a wonderful thing, that speech was afraid to approach the thought of the divine nature, since it does not comprehend the wonder even of one of its external attributes! For it does not say that there is no end to the Being of God, deeming it presumptuous even to consider it at all, but it expresses in words wonder at the splendour observed in the glory.   Again, it was unable even to see the glory of the Being itself, but was astonished to observe the glory of his holiness.   How far is it therefore from investigating what the Nature is, when it has not the capacity to wonder at the outskirts of its manifestation?   It did not wonder at his holiness, nor at the the glory of his holiness, but after first setting down that it wondered only at the splendour of the glory of the holiness, it was then overwhelmed at the wonder of this;   for it did not grasp in the mind the end of what was wondered at.   This is why it says, *Of the splendour of the glory of his holiness there is no end.*

415,17.   Therefore, in words about things concerning God, when the discussion is about his Being, that is the moment for keeping silent, but when it is about some good activity, of which the knowledge reaches down even to us, then is the moment for speaking of the powers, to proclaim the wonders, to recount the works, to use language thus far; but in matters which lie beyond, it is the moment not to allow the creation to overstep its boundaries, but to be content to [p416] know itself. For in my reckoning the creation does not yet know itself, nor does it understand what is the Being of the soul, what is the nature of the body, where existing things come from, how things are produced from one another, how what is not takes being, how what is is dissolved into what is not, what is the harmonious unity of opposites in this world. If the creation does not know itself, how will it explain what is beyond it? A moment, then, for keeping silent about these things; for in these matters silence is better. But there is a moment for speaking of the things through which our life increases in virtue, in Christ Jesus our Lord, to whom be the glory and the power for ever. AMEN.

The Eighth Homily

The text of Ecclesiastes 3,8–13

3,8   moment for loving and a moment for hating,
                a moment for war and a moment for peace.

9   What advantage is there for the doer in the things
                                at which he toils?

10   I saw the distraction which God gave
                to the sons of men to be distracted in it.

11   All things which he made are good at his right
                                moment,
                he also gave time together in their heart,
                so that a man may not find
                the making which God made from beginning to end.

12   I know that there is no good in them,
                except for rejoicing and doing good in his life.

13   And every man who shall eat and drink,
                let him also see good in all his toil;
                that is the gift of God.

416,11 – 417,9   Eccl 3,8

Loving and hating

416,12. **A moment for loving and a moment for hating.** Who will there be whose hearing is so purified that he receives in a pure form the saying about loving, without acquiring at the same time any impure love? Perhaps our ears too need the [p417] fingers of Jesus (Mark 7,33), so that by the divine touch of the true Word the hearing power of our soul may be set free from all the filth which stops up its ears, to make us understand the love which is praiseworthy, and receive in our soul what is the **moment for loving** and what the **moment for hating.** I do not think this moment is any other than the expedient one.   For the benefit to be gained from each, in my judgment, determines the right moment to use it;   if what is done falls outside what brings advantage, it falls also outside the right moment.

417,10 - 426,7   Eccl 3,8

Loving

417,10.   First however we must, I think, consider the connotation of these two words, I mean 'love' and 'hate', so that we may thus also logically apprehend their timely use.   The inner disposition towards what is desired, functioning through pleasure and passionate feeling, produces love;   but aversion from what is unpleasant, and turning away from what is painful, is hatred.   Each of these dispositions can be used both profitably and unprofitably, and on the whole the life lived for good or ill takes its origin from this.   The place we are drawn to by affection is the one we adapt our souls to, and what we are disposed to hate we become alienated from.   Whether the disposition of the soul is towards good or evil, the object of affection infiltrates the soul.   But whichever it is, [p418] and in whichever case hatred intervenes, it effects separation, whether it be from a good or bad thing.

418,3.   We should therefore enquire what is by nature lovable and what is hateful, so that by employing this disposition of soul at the right moment we may become strangers to evil things through hatred, and blended with the nature of the good.   If only human nature were trained in this above all things — I mean discrimination between what is good and what is not!   The passions would make no headway throughout our lives, if from the outset we recognized the good.   But as it is, making irrational sensation our criterion of the good from the beginning, we grow up habituated to our original judgment of reality, and because of it we find it hard to tear ourselves from things judged good by sensation, since we have reinforced in ourselves the attitude towards them, to which we have become habituated.

418,15. A thing seems beautiful to human beings if it gives pleasure to the eyes by its pretty colour, whether it is made of a lifeless material or is among the living wonders. A piece of music is beautiful to the hearing, and among liquids and vapours beauty of that kind is defined by the sense of taste or smell. The most brutish and mindless of all is the sense of touch, through which unbridled pleasure naturally prevails in the choice of the good. Since therefore the senses are engendered in us as soon as we are born, and [p419] we become habituated to them from the beginning of our life, and the attachment to the irrational life is strong in our sensual power (for all this kind of thing is to be seen also in irrational creatures), and the mind is hampered in its proper activity, being allowed no scope by its infant status, but is somehow cramped by the dominance of less rational sensation — for these reasons the haphazard and mistaken use of the loving disposition becomes the source and the pretext for the life of evil.

419,9. Since our nature is a double one, a combination of mind and sense, it follows that our life too is double, taking a separate form in each of our two parts, physical in the sensing part and in the other mental and non-physical. Similarly, good and non-good are not the same thing for each aspect of our life, but mental for the mental part, and for the sensual and bodily part, whatever sense desires. Thus, since sense is part of our nature right from birth, but the mind waits for a proper age to be reached, to be able to reveal itself gradually in the person, the mind, which develops slowly, is for this reason dominated by the sense, which is complete, and by compulsion grows habituated to the perpetual superiority, so that it submits to sense, judging good or bad according to whatever sense selects or rejects.

419,23. The reason why [p420] discernment of the true good is difficult, and hard for us to achieve, is that we are prejudiced by sensual criteria, and we define good as what is enjoyable and pleasant. For just as we cannot see the beauties of the heavens when a cloud fills the air above our heads, so neither can the soul's eye have a clear view of virtue when it is dulled through pleasure as by a mist over the eyes. When sense looks towards pleasure, but the mind is prevented by pleasure from looking towards virtue, that is the beginning of evil, because when the mind is dominated by sense it too favours the irrational judgment of what is good, and if the eye says that goodness lies in superficial attractiveness, the understanding goes along with it; and in the other cases likewise what pleases the sense wins the verdict as good. But if somehow it had been possible for the true discernment of the good to be present in us from the beginning, with the mind assessing goodness by its own standard, we should not by servility to irrational sense become like animals, and be enslaved.

420,18. So that this confusion might be resolved in us and what is naturally lovable and its contrary clearly recognized, the Ecclesiast makes this point in his text, that there is **A moment for loving and a moment for hating;** he thereby distinguishes the nature of things, pointing out what [p421] is to be loved with advantage and what is to be hated. In the heat of the passions which belong to its time of life, youth says that it is the moment for it to love the things which are dear to youth. But the Ecclesiast replies to youth by setting a different moment for pure love, implying that the mistaken disposition of the soul towards bad things is not love. Just as in a healthy person thirst affects the body at a proper moment, but in the case of those in whom the bite of the thirst-adder has produced such a condition, no one would say that thirst was operating at the right moment (for in these people thirst is not a natural appetite, but has become a disease), in the same way the sordid affection of youth is not affection at all but a disease which is caught through the burning and poisonous bite of its age. Not every love has its right moment, but love for the only Lovable has.

421,15. It it however not possible to come to a clear understanding of these things unless in our investigation we make the following logical distinction: of the good things sought among humans, some are really what the word suggests, and some are falsely so named. All the things which give a satisfaction which is not transient, and which do not seem good to one person and useless to others, but are good

always, at all times, and in all people whom they affect [p422] —
these are the truly good things, since they always remain as they are
and admit no admixture of what is bad; and for precise thinkers they
are attributed only to the divine and everlasting nature. All the
other things which are in sensual terms good, though they may seem
good because of deluded thought, have no real being or existence;
although they are naturally subject to flux and transient, through
some delusion and idle preconception they are regarded by the
uninformed as truly existing. Those who cling to what is unstable do
not reach out for what stands for ever.

422,9. As if he were standing on a high watchtower, the Ecclesiast
seems to cry aloud to the human race through these words, **A moment
for loving and a moment for hating**, that the truly good things are
different, and they are good in themselves and make those who share
in them good. Whatever may be the nature of what is shared, what
shares in it must conform. For instance, the mouth of one who
takes a mouthful of something spicy smells sweet, and likewise smells
unpleasant when he eats garlic or something else with a strong
flavour. Surely then, since all the filth of sin stinks, but conversely
the virtue of Christ is *a sweet smell*, and the loving disposition
naturally brings about assimilation to what is loved, so whatever
[p423] we choose in love we become, either the *sweet smell of Christ*
or a foul stench (II Cor 2,15). The one who loves the good will also
be good himself, as the goodness generated in him changes into itself
the one who receives it.

423,4. The reason why the one who eternally is offers himself to us
to eat, is that taking him into ourselves we may become that which
he is; for he says, *My flesh is really food, and my blood is really
drink* (Jn 6,55). The one who loves this flesh will not become a
flesh-lover, and the one who regards the blood in this way will be
pure from sensual blood. For the flesh of the Word and the blood
which is within that flesh has not one particular grace, but is sweet
to those who taste it, and desirable to those who long for it, and to
those who love, it, adorable. If someone directs his affection to
things which do not exist, it is inevitable that he too will become

that which by nature they are. Thus since among the things that are one thing is real and another futile, we ought to recognize the futile, so that by contrast with it we may understand the nature of what really is.

423,18. This is what all the holy ones do, who lead back those who have strayed from the right road and are wandering along a winding path, to the Way from which they have turned aside, calling from afar, 'Flee from the road you are travelling on, [p424] for there are robbers and highwaymen and murderers' ambushes along it', so that the traveller, perceiving his danger, may turn from the way of destruction; to turn back from that way is to be taught the way of salvation. Thus the great Ecclesiast too calls from above to humankind, as it wanders *in untrodden places and not in the way* (Ps 107/106,40), as the prophet says, expressing this directly in the words he uses: 'Why do you human beings constantly go astray? Why do you love futile things, and grow fond of the unreal, and why have you become deeply attached to things which have no existence? There is another way, which does not wander and which leads to salvation. That is the one to love, that is the one to travel along with strong affection, whose name is *truth and life* (Jn 14,6) and *light* (Jn 12,46) and immortality and the like. This way along which you are now running deserves to be hated and shunned; for it is without light and shrouded in darkness, and leads to precipices and chasms and the haunts of wild beasts and robbers' ambushes.'

424,15. When therefore he says, **A moment for loving,** he indicates what is truly loved and yearned for, and when he adds the moment for hatred he is teaching what we ought to turn away from. So let us learn what is intrinsically desirable and embrace this with love, not at all [p425] diverted by misjudgment of the good, wasting our affection on those things which great David forbade, saying, *O sons of men, how long will you be dull of heart? for what purpose do you love futility and seek falsehood* (Ps 4,3/2)? What truly exists is the one and only intrinsically Lovable, of whom also the rule of the Ten Commandments says, *You shall love the Lord your God with all your heart and with all your soul and with all your mind* (Deut 6,5; Mat

22,37 and par.); and again the only thing to be hated in truth is the Inventor of evil, the Enemy of our life, about whom the Law says, *You shall hate your enemy* (see Mat 5,43).

425,10. The love of God becomes a strength for the one who loves, but the disposition to evil brings destruction on the one who loves what is evil. The prophecy says this: *I will love you, O Lord my strength; the Lord is my firmness and my refuge and my deliverer* (Ps 18,1-2/17,2-3), but of the contrary it says, *The one who loves injustice hates his own soul; he will rain down a snare on sinners* (Ps 11/10,5-6). The whole life, then, is the moment for affection for God, and all one's career the moment for estranging oneself from the Enemy. The one who is without the love of God in a small part of his own life becomes utterly without him from whose [p426] love he has become separated. The one who is now outside God must be outside the light, because God is light, but he must also be outside life and immortality and every thought and concept which refers to the transcendent; for God is all these things. The one who is not within these is surely within their opposites. Darkness and ruin and utter destruction and death await such a one.

426,8 – 428,19   Eccl 3,8

The consequences of loving and hating

426,8. The saying of the Ecclesiast draws attention to this by making the contrast in a pithy phrase. He reveals through timely love and hate operating at the right moment the nature of the two things thought of as opposites. A moment, he says, for loving — you must add 'the good' — and then he says, A moment for hating — you have to understand that the word refers to 'evil'. For the *confused and erroneous disposition in our soul is the root and source of sin.

426,15. *No one*, it says, *can serve two masters; #for surely he will hate one and love the other* (Mat 6,24). The distinction shows who is the bad master, from whom one should separate oneself by hatred, and who is the one who rules his subject for good, to whom one should attach oneself with love. Anyone who clings to the hateful and despises the lovable, is reversing the occasions for love [p427] and hate to his own harm. For one who despises something will be despised by it, and one who clings to destruction will gain for himself the very thing he clings to.

427,3.   If you make a distinction in your mind between things thought of as virtue and vice you will recognize the moment for the right attitude to each of them.   Restraint and pleasure, self-control and indulgence, humility and pride, goodwill and perversity, and all that are regarded as opposites of one another, are plainly set out for you by the Ecclesiast, so that by adopting attitudes about them in your soul you may make profitable decisions.   Thus there is a **moment for loving** restraint, and **for hating** pleasure, so that you do not become pleasure-loving rather than God-loving, and likewise in all the other cases, quarrel-loving, gain-loving, glory-loving, and all the rest, which through the use of affection for improper ends separate us from the disposition to good.

427,15.   Somewhat incidentally we have learned the lesson, that every impulse of the soul was framed for good by the One who created our nature, but the mistaken use of such impulses produces the [p428] drives towards evil.   Though our power of free will is a good, when it is active for evil it becomes the worst of evils.   Conversely, the power to reject unpleasant things, whose name is hate, is an instrument of virtue when it is deployed against the enemy, but becomes a weapon of sin when it is opposed to the good. Surely then, *everything God created* of the things framed in us *is good, and nothing is to be rejected that is accepted with thanksgiving* (I Tim 4,4), but the ungrateful use of these things turns into a passion the created means by which fellowship with God comes about;   contrary things enter and are set up in God's place, so that for such people their passions become gods. Thus for gluttons *the belly* becomes *God* (Phil 3,19).   Thus the covetous make their disease into an idol for themselves (Col 3,5).   Thus those whose soul's eyes are blinded by error in this present age have made vanity their God.   To sum up, whatever a person submits his reason to, making it slave and subject,

he has in his sickness made that into a god, and he would not be in
this state if he had not attached himself to evil by love.

#428,19 - 433,15   Eccl 3,8

War and peace

428,19.   If therefore we have identified the right moment for love
and hate, let us love the one and go to war with the other. [p429]
#For there is, he says, A moment for war and a moment for peace.
You see the ranks of the opposing passions, the law of the flesh *at
war with the law of* your *mind and taking prisoners with the law of
sin* (Rom 7,23).   Notice the variety of weapons of war, the many
different forms the enemy's campaign takes against your city.   He
sends out spies, he suborns traitors, he lies in wait on the roads, he
sets up traps and ambushes, he finds himself allies, he builds
battering-rams, he provides himself with slingers and archers and
hand-to-hand troops for close fighting, and a cavalry force and
everything else of the kind against you.   You cannot be unaware of
the meaning of the words, of who the traitor is, who the spy is, who
the men in ambush are, who the slingers and javelin-men and archers
are, and who the hand-to-hand fighters and the troop of horse, and
what sort of battering-rams they are, with which the wall of your
soul is shattered.

429,15.   With all this in view we must provide weapons for ourselves
also, and call up our allies and make a selection of recruits from our
subjects, [p430] in case anyone is in league with the enemy;   and we
must take precautions against ambushes along the road, and ward off
missiles with shields, and hold out against those who fight against us
hand-to-hand, and dig trenches across the cavalry's route against us,
and fortify the walls with defences and jutting bulwarks, so that they
are not shattered by the battering-rams.

430,6.   There is surely no need at all for us to explain in detail how
the enemy of the city of each one of us, founded in the soul by God,
tries out our strength with spies, and whom he has in our own selves
to betray our strength.   To demonstrate the idea more clearly, such

is the first onslaught of temptation, from which passions take their rise, and this becomes the spy of our strength, the sort of sight which meets the eye and is able to arouse desire. Through this the enemy spies out the strength within you, whether you are firm and well-prepared, or slack and easily captured. For if you did not give way at the sight, and the sinew of your understanding did not slacken at what you saw, but you dismissed the incident without being affected by it, you frightened away the spy at once [p431] by showing him as it were a phalanx of hoplites bristling with spears, I mean the armed mass of the thoughts. But if your senses were softened by pleasure at the sight, and the image of the shape made its way inside your understanding through the eyes, then the mind, the commander of those inside, is worn out by the war, as he has nothing manly or youthful about him, but is lazy and weak, and a great number of traitors from the population of thoughts is gathering round the spy. These are the traitors of whom the Lord says, *A man's enemies are those under his own roof* (Mat 10,36), the ones which come from the heart and defile the man (Mat 15,11.18-19), whose names can be clearly learnt from the Gospel (cf Plato, *Resp.* VIII 559-560).

431,10. Following this it should no longer be difficult for you to understand the details of this warlike preparation one by one: those who lie in a hidden ambush, whom people encounter as they travel unsuspecting along the way of life. For those who on the pretext of friendship and goodwill drag anyone who is persuaded by them down to the destruction of sin, are those who lie in wait along the roads, and they are those who sing the praises of pleasure, who lead you by the hand towards theatres, who tell you about the fun of evil, and when they challenge you to imitate the same things through what they do, [p432] they call themselves brothers and friends for the destruction of the lost. Of these it is written, *Every brother will kick you with his heel, and every friend will come* with a trick (Jer 9,4/3).

432,3. If we have understood the ambushes, the company of slingers and archers and javelin-men should also be clear. The proud and the passionate and the slanderers who by starting insults shoot provocative words instead of weapons and stones from their bows and slings, and throw their javelins, wound to the core the hearts of those who travel without breastplate and without vigilance. It would not be wrong to compare the qualities of pride and arrogance with the prancing of horses. #For those who use exaggerated words of bombast like hollow hooves to lash out at gentle people, are quite simply horses with arching neck and tossing head; and scripture says of these, [p433] *Let not the foot of pride reach me* (Ps 36,11/35,12). The battering-ram by which the structure of the walls is undone might reasonably be called the love of possessions. For nothing in the enemy's armament is as heavy and dangerous as the battering-ram of the love of money. However much people surround their souls by building up the other virtues in a close-knit structure, nonetheless even through such things as these the battering-ram often penetrates.

433,8.   One can also see the love of possessions making an attack even through prudence, and this violent and irresistible onslaught of evil getting inside faith and observance of the sacraments and chastity and humility and everything of that kind, so that some people, chaste and prudent and on fire with faith, and restrained in conduct and moderate in behaviour, can put up a resistance to all but this disease.

433,16 - 434,21   Eccl 3,8

The armour of God

433,16. If we have taken stock of the enemy's forces, this would be the right moment to make war on them. But one would have no confidence against the ranks of the opponents unless he were protected by the *whole armour* of the Apostle. Everyone, surely, knows the scheme of that divine arming, by which he makes the one who stands against the phalanx of his enemies invulnerable to the darts shot at him (Eph 6,13-17). By dividing the virtues into different types the Apostle has made each type of virtue into the particular piece of armour for each of the crucial moments in our lives. Entwining justice with faith and plaiting them together he constructs with them the hoplite's breastplate, [p434] protecting the soldier's body thoroughly and securely with them both.   One piece of armour separated from another cannot by itself be a protection for the one who handles it.   Faith without the works of justice is not enough to save one from death, nor again is the justice of one's life a guarantee of salvation if it is on its own, divorced from faith. Thus by weaving together faith and justice as raw materials for this armour he protects the hoplite's body completely over the heart;   for the heart is understood as in the breast.   He protects the warrior's head with hope (I Thess 5,8), signifying that it should be the good soldier's business to wave aloft his hope of things above like a plume. The shield, the armament of protection, is the unbreakable faith, which the point of the arrow cannot pierce.   We must surely take the arrows shot by the enemies as the various assaults of the passions. The protective weapon with which the warrior's right hand is armed against the enemy is the Holy Spirit, terrible to his opponent, but to the one who wields it, salvation.   The whole teaching of the Gospel makes a safe covering for the feet, so that no part of the body is left naked and liable to blows. [p435]

435,1 – 436,20   Eccl 3,8

Peace with God

435,1. If we have learnt, then, whom we should go to war with and how to carry on the fight, we must also learn the other part of the lesson, with whom the scripture solemnly warns us to make a peaceful alliance.   What is the good army, with which I am to join forces through peace?   Who is the king of such an army?   It is clear, from what we are taught by the inspired scriptures, that it is the array of the angels of the host of heaven. For *There was*, it says, *a multitude of the heavenly host praising God* (Luke 2,13).   And Daniel observes ten thousand times ten thousand in attendance, and sees thousands of thousands of ministers (Dan 7,10).   The prophets too bear witness to something similar, naming the Lord of all *Lord of hosts*, and *Lord of Powers* (Ps 24/23,10 etc?).   And to Joshua the son of Nun the one mighty in war says *I am the Commander-in-chief of the force* (Josh 5,14).

435,14.   If we have learnt what the good alliance is and who is the Commander of these allied troops, let us make a treaty with him, let us run to join his command, let us make friends with the one who has gained such power.   The way to be attached to him is taught by the assembler of this league, the great Apostle, when he says, [p436] *Therefore, since we are justified by faith, let us have peace with God* (Rom 5,1), and again, *We are ambassadors for Christ, as though God were urging through us;   we implore you on Christ's behalf, be reconciled with God* (II Cor 5,20).   As long as we were *by nature children of wrath* by doing what is wrong (Eph 2,3), we stood in the ranks of those who resist the right hand of the most high (Ps 77,10/76,11);   but if we lay aside ungodliness and worldly desires, in holy, just and godly living, by making this peace we shall be joined to the true Peace.   For so the Apostle says of him, *He is himself our peace* (Eph 2,14).

436,10.   This statement is the final summary of everything timely done.   We have learned to do everything at the right moment, so that we may achieve this: to be at peace with God by being at war with the Adversary.   Even if the virtues, with which we must be friends, are also called the army of peace, it will surely not lead the argument outside the interpretation we have given, because every name and thought of virtue leads back to the Lord of virtues.   And why should we prolong the discussion of such matters, when what has already been said is enough to make clear the meaning contained in the words?

436,20 – 437,19   Eccl 3,9

Profit from the world

436,18.   When he has through these words kindled the soul of one initiated in these sublime teachings, he once more leads up to a sublime height the soul of the person following his text, and says, **What advantage is there for the doer in the things at which he toils?**

which is the same as saying, 'What [p437] profit is there for the person from works, from which there is no profit?   He tills the ground, he goes to sea, he endures the hardships of military service, he sells, he buys, he makes a loss, he makes a profit, he goes to court, he fights his case;   he loses the case, he wins the verdict; he is pitied, he is congratulated;   he stays at home, he travels abroad;   whatever things we see in life, in all its diverse affairs, as they variously affect each person — what profit does the pursuit of these things bring to the one who spends his own life in this sort of way?'

437,8.   *Is it not the case that, as soon as he ceases to live, all things are   shrouded in oblivion, and he departs, stripped bare of the things he strove for, taking with him none of his present possessions, but only the conscience about them?   From this conscience, hereafter, this voice seems to come to the person whose life has gone astray through such occupations, 'What advantage have you had from those many labours, in which you toiled?   Where are your splendid houses?   Where are your buried purses?   Where are your bronze statues, and the words of praise?   Here are fire, and whips, and impartial judgment, and the scrutiny of things done in life which cannot be deceived.   **What advantage is there for the doer, in the things at which he toils?**

*437,20 – 440,19   Eccl 3,10-11

God's goodness turned to bad uses

437,20.   After that he says, **I saw the distraction which** [p438] **God gave to the sons of men to be distracted in it.   All things which he made are good at his right moment;   he also gave time together in their heart, so that a man may not find the making which God made from beginning to end.**   What does this mean?   'I know', he says, 'the source in life of the distraction of human nature, which takes its origin from the good works of God.   For he made all things for good (Gen 1,3), and gave to those who participate in reality a mind able to discern the good, by which the right moment for each activity, once recognized, bestows the perception of the good on those who use them. But when the reason, perverted from what is right by evil counsel (Gen 3,1), fell away from correct judgment of reality, the reversing of the right moment turned what is useful in each case into the opposite experience.

438,14. 'It is as if someone who has set out on a table all the preparations for a banquet were to put certain implements alongside suitable to help with eating, the sort of thing manufactured by specialized craftsmen, small knives with which the diners cut up some of the food offered them, or silver prongs made with a hollow part attached to one end [p439] convenient for holding soup; then one of the guests at the dinner changes the function of what lies before him and uses each for the wrong purpose, and cuts with his knife either himself or one of the people sitting next to him, and with his prong pierces his neighbour's eye or his own; you might say that this person misused his host's cutlery, not because the one who provided it prepared befoerehand the cause of what happened, but because the wrong use of the things laid out led to this disaster the one who used stupidly what lay before him.

439,10. 'In just the same way', he says, 'I too know that each thing comes from God for all good, as long as use is made of it at the right moment for a proper purpose, but the perversion of right judgment about reality turns good things into the beginning of evils. What sort of thing do I mean? What is more pleasant than the activity of the eyes? — yet when the sight becomes an agennt of passion to such persons, what was made as a benefit is said to have become the cause of evil; this is tantamount to saying that anyone who uses the good in a bad way makes his use into a disease. It is the same with everything else which nature gets from God — it depends [p440] on the choice of persons concerned whether it becomes the material for good or evil. Therefore', he says, all things which he made are good at his right moment.

#440,2. He also gave together time in their heart. Time, which is a dimensional idea, by itself signifies the whole creation which comes about in it. Therefore by referring to the container the sentence points to everthing contained in it.   Thus everything which exists in time God gave to the human heart for good, so that by the greatness and beauty of created things it may contemplate thereby the Creator (Wisdom 3,5).   But through the very benefits given them humans were damaged by not using each one rightly and profitably.

440,11.   For this reason he says, So that a man may not find the making which God made, which means that for this reason falsehood took control of the human soul, so that he might not recognize the good making which God made with the aim of benefiting him, since in all that has come to be from the beginning of creation and until the consummation of all there is nothing evil in reality;   for it is not natural for evil to arise out of good.   If the cause of all things is good, then everything which has its existence from good is certainly good. [p441]

441,1 - 442,4.   Eccl 3,12-13

Joy in the Good

441,1.   Then he says, I know that there is no good in them, except for rejoicing and doing good in his life.   These words sum up the argument.   For if the use of God's creatures at the right moment determines what is good in human life, there should be one good thing, the perpetual joy in good things, and that is the child of good deeds. Keeping the commandments gives joy now through hope to the one who promotes good deeds, but hereafter the enjoyment of good things when hopes are fulfilled holds out everlasting joy to the worthy, when the Lord says to those who have done good, Come you blessed ones, inherit the kingdom prepared for you (Mat 25,34).

441,12.   What food and drink are to the body, the means by which natural life is preserved, that, for the soul, is to look towards the Good;   and that truly is a gift of God, to gaze upon God.   This is the idea which is explained in the following words.   The text runs like this: And every man who shall eat and drink, let him also see good in all his toil, that is the gift of God.   For as the fleshly man, he says, gets strength by eating and drinking, so the one who looks at the good (the true Good is he who alone is good) [p442] has the **gift of God in all his toil,** just this, to look upon the Good for ever, in Christ Jesus our Lord, to whom be the glory and the power for ever and ever.   AMEN.

Homily I

Anthony Meredith

277-299,3 Introduction: Higher meaning in Ecclesiastes than in Proverbs

From the outset Gregory insists on the importance of labour, sweat, toil for those embarking on a study of Ecclesiastes. The book of Proverbs had been a preparation for Ecclesiastes in two senses. Not only had it come before Ecclesiastes in sequence and so prepared the reader for it — the exact force of this type of προγύνασμα is elaborated in the next section —, it had also done so by accustoming the mind to exercise itself on a hard topic. The effort of penetrating the meaning of Ecclesiastes is compared to a contest or a struggle and the tools without which success is impossible are πόνος (4 times) and ἰδρώς (twice). All this intellectual labour is justified as done in obedience to the Lord's command at Jn 5,39: 'Search the scriptures'. Lines 12 and following of page 278 express vividly enough the difficulty and effort of the enterprise of understanding Ecclesiastes. The exegete is like an athlete searching for a foothold for his thoughts.

The idea that the understanding of a text, sacred or otherwise, demands so high a degree of mental exercise can be paralleled in St Augustine. There also exists a treatise on the subject of προγυνάσματα in Spengel's *Rhetores Graeci* III,449 from Nicholaus Sophista. Doubtless, also, the idea that truth needed for its

discovery mental acuity and a good deal of training occurs in Plato's
Republic.[1]   In Christian writers, however, prior to Gregory, only in
Clement and Origen do we find a like stress on 'exercise'.   Usually,
even in Gregory, the notions of πόνος and ίδρώς are confined to the
moral life as in Hesiod, *Works and Days* 289.[2]   It is the use of such
ideas for intellectual endeavour that is less common.

1.   279,4–281,2 = Eccl 1,1. The meaning of the title *Ecclesiastes.*

This section subdivides at 280,5 into two halves. In the first
Gregory identifies the σκοπός of the work; in the latter the identity
of the speaker. Unlike the other books of the bible, the purpose of
Ecclesiastes is solely the conduct of the church (279,20). If it be
asked how precisely the book furthers the needs of the church, the
answer is by instruction in the life of virtue and that itself is
achieved by freeing the mind from the dominion of sense and at the
same time inspiring it with the love for things unseen (280,6). The
close connexion between the love of and discovery of truth on the
one hand and the reformation of life on the other owes much to the
Platonic tradition, above all in the language which is used to express
the upward search for the transcendent. The relation, however,

---

1   Plato, *Republic* 7, 532b ff. and especially 533c, where the 'eye
    of the soul' is purified and prepared by dialectic for the vision
    of the Good. Plotinus appears to regard such purification as
    partly a moral (cf. *Enn.* 1,6,9,25) and partly an intellectual
    progress (cf. *Enn.*1,3,1,28). That the later Platonists, above all
    Proclus, saw the need for such logical exercise as a propaedeutic
    for seeing the truth is clear from his treatment of the
    Parmenides in *Theologica Platonica* 1,8.9). On the Christian side
    Origen stresses the need for mental *exercitium* for the penetra-
    tion of the creed at *De Principiis* Praef. 3 and in the prologue
    to his *Commentary on the Canticle* GCS 8, 76,9ff. St Augustine
    also lays great stress on the importance of *exercitium* for the
    acquisition of spiritual understanding. So at *Sol.* 1,12,23 the
    search for the light demands *exercendi sunt prius,* and similar
    remarks at *de quantitate animae* 15,25, and *de Trinitate* 15,1.1
    and for a discussion cf. H.I. Marrou, St Augustin et la fin de la
    culture antique, Paris, 1938, pp. 141 ff.

2   For the popularity of this quotation see the parallels assembled
    by Rzach in his commentary; the earliest seems to be at Plato,
    Protagoras 340 D. Gregory uses the idea of sweat as a
    necessary pathway to virtue, *De Instituto* GNO VIII/I 45,3; *De
    Vita Moysis* 2,305.

between these two elements, the intellectual and the moral, has been significantly modified. For, although it is true that Plato's interest in the *Apology*[3] is 'how should one live one's life'and in the *Republic* the pursuit of truth is subordinated to severely political considerations, the more 'mystical' treatises of Plato, the *Phaedrus*, *Phaedo* and *Symposium*[4] regard the vision of beauty and ultimate reality as the goal to which the life of virtue is a means. The ambiguous position of Plato on this issue is resolved in the same direction by both Aristotle and Plotinus,[5] who place the life of the mind and mystical union as the ultimate goal of at least philosophic endeavour. How precisely Gregory here conceives the interrelation of virtue and contemplation is not *absolutely* clear, but the balance probably is in favour of the reverse position to that advocated by the *Symposium*. If this is true it will be in accord with the teaching of the *Life of Moses*.[6] The Platonic subordination of sense to intellect has been made to subserve a Stoic search for moral perfection.

---

3 For the pursuit of virtue and the cure of the soul as the primary aims of both life and philosophy see *Apology* 29 E ff. and this, being a τεχνή demands knowledge as at *Laches* 185 E.

4 The most emphatically mystical passages, and those which seem to locate the vision of reality/beauty *above* the acquisition of virtue at *Phaedrus* 249 D, which likens the vision of ultimate reality to a recovery of lost blessedness, and *Symposium* 210 A-211 C, where the upward ascent depends rather on desire than on memory.

5 Aristotle *Nicomacean Ethics* 10,7, where the life of thought comes after the life of moral virtue and makes us truly divine; and for Plotinus cf. *Ennead* 6,9,11.

6 Gregory's understanding throughout the *De Vita Moysis* sees knowledge of the nature of God, truly real, incomprehensible and infinite, as a prelude to and condition of the possibility of the life of virtue, cf. especially preface ss. 5-7. It is instructive in general to compare the position of Gregory on Ecclesiastes with that of Origen, who in the prologue to his *Commentary on the Song* (p.78,28) compares Proverbs, Ecclesiastes and the Song to the three patriarchs, Abraham, Isaac and Jacob, who stand respectively for moral philosophy, natural philosophy and theology, a progress which owes something to the Stoics (cf. Seneca *ep.* 89,8) and to Albinus (*Did.* 3) and which in its turn influenced Evagrius' account of the spiritual life in the prologue 9 to the *Praktikos*.

Who, then, is the author of the work, the Ecclesiast? By two
lines of argument Gregory concludes that he is the Christ. (1) The
Ecclesiast is the one who gathers together and so, pre-eminently, is
Christ. Surely there is an allusion at 280,9 to Jn 11,52, '(Jesus
came) to gather into one the children of God who are scattered
abroad.' (2) By putting together Jn 1,49 and Eccl 1,1 Gregory
concludes that as Jesus is the Son of David and Solomon is also the
Son of David, Jesus must be Solomon and therefore the author of
Ecclesiastes. This arguably rabbinic method seems to me unusual,
even in Gregory, but its conclusion leaves no important trace on the
development of the exposition.

2.   281,3-285-13 = Eccl 1,2. **The meaning of 'futility of futilities'.**

The first two paragraphs of this section are primarily verbal in
interest (283,3-17). To begin with, Gregory distinguishes three
differing senses of the word 'futile', which are conveniently
summarized at 282,7-9 as 'a meaningless word, an unprofitable
activity, or an unrealized plan, or unsuccessful effort, or in general
what serves no useful purpose at all', meaninglessness, therefore,
pointlessness and frustration. One of the illustrations of pointlessness at 281,13 (children building sandcastles) is taken up again at
290,2/3, where, as the note indicates, the allusion is to Iliad 15,363.

The second paragraph explores the meaning of the intensified
form 'futility of futilities', solely with references to scriptural
parallels. The conclusion arrived at (283,5) is 'exaggerative intensity'.
This appeal in search of meaning to γραφική συνήθεια (282,12/13), and
is a good example of the point made by Professor Young, who in an
article on 'The rhetorical schools and their influence on patristic
exegesis' (195) writes 'How can their (sc. the Cappadocians') exegesis
be explained? ... They had all been trained according to the classical
paideia, and naturally used rhetorical techniques in commenting upon
literature, in spite of their philosophical interests.' Origen's analysis
of the meaning of ἀρχή in the first volume of his *Commentary on*

John is a good example of the practice and of the fact that it was not restricted to 'Antiochenes' as opposed to 'Alexandrians'.[7]

At 283,8 Gregory applies the expression 'futility of futilities' to the physical universe. But this identification seems to leave him in the role of a critic of the work of God; and it is to counter this objection that the rest of section 2 (283,18-285,12) is devoted. His first move is to argue that the dual composition of man into soul and body is parallel to a further distinction in the order of things between the unseen and the seen. The lives of these two elements in our make-up are quite distinct. The life of the body is mortal and orientated towards the present, that of the soul is deathless and looks to eternity. The conclusion is that the aim of the author is to disengage our attention from things seen and concentrate them upon things unseen and 'real'.

This contrast, familiar from Plato and stated at 280,5 to be the aim of the whole work, still leaves a problem for those who believe in the creation of the whole world, seen and unseen, by God, a problem isolated by Gregory himself and addressed in the ensuing paragraph (284,12-285,12). His main answer comes in the form of a distinction between two contrasted attitudes towards the visible universe. There are some, who through human stupidity (ἀβουλία)[8] (285,4) allow their gaze and their wonder to stop at the surface of this world, at things visible and tangible. Others, however, follow the advice of Wisdom 13,5 (285,2) and treat the world of sense as a gateway to the unseen world. This ability to rise above the seen to the unseen, to go through the changing to the changeless, is outlined in a passage full of Platonic echoes, above all in its identification of God with the good that really is. The language of 284,17ff is like

---

7   For Origen, cf. *Comm. in Joannem* 1, XIV,90-XX,124.

8   For the dispute about the meaning of ἀβουλία and the hesitations of translators cf. the discussion by Aubinae at *De Virginitate* 23 (336,10) and of Daniélou on *De Vita Moysis* 2,175; the former sees the stress as lying on the intelligence, the latter more on the will. It seems doubtful if Gregory had developed the idea of will as a distinct faculty from that of the intellect at this date.

that of 280,5ff and owes a good deal to Plato's *Phaedrus*[9]. Further
the close connexion drawn by Gregory between knowledge of divine
mysteries and becoming like God is a familiar Platonic trope (cf. esp.
284,20) and *Theaetetus* 176 B), though it is perhaps fair to add that
such a way of thinking is expressed in the New Testament in 2 Cor
3,18 and 1 Jn 3,2. More unmistakably Platonic is the language used
of God at 285,10-12, especially the preference for the neuter over
the masculine. Two further points are in order. 'To know this good
is to possess it' at 285,12 seems to endorse a less cataphatic and
epectatic approach to the problem of the knowledge of God than is
found in either the *Contra Eunomium* or in the *De Vita Moysis*, or
indeed in the sixth homily *On the Beatitudes*[10]. Secondly the
description/definition of God at 285,11 as 'the good that really is' is
not, as the late Professor Dörrie has argued, the identification that
Plotinus would have been prepared to endorse, with his (Plotinus')
distinction between 'The Good' and the 'Really real'.

3.   285,13-291,14 = Eccl 1,3-7. The futility of worldly pleasures
       and the advantages of stability.

The central purpose of this section is to demonstrate the
futility of human success, life and prospects, if it allows itself to
become immersed in the unreality and suitability of the visible world.
If we devote all our energies to this passing world it is hardly
surprising that we ourselves become like the object of our love.
Gregory illustrates his theme by pointing to the fragility of the
sensory universe, all caught in a cycle of endless motion and no
achievement. This is eminently true of the sun and the rivers and the
sea, all of which despite their endless labour (286.19, cf. Theocritus
[?], *Idyll* 1,38), never come to an end and never achieve anything
lasting or any increase. Even though it be true that the earth itself
is more stationary (286,4/5), this does not seem to count as an

---

9   For ἀνακύπτω, *Phaedrus* 249 C.

10   *De Beatitudinibus* 6, PG 44,1268 B ff;   *Contra Eunomium* 2.69-70;
     De Vita Moysis 2,236.

exception while it, like the remainder of visible creation never acquires any newness (286,8). And all this is a symbol of the life of man (287,3-8).

In elaborating the theme of the parallel between the cyclic character of the universe and of human life (287,3ff), it is hard to avoid the conclusion that Gregory presses his point so hard and so far that he seems to affirm some doctrine of pre-existence. The sun circles and the human spirit circles. If the cyclic order is the pattern under which all created reality lives, it is surely the case that we are caught up into it and replicate it in our own eyes. It is, admittedly, strange to find Gregory here endorsing a view which he elsewhere consistently rejects, though his treatment of the lost sheep of Lk 15,3-7 makes better sense on some sort of theory of pre-existence.

The everlasting cycle of the seasons and the elements ought to lead mankind to a more sober frame of mind, as in its own way, should the weary stability of the earth. Contrast with this endless round or this tedious stability the admirable, steadfast stability of which St Paul writes at 2 Tim 3,14 'Continue in the things you have learnt and been convinced of.' Clearly Gregory wishes us to understand that the condition of the steadfast believer is superior both to the sea and the land, though how precisely this is true is not made clear. The distinction made at *De Vita Moysis* 2,244 between cyclic change (bad) and endless upward change (good), has not yet appeared. The sea at 289,3 provides Gregory with an instructive example of the pointlessness of greed. The sea is never able to say enough to the continuous contributions of the rivers, any more than our own insatiate greed is set to rest by the food we offer it. Gregory concludes this paragraph by a verbal reference to the discussion of the three senses of 'futility' at 281,3-282,9. The pointlessness of an hour wasted upon things visible is also likened to the sandcastles of *Iliad* 15,363 again already alluded to at 281,13.

Section 3 ends (290,7-291,14) with a highly wrought rhetorical passage, in which the hearer is exhorted to leave the futile, unreal conditions of the seaside and turn inland, in order to grasp the immaterial life (290,17-22), retaining only a memory of those things people here strive after. In a passage of high rhetoric (291,3ff) Gregory urges the claims of the higher life. Two conditions are envisaged. First there is that of those who have been successful in transferring their allegiance from the life of sense to that of the spirit; second that of those who are warmly attached (291,8) to things of the body and though they realise the profitlessness of the things of sense all they can do is cry out 'futility of futilities'.

Despite the fact that especially at 284,12ff Gregory had tried to avoid the conclusion that part of the created order was either evil or very seriously flawed, the whole logic of his argument in the paragraph 298,7-291,14 sounds very dualist. It bears in tone a marked resemblance to the celebrated, world-weary epigram of Palladas which likens the whole of life to a stage or a game, not to be treated seriously, a view which Plotinus on several occasions endorses.[11] Again the notion that one must detach oneself from things earthly in order to attach oneself to things heavenly owes something in general tone to the upward ascent of the *Symposium*, but in language Gregory himself frequently speak of the need to free oneself from προσπάθεια and in this language his is close to Porphyry.[12]

4.   291,15-294,17 = Eccl 1,8. The difficulty of using words either to exhort to virtue or to express adequately the divine nature.

What is the meaning of the text of Eccl 1,8: 'All words are laborious and a man will not be able to speak'? Gregory's treatment begins with the assertion that in fact nothing is easier than speaking.

---

11   For the depressing pessimism of Palladas cf. *Anth. Pal.* X,72 = *OGBV* 639 and for similar sentiments cf. Plotinus *Enn.* 3,2,15; though the idea that this life is a game, unworthy the attention of the serious can be paralleled in Teles. For the religious affiliation of Palladas cf. Averil Cameron, Palladas and Christian polemic: *JRS* 55 (1965) 17-30, cf. note 3.

12   προσπάθεια or 'disordered affection' is defined at *SVF* 3,397 as desire enslaved and is equivalently all that troubles peace of soul; it is censured alike by Porphyry at *Abst.* 1,30/31 and *Marcellam* 32, and by Gregory especially in *De Virg.* 4 (276,8); 6 (279,17); 8 (285,25); 11 (293,19); in all cases negatively.

To breathe, to form words, to use the tongue is no trouble at all. To say what we think is incomparably easier than digging and dislodging stones. He finds the solution to his problem with the help of 1 Tim 5,17. 'Let the elders be deemed worthy of double honour, especially those who labour in the word.' The exegesis of an unpromising passage by means of another scriptural quotation occus also at 281,1, Exhortation to virtue is something which calls from the speaker sweat and labour language reminiscent of the introduction to this sermon (cf. e.g. 278,5), though the reference is different here. Part of the labour entailed in leading others to a virutous life derives from the fact that effective communication of the value of virtue demands the practice of virtue on the part of the instructor; and that virtue itself requires labour was a standard part of Greek popular morality from Hesiod onwards.

A second explanation of the verse and above all of the reason for describing words as difficult is now offered. Once the soul has freed itself from the futility of sense, and risen upwards to the contemplation of things unseen, then the frailty of language is discovered (293,7/8). The argument that follows is *a fortiori*. Although we are familiar enough with the four elements, we would be unable except with difficulty either to define the nature of the elements, or to explain how they derived their existence. But if the human power of speech is defeated by the natures of the four elements, how much more will our powers of reason and speech be defeated by the nature of the Word and the Father (293,19). Speechlessness and silence are the only appropriate respsonses in the face of the mystery of God. Any expression necessarily falls short of the desired goal.

This form of argument is not isolated in Gregory and occurs also in *Contra Eunomium 2*,[13] usually asserted to come from the same period. Where it appears to differ from that work is its failure to

---

13 The *a fortiori* argument, from the difficulty of understanding the heavens to the greater difficulty of understanding their maker occurs at *Contra Eunomium* 2,71.

argue to the divine inexpressibility from either infinity or incomprehensibility. The argument here put forward could be seen as more of
an expansion of the hackneyed dictum of Plato, *Timaeus* 28C, than as
proceeding from a form of negative theology that has its roots in
Philo. This observation is to some extent reinforced by the apparent
availability of the divine nature at 285,8-12. If, as Mühlenberg and
others[14] argue, Gregory learnt the divine darkness less or not at all
through experience and largely or solely as a result of his anti-
Anomoean conviction in the non-definability of God, and if the *Contra
Eunomium* is the first text where the doctrine is clearly enunciated
and if this 'discovery' is the cause of the difference in vision
between acknowledged early works, like the *De Virginitate* and later
ones like *De Vita Moysis*, it would seem to follow that *In Ecclesiasten*
must either predate the *Contra Eunomium* (more probable) or come
very soon after, before Gregory has had time to fit his spiritual
vision to the austere demands of his theology.

5.   294,18-298,3 = Eccl 1,9-11. Body and soul; resurrection and the
      final abolition of evil with the universal restoration of all
      things.

      Gregory divides Eccl 1,9 into three sections, the first of which,
- 'What is it that has come to be? The same that shall be,' - is
dealt with from 294,18 till 296,3; the second, - 'And what is it that
has been made? The same that shall be made' - from 296,3 till
296,17, and the third - 'And there is nothing fresh under the sun', -
is discussed with verses 10 and 11 for the remainder of the homily
from 296,18 till 298,3.

      In dealing with verse 9,1 by envisaging an interlocutor (295,1-5)
who asks how it is possible to speak of 'having been' and of 'coming
to be' in the future, if there is nothing permanent and everything is
futile. Gregory answers at 295,8ff that the enduring subject is the

---

14 H. Langerbeck, Zur Interpretation Gregors von Nyssa': TLZ 82
    (1957) 81-90, argues against the idea that Gregory's apophaticism
    is a type of religious experience; rather does it spring from his
    conviction of the divine infinity, which was developed in response
    to a doctrinal challenge.

human race, or more properly individual human beings, by raising themselves by virtue, adorning and forming themselves with good characters and freeing themselves from the defilement of sin, have restored the image and likeness which was theirs in the beginning (cf. Gen 1,26). The very fact that this condition of likeness to God is not at present realised, is clear proof of the vanity of the present situation.

There are several characteristic Platonic and Gregorian ideas in this passage.   (1) It is the soul that is to be adorned and is regarded as the true self; and it is the soul that is in the image and likeness of God.   (2) The perfection of the soul in the future uses the language of forming, 'morphosis', which has roots in Rom 12,2 and has been singled out by Jaeger[15] as the principal feature in which it is possible to trace the continuity of Greek and Christian ideas of human perfection.   (3) The language of dirt and defilement with which Gregory describes the present condition of the human spirit has parallels elsewhere in Gregory, possibly echoes Plotinus and goes back ultimately to the image of the sea Glaucus of *Republic*.[16]   (4) Gregory here, as elsewhere, draws no distinction between 'image' and 'likeness', a feature which he shares with Athanasius, but which serves to distinguish him from Origen.[17]

Gregory begins his treatment of Eccl 1,9,2 by insisting that it is not simply a repetition of the first part of the verse, as though there were no distinction in sense between 'what has come to be' and

---

15   Werner Jaeger, Early Christianity and Greek Paideia, Oxford 1962, section VII and note 1, p. 140; for further examples cf. esp. *In Inscriptiones Psalmorum* GNO V, 101,17; 117,4; 173,21.   The similarity with *Ennead* 1,6,9 and through that with *Phaedrus* 252 D hardly needs stressing, though the influence of Rom 12,2 should not be overlooked.

16   *Republic* 10,611 and for the idea of the 'inner man' cf. *Rep.* 9,589 A;   though cf also Rom 7,22 and 2 Cor 4,16;   the idea of defiling dirt occurs also at *De Virginitate* 12,3 (GNO VIII/I 300,13 ff) and *Ennead* 4.7.10.46.

17   For the distinction of image and likeness cf. Origen *Contra Celsum* 4,30 and Chadwick *ad loc*, and for Gregory's identification of the two, Or. Cat. 5 and Srawley's note (p. 24,5).

'what has been made'.   The soul came to be, γέγονεν, the body has
been made, πεποίηται.   Not, Gregory adds, that there is any semantic
difference between the two words;   the different words are used in
order to bring out different points.   The soul 'came to be' as it shall
be in the future.   The nature of the body, made by God's hands, will
only become clear at the resurrection.   This looks as though Gregory
is drawing a distinction between the primal creation of the body and
its future post resurrection condition.   The next sentence, however,
appears to rule that idea out.   The translation of 296.15/16 reads:
'For however you may see it after the resurrection of the dead, just
such it was made at the first.'   The final sentence confirms this by
identifying resurrection with the restoration of the original state, a
regular identification with Gregory.   But if he makes this identification then the distinction between soul and body made on the basis of
a distinction between restoration of soul and realization of body
hardly makes any sense.   I suggest that we have here an inelegant,
perhaps even inept, fusion of two different ideas.   It would be much
easier for his argument if Gregory could ignore the body and the
resurrection.   Unfortunately for his Christianity, he cannot do that;
therefore he juxtaposes the view of Origen that the beginning and end
of the soul will be the same and an Athanasian view of a body, made
indeed for immortality, but initially possessing it only prospectively or,
perhaps, conditionally.[18]   At this stage Gregory shows no indication
of believing in a primal, sexless creation, to be restored at the end,
a view he explores in De Hominis Opificio.[19]   In this passage there
seem to be vestiges of a Platonic/Origenist doctrine of pre-existence
of soul perhaps alluded to at 287,21 ff.[20]   The third part of section

---

18   For the original possession by the soul of all beauty cf. Origen,
     De Principiis 1,6,1 and, though less clearly, St Athanasius De
     Incarnatione 3,4.

19   On the double creation of man, the former perfect and sexless,
     the latter 'flawed' by passion and sexual difference cf. De
     Hominis Opificio 16 ad finem.

20   Gregory officially rejected the doctrine of pre-existence and
     probably attributed it to Origen at De an. et res., PG 46,112 C
     and Hom. Op. 28,3/4.   However it makes a good deal more sense
     of his teaching at Adv. Apoll. 16 (GNO III/I, 152,2ff).

5 and the last section of the first homily stretch from 296,19 to
298,3. It discusses Eccl 1,.9.3 and then verses 10 and 11. It consists mainly of an elaboration of the idea of universal apocastasis
with the help of Eccl 1,9 'There is nothing fresh under the sun'. In
elaborating this theme Gregory does little more than repeat the text
of Eccl with minimal comment; indeed the passage from 296,19-297,10
is no more than quotation and minimal paraphrase. The remainder
(297,11-298,3) is occupied with Eccl 1,11: 'There is no memory for
the first, and indeed for those who come last there will be no memory
of them.' Gregory gives to the verse a moral meaning, by means of
identifying being and good and conversely non-being and evil. In this
we 'having no memory of the first' comes to mean 'inclining to evil
and forgetting the good'. Again when we return to good, evil will be
covered with oblivion. The primal forgetfulness of good is here
clearly taken to mean the fall, and the ultimate forgetfulness of evil
coincides with the ultimate disappearance of the memory of evil. In
other words the destruction of evil (= non-being) will issue in the
triumph of good (= being). In such a Platonic scheme it is hard to
know what can be meant by the disappearance of evil, especially
where evil and non-being are identified. But this is a problem in any
theodicy where God's power and goodness are protected by the
assertion that evil is insubstantial.

This Platonic picture is reinforced partly by the language in
which the slant to vice is expressed 'ἔρρεψε[21] (297,13), and partly by
the intellectualist attitude adopted towards the problem of wrong
choices. At 285,4 and 291,12 Gregory connects them with ἀβουλία,[8]
a word which is sometimes rendered 'foolishness' or 'stupidity' – an
intellectual error, in other words, and sometimes as 'wrong choice',
where the overtones are more voluntarist. I have recommended the
expression 'misjudgment', to bring out the primarily intellectualist

---

21 The use of the word ῥέπω in the sense of downward tilt occurs
    for the first time at Phaedrus 247 B, from which it passes to
    Ennead 2,1,3,22; 4,8,5,24, and thence to Porphyry Abst. 1,30 and
    Gregory De Virginitate 5 (277,15) on which see Aubineau ad loc.

character of Gregory's treatment of bad choices, where the
translators originally wrote 'folly', 'foolish deeds'.

There are many areas in this homily which betray the extent to
which Gregory's 'Platonism' has been imperfectly integrated into either
his own later held views about the nature of God, human progress and
change or into a rich understanding of the place of the body in the
divine design.   As we have seen Gregory came close to endorsing a
programme of pre-existence, and even if he avoids that, he hardly
seems to have a coherent attitude to the body, a fact which is
evident from the confusing passage at 296,3ff.   The homily's
treatment of the divine nature seems to show nothing of Gregory's
later preoccupation with the infinity and incomprehensibility of God
and the treatment of change seems to find no room for the doctrine
of endless upward mobility, which is also a feature of the later
writings of Gregory.   Indeed the close connexion between the two
ideas is quite lacking in this homily and, I would suggest, in the work
at large.   Gregory also seems to be happy with the understanding of
sin as ἀβουλία[8] (285,4; 291,12) and also at 295,11 with the notion
of sin as dirt which defiles the soul, without, apparently inwardly
corrupting it.   Even Gregory's habit of interpreting one piece of
scripture with the help of another is not totally foreign to the later
commentators on Plato, who assumed, if Proclus' practice is anything
to judge by, that Plato speaks with a coherent voice.   On only one
point of substance can Gregory be seen as departing from the later,
if not from the genuinely Platonic position.   For Gregory the pursuit
of truth about the universe was seen not as something to be aimed
at for itself, but as a means to the growth in virtue, to which all
else is subordinated (280,1).

Homilie II.   Eccl 1,12–2,3

Ekkehard Mühlenberg

I.   **Textkritische Beobachtungen:**

1.   306,24 lies εἰπὲ und nicht εἶπε – so Praefatio p. 197;
308,8 vielleicht φησὶ nach γὰρ mit EYG P gegen WS;
310,7 Komma vor καὶ halte ich für besser.

2.   P. Alexander setzt keine Parenthesen.   Ich halte sie für nötig:

300,6–11 (τὸ γὰρ – ἀπολέσασι), διὰ τοῦτο ...

300,17–18 (οὕτω – ἐταπεινώθησαν), τοῦτο ...

303,10–11 (ἥ γὰρ – ἐγένετο). ἀλλ᾿...

306,11–307,4 Die Konstruktion ist: ὡς οὖν οὐδενὸς ...
κωλύματος (ἥ τε γὰρ ... ἦν, οὐδενὸς ... ἐπικόπτοντος), τά τε
ἄλλα σοφὸς ὢν ... δι᾿ αὐτῆς εἶπε ...

II.   **Formale Beobachtungen**

1.   Homilie II ist die kürzeste Predigt!

Sie hat 348 Textzeilen, Hom. VI hat 367; die längste ist Hom.
VII mit 530.   Wenn man Hom. V ausnimmt (sie ist über 59 Verszeilen),
dann hat Homilie II die längste Textgrundlage mit 35 Verszeilen.   Aus
Statistik soll man bekanntlich nur sehr vorsichtige Schlüsse ziehen,
wenn überhaupt.   Es läßt sich vermuten, daß Gregor 35 Verszeilen
kaum auf ein einziges übergreifendes Thema reduzieren wird.   In der 3.
Homilie faßt Gregor den Inhalt seiner 2. Homilie zusammen (315,2–7).
Er bezieht sich dabei nur auf die zweite Hälfte.   Was er dagegen als
das Thema 'im ersten' (314,13) angibt, bezieht sich auf die erste

Hälfte der *zweiten* Homilie (314,16-315,1; Stichwort: ἐπισκέπτεται, cf. Eccl 1,13,2-3 und 299,14 sqq).

2.   *Formal läßt sich feststellen, daß Hom. II in zwei Teile gegliedert ist.*   305,14-16 wird ein neues Thema angekündigt: 'Im folgenden erfahren wir, welches der Rückweg des Verirrten ist und auf welche Weise die Rückführung aus dem Übel zum Guten geschieht.' Dazu gibt Gregor einen Überblick, der das Ziel der Verse 1,16 sqq vorweg zusammenfassend formuliert.   Denn zwei Seiten weiter (307,15-18) sagt Gregor: 'Das ist also das Ziel des Textes, der auf den vorherigen Abschnitt folgt.'   Und jetzt wolle er Wort für Wort auslegen.   Die Predigt wird also geteilt: Eccl 1,12-15 liegt dem ersten Teil (298,5-305,13) zugrunde, der zweite Teil (305,14 sqq) ist der Auslegung von Eccl 1,16-2,3 gewidmet.   Formal gesehen behandelt das Überleitungsstück (305,14-307,14) die Frage nach dem Ziel (σκοπός) des Textes, und ein solcher Arbeitsschritt geht der Auslegung Wort für Wort gewöhnlich voraus.   Der Übergang vom ersten zum zweiten Teil ist auch ein Wechsel der Person, die den Text spricht.   Die Bestimmung der sprechenden Person ist auch ein Arbeitsschritt, der vorweg zu erledigen ist.   Jedoch gibt der Bibeltext selbst nicht den geringsten Hinweis, daß ab Vers 16 des 1. Kapitels eine neue Person auftritt. Gregor ist also gezwungen, sein Textverständnis durch einen allgemeinen Gedanken plausibel zu machen.   Außerdem behandelt er die Frage nach Anordnung des Berichts (τάξις).   Der ganze Abschnitt (305,14-307,14) ist also ein philologisches Vorwort.

3.   *Gregor vermerkt gelegentlich Auslegungsprobleme, aber nur einmal ausdrücklich.*

a)   Zu Eccl 1,13,4-6 ('Gott gab den Menschenkindern eine böse Zerstreuung, um sie darin zu zerstreuen') sagt er, daß ein wörtliches und vordergründiges Verständnis des Textes gottlos sei.   Das begründet er zuerst allgemein aus dem Gottesgedanken, dann bietet er eine Sammlung von Schriftstellen für 'Gott gab', die seine Auslegung bestätigen sollen (301,8-303,2).

b)   An zwei Stellen sagt Gregor, daß ein *Wort* in der Bibel einen bestimmten Sinn hat.   Der Gedanke, der dieser Methode zugrunde liegt, ist die Übereinstimmung der Bibel mit sich selbst, also die Bibel durch die Bibel zu erklären; konkret ist es die Konkordanzmethode, 'der Sprachgebrauch der Bibel' (ἡ γραφικὴ συνήθεια 304,7-9; σύνηθες ... τῇ ἁγίᾳ γραφῇ 302,8-9).

Zu περιφορά = 'Zu dem Lachen sagte ich: Schwindel' (Eccl 2,2,1) weiß Gregor keine Bibelstelle; da bezieht er sich auf die semantische Nähe zu παραφορά und schmückt eine antike Definition des Lachens aus (310,6-16), so daß er am Ende sagen kann: Lachen ist παράνοια.

c) Andere Bibelstellen führt Gregor verschiedentlich an, um den *Gedanken* eines Satzes zu erklären, zu Eccl 1,12,2 (299,10 sq): 'Ich wurde König über Israel in Jerusalem'. Frage: 'Wann geschah das?' Antwort durch Psalm 2,6+7; zu Eccl 1,17,2: 'Gleichnisse und Wissen erkannte ich' — die Gleichnisse Jesu werden herangezogen (309,1-8).

d)   Sacherklärungen

Zu Eccl 1,12,1-3 (300,5-11): 'Da also die Übel mit der Erde verbunden sind.' In biblischer Reminiszenz denkt Gregor bei den Übeln an die Schlange (Gen 3) und erklärt, daß die Schlange Erde frißt. Sicher hat er in keinem naturwissenschaftlichen Werk nachgeschlagen; er weiß eben, daß die Schlange zu den Kriechtieren (τὸ ἑρπυστικὸν θηρίον) gehört.

Im Zusammenhang mit Eccl 1,13,4-6 (301,11-17): Vom Guten geht nur Gutes aus. Beweise sind ihm Mt 7,17 ('Der gute Baum bringt gute Früchte'), Mt 7,16 sowie Lk 6,45.

Zu Eccl 1,14 (303,4-6): 'Alles, was im Leben unter der Sonne geschehen war, das alles war Nichtigkeit' erklärt Gregor mit den Psalmworten Ps. 13,2-3: Es gab keinen Verständigen und niemanden, der Gotte suchte ... .

Zu Eccl 1,15 (303,14-304,4): 'Was verdreht ist, kann nicht wieder ausgerichtet werden' — Beispiel von der Arbeit eines Tischlers, der seine Werkstücke gerade vermißt, damit sie sich ineinander fügen lassen.

Zu Salomo (Eccl 1,16 sqq): Die geschichtliche Stellung des dritten Königs über Israel und der Höhepunkt israelitischer Macht (306,11-19).

Vielleicht noch zu Eccl 2,3,1-2 (312,2-5) die Illustration des Trinkvorganges.

e) Προσωποποιία (Charakterdarstellung)

Gregor benutzt in der Auslegung die Paraphrase in Nachahmung der Ich-Rede, die in den Bibelworten vorliegt. Im Prinzip ist es eine wichtige Auslegungsregel, daß bei der Interpretation von Dichtung die sprechende Person, aber auch ihr Charakter und die Angemessenheit der Rede aus ihrem Munde beachtet werden müssen. Gregor nimmt nun an, daß Salomo richtig und gut spricht, und um das zu verdeutlichen, gibt Gregor dessen Worte in Ich-Form wieder, damit sie verständlich werden (307,19-308,9; 309,10-12; 312,6-10; 313,8-314,2). An einigen Stellen gibt Gregor an, daß er sich dieser Methode bedienen will: 310,16 sq (310,17-311,2); 311,3 (311,3-14); 312,10 sq (312,11-17).[1]

III. Behandelte Einzelthemen

Der vorgegebene Text veranlaßt Gregor an vier Stellen, für seine Erklärung weiter auszuholen und einen Gedanken zu thematisieren. Dazu zähle ich die Ausführungen darüber,

1. daß Gott nicht die Ursache des Bösen ist (301,7-303,2);

2. daß das Verdrehte aus dem Kosmos ausgeschlossen ist (303,13-304,6);

3. daß der Kosmos durch den Verlust der menschlichen Natur unvollständig wurde und seine Ganzheit wieder- hergestellt werden muß (304,23-305,13);

4. daß Freude und Lust bei körperlichen Empfindungen kurzfristig sind (312,9-313,8); im Hinblick auf dieses letzte Thema meine ich eine sprachliche Nähe zu De beatitudinibus or. IV (44,1244/5) und ep. 18 (VIII 2 58/9) beobachtet zu haben.

---

1. Zu meinem Teil II habe ich mit Gewinn benutzt: Bernd Neuschäfer, Origenes als Philologe, Basel 1987, Schweizerische Beiträge zur Altertumswissenschaft Heft 18).

IV. Gedankengang der Homilie II

Grundsätzlich gilt für Gregor, daß der Bibeltext, hier Eccl 1,12-
2,3, eine Einheit ist und ihm ein geschlossener Gedankengang zugrunde
liegt. Gregor erklärt nicht nur die Verse nacheinander, sondern die im
ersten Vers begonnene Erklärung wird in der Weise fortgeführt, daß
sich die folgenden Verse jeweils als Bestätigung des schon
ausgeführten Gedankens ergeben und meist so eingeführt werden
können: 'Denn es heißt' oder 'Denn er sagt ... ' Gregors
Auslegungsaufgabe besteht also darin, das Thema, besser die
gedankliche Ebene zu finden, auf der sich Texte in ihrer vorgegebenen
Reihenfolge wie die Trittsteine im unwegsamen Gelände nahtlos
aneinanderfügen. Ich denke, daß Gregor darin erfolgreich ist. Und
ich frage, wie ihm das gelingt.

Der Ausgangspunkt ist der erste Vers (Eccl 1,12,1): 'Ich bin
der Kirchenführer.' Gregor erklärt ἐκκλησιάστης erstens von seinem
verbalen Sinn her: 'zu einer Versammlung zusammenführen', und
zweitens identifiziert er den ἐκκλησιάστης mit Christus. Die
Begründung gab er schon in Homilie I (280,8-281,2). Er benutzt den
Rückgriff als Einleitung in der Weise, daß der ἐκκλησιάστης 'das
Verirrte und Zerstreute' durch seine Worte zu einer Gemeinschaft
zusammenführt. Die Worte, die die Zusammenführung bewirken, findet
Gregor — das ist sein Einfall — in Joh 6,63 beschrieben: 'Die Worte,
die ich rede, sind Geist und Leben.' Ihre Wirkungsweise wird durch
Gleichsetzungen, die in den Evangelien begegnen, beschrieben (Stimme
des Arztes, Wort des Lebens, Stimme der Auferstehung, Wort des
Lichtes etc.). Dann (299,3-9) erfolgt die applicatio: So spricht der
Kirchenführer zur Kirche, und die sind wir.

Nach dieser Einleitung, die eine Erweiterung des schon in Homilie
I Gesagten ist, macht Gregor einen abrupten aber naheliegenden
Übergang: 'Was also sagt der Kirchenführer?' (299,10). Dazu führt
Gregor den nächsten Vers an, d.i. Eccl 1,12,2: 'Ich wurde König über
Israel in Jerusalem.' Dieser Vers wird nur durch die Frage nach dem
Zeitpunkt erläutert; Psalm 2,6+7 beantwortet die Frage, bedarf aber
der weiteren Klärung, daß hier die Inkarnation gemeint sei ('Heute habe

ich dich gezeugt', Ps 2,7). Den Psalmvers auf die Inkarnation zu beziehen, hatte schon Origenes vorgegeben.[2]

Da Gregor nun die Inkarnation, also das Geschehen zur Erlösung der Menschheit eingeführt hat, versteht er die folgenden Verse als die Aussagen über Grund und Ziel der Inkarnation (Eccl 1,13-15). Gregor weist darauf hin, daß nun 'das große Geheimnis der Errettung' dargestellt werde. Nach Einleitung (298,5-299,9) und Überleitung (299,10-19) wird der Predigt eine erste Überschrift gegeben. In vier Schritten gelangt Gregor dann zu dem Bild einer kosmologischen Soteriologie, zur Apokatastasis der ursprünglichen Schöpfung Gottes. Das Bild der kosmologischen Soteriologie ist origenistisch.[3] Gregor braucht es nicht wie ein geliehenes System heranzuziehen, sondern er findet die Vorstellung von der Wiederherstellung des Alls im Ecclesiastestext 1,13-15 bestätigt, richtiger noch, es drängt sich ihm auf, nachdem er festgestellt hat, daß die Worte das Ziel der Inkarnation behandeln.

Erster Schritt (299,24-301,2): 'Um alles, was unter dem Himmel geschehen ist, zu erfahren' (Eccl 1,13,1-3). Dies will Gregor auslegen: 'Was unter dem Himmel geschehen ist.' 'Unter dem Himmel', also nicht das Himmlische selbst. Da Gregor κατασκέψασθαι als ἐπισκέψασθαι = ἐπισκέψεσθαι versteht (was sprachlich nicht korrekt ist), d.h. 'sich kümmern um' (300,2+4; cf. 300,19 und 314,16), ist für ihn der Sinn klar. Über dem Himmel bedarf nichts der Fürsorge, da sei nichts geknechtet, aber unter dem Himmel, auf der Erde ist Neues aufgetreten, dort herrscht die Nichtigkeit, neues Geschehen ist eingetreten, das Nichtseiende hat die Macht auf der Erde gewonnen. Um diese Auslegung noch einmal nachzuzeichnen:

a)   κατασκέψασθαι ist ἐπισκέψασθαι = sich kümmern um;

---

2   Cf. PG 23,88A14-B15; Identifizierung nach PTS 19 Seite 135.

3   Vgl. R. Hübner, Die Einheit des Leibes Christi bei Gregor von Nyssa, Leiden 1974, Philosophia Patrum 2, 44 f. 58-61; 96; 125-129.

b)   die vom Text aufgegebenen Fragen sind, warum unter dem Himmel,
weiterhin, warum dort ein neues Geschehen eingetreten ist;

c)   das Ergebnis des neuen Geschehens auf der Erde ist die Herrschaft der Nichtigkeit; das weiß Gregor vom Anfang (Eccl 1,2)
her und hatte es schon in der 1. Homilie platonisch als die
Macht des Nichtseienden gedeutet.

Zweiter Schritt (301,3-303,11).   Im Text Eccl 1,12,1 stand auch
ἐκζητῆσαι = untersuchen.   Also muß der weitere Vers (Eccl 1,13,4-6)
angeben, wie es zur Herrschaft des Nichtseienden gekommen ist.   Daß
die Herrschaft des Nichtseienden über das Seiende nicht ursprünglich
sein kann, wußte Gregor schon; es hieß ja: 'zu untersuchen, was ...
geschehen ist.'   Nun also die Ursache, wofür Gregor weiter ausholen
muß, da der Bibeltext sagt: 'Gott gab den Menschenkindern eine böse
Zerstreuung, um sie darin zu zerstreuen.'   Gott als die Quelle des
Guten kann Böses nicht verursacht haben.   Vielmehr, so Gregor, 'ist
es angemessener, an dem Grundsatz festzuhalten, daß die gute Gabe
Gottes, d.h. die selbstmächtige Bewegung durch den verfehlten
Gebrauch, den die Menschen davon machten, zum Werkzeug für die
Sünde wurde' (301,19-22).   Also das Festhalten an der Überzeugung,
daß Gott der Geber des Guten ist — ich denke dieses Festhalten ist
Glaube und sein Gegenteil gottlos —, führt Gregor zu einer anderen
Ursache für die Schlechtigkeit, zum verkehrten Willen des Menschen.
Solche Auslegung ist gegen den Wortlaut dieses wie auch anderer
Texte, die Gregor getreulich anführt (302,10-15).   Aber seit Clemens
und Origenes, ja seit Plato (Resp 617 e) stand fest, daß Gott nicht
die Ursache des Bösen ist.   Gregor kann denn auch den Ecclesiastestext selbst als Bestätigung anführen, weil dort προαίρεσις πνεύματος
(1,14,3) wirklich steht, und zwar so steht, daß 'die Entscheidung des
Geistes' angeklagt wird.   Daraus zieht Gregor den Schluß: erstens, daß
wirklich die Schuld hier in der Entscheidung des Menschen liegt, aber
zweitens, daß ein nachträgliches Geschehen vorliegt, da eine
Schuldzuweisung ausgesprochen ist: 'Er wäre ja ohne Schuld, wenn er
schon so ins Sein gekommen wäre' (303,10 sq).   Zu bemerken ist, daß
Gregor aus seinem Gedankengang heraus annimmt, hier liege eine
Anklage vor; genau genommen trägt er es ein.

Dritter Schritt (303,10/12-304,6). Nun wird der Zustand des eingetretenen Geschehens beschrieben. 'Denn was verdreht ist, kann nicht wieder ausgerichtet werden' (Eccl 1,15,1). ἐπικοσμηθῆναι – Gregor liest heraus, daß es sich um den Kosmos handelt, um die von Gott der Schöpfung eingestiftete Ordnung. Der kosmische Zusammenhang liegt nicht auf der Hand. Aber hat man den Blick einmal auf kosmische Ausmaße geweitet, dann ist die sprachliche Anknüpfung nicht mehr fremdartig. Zugunsten Gregors ist auch anzuführen, daß er der Grundsätzlichkeit der Aussage (οὐ δυνήσεται) gerecht wird. Also: die menschliche Entscheidung zum Schlechten hat die Menschheit 'aus dem Kosmos herausgedreht' (303,11), und zwar irreparabel (304,4-6).

Vierter Schritt (304,6-305,13) zu Eccl 1,15,2: 'Und ein Mangel kann nicht gezählt werden.' Zunächst scheint uns das Vorgehen Gregors ganz arglos zu sein. Denn er erklärt, daß ein Mangel in der biblischen Sprache das Fehlen bedeute, und Fehlendes könne auf der Habenseite kein Posten sein (cf. 304,16 sq). Aber: 'Was will er durch diesen Spruch sagen?' (304,23). Gregors Antwort ist die Zusammenfassung des bisherigen Gedankenganges: 'Daß auch wir einst der Ganzheit zugezählt wurden' (304,23-305,1). Hat man noch im Ohr: 'aus dem Kosmos herausgedreht' (303,11), dann ist die Erläuterung stimmig. Aus dem Kosmos ist die menschliche Natur herausgefallen; also, so Gregor, fehlt der ursprünglichen Ganzheit, die der Kosmos als Gottes Schöpfung ist, ein Glied. Und nun greift Gregor auf das Bild zurück, das er in seiner Einleitung nur angedeutet hatte: das Verirrte einzusammeln (cf. 280,8-11 und 299,6-8), das ist das eine Schaf der hundert Schafe zurückbringen und so die ursprüngliche Ganzheit der Hundert wiederherstellen (305,1-13; cf. Mt 18,12+13). Auf den himmlischen Weg soll die menschliche Natur zurückgebracht werden (cf. 305,4); man ist versucht hinzuzufügen, auch an den himmlischen Ort, wo die neunundneunzig Geistwesen immer geblieben sind. Jedoch ist Gregor vorsichtig; er benutzt die örtlichen Vorstellungen nur als Metapher: Die sündige Menschheit befindet sich in der 'salzigen und bitteren Region' (305,4-5; cf. Hiob 39,6 — auch Plato, Pol 273d und Plotin I 8,13,16: Region der Ungleicheit).

Nachdem Grund und Ziel der Errettung, d.h. der Inkarnation festgestellt sind, beginnt die zweite Hälfte der Homilie. Gregor gibt ihr das Thema: 'Welches ist der Rückweg des Verirrten und auf welche Weise geschieht die Rückführung aus dem Übel zum Guten' (305,14 sq). Im Grunde ist dies das Thema aller noch folgenden Homilien, aber wir werden sehen, zu welchem Ende Gregor sein Thema in dieser Homilie führt.

Nun würde man eine Christologie erwarten, aber gar nichts davon! Vielmehr ändert Gregor die gedankliche Ebene, und man könnte sagen, daß es im Getriebe knirscht. Ab hier, d.h. ab Eccl 1,16 werden wir unterrichtet 'über den Rückweg des Verirrten ... ' Ohne schon auf den nächsten Bibelvers einzugehen, versucht Gregor seinen Hörern den Themenwechsel plausibel zu machen. Sein Überleitungsstichwort heißt: Erfahrung. 'Der nämlich, der Erfahrung hat, "allenthalben gleich wie wir, doch ohne Sünde" (Hbr 4,15), spricht uns aus unserer Situation her an' (305,16 sq). Würden wir das Folgende nicht kennen, so wäre die Anknüpfung an den bisherigen Gedankengang bruchlos. Denn um die menschliche Natur wieder in die Hundertschaft der geistigen Schafe einzugliedern, 'nahm Christus das Verlorene auf seine Schultern' (305,10; cf. Lk 15,5). Mit einer anderen biblischen Wendung (Mt 8,17 = Jes 53,4) nimmt Gregor das Bild auf: 'Der unsere Schwachheiten auf sich nahm, zeigt uns durch die Schwächen unserer Natur den Weg, der aus der Schlechtigkeit herausführt' (305,18 sq). Auch jetzt könnte der Hörer noch erwarten, daß eine Christologie folgt, d.h. Ausführungen über den Christus der Evangelien. Aber dem ist nicht so, sondern Gregor überrascht seine Hörer mit der Veränderung: 'Jetzt aber aufgepaßt: Die Weisheit aus Salomo nach dem Fleisch spricht uns an' (305,19-21). Philologisch gesehen ist das die Feststellung, daß nun ein Wechsel der sprechenden Person anzunehmen ist. Von der Sache als Thema ist ein Personenwechsel nicht nötig; er widerspricht dem Gedankengang. Gregor hätte philologisch begründen können, daß die folgenden Verse nicht mehr Christus als dem direkten Sprecher angemessen sind, sondern vielmehr Salomo. Aber erstens ist die Predigt in ihrer Darstellungsform kein Kommentarwerk, und zweitens will Gregor ja gar keinen ganz anderen Sprecher haben. 'Der nämlich, der unsere Schwachheiten auf sich nahm,' sagte Gregor, 'der zeigt uns durch die Schwäche unserer Natur den Weg, der aus der Schlechtigkeit herausführt.' Warum also der Wechsel der sprechenden Person? Mir scheint, daß Gregor sich der Auslegungstradition beugt, aber erst ab hier. Er tut es, so vermute ich, weil er die folgenden Verse eben nicht mehr in den Mund des menschgewordenen Christus legen kann. Denn die folgenden Erfahrungen, die unsere Schwächen sind, hat der inkarnierte Christus eben nicht erfahren. Und doch bleiben die folgenden Erfahrungen mit Christus verbunden, da die Weisheit aus Salomo spricht. Man kann die Form, in der der Ekklesiastes der durch Christus geschehenen Erlösung subsumiert wird, bewundern. Aber man kann auch fragen, ob die nun aus Salomos Worten herausgelesene 'Rückführung aus dem Übel zum Guten' (305,14 sq) noch christlich ist, d.h. ob christliche Erlösung darin besteht, daß, wie Gregor sagt, 'wir dazu geführt werden, das zu verachten, was bei den Menschen als erstrebenswert gilt' (305,21-23).

Die zweite Hälfte der Predigt gliedert sich in ein Proömium (305,14-307,14) und drei weitere Teile:

1. Tugend wird durch Anstrengung erworben (307,15-309,18).

2. Lachen und körperliches Vergnügen berauben den Menschen der Vernunft (309,19-311,14).

3. Die Erfahrung der Nichtigkeit der Sinneslüste führt zur Suche nach dem wahrhaft Guten (311,15-314,10).

Die Überleitung zum neuen Thema und zu einem neuen Sprecher macht sich einen Topos zunutze. Es ist der Gedanke der Erfahrung, deren Besitz das Lehren glaubwürdig macht. Mit Hilfe dieses Gedankens (übrigens auch bei Didymus, vgl. bes. EcclT 45,10-15) leitet Gregor vom inkarnierten Christus zu Salomo über und führt dann breit aus, inwiefern Salomo die Erfahrung machen konnte, daß Sinnesvergnügen nichtig sei. Salomo, der dritte König, war der reiche Friedenskönig (306,11-19): 'Für seine Wünsche gab es kein Hindernis' (306,19 sq).

Jedoch steht Gregor vor der Schwierigkeit, Salomo trotz des Verweises auf dessen Lusterfahrung nicht zum Lüstling zu machen.

Deswegen trägt Gregor einen Gedanken ein, der nur zwei textliche Anhaltspunkte hat. Der erste Teil über Eccl 1,16-18 sagt einmal, daß Salomo über den Besitz, der ihm zugefallen war, hinaus 'Weisheit hinzufügte' (1,16,3), und zum andern, daß mit dem Zuwachs von Erkenntnis auch 'Zuwachs von Pein' (1,18,2) kam. Dies und nichts anderes hat Gregor im Sinn: Salomos Weisheitserfahrung ist der Ertrag von Mühe und Schweiß, nur durch Mühe und Schweiß ist der Erwerb von Weisheit möglich (cf. 307,24 sq; cf. Hesiod, Opera 287-290; Aristo der Stoiker SVF I 85, 18/9; Epiktet III 12,7; Clemens, Stromata passim, bes. IV 5; bei Gregor cf. Cant. p. 188, 1-4).

Dann, im zweiten Teil zu Eccl 2,1-2, hat Gregor das Problem, wie sich Salomo denn die Erfahrung der Sinneslüste aneignete. Natürlich, müßte man sagen, läßt sich Salomo nicht verführen, sondern nur studienhalber probiert er die Sinnesfreuden aus (cf. 310,3-6). Und Lachen und Vergnügen konfrontiert er sofort; daß er sie ausprobiert hätte, vermeidet Gregor zu behaupten.

Im dritten Teil schließlich deutet Gregor vorsichtig an, daß Salomo Sinneslüste ausprobierte, um, wie Gregor Eccl 2,3 insgesamt deutet, das Gute zu suchen, das nicht nur momentane Freude bereitet. Sein Ziel, das Andere, das dauernde Gute von Sinnesfreuden zu unterscheiden, erreicht Gregor durch zwei Vorstellungsreihen: Einmal beschreibt er am Beispiel von Trinken und Essen, daß die Lust mit der Sättigung vergeht (cf. 312,23 sq); zum andern behauptet er, das lustbereitende Gute sei bei den Menschen je nach Altersstufe verschieden (cf. 313,5-8). Dem stellt er das Gute gegenüber, das allen Altersstufen und jeder Lebenslage genüge (313,17-314,2), das sich immer gleichbleibe und im Genuß die Begierde danach nicht mindere (313,10-15). Im Unterschied zu den Homilien zum Hohenlied und zur Vita Mosis fehlt in dieser Beschreibung die fortschreitende Bewegung, die Gregor meist in Anlehnung an Phil 3,13 formuliert (cf. e.g. Cant. p. 158 oder 174). Gregor beendet die Homilie fast unvermittelt. Er faßt zusammen: 'Nach meiner Überzeugung ist es das wirklich seiende Gute, das Salomo zu sehen suchte' (314,2-3). Und gleich wieder setzt er sein Ich: 'Das scheint mir nichts anderes zu sein als das Werk des Glaubens' (314,5 sq; 'Werk des Glaubens' sonst nirgends bei Gregor).

Daraus macht er dann 'das gute Werk, das auch bei uns geschehen möge in Christus Jesus, unserem Herrn, dem sei Ehre bis in Ewigkeit. Amen' (314,8-10).

An introduction to Homily III

Adolf Martin Ritter

The text to be interpreted is Eccl. 2,4-6. The Greek, quoted by
Gregory in the course of his exegesis in a quite distinctive way, runs
as follows:

ἐμεγάλυνα ποίημά μου,

ᾠκοδόμησά μοι οἴκους.

φύτευσά μοι ἀμπελῶνας

(the next line, corresponding to ἐποίησά μοι κήπους καὶ παραδείσους in
Rahlfs' edition of the LXX, is not formally quoted, but only alluded
to: only the words κήπων καὶ παραδείσων are certain. Then follows
the full text)

ἐφύτευσα πᾶν ξύλον καρποῦ·

ἐποίησα γάρ μοι κολυμβήθρας ὑδάτων

τοῦ ποτίσαι ἀπ' αὐτῶν δρυμὸν βλαστῶντα ξύλα.

In this homily Gregory quotes the Bible text *en bloc* neither at the
beginning nor in the course of his exegesis. After a short systematic
introduction to the whole of the Bible text and its σκοπός (as German
exegetes would say), Gregory interprets the text phrase by phrase.
Nevertheless, he uses incidentally in our homily a phrase which sounds
nearly technical: διὰ τῆς νῦν ἀναγνώσεως ('the present reading',
317,13), which gives the impression of a solemn reading of the text
(by Gregory himself or by another) before the sermon began.

The homily begins by summarizing very briefly the two preceding homilies. The first let us understand that the real author of the Book of Ecclesiastes is the Logos himself, he who combines the divine work of creation with that of salvation: ὁ πᾶσαν ἐκκλησιάζων τὴν κτίσιν ('who calls together the whole creation'; cf. the ἐκκλησιαστικὴ φωνή of the first line) καὶ ... — allusions to the gospel follow, e.g. Lk 19,10; Mt 18,11, so that we have paraphrases of creation 'by the word' and of salvation before us. It also let us understand that life 'under the heaven' (Eccl. 1,13,3) is the subject of the author's investigation (ἐπισκέπτασθαι) in the Book of Ecclesiastes, a life in which deceit, futility and unreality or nothingness, that which has no ὕπαρξις (in German: 'das Nichtige') prevail.

Homily II taught us, according to Gregory's summary, that the indictment (κατηγορία) of an attitude to life (διάθεσις) based on enjoyment and passion or emotion (πάθος), comes from the mouth of Solomon (and not of the Logos or Word himself). Gregory follows here the tradition of 'prosopographical' (or prosopological) exegesis, characterized by the assumption that the Spirit or the Logos as the real author of Holy Scripture uses different πρόσωπα to speak to us. The main criterion for differentiating between the various πρόσωπα is the content of the given passage (see, for example, C. Andresen's fine Marburg inaugural lecture, Zur Entstehung und Geschichte des trinitarischen Personenbegriffes: ZNW 52, 1961, 1-39; résumé in StPatr 6, 1962, 3-5). In this case, the content, demanding to see in Solomon the πρόσωπον speaking, is the obvious intention of the text, which is to make the indictment (κατηγορία) of the wrong disposition (διάθεσις) convincing to us. Because (or better, although) Solomon *had* the full (absolute) freedom (πᾶσα ἐξουσία) to enjoy what serves for pleasure (ἡδονή), he nevertheless believes all that seems to be desired by mankind to be nothing!

As the main content of Homily III Gregory announces in his introduction, 'What follows', i.e. what follows logically (τὸ ἀκόλουθον — Gregory always likes ἀκολουθία[1]), and, as he sees it, 'particularly

---

1. See below, S. Leanza pp. 346-348.

appropriate to the members of the church' (μάλιστα ... κατάλληλον ... τοῖς ἐκκλησιάζουσι). Gregory continues, as we see, to play on words: after ἐκκλησιαστής, ἐκκλησιαστικός and ἐκκλησιάζω in the sense of 'summon', 'convene', 'convoke', we meet the last word in another sense, 'to belong (or adhere) to the church' (PGL gives references enough for both meanings). And what is it that Gregory regards as especially appropriate for Christians)? It is the ἐξομολόγησις, the confession of things 'not rightly done', i.e. not in accordance with reason (περὶ τῶν μὴ κατὰ λόγον γεγεννημένων). Gregory uses here the technical term ἐξομολόγησις, which could at the same time, as naming the most important part, the oral confession, serve as designation of the whole 'penitential' procedure, and could even be taken over by the Latin-speaking western church (as Tertullian testifies). It is a confession which makes the soul feel ashamed (πάθος in this case not in the sense of 'passion' or 'burning indignation', but 'feeling' or 'emotion'), by — publicly! — expressing or pronouncing things foolish or unreasonably done (διὰ τῆς τῶν ἀτόπων ἐξαγορεύσεως — in the translation, 'the public acknowledgement of sins'). ἐξαγόρευσις, used here as an explanation of ἐξομολόγησις, serves further on to replace it.

With αἰσχύνη or τὸ τῆς αἰσχύνης ... πάθος (translated 'shame', 'feeling/emotion of shame') we meet the catchword which Gregory reflects upon in a first section of the Homily's main part (315,13- 317,12), complemented by the cognate term αἰδώς (translated 'modesty'), which Gregory seems to need for a full-scale discussion. Or is the introduction of αἰδώς beside αἰσχύνη influenced by Aristotle's Nicomachean Ethics IV and other works? At any rate, in this first section Gregory reflects upon the relation between αἰδώς and αἰσχύνη (following, but not strictly quoting, Aristotle and others [see the apparatus testimoniorum]; the substance of the discussion is different in Gregory and in Aristotle), and he tries to determine their bearing on and contribution to the virtuous life. αἰδώς and αἰσχύνη have in common that they are placed in our nature by its Creator and can therefore be regarded as a certain disposition (διάθεσις) of the human soul. The aim of this disposition is to serve as a means to deter us from worse things (ἀποτροπὴ τῶν χειρόνων) and to prevent sin, provided, it is true, one is willing to use this psychic disposition in an appropriate way.

αἰδώς and αἰσχύνη are distinguished from each other insofar as the one appears or arises before, the other after, sins have been done and detected! They are cognate with each other insofar as both are apt to prevent sin, even if it is the repetition of past sin. According to their different relation to reality αἰδώς may be defined as a reduced form of αἰσχύνη, and αἰσχύνη as an intensified form of αἰδώς. Identity and difference of both feelings find their expression also by the colour in a person's face. αἰδώς reveals itself only by a blush (ἐρυθρήματι μόνῳ), whereas he who has been convicted of a fault and therefore has been filled with αἰσχύνη, becomes ashen and pale red (πελιδνὸς γίνεται καὶ ὑπερυθρός — in the translation, 'becomes livid and reddish') — Aristotle gives the necessary explanation of the psychological reasons for this alarming phenomenon (see again the *apparatus testimoniorum* in Alexander's edition).

Gregory illustrates the result of his reflections by an example, taken, as often, from the medical sphere. In the next section, which is unambiguously delimited by Ταῦτα τοίνυν ('This therefore' in 317,13) and Ἴδωμεν τοίνυν ('Let us see then' in 319,11), Gregory goes on to say that it is not easy to decide with certainty whether Solomon really did those things which he blames himself for, or whether he made the story up for our benefit — a repetition of an analogous discussion in Homily II. Whether Solomon discusses these things οἰκονομίας χάριν, i.e. intending to meet our specific situation and to accommodate himself to it (in the translation, 'by benevolent design'; cf. the usual distinction in canonistics between a procedure or decision κατ' οἰκονομίαν and κατ' ἀκρίβειαν), — or whether he deliberately lowered himself to enjoy such things in order to train his senses δι' ἀκριβείας (translated 'rigorously'; here we meet the corollary of οἰκονομία!), and by means of the 'opposite' (or 'alien things', τῶν ἐναντίων), anyone who wishes is free to decide according to the speculation he wishes to make.

Even to suppose that Solomon really made experiences with earthly pleasures his own is quite acceptable. Gregory illustrates this by the example of a pearl-fisher or diver, to whom the exertions under water cause not the least pleasure; only the hope of gaining the pearl lets him endure till the end. So Solomon submerged himself, maybe, in luxury and lust, with the intention of finding something useful to reflect upon (τι τῇ διανοίᾳ χρήσιμον, 'something useful to the mind'), not to fill himself with the salt of the sea, that is, with pleasure. This discovery, useful to reflect upon, could perhaps be the attenuation of carnal desire ('blunted the body's appetites', τό ἀμβλῦναι τὰς τοῦ σώματος ὁρμάς), by making freely accessible whatever the body wants; for as experience teaches us, nature always moves more eagerly towards what is forbidden. The other justification might be that the teacher engages in temptations, in order to increase the plausibility of his teaching and warnings, like the physician, whose reputation increases if he himself has suffered the same complaints which he is later asked to diagnose and treat.

So far Gregory has given an introduction and preliminary systematic treatment of the Homily's main content or σκοπός. What he does in the rest is to interpret line by line, κῶλον after κῶλον, the Bible text (Eccl. 2,4-6), a procedure similar to that of Homilies I and II. It is, however, not necessary to follow here his interpretation in detail. I should like only to mention the following:

(1)   By far the most extensive explanation is given to the fourth verse of Eccl. 2 (319,11-331,11), whereas the last two verses of 'today's reading' (τῆς νῦν ἀναγνώσεως, 'the present reading') are passed through in less than three pages, the last verse in exactly 11 lines of Alexander's edition.

(2)   Gregory's interpretation aims at making evident a negative sense, being in harmony with the statement from which he proceeded when beginning his interpretation of the Bible text in detail, namely: 'The text starts from a charge' or 'begins straight away with an indictment' (εὐθὺς ἐκ κατηγορίας ὁ λόγος ἄρχεται, 319,13-14; cf. the beginning of Homily II).

(3)   Gregory reaches his goal by stressing:

(a) the dynamism of μεγαλύνω ('enlarge', in Eccl. 2,4,1), and the antithesis, 'my creation or product/God's creation' (ποίημά μου/ποίημα θεοῦ, 'my doing/God's doing');

(b) the plural οἴκους, 'houses', and not the one house which the human being needs, — this 'physiological premature birth', this 'animal', who is, he says, 'too weak to bear the extremes of heat and cold' (320,6-7; here the man from Cappadocia is speaking!);

(c) the association of vineyards with their consequence (τέλος), drunkenness (327,21-330,11), and of vegetable-plots (κῆποι) with the production of 'plants, the food of the weak in health' (331,16);

(d) the antithesis of the many gardens (παράδεισοι) and the one heavenly Garden of Paradise (331,14-15), and also of the earthly water and the one source of spiritual power (333,4-334,3).

(4)   In doing this Gregory lives in grand rhetorical style, especially in his lengthy interpretation of Eccl. ·2,4. We meet here fine examples of chiasmus, a big three-fold climax (328,18-329,13), and some fine and effective ἐκφράσεις (descriptive passages) of the kind which Gregory likes very much, as all Gregorians know, and which his original audience would have appreciated (e.g. within the context of 319,11-324,2 and 327,21-330,11). I would certainly try to emulate Gregory's rhetoric where the climax of 328-329 is concerned, and to give the translation more brilliance.

Homily II, I conclude, does not come up with philosophical or theological sensations. In this respect its substance is fairly restricted. One may even ask what in this Bible interpretation is really Christian or biblical at all. Its main interest lies, as I see it, in the realm of rhetoric.

Homily 4

Lionel Wickham

Homily 4 is a fine, bold piece, rich in striking imagery, particularly in the last section where Gregory speaks about the snake of passion (348,15 ff.) and, in his last paragraph, likens the futility of the pursuit of pleasure to tracing out the shapes of letters on water. These rangings of poetic fancy are very characteristic of the author and were much admired. If the brilliant paradox is the typical feature of the other Gregory (of Nazianzus) and the judicious analysis of the Bible that typical of Basil (I am thinking of *De Spiritu Sancto*), it is the haunting image, elaborated often to the point of a literary conceit, which betrays the particular style of our Gregory. Moreover, Gregory speaks here about slavery and usury: public issues of conscience and morality where the attitudes of the Church in his day differ widely from our own. The Church, upon the whole, accepted slavery and rejected usury in his day. We reverse the attitudes. But does not Gregory here go beyond the usual acceptance (of course, always qualified) of slavery as an institution to something that amounts to condemnation of it? And what is he actually saying about usury? These are questions I would like to raise. They lead me to some tentative suggestions about the context of the sermon and the character of the audience addressed. What I want to say will not, I think, contradict the main conclusions of Professor Bergadá on this Homily 4, but I want to approach the interpretation in a slightly different way which puts what Gregory intends in another perspective. I will go through the text, trying the recapture Gregory's train of thought and make it explicit. The general divisions introduced by the translators seem to me sound and helpful, and I shall follow them.

1.   334,4-338,2. The evils of slave-owning.

We are hearing now from King Solomon a confession of his guilty acts, as Gregory interprets the passage. This is the model of what we are to avoid. Solomon has now got to an indictment of himself for ὑπερηφανία ('pride'). This is the attitude of 'overweening arrogance' (if I ctch the correct nuance of the word). It is the arrogance which leads to treating other persons with contempt. This attitude is exemplified at its most vain, nonsensical and deluded (τυφός). When Solomon says, 'I got me slaves and slave-girls, and homebred slaves were born for me', that is to make a pretentious claim (ἀλαξονεία) to a status that belongs only to God. For all things are slaves of God. Only God has property-rights over all things and anyone who attributes such rights to himself over another portion of the human species, so as to claim to be owner or lord over them, is guilty of overweening arrogance. For all men are of one stock and the κυριοτησ, which belongs absolutely to God and relatively to man over the rest of earthly creation, cannot be claimed by one part of mankind absolutely.

I will not now go into the details of Gregory's arguments here, which have been most carefully set out by Professor Bergadá. The unity in essential status of the human race, the dignity of man as free, in the image of God's freedom, the artificiality of the title κύριος or δεσπότης when applied to one human being over another: all combine to reinforce the arrogance of the claim by Solomon ἐκτήσαμην δούλους καὶ παιδίσκας. By talking of cattle and sheep in the same breath with slaves and slave-girls (Gregory ends) Solomon implies that they were all subject to himself in the same way.

I make three small notes. (a) p. 336,21f: ἀνάγκη γὰρ πᾶσα καὶ τὸ κτῆμα τοῦ πωλουμένου συναποδίδοσθαι, 'For the property of the person sold is bound to be sold with him too.' The editor of the Greek text records (p. 337) that this does not square with Roman

Law, which rules that a slave's property is not sold along with him
unless expressly stipulated.   There might be a variety of explanations
of the discrepancy.   But it would be fair to conclude that Gregory's
hearers are not lawyers.   And I would suggest that they are not
people with experience of buying or selling slaves.   (b) The translation
is too heavy of the sentence beginning p. 337,19.   I would render: 'I
see nothing further (apart from the name) than a subordinate accruing
to you from a name'.   Gregory's language is loose, but he means that
the word 'slave' does not make any difference in reality to the one
who has acquired a ὑποχείριον: it gives him no right or actual
authority.   (c) There must be many parallels for the lines which
follow.   Shakespeare's Shylock is a fine example of the genre.   But
what are the precise ancient models here?

On the passage as a whole I would observe that in context it is
not so much a condemnation of slavery or about the evils of owning
slaves, as a condemnation of pride in the sense of overweening
arrogance.   Slavery is, of course, an issue for public conscience and
morality, and Gregory's arguments are, in the end, arguments for the
abolition of slavery.   But Gregory treats the matter in the domain of
private conscience.   This is an example of the kind of arrogance
against God and Man of which we each individually may be guilty.
Gregory is not generalizing to the condemnation of a social system as
such, so far as I can see.   What he has to say is consistent with
the toleration of the system, provided that the absolute claims of
God are recognized.   To put it another way, Gregory's arguments are
against the *use* of one person by another, where that use implies the
assumption of divine superiority; they are not against employment as
such.   I do not think Gregory goes beyond the usual view of his time,
therefore.   At least not by direct intention.   My guess would be that
Gregory's words would encourage his hearers to free their slaves, if
they had any.   There are plenty of examples of devout Christians
doing that.   Gregory Nazianzen, for instance, did so, as his will
shows.   But the congregation is not being invited, as it were, to
campaign for a change in the law.   My speculation would be that
Gregory's congregation at a mid-week service where this Homily was

delivered would consist mainly of clergy and devout lay people who did not have slaves and would not feel threatened by what they heard. I think one could add that the sermon is not the place where the preacher attempts, in ancient or modern times, to change people's basic assumptions, whether doctrinal or moral. Convictions are reinforced (with, it may be, one played off against another) but not profoundly altered. Naturally, that leaves open the question of whether Gregory's arguments are consistent with the continued existence of slavery as an institution at all. And any consideration of that would have to take into account the very varied forms assumed by that institution in ancient times.

2.   338,23-343,9. The uselessness of gold.

I pass now to the second section. Solomon, according to Gregory, now moves on the describe the greatest sins of his. 'He denounces himself for *the root of all evils*, which is *the love of money.*' I find the movement of thought disconcerting on Gregory's part. It is occasioned by the text he is commenting upon and Gregory's interpretation of it as a progressive ἐξομολόγησις. The text from 1 Tim 6,10 gives him his cue. But it is surely odd to make love of money a greater sin than pride or than pretension to God's rights over other human beings. Perhaps Gregory means to distinguish the πάθος of ὑπερηφανεία from the ἁμαρτήματα or actual transgressions of Solomon. Or perhaps he might say he is not answerable for Solomon's way of putting it. However that may be, the gathering of silver and gold is a sin, because it oversteps the bounds of human authority. Mankind has been given what lies on the surface of the ground, but has no right to mine. Gregory makes the last point, by rhetorical questions. He recognizes it as offered ἀγωνιστικῶς not δογματικῶς. Perhaps a right to mine *may* be allowed. But Solomon has used force to exact money from his subjects for personal aggrandisement. There we touch upon sin. But to what end? Gold does not secure happiness either of soul or body even in vast quantities. 'If therefore the abundance of gold proposed in our argument offers no benefit in body or soul, it is far more likely that when it is available on a small scale it will prove useless to those

who possess it.'   Of course, gold is used to buy things that are
useful.   But the mere acquisition of the stuff for its own sake is
futile.   If you answer that gold is beautiful, it can be pointed out
that it is not more beautiful than other things which are available for
all.   If you use it for jewellery it will not compensate for defects in
the appearance of the wearer.

There is an interesting parallel passage to the present in Pliny
N.H. 33 ad.init. where Pliny castigates the practice of mining, then
moves on to gold and silver, and ends by blessing the epoch when
exchange was normal before the invention of coinage.[1]   Gregory takes
no note of the Biblical approval of mining in Deut 8,9.   I think it
possible that he follows here some source which linked condemnation
of mining, of precious metals, of coinage and then of usury.   Let me
make a few comments.   Gregory tells his congregation three facts: (1)
there are things money cannot buy; (2) the substance which forms the
basis of exchange is useless if it does not lead to exchange; (3) gold
has no special beauty or utility in itself.   And he draws the important
lesson that it does not matter whether you have any or not.   But
notice how these matters are put together, in a 'jerky' way, without
regard to a defined economic theory.   Of course, it can truly be said
that a sermon is not the place for a discussion of issues of that
kind, and that Gregory's aim is to elevate his hearers beyond such
things.   It seems to me odd that he says nothing to distinguish
currency from gold/silver, though Gregory must have been aware of it,
and an understanding of economic theory lies behind his comments, as
a parallel will show.   Perhaps one might speculate that Gregory's
congregation is not made up of people for whom currency was of
special importance: it was used, of course, but it stood for savings
in people's minds; what was hoarded, especially if it came in the form
of precious metals, rather than used.   This is, perhaps, a
congregation dependent upon farming rather than trade.   The same
sort of speculation comes to mind with the next section.

---

1.   C.Nicolet, Pline, Paul et la théorie de la monnaie: *Athenaeum*
1984, 105-135.

3.   343,10–346,14. Against usury.

Gold has, Gregory continues, been proved useless and its acquisition irrational and leading to acts of violence. Violence by way of outright robbery but also by way of the immoral exaction of interest on loans. 'What is the difference between getting someone else's property by seizing it ... and acquiring what is not one's own by exacting interest?

Interest is money generating money, which is an absurdity. The lender offers a loan to the farmer whose crops fail. The loan lands the borrower in even worse straits. The debtor cannot repay loan and interest, and the lender strips his debtor naked. This is legally enforced crime, not philanthropy. Interest (τόκος) 'is the "child" with which greed was in labour, and to which wickedness gave birth, and whose midwife is miserliness.' There is an important parallel in Aristotle *Pol.* 1,9f (with which cf. *Eth.Nic.* V) which is no doubt the ultimate source for this condemnation of usury.[2]

I comment: this is a tissue of commonplaces. Which is not to say that it did not come home as real to the congregation. It represents stereotypes and caricatures which would surely have re-inforced reasonably grounded prejudices. It offers a suitable object of common abomination: the money-lender. Perhaps Gregory's picture is meant to stand as well as an awful warning of the dangers of debt in a rural community. I have not met with any arguments in favour of usury in patristic writings, or any technical discussion of its basis. Church law forbade it both to laity and clergy and many collections of canons (e.g. Canon 17 of Nicaea) mention it. Clearly too it went on and could not be stamped out. Public law in Gregory's time allowed it, moderating the rates at which interest might be charged.[3] According to John Chrysostom (*Hom.* 56 *In Matth.* c.6, PG

---

2.   See the article by Nicolet, n. 1.

3.   See E. Bianchi, 'Il temam d'usura. Canone conciliare e legislazione imperiale del IV secolo' (second part of a two-part essay): *Athenaeum* 1984, 136–153.

57,557) senators and dignitaries were forbidden to lend on interest. Justinian's code has detailed provisions on the subject: 12% p.a. is the highest rate sanctioned (paid monthly). Gregory, of course, does not dispute the public legality of usury (contracts can be enforced in a court of law — it is legally sanctioned theft) but his language is that of absolute condemnation. I think there is a subtle difference here from his treatment of slavery. From usury Gregory now passes to personal sins and vices.

4.   346,15-348,14. Drunkeness aggravates the pleasures of sound and sight.

Money-loving is the *root of all the evils* and Solomon, having talked about the root of his sins, now goes on to describe the outward symptoms of the diseased condition. The luxury money brings leads to revelry, the false gratification of hearing and sight, to sensuality and indecency made worse by wine. I do not think the passage requires my comment. The theme has been dealt with by preachers from time immemorial.

5.   348,15-353,9. The serpent as the symbol of passion; the Ecclesiast's experience of pleasure.

Gregory now draws together what Solomon has been saying. He starts with a comparison. Pleasure is like a snake; it slips into the soul secretly and is then difficult to dislodge. Best deny any entry. What Solomon acknowledges to us is that he has explored every avenue of enjoyment and has come to realise its frivolity. He teaches us to set no store by wealth, ambition and all the rest, for all these things are utterly transient and insubstantial. I have only two comments to make upon an eloquent passage. (a) I think the translation 'choice of spirit' sounds very odd. Regardless of what the phrase means in Homily 2 (303,6-11), here the sense must be not of human 'spirit' but natural 'wind', i.e. a seeking after what is as empty as the wine. (b) I ask what the function of the two brilliant illustrations (the snake of pleasure and writing on water) is. The editor signals that the snake image figures elsewhere in Gregory, so it is clearly one he found useful and no doubt his congregation enjoyed

hearing.   He is able to link it with a Biblical text (watching out for
the head) and a biblical idea (the snake as a symbol of evil).   That
gives it a spiritual 'tone' it might otherwise lack.   The basic idea is
straightforward, indeed commonplace, enough: just as it is difficult to
get rid of a snake in the wall of a house, so it is difficult to rid of
the desire for pleasure once it has been gratified.   But as the image
is elaborated it becomes hard to follow.   That is not true of the
second illustration, which is plain and unadorned.   My guess is that
the function of both is the same: to make a hackneyed point
memorable.

La condamnation de l'esclavage dans l'Homélie IV

Maria Mercedès Bergadá

L'Homélie IV sur l'*Ecclésiaste* — parmi les huit discours que Grégoire de Nysse a consacrés au livre de Qohélet — commente le texte qui va du verset 2,7 jusqu'au verset 2,11.

Trois thèmes vont attirer successivement l'attention de Grégoire, à commencer par celui qui sera l'object de cette communication: la condamnation de l'esclavage, qui prétend faire d'un homme le maître et le propriétaire d'un autre homme.

1. L'argumentation prend son départ, dès le premier paragraphe de cette homélie, en faisant allusion aux précedents versets 4-7 dans lesquels le personnage qui parle, déjà désabusé des nourritures terrestres et ayant connu d'expérience la vanité de tous les biens de ce monde, fait une énumération retrospective de tous ces biens de fortune dont il a joui: 'J'ai fait grand. Je me suis bâti des palais, je me suis planté des vignes, je me suis fait des jardins et des vergers, et j'y ai planté tous les arbres fruitiers. Je me suis fait des citernes pour arroser de leurs eaux les jeunes arbres de mes plantations. J'ai acquis des esclaves (au masculin, δούλους) et des servantes (παιδίσκας), j'ai eu des domestiques et des troupeaux, du gros et du petit bétail en abondance, plus que quiconque avant moi à Jérusalem.' La première phrase du verset 7, citée littéralement, c'est la texte dont Grégoire va faire son leit-motiv dans les paragraphes qui vont suivre et dans toute cette première partie de l'homélie: ἐκτήσαμεν δούλους καὶ παιδίσκας.

Une fois ainsi attirée l'attention sur ce texte, il entre de plein
pied dans le coeur du problème: dans toute cette longue et
présomptueuse énumération il n'y a rien qui mette si fortement en
évidence la superbe et la folie de celui qui parle — 'la phrase a pour
nous la valeur d'une confession', signale Grégoire au début (334,4) —
comme cette affirmation qui énonce un fait vraiment monstrueux: τὸν
ἄνθρωπον ὄντα, δεσπότην ἑαυτὸν τῶν ὁμοφύλων οἴεσθαι.   C'est à dire,
que quelqu'un qui n'est qu'un simple homme se croie maître de ceux qui
lui sont semblables, qui partagent sa même nature, qui appartiennent à
la même espèce que lui.

C'est à remarquer ici le mot ὁμόφυλος employé par Grégoire pour
signaler cette condition: ils partagent tous, le maître et ses prétendus
esclaves, ce qu'on dirait un même φῦλον (mot qui peut avoir pour
quelques uns d'entre nous des résonnances teilhardiennes, ce qui ne
serait pas certainement la seule coïncidence qu'on pourrait signaler
entre la pensée de Teilhard de Chardin et celle du nyséen).   Nous
retrouverons une fois encore ce terme ὁμόφυλος dans les paragraphes
qui suivent, et on le trouve aussi p.ex. dans le *Traité de la Virginité*
(XVIII,3), du même Grégoire.   Cependant le *PGL* de Lampe ne le
régistre pas, tandis qu'on peut le trouver au Liddell/Scott avec des
exemples de l'époque classique, tels que Thucydide et Xénophon,
toujours avec le sens 'of the same race or stock, akin'.

Après quoi il signale avec force: 'Voila la tumeur de la
vantardise: cette voix s'insurge ouvertement en face de Dieu.   Car
tout ce qui existe est soumis (δοῦλα) au pouvoir (ἐξουσία) de Celui
qui est au dessus de tout.   Celui donc qui fait sien ce qui est la
propriété de Dieu, en assignant à sa propre espèce la souveraineté, de
sorte qu'il arrive à se croire seigneur d'hommes et de femmes, qu'est-
ce qu'il fait, sinon outrepasser par sa vantardise les limites de sa
propre nature, en se regardant soi-même comme s'il était différent de
ceux qui lui sont soumis?' (334,16-335,4).

Voici donc un premier argument, qu'on pourrait dire d'ordre
strictement naturel et même philosophique: l'homme ne peut pas avoir
des droits de propriété sur une autre créature humaine parce que

celle-ci appartient au même genre que lui, lui est ὁμόφυλος, son semblable.

Nous pensons qu'il est utile encore une fois de faire attention aux mots dont Grégoire se sert pour exprimer ses idées: le terme δοῦλος, 'esclave', est délibérément employé pour dire la soumission de toutes les créatures au pouvoir (ἐξουσία) de Dieu. C'est donc le Créateur, qui est au dessus de tout, le seul qui peut avoir en propriété tout ce qu'il a créé et qui évidemment, par ce fait même, est au dessous de lui. Mais l'homme, la plus haute de toutes les créatures visibles, pourra certainement avoir quelque autorité sur d'autres hommes, dans les conditions établies par l'organisation sociale et de conformité avec ses lois, mais il ne pourra jamais être le propriétaire d'aucun de ses semblables. Des droits de propriété, il ne peut les avoir que sur des êtres qui sont au dessous de lui, qui lui sont inférieurs, que ce soient des bêtes, des oiseaux ou des poissons, des arbres avec leur bois et leurs fruits, des terres avec leurs récoltes, des objets manufacturés par lui-même ou par d'autres hommes, — enfin, il ne peut être que le propriétaire de tout ce qui existe sur la face de la terre à la seule exception des créatures humaines, qui sont ses semblables, qui lui sont ὁμόφυλοι.

2.   ἐκτησάμην δούλους καὶ παιδίσκας, 'J'ai acquis des esclaves et des servantes,' répète Grégoire pour introduire un second argument, celui-ci d'une allure plus théologique et fondée sur l'Ecriture: 'Tu condamnes l'homme à l'esclavage,' — écrit-il — 'cet homme qui a une nature *libre* et *maîtresse d'elle même* (ἐλευθέρα ἡ φύσις καὶ αὐτεξούσιος, il faut bien faire attention à ces deux mots, sur lesquels nous allons revenir), et tu te permets de donner une loi qui s'oppose à Dieu, en renversant la loi naturelle. Car ce même homme, qui fut créé pour être le maître de la terre, celui que le Créateur constitua comme seigneur de toute la création visible, tu le soumets au joug de la servitude en faisant résistance et opposition à l'ordre divin' (335,5-11).

Il est très important, à notre avis, le fait que, dans ce passage que nous venons de citer, ἐλεύθερος et αὐτεξούσιος ne sont pas pour Grégoire des synonimes; bien au contraire, il les énumère comme deux

choses différentes.   Car par le mot d'ἐλεύθερος, comme on le verra
après, on désigne d'ordinaire celui qui jouit de la liberté extérieure,
civile ou politique, par opposition au δοῦλος, qui est assujetti à
servage, l'esclave.   Le mot αὐτεξουσία, d'autre part, est celui dont
Grégoire se sert presqu'invariablement et dans ses ouvres les plus
importantes, tels que le traité *De hominis opificio*, l'*Oratio
catechetica* et bien d'autres, pour désigner la liberté intérieure de la
volonté, c'est à dire le *liberum arbitrium*.   On verra plus tard, quand
nous serons arrivés à la considération du troisième argument, l'importance de cette précision.

        La force de l'argument que Grégoire vient d'exposer procède de
l'autorité de l'Écriture qui nous enseigne (Gen 1,26) que Dieu, en
créant l'homme à son image, comme sa ressemblance, a établi 'qu'ils
dominent sur les poissons de la mer, les oiseaux du ciel, les bestiaux,
toutes les bêtes sauvages et toutes les bestioles qui rampent sur la
terre'.   C'est à cause de cela que Grégoire interroge et incrèpe:
'Est-ce que tu a oublié les limites de ton pouvoir, non obstant que
jusqu'à présent ton empire était restreint aux seuls irrationnels? ...
Comment est-il possible que, en allant bien au delà de ce qui est
soumis à ton pouvoir, tu t'exaltes face à cette même nature qui est
libre (κατ' αὐτῆς ἐπαίρῃ τῆς ἐλευθέρας φύσεως), en mettant dans le
nombre des quadrupèdes, ou même de ceux qui n'ont pas de pieds, celui
qui est de ta même espèce (τὸ ὁμόφυλον)?' (335,12-17).

        Et en faisant appel encore une fois à l'autorité de l'Écriture,
qui dit que Dieu a mis sous la domination de l'homme 'toutes les
choses: le bétail, les juments, les brébis', voici que Grégoire
interroge, dans le meilleur style de la rhétorique de sons temps:
'Est-ce que, par hasard, des hommes te sont nés du bétail?   Est-ce
que les vaches ont engendré pour toi une descendance humaine?' —
parce que, évidemment, si un homme est le propriétaire d'un animal il
le sera aussi de ses rejetons.   Ce cas absurde — qu'une bête
irrationnelle puisse mettre au monde un être humain — serait donc,
dans l'infléxible logique dont Grégoire fait preuve, le seul cas où un
homme aurait pu invoquer des droits de propriété sur un autre homme.
'Car la seule possession des hommes est la nature irrationnelle. ...

"Celui," — dit-il — "qui produit le foin pour les bêtes et la verdure pour le service [= pour les esclaves] de l'homme." — Mais toi, au contraire, en déchirant la nature même de l'esclavage et de la seigneurie, tu fais que *le semblable domine à son semblable* et se constitue en maître de son égal' (335,20-336,5).

Comme on le voit, après avoir eu recours à l'argument théologique et scripturaire tiré de la création de l'homme fait à l'image et ressemblance de Dieu et constitué seigneur de la création visible, Grégoire boucle son argument en retournant au plan de la pure raison naturelle qui était le sien dans l'argument précedent: c'est faire violence à la fois à la notion d'esclavage et à celle de seigneurie, que de prétendre qu'un homme puisse dominer celui qui est son semblable et se constituer ainsi en maître de son égal.   Conclusion à laquelle il avait arrivé déjà dans le premier argument.

3.   Grégoire répète encore une fois le texte qu'il commente: 'J'ai acquis des esclaves et des servantes,' pour en déduire une troisième argumentation — qu'on pourrait penser, à première vue, un corollaire de l'antérieure — exprimée à travers une chaîne d'interrogations rhétoriques visant à l'effet facile sur les possibles auditeurs.   Car, face à cet homme qui se vante d'avoir eu en possession un si grand nombre d'esclaves et de servantes, on a bien le droit de lui demander combien il les a payés, à quel prix il les a achétés.

De fait, l'interpellé pourrait bien lui répondre avec une chiffre quelconque, en monnaie courante, qu'il aurait payée au marché des esclaves.   Mais évidemment la question vise à souligner que, si l'on a bien compris ce que c'est une créature humaine, créée par Dieu à son image et destinée à avoir le domaine de la terre et de tout ce qu'elle contient, il est alors tout à fait absurde de vouloir lui assigner un prix.   Car ce serait de vouloir mettre un prix au monde entier et à un être qui n'est rien d'autre que l'image de Dieu.

Toute une cascade de questions va mettre en relief l'absurdité d'une telle prétention: 'Qu'est-ce que tu as pu trouver, dans le monde entier, qui puisse être mis en rapport avec la valeur d'une telle nature?   Quel prix as tu fixé à la raison?   Combien de sous as tu dépensés pour l'image de Dieu? Par combien de pièces as tu achété cette nature faite par Dieu lui-même? Car Dieu a dit: "Faisons l'homme à notre image, selon notre ressemblance."' Et l'interrogatoire continue, sans trève et implacable: 'Dis-moi, si tu le peux, qui est-ce qui peut vendre, qui est-ce qui peut achéter celui qui est fait à la ressemblance de Dieu et qui a été doué par Dieu du pouvoir de régir tout ce qui existe sur la terre?' (336,7-15).

Il avance une première affirmation: 'Il n'y a que Dieu qui puisse faire cela.' Mais aussitôt il hésite, comme ayant fait une attribution excessive, même s'il s'agit du pouvoir de Dieu: 'Plus encore, on dirait que *ni Dieu même peut le faire*. Car "ses dons sont sans répentir" (Rom 11,29), et pourtant *il ne réduira pas à servitude cette nature qu'il a confirmée dans sa liberté même quand nous nous sommes assujettis à la servitude du péché*. De la sorte, si Dieu lui-même n'a pas réduit à servitude celui qui est libre (ὁ θεὸς οὐ δουλοῖ τὸ ἐλεύθερον), qui est-ce qui osera étendre son propre domaine même au délà de celui de Dieu?' (336,15-20).

Tel est l'argument qu'on pourrait dire le plus cher à Grégoire et qui réflète l'une des thèses les plus caractéristiques de son anthropologie. Car il voit dans le *liberum arbitrium* — plus encore que dans l'intellect, comme c'était le cas chez Philon, Origène et toute la ligne d'inspiration platonicienne — le trait principal de cette ressemblance de l'homme à Dieu: l'homme est αὐτεξούσιος comme Dieu est αὐτεξούσιος — nous dit Grégoire dans le *De hominis opificio* (ch. IV) — et cette αὐτεξουσία, c'est à dire cette condition d'être maître de soi, de ses actions, de ses vouloirs, c'est le propre de la condition *royale* qui est celle de l'homme.

Mais voici un argument qu'il faut examiner de près, dans son fond et dans sa terminologie. Avant tout il faut signaler un détail un peu surprenant, bien qu'ordonné à son propos démonstratif. Car dans ces textes si bien connus du *De hominis opificio*, et partout ailleurs dans ses autres écrits, c'est toujours ce mot d'αὐτεξουσία qui est employé par Grégoire quand il parle du *liberum arbitrium*, de cette liberté de choix qui est le propre de la volonté. Mais voici que dans cet argument que nous venons d'exposer, et en se référant sans aucun doute à cette liberté de la volonté, cette faculté que l'homme a conservée même après la chûte originelle, notre bon Grégoire a parlé d'ἐλευθερία (336,18) et d'ἐλεύθερον (336,19), tandis que ce dernier mot, dans tout ce que nous venons de voir, est constamment contraposé à celui de δοῦλος pour signifier la condition de 'libre' en tant que pas soumis au domaine extérieur d'un maître. (Ce qui est, d'ailleurs, le sens ordinaire de ce mot, qui surgit dans le vocabulaire de la Grèce classique — par opposition à celui de δοῦλος qui lui est antérieur, comme l'a bien montré M. Max Pohlenz dans son beau livre[1] — pour désigner la condition de l'homme qui jouissait de tous ses droits civiles ou politiques, le citoyen dans la πόλις, à la différence de l'esclave, du serf, de l'homme assujetti extérieurement à une servitude ou à une limitation quelconque de ses droits.

Il est vrai, bien sûr, que le contenu sémantique de ce mot a subi une évolution, et que dans le grec des Pères on peut trouver bien d'exemples de l'emploi des mots ἐλεύθερος et ἐλευθερία en faissant référence au libre arbitre, à la liberté des propres décisions. Mais ce n'est pas le cas de Grégoire de Nysse, car chez lui ce sont les mots αὐτεξούσιος et αὐτεξουσία, comme nous venons de la signaler, ceux qui sont employés d'ordinaire à ce propos. Tandis qu'on peut aussi trouver un peu partout dans ses écrits les mots ἐλεύθερος et ἐλευθερία avec deux significations possibles: d'une part celle du grec classique que nous venons de renseigner, c'est à dire la condition de celui qui n'est pas sujet à une servitude extérieure; d'autre part — à l'autre bout de l'échelle, pourrait-on dire — la condition intérieure de celui qui, ayant réussi à dompter la tyrannie de ses passions et de ses mauvaises inclinations, s'est affranchi de leur joug et a acquis cette disposition de spontanéité pour le bien que saint Augustin, dans sa langue latine, nommera du nom de *libertas* et que d'autres Pères grecs bien avant Grégoire ont désignée avec un mot emprunté au vocabulaire stoïcien mais revêtu maintenant d'un autre sens, ἀπάθεια, 'impassibilité'. Grégoire lui aussi l'emploie parfois, mais c'est plus

---

1   Max Pohlenz, Die griechische Freiheit. Wesen und Werben eines Lebensideals, Heidelberg 1955.

fréquent chez lui le mot ἐλευθερία pour exprimer ce concept, comme nous pouvons le constater p.ex. dans plusieurs passages de la *Vie de Moïse* et du *Traité de la Virginité*. Il paraît utile de signaler un texte de ce dernier qui réunit, tout à fait à notre propos, et les deux significations que le mot a pour notre auteur et la logique du passage de l'une à l'autre: 'Et de même que les serviteurs affranchis (οἱ ἐλευθερωθέντες) cessent de servir leurs propriétaires lorsq'ils sont devenus leur propres maîtres, ... ainsi, je pense, l'âme affranchie du culte du corps et de ses tromperies reconnait désormais l'activité qui lui est propre et naturelle: la liberté (ἐλευθερία), comme nous l'avons appris de l'Apôtre, consiste à n'être pas assujetti à un joug d'esclave ... .'[2] Dans aucun cas, on le voit bien, c'est le *liberum arbitrium* ce qu'on vise dans ce texte. Par ailleurs, dans ce même *Traité de la Virginité* (XII, 2.11-14) et en parlant précisément de la création et de la chûte de l'homme, Grégoire écrit qu'il était 'image et similitude de la puissance qui règne sur tous les êtres, et pour cette raison possédait aussi, *dans sa souveraine liberté de choix* (ἐν τῷ αὐτεξουσίῳ τῆς προαιρέσεως), la ressemblance avec le maître universel ... .'

Nous avons cru utile de préciser ainsi les sens que ces mots ont presque invariablement dans le vocabulaire de Grégoire de Nysse, afin de souligner qu'il nous semble pleinement délibérée, aux fins de l'argumentation, la substitution du terme αὐτεξουσία (qu'il aurait employé dans n'importe quel autre cas similaire) pour ceux d'ἐλευθερία et ἐλεύθερον (que jusqu'à ce moment dans le texte de cette homélie venaient constamment employés pour désigner la condition opposée à celle du δοῦλος, de l'esclave). Mais même avec cette petite argutie terminologique, cet argument, si on l'examine avec attention, n'est pas concluant. Car ce qu'on ôte à un homme, quand on le réduit à l'esclavage, c'est sa condition d'ἐλεύθερος, c'est à dire sa liberté extérieure, civile ou politique. Tandis que ce que Dieu a respecté dans son image même déchue c'est l'αὐτεξουσία, c'est à dire le *liberum arbitrium* ou liberté du vouloir. Et celle-ci, l'esclave lui aussi la conserve comme son bien inviolable, et en ce sens il n'est pas moins

---

2   *De virg.*, XVIII, 4.16-23 (trad. M. Aubineau, SC 119).

libre que son maître, et aucun maître ne pourra jamais lui ôter sa faculté de vouloir ou de ne pas vouloir, de vouloir ceci ou cela, même si les circonstances extérieures dans lesquelles il vit ne lui permettent pas toujours de mettre en oeuvre ses volontés.

4.   Pour finir, Grégoire va développer une autre argumentation quelque peu artificieuse et rhétorique, que l'on pourrait résumer ainsi: Quand on achète quelque bien, on l'achète avec tous les droits qui lui sont connexes. Or, si Dieu a donné à l'homme le domaine sur tout ce qui existe sur la terre, quand on prétend acheter un homme on achète la terre entière avec tout ce qu'elle contient. Et alors, le prix serait évidemment incalculable; il n'y aurait pas de richesses assez abondantes, au monde entier, pour payer d'un prix équitable la terre et tout ce qu'elle contient, et moins encore il y en aura pour acheter celui qui est au dessus d'elle (336,20-337,5). Mais il y a encore plus: pour quelqu'un qui connaisse bien la nature humaine, même le monde tout entier avec toutes ses richesses ne sera jamais un prix adéquat pour l'*âme* de l'homme (337,5-7).

Grégoire n'insiste pas sur ce dernier aspect, comme on l'aurait attendu (et il aurait eu beau jeu à s'appuyer sur l'immense supériorité de l'âme par rapport aux êtres matériels, pour montrer combien elle est, à elle seule, plus précieuse que mille mondes avec tout ce qu'ils pourraient contenir). Au contraire, il revient à l'argumentation déjà esquissée: 'Si l'on admet que l'être humain soit vendible, dans ce cas on porterait au marché rien d'autre que le seigneur de la terre et avec lui on mettrait à l'enchère tout ce qui lui appartient, c'est à dire la création entière: la terre, la mer avec ses îles et tout ce qu'elles contiennent. Quel prix devra donc payer celui qui achète? Combien devra-t-il recevoir celui qui vend, puisque le contrat lui assure la possession de tant de choses?' (337,7-14). Et cependant — continue-t-il — dans la pratique quotidienne ce n'est pas question de fabuleux trésors (qui encore seraient tout à fait insuffisantes). Il suffit d'un petit bout de papier, de quelques mots d'un contrat, de quelques monnaies qu'on compte, pour qu'un homme puisse se figurer qu'il est le maître de l'image de Dieu. 'O folie!', s'écrie Grégoire. 'Si ce contrat venait à être détruit; si la rouille venait à corroyer les lettres, si une goute d'eau tombée de quelque part vient les effacer, qu'est-ce qu'il en reste de l'attestation de ce servage? Où est le titre de ton domaine?' (337,15-19).

Et il réfléchit sur un ton tout à fait accord avec l'*Ecclesiaste* qu'il commente: 'Je ne vois rien que t'appartienne comme propre en vertu de ton nom (d'homme), sauf ce même nom. Car, est-ce qu'il y a quelque chose qui t'appartienne en raison de ta nature? Ni le temps, certainement, ni aucun privilège.' Et c'est l'occasion de mettre en évidence l'égalité foncière entre l'esclave et son prétendu maître, car pour l'un aussi bien que pour l'autre 'un seul est l'origine, un seul le procès de la vie; tous deux ils sont de même soumis aux affections de l'âme et du corps, aux peines et à la joie, ... à la maladie et à la mort' (337,19-338,8). Aucune différence, en toutes ces choses, entre le maître et l'esclave: c'est le même l'air que tous deux aspirent en respirant; c'est aussi le même soleil que tous deux regardent; c'est une même construction celle de leurs corps avec ses organes et ce sont aussi les mêmes leur procès physiologiques, et, finalement, c'est une même poussière qu'ils seront après leur mort, et ce sera pour tous deux un même jugement, un même ciel, ou l'enfer commun. Après cette énumération qui sent un peu les lieux communs des exercices des rhéteurs, c'est le moment pour Grégoire d'interroger son interlocuteur imaginaire: 'Si donc vous êtes égaux en tout, dis-moi en quoi penses-tu fonder ta supériorité pour arriver à te croire seigneur d'un homme quand toi même tu n'est rien d'autre qu'un homme?' (338,15-16).

Et voici que, pour finir avec ce thème de l'esclavage et passer avant dans le commentaire du texte, il réprend à nouveau son refrain, 'J'ai acquis des esclaves et des servantes,' pour faire à ce propos une considération qui n'ajoute rien de nouveau au déjà dit: 'En parlant de cette sorte, en ajoutant tout de suite combien grande avait été sa fortune en matière de bétail et de brébis, cet homme parle de ses esclaves tout comme s'il s'agissait de troupeaux de vaches ou de porcs, et il met dans le même plan de subordination les bêtes et l'être humain' (338,17-22).

A vrai dire, toute cette longue tirade finale (336,20-338,22), qui réflète la rhétorique de son temps, n'ajoute que peu de chose aux trois premiers arguments, qui sont, à notre avis, les seuls qui méritent d'être retenus et que l'on pourrait synthétiser ainsi:

1) l'argument philosophique, fondé sur l'égalité naturelle de tous les hommes, en tant qu'ὁμόφυλοι, c'est à dire appartenant tous à la même espèce;

2) l'argument théologique, fondé sur le récit de Gen 1,26, qui montre l'homme créé par Dieu comme son image et à sa ressemblance, et destiné par lui à avoir la domination sur toute la terre;

3) un argument que nous dirions le plus personnel de Grégoire et directement inspiré dans sa conception anthropologique qui voit dans le libre arbitre de la volonté le trait principal de la ressemblance à Dieu. C'est absurde qu'un homme prétende réduire à servitude cette créature dont la liberté a été à tel point respectée par Dieu lui-même, qu'il la lui conserva encore quand l'homme en abusa pour l'offenser. L'argument a son effect, bien sûr. Mais il faut bien signaler, comme nous l'avons déjà fait, que dans cette argumentation le Nyséen, en altérant sa terminologie habituelle qui réserve les mots d'αὐτεξούσιος et αὐτεξουσία pour se référer au libre arbitre, ici lui applique les termes ἐλεύθερος et ἐλευθερία qui partout ailleurs, dans cette même homélie, ne désignent que la condition de celui qui jouit de sa liberté extérieure, civile ou sociale. Ce qui est bien autre chose que le libre arbitre de la volonté. Et dans cette même homélie Grégoire savait en faire la distinction quand, au début du second argument, il écrit que Dieu créa l'homme ἐλεύθερος καὶ αὐτεξούσιος.

Résumé by the Author

Translated by the Editor

Taking as his *Leitmotiv* the words 'I got me slaves and slavegirls' (Eccl. 2,7), Gregory indicates the absurdity of slavery by three chief arguments:

1.   At the level of mere natural reason, a human being cannot be master of one of his own kind or species, ὁμόφυλος with himself.

2.   At the theological level, Genesis 1,26 tells us that God made man in his own image and appointed him lord of all the rest of the visible creation.   Another human being therefore can hardly pretend to reduce to slavery one who is in the image of God and who has dominion over the whole earth.

3.   A third argument, which might be thought more characteristic of Gregory, who sees in free will the chief mark of the likeness between human beings and God, amounts to this: A person could hardly pretend to reduce to slavery one whose freedom is so far respected by God himself that he preserves it, even when it is misused to offend against him.   The argument seems powerful.   It should however be noted that it concerns two different things: one is the external freedom, the civic or political liberty (ἐλευθερία) of the person who is not δοῦλος, not a slave in bondage; the other is the liberty which is a function of will, i.e. freedom of the will, *liberum arbitrium*. Usually, and in his most important works, Gregory refers to free will by the term αὐτεξουσία; in Homily IV this freedom is referred to by the terms ἐλεύθερος and ἐλευθερία, which elsewhere in the same homily are also used for external liberty.   Notwithstanding this verbal trick, which facilitates the slide from one notion to the other, we ought to observe that the two cases are distinct: if it is a matter of freedom of the will, that *liberum arbitrium* which God honours for all mankind even in its fallen condition, then the slave still possesses it as well as his master, even though he might not be able always to put his free choices into practice.

9

Exegesis and Theology in Gregory of Nyssa's
Fifth Homily on Ecclesiastes

Ronald E. Heine

The influence of Origen on Gregory's exegesis is more apparent in Hom. V than in any of the other homilies on Ecclesiastes. This is true because Eccl 2,14 falls in this homily, and Origen's interpretation of this verse, as S. Leanza has shown, was well known and exceptionally extensive in its influence.[1] Origen's general work on Ecclesiastes has perished, except for bits and pieces scattered about in some of his other works, in catenae, and in citations in other Fathers.[2] This makes it impossible to ascertain the extent of Gregory's indebtedness to Origen in his overall interpretation of Ecclesiastes.

I shall attempt to show in this essay not only how Gregory is indebted to Origen for particular meanings given to texts in this homily, but how thoroughly his way of approaching texts reflects Origen's influence, and also how he correlates exegetical insights derived from Origen with emphases belonging to his own moral theology.

---

1   L'esegesi d'Origene al libro dell'Ecclesiaste (Regii Calabrorum 1975), 112.

2   These bits and pieces have been conveniently collected in Leanza's work mentioned in note 1.

'Comparing Spiritual Things with Spiritual'

> These are all the passages of Scripture about the hart that
> we are able to recall at present. We have quoted them that *we*
> *may speak not in the doctrine of human wisdom, but in the*
> *doctrine of the Spirit, comparing spiritual things with*
> *spiritual*.[3]

In this passage in the *Commentary on the Song of Songs* Origen uses
the principle, well known in ancient exegesis among interpreters of
Homer as well as Jewish and Christian interpreters of Scripture,[4] of
interpreting one passage by comparison with other passages. The
whole of the Greek Bible was considered to be a kind of lexicon for
defining the meaning or implications of a word in any given passage.
On the basis of 1 Cor 2,13, Origen called this 'comparing spiritual
things with spiritual'. He explains what he means in at least three
different passages. In the first, from his commentary on the first
Psalm, in a selection which Basil and Gregory of Nazianzus included in
their *Philocalia*, he claims to get the principle from a Jewish teacher.
This teacher compared Scripture to a house containing many locked
rooms. Before each door lay a key, but it was not the key to that
door. It is a great piece of work, the Jewish teacher had said, to
discover the right key for the right door. So, he said, it is with the
Scriptures, because of their obscurity. 'We take our points of
departure to understand them from no other source than other
Scriptures since they hold the explanation scattered among
themselves.'[5] Origen then adds, 'The Apostle, I think, suggested such
a way of coming to a knowledge of the divine words when he said,

---

3   Origen, *Cant.* 3,12; trans. R.P. Lawson (ACW 26): 218.

4   See Philip Sellew, Achilles or Christ? Porphyry and Didymus in
     Debate over Allegorical Interpretation: HThR 82:1 (1989) 83;
     and N. Delange, *Origen and the Jews* (Cambridge, 1976), 194–196,
     notes 41 and 48.

5   Origène, *Philocalie, 1–20*, ed. M. Harl (SC 302) II 3,244.   Cf.
     Origenes, *In librum Regum Homilia* I,5, 'Cognata quippe est sibi
     Scriptura divina' (PG 12,1000B).

Which things also we speak, not in words taught by human wisdom, but in words taught by the Spirit, comparing spiritual things with spiritual.'[6]

In the fragments remaining of his comments on 1 Corinthians Origen explains 1 Cor 2,13 by saying 'By comparing one text with another and bringing the similarities together, the mind, as it were, of Scripture is revealed. For in this way I understand the things of God and am taught by the Spirit. For not only [must I] have learned the things of the Spirit who moved Isaiah, but [I must] also have had the same Spirit which closed and sealed Isaiah's words. For unless the Spirit opens the words of the prophets, the things which have been closed cannot be opened.'[7]

This latter passage does not refer to a kind of charismatic exegesis by which the meaning of the text is assumed to be given to the interpreter in much the same way that the words were assumed to be given to the author of the text. Origen intends something that involves the intellectual activity of the interpreter. He, as all the Fathers, held the view that every word in Scripture was given by the Spirit. When, therefore, he arrives at a meaning for a particular text, by comparing texts containing the same key terminology, it is the Spirit, speaking by means of the other texts, that teaches him (or unlocks for him) the meaning of the mystery in his text. And, if we assume that he took the words of his Jewish teacher seriously, he too must have thought that the Scriptures themselves 'hold the explanation scattered among themselves'. In fact, Origen introduces his explanation of 1 Cor 2,13 with the question, 'But how is one taught by the Spirit?' He answers by saying that it is by 'comparing one text with another'.[8]

---

6   Harl, 244.

7   C. Jenkins, ed., 'Origen on 1 Corinthians', JThS 9 (1908), 240. Cf. Philocalie II,1-2, and Harl's comments on the closed Scriptures, 251-254.

8   Ibid.

One other passage confirms this view of Origen's understanding of 1 Cor 2,13. Celsus had asserted that the obscure utterances of the Old Testament prophets were meaningless. Origen agreed that many of the utterances were obscure, but objected that they were not meaningless. The key to their interpretation, he asserted, lay in the interpreter and his methodology. 'It is only a person who is wise and truly in Christ,' he says, 'who could give as a connected whole the interpretation of the obscure passages in the prophet by "comparing spiritual things with spiritual" and by explaining each phrase he found in the text from the common usage of that phrase elsewhere in Scripture'.[9]   Origen certainly thought that only a spiritual person could understand the spiritual meaning of the Bible. The way, however, that such a person arrived at the spiritual meaning of the various passages of the Bible was by allowing the Spirit to instruct him through other passages in the Bible. The principle of interpreting Scripture by Scripture lies at the heart of Origen's spiritual exegesis.[10]

My purpose in this section is not to argue that Gregory is dependent on Origen for each interpretation he gives to the text of Ecclesiastes in Hom. V, but to show how he makes use of the principle of comparing Scripture with Scripture at certain key passages in the homily.   I have attempted to show elsewhere how Gregory was indebted to Origen for his general approach to exegesis, and how certain key texts of Paul used by Origen to explain and defend his approach to the Bible were taken up by Gregory.[11]   While Gregory does not appear to have used 1 Cor 2,13 to explain his exegetical method, the principle of interpreting Scripture by Scripture is common in his works.   He is not slavishly dependent on Origen either in meanings he gives to the text or in the use he makes of this principle of exegesis, but it is obvious that he has learned from Origen.

---

9   *Cels.*, 7,11 (GCS II 163,1-5; trans. H. Chadwick 404).

10   For examples, see *Cant.* 3,12;   *Comm. Jn.* 1,90ff.; 19,12-15.

11   Gregory of Nyssa's Apology for Allegory: VigChr 38 (1984) 360-370.

Gregory differs from Origen most notably in his use of this principle in that he usually makes no effort to collect all the passages where a term appears in the Bible, but interprets his passage on the basis of one, or, at most, only a few other Biblical texts.   Perhaps the difference is due to the difference in genre, i.e. Origen, in most cases, was writing commentaries, whereas Gregory was addressing a congregation.   The difference might also be due to the fact that certain words and verses in the Bible had become fixed in the tradition as pointing to one another, or, as we can demonstrate in a few instances, that he is relying on an identification already made by Origen.   It is also quite possible that Gregory's mind was not so thoroughly saturated with the Bible as was Origen's, so that multiple passages did not come so readily to his mind.

We shall look at five key passages in this homily where Gregory arrives at the meaning for his text in Ecclesiastes by a comparison with terminology in other Biblical texts.

GNO V, 355.1-16 on Eccl 2,12

'I looked myself to see wisdom, and dizziness and folly; for what man is there, who will go after counsel, the many things she has made.'

The word on which Gregory focuses his exegesis in this verse is wisdom.   There are two important points to note, however, which are preparatory to his adducing other passages from the Bible to define wisdom here.   The first is the Biblical text itself which he is explaining.   The Rahlfs edition of the LXX has, in the second clause of the verse, τὰ ὅσα ἐποίησεν αὐτήν, which must mean something like 'he has made her (i.e. counsel) so many things'.   Gregory's text has τὰ ὅσα ἐποίησεν αὕτη, 'she (i.e. counsel) has made so many things'. The significant difference is the change of the pronoun from the accusative to the nominative case.   Counsel, in Gregory's reading of the text is a 'maker'.   This is significant for the way he interprets the text.   Codex Sinaiticus preserves the reading αυτη,[12] and Didymus

---

12   The LXX differs so much from the Hebrew text of Eccl 2,12 as to make comparisons fruitless for our purposes.

the Blind has a text that is similar to Gregory's, [σ]ὺν τὰ πάντα ἐποίησεν αὐτῇ.[13]   Here counsel is again the subject of the verb 'made'. A similar reading is also preserved in some catena texts.[14] We need not assume that Gregory has altered the Biblical text for the sake of his exegesis here, but either that the text of the LXX he knew had the reading that he quotes, or that he knew the reading he quotes as an alternative reading and deliberately chose the alternative because of what he understood the verse to mean.

The second point to note as preparatory to Gregory's main interpretation of this verse is that he identifies counsel with wisdom (355,5-7). This move then allows him to apply the phrase descriptive of counsel, 'she has made so many things', to wisdom.   He paraphrases the second clause as follows: 'wisdom, which he also calls counsel, creative (ποιητικήν) of the things that truly are and exist and are not contemplated in vanity' (355,8-10).   Gregory perceives Eccl 2,12 to be speaking of wisdom as God's agent in creation.

On the basis of his perception that Eccl 2,12 refers to the activity of wisdom in creation, Gregory proceeds, by references to four passages of Scripture,[15] to identify wisdom in this verse with Christ.   The first is a very loose allusion to Prv 8,22[16] which was a standard Christological text for the Fathers: 'The Lord created me (i.e. Wisdom) as the beginning of his ways for his works.'   Gregory glances at it, so to speak, with the words, 'the real wisdom and counsel ... is nothing other than that wisdom which is thought of as

---

13   G. Binder/L. Liesenborghs, Didymos der Blinde. Kommentar zum Ecclesiastes (Tura-Papyrus), Teil I,1 (Bonn: Rudolf Habelt, 1979), 234.   There are no similarities between Gregory's exegetical comments and those of Didymus.   Didymus makes none of the Christological connections that Gregory makes with this verse. He is more interested in periphora than sophia here.

14   See CChr.SG 4,18 and 11,15, both of which read σύμπαντα ὅσα ἐποίησεν αυτη.   The first treats αυτη as the demonstrative pronoun, and the second as the personal pronoun.

15   The apparatus in GNO V notes only Ps 103,24 and 1 Cor 1,24.

16   For the looseness of some of Gregory's scriptural allusions, cf. his allusion to Ps 1,1,3 on the preceding page 354, 5-10.

before the universe (τῆς τοῦ παντὸς προεπινοουμένης σοφίας) (355, 12-13).

This is followed immediately by an introduction to and quotation of Ps 103,24. 'Now this is she in whom God made all things, just as the prophet says, "You made all things in wisdom"'.[17]   He next turns, in the same sentence, to identify this wisdom in Ps 103,24, who was active in creation, with Christ, by means of 1 Cor 1,24, 'but Christ is the power of God and the wisdom of God in whom all things came to be and were set in order' (355,15-16). Finally, I take the words, 'in whom all things came to be' (ἐν ᾗ τὰ πάντα ἐγένετο) to be a reference, not back to Ps 103,24, where the verb is ἐποίησας (πάντα ἐν σοφίᾳ ἐποίησας), but to Jn 1,3, where the verb is ἐγένετο (πάντα δι' αὐτοῦ ἐγένετο).   I think Gregory is here blending Logos and Wisdom, both of which are cited in the Bible as agents of creation, and both of which are applied to Christ.   These three Scriptures (Ps 103,24, 1 Cor 1,24, Jn 1,3) are again brought together by Gregory, though in a freer fashion, and applied to Christ in perf., where he says of 1 Cor 1,24, 'For since the whole creation, both as much as is known by sense perception and that which lies beyond the observation of the senses came to be through him (δι' αὐτοῦ γέγονε, Jn 1,3) and consists in him (Col 1,17), wisdom, of necessity, is intertwined with power (ἡ σοφία ... 1 Cor 1,24) in reference to the definition of the meaning of Christ who made all things' (τοῦ τὰ πάντα ποιήσαντος, Ps 103,24).[18]   Gregory explicitly links Jn 1,3 with 1 Cor 1,24 in Contra Eunomium, 'But Christ', he says, is 'the power of God and the wisdom of God', through whom all things came to be (δι' οὗ τὰ πάντα ἐγένετο) and without whom is no existent thing, as John testifies.'[19]

---

17   This was not a verse that Gregory always used of Christ.   In two other citations in other treatises Gregory does not identify wisdom in Ps 103,24 with Christ (PG 46,168A.548D).   In the latter reference he refers to Ps 103,24 as 'that vèrse which is sung by all' which suggests that the verse was regularly used in worship.

18   GNO VIII,1, 182,7-11.

19   GNO II, 24-26.

Origen had joined Ps 103,24 with Jn 1,3. '"All things were made by him" who was "in the beginning" for according to David, God made "all things in wisdom".'[20]   He also frequently loosely links Jn 1,1-3 with 1 Cor 1,24 by referring to Christ as the Word and Wisdom of God.[21]   Athanasius, however, may have been Gregory's more immediate source for joining Jn 1,1-3 with 1 Cor 1,24.   He, too, frequently speaks of Christ as the Wisdom and Word of the Father.   He also, however, uses the verb διακοσμεῖν,[22] which Gregory uses here,[23] of God's creative activity.   In a very free conflation of 1 Cor 1,24 and Jn 1,1-3, Athanasius refers to the son as 'the power of the Father and his Wisdom and Word"[24] and in another passage he speaks of the Father of Christ who ... through his own Wisdom and his own Word guides and sets in order (διακοσμεῖ) the universe for our salvation.[25]

Gregory's exegetical procedure in treating Eccl 2,12, then, is first to make clear that σοφία is the subject of ἐποίησεν, thereby stressing that wisdom in her creative role is to be understood in this verse.   He then looks at this concept through the prism of four other passages of Scripture, all of which were connected with Christ, and several with one another, in the exegetical tradition of the Church.   By the use of these four passages of Scripture he successively identifies (1) wisdom as God's creative agent (Prv 8,22, Ps 103,24), (2) Christ as God's wisdom (1 Cor 1,24), and (3) Christ as

20   *Comm. Jn.* 1,290; trans. FOTC 80:94; cf.II.188; FOTC 80:221.

21   See, for example, GCS IX,112,24-25; 117,20; 131,12; XI,56,28; 96,2; 184,14; and XII, Fr.317.

22   Hippolytus, *Haer.* (1,19 GCS XXVI, 19,4-6) links this verb with Plato's description of God as τὸν ποιητὴν καὶ διακοσμήσαντα τόδε τὸ πᾶν.   It had, however, become firmly established as a verb descriptive of God's work in creation in the exegetical tradition of the Church long before Gregory.   See 1 Clem 33.22; Athanasius, *C.Gentes* 40; 43; 47; *De Inc.* 1.   Josephus (*Ant.* I,1,31) uses it of the creation of the sun, moon, and stars, and it is used frequently of various aspects of the creation by Philo (see L. Cohn/P. Wendland, *Philonis Alexandrini* VII *Indices ad Philonis Alexandrini Opera* [Berlin 1927] 178).

23   GNO V, 355,15-16.

24   *C.Gentes* 46.

25   Ibid., 40

God's creative agent (Jn 1,3).   By this procedure Gregory establishes that it is Christ to whom the Ecclesiast looks when he looks 'to see wisdom'.   Christ is, therefore, 'the real wisdom'.26   The goal of human wisdom, he asserts on the basis of Eccl 2,12c, is 'to follow the real wisdom'.27   We will treat the significance of this introduction of Christ into Eccl 2 in a later section of the paper.28

GNO V, 357,1.21–358,10 on Eccl 2,14a

'The eyes of the wise man are in his head.'

I am concerned at this point only with Gregory's use of other passages of Scripture to interpret Eccl 2,14a.   I shall return later to discuss other aspects of his exegesis of this verse.

While Gregory does not state it as such, we should probably assume that he understands the wise man mentioned here to be the man who follows 'the real wisdom',29 which he identified with Christ in his exegesis of Eccl 2,12.   The exegesis here then reflects and reinforces that earlier exegesis.

The word 'head' in Eccl 2,14a leads Gregory's thought to 1 Cor 11,3 where Paul says, 'Christ is the head of every man'.30   We need not search far to find his source for this connection.   Origen had said on this verse, '"The wise man has his eyes in his head," in The key term for Gregory's exegesis here is darkness (σκότος).   He has earlier, in his discussion of Eccl 2,13b, identified darkness as symbolic of evil.   He then asserts that evil is like darkness, in Christ, since "Christ is the head of a man," the apostle says.'31

---

26 GNO V, 355,15–16.

27 GNO V, 355,7

28 Gregory begins his homilies on Ecclesiastes by establishing with the same method of exegesis that it is Christ who speaks in this book (GNO V, 280,8–281,2;   cf. 298,5–13).

29 GNO V, 355,7–16.

30 GNO V, 357,20–22

31 *Dial.*, 160–162;   tr. Chadwick LCC II, 450–451; cf. Leanza, 35–36.

Gregory then paraphrases Acts 17,28, changing the third person pronoun, which in Acts refers to God, to Christ, and says that all 'who live and move and are in Christ' have their eyes in their head.[32].

GNO V, 358,11-16 on Eccl 2,14b

'But the fool walks in darkness.'

The key term for Gregory's exegesis here is darkness (σκότος). He has earlier, in his discussion of Eccl 2,13b, identified darkness as symbolic of evil. He then assert that evil is like darkness, in

contradistinction to good and light, in that the former have no essence in and of themselves, but depend for their existence on the deprivation of good and light.[33]

In our passage he elucidates what it means to walk in darkness by an allusion to the words of Jesus about putting a lamp on a lampstand. I think, however, that rather than the passages referred to in the GNO edition, Gregory has in mind primarily Lk 11,33-36, where, immediately following the saying about the lampstand (Lk 11,33), the eye is identified as 'the lamp of the body' (Lk 11,34), and the warning is given, 'Beware, lest the light in you be darkness (τὸ φῶς τὸ ἐν σοὶ σκότος),' i.e. because your eye is evil (Lk 11,35).

Gregory glosses Eccl 2,14b with the statement, 'For the one who does not display his light on a lampstand [i.e. the wise man who has his eyes in his head], but puts it underneath the bed makes the light head to its βάσις. The Biblical imagery of the lamp (= the eye) either on the lampstand (= the head) or under the bed (= the heel) is, therefore, a way of restating what he has previously said, but with the emphasis transferred from the head to the heel. The person in himself darkness' (τὸ φέγγος ἑαυτῷ σκότος).[34] The σκότος of Eccl

---

32 GNO V, 358,3-4.

33 GNO V, 356,4-16.   Cf. G.C. Stead, Ontology and Terminology in Gregory of Nyssa: Gregor von Nyssa und die Philosophie, hg. v. H. Dörrie/M. Altenburger/U. Schramm (Leiden, 1976) 114-115.

34 GNO V, 358,12-14.

2,14b is identified with the σκότος of Lk 11,35. In addition, Gregory does not use the simple phrase from the Gospels, ὑποκάτω κλίνης,[35] but says the lamp is put under τῇ βάσει τῆς κλίνης. In his earlier discussion of the head and the heel of the soul, the heel is referred to as the βάσις of the soul.[36] Putting the lamp under the βάσις of the bed, therefore, is like transferring the eyes of the soul from its head to its βάσις. The Biblical imagery of the lamp (= the eye) either on the lampstand (= the head) or under the bed (= the heel) is, therefore, a way of restating what he has previously aid, but with the emphasis transferred from the head to the heel.   The person who does this, Gregory says, 'has become a creator of what is non-existent',[37] for darkness, as he established earlier, like evil, is non-existent.

Gregory's use of this passage in Luke to interpret Eccl 2,14b appears to be unique. No comments by Origen on Eccl 2,14b have been preserved.[38]

GNO V, 365.13-18 on Eccl 2,16a

'For the memory of the wise is not with the fool for ever.'

Gregory understands Eccl 2,14c-26 to be a debate between a fool and a wise man. The Ecclesiast presents the arguments from both sides

---

35 Lk 8,16. κλίνη occurs only in the accounts in Lk 8,16 and Mk 4,21 (ὑπὸ τὴν κλίνην). Gregory has, perhaps, fused vocabulary from the various accounts in his argument.

36 GNO V, 357,13.

37 GNO V, 358,14-15.

38 Gregory may have found some suggestive comments by Origen on Lk 11,33-36, however, especially in Origen's identification of the 'darkness' in Lk 11,34 with 'the passionate part of the soul' (Fr. 187 on Luke, GCS 49, 307,8-10. Cf. ibid. 305-306, and Fr. 128 on Matthew, GCS 41, 66). Origen also refers to Jesus' washing of the disciples' feet as 'symbolic of the feet (baseis) of your souls being purified' (Comm. Jn. 32,87).   Philo (de somniis I, 23,146) interprets the ladder in Jacob's dream as the soul, and says 'Its foot (basis) is sense-perception, which is as it were the earthly element in it, and its head (kephale), the mind (nous), which is wholly unalloyed, the heavenly element, as it may be called' (trans. Colson & Whittaker, Loeb V, 375).

as if he were himself the speaker in each case.[39]   The Ecclesiast's
own position, of course, is to be identified with the wise man.
Gregory takes Eccl 2,14c-15b to be an objection to the virtuous life
put forward by the fool.   Since every life, including the virtuous one,
ends in death, there is really no difference between the virtuous and
the wicked.   Gregory identifies the 'one fate' of Eccl 2,15a with
death.   In this he was independent of Origen, for the latter glosses
the word as plural and takes it to refer to 'poverty, wealth, sickness,
health, death'.[40]

   Gregory then takes Eccl 2,16a as the response of the wise man
to the fool's assertion that the fact of death eliminates any
supposed advantage in the virtuous life.   He asserts that the fool's
assumption that the virtuous life should deliver one from physical
death shows that the fool understands neither in what the immortality
of virtue consists, nor what the death of those who live in evil is.[41]
'For the memory of the wise', he says, 'lives for ever and lasts as
long as eternity, but even the memory of the fool is extinguished with
him'.[42]   Ps 9,7 is then introduced to show that 'memory' in Eccl
2,16a should be understood in this way.   'On such matters the prophet
also says "Their memory has perished" — conspicuously and plainly;
for that is what the addition of "their sound" shows.'[43]

   Here Gregory is clearly following Origen's lead.   Origen says on
this verse,

> For granting that visitations in this life are common to the
> wise and the foolish, in the coming age, however, the wise man
> is held in everlasting memory and has unending enjoyment.   But
> even the memory of the fool is obliterated, as it says in the

---

39   See GNO V, 361,7-8; 363,10-14; 364,13-14.

40   Cod. Vat. gr. 1694, ff. 20r-20v, quoted in Leanza, 12.

41   GNO V, 365,9-13.

42   Ibid., 365,13-15

43   Ibid., 365,16-18.

Psalm, 'Their memory has perished with sound'. In other words,
they are not even worthy of memory with God.[44]

The use of the verb 'obliterate' suggests that Origen may have
pondered a larger portion of the ninth Psalm in relation to Eccl 2,16,
for the same verb appears in Ps 9,6, where it is said of the wicked,
'You have obliterated their name for ever and ever'.   Gregory's
discussion betrays no further contact with Ps 9 beyond the verse
quoted. His discussion at this point is little more than a paraphrase
of Origen's words.   It appears that Origen, on the basis of the
appearance of the word 'memory' in Eccl 2,16a looked to Ps 9 as the
key to understand the verse, and that Gregory, in turn, looked to
Origen.

GNO V, 371.9-372.3 on Eccl 2,24-26a

'There is no good in a man; what he eats and drinks and will
show to his soul is good in his toil. This also I saw, that it
is from God's hand; for who eats and who drinks apart from
him? For to the man, the good one before his face, he has
given wisdom and knowledge and joy.'

Gregory takes Eccl 2,24-25 to be another objection to the virtuous
life put forward by the fool.[45]   The objection is that only what may
be received into oneself, namely food and drink, is good.[46]   The reply
of the wise man, as Gregory understands it, is found in Eccl 2,26a.
Since the objection has involved food, Gregory takes the reply also
to be made in terms of food.   God has given the good man 'instead
of food, wisdom and knowledge and joy', or, as he states it in his
earlier summary, food and drink 'are not the things through which
mankind is nourished and cheered, but wisdom and knowledge.'[47]

Gregory shows what this means by a citation and short
exposition of Mt 4,4 and Rom 14,17. There is a short exposition of

---

44   Cod. Vat. gr. 1694, ff. 20r-20v, quoted in Leanza, 12.

45   GNO V, 363,10-14; 370,12-19.

46   Ibid., 363,14-16; 370,12-371.2.

47   Ibid., 371,9-10; 363,17-18.

Mt 4,4 in the catena fragments of Origen on Matthew that is almost exactly parallel to Gregory's exposition:

Origen Fr. 64   Gregory

οὐ τρέφεται ἄρτῳ ἡ ἀρετή   οὐ τρέφεται ἄρτῳ ἡ ἀρετή,

οὐ διὰ κρεῶν καὶ τῶν ἄλλων   οὐ διὰ κρεῶν ἡ τῆς ψυχῆς

τῆς σαρκὸς ἐδωδίμων ἡ τῆς   δύναμις εὐεκτεῖ καὶ πιαίνεται.

ψυχῆς δύναμις εὐεκτεῖ.   ἄλλοις ἐδέσμασιν ὁ ὑψηλὸς βίος

ἄρτος δὲ πνευματικός ἐστι καὶ   τρέφεται καὶ ἀδρύνεται τροφῇ

ζωὴ τοῦ κατὰ ἀλήθειαν ἀνθρώπου   τοῦ ἀγαθοῦ ἡ σωφροσύνη,

ἡ ἀρετή, σωφροσύνη, σοφία,   ἄρτος ἡ σοφία, ὄψον ἡ

δικαιοσύνη, ἀπάθεια.[48]   δικαιοσύνη, ποτὸν ἡ ἀπάθεια ...

Unfortunately, it seems to me that the parallels are too precise, including the same list of virtues in the same order, for this to be a case of Gregory referring to Origen. Gregory rarely quotes anything verbatim. It seems more likely to me that the fragment has been incorrectly attributed to Origen in the Catenae, and that it is actually from this passage in Gregory, having been slightly condensed and rewritten, as was commonly done in the Catenae.[49] We must, at best, I think, leave the possibility of Gregory's dependence on Origen for this exposition of Mt 4,4 an open question.

I note again the virtues Gregory lists in his exposition of Mt 4,4 as the food for the sublime life — prudence, widsom, justice, and freedom from passion — for they are related to his citation of Rom 14,17. 'We should learn from this instance too', he says, 'as we have also heard from the Apostle, that 'the kingdom of God is not

---

48   GCS 41, 41.

49   See R.E. Heine, Can the Catena Fragments of Origen's Commentary on John be trusted?: VigChr 40 (1986) 118-134, esp. 126-128. Even the phrase τῶν ... τῆς σαρκὸς ἐδωδίμων in Fr. 64, which is not parallelled in the passage from Gregory I have quoted, can be found two lines above it (371,11). Origen's commentary on Matthew provides no help, for the books that are extant begin in Chapter 13 of the Gospel. The rare verb, εὐεκτεῖν, does not appear in any of the works of Origen extant in Greek (it does occur once in Clement, q.d.s. 18,4), nor have I found any instance of his speaking of virtue 'being nourished'. These, of course, are far from conclusive arguments against this fragment being from Origen, but they at least support rather than go against my suspicion.

food and drink, but justice', and 'freedom from passion (ἀπάθεια) and blessedness (μακαριότης).' Gregory has substituted 'freedom from passion and blessedness' for 'peace and joy in the Holy Spirit' in the text of Rom 14,17. There is a very free citation of Rom 14,17 in *De virginitate* which contains the words 'joy and peace'[50] This shows, at least, that Gregory knew the text of Rom 14,17 to contain the words 'peace and joy', and not 'freedom from passion and blessedness'. The only other citation of Rom 14,17 in Gregory's works that I have found is in *De hominis opificio* 18. Here he cites only the first half of the verse. The citation is of interest, however, for it is joined with a citation of Mt 4,4, and in the exposition contains some hints that are helpful for understanding the working of his mind in this section of Homily V.

> It may be, however, that some one feels shame at the fact
> that our life, like that of the brutes, is sustained by food,
> and for this reason deems man unworthy of being supposed to
> have been framed in the image of God; but he may expect that
> freedom from this function will one day be bestowed upon our
> nature in the life we look for; for, as the Apostle says, 'the
> kingdom of God is not meat and drink' (Rom 14,17); and the
> Lord declared that 'man shall not live by bread alone, but by
> every word that proceeds out of the mouth of God' (Mt 4,4).
> Further, as the resurrection holds forth to us a life equal with
> the angels (cf. Lk 20,36), and with the angels there is no
> food, there is sufficient ground for believing that man, who
> will live in like fashion with the angels, will be released from
> such a function.[51]

Here Mt 4,4 and Rom 14,17 are joined in an eschatological setting with the additional theme, based on Lk 20,36 and parallels, of living like the angels, which here means primarily having no need for food.

What shall we make of Gregory's citation of Rom 14,17 in Hom. V?   First, I think we must conclude that he has deliberately

---

50   GNO VIII/1, 314,16-17.

51   PG 44 196A-B; tr. NPNF V, 409.

introduced 'freedom from passion and blessedness' into the citation. These were important and interrelated themes in his moral theology. In the first chapter of *Pss.titt.* he says 'the goal of the virtuous life is blessedness',[52] and later he defines human blessedness as 'likeness to God'.[53]

Gregory believed that man had been created in a state of blessedness, but came into fellowship with evil by his free will and fell from that blessedness which, he says, is conceived as freedom from passion.[54] Here the important link between blessedness and freedom from passion becomes apparent. Blessedness is to be free from passion. It also points to the important link in Gregory's mind between blessedness and living like the angels, and shows the way, I think, from the eschatological setting given to Rom 14,17 in the passage in *De hominis opificio* to the non-eschatological emphasis the verse is used to make in our text.

What Gregory means by living like the angels is to be free from passion.[55] This is an eschatological promise held out to the saints on the basis of Lk 20,36 and the parallel texts in the Gospels.[56] Since this is what our life is to be like after the resurrection, Gregory argues in *hom. in Cant.* it would follow that we should prepare ourselves for this anticipated life, and practice it in advance by not living according to the flesh or being conformed to this world, but imitating the angelic purity by means of freedom from passion.[57]

---

52   GNO V, 25,11

53   Ibid., 26,10-11. Cf. further the whole first chapter (GNO V, 25-26) which relates the theme of blessedness to the first Psalm, and especially to Ps 1,3, with the introductory section of Hom.V on Ecclesiastes which also alludes to blessedness in relation to Ps 1,1,3 (GNO V, 354.1-12).

54   *Or. catech.* 8 (PG 45 33B); cf. GNO VI, 28,21-22.

55   GNO VI, 30,6-8.

56   Ibid. See also 134,9-11

57   Ibid., 134,9-135,2. Gregory reflects a Platonic concept when he speaks of 'practising the anticipated life in advance' (προμελετᾶν τὸν ἐλπιζόμενον βίον) (GNO VI, 134,16). Socrates asserted that the soul, in this life, is always training (μελετῶσα) for the time

This, it appears, is what Gregory intends here also, though it is not so clearly stated. The good man sets his eyes on things above and is nurtured by the virtues that correspond to that higher life. He, in effect, lives now as he anticipates living later. He does not consider food and drink, or any of the other things which serve the desires of the body, to be among the things to be zealously pursued in this life because 'the kingdom of God is not food and drink, but justice and freedom from passion and blessedness.'[58]

The importance of this exposition in Gregory's mind for his homily may be ascertained by noting that in the introduction to Hom. VI, he singles out two things which he considers himself to have accomplished in Hom. V. One was to indicate what the good is 'to which one must look by means of the eyes which are in the head', and the other was to contrast 'the nourishment in accordance with wisdom' with those who look to physical enjoyment.[59]

The Outer and Inner Man

Just as these different ages that we have mentioned are denoted by the same words both for the outer man and for the inner, so also will you find the names of the members of the body transferred to those of the soul; or rather the faculties and powers of the soul are to be called its members. We read in Ecclesiastes, therefore: *The eyes of a wise man are in his head* ... The members have the same names, yes; but the names plainly and without any ambiguity carry meanings proper to the inner, not the outer man (Origen, *Cant.* Prologue 2; trans. Lawson, 27-28)

when it will be without the body, and that true philosophy is, in fact, the soul's training of itself to die readily (τεθνάναι μελετῶσα ῥᾳδίως) (*Phaed.* 80e-81a).

58 GNO V, 372,1-3. Cf. Origen, *comm. in Mt.* 12,14 (GCS 40, 96,6-97,21), where he asserts that the one who lives in accordance with the virtues is already in the kingdom of heaven.

59 GNO V, 373,6-13.

'Why does he say here,' Gregory asks of Eccl 2,14a, 'that only the wise man's head is equipped with eyes?'[60]   Although all three of the nouns in Eccl 2,14a are important in Gregory's exposition, his interpretation hinges on the noun 'head', which he interprets in two ways.   He first takes the term in a psychological sense and identifies it with the rational faculty of the soul.   A little later he identifies it with Christ.   I treat the psychological sense Gregory gives to the term in this section, and return to the identification with Christ in the final section.

Gregory begins by asserting, in obvious dependence on Origen's comments on this verse quoted above, that the Ecclesiast must mean by this statement 'that there is an analogy between what is thought to belong to the soul and parts of the body.'[61]   Just as in the body that which projects over the rest is called the head, so in the soul that part which rules and is foremost is thought of as the head. And, if the highest part of the soul can be called the head, it may be proper to refer to its lowest part, i.e. the part that has contact with the body and deals with the senses, as the heel.   The proper place for the eyes is in the head, where they contemplate the sights that are above, but it is possible for 'the soul's power of vision and contemplation' to become engaged with objects of sense, so that 'its eyes are transferred to its heels.'[62]

The thought of the entire homily revolves around this paragraph. While Gregory never states the contrast in quite these words, what he argues is that the wise man's eyes are in his head, and the fool's eyes are in his heels.   This division corresponds to Gregory's understanding of the soul.

---

60   Ibid., 357,6-7.

61   *Ibid.*, 357,7-9.   The assertion of such an analogy, but without explicit reference to Eccl 2,14 occurs also in Origen, *In Exod.* 10,3; *princ.* 1,1,9; *Cels.* 7,34.

62   Ibid., 357,9-19.

Gregory's basic view of the soul was Platonic, although he tried to express it in Biblical images and terminology.[63] In *v.Mos.* he compares the structure of the soul to the lintel supported by the two door posts of the Israelites' homes in Egypt, and says the Bible is referring symbolically to what 'the foreign teaching imagines when it divides the soul into the rational, appetitive, and spirited faculties'.[64] The doorposts represent the appetitive and spirited faculties which underlie and support the lintel, the rational faculty of the soul. This structure, with the rational faculty over and supported by the appetitive and spirited faculties, is the way Gregory conceived the soul to function properly.[65] The soul should always be under the control of the rational faculty. When this is not the case, the result is chaos and destruction. If we could imagine, he says, a hoplite putting all his armor on backwards, 'then we should have an idea of the fate in life which is sure to await him whose confused judgment makes him reverse the proper uses of his soul's faculties.'[66]

By a reversal of the soul's faculties Gregory means that the appetitive faculty gets control of the soul. The spirited faculty has only a supportive role in the soul, never a leading role. The opposites which struggle for control against one another are the

---

63 See H.F. Cherniss, The Platonism of Gregory of Nyssa, UCPCP XI/1 (Berkley, 1930) 12-25; E.G. Konstantinou, Die Tugendlehre Gregors von Nyssa im Verhältnis zu der antikphilosophischen und jüdisch-christlichen Tradition (Würzburg, 1966), 99-106, and the relevant works cited by A.J. Malherbe and E. Ferguson, Gregory of Nyssa. The Life of Moses (New York, 1978), 169 note 116. Gregory could also use Aristotelian terminology in describing the soul (see *hom. opif.* 8). On his use of scriptural terminology see PG 46 52Aff), and cf. F. Young, Adam and Anthropos: VigChr 37 (1983) 115.

64 GNO VII, I, 62,10-11.

65 Ibid., 62,18-63,3. For other passages in Gregory which discuss the structure of the soul and make this same point, see R.E. Heine, Perfection in the Virtuous Life (PatMS 2 Philadelphia, 1975) 221-228.

66 GNO VIII, I, 319,16-25; trans. NPNF V, 364. Cf. his vivid depiction of the soul being dragged to destruction by the passions in his blending of the imagery of the *Phaedrus* myth with the Egyptian charioteers in the Exodus story (GNO VII, I, 71).

rational and appetitive faculties.   The spirited faculty, however, is
always joined with the appetitive in Gregory's thought.   The two
faculties together are perceived as basically different from the
rational faculty.   In effect, Gregory thinks of a rational and
irrational division within the soul, the further division of the
irrational into the appetitive and spirited being only a sub-point in his
psychology.[67]

This understanding of the soul underlies the exposition of Eccl
2,12-26.   Gregory makes no attempt in the homily to explain or
develop his doctrine of the soul.   It is present, however, as the
foundation on which he erects his exposition.

The two-tiered structure of the soul appears as Gregory sets
forth the possibility of the eyes of the soul being located either in
its head or in its heels.[68]   Not only does he see the structure of
the soul reflected in Eccl 2,14a, but also the proper function of the
respective parts and the possibility of them functioning improperly.
The eyes should be located in the soul's head, i.e. its rational
faculty, but it is also possible for them to be transferred to its
heels, that part of the soul which deals with the body.

It is this understood structure of the soul which underlies his
citation and exposition of the saying about a lamp being put either on
a lampstand or under a bed which we discussed in the first section of
the paper.[69]

His understanding of the soul is reflected also in the delightful
description of lawyers who cleverly manipulate evidence to their own
advantage.   Such men are admired for their perspicuity, but if
examined from the perspective of that eye which is situated in the

---

67   Both Origen (princ. 3,4,1) and Basil (PG 31, 213C) also spoke of
     the appetitive and spirited faculties of the soul as one, in
     opposition to the rational faculty.

68   GNO V, 357,1-18.

69   Ibid., 358,11-16.

head, it is apparent that such men are 'utterly blind', and are adorning their heel, 'which is torn by the fangs of the serpent'.[70]

Those whose eyes are in their heels, who appear to see but are in reality blind, are then contrasted with those whose eyes are in their head. These latter may appear to be fools, but are in reality wise.[71]   Paul is cited as the prime example. Gregory alludes to Paul's many afflictions, which made him appear foolish, and quotes Rom 8,35 as the summation of the Pauline example.   'This', he asserts, 'is equivalent to saying, "Who shall gouge my eyes out of my head and remove them to the trodden and earthy part of me?"' i.e. to my heels.[72]

Gregory's concept of the structure of the soul and the proper function of its faculties also lie beneath the surface of his exposition of Eccl 2,18-19.   This passage asserts the folly of laboring for what will be left to another at death, when one cannot know how the recipient will use the things inherited. The key terms for Gregory's exposition are the verb ἐξουσιάσεται and the noun μόχθος.   These terms in Ecclesiastes provide the basis for Gregory's assertion that the Ecclesiast did not 'passively slip into the life of enjoyment, but came to it by reason of wisdom.'[73]

The fact that he calls luxurious living 'toil', Gregory says, shows 'that he had approached participation in pleasure with effort, like some difficult contest.'[74]   The use of the verb 'to be controlled by' of the one who succeeds the Ecclesiast suggests, Gregory thinks, that the latter was not mastered by pleasure, as the verb suggests

---

70 Ibid., 358,19-359,5. I take the reference to the heel 'torn by the fangs of the serpent' to be an allusion to Gn 3,15.

71 Origen makes such a contrast between wisdom and folly in his eighth homily on Jeremiah. It was later to be a favorite theme of Erasmus. See M.A. Screech, Erasmus, Ecstasy and the Praise of Folly (London, 1988).

72 GNO V, 360,9-13.

73· Ibid., 368,9-11. Gregory reflects on the problem of Solomon's participation in the life of enjoyment also in Homilies II-IV.

74 Ibid., 368,15-17.

his successor might be, but was himself in control of it.[75]   It seems clearly to have been problematical for Gregory that the Ecclesiast had partaken of the life of enjoyment.   He asserts three times that the Ecclesiast came to the life of enjoyment at wisdom's request.[76] In addition, it was not the usual participation in the pleasurable life. The Ecclesiast's romp through the life of enjoyment was (1) for a limited period, (2) for the sake of knowledge, and (3) was carefully monitored by the intellect.[77]   After a while he 'bridled it with the harness of reason and curbed it with the force of intellect (νοῦ).[78] Gregory asserts that such a controlled tour of the life of the senses is not for everyone, and that a lesser person may be mastered by the life of pleasure and bow to its domination like a slave.[79]

The interesting aspect of this exposition is that here the rational faculty of the soul voluntarily gives free rein temporarily to the irrational faculty but without ever, it seems, fully losing control of the soul.   Reason has not here dropped the reins and been 'dragged behind like a charioteer who has got entangled in his car.'[80] This appears to be neither a case of the irrational faculties of the soul cooperating with and supporting the rational faculty under the latter's control, as Gregory conceived the proper state of the soul to be, nor a case of the irrational faculties upsetting the normal structure of the soul and seizing control.   Perhaps it is best to leave it, as Gregory seems to do, as an exceptional case which he was led to posit because of what he understood the text of Ecclesiastes to mean in relation to his own understanding of the soul.

---

75   Ibid., 368,1-4.

76   Ibid., 367,17; 368,10-11.14-15

77   Ibid., 367,19.16.20-368,1.

78   Ibid., 367.20-368.1

79   Ibid., 368,1-4.

80   *De anima.* (PG 46,61C; trans. NPNF V, 442).   Cf. *Ps.titt.* I.8 (GNO V, 62.2-5 where Gregory speaks of ἐπιθυμία being kept in control by 'the reins of thought'.

'The Thinking Faculty is in Christ'

> There is a curious saying in Ecclesiastes. To anyone that does not understand it, it will seem meaningless, but it is for the wise man that Ecclesiastes says: 'The wise man has his eyes in his head'. In what head? Every man, even the blockhead and the fool, has his bodily eyes in his bodily head. But 'the wise man has his eyes ... in his head,' in Christ, since 'Christ is the head of a man,' the Apostle says. The thinking faculty is in Christ (Origen, *dial.* 20, trans. Chadwick, LCC II, 450-451).

> The outward man has eyes, and the inward man also is said to have eyes ... Our eyes are our mind (ibid., 17; 448-449).

I come now to the identification which Gregory makes, again in obvious dependence on Origen, between the term 'head' and Christ in Eccl 2,14a, and also to the identification he makes of Christ with wisdom in Eccl 2,13. I have already discussed Gregory's exegetical procedure in treating these two verses and the ways in which he was dependent on Origen in this.[81] I wish here only to suggest the significance of these identifications for Gregory's thought in this homily.

In his concluding remarks in Hom. V, Gregory says that he hopes the homily will be an aid for fleeing the things that are condemned and a resource for the achievement of what is superior.[82] It is, in other words, a homily about the successful accomplishment of the virtuous life.

Gregory understands the virtuous life to be an imitation of the divine nature as that has been revealed in Christ.[83] In his treatises *de perfectione* and *de professione Christiana* he sets forth the virtuous life as a participation in and practising of the concepts that

---

81 See the discussions above in the sections on GNO V, 357,1.21-358,10 and GNO V, 355,1-16.

82 GNO V, 372,15-18.

83 GNO VIII, I, 136,7-8. Cf. Origen, *Cels.* 8,17

are applied to Christ in the Bible.[84]   In a discussion of the
significance of looking to Christ as 'the head'[85] in *perf.*, he argues
that there must be a continuity of nature between the head and the
body.   'The word, therefore, teaches us through these things that
what the head is (ἐστίν) in its nature, this also the individual parts
are to become (γενέσθαι) in order that they may be proper to the
head.'[86] 'If we suppose,' he goes on, 'that the head of the essence
is purity ... , it is certainly necessary that the parts which belong
under such a head be pure; if we think the head is incorruption, the
parts must certainly exist in incorruption.   In like manner also the
other concepts which the head is considered to be are accordingly to
be observed in the parts, namely peace, sanctification, truth, and all
such things.'[87]

The key to generating these qualities in the virtuous life lies in
the mind. 'There are three things,' Gregory says, 'which characterize
the life of the Christian: action, speech, and reflection. Of these,
reflection is more primitive than the others, for thought is the source
of all speech, and speech is second after reflection ..., and action is
third in rank after reason and speech, bringing what was thought into
actuality'.[88]   Herein lies the importance of having one's mind focused
on Christ.

That which is pure of every passionate condition looks to the
founder of impassibility (ἀπαθείας), who is Christ, from whom
someone drawing the concepts into himself as from a pure and
uncorrupted spring will demonstrate such a likeness in himself
to the original as exists between the gushing spring water and
that water in a jar which has come from the spring. For the

84   See, especially, GNO VIII, I, 175-176.
85   He is referring here to Christ as the head of the Church (Eph
      5,23), but he is thinking of the life of the individual.
86   GNO VIII, I, 198,1-3.
87   Ibid., 198,13-199,6; cf. 136,2-6.
88   Ibid., 210.4-11.

purity which is beheld both in Christ and in the one who participates in him is one in nature.   The one, however, gushes
forth like a spring, and the other draws water for himself by
participating, by transferring to his own life the beauty in the
concepts.   Consequently there is a harmony between the hidden
man and the manifest, a gracefulness of life which corresponds
to the concepts set in motion in relation to Christ.[89]

When we bring this basic framework of Gregory's understanding
of what the virtuous life is and the means for its accomplishment to
the sections in Hom. V which speak of Christ, it can be seen that
these sections reflect his theology of the virtuous life.   The
differences in the way he states things here and in the treatises
perf. and *prof. Chr.* lie in the different genres of the treatises.   In
the latter Gregory is working systematically, more or less, so that his
doctrine structures the material.   Here he is working exegetically
(again, more or less!) so that the text puts certain constraints on
what he says and how he says it.   Nevertheless, some of the key
issues of his theology of the virtuous life shine through.

First, the virtuous life is centred on Christ, who is (1) the
source of all virtue,[90] and (2) himself absolute virtue.[91]   Second, the
importance of the thinking faculty in relation to the virtuous life is
stressed.   This is the importance of the eyes being in the head for
Gregory.   This is somewhat obscured by his double identification of
the term 'head', as both the ruling faculty of the soul and Christ.
When he speaks of 'head' in the former sense, there is a certain
overlapping of the way he uses the terms 'head' and 'eyes', for he
can still speak of the eyes as 'the soul's power of vision and contemplation'.[92]   When, however, 'head' means Christ, the eyes are

---

89   Ibid., 212,4-16.90 GNO V, 358,7-8.

91   Ibid., 358,9. Cf. GNO VII, I, 118,20, and Origen, GCS 40, 97,21-
22.

92   GNO V, 357,16.   .

clearly the thinking faculty of the soul, and are to be focused on Christ.[93]

These same themes can be seen in his identification of wisdom with Christ, when the Ecclesiast says he looks 'to see wisdom'. Real wisdom is Christ, Gregory argues, and, if human wisdom is 'to have pondered the true works of real Wisdom and Counsel', again emphasizing the role of the thinking faculty, 'and if' he continues, stressing the centrality of Christ in the virtuous life, 'the work of that ... Wisdom is immortality, the blessedness of the soul, courage, justice, prudence, and every name and concept applied to virtue, then perhaps in consequence we are being brought nearer to the knowledge of good things'.[94]

What we have seen in Homily V so far as exegesis and theology are concerned is twofold. First, the influence of Origen on Gregory's exegesis was extensive, both in the approach he took to establish the meaning of a text, and also, in some instances, in the meaning he understood a text to have. On the other hand, Gregory's own creativity is also apparent. He could use Origen's approach to exegesis independently, and he could also take meanings Origen had given to texts and use them to make points that derived from his own moral theology.

---

93   See ibid., 358,2-10.
94   Ibid., 355,16-356,1.

10

Grammatik und Rhetorik

in Gregors von Nyssa Exegese des Buches Prediger

Beobachtungen zur fünften Homilie

Henriette M. Meissner

Die exegetischen Homilien Gregors von Nyssa sind zweifach der heidnischen Schultradition verpflichtet.[1] Zum einen — als Rede — der Rhetorik, zum anderen — als Auslegung eines Textes — der Grammatik. Im antiken Grammatikunterricht, der Vorstufe des Rhetorikunterrichts, wurde das Instrumentarium heidnischer Texterklärung vermittelt. Diese umfaßte, soweit man dies erschließen kann,[2] nach dem Vorlesen die textkritische Behandlung (διορθωτικόν), die sprachliche Erklärung, die jedes Wort und jeden Satz zu verstehen suchte, die Sacherklärung und die grammatisch-rhetorische Exegese (ἐξηγητικόν). Abschließend folgte eine ästhetische und moralische Würdigung (κρίσις ποιημάτων).[3] Wie sehr die christliche Bibelexegese dem heidnischen Grammatikunterricht

---

1   Überarbeitete Fassung eines Vortrags vor dem 'Seventh International Colloquium on Gregory of Nyssa' am 7. September 1990 in St Andrews, Schottland. Meinem verehrten Doktorvater, Herrn Prof. Dr. Spira, verdanke ich die Anregung zu dem Thema — ihm seien die vorliegenden Ausführungen gewidmet. Herrn Prof. the Revd. S.G. Hall danke ich für die Möglichkeit, auf dem Kongress vortragen zu dürfen.

2   Grundlegend: Chr. Schäublin, Untersuchungen zu Methode und Herkunft der antiochenischen Exegese (Theophaneia 23), Köln-Bonn 1974, 34 f.; B. Neuschäfer, Origenes als Philologe. Bd. I u. II (SBA 18), Basel 1987, 35 f.

3   Zur Problematik der κρίσις ποιημάτων, über deren Inhalt nur Vermutungen möglich sind, cf. Neuschäfer, 247-263.

verpflichtet ist, hat die neuere Forschung sowohl für die antioche-
nische Schule — ich nenne das Buch von Schäublin — als auch für die
alexandrinische — hier genügt es, das Buch von Neuschäfer, Origenes
als Philologe, zu erwähnen — gezeigt.[4]   Für Gregor ist der
grammatisch-rhetorische Hintergrund seiner exegetischen Schriften
bisher kaum verfolgt worden.[5]   Die folgenden Ausführungen sollen ein
Versuch in dieser Richtung sein.

1.   Die Topik des Kommentarprologes und die Einleitung zur fünften
      Homilie (In Eccl. V, 353,11-354,23).

      In der Einleitung zur fünften Homilie nimmt Gregor den Anfang
der ersten Homilie auf, wo er Ziel und Nutzen des Predigerbuches
bestimmt.   Dabei greift er auf einige Topoi des antiken Kommentarprologes zurück, die zuerst kurz vergegenwärtigt werden sollen.[6]

      In Gregors erster Homilie lassen sich mehrere Topoi, die
traditionellerweise im antiken Dichter- oder Philosophenkommentar
behandelt werden konnten, fassen.   Gregor ordnet zunächst das
vorliegende Werk sozusagen in das 'Lehrgebäude der Philosophie' ein
(τάξις); bei der ebenfalls topischen Besprechung der Überschrift (αἰτία

---

4   Grundlegend zur exegetischen Methode sind die Monographien von
     Schäublin und Neuschäfer.

5   Einiges Material — allerdings ohne dessen grammatisch-rhetorische
     Tradition zu würdigen — hat für die Kappadokier H. Weiss (Die
     grossen Kappadocier. Basilius, Gregor von Nazianz und Gregor von
     Nyssa als Exegeten. Ein Beitrag zur Geschichte der Exegese,
     Braunsberg 1872) zusammengetragen: zum ἱστορικόν 26 ff.; zur
     Textkritik 35 ff.; zur sprachlichen und grammatisch-rhetorischen
     Erklärung 50 ff.

6   Zum folgenden ausführlich mit allen notwendigen Belegstellen:
     Schäublin, 66-83; Neuschäfer, 57-84.   Neuschäfer behandelt
     a.a.O. auch die Problematik der Entwicklung und Schematisierung
     des Kommentarprologes.   Sehr deutlich die Ausführungen von
     I. Hadot, Les introductions aux commentaires exégétiques chez les
     auteurs néoplatoniciens et les auteurs chrétiens: M. Tardieu (ed.),
     Les règles de l'interprétation (Patrimoines), Paris 1987, 99-122.
     Zum σκοπός in den neuplatonischen Kommentaren, s. jetzt auch M.
     Heath, Unity in Greek Poets, Oxford 1989, 124-136.

τῆς ἐπιγραφῆς) bestimmt er dann den σκοπός des Predigerbuches und dessen Nutzen (χρήσιμον).

Die Einordnung in ein größeres Ganzes (τάξις) wird gleich zu Beginn sehr kurz angedeutet. Gregor sagt nur, daß sich das Buch Prediger an die Proverbien anschließe (In Eccl. I, 277,3-278,1). Aus der ersten Homilie des Hoheliedkommentars wissen wir, daß das Buch Prediger auch für Gregor das Mittelstück der Reihe Proverbien—Prediger—Hohelied bildete.[7]   Für ihn stellt das Buch Prediger im Vergleich mit den Proverbien einen Aufstieg dar (ἄνοδος), der dem Zuhörer offensteht, der schon für ein vollendeteres Wissen vorbereitet ist (In Eccl. I, 277,8-278,1).   Zu Beginn der achten Homilie fragt Gregor, wer von den Zuhören schon so 'rein' ist, daß er das Wort φιλέω angemessen verstehen kann (In Eccl. VIII, 416,12-15): damit ist der Zustand angesprochen, den seine Zuhörer nach der Vorbereitung durch das Buch Prediger haben sollten, um das Hohelied zu verstehen. Im Hohelied selbst erfolgt dann der Aufstieg (ἄνοδος, ἀνάβασις) bzw. die μυσταγωγία zu den innersten Geheimnissen des Glaubens (In Cant. I, GNO VI 22,16-17).   Am Ende der Homilienreihe klingt also zumindest der Gedanke an das Werk an, auf das der Prediger vorbereitet.[8]

Mit dieser Einordnung des Predigers als Vorbereitung für die Mysterien des Glaubens hängt eng die Bestimmung des σκοπός, des Wirkungszieles des Werkes, zusammen.   Das Ziel (σκοπός) des Buches Prediger ist für Gregor, den menschlichen νοῦς von den weltlichen Dingen, die in den Bereich der Wahrnehmung (αἴσθησις) fallen, wegzuführen und ihm ein Verlangen (ἐπιθυμία) für den Bereich

---

7   Greg. Nys. In Cant. I, GNO VI 17,7-25,1; cf. I. Hadot, Introductions, 115-117 zum Topos der τάξις im Prolog von Origenes Comm. in. Cant.; zu der Reihenfolge und Bedeutung der ersten drei Bücher Salomons in den Prologen der patristischen Hoheliedkommentare cf. M. Harl, Les trois livres de *Salomon* et les trois parties de la philosophie dans les Prologues des Commentaires sur le *Cantique des Cantiques* d'Origène aux Chaînes exégétiques grecques: J. Dummer (Hg.), Texte und Textkritik.   Eine Aufsatzsammlung (TU 133), Berlin 1987, 249-269.

8   Das heißt nicht, daß Gregor schon an eine Homilienreihe In Cant. gedacht haben muß.   Denn die vorbereitende Funktion des Predigers und der Rahmen, in dem das Hohelied verstanden werden mußte, waren z.B. durch die Erklärung des Origenes bekannt.

einzuflößen, der jenseits der αἴσθησις liegt (In Eccl. I, 280,2-7). —
Denn mit dieser Geisteshaltung ist er, wie wir folgern können, für die
Lehren des Hoheliedes vorbereitet.

Ziel des Werkes und dessen Nutzen sind eng miteinander
verbunden. Der Nutzen des Werkes (χρήσιμον) liegt, wie Gregor
ausführt, darin, daß es über die Dinge belehrt, die für einen sittlichen
Lebenswandel (ἀρετὴ τοῦ βίου) nützlich sind. Damit diene es in
besonderem Maße der Kirche (ἐκκλησία) und habe auch deshalb die
Überschrift Ekklesiastes.⁹ Denn zum Christentum, zur εὐσέβεια, genügt
nicht allein, wie Gregor nicht müde wird zu betonen, die rechte Lehre,
sondern es muß auch der rechte Lebenswandel hinzukommen.¹⁰

Soweit also hält sich Gregor durchaus an die gängige Topik der
Kommentarprologe. Die Frage nach dem σκοπός eines Werkes hat
allerdings bei ihm eine weit größere Bedeutung als sonst in der antiken
Literatur. Dies haben Rondeau und Le Boulluec am Beispiel von
Gregors Schrift In Inscriptiones Psalmorum deutlich gezeigt.¹¹ Gregor
ordnet nämlich dem einmal bestimmten σκοπός gewöhnlich seine gesamte
Auslegung unter; der Text wird mit Blick auf dieses Ziel hin
interpretiert, wobei für ihn die einzelnen Teile folgerichtig (κατ'
ἀκολουθίαν) miteinander verbunden sind. Denn für die Interpretation
eines Werkes gilt, wie er andernorts sagt, folgendes:

9   In Eccl. I, 279,5-280,2; χρήσιμος cf. ibid 279,12.

10   Cf. Ep. 24,2, GNO VIII 2 75,13-14: ... διαιρῶν γὰρ εἰς δύο τὴν
     τῶν Χριστιανῶν πολιτείαν [cf. In Eccl. I, 279,21: τὴν
     ἐκκλησιαστικὴν πολιτείαν], εἴς τε τὸ ἠθικὸν μέρος καὶ εἰς τὴν ⟨τῶν⟩
     δογμάτων ἀκρίβειαν, ...; cf. In Cant. XIII, GNO VI 393,21-394,6;
     VMoys. II, 166 (SC 1) u.a.

11   M.-J. Rondeau, Exégèse du psautier et anabase spirituelle chez
     Grégoire de Nysse: Epektasis. Mélanges J. Daniélou, Paris 1972,
     517-531; ders., D'où vient la technique exégétique utilisée par
     Grégoire de Nysse dans son traité "Sur les titres des Psaumes"?:
     Mélanges H.-Ch. Puech, Paris 1974, 263-287; A. Le Boulluec,
     L'Unité du texte. La visée du psautier selon Grégoire de Nysse:
     Le texte et ses representations. Etudes de litt. anc. III, Paris
     (Pr. de l'Ecole normale superieure), 1987, 159-166.

παντὶ γὰρ τῷ κατά τινα σκοπὸν κατορθουμένῳ τάξις τις ἔπεστι
φυσική τε καὶ ἀναγκαία ἡ δι'ἀκολούθου κατορθοῦσα τὸ
σπουδαζόμενον.

Jeder Sache, die nach einem bestimmten Ziel (σκοπός) ausge-
richtet ist, wohnt eine gewisse natürliche und zwingende
Anordnung (τάξις) inne, die folgerichtig (δι' ἀκολούθου) das
Erstrebte zu Wege bringt.

In Inscr. Ps. II,11, GNO V 115,22-25

Dieser Grundsatz ist immer wieder in seinen exegetischen Homilien zu
spüren, wenn er von der ἀκολουθία oder der Abfolge (τάξις)[12] der
einzelnen Teile eines Textes spricht. Der σκοπός ist meist identisch
mit einer Hinführung bzw. einem Aufstieg zu einer höheren Wissens-
oder Verhaltensebene. Gregors Auslegung erhält durch seine Hinweise
auf dieses höhere Ziel und die Abfolge, die zu diesem Ziel hinführt,
eine besondere, dynamische Qualität, die den Zuhörer packt und 'nach
oben' mitreißt.[13]

Die fünfte Homilie beginnt Gregor mit der Ankündigung, daß

νῦν ἡμῖν παρὰ τοῦ μεγάλου τῆς ἐκκλησίας καθηγεμόνος ἡ ἐπὶ τὰ

ὑψηλότερα τῶν μαθημάτων γίνεται μυσταγωγία.

jetzt für uns vom großen Führer der Kirche eine μυσταγωγία zu
den höheren Lehren erfolge.

In Eccl. V, 353, 11 f.

War zunächst nur ein Aufstieg zwischen den Proverbien und dem Buch
Prediger festgestellt worden, so wird dieser Gedanke nun auch in die
Schrift Prediger selbst hineingetragen. Die bisherigen Ausführungen
des Predigers galten nämlich, wie Gregor ausführt, dem Thema der

---

12 Zur ἀκολουθία in den Schriften Gregors, s. J. Daniélou, L'être et
le temps chez Grégoire de Nysse, Leiden 1970, 18-50; zur
Exegese, bes. 37 ff.; ebendort zur ἀκολουθία.

13 In den Homilien In Eccl.: Verweis auf den Aufstieg In Eccl.I,
277,8-9; 278,1; In Eccl. V, 353,12-13; In Eccl. VII, 406,12; In
Eccl. VIII, 436,20-24; zur ἀκολουθία u.a. In Eccl. V, 355,22; In
Eccl. VI, 373,6; In Eccl. VII, 397,16 ff.; 403,21-22; 406,12; zur
τάξις In Eccl. II, 307,4-5; In Eccl. VII, 409,10 f.; cf. 411,2-3.
Cf. Daniélou, Être, 37 ff.

Nichtigkeit (ματαιότης), um so das Verlangen nach dem körperlichen Genuß auszulöschen (In Eccl. V, 353,13-15). Im folgenden darf dagegen eine Hinführung (προσάγειν, μυσταγωγία) zum wahren Guten erwartet werden (In Eccl. V, 353.15-17).[14] Der anfangs formulierte σκοπός des Werkes wird also in zwei Schritten vom Prediger vorgetragen, wobei eine Hinführung zum höheren Wissen erfolgt.

Damit ist zumindest ansatzweise die Frage nach einer Gliederung des kommentierten Werkes angesprochen, technisch gesehen also die εἰς κεφάλαια διαίρεσις.[15] Dieser Punkt gehörte ebenfalls zu den Topoi des Kommentarprologes und Gregors Schrift In Inscr. Ps. macht deutlich, wie er diesen Topos für seine Zwecke zu nutzen weiß. Dort zeigt er nämlich, daß die Gliederung der Psalmen in fünf Teile identisch ist mit den fünf Stufen eines Aufstieges.[16] In der vorliegenden fünften Homilie sagt Gregor nun, daß die erste Stufe der Psalmen mit dem, was der Prediger mit seinen Ausführungen über die Nichtigkeit erreichen will, übereinstimmt (In Eccl. V, 354,1-23). Der Beginn des Buches Prediger, besprochen in den Homilien I-IV, und der Beginn der Psalmen stellen in Gregors Augen eine Einführung (εἰσαγωγικὴ ὑφήγησις)[17] zu einem reinen Lebenswandel dar. David in den Psalmen ebenso wie Salomon im Buch Prediger handelten richtig, wenn sie zunächst als Vorstufe einer Hinwendung zum Guten die Abwendung vom Schlechten lehrten. Dies entspreche nämlich, wie man aus dem Vergleich mit dem Vorgehen des Arztes (In Eccl. V, 354,13-16) folgern darf, der ἀκολουθία der Dinge.

Die in der fünften Homilie vorgetragene Gliederung bestätigt Gregor nochmals in Hom. VI (In Eccl. VI, 373,6-11): zunächst

---

14 προκαθήρας γὰρ τὰς ψυχὰς διὰ τῶν προλαβόντων λόγων καὶ πάσης ἀποστήσας τῆς κατὰ τὸ μάταιον ἐγγινομένης τοῖς ἀνθρώποις ἐπιθυμίας (das bisherige Thema des Predigers und der Homilien I-IV) οὕτω προσάγει τῇ ἀληθείᾳ τὸν νοῦν (das neue Thema des Predigers, nachdem die ματαιότης hinreichend behandelt ist) ... (In Eccl. V, 353,13-15).

15 Cf. Anm.6.

16 Cf. Rondeau, 519 ff.; Le Boulluec, 159-164.

17 In Eccl. V, 354,1-2; cf. In Inscr. Ps.II,8, GNO V 92,12 (zum ersten Psalm), cf. ibid. I,1 26,23 f.; I,2 29,2 ff.

erfolgen die Ausführungen über die Nichtigkeit, dann wird das wahrhaft Gute gezeigt; in Hom. VI bleibt als ζητούμενον die Frage nach dem Weg ⟨τέχνη καὶ ἔφοδος⟩ zu diesem Guten ⟨In Eccl. V, 373,12-13⟩.[18]

2. Leitgedanke und Gliederung der fünften Homilie

Das neue Thema, das Gregor in der Einleitung zur fünften Homilie formuliert, beherrscht als Leitgedanke die Auslegung des Textes, der der fünften Homilie zugrundeliegt. Den Textabschnitt Eccl. 2,12-26 bespricht Gregor in drei Abschnitten, wobei sich jeweils zeigt, daß nicht mehr allein, wie bisher, die Nichtigkeit, sondern nun auch die Erkenntnis und die Hinführung zum Guten Themen des Buches Prediger sind:

1. Die Auslegung von Eccl. 2,12-13 (In Eccl. V, 355,1-356,19)

Aus der näheren Bestimmung des Begriffes σοφία ergibt sich nach Gregor, 'daß wir vielleicht folgerichtig zur Erkenntnis der guten Dinge hingeführt werden' ⟨... τάχα δι' ἀκολούθου τῇ γνώσει τῶν ἀγαθῶν προσαγόμεθα In Eccl. V, 355,22 f.⟩. Mit dieser Formulierung nimmt er den Gedanken der Einleitung auf, in der von einer Einführung in die Mysterien ⟨μυσταγωγία In Eccl. V, 353,12⟩, einer Hinführung zur Wahrheit ⟨προσάγειν τῇ ἀληθείᾳ In Eccl. V, 353,15⟩ und einer Einführung ⟨εἰσαγωγικὴ ὑφήγησις In Eccl. V, 354,2-3⟩ die Rede war.[19]

Der anschließende Vergleich von Weisheit und Torheit mit Licht und Dunkelheit ⟨Eccl. 2,13; In Eccl. V, 356,1-19⟩ hilft seiner Meinung

---

18 κατεγνώσθη τὰ πάντα ἐν τοῖς προλαβοῦσι λόγοις ὡς μάταια, ὅσα κατὰ τὸν ἀνθρώπινον βίον ἐπ'οὐδενὶ ψυχικῷ κέρδει σπουδάζεται. ὑπεδείχθη τὸ ἀγαθόν, πρὸς ὃ χρὴ διὰ τῶν τῇ κεφαλῇ ἐγκειμένων ὀμμάτων βλέπειν, τοῖς δὲ τὴν σωματικὴν προϊσχομένοις ἀπόλαυσιν ἀντετέθη ἡ κατὰ σοφίαν τροφή. πῶς ἄν τις κατ' ἀρετὴν βιῴη καθάπερ τινὰ τέχνην καὶ ἔφοδον πρὸς τὴν τοῦ βίου κατόρθωσιν διὰ τοῦ λόγου λαβών. ταῦτα οὖν ἐστιν, ἃ ἐπαγγέλλεται ἡμῖν ἐν προοιμίοις ἡ προκειμένη τῶν λογίων ἐξέτασις, ... ⟨In Eccl.V, 373,6-15⟩.

19 Zur Bedeutung der Komposita von ἄγειν, besonders aber des Ausdrucks λόγῳ προσάγειν, für Gregors Vorstellung von einer rhetorisch korrekten Argumentation, H.M. Meissner, Rhetorik und Theologie. Der Dialog Gregors von Nyssa De anima et resurrectione. (Patrologia 1) Frankfurt a. M. u.a. 1991, 127-170.

nach bei der Beurteilung des Schönen und Guten (πρὸς τὴν τοῦ καλοῦ κρίσιν In Eccl. V, 356,4-5).

2. Die Auslegung von Eccl. 2,14 'Die Augen des Weisen sind in seinem Kopf, der Tor wandelt im Dunkeln' (In Eccl. V, 356,20-360,22)

Gregor beginnt diesen Abschnitt mit einer Frage:

'Αλλὰ τί κέρδος ἡμῖν ἐκ τοῦ θαυμάσαι τὸ ἀγαθόν, εἰ μή τις καὶ ἔφοδος παρὰ τοῦ διδασκάλου πρὸς τὴν τούτου κτῆσιν ὑποδειχθείη;

Welchen Nutzen aber ziehen wir daraus, daß wir das Gute bewundern, wenn uns nicht auch ein Weg (ἔφοδος) vom Lehrer zu dessen Besitz angedeutet wird?

In Eccl. V, 356,20-22

Wieder thematisiert Gregor den Weg, die Hinführung zum Guten. Eine Antwort erwartet er von der nächsten Äußerung des Predigers:

πῶς οὖν ἔστι καὶ ἡμᾶς ἐν τῇ τοῦ καλοῦ μετουσίᾳ γενέσθαι, ἀκούσωμεν τοῦ διδάσκοντος.

Wie es nun möglich ist, daß auch wir am Guten teilhaben, dazu wollen wir den Lehrer hören.

In Eccl. V, 356,22-23

Der Text zeigt seiner Meinung nach, daß der, der seine Augen auf Christus, die ἀρχή von allem, richtet (ἀνάγειν In Eccl. V, 357,20), seinen Blick auf jegliche Tugend und jegliches Gute gerichtet hat (In Eccl. V, 358,7-10). Dies sei gleichbedeutend mit der Forderung τὸ ἄνω φρονεῖν (In Eccl. V, 360,13-16).

Wie im vorhergehenden Abschnitt zeigt er zuerst am Text 'Die Augen des Weisen sind in seinem Kopf' die Ausrichtung auf die Tugend auf (In Eccl. V, 356,23-358,10), um dann darauf hinzuweisen, daß der Prediger am Text 'Der Tor wandelt im Dunkeln' den Gegensatz zwischen dem, der seine Augen nach oben, auf Christus, gerichtet hat, und dem, der nach unten auf den Bereich des Nichtigen schaut, herausarbeitet (In Eccl. V, 358,11-360,16).[20] Sowohl im ersten als auch im zweiten Abschnitt seiner Auslegung weist Gregor also nach, daß zunächst jeweils der Zugang zum Guten und anschließend der Gegensatz zwischen dem Guten und Schlechten, bzw. dem, der dem Guten bzw. Schlechten folgt, aufgezeigt wird.

Seine Folgerung aus der bisherigen Exegese ist φύγωμεν τὴν ἀφροσύνην (In Eccl. V, 360,18). Diese Aufforderung greift die prägnant formulierte Aussage der Einleitung zur fünften Homilie wieder auf: 'Der Anfang des Tugendlebens ist es, außerhalb des Schlechten zu kommen' (In Eccl. V, 354,1). Die Flucht vor der Torheit ist also zugleich der gesuchte Zugang zum Guten.

3. Die Auslegung von Eccl. 2,14-26 (In Eccl. V, 360,22-372,19)

Gregor begreift, wie wir unten noch genauer sehen werden, diesen Textabschnitt als Diskussion zwischen Lehrer und Schüler. Der Lehrer wehrt dabei die Einwände gegen ein tugendhaftes Leben ab. Für ihn behandelt (θεραπεύει In Eccl. V, 361,1) der Lehrer, wie ein Arzt, die Kleinmütigkeit des Schülers, der noch nicht den Vorteil (κέρδος In Eccl. V, 361,3) des Tugendlebens sieht. Diesen belehrt er über den Unterschied (διαφορά) zwischen dem tugendhaften und dem nicht tugendhaften Leben und zeigt den Vorteil der Arete gegenüber der Schlechtigkeit auf (In Eccl. V, 361,10-13). Auch dadurch wird ein Zugang zum Guten geschaffen, wie Gregor noch einmal klar am Ende dieser langen Auslegung zum Ausdruck bringt:

> ὅσα τοίνυν ἐκ τῆς παραλλήλου ταύτης συνεξετάσεως τοῦ τε καλοῦ καὶ τοῦ χείρονος διὰ τῆς νῦν μεμαθήκαμεν ἀναγνώσεως, γένοιτο ἡμῖν βοήθεια πρὸς ἀποφυγὴν μὲν τῶν κατεγνωσμένων, ἐφόδιον δὲ τῶν πρὸς τὸ κρεῖττον κατορθουμένων, ...

> was wir also aufgrund dieser parallelen Untersuchung des Guten und des Schlechteren durch die heutige Lesung erfahren haben, möge uns eine Hilfe zur Flucht (βοήθεια πρὸς ἀποφυγήν) vor

---

20 Während Gregor also In Eccl. V, 356,1-19 mit einem Vergleich aufgrund der Ähnlichkeit seinen Gedankengang schließt, arbeitet er an der vorliegenden Stelle mit einem Vergleich aufgrund der Unähnlichkeit (exemplum contrarium). S. dazu im folgenden die Ausführungen zu In Eccl. V, 355,1-5 mit Anm. 36-37; Meissner, Rhetorik und Theologie, 155-160 (zur Induktion) und 215 Anm. 111.

dem, was verdammt ist, und zugleich Zugang (ἐφόδιον) zu dem, was auf das Bessere gerichtet ist, sein ...

In Eccl. V, 372,15-18

Es zeigt sich also, daß das in der Einleitung der Homilie formulierte Thema: Hinführung zum Guten durch Abkehr vom Schlechten sozusagen das Leitmotiv ist, anhand dessen Gregor die vorliegende Textperikope erklärt. Dieses Leitmotiv wiederum ist dem zuvor ermittelten σκοπός des Werkes untergeordnet.

3.   Der pädagogische Charakter des Buches Prediger

Die Schrift Prediger belehrt nach Gregor den Zuhörer und erzieht ihn zu einem tugendhaften Leben (In Eccl. I, 279,20-280,2). Darin liegen für ihn das Ziel (σκοπός) und der Nutzen (χρήσιμον) des Werkes. Dadurch, daß das Werk in besonderem Maße einen moralischen Nutzen bringt, unterscheide es sich seiner Meinung nach von den anderen, eher historisch ausgerichteten Schriften des Alten Testamentes; weil es der Kirche so mehr nütze als die anderen Schriften des Alten Testamentes, habe das Buch Prediger, nach Gregors Auffassung, den Titel Ekklesiastes erhalten (In Eccl. I, 279,5-280,2).

Die Frage nach dem Nutzen (ὠφέλεια) einer Schrift nahm auch im antiken Grammatikunterricht eine hervorragende Stellung ein.[21] Der antike Streit, ob die Dichtung erfreuen und/oder nützen solle, ist hinreichend bekannt. Wahrscheinlich unter stoischem Einfluß wird in den Scholien und theoretischen Schriften vor allem die Frage nach dem moralischen Nutzen der kommentierten Schrift behandelt. So trifft man in den Homerscholien häufig die formelhafte Wendung διδάσκει ἡμᾶς ὁ ποιητής, mit der die Homererklärer zu der moralischen Belehrung überleiten, die einer Textpassage abgewonnen werden kann.[22] Hier wirkt die alte Vorstellung fort, daß der Dichter Lehrer und Erzieher

---

21 Zu dem folgenden s. ausführlich mit Belegen: Neuschäfer, 247-263; Schäublin, 161-164.

22 Cf. Neuschäfer, 252 f.; Schäublin, 162 f.

seines Publikums ist.[23]   Auch in der Schrift Plutarchs, wie die
Jugendlichen die Gedichte hören sollen, und bei Basileios, in seiner
Schrift Ad Adulescentulos, steht das Nützliche (ὠφέλιμον, χρήσιμον) bei
der Interpretation der Dichtungswerke im Vordergrund.[24]   Eine
Betrachtung der auszulegenden Schrift unter dem Gesichtspunkt des
moralischen Nutzens hatte also einen festen Platz in der heidnischen
Texterklärung und im antiken Grammatikunterricht.

Die pädagogische Sicht des Buches Predigers durchzieht Gregors
Homilien.   Häufiger ist, wie z.B. in der fünften Homilie, von der Lehre,
dem Lehrer, der Erziehung oder dem Lernen die Rede.[25]   Diese
pädagogische Terminologie muß, wie das Vorhergehende gezeigt hat, in
enger Verbindung mit Gregors Bestimmung von Ziel und Nutzen des
Werkes gesehen werden.   Denn der Lehrer führt zum Ziel, der Wahrheit
bzw. der Erkenntnis des Guten (προσάγειν In Eccl. V, 355,22; 353,15/
ὁδηγέω In Eccl. II, 305,22/ὑφηγητής In Eccl. V,   371,2).[26]   Er ist
schon weiter vorangeschritten als der Zuhörer und kennt so das Ziel,
das er 'von oben' dem Hörer zuruft (In Eccl. I, 290,15-18; cf.
284,16-19; In Eccl. VIII, 424,4).   Auffällig ist, wie sehr die Person
des Exegeten in den Hintergrund rückt; es ist der Prediger oder dessen
λόγος[27], der scheinbar direkt zu den Zuhörern spricht.

4. Die Frage nach dem Sprecher (τὸ πρόσωπον τὸ λέγον)

Wer aber ist der Lehrer?   Wer ist der Führer der Kirche, der
uns zum höheren Wissen, wie am Anfang der fünften Homilie gesagt
wird, führen soll?   Wer spricht im Buch Prediger?   Damit ist die

---

23 Cf. Schäublin, 162.

24 Schäublin, 163; Neuschäfer, 259.

25 In Eccl.V, 355,7; 356,23; 361,10 (διδάσκει); 356,21; 370,13 f.;
    371,1-2 (διδάσκαλος); 360,17; 371,21; 372,16 (μανθάνειν).   Zu
    παιδεύειν s. z.B. In Eccl. III, 317,13-14; IV, 352,12; In Eccl. VI,
    382,10; In Eccl. VII, 409,4.

26 Zur Bedeutung des προσάγειν bei Gregor, s. Meissner, Rhetorik und
    Theologie, 127-170; dort auch zur Rolle des Lehrers in der
    Hinführung zur Wahrheit (138 ff.).

27 Cf. z.B. In Eccl. V, 260,22; In Eccl. VI, 374,13; 375,1-2; 376,9-
    11.

traditionelle Frage der Kommentatoren nach dem πρόσωπον τὸ λέγον,
also nach dem jeweiligen Sprecher, gestellt.[28]   Gregor findet im
vorliegenden Fall zwei Antworten.   Zum einen kann es sich um den
historischen Salomon handeln, zum anderen um den wahren Ekklesiastes,
Christus selbst.[29]

Schon bei der Besprechung der Überschrift 'Ekklesiastes' nennt
Gregor die Möglichkeit, die er nachfolgend begründet, daß unter dem
Titel Ekklesiastes der wahre Führer der Kirche, Christus, zu verstehen
ist (In Eccl. I, 280,7-281,2).   Der Sinn des Titels sei, daß 'wir
dadurch lernen, daß auf ihn, der durch das Evangelium die Kirche
zusammengefügt hat, die Kraft dieser (im Buch Prediger stehenden)
Worte verweist'[30] (In Eccl. I, 280,16-20).   Für Gregor ist es also die
Weisheit, d.h. Christus, die, wie Gregor an anderer Stelle betont, durch
den historischen Salomon, den Salomon 'nach dem Fleische' (ὁ κατὰ
σάρκα Σαλομών), spricht.   Ebenso betont Gregor in seiner ersten
Homilie In Cant., daß Christus Salomon als Werkzeug benutze, um mit
dessen Stimme zu sprechen.[31]

In den Predigerhomilien nimmt Gregor als sprechende Person meist
Salomon an.   Aber zu Beginn der zweiten Homilie (In Eccl. II, 298,5
ff.) weist er ausdrücklich die Verse Christus zu, der über das Myste-
rium der Inkarnation spreche.   Gregor nennt hier nicht das Kriterium,

---

28   Zum πρόσωπον τὸ λέγον s. Neuschäfer, 263-276; Schäublin, 86-
     88.

29   In den Homilien zum Prediger erwähnt er noch häufiger diese
     Technik: In Eccl. VI, 383,15 f. meint er, daß Deut. 32,39 ἐκ
     προσώπου τοῦ θεοῦ gesprochen sei, und In Eccl. VI, 385,21-386,1
     nimmt er an, daß Matth. 5,4 ἐκ προσώπου τοῦ κυρίου zu verstehen
     sei.

30   τάχα δὲ οὐκ ἔξω τοῦ εἰκότος εἰς ταύτην τὴν διάνοιαν τὴν τῆς
     ἐπιγραφῆς ἀναφέρομεν σημασίαν, ἵνα διὰ τούτου μάθωμεν, ὅτι εἰς
     αὐτὸν τὸν διὰ τοῦ εὐαγγελίου τὴν ἐκκλησίαν πηξάμενον ἡ τῶν
     ῥημάτων τούτων ἀναφέρεται δύναμις (In Eccl. V, 280,16-20).   Zu
     der vorsichtigen Formulierung τάχα δὲ οὐκ ἔξω τοῦ εἰκότος, die
     eine Denk- oder Interpretationsmöglichkeit offenhält, s. auch
     Meissner, Rhetorik und Theologie, bes. 373 mit Anm. 8.

31   In Eccl. II, 305,19-21; In Cant. I, GNO VI 17,7-12; In Inscr. Ps.
     ist es der Heilige Geist, der durch David spricht (In Inscr. Ps.
     II,10, GNO V 114,15 ff.; II,11, GNO V 115,17-19).

das ihn einen Sprecherwechsel annehmen läßt. Doch kennen wir dieses Kriterium z.B. aus Origenes: der Inhalt der Verse ist nicht Salomon als Sprecher angemessen, sondern Christus. Wie Schäublin und Neuschäfer gezeigt haben, ist die Frage, ob eine bestimmte Rede einer bestimmten Person angemessen ist, ein Thema der Rhetorik, das unter dem Stichwort Prosopopoiia breit abgehandelt wurde.[32] Die Überlegung, daß eine Aussage über die Inkarnation eher Christus als Salomon angemessen ist, muß also der Zuweisung der Rede zu Anfang der zweiten Homilie zugrundeliegen, ohne daß Gregor an dieser Stelle explizit darauf verweist. In einem Kommentar hätte er dies vielleicht genauer begründet, in der Homilie begnügt er sich mit der einfachen Feststellung.

War zu Anfang der zweiten Homilie Christus als Sprecher angenommen worden, ist es für die Interpretation von Prediger 1,16 ff. von Bedeutung, daß der historische Salomon (ὁ κατὰ σάρκα Σαλομών) der Sprecher ist. Deshalb macht Gregor ausdrücklich darauf aufmerksam, daß nunmehr die Weisheit durch den historischen Salomon spreche (In Eccl. II, 305,19-21). Diese Zuweisung gebe dem Gesagten nämlich eine höhere Glaubwürdigkeit (ἀξιοπιστία).[33] Das Ziel des Predigers, die Menschen zur Abkehr vom weltlichen Vergnügen zu bewegen, kann also leichter erreicht werden. Gregor argumentiert dabei folgendermaßen mit der Person des Sprechers: Wenn Salomon, dem alle Möglichkeiten des Genusses offenstanden und der diese ausprobiert hat, das Wohlleben zurückweist, dann kann ihm nicht vorgeworfen werden, er lehne nur das ab, was er nicht kenne oder sich nicht leisten könne. Weil Salomon aus eigener Erfahrung (πεῖρα) die Genüsse des Lebens kenne, sei er glaubwürdig, wenn er diese aufgrund seiner Erfahrung ablehne (In Eccl. III, 315,2-7).

Dies ist eine durchaus rhetorische Überlegung. Auch in den Iliasscholien finden wir die Bemerkung, daß eine Rede aufgrund der Besonderheiten der Person, die sie vorträgt, besonders glaubwürdig (ἀξιόπιστος) ist. Den Gedanken, daß die Person des Sprechers selbst

32 Neuschäfer, 263-276;   Schäublin, 86-88.
33 Cf. In Eccl. II, 306,2 und die Zusammenfassung zu Anfang der dritten Homilie In Eccl. III, 315,4-7.

zur Glaubwürdigkeit einer Rede beiträgt, führt Aristoteles unter den Überzeugungsmitteln auf.[34]   Gregor greift an dieser Stelle also Überlegungen auf, die in Rhetorik und Grammatik üblich waren.

Allerdings stellt sich nun für Gregor die Frage, ob Salomon tatsächlich all das getan hat, zu dem er sich bekennt.   Denn ein solches Bekenntnis könnte seine Glaubwürdigkeit durchaus erschüttern. Rhetorisch gesehen ist aber, wie wir gesehen haben, die Glaubwürdigkeit des Sprechers von größter Bedeutung.   Gregor kann diese Frage nicht genau beantworten, legt jedoch zwei Vermutungen vor.   Entweder führe Salomon dies nur aus, um uns zu überzeugen, oder aber er handele aus dem Interesse heraus, seine Sinne abzustumpfen (In Eccl. III 309,14-311,14).

Auf diese Überlegungen zum Sprecher (πρόσωπον) Salomon, die Gregor in der dritten Homilie anstellt, kommt er noch einmal in Hom. V zurück, wo er darauf hinweist, daß Salomon das Vergnügen nicht aus πάθος, sondern aufgrund einer bestimmten Überlegung erprobt hat (In Eccl. V, 367,15-368,18).

Auch die Person des Sprechers dient also in Gregors Augen dazu, das Ziel (σκοπός) des Werkes zu erreichen.   Die Reflexion über die Person Salomons deckt auf, daß durch das πρόσωπον die Glaubwürdigkeit der Worte des Predigers erhöht werden soll und dies somit eine Hilfe darstellt, um den Zuhörer zu überzeugen.

5.   Rhetorische und grammatische Bemerkungen in Gregors Exegese (In Eccl. V, 355,1-356,19)

Wenden wir uns der Auslegung von Eccl. 2,12-13 in der fünften Homilie zu.   Gregor hatte in der Einleitung zur fünften Homilie ange-kündigt, daß der Prediger, nachdem er die Nichtigkeit der weltlichen

---

34 Sch.II.P 328-30a Erbse (Die Worte sind glaubhaft, weil sie von einem Herold gesprochen werden, der viel in der Welt herumkommt); Arist. Rhet. I,2 1356a1-13; cf. I,11 1371a8-17.

Dinge 'vor ʌugen geführt habe' (ὑπ' ὄψιν ἄγειν),[35] nun das wahrhaft Gute andeuten werde (ὑποδεικνύειν In Eccl. V, 354,20). Diese Behauptung sieht er durch die Auslegung von Eccl. 2,12-13 begründet (γάρ In Eccl. V, 355,1). Denn durch diese Aussage des Predigers werden wir, wie Gregor sagt, 'vielleicht zur Erkenntnis des Guten hingeführt' (In Eccl. V, 355,22 f.). Damit ist diese Stelle, wie wir schon sahen, dem σκοπός des Werkes untergeordnet.

Mit Blick auf die grammatisch-rhetorische Tradition sind m.E. mehrere Punkte an dieser Auslegung erwähnenswert.

(1) Gregor gibt den auszulegenden Vers 'Ich blickte mich um, um die Weisheit zu sehen und die Tollheit und die Torheit' mit einer rhetorischen Zwischenbemerkung wieder:

> Ἐπέβλεψα γὰρ ἐγώ, φησί, τοῦ ἰδεῖν σοφίαν. ὡς δ'ἄν ἀκριβῶς ἴδοιμι τὸ ποθούμενον, εἶδον πρότερον καὶ τὴν παραφορὰν καὶ τὴν ἀφροσύνην. ἐκ γὰρ τῆς πρὸς τὸ ἀντικείμενον παραθέσεως ἀκριβεστέρα γίνεται τῶν σπουδαζομένων ἡ θεωρία.

> Denn ich blickte mich um, sagt er, um die Weisheit zu sehen. Damit ich genau sähe, was ich erstrebte, sah ich zuerst Tollheit und Torheit an. Denn aufgrund der vergleichenden Nebeneinanderstellung mit dem Entgegengesetzten wird eine genaue Kenntnis des Erstrebten erreicht.

> In Eccl. V, 355,1-5

Er unterstellt also dem Prediger, daß er zur Verdeutlichung des Gesagten die rhetorische Technik des Vergleichs mit dem Entgegengesetzten (exemplum contrarium) gebraucht habe.[36] Diese

---

35 In Eccl.V, 354,18. Dies ist m.E. ein Hinweis darauf, daß Gregor annimmt, daß der Prediger hier die rhetorische Technik der Ekphrasis oder Evidentia benutzt. Denn ὑπ' ὄψιν ἄγειν ist der Terminus technicus für dieses Vorgehen: s. H. Lausberg, Handbuch der literarischen Rhetorik. Eine Grundlegung der Literaturwissenschaft, München ²1973 § 810; weitere Beispiele De Beat. III, PG 44, 1220B9; In Inscr. Ps. I,8, GNO V 53,4-6 u. 56,5-8.

36 Cf. Lausberg, Handbuch, § 420,3; 423,3. Dahinter steht der von Aristoteles häufiger zitierte Grundsatz, daß Gegensätze derselben Wissenschaft unterliegen: τῶν ἀντικειμένων ἡ αὐτὴ ἐπιστήμη (Arist. Top. I,14 105b33; II,2 109b17).

Vergleichstechnik findet sich seiner Meinung nach häufiger im Prediger.[37]

(2) Er begründet seine Interpretation, daß 'σοφία' die wahre Weisheit, also Christus, meine, mit Stellen aus dem Alten (Ps. 103,24) und dem Neuen Testament (1. Cor. 1,24). Dahinter steht ein Gedanke aus der antiken Auslegungstradition, daß nämlich die Heilige Schrift mit Hilfe der Heiligen Schrift erklärt werden müsse. Dies ist der von Porphyr für Homer prägnant formulierte Grundsatz, 'Homer aus Homer zu erklären'.[38]

Dies gilt vor allem auch für die Worterklärung, dem γλωσσηματικόν, bei der die christlichen Exegeten wiederum die Methoden der heidnischen Grammatiklehrer aufgreifen. Am häufigsten trifft man in Gregors Homilien zum Prediger den Rückgriff auf den biblischen oder alltäglichen Sprachgebrauch. Der dafür gebrauchte Terminus technicus lautet συνήθεια; diese Methode ist bei Origenes wie in den Homerscholien sehr häufig anzutreffen.[39]

Die Beachtung des Sprachgebrauchs der Heiligen Schrift dient dazu, die Bedeutung des Wortes aus seiner sonst üblichen Verwendung herzuleiten oder auf den häufig anzutreffenden Sinn eines Begriffes hinzuweisen. Dies wendet Gregor an der vorliegenden Stelle der fünften Homilie an. Mehrmals verweist Gregor explizit auf diese Methode. Zum Beispiel bestimmt er unter Heranziehung der γραφική συνήθεια (In Eccl. I, 282,12 f.; 283,4) die Bedeutung von ματαιότης ματαιοτήτων in der ersten Homilie (In Eccl. I, 282,10-283,17); in der zweiten Homilie zeigt er, was die Heilige Schrift unter ὑστέρημα versteht (In Eccl. II, 304,7 ff.); in der sechsten Homilie wendet er diese Technik auf das Wort κοπετός an (In Eccl. VI, 388,17 ff.), in der achten auf περίληψις (In Eccl. VIII, 398,1 ff.).

---

37 Cf. In Eccl. VII, 406,17-407,5 (ἀντιθεωρεῖται, ἀντιδιαιρεῖται); In
    Eccl. VIII, 423,15-18 (ἀντιπαράθεσις); ibid. 426,17 (ἀντιδιαστολή);
    cf. In Eccl. V, 356,1-2 (s. Anm.41); cf. De Beat. I, PG 44,
    1196D10-12 u. 1200A13-B1; cf. Anm.20.

38 Dazu ausführlich Neuschäfer, 277-285; Schäublin, 159-160. Zu
    Gregor s. den Vortrag von R.E. Heine, s.u. 205-230.

39 Zur συνήθεια s. Neuschäfer, 143-145.

Auch ein Beispiel für das Heranziehen des täglichen Sprach-
gebrauchs ist bei ihm zu finden. So gelangt er zu einer genauen
Bestimmung des Begriffes μάταιος durch eine sorgfältige Analyse des
Sermo cotidianus. Dabei führt er ebenfalls Belege und Beispiele an,
wie er es auch im Falle des biblischen Sprachgebrauchs machte (In
Eccl. I, 281,3-282,9).

Gleichfalls   in   den   Bereich   der   Worterklärung   gehört   die
Unterscheidung von Synonymen. In den Scholien und den spätantiken
Synonymenlexika wird sehr genau auf den Gebrauch der Wörter und
deren Differenzierung geachtet.[40] Dieses Streben nach genauer
Begriffsdifferenzierung hat schon Origenes aus der paganen Auslegung
übernommen. Ein Beispiel findet sich in den hier untersuchten
Homilien: Gregor besteht darauf, daß es sich bei der Nennung von
γεγονός und πεποιημένον in Eccl. I, 9 nicht um eine bedeutungslose
Wiederholung (ματαία ἐπανάληψις In Eccl.I, 296,5) handele, sondern daß
ein Unterschied (διαφορά) zwischen diesen Wörtern bestehe. Diese
Unterscheidung macht er theologisch fruchtbar, genauer gesagt, soll
diese Unterscheidung den Zuhörer auf den darin verborgenen nützlichen,
theologischen Gedanken bringen (In Eccl. I, 296,4 ff.). Dahinter steht
letztlich die Überlegung, daß die Heilige Schrift in jeder Einzelheit
inspiriert und zu unserem Nutzen geschrieben ist.

(3) Auch Eccl. 2,13 'Da sah ich, daß die Weisheit die Torheit
übertrifft wie das Licht die Finsternis' gibt Gregor in eigenen Worten
interpretierend wieder, wobei er wie zuvor auf die gegenüberstellende
Untersuchung zweier Begriffe verweist.[41]   Dabei unterzieht er den
Vergleich einer rhetorischen Beurteilung. Für ihn gebraucht der
Prediger diesen Vergleich angemessen (προσηκόντως In Eccl. V, 356,4).
Er begründet dies durch eine nähere Betrachtung der verglichenen Dinge
und kommt abschließend zu dem Urteil:

---

40 Neuschäfer, 141 f. zu dieser Frage.

41 In Eccl. V, 356,1-2 ἐν ζυγῷ διέκρινα τὸ ὂν τοῦ μὴ ὄντος.

ἴση τοίνυν ἡ διαφορὰ τοῦ φωτὸς πρὸς τὸ σκότος καὶ τῆς σοφίας
πρὸς ἀφροσύνην ἐστίν.

Also ist der Unterschied zwischen Licht und Finsternis ebenso
groß wie der zwischen Weisheit und Torheit.

In Eccl. V, 356,16-17

Rhetorisch gesehen stellt Gregor also den Grad der Ähnlichkeit in dem
Vergleich fest.[42]

Ebenso spricht die Auslegung von Eccl. 1,17 'Ich erkannte die
Vergleiche und das Wissen' in der zweiten Homilie den Rhetor in Gregor
an. Dieses Lemma führt ihn dazu, anzunehmen, daß der Prediger auf
die rhetorische Induktion verweise, die auch der Herr selbst, also
Christus, im Evangelium anwende. Sie diene dazu, das über dem
menschlichen Begreifen Liegende durch einen Vergleich mit dem
Bekannten 'vor Augen zu führen' (In Eccl. II, 308,17-309,8).[43] Dies
mag genügen, um zu zeigen, daß Gregor eine rhetorische Schulung bzw.
Vorgehensweise des Predigers wie auch Christi selbst annimmt.

(4) Damit ergibt sich eine letzte Bemerkung zur exegetischen
Methode Gregors. Denn die zuletzt vorgetragene Interpretation des
Begriffes σοφία pars pro toto oder ἀπὸ τοῦ μέρους τὸ πᾶν für das
Gute insgesamt ist nur eine von vielen methodischen Möglichkeiten, die
zum dritten Arbeitsgang der antiken Textauslegung, dem sogenannten
τεχνικόν, gehörte. Darunter fällt neben grammatikalischen Bemerkungen
z.B. zu Artikel- oder Modusgebrauch auch das Erklären der rhetorischen Stilmittel, wie in unserem Fall die Synekdoche.

---

42 In der Rhetorik wird gewöhnlich der Grad der Ähnlichkeit zwischen
    den verglichenen Dingen festgestellt: Lausberg, Handbuch, § 420 u.
    423.

43 Zur Induktion bei Gregor s. Meissner, Rhetorik und Theologie, 155-
    160; zur Formulierung ὑπ' ὄψιν ἄγειν (In Eccl. II, 309,3) s.o. Anm.
    35.

An rhetorischen Stilmitteln erwähnt Gregor in den Predigerhomilien explizit die Synekdoche, die Epitasis bzw. Hyperbel und die Epanalepse.[44] Wirklich grammatikalische Bemerkungen sind hingegen selten. Eine Bemerkungen zur Benutzung des Demonstrativpronomens findet sich in De Beat. V, PG 44, 1261A6-7. Bei Gregor von Nazianz und vor allem bei Basileios gibt es mehr Belege für solche grammatikalischen Vermerke.[45] Das kann allerdings auch damit zusammenhängen, daß Gregor von Nyssa keinen Kommentar sondern Homilien verfaßt.

6. **Das methodische Vorgehen bei der Exegese von Eccl. 2,14-26: προθεωρία, ἀντίθεσις-λύσις (In Eccl. V, 360,22-372,19)**

Bei der Auslegung dieses Textabschnittes lassen sich zwei Teile unterscheiden. Gregor beginnt mit dem, was er eine προθεωρία nennt, um dann den Text im einzelnen auszulegen. Zu Beginn des zweiten Teiles nimmt er Stellung zu seiner Vorgehensweise:

'Η μὲν οὖν διάνοια τῶν ἐφεξῆς γεγραμμένων καὶ ἡ κατὰ τὸ ἀκόλουθον προθεωρία αὕτη ἐστίν, ἣν δι'ὀλίγου νῦν παρεθέμεθα. καιρὸς δ'ἂν εἴη πάλιν ἐπαναλαβεῖν τὴν λέξιν καὶ προσαρμόσαι δι' ἀκριβείας τοῖς ῥητοῖς τὰ νοήματα.

Der Sinn (διάνοια) also des anschließenden Textabschnittes und die folgerichtige Vorbetrachtung (προθεωρία) ist dies, was wir gerade knapp dargelegt haben. Es ist aber wohl Zeit, wiederum den Wortlaut (λέξις) aufzunehmen und sorgfältig die Gedanken (νοήματα) mit dem Gesagten zusammenzupassen (προσαρμόσαι).

In Eccl. V, 364,7-10

---

44 *Synekdoche* (ἀπὸ μέρους): In Eccl. I, 287,22; In Eccl. VII, 399,4-5; cf. De Beat. IV, PG 44, 1241B8-10 (Synekdoche als συνήθεια der Heiligen Schrift); cf. zu diesem Stilmittel Neuschäfer, 224 f.; Schäublin, 111 f. *Epitasis/Hyperbel*: Zur problematischen Bestimmung der Epitasis s. Neuschäfer, 229 f.; zur Hyperbel ders. 235; In Eccl. I, 282,10-283,17 (καθ' ὑπέρθεσιν ibid. 283,3/8/14; ἐπίτασις 283,11; ὑπερβολή 283,17); In Eccl. VI, 388,15-22 (ἐπίτασις): diese Stelle (Eccl. 3,4) interpretiert auch Origenes unter Zuhilfenahme der Epitasis (s. Neuschäfer, 229); cf. De Beat. V, PG 44, 1252C8. *Epanalepse*: In Eccl. I, 296,5; In Eccl. VI, 388,13.

45 Einige Stellen bei Weiss, 50-58.

Was meint Gregor, wenn er von einer προθεωρία spricht?

Die Technik der προθεωρία benutzt Gregor in seinen Schriften häufiger. Scheinbar losgelöst von der unmittelbar vorliegenden Frage oder Textstelle behandelt er zunächst ein allgemeines Philosophoumenon oder Theologoumenon, dessen Bezug zur vorliegenden Frage sich für den Leser erst später herausstellt. Mit Hilfe dieser Vorbetrachtung bereitet er seinen Hörer auf die Deutung vor.

Ein typisches Beispiel findet sich zu Beginn der sechsten Homilie In Cant., wo Gregor selbst seine Vorgehensweise kommentiert:

1. Schritt: Damit der Zuhörer die Textpassage versteht, hält er es für nötig, ihm zunächst den Sinn (διάνοια In Cant. VI, GNO VI 173,4-5; 175,5; νόημα 175,17) der Passage vorzutragen. Dies geschieht durch eine προθεωρία (In Cant. VI, GNO VI 173,4-5; 175,4-5 u. 17; cf. προέκθεσις In Cant. VI, GNO VI 173,3) über die Zweiteilung der Natur des Seienden in Aistheta und Noeta und des letzteren in Aktista und Ktista (In Cant. VI, GNO VI 173,1-174,20).

2. Schritt: Er wiederholt den Wortlaut (λέξις In Cant.VI, GNO VI 175,3) der Textpassage (In Cant. VI, GNO VI 175,1-15).

3. Schritt: Schließlich fügt er den Wortlaut des Bibeltextes mit dem vorher Betrachteten zusammen. Das Wort, das er dafür benutzt, ist ἐφαρμόζειν (In Cant. VI, GNO VI 173,4 u. 175,4).

Gregor nennt dieses Vorschalten einer allgemeineren Untersuchung προέκθεσις[46] und häufiger noch προθεωρία, eine Vorüberlegung. Sein Vorgehen ist m.E. mit der rhetorischen Technik der προκατασκευή, der Vorbereitung der späteren Beweisführung in der Narratio einer Gerichtsrede,[47] verwandt. Denn auch in der vorbereitenden Narratio

---

46 προέκθεσις: In Cant. VI, GNO VI 173,3; προθεωρία: In Eccl. V, 364,8; In Eccl. VI, 376,12; In Cant. VI, GNO VI 173,4-5; 175,4-5 u. 17.

47 Während der Terminus προθεωρία fast ungebräuchlich gewesen zu sein scheint (cf. Io. Chr. Th. Ernesti, Lexicon technologiae Graecorum rhetoricae, Leipzig 1795, s.v., 291: 'introductio, et praefatio, qua Rhetores declamationum suarum argumenta, partes et, artificia enarrare solebant'; cf. O. Immisch, Zu Martial,

werden — vom Zuhörer noch unbemerkt — die Samen für das Verständnis des folgenden gelegt (*semina spargere*). Der Redner weiß schon vorher, was er beweisen oder zeigen will. Mit Blick auf dieses Vorwissen bereitet er den Zuhörer auf das Folgende vor. Ebenso geht Gregor vor, der hier, wie an vielen anderen Stellen seines Werkes, den Leser durch eine Protheoria auf das richtige Verständnis einer schwierigen Textpassage oder Frage vorbereitet.

Das Zusammenfügen von ermitteltem Textsinn und dem Wortlaut des Textes wird hier, wie an anderen Textstellen, ἐφ- oder προσαρμόζειν genannt. Durch dieses Zusammenfügen kann, wie Gregor selbst sagt, überprüft werden, ob der Ausleger tatsächlich den richtigen Sinn getroffen hat[48]. Denn erst, wenn die Schrift selbst die Auslegung bezeugt (μαρτυρία) bzw. besiegelt (σφραγίς),[49] ist diese gültig. In diesem Sinne ist auch die Bemerkung am Ende der fünften Homilie zur Auslegung von Eccl. 2,26 zu verstehen. Dort sagt Gregor:

Hermes 46, 1911 (481-517), 488 Anm. 1), führt die προέκθεσις weiter. Nach Ernesti (s.v., 288-289) ist darunter Folgendes zu verstehen: 'expositio rerum et capitum, de quibus deinceps argumentandum sit: quam alii πρόθεσιν et πρόφασιν dixere.' Proekthesis wird oft synonym mit Prokataskeue und Prodiegesis gebraucht. Hermog. Meth. 12 427,12-14 Rabe bemerkt: Τὸ ἐν ἀρχῇ τι λέγειν ἐπὶ κεφαλαίων, περὶ ὧν τις μέλλει κατασκευάζειν ἢ διδάσκειν, οἱ τεχνικοὶ καλοῦσι προέκθεσιν, ... Die Alten nannten diese Technik auch ὑπόσχεσις (ibid. 427,16 f.). Eustathius findet diese Technik in der Ilias verwendet: ἐνταῦθα δὲ ἰστέον καὶ ὅτι σχῆμα εὐκρινείας καὶ σαφηνείας παρὰ τοῖς παλαιοῖς ἡ προέκθεσις, προδιδάσκουσα κεφαλαιωδῶς καὶ προεκτιθεμένη τὸν τοῦ ἐφεξῆς λόγου σκόπον (Comm. II,A1 7 = 12,44-46 van der Valk). Während die Rhetoren anstatt von Prokataskeue von Proekthesis oder Hyposchesis sprechen, verwenden die Philosophen, so Eustathius, den Begriff Skopos (ibid. A4 18 = 29,25-27).

48 In Inscr. Ps. II,8, GNO V 93,7-10: ἔξεστι τῷ βουλομένῳ δι' αὐτῶν τῶν θείων ῥημάτων δοκιμάσαι τὴν ἡμετέραν ὑπόληψιν, εἴπερ ἐφαρμόζει τὰ παρ' ἡμῶν εἰρημένα τῇ θεοπνεύστῳ γραφῇ.

49 Cf. B. Studer, Der geschichtliche Hintergrund des ersten Buches "Contra Eunomium" Gregors von Nyssa: L.F. Mateo-Seco/J.L. Bastero (Hg.), El "Contra Eunomium I" en la produccion literaria de Gregorio de Nisa. VI Coloquio Internacional sobre Gregorio de Nisa, Pamplona 1988 (139-171) 153 f. zur μαρτυρία; σφραγίς der Heiligen Schrift, cf. De An. Res. PG 46, 64B4-7. Ausführlicher zu Gregor s. Meissner, Rhetorik und Theologie, 145 ff.

ταῦτα εἶπον ἐγὼ τῇ ἐμαυτοῦ φωνῇ, ἐπισφραγίσει δὲ τὴν διάνοιαν
ταύτην ἡ τῶν θείων ῥημάτων παράθεσις.

Dieses habe ich mit meinen eigenen Worten gesagt. Ein
Vergleich mit den göttlichen Worten besiegelt (ἐπισφραγίζεται)
aber diesen Sinn (διάνοια).

In Eccl. V, 372,10-11

Es folgt der Wortlaut der Stelle. — Dies mag genügen. Im Rahmen
dieser Ausführungen würde es zu weit führen, den für Gregors Denken
zentralen Gedanken darzulegen, daß die Heilige Schrift Maßstab
jeglicher Untersuchung sein muß.[50]

In der fünften Homilie besteht die Protheoria, die den Sinn
(διάνοια) des Textes aufdecken soll, aus jeweils einer freien Nacher-
zählung des Textes und einer Wiedergabe im Wortlaut (λέξις). Die
freiere Textparaphrase, die den Sinn aufdecken soll, lehnt sich an die
rhetorische Technik der Paraphrasis[51] an. Diese Technik wird im
Rahmen der Progymnasmata geübt. Der Schüler hat die Aufgabe, einen
Text, z.B. eine schwierige Dichterpassage, in anderen Worten wieder-
zugeben. Dabei werden vor allem ungewöhnliche Wörter und Formen
ersetzt; die Vorlage kann je nach rednerischer Begabung verändert
werden. Wichtig für Gregor ist, daß der Sinn der Passage beibehalten
wird, also eine Tractatio der Vorlage vorliegt.

Dieses Abwechseln von interpretierender Paraphrase und Anführen
des Wortlautes ist nicht nur auf die Protheoria beschränkt, sondern
wird von ihm auch in der folgenden genaueren Untersuchung eingesetzt.

---

50 Zu diesem Konzept s. Meissner, Rhetorik und Theologie, 145 ff.;
    cf. Ad. Abl. GNO III,1 38,19-39,7; Ref. Eun. 2, GNO II 312,12-
    20; De An. Res. PG 46, 49C3-8; Ad Eusth., GNO III,1 6,3-6; cf.
    C.Eun. III,1,5, GNO II 5,14-19.

51 Zur Technik der Paraphrase und Metaphrase s. ausführlich
    F. Vinel, La Metaphrasis in Ecclesiasten de Grégoire le
    Thamaturge. Entre traduction et interprétation, une explication de
    texte: Lectures anciennes de la Bible (Cahiers de Biblia Patristica
    1), Strasbourg 1987, 191-216 bes. 194-197; cf. Lausberg,
    Handbuch, § 1099-1103.

Gregors Versuch, den Textsinn zu ermitteln, geht von einer Inter-
pretationsvoraussetzung aus, die er gleich zu Beginn in der Protheoria
erwähnt und auf die er in beiden Teilen seiner Auslegung immer wieder
hinweist.

Für ihn setzt der Prediger nämlich in diesem Textabschnitt die
Methode ein, mittels Antithesis und Lysis vorzugehen. Der Prediger
trägt in seiner eigenen Person zunächst die Einwände gegen die Tugend
vor und löst dann die vorgetragenen Probleme:[52]

ἐν τῷ ἰδίῳ προσώπῳ διεξιὼν ἑκάτερα, καὶ τὴν λύσιν καὶ τὴν
ἀντίθεσιν.

In seiner Person geht er beides durch, sowohl die Lysis als
auch die Antithesis.

In Eccl. V, 363,13-14

τοῦτο δὲ ἐστιν ἡ ἀντίθεσις, ἣν αὐτὸς ἑαυτῷ ἀντιτίθησι λέγων·...

Dies ist der Einwand (ἀντίθεσις), den er sich selbst
entgegenstellt, wenn er sagt: ...

In Eccl. V, 364,13-14

Besonders an einer Stelle wird deutlich, wie sich der Zuhörer
sozusagen die kommunikative Situation vorzustellen hat. Um ἀντίθεσις
und λύσις zu verdeutlichen, fingiert Gregor eine kleine dramatische
Szene, in der sich der Schüler an den Lehrer wendet und ihm seinen
Einwand nennt (In Eccl. V, 370,13 ff.). Zur Veranschaulichung läßt
Gregor den, der die ἀντίθεσις vorträgt, eine kleine Rede halten, er
bedient sich also der Sermocinatio. Dabei ist die Gegenthese
(ἀντίθεσις) des Schülers übrigens recht spitzfindig:

εἰ τὸ ἔξω ἡμῶν ἐν ματαίοις ἀριθμεῖς, ὦ διδάσκαλε, ὅπερ ἂν εἰς
ἑαυτοὺς ἀναλάβωμεν, οὐκ ἂν εἰκότως καταγνωσθείη ὡς μάταιον.

Wenn du, Lehrer, das, was außerhalb von uns liegt, unter die
nichtigen Dinge zählst, dann wird doch wohl das, was wir (beim

---

52 In Eccl. V, 361,7-14; 363,10-20; 364,13-14 u. 21-23; 370,12 f.
    u. 18 f.; 371,1-3.

Essen und Trinken) in uns aufnehmen, wahrscheinlicherweise nicht als nichtig verdammt werden können ...

In Eccl. V, 370,13-15

Nachdem Gregor durch die Sermocinatio den Sinn (διάνοια In Eccl. V, 370,18) und anschließend den Wortlaut des Textes wiedergegeben hat (In Eccl. V, 370,19-22), fährt er fort mit der Frage:

τί δὲ πρὸς ταῦτα ὁ τῆς σοφίας ὑφηγητὴς τῷ ἀνθρώπῳ φησὶ τῷ ἀγαθῷ;

Was aber antwortet auf dieses der Führer zur Weisheit dem Menschen, 'und zwar dem guten'?

In Eccl. V, 371,2-3

Damit ist die Situation klar, die sich Gregor und sein Zuhörer vorstellen. Der Prediger geht an dieser Stelle dialektisch vor und zwar so, wie es im philosophischen Unterricht üblich war. P. Hadot[53] hat dieses Vorgehen folgendermaßen beschrieben: Der Unterricht erfolgt immer gegen eine bestimmte These, also *contra thesim*. Die Antwort des Lehrers, seine Lösung des Problems, kann entweder in dialektischer Weise, also in Rede und Antwort mit dem Schüler, erfolgen oder so, daß der Lehrer eine Gegenrede hält.

Die Methode, in Frage und Antwort vorzugehen, wobei die Frage eine ἀντίθεσις enthält, hat Gregor schon im Text der ersten Homilie zur Auslegung angewandt. Auch dort stellt der Prediger sich selbst eine Frage, die er anschließend beantwortet, bzw. er stellt die Fragen, die sich dem Zuhörer aufdrängen (In Eccl. I, 294,18-296,4).

Gregor setzt häufiger die Methode ein, mittels ἀντίθεσις und λύσις zu argumentieren, bzw. geht dialogisch in Auseinandersetzung mit den oft fiktiven Einwänden eines Zuhörers vor. Die nächste Parallele zur im Prediger konstatierten Methode findet sich am Anfang der Schrift De Professione Christiana (GNO VIII,1 129,14-130,15). Dort erinnert er Harmonios an die Unterhaltungen, in denen dieser die Einwände vorbrachte, während Gregor die λύσις übernahm. Da jedoch

---

53 P. Hadot: Philosophie, Dialectique, Rhétorique dans l'Antiquité. in: Studia Philosophica 39, 1980, (139-166) bes. 149-150.

im Moment eine Zusammenkunft der beiden Gesprächspartner unmöglich ist, kündigt er an, daß im folgenden er selbst, Gregor, sowohl die Rolle (πρόσωπον) des Gegners als auch die des Lehrers übernehmen werde.[54]

Gregor nimmt also an, daß der Sprecher (τὸ πρόσωπον) des biblischen Textes nach der dialektischen Methode, mittels Antithesis und Lysis zu argumentieren, vorgeht. Im Grunde strebt er also eine Interpretation des schwierigen Textes aufgrund einer genauen Analyse der Person des Sprechers an. Dies ist ein Rückgriff auf die Kommentartechnik des πρόσωπον τὸ λέγον, bei der, wie wir sahen, untersucht wird, wer spricht bzw. ob die Rede dem jeweiligen Sprecher angemessen ist. In diesem Falle ist das, was der Prediger vorbringt, nicht immer seiner Rolle als Lehrer der Weisheit angemessen. Die Lösung dieses Problems bringt die Erkenntnis, daß der Prediger hier zwei Rollen zugleich übernimmt: er trägt die Einwände gegen das Tugendleben vor und widerlegt diese dann. Vergleichbar ist damit das Vorgehen des Origenes im Römerkommentar, der feststellt, daß Paulus die Rolle des *advocatus diaboli* übernehme, und nicht mehr als Apostel Paulus im eigentlichen Sinne spreche; ebenso spricht Hieronymus in seinem Kommentar zum Buch Prediger ein solches Vorgehen dem Prediger zu.[55]

Zusammenfassung

1. Gregor gebraucht in seinen Homilien zum Buch Prediger, wie in der christlichen Exegese allgemein üblich, die Techniken der heidnischen Texterklärer. Es finden sich die Topoi des Kommentarprologes, wie σκοπός, Besprechung des Titels, Einordnung des Werkes in einen

---

54 Zur Methode von ἀντίθεσις und λύσις in den Werken Gregors s. ausführlicher Meissner, Rhetorik und Theologie, 115–121.

55 Origenes, In Rom. Comm. 7,13 PG 14, 1144A12–B12; Hieronymus, Comm. In Eccl. 9,7/8 CCh.SL 72,325–326, bes. 126 ff. u. 161–164. Cf. Neuschäfer, 270; zum advocatus diaboli bei Gregor s.o. Anm. 54.

größeren Zusammenhang (τάξις) und vielleicht auch die Einteilung des Werkes in größere Abschnitte.

Er untersucht die Wortbedeutungen, verweist auf den gewöhnlichen Sprachgebrauch der Heiligen Schrift oder der Umgangssprache. Er beachtet den Einsatz rhetorischer Stilmittel und macht sich Gedanken zur Person des Sprechers (τὸ πρόσωπον τὸ λέγον).

Damit steht er in der Tradition der heidnischen Texterklärung. Charakteristisch für Gregor ist, wie er den Topos des σκοπός und den des χρήσιμον benutzt. Für ihn ist das ganze Buch Prediger auf ein Ziel ausgerichtet, ebenso wie sein Auslegungsversuch in den Homilien. Auffallend ist die Betonung des pädagogischen Aspektes der Heiligen Schrift: Der Lehrer, also der Prediger, führt zum Ziel, zum moralischen Nutzen. Der Gedanke des Aufstiegs, so prominent in den Hohelied-homilien, den Predigten über die Seligpreisungen oder der Vita Moysis, tritt in seinen Homilien zum Buch Prediger gegenüber der Pädagogia der Heiligen Schrift etwas in den Hintergrund.

2. Gregors Bildung ist eine rhetorische Bildung. Dies kommt, wie wir sahen, immer wieder auch in der Exegese zum Vorschein. Gregor geht zum einen ganz selbstverständlich davon aus, daß sich auch der Prediger, wenn er durch die Bibel zu uns spricht, an die rhetorischen Regeln hält. Zum anderen beurteilt er die 'Redekunst' des Predigers als Rhetoriklehrer.

Time For All and a Moment for Each:

The Sixth Homily of Gregory of Nyssa on Ecclesiastes

Alden A. Mosshammer

I.   Introduction

'For all things the time and a moment for every activity under the heaven.' In commenting on the introductory sentence of the third chapter of Ecclesiastes, Gregory of Nyssa begins for the first time to explore some of the ideas that we associate with the distinctive philosophy of being and becoming in his most mature works.   His earliest works are marked by an almost unrelieved contrast between the intellectual and the material natures.   The distance between the two is spatial, and perfection would consist in a vertical rising away from sensory experience towards a purely intellectual apprehension of the intelligible nature.   Having been joined to a mortal body, the human soul is trapped in an alien environment.   There is a physical barrier separating the material from the intellectual, through which nothing bodily can pass.   The *Homilies on the Beatitudes* (PG 44,1209A) offer an excellent sample of this vertical structure. If we could take wings from the Lord's saying, Gregory says, and stand on the back of heaven's shell, there we would find the supercelestial land whose inheritance awaits those who have lived in accordance with virtue.   To the extent that there is an historical or an horizontal dimension in Gregory's thought, his attitude is largely negative. Historical time is a regressive degradation of an original state of perfection, and man must move backwards in time so as to remedy the deficiency.   In the essay *On Virginity* (GNO VIII/1, 299,13; 302,19)

Gregory remarks that the first sin was the small beginning of an
endless stream of evil that floods human life; the path towards virtue
is a palindrome, he says — one must reverse the sequence of events.

In his later works Gregory speaks more positively of the union
of body and soul as the essential link between the intellectual and
material natures.[1]   Sin is a deformation of this link; and time offers
the possibility of change for the better through an historical process
of building the body of Christ until God is again 'all in all'.[2]   The
debate with Eunomius marks the critical turning point in Gregory's
intellectual development.   Ekkehard Mühlenberg has shown how Gregory
enunciated a new understanding of the divine infinity in the first book
against Eunomius.[3]   Mariette Canévet has argued that Gregory
developed a new method of Biblical exegesis in the first book against
Eunomius, which differentiates the commentaries of his later period
from those of his earlier works.[4]   Gregory's understanding of time
offers yet another example of new directions clearly evident for the
first time in the first book against Eunomius.[5]   Yet, as important as

---

[1]   So *Or. Cat.* PG 45,25C-D.   Gregory anticipates the idea in *De
Hom. Opif.* (PG 44,145C; 161D), but the fully developed view
appears only in the later works.   Eugenio Corsini has discussed
this aspect of Gregory's thought in a series of studies.   See
'Plérôme humaine et plérôme cosmique chez Grégoire de Nysse':
*Écriture et culture philosophique dans la pensée de Grégoire de
Nysse*, ed. M.Harl, Leiden 1971, 111-126; 'L'harmonie du monde et
l'homme microcosme dans le De Hominis Opificio': *Epektasis:
Mélanges patristiques offerts au Cardinal J. Daniélou*, ed. J.
Fontaine/Ch. Kannengiesser, Paris 1972, 455-462; 'La polemica
contra Eunomio e la formazione della dottrina sulla creazione in
Gregorio di Nissa': *Arché e Telos. L'antropologia di Origene e di
Gregorio di Nissa*, ed. Ugo Bianchi, Milano, 1981, 197-213.
Corsini believes that the first book against Eunomius predates the
De Hominis Opificio, thus reversing the usual chronology; but this
view has not prevailed.

[2]   E.g. *In Cant.* GNO VI, 384,21-386,17.

[3]   Ekkehard Mühlenberg, *Die Unendlichkeit Gottes bei Gregor von
Nyssa* (FKDG 16), Göttingen 1966.

[4]   Mariette Canévet, *Grégoire de Nysse et l'herméneutique Biblique*,
Études Augustiniennes, Paris 1983.

[5]   See Paul Zemp, *Die Grundlagen heilsgeschichtliche Denkens bei
Gregor von Nyssa*, MTS.S 38), München 1970.   Zemp discusses the
change in perspective between earlier and later works, but doesn't

it was for Gregory's intellectual development, it was not only the debate with Eunomius that led Gregory to develop his new philosophy about the structure of existence in time. Even in his earlier works, Gregory is reaching for some strategy to accommodate his negative and essentially Platonic view about the physical world as men experience it to his more positive and Christian view that as a creation of God the visible universe and man's place within it must somehow be understood as good. Examples of this tension abound in Gregory's earlier works. In his essay *On the Profession of the Christian Name*, for example, while Gregory speaks of the impossibility of assimilating the earthly nature to the heavenly, he also maintains that a heavenly sojourn is possible for anyone who wants it, even here on the earth, by means not of a change of place but of will (οὐ διὰ τοπικῆς μεταβάσεως, ἀλλὰ διὰ προαιρέσεως μόνης GNO VIII/1, 140.4).

The significance of the *Homilies on Ecclesiastes* lies in its testimony to a transitional stage in Gregory's thought. In this work we can see Gregory responding to the tensions in his own thought with new strategies that he will shortly develop into powerful weapons for the debate with Eunomius. The homilies cannot be dated with precision from any external evidence, but their composition certainly belongs to the period between 378 and 381. The reference in the sixth homily to the prevailing ἀπιστία (382,16) points, as Jaeger suggested, to a date before the Council of Constantinople in 381.[6] The composition of the work may be roughly contemporary with that of the first book against Eunomius, written in the latter part of 380.[7] There are many verbal similarities, the first book against

---

emphasize the first book against Eunomius as a critical turning point in the same way that Mühlenberg and Canévet do. Cf. also David Balás, 'Eternity and Time in Gregory of Nyssa's Contra Eunomium', *Gregor von Nyssa und die Philosophie*, ed. H. Dörrie, M. Altenburger, A. Schramm, Leiden 1976, 128-153.

6   See Paul Alexander's comment *ad locum*.

7   On this point and the chronology of Gregory's works in general see Gerhard May, 'Die Chronologie des Lebens und der Werke des Gregor von Nyssa', *Écriture et Culture Philosophique dans la*

Eunomius presenting more highly developed versions of ideas expressed
in the homilies on Ecclesiastes.   In the sixth homily, for example,
Gregory defines time as the common measure of all things that come
into being.   In the first book against Eunomius (GNO I 135,1; cf.
79,2), Gregory argues that there can be no notion of measure in the
divine nature.   For the divine is not in time, but time is from the
divine.   The more fully developed argument may be a consequence of
the polemical context, but it is difficult to believe that Gregory would
have already written the first book against Eunomius when he came to
comment on the Ecclesiast's verses about time.   The *Apologia in
Hexaemeron*, written after the spring of 378 at the earliest, provides
a *terminus post quem*, since, as I shall show, that work reflects a
different understanding of the structure of reality.[8]   If, as I will
also suggest, the dialogue on the soul also reflects the earlier
understanding, then we are brought to a date after the death of
Macrina in the summer of 378 at the earliest.[9]   By this time the
first two books of Eunomius's *Apologia Apologiae* had certainly been
published[10].   Gregory was therefore probably working on these homilies
shortly before he wrote his first book against Eunomius, perhaps while
waiting to get his hands on that copy of Eunomius's book which was

---

Pensée de Grégoire de Nysse, ed. Marguerite Harl, Leiden 1971,
51–67, where references to earlier work may be found.

8   The *Apologia* (PG 44, 124A) refers to *De Hominis Opificio* as
     having already been written.   The latter Gregory says (PG 44,
     125B) he wrote as an Easter offering for his brother Peter to
     supplement the work of Basil.   The discussion of Basil seems to
     presuppose his death, and the inscription to the work makes this
     supposition explicit.   Basil died, according to the usual
     reconstruction, in January 379.   See now Pierre Maraval, 'La
     date de la mort de Basile de Césarée', *REAug 34* (1988) 25–38,
     who argues for a date as early as September of 377.

9   On the date of the death of Macrina see Pierre Maraval (see
     above, note 8), and the introduction to his *Vie de Sainte Macrine*
     (SC 178), Paris 1971.   Maraval would now date the death of
     Macrina to July 19, 378, rather than to July 19, 390, as he had
     argued in his edition.   Maraval's arguments, which are persuasive,
     require a thorough reexamination of the chronology of Gregory's
     career between 378 and 381.

10   On the chronology of Eunomius's works, see Richard Paul
     Vaggione, *Eunomius: The Extant Works* (OECT), Oxford 1987.

recalled by its owner after only seventeen days (*Ep*. 29, GNO VIII, 87.13). It was while writing this commentary, with perhaps the task facing him in responding to Eunomius very much on his mind, that Gregory first conceived of the relationship between time and measure that he was to use so effectively in that debate.

2.   The General Theme of the Homilies

Gregory brought to his commentary on Ecclesiastes an unresolved tension between his vertical structuring of the universe with its impassable barrier separating the material from the intellectual natures and his conviction that the Christian could somehow rise to the heavenly life through a change not of place but of will. The juxtaposition in the text of the first three chapters of Ecclesiastes of two frequently repeated phrases forced Gregory to focus on this tension. The phrase 'futility of futilities' suggests the negative point of view, while 'a time for every activity under the heaven' might have more positive implications.

The main theme of the homilies on Ecclesiastes is that suggested by the opening lines of the text — futility of futilities, all is futility. Gregory defines futility as insubstantiality — that is, the lack of real being — and he defines the futility of futilities as a rhetorical hyperbole referring to the visible universe within which man, as a compound of body and soul, must live. The idea that the visible world is not finally real is a Platonizing point of view consistent with a vertical structuring of reality and with a depreciation of the visible cosmos and the bodily life. The homilies offer many examples of Platonizing expressions about the superiority of the permanent intellectual nature to the transitory nature of sensibles.[11] What is distinctive about Gregory's approach, however, and what stands in tension with this vertical distancing, is his claim that the unreality of the visible cosmos does not derive from its material nature as such, but from distortion of the world as it was meant to be. Unless

---

11   See, for example, 325,1, where Gregory contrasts the archetype of beauty with its visible representatives, and 352,2-11, where he characterizes sensory perception as futile, unable to cross the heavenly boundary to contemplate the goods that lie beyond.

anything exists in its original state, Gregory says (Homily 1, 296,21), it does not truly exist at all. The purpose of the Book of Ecclesiastes is not to teach that the visible world as such is the futility of futilities, but that the distortion which sin has introduced has deprived the world of substance and caused it to become futile instead of productive. Thus (Homily 2, 301,3) the true Ecclesiast is the incarnate Christ who searched out the area beneath the heavens to find out how it is that non-being has become dominant over being, futility over substance.

Such passages belong to a now well established tradition, shared for example by Origen and Basil and to be adopted also by Augustine, that exculpates God from any responsibility for evil by defining evil as an absence. Gregory goes beyond this tradition, however, by developing the idea already suggested in his earlier works that what man requires is a change of will, not of place. The cause of evil, futility, and unreality, Gregory says in his second homily (301,17ff), lies in the free choices of the created will. This too is not an entirely original idea, but Gregory goes further still in claiming that evil is not merely an object of choice, but its product.[12] Whoever puts his lamp under the bed turns light into darkness, becoming himself the manufacturer of the unreal (358,14). The insubstantial nature of evil is given being in those who have fallen away from the good (407,9).

The possibility that the human will might itself be the author and receptacle of evil Gregory had already entertained in the *Homilies on the Beatitudes* (PG 44,1256B). It is the Ecclesiast's second theme — time and moment — that leads Gregory to develop these ideas and to find both the explanation and the remedy for the enslavement of being to non-being. If the futility of futilities is a perversion of nature and if created intelligence is responsible for the deformation of reality, then created intelligence also has the power to turn the process around. It is not space that defines and measures all things,

---

12 On this subject see my paper, 'Non-Being and Evil in Gregory of Nyssa', *Vigiliae Christianae* 44 (1990) 136-167.

but time.   Within the dimension of time the material and intellectual
natures share a common structure of being.   What the physical
barrier of space denies, the moral dimension of time makes accessible.

3.   Time and Measure in the Sixth Homily

Gregory addresses himself to the Ecclesiast's second theme in
the sixth homily.   Here he begins a commentary, which extends through
the remainder of the homilies, on the series of statements in
Ecclesiastes that speak about 'times' and 'seasons'.   The first is a
general statement.   'For all things the time', says the preacher, 'and
a moment for every activity under the heaven'.   According to
Gregory, the purpose of all that has preceded is revealed most clearly
in the section introduced by this text.   In the preceding verses, he
says, everything pursued in life without advantage to the soul was
condemned as futile.   The good was demonstrated, towards which one
should look with eyes in his head; and the nourishment of wisdom was
contrasted with the things that offer bodily enjoyment.   What remains
is to obtain from the text some kind of art and method for the
correction of life in accordance with virtue.   Gregory claims that
such a method is just what the Ecclesiast teaches when he says 'for
all things the time, and a moment for every activity under the
heaven'.   Gregory urges the reader to look into the depths of meaning
here, for he will find much philosophy, both theoretical and practical.

Gregory seems to find the theoretical philosophy in what the
Ecclesiast says about time (χρόνος), the practical philosophy in the
long series of verses about season or moment (καιρός).   He discusses
the meaning of 'time' in this text at some length, but leaves 'moment'
less well defined.   Gregory begins, as he so often does when
expounding what he takes to be a philosophical text, by dividing
existing things between the material and sensory on the one side and
the intellectual and immaterial on the other.   The immaterial nature
lies above sensory apprehension, and we shall know it only when we
have doffed the senses.   Sensory perception has the material nature
as its object, but it cannot cross the heavenly body so as to slip
through to the things that lie beyond phenomena.   It is for this
reason, Gregory says, that the text deals with things 'under the

heaven', so that we might get through life in this lower region without stumbling. Contemplation of the good is obscured by sensible things. We need some kind of science for the discernment of the good, something like a carpenter's rule against which to measure the correctness of everything that happens. Therefore the text shows us such a rule by means of which life may be kept straight along just the right line. The Preacher sets forth two criteria of the good for each thing pursued in this life — the commensurate and the timely.

This passage evokes the vertical structuring that dominates Gregory's earlier works. The intellectual nature lies literally and spatially above the material cosmos, separated from it by the body of heaven. Sensation cannot poke a hole through that barrier so as to reach intelligible reality. Since we live in the sensible world, the Ecclesiast gives us a rule for measuring the good within that world. Gregory says that the division between intelligibles and sensibles will be his 'method' for interpreting the text. We expect him therefore to go on to discuss further this distinction and to obtain from the text a method for moving from the multiplicity of sensible objects towards the apprehension, however dim, of the archetype of all good. Such a discussion would continue the line of argument, begun in the fifth homily and recalled in the opening sentences of the sixth, about those who have eyes in their head. Instead, Gregory abruptly drops the line of argument based on the division between intelligibles and sensibles and begins an extensive defense of his introduction of the notion of measure into the discussion of a text that speaks of time.

Gregory claims that the Ecclesiast makes the commensurate (σύμμετρον) and the timely (εὔκαιρον) the two criteria of the good. By mentioning 'time' (χρόνος) the Ecclesiast implies 'measure' (μέτρον); because, Gregory says, time stretches out alongside everything that happens. Measure and season are therefore the two criteria of the good. 'These then are the criteria of the good,' Gregory continues. 'Whether they apply appropriately and absolutely for the correct establishment of every virtue I do not yet decide until the text in its course shall make clear. Nevertheless that the greater part of our assigned life is straightened by such an observance is clear for anyone to see.' Gregory then proceeds with a discussion of virtue as a golden mean between excesses that is reminiscent of the Nico-machean Ethics.[13] Virtue is the exercise of a faculty in the right quantity, as courage is a mean between cowardice and rashness. Similarly, Gregory explains καιρός or timeliness as the exercise of the right quantity at the right moment, neither too early nor too late. He uses the examples of harvesting, sailing, and administering medical treatment. The good and the right must be perfect in both respects, adhering to both measure and moment. To observe the one without the other would be like trying to hop on one foot.

The purpose of this very traditional discussion has little to do with the definition of virtue. Gregory's real interest is measure. The discussion of virtue serves only to demonstrate, on a common-sense basis of what is 'available for everyone to know' (375,3), that Gregory is justified in substituting μέτρον for χρόνος in the Ecclesiast's text. Whether it is true universally that measure and moment are the criteria of the good remains to be seen in the course of the analysis of the specific 'moments' of the text. Gregory does not conclude the argument and make his decision on this question until he comes to comment at the end of the eighth homily on the text 'All things which he made are good at his right moment'. Meanwhile, according to Gregory, there is certainly justification in supposing that by 'time' the preacher means 'measure', since even the outer philosophers have recognized this truth and divided it among themselves, the one saying 'Nothing too much', the other 'Measure is best'.

After this common-sense argument in support of his conclusion, Gregory returns to his own more philosophical analysis. He expands on his earlier claim that 'time' means 'measure' in this text, because time is co-extensive with all that happens. Time is an expression of measure, he says (376,23), because time is the measure of everything that is individually measured. Every particular thing has its own measure or quantity and these are different for every individual thing

---

13 Aristotle, *Eth.Nic.* II 6,1106 a 26, cited by Alexander *ad locum.*

that is measured.   Time itself, however, is the common measure
(γενικὸν μέτρον) because time contains all things within itself.   The
preacher did not say there is 'measure' for all things, because of the
vast inequality of more and less among the things measured.   Instead
he said that time is for all things the common measure, by which
every thing that comes into being is measured.

Gregory claims that the Ecclesiast is here defining virtue in a
classical Aristotelian sense as a golden mean between excess and
lack, between haste and tardiness.   He himself echoes this traditional
definition of virtue in other works.   Gregory frequently uses καιρὸς
and μέτρον, or their cognates, as closely connected pairs, sometimes
when speaking of virtue, sometimes when discussing the harmony of
disparate elements that come together to form material bodies.[14]
Yet his subsequent exposition of individual verses makes no use
whatsoever of this definition.   Furthermore, while he lavishes his
attention on defining χρόνος, he offers no definition of καιρὸς,
although it is the latter word that the Ecclesiast uses in the
following verses.   Gregory is far more interested in the idea that
virtue is a mean.   In fact, Aristotle had not defined virtue as a
μέτρον, but as τὸ μέσον.[15]   Gregory's real interest in this passage
has more in common with the Aristotelian definition of time as the
measure of motion (μέτρον κινήσεως).[16]   His understanding of time is,
however, quite different from Aristotle's, even if his definition
suggests an Aristotelian influence.   The origin and paradigm of all

---

14   In *De Virginitate* GNO VIII.1,25, he defines virtue as being 'in the
middle' and adduces examples similar to those that appear here.
In *De Hominis Opificio* PG 44,165A, he attributes the human
body's very ability to survive to a measured balance of opposites
conjoining at the right moment.   In the commentary on the
Inscriptions to the Psalms (GNO V, 33,13–25) he likens virtue to
a musical harmony neither beyond nor beneath the right measure.

15   Cf. the comments of Rachel Moriarty above, p. 32.

16   Aristotle, *Phys.* 220b25.   See John F. Callahan, *Four Views of
Time in Ancient Philosophy* (Cambridge, Mass. 1948) esp. 50–82.
Paul Zemp (see above note 5, p. 91) has drawn attention to the
parallel between Aristotle and Gregory.

motion is for Gregory the motion from non-being to being.[17]   Thus
Gregory here defines time not simply as the measure of motion
through physical space, but the measure that accompanies and defines
all things that come into being.   For Aristotle, time and motion are
reciprocal relationships that numerically represent one another through
the common attribute of the distance traversed.   For Gregory,
however, time is rather a kind of space in itself than a numerical
representation of motion across space.   One of the most interesting
aspects of Gregory's all too brief discussion of time as measure is
his use of spatial metaphors.   He begins by stating that the
Ecclesiast is instructing the reader about the material division of
existing things.   He makes little use of this distinction in the
subsequent argument, but his discussion retains the spatial categories
associated with the material nature.   In effect, he applies the
categories of place to time so as to generate a new understanding of
space.

        Already in his opening remarks Gregory had said that the
Ecclesiast's text offers the reader something like a carpenter's rule
or a chalk-line.   For Gregory a μέτρον is not an abstraction like
Aristotle's 'number', but something having a definite size.   He often
uses the word in reference to a defined and limited space.   In the *De
Hominis Opificio* (PG 44,201C-D), Gregory says that motion in evil is
contained within a definite μέτρον.   In a famous analogy, he then
compares this measure of evil with the conical space of darkness
formed by the interposition of the earth's body athwart the light of
the sun.   If one could cross the μέτρον of this shadow, Gregory
says, he would again come out into the light.   To speak of time as a
μέτρον is to conceive of time as a kind of space.

        In both passages of the sixth homily where Gregory says that
χρόνος is the μέτρον that accompanies all things, he uses a word of
spatial extension, of stretching along (συμπαρατείνεται, 374,20;
377,3).   In the first passage he says that χρόνος stretches along

---

17   *De Hom. Opif.* PG 44,183C.   Gregory repeats this idea frequently
    in the *Catechetical Oration* (e.g. PG 45,28D.40A.57D.100D).

together with each thing coming into being. In the second it is the interval of time (τὸ διάστημα τοῦ χρόνου) that stretches out alongside the position of each of the things that come to be. Gregory uses this word of chronological extension in earlier works also. In the *De Hominis Opificio* (PG 44, 205C; 208A), he says that God foreknew the time commensurate (σύμμετρον) with the making of men; and he urges the reader to await the fulfilment of this time which is necessarily coextensive (συμπαρατείνοντα) with the increase of humanity. In his commentary on the sixth Psalm, Gregory says that the seventh day, being the end (πέρας) of creation, circumscribed within itself the time that stretches out alongside (συμπαρεκτεινόμενον) the construction of the cosmos. For this reason we measure the whole διάστημα of time by sevens.[18] In the homilies on Ecclesiastes, the spatial language which it is so natural to use when measuring intervals of time lead Gregory to conceive of time itself as a kind of measured space.

The merging of spatial with temporal categories in the sixth homily reflects a fundamental shift in Gregory's understanding of the nature of reality. The key concept is measured differentiation. The key word is διάστημα, which literally means a 'standing apart'. Gregory often uses διάστημα as a spatial term. The word is virtually synonymous with μέτρον in the passage of the *De Opificio* where Gregory speaks of the extension of evil. But he just as often in his earlier works uses διάστημα to refer to an interval of time.[19] Both are well established usages. Polybius, for example, uses the word to refer both to the four-year length of an Olympiad (9.1.1) and to the geographical space separating one place from another (4.39.5). Methodius of Olympus gave the notion of chronological interval a specifically Christian content by characterizing ordinary time as divided into intervals of past, present, and future, whereas the time after the general resurrection will be more like God's time, in which

---

18   *In Sextum Psalmum* GNO V 188,20-189,4. That this work belongs to a group of commentaries to be dated before 381 is the general consensus. E. Mühlenberg (see note 3 above, p. 94) has suggested that this piece presupposes both the Homilies on the Beatitudes and the commentary on the Inscriptions to the Psalms.

19   E.g. *In Hexaemeron* PG 44,77B; *De Anima* PG 46,101B.

everything is simultaneously present with no such διαστήματα.[20]   As Gregory's commentators have often pointed out, his use of the word is reminiscent of the Stoic definition of time as the διάστημα of the motion of the cosmos.[21]   Plotinus (III 7,7.8.35) criticized this definition as yielding a spatial measurement of motion from one point to another, but not a satisfactory definition of time itself.   Plotinus himself (III 7,11) thought of time as an image of eternity produced by the soul in its motion towards multiplicity.[22]

Some scholars have seen in Gregory's usage a synthesis of the Stoic with the Plotinian understandings.[23]   It is difficult to assess what influence, if any, earlier philosophical views of time may have exercised on Gregory.   In fact, Gregory's understanding is distinctively his own and bears little relationship to Aristotle, the Stoics, Methodius, or Plotinus.   For Gregory, time is not, as for Aristotle and the Stoics, the measurement of motion across the extension of bodily space.   Nor does he share the view of Plotinus that time is the image of eternity under the conditions of multiplicity.   In the homilies on Ecclesiastes he goes beyond his own earlier usage, which he shares with Methodius, Basil, and the common language of the period, that the διάστημα of time is a measurable interval or gap between one event and another.   For Gregory, time is itself a kind of defined space like the conical shadow of the earth.   Time is the μέτρον, Gregory says, containing all things in itself (377,14).   In the eighth homily he makes the metaphor more explicit, saying that time is an extensional idea (διαστηματικόν, 440,3) which signifies the creation that comes to be within it.   By mentioning the container the

---

20 Methodius, *De Resurrectione* II 25 (380-82 Bonwetsch).   Gregory perhaps echoes this definition of time in the homilies on the Lord's Prayer, PG 44,1125A.

21 Chrysippus apud Simplicium, *Stoic. Vet. Fr.* II, n. 509; cf. *Zeno Stoicus Fr.* i, n. 93.   See especially H.U. von Balthasar, *Présence et pensée. Essai sur la philosophie religieuse de Grégoire de Nysse*, Paris 1942, 6-7.   Cf. also Brooks Otis, 'Gregory of Nyssa and the Cappadocian Concept of Time': *StPatr* 14 (1976) 327-57.

22 See John F. Callahan, *Four View of Time* (above, note 16).

23 Von Balthasar, *Présence et pensée* ... , 6, note 1.

Ecclesiast therefore includes all that is contained therein. This language anticipates a famous passage of the first book against Eunomius (GNO I, 136,8-12), where Gregory says that God prepared the aeons and the place (τόπον) within them as a kind of space to be a receptacle (χώρημα δεκτικὸν) for things that come into being. The metaphor echoes a well known passage of the *Timaeus* (52B), where Plato speaks of space as the receptacle of sensible being. Gregory goes beyond both Plato and the text of the Ecclesiast. Time is a receptacle that provides a home not only for all sensible being 'under the heaven', but for all things that come into being. As the measure that contains all things, the διάστημα of time is the essential characteristic that distinguishes created reality from the unchanging and unmeasured being of God. Gregory takes this next step in the seventh homily, where he says that the creation is nothing other than διάστημα (412,14). Having in the sixth homily conceived of the διάστημα of time as a kind of measured space, he now generalizes further and makes the idea of dimension itself an ontological category. What is most significant about his discussion in the sixth homily is not that time is the measure of all things, but that all things are measured.

This is not the place to essay a comprehensive discussion of the use of the word διάστημα in Gregory's works or of the interpretative significance of his usage.[24] The interest of the sixth homily on Ecclesiastes lies in its witness to a transitional stage in Gregory's thought, when he had not yet invested the word with the full significance which it carries in his most mature works. Gregory

---

24   For discussion see in addition to von Balthasar, Otis, and Zemp (above, notes 21 and 5), John F.Callahan, 'Gregory of Nyssa and the Psychological View of Time': *Atti del XII Congresso Internazionale di Filosofia* vol 11 (Firenze 1960) 59-66; Lloyd G. Patterson, 'The Conversion of Diastema in the Patristic View of Time': *Lux in Lumine*, ed. Richard A. Norris, New York 1966, 93-111; and T. Paul Verghese, 'ΔΙΑΣΤΗΜΑ and ΔΙΑΣΤΑΣΙΣ in Gregory of Nyssa': *Gregor von Nyssa und die Philosophie*, ed. H. Dörrie/M. Altenburger/A. Schramm, Leiden 1976, 243-258. A comprehensive study which would analyze the nuances among Gregory's usages and seek to trace the development of his thought through an examination of this verbal cluster is still lacking. Attention has focused instead on Gregory's mature usage. Zemp's is the most

arrives at his new usage not through philosophical speculation on the nature of time in the manner of a Plotinus or an Aristotle, but by a process of fusing, perhaps indeed of confusing, the spatial and temporal connotations that the word διάστημα carries in ordinary usage. This fusion permits Gregory to unite once separate aspects of his own thought. The text of Ecclesiastes confronts Gregory with the unresolved tension between his understanding of the sensible order as the source of a physical limitation which prevents the human soul from rising to its true home among intelligibles and his teaching that, as he puts it in the second homily (302,1), the sovereign motion of the human mind is itself the cause of this separation. He finds in the Ecclesiast's emphasis on time an art and a method not only for escaping the futility of futilities, but also for resolving this tension in his own thought. By making time, rather than place, the essential dimension of all becoming, Gregory is able in the seventh homily to rise to a higher philosophy in which the distinction between sensibles and intelligibles is no longer supreme. This he accomplishes by combining the spatial and temporal usages of διάστημα to generate a new kind of space which imposes upon intelligibles the same kind of limits he had once applied only to the sensible order.

We can better appreciate the critical shift in perspective that seems to be under way in the sixth homily by briefly comparing Gregory's use of the term διάστημα in his earlier works with that which emerges from the homilies on Ecclesiastes. In the second homily on the Beatitudes (PG 44,1209A), commenting on the super-heavenly land that one would find if he were able to take wing and stand on the back of heaven's shell, Gregory says that all sensible phenomena are akin. However high anything might seem to be in spatial διάστημα, it remains nevertheless below that intellectual essence which reason cannot attain without crossing first all that sensation can reach. In the *De Opificio* (PG 44,209D), Gregory

---

satisfactory discussion of the earlier usage. See especially pp. 63-72. I have not had access to the unpublished dissertation (Louvain 1966) of Paul Dandelot, *La doctrine du diastêma chez S.Grégoire de Nysse*, cited by Verghese (p. 244) as leaving 'a great deal to be desired'.

discusses the problem of whether the material nature can be a product of the divine. The divine nature is simple and immaterial, uncompounded, without quality or size, whereas the material nature is apprehended in a dimensional arrangement (ἐν διαστηματικῇ παρατάσει) with its qualities of color, shape, weight, size, hardness, and so forth. How is it, Gregory asks, that matter can be fashioned from the immaterial, that which is dimensional from that which is not (ἐκ τοῦ ἀδιαστάτου τὴν διαστηματικὴν φύσιν)?   Gregory discusses the same issue in the *De Anima* (PG46, 124B-C). There is no difficulty, he says, in understanding how the intellectual part of creation comes from the divine nature, because the intellectual nature has a kinship with the divine in that it is immortal, uncompounded, and without dimension (ἀδιάστατον). The dialogue on the soul is difficult to date, except that it must have been written after the death of Macrina in 378 at the earliest. The absence of the new definition of created διάστημα that appears in the seventh homily suggests that the dialogue antedates the homilies on Ecclesiastes. In the *De Mortuis*, generally considered an early work, Gregory asks what qualities must characterize the soul in its likeness to God. It must not, he says (GNO IX 41,20-25), exhibit the qualities of body, shape, thickness, space, or time that characterize the material creation, but must rather assimilate itself to the intellectual, immaterial, and non-dimensional (ἀδιάστατον) qualities that are left when all notion of body has been removed. Again, Gregory is contrasting the material nature with the divine, but again it is as an intellectual nature, not as an uncreated nature, that the divine is without dimension; and it is noteworthy that time is among the dimensions associated with body. The most striking example of Gregory's earlier usage appears in the *Apologia in Hexaemeron* (PG 44,81C-D), where Gregory defines the firmament that divides the upper from the lower waters as the boundary between the intellectual and the sensible natures. The intellectual creation beyond the firmament is not characterized by shape, size, position in space, measurement by διαστήματα, color, figure, thickness, or any of the other things tht exist beneath the heaven.

A comparison between these passages and what Gregory says in the seventh homily shows the merging of spatial with temporal categories that is taking place in the sixth homily. Gregory generalizes the qualities that he had previously associated with the spatial dimensions of the material nature to include the more generic dimension of time and with it the whole of created reality, intellectual as well as sensible. Previously he had emphasized the kinship of all that is sensible and its estrangement from the undimensional nature of all that is intellectual. In the seventh homily he characterizes the whole created order as dimensional and therefore akin to itself (411,15). In the homilies on the Beatitudes it was not possible to escape the sensible order however far one travelled in spatial extension. In the seventh homily on Ecclesiastes it is the created intellect that cannot pass beyond its own boundaries (412,7-9). Just as in earlier works Gregory had said that sensory perception is possible only because of the finite qualities of shape and size that define objects and separate one thing from another, so now he says human intellection in general is possible only because the whole created nature is defined and marked off by limiting qualities. The physical definition of matter is what both makes sensory perception possible and prevents the senses from direct apprehension of intelligibles. Similarly the finite dimensions of the whole created order, summed up in the now general term διάστημα, make human thought possible and prevent the intellect from apprehending the uncreated nature in which there are no such demarcations. He uses the same phrase to characterize the activity in dimensional arrangement (ἐν διαστηματικῇ παρατάσει 412,13) of the human mind that he had applied in the De Opificio to sensory perception.

What makes this new understanding possible is Gregory's defi-nition of time as the common measure of all things that come into being. Within the text of the sixth homily we can almost detect the shift taking place in Gregory's thinking. His description of the differentiation between the intelligible and the sensible natures, separated by a physical boundary that sensation cannot cross, retains the vertical structuring of the earlier works. He states that the

Ecclesiast is here speaking about things under the heaven, that is about the sensible world, so that he might well have gone on to describe the measured limits of the sensible order in much the same way as in the earlier works. Measure is one of the attributes that Gregory associates with the spatial extension of the material order.[25] But it is time, not space, that the Ecclesiast makes the key to understanding the futility of futilities. Gregory has already attributed this futility to a distortion of nature caused by the created will. Virtue or its absence is a quality only of the intellectual nature, as Gregory says elsewhere.[26] If time is the measure of virtue, then measure must be an attribute of all things that come into being, the intellectual as well as the sensible, whether or not they are confined to the physical space beneath the body of the heavens. In the process of explaining why the Ecclesiast substitutes χρόνος for μέτρον, Gregory begins to move beyond his earlier understanding of the intellectual and the sensible as two distinct orders of reality and to see them instead as sharing a single order of reality defined by a common measuredness of which space and time are but different aspects. It is not until the seventh homily that Gregory explicitly states that this measuredness applies to the intellect as well as to the senses, and it is not until he wrote the first book against Eunomius that he explores the dimensions of time in any detail. Gregory's thinking on this point is in transition, and he may very well not have realized the full implications of his definition of time in the sixth homily as the measured extension of all things until he came to write the seventh. Gregory was beginning to think along new lines even as he himself peered into the depths of philosophy suggested by this text.

It is a mistake to suggest, as von Balthasar does, that Gregory distinguishes between the material διάστημα that separates the sensible from the intelligible and the created διάστημα that separates

---

25   See for example *De Hominis Opificio* PG 44, 185B.
26   See for example *De Hominis Opificio* PG 44, 135B-D, 184B-C.

all contingent being from God.[27]   It is true that Gregory understands
the intellectual and the sensible as limited in different ways, and he
discusses this problem in a well known passage of the sixth homily on
the Song of Songs (GNO VI, 173-174).   But the explanation for the
different understanding of διάστημα in the *Apologia in Hexaemeron* as
compared with the first book against Eunomius is that Gregory
changed both his usage and his whole way of thinking about the
nature of reality.   The homilies on Ecclesiastes reflect a crucial
stage in this intellectual development — the generalization of spatial
categories to include the measured differentiation of all contingent
being.   A passage in the homilies on the Lord's Prayer (PG 44,1145B)
may represent the immediately preceding logical step.   The separation
between the earthly life and the heavenly kingdom, Gregory says,
between God and man, is not a spatial gap (οὐ τοπικὴ ἡ διάστασις) so
that we require some kind of machine by means of which we might
elevate this heavy and material dwelling or change it into something
immaterial and intellectual.   The difference lies entirely within the will
(προαίρεσις) of man.   Whither it turns, there will it dwell.[28]

4.   A Moment for Everything

Gregory has indeed found much philosophy in the Ecclesiast's
phrase, 'Time for all, a moment for everything'.   In this verse
Gregory discovers a new understanding of the structure of created
reality as measured, bounded, characterized by difference.   Time is
the measure of all things, because all things are measured.   The
latter is the more important point.   Each material thing is different
and separate from every other thing that exists alongside it in space.
Generalizing these spatial categories to include time as a kind of
measured space, Gregory now sees each created thing as different

---

27   See note 21 above.

28   Scholars generally agree that the homilies on the Lord's Prayer
belong to the period between 379 and 381; see the discussion of
May (above, note 7).   Jean Daniélou has suggested a date during
the Lenten season of 379; see his 'Chrismation prébaptismale et
divinité de l'ésprit chez Grégoire de Nysse', *RechSR* 56 (1968)
177-98.   The homilies on Ecclesiastes may very well have been
written shortly after those on the Lord's Prayer.   There is a

from every other created thing and even as different from itself in
the constant motion from non-being towards being. On yet another
level of abstraction, difference itself is the distinguishing mark of
the whole created order. All created relaity is different from the
creator precisely because all created things are different from each
other. In the first book against Eunomius, Gregory will make the idea
he has discovered here, that time is the origin of all measure, his
most powerful weapon against all efforts to introduce an interval
between the Father and the Son.[29]

If time is the common measure for all things, the next question
is how Gregory understands the 'moment'. Gregory does not define
καιρὸς in the sixth homily, but he apparently takes the Ecclesiast's
sentence hypotactically. Because time is the common measure for all
things, therefore for each thing that comes into existence there is a
moment. Just as time is not merely chronological, so the right
moment is not merely an instant in the horizontal motion of time.
The διάστημα is the whole space between being and non-being, a space
through which created intelligence can move with a freedom that
physical space denies. Moment defines the character of every
particular point within that space and determines whether its motion
will be towards the fullness of being or the emptiness of non-being.
Time measures all things, differentiating one thing from another and
Timeliness means recognizing the essential differentiatedness of the
created order in time and acting in such a way as to effect the
right kind of difference. Although Gregory does not explicitly define
καιρὸς, it is clear from his subsequent discussion of the individual

---

striking verbal similarity between the two works in Gregory's
comparison of the beginnings of evil to the head of a snake
(Homily 4, 348,16; cf. De Or. Dom., PG 44 1172A). The metaphor
appears also in the Life of Moses (GNO VII 161,21). The
passage in the homilies on Ecclesiastes shares phraseology with
both of the others, which however have little verbal similarity
with each other. How far one can press such comparisons into
the service of chronology is of course problematic.

29   See for example Contra Eun. I, 365-375, GNO I, 134-137.
Ekkehard Mühlenberg has discussed this point in detail (above,
note 3: see especially pp. 106-111, 135-141).

verses that 'timeliness' measures not a quantity of time, but rather the quality of its motion.

Gregory proceeds to his commentary using καιρός in reference to his own exposition. Now, he says (378,6), would be the moment for us to proceed in logical order to the actual contemplation of the divinely inspired sayings. This is a common usage of καιρός for Gregory (e.g. *In Psalm.* GNO V, 34.17), and it is difficult to say whether in this context there is an intentional pun. However that may be, Gregory gives most attention to the first saying, 'a time to give birth, a time to die'. He comments first on the appropriateness of the Ecclesiast's pairing of birth and death at the head of the list of opposites. Birth necessarily entails death, and it was to remind the reader of this ineluctable condition of human existence that Moses entitled the first two books of the Bible 'Genesis' and 'Exodus'. If people would only wake up to this obvious fact, they would stop running around in circles with the godless and would seek the straight path instead. Blessed are they, Gregory says, who leave the circular deceits of this life and travel along the straight path of virtue. Virtue he now defines not as an Aristotelian mean, but as turning one's soul away from the futility that is here so as to stretch towards what lies ahead through faith in hope.

This passage recalls what Gregory says in the first homily (287,3ff) about the endless cycles of birth and death. There he encouraged the reader to recognize the futility of earthly existence. Here he expounds the Ecclesiast's method for breaking free from that cyclical futility and seeking the straight path. There came a moment when I was born, Gregory says, and there will come a moment when I will die. But this is not the kind of moment the Ecclesiast is talking about. Physical birth and death are involuntary and have nothing to do with finding the straight road of virtue. It is a timely birth when one is pregnant by the fear of God and through labor of the soul engenders his own salvation. For we become our own fathers when we fashion and bring ourselves to birth through a noble exercise of freedom (προαίρεσις). This we accomplish by receiving into ourselves the form (μορφή) of Christ. The moment for such birth is one,

Gregory says, not many. Whoever misses the right moment labors to destruction and is midwife to his own death.

Although Gregory says here that there is only one moment for birth, in the next passage he states that every moment is the right one for a good death, even as Saint Paul died every day. The timely death Gregory defines as the sponsoring agent (πρόξενος) of life. Thus the right moment for birth and the right moment for death are the same moment; and that moment is both one and many. It is one moment in that it is a decisive act of self-definition; it is many moments in that one must endlessly be giving new birth to himself in order to avoid the endlessness of running around in circles with the ungodly. That the one moment of the right decision is every moment of life Gregory explicitly states in the seventh and eighth homilies (401,4; 405,3; 425,16).

For the purposes of the present argument, what is most important about this passage is its emphasis on the creative powers of the human will. The straight path out of the circular futility of life lies in an exercise of human choice. The unseen realities that one is called upon to contemplate are not Platonic intelligibles lying above the celestial sphere where the senses cannot reach, but what lies ahead in hope through faith, whither the human will can reach through an act of self-regeneration. The straight path stretches horizontally through time and vertically towards real being, but not upward through space. Gregory is talking about right moments that transform the measured space within which everything comes to be, not about a flight from sensibles to intelligibles. To have eyes in one's head is to see reality as Christ sees it, not to see some other reality beyond the firmament.

Gregory interprets the next set of texts accordingly. In order to participate in reality as Christ sees it, one must first separate himself from the unreality that has come to mask it. There is a time for planting, a time for weeding. God is the gardener, Gregory says, and we are his garden. Only the Great Gardener knows how to plant good things. Whatever is not of his planting, Gregory says quoting Matthew (15,13), will be weeded out. Gregory makes faith his example of God's planting, contrasting it both with the evil weeds of the Pharisees and with the contemporary unbelief prevailing over the minds of many. It is this passage (382,16) that dates the work to the period before the Council of Constantinople. This unbelief, Gregory says, is not of the father's planting, but comes from the one who sows or plants alongside (παρασπείροντος, παραφυτεύοντος). What applies to faith applies to all the other virtues as well. To plant self-control is to weed license; the unjust growth is weeded out by the implant of justice. The plant of humility destroys pride; the blossom of love dries out the evil branch of hatred. Conversely, the growth of injustice freezes love, and so forth through all the virtues.

The moments for killing and healing, tearing down and building, convey a similar teaching. We must kill the enemy within' ourselves in order to heal the disposition of love which has become ill in us because of hate. Using the analogy of an intestinal parasite, Gregory says that when someone realizes that his soul has borne and nourishes a beast within itself he must make timely use of the killing medicine that brings health, namely the teaching of the gospel. Likewise there is a time to destroy the houses of evil within us and a time to find a broad space for the construction of the temple of God which is built within us from the timbers of virtue. Let the works of darkness first be torn down and then the brilliant houses of life constructed in their place.

In these passages Gregory uses language reminiscent of the earlier homilies. The whole discussion is informed by the major theme of the work — that the futility now prevailing under the heavens is not of God's making. The discussion of planting and weeding recalls the earlier discussion of Solomon's gardens in the third homily, where Gregory characterizes lavish horticulture as a violence of art against nature (332,18). The shining temple that replaces the buildings of darkness recalls the language of the fifth homily, where Gregory says that whoever puts his lamp under the bed turns light into darkness, becoming himself the manufacturer of the unreal (358,11).

The art and method that the Ecclesiast teaches in his series of moments is reversal. In the beginning of the fifth homily (353,13)

Gregory had said that as escape from evil is the beginning of virtue, so escape from futility is prerequisite to the experience of reality. Hence Gregory's emphasis in the sixth homily is on the negative — on weeding, killing, destroying. This separation from futility prepares us for the higher philosophy in the seventh homily about the nature of reality. Meanwhile, Gregory's point is that it is the perversion of the visible cosmos that one must escape, not the cosmos itself. As we will learn in the seventh homily, the cosmos lacks real being of its own, but is nevertheless real as long as it clings to the being of its maker. The origin of futility is not the sensible nature as such but, as Gregory has already suggested in the first homily (284,21-285,12), the delusion of supposing that the world has an existence of its own.

The right moments for weeping and for laughing, for beating and for dancing, prompt Gregory to a diatribe on the worst perversion of all — the fallen state of human nature in comparison with what it once was. Who would not spend his whole life in weeping if he knew his own situation — what he once had and now has lost, what his nature was in the beginning and what it is now. The passage recalls a similar lament in the homilies on the Beatitudes (PG 44,1225D), as Alexander points out in the apparatus. There is no need to rehearse the long list of Gregory's complaints. His central point is that in the beginning human nature enjoyed immortality and equality with the angels, in an unmediated contemplation of the hypercosmic goods. Now, however, our nature is plagued with an evil chain of passions that no one in this life can escape. Most mournful of all is the fearful judgment that awaits the enemies of God. Now therefore is the time to weep. A mournful attitude towards this life will help to minimize mistakes in it. The promised joy will therefore await us in hope. Human life is a compound, Gregory says, made up of body and soul. It would be well to beat upon ourselves in bodily life so as to prepare the dance of the soul. 'He who exhibits his life as thoroughly lamentable', Gregory concludes, 'will rest in the bosom of the patriarch; may we too rest in it, through the mercy of our Saviour Jesus Christ, to whom be the glory for ever. Amen.'

On this lugubrious note, Gregory ends the sixth homily. He has certainly found the moment for weeping, and his only hope seems to lie in a future beyond the grave. At the end of the homily Gregory's more pessimistic vertical structuring with its stark contrast between earth and heaven, body and soul, seems to have gained the upper hand. Life within the material order is worse than futile. We can only lament our fall into the body and the loss of the angelic ability we once had to contemplate what lies above the cosmos. Something better indeed awaits, but only if we have managed to pass the terrible judgment that awaits us when the course of this shadowy life has passed so as to be received into the bosom of Abraham. The contrast between the intellectual and the corporeal nature, between the world above and the world below dominates the closing paragraphs of the homily. The more optimistic idea of a horizontal ascent through time by seizing the right moment for a timely birth seems to have been completely overwhelmed.

We must remember, however, that this is only the sixth homily and that Gregory is proceeding through an ordered sequence of argument that correspsonds to the necessary sequence of progress in virtue. The true nature of reality cannot reveal itself until its opposite has been banished. The works of darkness must be torn down before we can build within us houses of light. It is the distortion of nature, the dominance of non-being over being, that Gregory here laments. This confessional dirge, like Dante's flood of tears in the 31st Purgatorio, prepares the way for the revelation of truth that the seventh homily will find in mending the rent fabric of reality. It is not until the eighth homily that Gregory concludes his discussion and answers the question left open at the beginning of the sixth — whether or not time and season are the right criteria for the establishment of all virtue. A few comments on the eighth are necessary here to complete this discussion of the sixth.

'All things which he made are good at his right moment,' says the Preacher; 'he also gave time together in their heart, so that a man may not find the making which God made from beginning to end'. Even if it is true, as I have suggested, that Gregory's thinking about

space and time was developing as he wrote these homilies, he must
have had in mind while he was exploring the depths of the philosophy
of time in the sixth homily these words of the Ecclesiast that he
would be commenting upon in the eighth.   In the sixth homily he
defines time as the common measure of all things and says that
measure and moment are the criteria of the good.   He does not
explicit define moment, but implies by example that the right moment
is the ability not only to distinguish between good and evil, reality
and futility, but also to alter the character of experience itself in
one direction or the other.   In the eighth homily we learn that the
right moment is in fact God's moment.   God made all things good in
his own moment.   He gave to those who participate in reality the
ability to distinguish the good.   The right moment (εὐκαιρία, 438,9) of
each thing's use bestows upon the user the perception of the good.
The reversal of the moment turns each thing into its opposite.   God
created all things good in his own moment and also gave time in their
hearts.   Here, following his text of Ecclesiastes, Gregory uses αἰών
rather than χρόνος, but he understands time in both homilies in much
the same way.   He said in the sixth homily that the extension of time
(377,2) stretches out alongside everything that comes into being and
that time is the measure containing (περιέχων, 377,14) all things within
itself.   Similarly, in the eighth homily he says that αἰών is an
extensional idea that signifies the whole creation that comes to be
within it (440,3-5).   God gave this time to men in their hearts, and it
is the heart of man that determines its quality.   It is the same with
all of the things that nature has to offer from God, Gregory says
(439,20); it lies within the choice of those who use them whether they
become material for good or for evil.   Thus time and moment are
indeed the criteria of the good.   For God gave to man the whole
measure of time and all that it contains for good.   The creation is
good in God's moment.   Whether or not it is good in man's moment is
within his own responsibility to determine.

4.   Some conclusions

The conjunction of the two phrases 'Futility of futilities' and 'A
moment for each thing that comes into being' leads Gregory in his

commentary on Ecclesiastes towards a new understanding of created reality and of the role of man within it. The διάστημα is no longer a physical barrier in space separating all that is material, including man, from all that is intellectual, including the angels, but the common receptacle of all creation, intellectual as well as material. This διάστημα is both the chronological space of development from beginning to ending and the ontological space that distinguishes created becoming from uncreated being. The διάστημα remains an uncrossable barrier, but it is a barrier between creator and creature, not between intellectual and sensible being. The character of man's double life of body and soul is indeed miserable. It is miserable, however, not because of that conjunction in itself, but because of the distortion of nature caused by sin. That distortion will not completely be repaired until the return of all things to their original state, but meanwhile each individual has the capacity to anticipate that restoration by choosing to experience reality in God's right moment rather than to miss the moment and to participate instead in the plunge back towards non-being. All things are created good in time and within time man can experience creation as good if he chooses to do so. The distinction between intellectual and sensible being is as much moral as it is ontological. The man who lives intellectually and for the soul is the man who experiences the making that God has made. The one who lives somatically is he who has chosen to judge the good by his own moment. Both men live the double life of body and soul. In one there is a civil war between the two, in the other a harmonious blend of opposites that is the measure of virtue.

These ideas, which inform the perspective of Gregory's most mature works, are of great interest in themselves. In the homilies on Ecclesiastes Gregory is moving towards something like the modern notion of the 'social construction of reality'.[30] If reality has any

---

30   See Peter L. Berger, *The Sacred Canopy. Elements of a Sociology of Religion,* New York 1969 and (with Thomas Luckmann) *The Social Construction of Reality. A Treatise in the Sociology of Knowledge,* New York 1967.

objective existence of its own, that objectivity can be known only to God, because only God can stand outside the διάστημα that contains it. Man shares the conditions of the reality that he seeks to know. He affects that reality in the very act of seeking to know it and to use it and is himself in turn affected by the effects he has caused. It is like eating garlic, Gregory says (422,17); what we choose we become. The idea that human beings create their own reality is one of the main theses of the homilies on the Song of Songs. A good example is the discussion in the twelfth homily (GNO VI, 348,12-352,5) of the two trees in the center of Paradise. By stating a geometrical impossibility the author of Genesis intends the reader to look beneath the literal meaning of the words for a deeper philosophy. There is in fact but one tree, which becomes life or death according as one chooses to appropriate it.

The interest of the Homilies on Ecclesiastes lies partly in their adumbration of these ideas, but primarily in their testimony to Gregory's own intellectual development. The sixth homily presents us with an excellent example of the mutual transformation of Platonism and Christianity. Contemplating the meaning of time from a Biblical point of view, Gregory comes to realize the inadequacy of his understanding of space from a Platonic point of view. Instead of abandoning the spatial categories that he now finds inconsistent with his Christian understanding of creation, he applies those categories to the dimension of time so as to define a new multidimensional space. However much Gregory might be shocked by the suggestion, his Platonism informs his Christianity, which would be much impoverished without it.

12

ʿΟ εὔκαιρος θάνατος

Consideraciones en torno a la muerte en las *Homilías al Eclesiastes*

de Gregorio de Nisa

Lucas F. Mateo Seco

La reflexión sobre la muerte humana aparece con cierta frecuencia en los *Homilías al Eclesiastés* de Gregorio de Nisa. A esta asunto dedica atención expresa en el comienzo de la Oratio VI,[1] comentando Eccl 3,2. El texto del Eclesiastés — 'hay un tiempo para dar a luz y un tiempo para morir' — , brinda al Niseno la posibilidad de detenerse en la consideración del tiempo oportuno para morir, es decir, de considerar la muerte humana en su relación con el momento y la forma en que acaece. Y lo hace con relativo detenimiento. De ahí que hable de una muerte en tiempo oportuno (ὁ εὔκαιρος θάνατος), considerando que para una 'buena muerte' todo momento de la vida terrena es oportuno[2].

Este aspecto de la muerte no es el único considerado por el Niseno en estas Homilías. Así, por ejemplo, la distinción entre mortal e inmortal aparece ya en la Oratio I[3], en correspondencia con la división de los seres tan subrayada por él[4]; en la Oratio IV,

---

1   GNO V, 372,20-381,18;   PG 44,696 C-704 C.

2   ... πᾶς τῷ ἁγίῳ Παύλῳ καιρὸς τοῦ ἀγαθοῦ θανάτου εὔκαιρος ἦν GNO V, 381,2-3].

3   GNO V, 284,3-11.

4   Cfr J. Daniélou, Éléments: L'être et le temps chez Grégoire de Nysse, Leiden 1970, 75-94, esp. 84-85; A. Mosshammer, The

apoyándose en la muerte — común a todos los hombres — argumentará contra la esclavitud, pues la igualdad ante la muerte nuestra que todos los hombres son iguales[5];   en la Oratio V dedicará unos párrafos a mostrar que el hecho de que la muerte acontezca al sabio y al ignorante no hace inútil la búsqueda de la sabiduría; en la Oratio VI, Gregorio dedicará un elocuente pasaje a hablar de la muerte en sentido espiritual, es decir, de la muerte al pecado — lo que se ha calificado como *muerte mística*[7] — , y ya casi al final de esta Oratio, volverá sobre la ausencia de la muerte en el Paraíso;[8] en la Oratio VII, considerará la oposición muerte-vida;[9] finalmente, en la Oratio VIII considerará el estar lejos de Dios como muerte.[10]

La variedad de aspectos de la muerte que considera Gregorio en estas Homilías es, pues, notable.   Todos ellos guardan relación entre sí y con lo que es el tema principal de mi aportación en este Coloquio: la muerte en tiempo oportuno, ὁ εὔκαιρος θάνατος.

Mortal e inmortal

La distinción mortal-inmortal aparece en un contexto de claro rechazo del maniqueismo, precisamente al commentar Eccl 1,2, es decir, al explicar el sentido en que ha de entenderse la afirmación en torno a la vanidad de las cosas.   En su traducción, Hall titula este

---

created and the uncreated in Gregory of Nyssa: L.F. Mateo-Seco y J.L. Bastero, edits., El 'Contra Eunomium I' en la producción literaria de Gregorio de Nisa, Pamplona, 1988, 353-380.5
GNO V, 338,8-14.

6   GNO V, 361,2-14; 364,14-366,6.

7   GNO VI, 379,14-381,18.   Theo Kobusch ha escrito sobre este tema, poniendo de relieve la especificidad cristiana de la muerte mística: 'Auf der Suche nach dem Ursprung der Lehre vom mystischen Tod wird man bis zur patristischen Philosophie zurückgeführt.   Das ist kein Zufall.   Diese Lehre ist christlichen Ursprung (...) Der mystische Tod ist die menschliche Form der Kenosis, die menschliche Form der Selbstentaüsserung, die Kenosis-Lehre selbst aber ist das Spezificum des Christlichen' (Theo Kobusch, ThQ 164 [1984] 187).

8   GNO V, 386,10-12.

9   GNO V, 403,1-4.

10   GNO V, 426,1-7.

trozo: *The futility of all things does not condemn God's creation.*
Gregorio tiene muy claro que toda acusación a las cosas creadas
cedería directamente en acusación a Aquel que las hizo,[11] y lo repite
con fuerza: no se puede vituperar la vida en la carne, porque es Dios
quien la hizo, como también El es el autor del cuerpo y del alma.[12]
La muerte, pues, y cuanto sobre ella diga Gregorio ha de entenderse
en este contexto de aprecio a toda la creación, también a la materia
y a la vida en carne, es decir, a la vida presente, revestida de
mortalidad.   Esto es verdaderamente importante.   Ni siquiera aquí, en
las *Homilías al Eclesiastés*, en las que el mismo texto sagrado le
brindaba la posibilidad de subrayar la vanidad de todo cuanto existe
bajo el sol, Gregorio se ha mostrado despreciativo por la inestable
vida mortal.

Como en otros lugares, también aquí subraya Greogorio la
diversidad existente entre el cuerpo y el alma.   Se trata de dos
elementos distintos, a los que corresponden distintas formas de vida:
la vida del cuerpo es mortal (θνητή) y sujeta a la muerte (ἐπίκηρος),
mientras que la del alma es impasible (ἀπαθής) e incontaminada
(ἀκήρατος); lo corporal mira sólo al momento presente; lo espiritual se
proyecta, en cambio, hacio lo eterno.   Y afirma categóricamente: es
grande la diferencia existente entre lo mortal y lo inmortal
(ἀθάνατον), entre lo temporal y lo eterno.[13]

A pesar de esta neta diferenciación, el Niseno no olvida que
ambos elementos — cuerpo y alma — forman una estrecha unidad por
la que concurren a una única vida.[14]   Lo que pasa es que cada uno

---

11   GNO V, 283, 18-21.

12   GNO V, 284, 14-17.

13   Cfr GNO V, 284,4-11.   Preocupado por defender la bondad de la
     creación, incluso en el estado actual, Gregorio puntualiza en este
     comentario a Eccl 1,2 que no es que las cosas sean vanas en sí
     mismas, sino que se las llama vanas con respecto a la vida
     futura, para poner de relieve que el hombre no se debe a la vida
     de los sentidos, la cual, comparada con la verdadera vida es
     irreal y carente de consistencia.

14   Daniélou ha descrito en un sugerente trabajo la profundidad con
     que Gregorio entiende este *concurso*, esta σύμπνοια, por la que
     elementos diversos *conspiran* acordes, como en una gran sinfonía,

de ellos lleva consigo la atracción hacia lo que le es cercano, hacia lo que le es más 'familiar':   el cuerpo hacio lo material y sensible; el alma, hacio lo espiritual y eterno.[15]   Es sin embargo propio del hombre mirar hacia una vida más sublime — la de Dios — , pues el conocimiento de los sentidos se le ha dado para que le guíe hacia el conocimiento de las cosas invisibles.[16]

La visión de Gregorio en torno a la naturaleza humana y a la misma condición mortal de la existencia es verdaderamente rica en matices.   Según Gregorio, la compleja composición del hombre — materia y espíritu —, que conlleva un difícil equilibrio, es el resultado

compuesta también de estabilidad y movimiento. 'Il serait intéressant' escribe Daniélou, 'de montrer comment ce rapport στάσις-κίνησις se retrouvera à nouveau au niveau de son anthro- pologie, suivant cette loi générale de sa pensée où les catégories de la cosmologie se retrouvent dans l'anthropologie, mais de façon seulement analogique.   La vie spirituelle sera ainsi pour Grégoire synthèse de stabilité et de mouvement' (J. Daniélou, Conspiration: L'être et le temps ... cit. 56-57).

15   A los hombres es familiar y conforme a su naturaleza una vida parecida a la vida divina; se les ha dado la vida sensible para que el mismo conocimiento sensible fuese su guía hacia el conocimiento de lo que no cae bajo los sentidos, de forma que, a través de las cosas pasajeras, conociesen la naturaleza estable (τὴν στάσιμον φύσιν) y vean lo que es verdaderamente bueno y lo posean por medio de la contemplación (Cfr GNO I, 284,19-285,12). Gregorio de Nisa es atraído fuertemente por la estabilidad, en la cual considera que reside la absoluta perfección.   Sin embargo, como ha puesto de relieve A. Spira, con respecto a la vida humana, Gregorio se aparta de la concepción según la cual todo movimiento implica imperfección, y piensa que en la misma mutabilidad reside una posibilidad de perfección: 'La perfection repose donc sur la mutabilité — la mutabilité vers le bien, le bon mouvement (ἀγαθὴ ἀλλοίωσις), ainsi que la qualifie Grégoire, dans un autre ouvrage.   Elle est un processus permanent qui n'admet aucun arrêt, un progrès infini, nécessairement infini, car son object — Dieu — est infini.   Telle est la thèse centrale, développée par Grégoire, sur la vie de l'homme dans le temps.   La stabilité cherchée se trouve, comme il le dit ailleurs, dans la course même' (A. Spira, Le temps d'un homme selon Aristote et Grégoire de Nysse. Stabilité et instabilité dans la pensée grecque, 'Colloques internationaux du CRNS' n. 604, Paris 1984, 288-289). Este planteamiento, indiscutiblemente, facilita a Gregorio la comprensión de las 'ventajas' que tiene para el hombre la vida mortal, entre cuyas caracterísas se encuentra la fugacidad.

16   Cfr GNO V, 284,19-285,2.

de un positivo querer de Dios.[17]   Como vemos por este texto de la
Oratio I que venimos comentando, tanto el alma como el cuerpo vienen
de Dios;   más aún, también la mortalidad viene de Dios y, en este
sentido, no carece de bondad.[18]

El problema de la mortalidad humana ha sido abordado por el
Niseno repetidamente.   Quizás el lugar más elocuente sea el largo
capítulo VIII de la *Oratio Catechetica Magna*.   En el, como ha hecho
notar Daniélou, no se trata propiamente de saber si la muerte, que
nos libra de la condición mortal, es un bien, sino si la condición
mortal, considerada en sí misma, es un bien.[19]   Gregorio, que con
tanta fuerza se lamenta en este mismo lugar de la situación del
hombre, sujeta al dolor, al cambio y a la muerte, defenderá con
fuerza que la mortalidad es un bien, precisamente porque nos ha sido
dada como camino para purificar a la naturaleza humana del pecado.
Es un bien venido de las manos *curadoras* de Dios.

En la visión nisena, la mortalidad aparece ligada al pecado de
origen.   Ha sido estudiado ya con profundidad el frecuente uso que
hace Gregorio de la metafora 'las túnicas de pieles', tomada de Gen
3,21: tras la caída, Dios hace túnicas de pieles y viste con ellas al
hombre y a la mujer.[20]   Las 'túnicas de pieles' designan en la pluma
nisena la condición mortal de la que es revestido el hombre por Dios
tras el pecado.

De la exégesis nisena a Gen 3,21, destaquemos lo siguiente como
trasfondo de este texto de la Oratio I in Ecclesiasten que venimos
comentando.   Según Gregorio, tras el pecado, Dios viste a los
primeros padres de estas túnicas hechas de pieles de animales; con

17   Así, p.e. el hombre ha side creado como unión de cuerpo y
     espíritu, para que sea como un pequeño microcosmo, como punto
     de unidad entre lo sensible y lo inteligible, entre lo material y los
     espiritual (cfr Or.Cat., esp. 5, PG 45,21B-25A).

18   Cfr GNO V, 284,14-15.

19   Cfr J. Daniélou, Mortalité: L'être et le temps. ... cit. 162-163.

20   Cfr J. Daniélou, Les tuniques de peau chez Grégoire de Nysse:
     Glaube, Geist, Geschichte (Festschrift E. Benz), Leiden 1967, 355-
     367;   Mortalité, cit. 154-164.

ellas reviste de mortalidad — tomada de los animales — a la
naturaleza humana, creada para la inmortalidad.[21]   Se trata de una
vestidura, es decir, de algo que es externo y que, por tanto, no
afecta a lo más íntimo del hombre, esto es, a la imagen de Dios que
hay en él y a su parte inmortal.[22]   Este revestimiento de mortalidad
está hecho por Dios en bien del hombre providencialmente, en orden a
su salvación[23].

Así pues, la condición mortal en que ahora nos encontramos,
aunque desde un punto de vista nos es contraria — va contra la
naturaleza humana, creada para la inmortalidad —, desde otro punto de
vista es buena, pues viene de las manos de Dios; Dios la ha impuesto
para librar al hombre — con la radicalidad que supone deshacer el
vaso de barro y rehacerlo de nuevo - de la maldad con la que se

---

21   Con respecto a este pasaje comenta Srawley: 'The δερμάτινος
      χιτών takes the place of the ἀπάθεια (J.H. Srawley, The Cate-
      chetical Oratio of Gregory of Nyssa, Cambridge 1956, 43 n. 4).

22   Cfr Or.Cat.Magn. 8, PG 45,33,B-D. El texto es claro: 'Puesto
      que toda piel separada del viviente está muerta, pienso
      ciertamente que aquel que cura (ἰατρεύοντα) nuestra maldad,
      providencialmente, después de esto imbuyó a los hombres fuerza
      para morir, tomada de la naturaleza irracional, para que no
      permaneciese siempre (l.c., C).   Dediqué a este asunto mi primer
      trabajo sobre el Niseno (La teología de la muerte en la 'Oratio
      Catechetica magna' de San Gregorio de Nisa: ScrTh 1 [1969] 453-
      473).   Cito esta parte del texto en la página 461.   En la
      traducción existe un error de sujeto, que, sin embargo, no influye
      en el comentario, que ahora vuelvo a repetir: 'Entiende el Niseno
      con esta imagen que la muerte no sólo es also extrínseco a la
      naturaleza humana primitiva, sino que la condición mortal de que
      ahora estamos revestidos ha sido impuesta por Dios a la
      humanidad con sentido transitorio, funcional: rehacer al hombre
      mediante la resurrección'.

23   En este mismo lugar - la Oratio Catechetica — Gregorio
      desarrolla esta misma idea al hilo de un sugerente ejemplo: el
      vaso de varro en el que dolosamente se ha vertido plomo líquido
      que, al enfriarse, ha cristalizado de forma que ya no puede
      vaciarse el vaso; como el dueño que hizo el vaso lo sigue
      queriendo, y sigue en posesión de la ciencia del alfarero, rompe
      el vaso con el plomo, y después lo rehace conforme a su
      primitiva figura, libre ya del plomo, que le es extraño; así, sucede
      con el hombre, vaso de barro; una vez que se mezcló el vicio a
      su parte sensible, es deschecha la materia, que ha recibido el
      vicio, y rehecha de nuevo por la resurrección, libre ya de la
      mezcla que le es ajena (Cfr Or.Cat. 8, PG 45,36A-C).

encuentra tan estrechamente unido. En la mente nisena, la comprensión del acontecimiento de la muerte està estrechamente ligada a su visión de la 'oeconomía de la salvación', es decir, el hecho de la muerte está vinculado tanto con la protohistoria — el pecado de origen —, como con la escatología: la resurrección. Ni la muerte, ni la condición mortal deben ser denostadas, 'pues si se acusa a la vida en la carne, siendo Dios autor de la carne, necesariamente este reproche se dirige contra El'.[24]   Esta breve frase que nos sale al paso en la Oratio I se apoya, pues, en un rico y bien meditado pensamiento.

Al mismo tiempo, esto no quiere decir que Gregorio no piense en el estado paradisíaco en el cual estaba ausente la muerte, y que no compare la vida presente con aquel feliz estado.   Así lo hace en la *Oratio Catechetica*,[25] utilizando como expresiones culminantes de su pensamiento las conocidas imágenes de los *vasos de barro* y el revestimiento de las *túnicas de pieles*, con las que designa, por una parte, que la condición mortal viene de las manos amorosas de Dios — 'que cura nuestra maldad'[26] — , y por otra, que esta condición mortal sigue siendo algo ajena no sólo al designio creador sobre el hombre, sino también a la misma naturaleza humana, como lo es el vestido con respecto a su portador y, finalmente que, en la providencia, el final de la muerte es la resurrección, rehacer el vaso de barro.

En las *Homilías al Eclesiastés* Gregorio alude de pasada a la inmortalidad paradisíaca por contraste con la mortalidad presente. Al hilo de Eccl 3,4 — 'hay tiempo para llorar y tiempo para reír' — , enumeraza razones por las que el tiempo presente es oportuno para llorar: ¿quién no lloraría al considerar lo que tuvo y lo que perdió, es decir, el estado en que en un comienzo estaba su vida, y el estado en que se encuentra en el presente? 'Entonces no existía la muerte, estaba ausente la enfermedad, mío y tuyo, — estas palabras perversas

---

24   GNO V, 284,14-16.

25   Cfr Or.Cat. 5, PG 45,24 A-B;   8, ibid., 33A-40C.

26   Ibid., 33C.

— estaban lejos de la vida de los primeros'[27]. En aquella bienaventurada vida, el hombre gozaba de honor similar al de los ángeles, del hablar confiado con Dios,[28] de la contemplación de los bienes supramundanos, de la consideración del propio honor de ser imagen de Dios.[29]

Por el pecado, el hombre ha perdido estos bienes y ha sido invadido por una caterva de males. La descripción que aquí hace Gregorio de estos males es amplia y elocuente, hasta el punto de llamar tenebrosa a esta vida[30]. Y, sin embargo, estos males han venido a los hombres de las manos de Dios 'para curar nuestra maldad'. De ahí que Gregorio diga con toda fuerza: 'Ahora es tiempo de llorar; el tiempo de reír está en esperanza, pues la actual tristeza se convertirá en la *madre* de la alegría que esperamos.'[31]

Muerte y vida

Muerte y vida forman un binomio de cosas opuestas. No son dos realidades positivamente existentes, sino que la una es negación de la otra. Encontramos esta afirmación como de pasada en la Oratio VII: De igual forma que el ciego en el Evangelio encontró lo que no tenía perdiendo lo que tenía, ya que en lugar de la ceguera

---

27 Oratio VI, GNO, 386,9-10. Y prosigue: 'Pues así como era común el sol y común el aire y, sobre todo, era común la gracia de Dios y su bendición, del mismo modo la participación en cada uno de los bienes estaba, sin reservas, a disposición de todos, y se desconocía la enfermedad de la avaricia, ni el que tenía menos odiaba al que tenía más' (Ibid., 10-15).

28 El Niseno utiliza aquí un término que le es muy querido y que tene en su pluma una gran riqueza: παρρησία. Esta confianza con Dios — este hablar de amigo a amigo — se pierde con el pecado de origen, siendo sustituida por la vergüenza. Este confiado hablar con Dios, recuperado por la gracia bautismal, es 'la estola' del cristiano, que le permite entrar en los santuarios celestes. Cfr J. Daniélou, Platonisme et théologie mystique, Paris 1944, 103-115; L.F. Mateo-Seco, Sacerdocio de Cristo y sacerdocio ministerial en los tres grandes Capadocios: VV.AA., Teología del Sacerdocio, IV, Burgos 1972, esp. 198-199.

29 Oratio VI, GNO 386, 18-387,1.

30 Ibid., 387,5-388,9

31 Ibid., 386,2-4.

recibió la visión, y en el caso del leproso, cuando fué removida la enfermedad retornó el don de la salud, 'y de igual forma que en aquellos que resucitan de la muerte, la mortalidad (νεκρότης) se aleja con la presencia de la vida ... '.[32]

Esta oposición implica que basta la presencia de la vida, para que desparezca la muerte, y al mismo tiempo, que la muerte ha de ser considerada como simple carencia de vida. Los ejemplos aducidos son claros: la ceguera y la visión, la salud y la enfermedad. Ambos coinciden en que, de los opuestos, el uno es carencia del otro; uno sólo de ellos, pues, tiene entidad positiva, el otro es, en consecuencia, negatividad. Gregorio repite este pensamiento — tan frecuente en la concepción clásica de mal — en diversos lugares. En forma verdaderamente gráfica lo hace en el capítulo 4 de la *Oratio Catechetica*: De igual forma que la visión consiste en ver — sintetizo el texto — , es decir, es una operación de la naturaleza, y la ceguera es privación de esta operación así la virtud es contraria al vicio; en consecuencia, no podemos pensar otro nacimiento del vicio que la ausencia de virtud.

En el caso de la muerte corporal, la concepción nisena de la vida como entidad positiva y de la muerte como lo contrario a ella, y la convicción de que el hombre es corporal por designio amoroso de Dios, que le ha hecho 'microcosmo', facilita al Niseno que capte con tanta fuerza la importancia de la resurrección en la oeconomía divina sobre el destino humano. Baste pensar en cuanto escribe sobre la acción salvadora del bautismo o del cuerpo eucarístico de Cristo,[33] o el mismo ejemplo utilizado de los 'vasos de barro'.

La muerte del sabio y la del insensato.

En la Oratio IV, Gregorio, luchando contra la esclavitud, argumenta que no se puede ser dueño de aquello a lo que se es igual en naturaleza y, por tanto, ningún hombre puede ser dueño de otro hombre. Entre las cosas a que recurre para mostrar esta igualdad de

---

32   Oratio VII, GNO V, 402,22-403,4.

33   Cfr Or.Cat. cps. 35 y 37.

naturaleza entre todos los hombres, es a la igualdad ante la muerte —
amo y esclavo se convertirán en polvo tras la muerte — , y ante el
juicio.[34] Esta igualdad ante la muerte será utilizada, sin embargo, en
la Oratio V como un argumento contra la vida virtuosa, argumento a
cuya solución dedica el Niseno amplio espacio.

El argumento es bien sencillo y debió ser muy frecuente an
ámbitos cercanos al paganismo: si ni el sabio ni el insensato pueden
evitar la muerte, ?qué bien se sigue de llevar una vida mejor?   La
igualdad de destino muestra la inutilidad de los esfuerzos por vivir
virtuosamente; la virtud es inútil, pues no sirve para librar de la
muerte.

Gregorio comienza su argumentación diciendo que la diferencia no
está en el *suceso* de la muerte, sino en el *más allá* de la muerte, es
decir, en los bienes o en los males que esperan después de ella.[35]
Distingue aquí entre el 'suceso de la muerte' (θανάτου συνάντημα),[36] y
una realidad más profunda.   El suceso de la muerte es lo visible de
ella; y este aspecto visible es común al sabio y al insensato.   El
insensato toma de esta igualdad la objeción que está resolviendo
Gregorio; y toma de aquí esta igualdad, porque sólo estima real
aquello que ve con los ojos de la carne.   La respuesta del
Eclesiastés — prosigue el Niseno — es que es vano ver las cosas
desde esta perspectiva, como si la distinción entre la vida virtuosa y
la malvada debiera percibirse en el mero acontecimiento de la muerte,
en el sentido de que sólo el perverso hubiese de soportar la muerte
corporal (ἐν τῷ σώματι), mientras que el virtuoso hubiese de
permanecer libre de esa muerte corporal (τοῦ σωματικοῦ θανάτου),
ignorando en qué consista la inmortalidad de la virtud y la muerte de
los que viven en la maldad[37].

No abunda más el Niseno en la distinción entre 'suceso de la
muerte', — común a virtuosos y perversos —, y en la inmortalidad

---

34   Oratio IV, GNO V, 338,12-13.

35   Cfr Oratio V, GNO V, 361,10-13.

36   Ibid., 364,15.

37   Ibid., 365,7-13

inherente a la virtud o en la muerte que conlleva la maldad.   El
interés apologético es muy concreto en este lugar, y Gregorio basa su
argumentación en que no se debe juzgar según las apariencias, cosa
que queda resuelta insinuando que la muerte no se agota en la
visibilidad del 'suceso de la muerte'; que hay otra clase de muerte y
también una inmortalidad, ambas no visibles a los ojos de la carne.
Al mismo tiempo, esta misma línea argumentativa le facilita subrayar
la igualdad entre el 'suceso de la muerte' y el 'morir en el cuerpo' o
la 'muerte corporal', dando a entender que existe otra clase de
muerte, y que es posible que el 'suceso de la muerte' pueda ser, en su
más íntima profundidad, apertura a un verdadero vivir.

Tiempo de dar a luz y tiempo de morir.

Todo cuanto va a decir Gregorio en torno a la muerte en la
Oratio VI, está dicho — como él mismo advierte — , teniendo como
marco la afirmación tomada de Eccl 3,1 de que cada cosa tiene su
tiempo y su oportunidad.   La bondad y la misma honestidad de una
cosa dependen de su oportunidad y de su medida.   Gregorio se ex-
tiende en una sabrosa digresión en torno a las relaciones entre
συμμετρία y εὐκαιρία con la bondad de cuanto sucede[38].   La
importancia del 'tiempo oportuno' radica en que no es bueno aquello
que se hace inoportunamente.

Los ejemplos aducidos para mostrar la importancia de la
εὐκαιρία en la acción son suficientemente expresivos: la siega — que
ha de hacerse en el momento preciso en que la mies está madura — ,
la navegación y la medicina.   Todo ha de hacerse con medida y
oportunidad.   La oportunidad — anota Gregorio — no es más que un
aspecto de la medida, pues el tiempo es medida de todo lo medido, ya
que todo lo que acontece, acontece en el tiempo.[39]

Este pensamiento será aplicado inmediatamente al nacimiento y a
la muerte, siguiendo Eccl 3,2, con un elogio a la edad madura, en el
que queda patente la sinceridad con que el Niseno mira la realidad.

---

38   Oratio VI, GNO V,374-375.

39   Ibid., 377,15-17.

Considera como perfecta la edad madura, es decir, aquella en que se
ha pasado lo inmoderado e insolente de la inmadurez, y aún no ha
llegado la decrepitud. Se trata de ese envidiable tiempo en que se
dan unidas fuerza y prudencia.[40]

Hay un tiempo para dar a luz y un tiempo para morir. '¡Ojalá
se me diese — clama el Niseno — el nacimiento a su tiempo y la
muerte en tiempo oportuno (εὔκαιρος).'[41] Gregorio subraya a
continuación lo que, en su aspecto fáctico, tienen estos sucesos de
involuntario: ni la mujer elige el momento del parto, ni la muerte
está en la libre elección (ἐν τῇ προαιρέσει) del moribundo.[42] Estos
sucesos — prosigue el Niseno — , en su materialidad, no son objeto ni
de virtud ni de vicio, ya que no están en nuestro poder. La
conclusión que deduce es la siguiente: cuando el Eclesiastés habla de
'tiempo oportuno' para nacer o morir — y, por tanto, se está
refiriendo a cualidades que hacen a las obras buenas — , no está
hablando del 'suceso' en cuanto tal, sino que se está refiriendo a
otra clase de nacimiento o de muerte.

Por nacimiento ha de entenderse un nuevo nacimiento de uno
mismo. Este sí que es un nacimiento oportuno (εὔκαιρον) no inmaduro.
Este nacimiento tiene lugar cuando, en cita de Is 26,17-18, 'cada
uno, concibiendo por el temor de Dios, se engendra a sí mismo para la
salvación por medio de los sufrimientos del alma; en cierto sentido,
nos hacemos padres de nosotros mismos, cuando por medio de una

---

40 Ibid., 377,20-378,2.

41 Ibid., 379,15-16.

42 Ibid., 379,19-20. En otro lugar, al referirse a la muerte de
    Cristo, Gregorio da a entender que esa muerte tuvo una
    voluntariedad especial y que no fue para El un suceso vivido
    pasiva, sino activamente. Al hilo de una cita de Jn 10,18,
    escribe 'Vuelve tus ojos hacia la grandeza del poder divino, y no
    ignorarás lo que se plantea en este lugar. Acuérdate de la
    declaración de Señor y conocerás qué revela acerca de su propio
    poder aquel que es dominador de todo; cómo separa el alma de su
    cuerpo con poder autocrático (πῶς αὐτοκρατικῇ ἐξουσίᾳ ...
    διαζεύγνυσι τὴν ψυχὴν ἐκ τοῦ σώματος) y no por necesidad de la
    naturaleza (οὐ φύσεως ἀνάγκη)' (De Tridui, PG 46,612 B). He
    estudiado por extenso este texto en mis Estudios sobre la
    cristología de Gregorio de Nisa, Pamplona 1978, 332 ss).

buena elección nos moldeamos a nosotros mismos (ἑαυτοὺς πλάσωμεν),
y nacemos, y venimos a la luz'.[43]

La consideración del hombre como hacedor de sí mismo mediante
sus elecciones morales es muy querida para el Niseno. El hombre se
engendra a sí mismo por su libre elección, porque, en cierto sentido,
se convierte en aquello que elige.[44] Esta afirmación de Gregorio —
que destaca la importancia del quehacer moral y la confianza en la
ascética — ha de conjugarse, como es obvio, con aquellas otras con
las que él mismo pone de relieve la teología sacramentaria, en
especial, la teología bautismal[45], y aquellos otros lugares en que dice
explícitamente que el buen actuar es don de Dios, pues es Él quien
hace morir al pecado.[46] Por lo que respecta al tema que nos ocupa
en este momento, baste notar que con esta forma de argumentar,
Gregorio nos traslada del significado de nacimiento y muerte en su
sentido físico a una consideración moral, es decir, a lo que se
califica justamente como 'muerte mística'. Se trata de una muerte
por la que uno nace a una nueva vida. Como escribe T. Kobusch,
tras citar este texto niseno, 'la muerte mística es esencialmente una
muerte por amor.[47]

A esta muerte al pecado, es decir, a esta muerte por amor,
Gregorio la llamará buena muerte: 'Si como está claro — prosigue —
nos hacemos nacer en un momento oportuno, también debería estar
claro cómo morimos oportunamente, pues para San Pablo cada

---

43   Oratio VI, GNO V,380,1–5.

44   Cfr Or.Cat. 8, PG 33, C.

45   Cfr p.e., Or.Cat. 35, ss. Cfr J. Daniélou, Platonisme et théologie
     mystique ... cit., 23–35.

46   Cfr p.e., Oratio VI, GNO V,381,13–17.

47   'Der mystische Tod is seinem Wesen nach ein personaler Vollzug,
     dur den der Mensch sein Sein in einem anderen neu gewinnt. Der
     mystische Tod ist wesentlich Liebestod. Nach Gregor stirbt der
     Mensch in der Taufe — versinnbildlicht durch das Begrabenwerden
     im mystischen Wasser — den willentlichen Tod, indem er mit dem
     für ihn freiwillig gestorbenen Gottessohn sterben will, so dass er
     auch mit ihm und in ihm das neue Leben haben wird' (T. Kobusch,
     l.c., 190).

momento es tiempo oportuno de una buena muerte (ἀγαθοῦ θανάτου).[48]
Morir cada día, como dice San Pablo de sí mismo (cfr I Cor 15,31),
quere decir morir al pecado, pues él no vivía para el pecado (cfr Rom
6,6),[49] pues mortificaba continuamente sus miembros (cfr Col 3,5) y
llevaba sobre sí mismo la muertel de cuerpo de Cristo (cfr 2 Cor
4,10), pues estaba crucificado con Cristo (cfr Gal 2,19-20), no
viviendo nunca para sí mismo, sino llevando en sí mismo la muerte de
Cristo'.[50]

Gregorio eleva el tono de cuanto viene diciendo hasta un fuerte
contexto cristológico y bautismal. Daniélou mostró brillantemente la
importancia de la mística bautismal en Gregorio de Nisa así como las
resonancias ascéticas que el binomio muerte-resurrección encuentra en
su pluma.[51] El pasaje que acabamos de resumir confirma lo atinado
de su apreciación. La thanatología nisena, en la que con tanta
insistencia se considera la muerte en el marco de la *oeconomía* divina,
incluye un amplio espacio a considerar esta muerte en el terreno
moral y ascético. La doctrina paulina — sobre todo, su doctrina
bautismal —, le es acicate para hacerlo.

La consecuencia prática en este lugar es clara: 'La muerte en
tiempo oportuno (εὔκαιρος θάνατος) es aquella que es agente de una
verdadera vida.' Se trata de un don de Dios (Θεοῦ δῶρον), pues es
El quien hace morir al pecado (νεκρωθῆναι τῇ ἁμαρτίᾳ) y ser vivificado
por el Espíritu.[52]

Generación y muerte.

También en este pasaje que nos ocupa, Gregorio aduce un
pensamiento que encontramos en otros lugares: la relación entre
generación carnal y muerte, entre γένεσις y φθορά. La muerte está

---

48   Ibid., 381,1-3.

49   Ibid., 381,9; μηδέποτε τῇ ἁμαρτίᾳ ζῶν.

50   Ibid., 381,9-12

51   J. Daniélou, Platonisme et théologie mystique ... cit., 19-45.

52   Oratio VI,381,13-17.

relacionada — como hemos visto — con la pérdida de inmortalidad paradisíaca; al mismo tiempo, es natural a la forma en que el hombre es engendrado.   Pienso que en la mente nisena se trata de dos aspectos de una misma realidad estrechamente relacionados.

En efecto, la inmortalidad se pierde, como se veía por las citas de la *Oratio Catechetica*, porque Dios reviste a los primeros padres de 'túnicas de pieles', significando precisamente que los reviste de mortalidad, tomada de la naturaleza animal.[53]   En cierto sentido, los ha revestido de animalidad, cosa que se manifesta también en la forma de engendrar.[54]   Esto no quiere decir que Gregorio tenga una visión peyorativa del sexo;   al hablar de Cristo que fué sexual y virginalmente engendrado por María, dirá con fuerza que sólo es indigna de Dios la afección viciosa (τὸ κατὰ κακίαν πάθος), cosa que no sucede con la generación carnal en cuanto tal[55].

---

53   Cfr Or.Cat. 8, PG 45,33C.

54   La cuestión aparece extensamente tratada en el cp. 17 del *De opificio hominis*.   Se plantea la pregunta siguiente: ¿Por qué Dios, al plasmar al hombre a su imagen, le añadió la diferencia de masculino y femenino?   Y tras notar modestamente que va a exponer su opinión, responde diciendo que *quizás sea útil* decir que Dios 'previendo que el hombre libremente no tomaría el camino del bien y, por tanto, había de perder el estado de vida angélica y con ello perder su modo de procreación, para que no dejase de haber el número completo de almas, encontró otro modo por el que se multiplicase el género humano, más acorde con la naturaleza de quienes habíamos caído en el vicio' (PG 44,189B-D). Sobre la cuestión de la división de sexos en el Niseno existe una amplia bibliografía entre la que cabe destacar.   F. Floeri, La 'division des sexes' chez Grégoire de Nysse: RevSR 27 (1953) 105-111; B. Salmona, Il progetto di Dio sull'uomo. Analisi del *De hominis opificio* di Gregorio di Nissa: Temi di antropologia teologica, Roma 1981, 343-376; P. Pisi, Genesi e phthorá. Le motivazioni protologiche della verginità in Gregorio di Nissa nella tradizione dell'enkrateia, Roma 1981, esp. 57-102; U. Bianchi, La doppia creazione dell'uomo negli Alessandrini, nei Cappadoci e nella gnosi, Roma 1978; E. Corsini, Plérôme humain et plérôme cosmique chez Grégoire de Nysse: M. Harl (ed.), Écriture et culture philosophique dans la pensée de Grégoire de Nysse (Actes du Colloque de Chevetogne), Leiden 1971, 111-126; L.F. Mateo-Seco, Masculinidad y feminidad en los Padres Griegos de siglo IV: VV.AA., Masculinidad y feminidad en la patrística, Pamplona 1989, 82-124.

55   Or.Cat. 9, PG 45,41A.

Ello no obsta para que considere que existe una conexión lógica
entre la forma en que el hombre es engendrado y su posterior
disolución por la muerte.   Aquí aduce dos autoridades.   Moisés 'el
amigo de Dios' escribió seguidos el Génesis — generación — y el Éxodo
— salida — , para que quienes los leyeran recordasen que la muerte
sigue inevitablemente al parto;[56] lo mismo hace el Eclesiastés al
colocar en el mismo orden generación y muerte, 'pués la muerte sigue
necesariamente   al   parto,   y   toda   generación   fluye   hacia   la
corrupción.'[57]

Se trata, pues, de una secuencia inevitable, que manifiesta que
la vida presente no es la verdadera vida, pues es una vida mortal,
mientras que en el proyecto originario de Dios el hombre debía ser
inmortal.   Por eso Gregorio exhorta aquí a que, abandonando los
engaños de esta vida, tomemos 'el camino de la virtud, luchando por
conseguir aquello que está prometido por la fe en la esperanza'.[58]

Y, sin embargo, esta vida mortal es de la máxima importancia:
en ella tiene el hombre el tiempo oportuno para nacer a la verdadera
vida, y el tiempo de la buena muerte, una muerte para la que siempre
hay tiempo oportuno en cualquier momento de la existencia terrena.[59]
Se trata de una ocasión única, pues 'hay un solo momento que engendra para la vida, no muchos,'[60] dice aludiendo al bautismo.

La generación natural y la muerte son un binomio inseparable,
porque la γένεσις está abocada a la φθορά; en el otro orden de
cosas — en el orden moral —, también se da una estrecha relación
entre el 'nuevo nacimiento' y la 'buena muerte'.   En efecto, 'la buena
muerte' esa muerte que está en nuestras manos y para la que siempre

---

56   Oratio VI, GNO V, 378,17-21.

57   Ibid., 378,10-11.

58   Ibid., 379,9-11.

59   Cfr Ibid., 381,2-3.

60   εἷς γὰρ καιρὸς ὁ εἰς ζωὴν τίκτων καὶ οὐ πολλοί (Ibid., 19-20).

es tiempo oportuno, no es otra cosa que un morir al pecado y ser vivificado por el Espíritu. De ahí que al 'dar la muerte' se le llame 'dar la vida'.[61]

Esta vida, resultado de la 'buena muerte', o lo que es lo mismo, resultado de un 'nuevo nacimiento', no es otra cosa que configuración con Cristo: llegar a ser hijos de Dios mediante la virtud, mediante la conformación con Cristo. Sin este nuevo nacimiento, el hombre es 'hijo de la ira', pues no se ha formado en él la forma de Cristo.[62] Así el comentario del Niseno a la sencilla frase de Eccl 3,2, 'hay tiempo de dar a luz y tiempo de morir', conduce al lector a una ferviente perspectiva cristológica.

La muerte de Macrina y de Moisés,

En las *Homilías al Eclesiastés*, la expresión 'buena muerta' está usada para designar con ella la muerte al pecado. De hecho, hablar de 'buena muerte' es lo mismo que decir nacimiento a una nueva vida, un nacimiento que, a su vez, consiste en la identificación con Cristo. Para esta muerte—vida, el tiempo de la existencia terrena es siempre 'tiempo oportuno'. A pesar de que, en estas Homilías, Gregorio utiliza las expresiones 'buena muerte' y muerte en 'tiempo oportuno', no entra sin embargo en la cuestión de lo que en siglos posteriores se daría en llamar 'una buena muerte'. La 'buena muerte' y el 'tiempo oportuno' están referidos aquí únicamente a la muerte al pecado.

¿No dijo nada más Gregorio en torno al momento en que acontece el 'suceso' de la muerte, ni en torno a la forma de vivir ese suceso, es decir, a la forma de morir bien? ¿Es que acaso en la mente del Niseno el hecho mismo de la muerte no puede también 'coronar' la existencia terrena, de tal forma que sea no sólo final de la vida terrena, sino también cumplimiento de esta vida?

En las *Homilías al Eclesiastés* no ocupa este asunto la mente de Gregorio. Sin embargo sí describió la belleza del acontecimiento de la

---

61   GNO V, 381,17-18.

62   Ibid., 380,9-10.

muerte en otros lugares, al presentarla como 'tránsito' a la otra vida y como 'coronamiento' de la lucha por la virtud.

Los lugares más explícitos — y, a mi parecer, más hermosos — se encuentran en *De Vita Moysis*. En la parte I, Gregorio describe la muerte de Moisés con estas inolvidables palabras: 'Entonces el legislador subió a un monte alto y desde lejos contempló la tierra que había sido preparada para Israel según la promesa hecha por Dios a los padres. Luego se alejó de la vida de los hombres, no habiendo dejado en la tierra, con la tumba, ninguna señal o recuerdo de su partida. El tiempo no mancilló su belleza, ni oscureció la luminosidad de sus ojos, ni disminuyó la gracia espendorosa del rostro, sino que permaneció siempre igual a sí mismo, conservando en la mutabilidad de la naturaleza la inmutabilidad de la belleza.'[63]

Quizás sin advertirlo, Gregorio ha descrito aquí su ideal del momento de la muerte, una muerte corporal llegada serenamente en la madurez, y que corone la constante muerte-resurrección que comporta la vida virtuosa. Esta muerte es 'oportuna' exactamente, porque llega cuando el hombre ha subido a la cumbre del monte de la virtud. La majestuosa y venerable figura de Moisés subiendo a la cima del monte, joven y anciano a un tiempo — pues la injuria de los años no ha conseguido ensombrecer el brillo de sus ojos — , con la serenidad de quien ha permanecido estable dentro de la mutabilidad de la naturaleza, es buena muestra de la muerte que Gregorio considera 'buena'.

Es lo mismo que encontramos en la parte II de *De vita Moysis*, cuando Gregorio realiza la exégesis de esta historia. En ella, desarrolla con inigualable belleza los pensamientos que le hemos visto exponer en torno a la muerte en las *Homilías al Eclesiastés*. El ideal de la virtud es ser siervos y amigos de Dios. A esto se le llama perfección o muerte viviente (τελευτὴν ζῶσαν) sobre la que no se alza ningún sepulcro y que no emsombrece los ojos, ni corrompe el rostro.[64]

---

63 *De vita Moysis*, I, ed. M. Simonetti, Gregorio di Nissa, La vita di Mosè, Fondazione Lorenzo Valla, Venecia 1984, n. 76, pp. 59-60.

64 Cfr Ibid., II, n.314, p. 248.

El final de *De vita Moysis* es una vibrante exhortación a la vida virtuosa, llamando a seguir el ejemplo de Moisés, a llevar — como él — una vida por la que uno pueda ser llamado 'amigo de Dios'. Moisés, después de una vida tan rica en luchas y acontecimientos, 'se acercó al monte del reposo', y, 'llegado a la cima del monte, como un hábil escultor que mira atentamente a la estatua de su vida, al final del trabajo puso no fin (τελευτήν), sino coronamiento (κορυφήν) a su trabajo[65].

Para Gregorio, el 'suceso' de la muerte, a ejemplo de Moisés puede ser — debe ser — no sólo término, sino coronamiento de la existencia tránsito a la luz y a la incorrupción. Este tránsito corona una vida según la virtud. En las *Homilías al Eclesiastés*, Gregorio tiene especialmente presente esta vida virtuosa el utilizar las expresiones 'buena muerte' y la muerte en 'tiempo oportuno'. Esta vida es la otra cara de la muerte al pecado. La muerte al pecado es la más importante, de tal forma que ella es denominada por Gregorio 'buena muerte'; al mismo tiempo no es otra cosa que un nuevo nacimiento por el que se destruye la más tremenda muerte, en cierto sentido, la más verdadera muerte: la muerte que comporta el pecado.

Para esta buena muerte, cualquier tiempo de la vida es tiempo oportuno, pues 'toda la vida es tiempo oportuno para amar a Dios, y toda la vida es tiempo oportuno para apartarse del enemigo, pues quien, aunque sea por un pequeño espacio de tiempo de su vida, está separado del amor de Dios, está totalmente fuera de aquel de cuyo amor se ha separado', y por tanto, está fuera de la luz, 'de la vida y de la incorrupción', y en consecuencia, está en manos de las cosas contrarias a ellas, es decir, 'de las tinieblas, de la corrupción, de la ruina total, y de la muerte'.[66]

Como hacía notar H. Meissner en el diálogo que siguió, parecida paz ante la muerte que 'consuma' una virtuosa encontramos en la narración de la muerte de Macrina. Junto a la hermana agonizante,

---

65 *Vit. Moys.*, II, 313, p. 246.
66 Oratio VIII, GNO V, 426,1-7.

Gregorio se encuentra entre la tristeza y el entusiasmo 'ante el
espectáculo de que ella había trascendido la naturaleza común', pues,
ante la perpectiva de la muerte, no padecía 'ningún sentimiento de
extrañeza, ni tenía miedo de abandonar esta vida', sino que 'hasta su
último aliento meditó profundamente con una sublime inteligencia sobre
lo que había sido el objeto de la elección de su vida terrena.'[67]   La
oración de Macrina contenida en el capítulo 24 explica esta serenidad
ante la muerte: 'eres tú, Señor, quien ha abolido para nosotros el
temor de la muerte.'[68]   Y finalmente, tras finalizar con la señal de
la cruz su plegaria de acción de gracias al encender las lámparas,
Macrina 'concluye con un profundo suspiro, a la vez, su oración y su
vida'.   Cuando Gregorio, cumpliendo su petición, va a cerrarle los
ojos, observa que, 'las pupilas los cubren con gracia, como en el
sueño natural.'[69]   La muerte en tiempo oportuno es pues, aquella que
sella para siempre con gracia, como en un sueño natural, la armonía
madura de la virtud.

Abstract by Stuart G. Hall

It is here argued that Gregory uses the text from Eccl 3,2 to
develop the idea that 'timely death' means dying spiritually.   Thoughts
about death are present in other works and in other Homilies on
Ecclesiastes.   Gregory's teaching is expounded in a series of themes:

Mortal and immortal: The body shares the futility of creation,
while the soul is impassible and pure.   The invisible should be seen by
means of the visible, and flesh and spirit are combined by a positive
act of God.   In *Or. cat.* Gregory considers whether mortality (not
death) is good, and concludes that the miseries of mortal life are
curative, God's treatment and cure for sin.   Death is itself an effect
of sin, signified by the coats of skin (Gen 3,21) which God put on
Adam and Eve: they are animal skins, representing the corruptibility

---

67   *Vita Macrinae*, 22.   Cfr P. Maraval, Grégoire de Nysse. *Vie de
     sainte Macrine*, SC 178, 1971, 212-214.

68   Ibid., 24, ed. Maraval, 218.

69   Ibid., 25, ed. Maraval, 226 y 228.

which clothes the immortal soul.   God is thus acquitted of creating
evil (cf. Hom. I GNO V, 284,14-16).   The paradisal state was
blissful, in communion with God and heavenly things (Hom. 6 386,9-15);
the present sorrow is good as the mother of future joys (386,2-4).

Death and life are a pair of opposites, and incompatible.   Death
is simply the negation of life (cf Hom. 8 402,22-403,4).

The death of the wise and that of the fool appear to be alike.
But Gregory argues in detail in Hom. 5 that this is only apparent, and
that a correct understanding of immortality sees it as transcending
bodily death (see 361,10-13; 365,7-13).

The 'moment for giving birth, and moment for dying' are likewise
spiritual, since physical birth and death are involuntary (379,19-20).
We freely choose to be born spiritually in virtue, in contrast with the
untimely birth of sinfulness (380,1-5).   Closely connected with this is
the 'timely death', εὔκαιρος θάνατος, which is a (presumably baptismal)
death to sin (381,13-17), chosen in love.   Paul was ready for death
at all times (381,1-12); timely death generates true life.

Birth and death, γένεσις and φθορά, are symbolized not only by
the coats of skins, but by the sequence of Moses' first 2 books,
Genesis ('birth') and Exodus ('death').   Birth and death belong
together, both physically, since all that is born also dies, and
spiritually, since good death and new birth go together; so, with
baptismal allusion, in 381,17-20, and implying conformity to Christ
himself (380,1-10).

The deaths of Macrina and Moses in Gregory's other writings
amply illustrate his understanding of 'timely death', especially that of
Moses who dies on the mountain-top, the pinnacle of virtue.

13

Zeit und Grenze. Zur Kritik des Gregor von Nyssa

an der Einseitigkeit der Naturphilosophie

Theo Kobusch

Gemäß dem Ziel eines Ecclesiastes-Kommentars das in einem ersten einführenden Abschnitt dargelegt wird, versucht Gregor von Nyssa in seiner Oratio 7, von der Welt der raumzeitlichen Gegenstände ausgehend, das Spezifische des Sittlichen und der metaphysischen Welt zu explizieren. Zunächst — und das ist Inhalt des zweiten Abschnitts — wird die Zeitlosigkeit des Sittlichen hervorgehoben. Die Dialektik von Finden und Suchen ist ein weiteres Merkmal der sittlich-metaphysischen gegenüber der physischen Welt. Schließlich — und das ist auch der Schluß der 7. Oratio — soll in einem vierten Abschnitt Gregors Kritik an der aristotelischen Vernunftkonzeption erläutert werden, die ebenfalls im Namen der Eigentümlichkeit der sittlich-metaphysischen Welt vorgebracht wird.

1. Der wissenschaftstheoretische Standort des Ecclesiasteskommentars

Will man ein Kapitel eines Ecclesiasteskommentars besonders behandeln, so muß zuvor der allgemeine Charakter eines solchen Kommentars gekennzeichnet oder, um es genauer zu sagen, der wissenschaftstheoretische Ort des Ecclesiasteskommentars klargemacht werden. Einen ersten Hinweis gibt schon die Einleitung der Gregor-Schrift selbst. Dort ist die Rede davon, daß der Geist durch die Gedanken der 'Sprüche' Salomons vorbereitet werde für das Erfassen der Schrift 'Ecclesiastes'. Diese Andeutung ist näher erläutert im Proömium und in der Oratio 1 des Canticum-Kommentars — schon bei

Origenes ist das der eigentliche Ort für wissenschaftstheoretische
Überlegungen.   Gregor begreift danach die Sprüche Salomons, den
Ecclesiastes und das Hohelied als Schriften, die zusammengehören und
zwar in dieser Ordnung und Reihenfolge.   Sie verkörpern die
Hauptdisziplinen der Philosophie, die in platonischem Sinne hierarchisch
geordnet sind als Stufen des 'Aufstiegs zum Volkommen'.[1]   Einzelne
Schriften des AT und später auch des NT können aber nur deswegen
als die christlichen Repräsentanten der philosophischen Disziplinen
gelten, weil der Inhalt der Hl. Schrift selbst auch als eine Form der
Philosophie verstanden wird.   Die Unterscheidung zwischen Philosophie
und Offenbarungstheologie ist dem patristischen Denken fremd und als
eine Entdeckung des 13. Jh. anzusehen.   Der Anspruch der christlichen
Autoren der ersten zwölf Jahrhunderte war demgegenüber, das
Christentum als die beste, als die 'wahre Philosophie' aufzuzeigen.[2]
Deswegen können in ihr auch einzelne philosophische Disziplinen
wiedererkannt werden nach der stoisch-aristotelischen Einteilung:
Ethik, Physik und Metaphysik/Logik.   Wie Origenes schon ausführt und
wie Gregor es andeutet, müssen nach diesem Modell die Sprüche
Salomons als die Ethik der christlichen Philosophie verstanden werden,
durch die die menschliche Seele von den Leidenschaften befreit und zu
einem tugendhaften Leben hingeführt wird.[3]   Das Ziel dieser
Entwicklung, die mit der ethischen Reinigung der Seele beginnt, ist die
Schau des wahrhaft Seienden,[4] die nach der mit Origenes beginnenden
Tradition im Hohelied thematisiert ist.   Gregor selbst nennt sie die
'mystische Theorie'.[5]   Das ist nicht eine Bezeichnung für einen
Zustand der Seele jenseits des Denkens, sondern ein traditioneller

---

1   Gregor v. Nyssa, Comm. in Cant. or.1, GNO VI, 17,7-11.

2   Zum Begriff der wahren Philosophie vgl. Gregor Nyss., De inst.
    Christ., GNO VIII 1, 48,13.

3   Vgl. Origenes, In Cant. ed. W.A. Baehrens GCS 5, 77-78. Gregor
    von Nyssa, a.a.O. GNO VI 1, 22,7; διὰ τῆς παροιμιώδους ἀγωγῆς
    ... εἰς τὴν τῶν ἀρετῶν ἐπιθυμίαν.

4   Zum Begriff des ὄντως ὄν im Sinne der göttlichen Realität bei
    Gregor vgl. bes. J. Daniélou, Theoria: L'être et le temps chez
    Grégoire de Nysse, Leiden 1970, 7f.

5   Vgl. Gregor v. Nyssa, GNO VI, 15,12; μέλλων ἅπτεσθαι τῆς ἐν τῷ
    Ἄισματι τῶν Ἀισμάτων μυστικῆς θεωρίας.

Ausdruck für die metaphysische Erkenntnis selbst, also für die höchste
Stufe des Denkens.[6]   Der Begriff des Mystischen oder auch der
mystischen Schau steht im Platonismus für die aristotelische Disziplin
der Metaphysik.   Clemens von Alexandrien und Origenes nennen sie
deswegen auch Epoptie.   Gregor verwendet diesen Begriff offenbar
nicht, spricht aber von der ἐποπτικὴ τῶν ὄντων φιλοσοφία[7].   Während
Ambrosius den griechischen Begriff des Mystischen beibehält, ist die
Rufinsche Übersetzung 'inspectiva' für ἐποπτικός später weitgehend
übernommen und so insbesondere durch Cassiodor und Alkuin dem
Mittelalter vermittelt worden.   Die disziplintheoretische Deutung des
Hoheliedes durch Origenes, die auch Gregor v. Nyssa übernimmt, hat
bis ins Hohe Mittelalter ihre Geltung behalten: Das Hohelied ist die
Metaphysik der Christlichen Philosophie.[8].   Zwischen den Proverbia und
dem Hohelied steht die Ecclesiastesschrift.   Gregor kennzeichnet ihren
Inhalt als die Erkenntnis der sichtbaren Welt, die die Seele zur
Erkenntnis des Unsichtbaren hinführt.[9]   Die sichtbare Welt als solche
zu erkennen bedeutet aber, sie in ihrer Bewegung, d.h. in ihrer

---

6   Zur Forschungstradition, die die 'Mystik' Gregors in Sinne einer
     überrationalen Gottesschau mißverstanden hat, und zur Kritik
     daran vgl. M.-B. von Stritzky, Zum Problem der Erkenntnis bei
     Gregor von Nyssa, Münster 1973, 67ff.

7   Zur Geschichte des Begriffs Epoptie vgl. P. Hadot, Epopteia:
     HWPh Bd. 2, hg. Ritter, Basel/Stuttgart 1972, 599 und vom Verf.
     Metaphysik: HWPh Bd. 5, 1197 ff.   Nach Gregor ist die Epoptie
     die eigentlich Gott zukommende Tätigkeit (vgl. C. Eun. I 397,8; II
     292,23; De sancta Trin. GNO III/1, 14,6; Quod non sint tres dei
     GNO III, 1, 44,10; ebd. 49,5; 50,1,13; In Inscr. Ps. I,6 GNO V
     40,20).   Nur an wenigen Stellen (vgl. In Inscr. Ps. I,6 GNO V
     41,15 und De anima et res. PG 45,57a) wird ἐποπτικός als
     Prädikat des Auges der menschlichen Seele gebraucht, so daß
     später (In Inscr. Ps. 76,1) von der Metaphysik als der Disziplin
     gesprochen werden kann, die das wahre Wesen 'des Seienden'
     erfassen kann.   Schließlich charakterisiert sie Gregor, De anima
     et res. PG 45,57A als die der Seele eigene und von Natur
     zukommende Kraft, durch die sie Abbild Gottes ist.

8   Vgl. dazu bes. S. Leanza, La classificazione dei libri salomonici e
     i suoi riflessi sulla questione dei rapporti tra Bibbia e scienze
     profane, da Origene agli scrittori medioevali: Aug. 14 (1974)
     651-666, und vom Verf., Origenes, der Initiator der christlichen
     Philosophie: Fschr. für H.J. Vogt, erscheint: Bonn 1993, sowie
     der in Anm. 37 genannte Aufsatz.

9   Gregor v. Nyssa, In Eccl. or. 1, 284,22-285,2.

Veränderbarkeit zu erfassen. Deswegen thematisiert der Ecclesiastes
eigentlich das Entstehen und Vergehen alles Sichtbaren. Man kann
mithin sagen, daß der Ecclesiasteskommentar als die 'Physik' im
aristotelischen Sinne — deren Gegenstand ja auch das Seiende ist,
insofern es sich bewegt — verstanden wird, genauer: als die Physik der
christlichen Philosophie. Allerdings ist sie keine rein theoretische
Wissenschaft wie bei Aristoteles, sondern erfüllt auch eine praktische
Funktion. Denn der Ecclesiasteskommentar hat nicht das Sichver-
ändernde der Naturdinge als solches allein zum Gegenstand, sondern
fragt nach der Wirkung auf die menschliche Seele. Was der Seele
eigentlich widerfährt, wenn sie sich dem Vergänglichen hingibt, und was
unveränderlich bleibt in der Welt des Veränderbaren, das ist das
eigentlich Thema dieser Schrift. Deswegen geht es in ihr nicht nur um
die Phänomene als solche, sondern genauer um das Verhältnis des
Menschen zu dieser sichtbaren, veränderlichen Welt. Auch ihr Ziel ist
— wie das der Ethik — propädeutischer Natur: sie reinigt die Seele von
der Beziehung zum Vergänglichen, damit sie dann durch die
metaphysische Erkenntnis des Hoheliedes in die göttlichen Geheimnisse
eindringen kann.[10]

2. Das Physische und das Sittliche

Nachdem die ersten vier Orationes die Lüge, Eitelkeit und Nichtigkeit
all dessen, was unter der Sonne ist, in verschiedener Weise betrachtet
und so - wie es am Anfang der fünften Oratio heißt - die menschliche
Seele von der Begierde nach den nichtigen Dingen befreit haben, indem
sie gleichsam eine Last von den Schultern abschüttelten, beginnt mit
der fünften Oratio die 'Mystagogie' zu den höheren Lehrgegenständen,
d.h. die positive Entfaltung der Wahrheit der Sache. Diese orientiert
sich in ihrem ersten Teil (390,1-400,9) an den Versen des
Ecclesiastes: 'Das Steinewerfen hat seine Zeit. Und das Steine-
sammeln hat seine Zeit' (3,5). Gregor interpretiert diese Verse des

10 Vgl. Gregor v. Nyssa, In Cant. or. 1, GNO VI 22,10: καὶ
διαβαλὼν ἐν τούτῳ τῷ λόγῳ τὴν περὶ τὰ φαινόμενα τῶν ἀνθρώπων
σχέσιν. ... ebd, 15: καὶ οὕτως ἐκκαθάρας τὴν καρδίαν τῆς περὶ τὰ
φαινόμενα σχέσεως ...

Ecclesiastes vor dem Hintergrund der in der 6. Oratio ausführlich dargelegten und in Oratio 7 wiederholten (390,7) These, daß das zeitliche Maß und die Rechtzeitigkeit Kriterien der Güte eines Seienden dieser Welt sind. Gregors Ziel ist es aber zu zeigen, daß die vollendete Gutheit, Gott selbst, von ganz anderer Art als das innerweltlich Seiende ist und deswegen auch nicht diesen Kriterien unterliegt. In diesem Sinne heißt es 407,1: Gott ist die παντελὴς ἀρετή, außerhalb derer das Böse ist. Im Hinblick auf den Begriff des Guten bzw. der Tugend muß man nach Gregor zwischen dem göttlichen und dem menschlichen Bereich unterscheiden. Die einfache, unveränderbare, eingestaltige göttliche Natur, die ganz unempfänglich ist für die Gemeinschaft mit dem Bösen, verharrt immer ohne Grenze im Guten. Das menschlich Gute dagegen, das immer in und aufgrund der Willensentscheidung ist, die auch zum Gegenteil tendieren kann, hat als seine einzige Grenze das Böse.[11] Im selben Sinne erklärt Gregor in De vita Moysis (GNO VII,1,4), daß es außer dem Bösen keine 'Grenze der sittlichen Gutheit gibt'; deswegen heißt Gott die παντελὴς ἀρετή, die ein völlig Unbegrenztes und Unendliches ist. Umgekehrt bedeutet das aber auch, daß all das, was unter dem Aspekt und dem Kriterium des Maßes, der Grenze, der zeitlichen Bestimmtheit usw. betrachtet werden kann, nichts mit dem sittlich Guten zu tun haben kann. Ἐδείχθη γὰρ ὅτι τὸ διαλαμβανόμενον πέρασιν ἀρετὴ οὐκ ἔστι (De v. Moys. 4,1f.).

Aber nicht nur Gott als die vollendete Gestalt sittlicher Gutheit ist so der Welt des Raumzeitlichen enthoben, sondern auch der Bereich des Menschlich-Sittlichen. Gregor drückt das in der 7. Oratio des Ecclesiastes-Kommentars durch die Frage aus: 'Was hat die zeitliche Ausdehnung mit dem aufgrund unseres Willens Ausgeführten zu tun?' (392,13f.) Das, was heute als widergesetzlich und sittlich schlecht beurteilt wird — ob es nun Mord, Ehebruch oder Diebstahl ist —, kann nicht morgen als sittlich gut angesehen werden. Das Sittliche überhaupt, die Norm des Guten und Bösen selbst, ist somit dem zeitlichen Wandel nicht unterworfen. Deswegen müssen solche

---

11   Vgl. Gregor v. Nyssa, In Cant.or.5, GNO VI, 158. Ähnlich auch Contra Eun. I 168, GNO I, 77,7 ff.

Geschichten wie die im Buch Numeri überlieferte von der Sabbat-
schändung eines Mannes vor dem Hintergrund dieser philosophischen
Überlegungen vom Wesen des Sittlichen verstanden werden.   Sowohl
diese Geschichte wie auch das Gebot der Sabbatruhe, bzw. der ἀπραξία
konnen gar nicht wörtlich gemeint sein, das heißt sie können gar nicht
auf den Bereich des Naturhaften bezogen sein, sonst ergäben sich
nach Gregor unerträgliche Absurditäten.   Deswegen muß vom Bereich
der φυσικὴ ἐνέργεια (393,17), die die Physik thematisiert, zum Bereich
des Ethischen aufgestiegen werden, um das Gesetz der ἀπραξία
verstehen zu können.   'Die unvernünftige Untätigkeit aber ist keine
Tugend' (395,2).   Gregor distanziert sich aus diesen Gründen von einer
die Ecclesiastesworte wie auch das Gebot von der Sabbatruhe wörtlich
verstehenden Tradition (390,13-391,14 und 395,16f.).   Nach dieser
Interpretationsrichtung werde mit den Ecclesiastesworten auf bestimmte
mosaische Sätze angespielt, die bei Zuwiderhandlung die Strafe der
Steinigung nach sich ziehen.   Wen Gregor damit genau meint, ist
schwer zu sagen.   Vielleicht handelt es sich um Gegner der Lehre vom
geistigen Sinn der Schriftworte, wie das von der antiochenischen
Schule bekannt ist.   Aber auch Apollinaris von Laodizea hat nach dem
Zeugnis des Didymus — genau wie bestimmte Stoiker und Porphyrios —
die allegorische Methode der Bibelinterpretation abgelehnt.[12]
Wahrscheinlich aber ist, daß sich Gregor von solchen Interpreten
distanziert, die von Hause aus als Origenisten Sensibilität für den
tieferen Sinn der Schriftworte haben, in diesem Falle ihn aber nicht
erkennen konnten.   Didymos der Blinde z.B. hat den Ecclesiastesvers im
wörtlichen Sinne verstanden und als Ankündigung der Strafe der
Steinigung für den, der gewisser verbotener Taten überführt ist,
gedeutet.[13]   Nach Gregor ist das aber unmöglich, da so von einer
Bewegung des Geistes, genauer des sittlichen Geistes die der zweite
Teil des Satzes, der vom Sammeln der Steine spricht, keinen Sinn hat.
Er erhält nur dann einen Sinn, wenn vorausgesetzt wird, daß Rede ist.

---

12 Vgl. Didymos der Blinde, Kommentar zum Ecclesiastes Teil III,
    Komm. zu Eccl. Kap. 5 u. 6, hg., übers. u. erl. v. J. Kramer,
    Bonn 1970, 20f. u. 88f.

13 Didymos der Blinde, Kommentar zum Ecclesiastes, Teil II, hg. u.
    übers. v. M. Gronewald, Bonn 1977, 46 f.

Damit kommt wiederum die grundlegende, von Origenes erstmals massiv vorgebrachte Unterscheidung zwischen dem natürlichen Sein, das Raum und Zeit unterworfen ist, und dem Sittlichen zur Geltung.[14] Denn während die Begriffe des Werfens und Haltens bezogen auf den Bereich der Natur sich schlechterdings widersprechen, ist im Bereich des Moralischen ein 'Wurf' denkbar — z.B. ein Tugend wie der Gerechtigkeit gegen den Feind, die Ungerechtigkeit —, der sich durch die 'Bewahrung' im Busen des Menschen vollzieht (397,4ff.). Diese, wie auch die dann (399,20ff.) folgende Zurückführung bestimmter Begriffe auf den Bereich des Moralischen geht von der These aus, daß das Gute und das Schlechte im eigentlichen Sinne moralischer Art sind. Dies ist eine ursprünglich stoische These, die Origenes selbst uns überliefert hat: καὶ οἱ ἐπιτυγχάνοντές γε αὐτῶν τὰ μὲν ἀγαθὰ καὶ κακὰ τίθενται ἐν τῇ προαιρέσει μόνῃ (C. Cels. IV,45).

Der stoische Hintergrund ist auch in dem Begriffspaar οἰκείωσις-ἀλλοτρίωσις erkennbar, durch welches das Sich-Ausschließende und Disjunktive von Gut und Böse im Bereich des Willensmäßigen am deutlichsten ausgedrückt wird. Derjenige, der sich die Tugend zu eigen macht, vollzieht notwendig den Akt der 'Entfremdung' gegenüber der Schlechtigkeit (399,9ff.), und umgekehrt ist jedes Fremdwerden gegenüber der Tugend eine Annäherung an das Böse.[15]

3. Suchen und Finden

Das Grundthema der Oratio 7 — die wesentliche Verschiedenheit des Bereichs der Dinge dieser Welt und des Moralischen (τὰ ἐκ προαιρέσεως) — kommt auch bei der Interpretation des Verses 'Es gibt

---

14 Vgl. dazu meinen Aufsatz: Die philosophische Bedeutung des Kirchenvaters Origenes: Theol. Quartalschrift 165 (1985) 94-105.

15 Zu den stoischen Termini vgl. bes. SVF III 178, III 229a. Ähnlich auch Philo v. Alexandrien, De post. Caini 135: ἡ πρὸς τὸ γενητὸν ἀλλοτρίωσις πρὸς θεὸν οἰκείωσιν εἰργάσατο,... Zu Gregor vgl. In Cant. or. 1, GNO VI, 28,23 und bes. Contra fatum ed. J.A. McDonough, GNO III/2, Leiden 1987, 44,21: ἡ γὰρ τοῦ ἀγαθοῦ ἀλλοτρίωσις τὴν πρὸς τὸ κακὸν οἰκειότητα σαφῶς ἐπιδείκνυσιν. Zu ähnlichen Begriffskombinationen vgl. In Cant. 60,5; 395,19. Vgl. dazu J. Stelzenberger, Die Beziehungen der frühchristlichen

eine Zeit zu suchen, und es gibt eine Zeit zu verlieren' (400,10 ff.)
zum Ausdruck. Denn nach dem tieferen Sinn dieser Worte geht es um
eine besondere Art der Suche, um eine Suche, die nicht durch ein
Finden am Ende abgeschlossen wird. Gregor sagt wörtlich, es sei ein
Suchen, 'dessen Finden das ständige Suchen selbst ist. Denn es ist
nicht eine Sache zu suchen und eine andere zu finden, sondern der
sich aus dem Suchen ergebende Gewinn ist das Suchen selbst (400,21-
401,2). Ein solcher Satz ist nur verstehbar vor dem Hintergrund des
Gregorschen Gottesbegriffs, wie er beispielhaft im Hoheliedkommentar
entwickelt wurde. Ebenda werden auch die Begriffe des 'Suchens' und
'Findens' im philosophischen Sinne gebraucht. Das göttliche Sein ist
nach Gregors Konzeption in dem Sinne 'unbegrenzt', daß 'das jeweilig
Erfaßte zwar in jedem Fall größer ist als das zuvor Begriffene, es
gibt jedoch dem Gesuchten in sich keine Grenze, sondern die Grenze
des Gefundenen wird denjenigen, die aufsteigen, zum Anfang für die
Auffindung des Oberen'.[16] Das Finden besteht also in der Entdeckung
des weiter zu Suchenden. Die Suche ist weder ein orientierungsloses
Herumirren, das noch nichts gefunden hätte, noch ein Streben nach
einem Bestimmten, das durch das Finden zum Stillstand käme. Gregor
hat deswegen das 'Stehenbleiben' als den Gegenbegriff zum Suchen
festgelegt, um anzudeuten, daß das Suchen als Annäherung an die
göttliche Wesenheit nicht dinghaft gedacht werden kann.[17] Während im
Canticum-Kommentar und an den meisten Stellen sonst diese das
göttliche Wesen bestimmende Grenzenlosigkeit und das dadurch bedingte
unaufhörliche Sichausstrecken der Seele in erkenntnistheoretischem
Sinne als unaufhörliche Schau erläutert wird, zeigt die Schrift 'De vita
Moysis' — die unserer 7. Oratio in besonderem Maße nahesteht — den
Zusammenhang auf, der zwischen dem ständigen Weitersuchen der
menschlichen Seele und Gott als moralischem Wesen (παντελὴς ἀρετή)
besteht. Die Vollkommenheit im Bereich des Moralischen darf nach

---

Sittenlehre zur Ethik der Stoa, ND der Ausgabe München 1933,
Hildesheim/Zürich/New York 1989, 332.

16 Vgl. Gregor v. Nyssa, In Cant. or. 8, GNO VI, 247,9ff.

17 Ebd. GNO VI, 352,15: ... οὐ τὸ στῆναι περὶ τὸ κατειλημμένον ἀλλὰ
τὸ ἀεὶ ζητοῦντα τὸ πλεῖον τοῦ καταληφθέντος μὴ ἵστασθαι. Vgl.
Langerbecks Anmerkung zu or. VI, GNO VI, 180,3!

Gregor nicht nach dem Modell der Naturdinge gedacht werden. Alles sinnfällige, quantitativ bestimmbare Sein hat bestimmte eigene Grenzen, die wir als Anfang und Ende bezeichnen können. Von einem bestimmten Punkt anzufangen und bei einem Bestimmten aufzuhören, macht die Vollkommenheit einer endlichen Sache aus. Ganz anders die Vollkommenheit im Bereich des Moralischen (ἐπὶ δὲ τῆς ἀρετῆς): hier bedeutet, an eine Grenze zu kommen und stillzustehen schon Unvollkommenheit. Denn 'alles Gute hat von seiner Natur her keine Grenze, wird aber durch die Gegenüberstellung des konträren Gegenteils begrenzt, wie das Leben durch den Tod und das Licht durch die Finsternis'.[18] Wie das eine nur sein kann, wenn das andere verschwunden ist, so 'ist es auch bei der uns vorliegenden Philosophie nicht möglich, etwas von den hohen Gegenständen zu erwerben, wenn man nicht das Interesse am Irdischen und Niedrigen verloren hat' (403,4ff.). Hier kommt das dialektische Verhältnis von Gewinn und Verlust im Bereich des Moralischen zum Ausdruck: Derjenige, der die Güter dieser Welt verloren und auf den Erwerb derselben verzichtet hat, ist nicht ärmer geworden, sondern reicher, denn 'der Mangel und Verlust dieser Dinge bedeutet die Existenz oder den Besitz des Erhofften' (403,14). Ein solcher hat gefunden, nicht obwohl er etwas verloren hat, sondern weil er etwas verloren hat.

4. Kritik an Aristoteles

Der letze Teil der Oratio 7 vollendet die Gegenüberstellung zwischen dem endlichen vergänglichen Sein und dem eigentlichen Gegenstand des menschlichen Suchens. Gregor entfaltet diesen Vergleich in einer besonderen Seinslehre (406,1: εἰς μείζονά τινα τὴν περὶ τῶν ὄντων φιλοσοφίαν). Inhalt dieser Seinslehre ist neben dem stoischen Gedanken von dem Zusammenhang aller Dinge[19] vor allem die theistische

---

18 Gregor v. Nyssa, De vita Moysis, GNO VII 1, ed. H. Musurillo, Leiden 1964, 3,6 ff.

19 J. Daniélou, Conspiration: L'être et le temps ... 63, spricht im Hinblick auf den stoischen Begriff der σύμπνοια in der 7. Oratio von einer 'transposition que lui-même opère de l'usage physique du mot à l'usage métaphysique'.

Idee des wirklich Seienden, das Gregor auch die Gutheit selbst nennt,[20] das alles zusammenhält und alles, was geworden ist, im Sein erhält. Alles vom wahrhaft Seienden im Sein Gehaltene ist mithin ein Seiendes und, da dieses wahrhaft Seiende zugleich die Gutheit selbst ist, auch ein Gutes. Nun aber gibt es auch das Schlechte bzw. das Böse. Was soll dieses 'es gibt' besagen? Was ist die Seinsweise des Bösen? Zunächst muß festgehalten werden, daß Gregor das Schlechte nur in der Form des moralisch Schlechten, d.h. des Bösen, meint. Das besagt der Satz: κακὸν γὰρ ἔξω προαιρέσεως ἐφ'ἑαυτοῦ κείμενον οὐκ ἔστιν (407,14f.).[21] Das Schlechte ist also nur als Gewolltes, und zwar als durch den menschlichen Willen Gewolltes. Mithin kann es selbst überhaupt nur so lange sein, als der Mensch es will, d.h. als der Mensch sich vom Guten abgewandt hat (407,10). Dem Schlechten als dem Bösen kommt deswegen nach Gregor die Seinsweise des Nicht-seins (ἀνυπαρξία 406,16; 407,9) zu, d.h. es ist nicht überhaupt nicht, sondern es ist nur als Abfall vom Guten.[22] Nun ist diese Lehre vom Schlechten im Sinne der privatio boni schon sehr alt. Aristoteles, der Mittelplatonismus und der Neuplatonismus haben sie vertreten, und viele von diesen Schulen Abhängige haben sie rezipiert. Doch man muß bei aller Ähnlichkeit zu diesen Vorstellungen der griechischen Metaphysik auch den besonderen Akzent des Gregor-Texte hervorheben. Das Schlechte ist nicht irgendein naturhaft bedingter Mangel an Gutem, sondern ist überhaupt nur in der Form des Bösen als ein Abweichen des menschlichen Willens von dem Guten, als dem eigentlich Gewollten. Es ist das αὐτεξούσιον, der freie Impuls, durch den der Mensch vom Guten abfällt. Deswegen ist das αὐτεξούσιον nicht als solches

---

20 Zu den platonisierenden αὐτό-Bildungen bei Gregor vgl. schon Origenes, In Matth. XIV, 7, GCS 10, hg. E. Klostermann, Leipzig 1935, 289,17: καὶ ὥσπερ αὐτός ἐστιν ἡ αὐτοσοφία καὶ ἡ αὐτο-δικαιοσύνη καὶ ἡ αὐτοαλήθεια.

21 Vgl. auch Gregor v. Nyssa, De anima et res. PG 45,101A

22 Wie hier das Böse als ein Produkt des vom wahren Sein abfallen-den menschlichen Willens ein Nichtseiendes genannt wird, so stellt Gregor in Ref. 29, GNO II, 323,9 ff. auch dem ὄντως ὄν die Phantasieprodukte der menschlichen Vernunft als μὴ ὄντα gegenüber. Zu dieser Problematik vgl. vom Verf., Sein und Sprache. Historische Grundlegung einer Ontologie der Sprache, Leiden 1987, 52ff.

schlecht, sondern vielmehr das, wodurch nach Gregor der Mensch 'gottgleich' ist.[23]   Das Schlechte ist also nur als Böses.   Just das entspricht wiederum der stoischen Lehre.[24]   Alles, was der gemeine Verstand sonst noch 'schlecht' nennt — Leid, Schmerzen, Unglück —, hängt nach Gregor mit diesem moralisch Schlechten zusammen, denn 'jeder wird sich selbst zum Urheber der   Schläge durch den eigenen Willen'.   Deswegen 'dürfte es wohl klar sein, daß keines der Übel getrennt von unserem Willen bestehen kann'.[25]

Der Mensch ist also Demiurg des Bösen, aber nicht des Guten, denn das absolut Gute ist unabhängig von seinem Wollen.   Gleichwohl ist die Prohairesis nach Gregor das das menschliche Sein schlechthin determinierende Element.   Durch seinen Willen macht sich der Mensch zu dem, was er ist.   'Nicht von oben stellt irgendeine zwingende Macht den einen ins Dunkle, den anderen ins Licht, sondern wir haben von Hause aus in unserer Natur und in unserem Willen die Ursachen des Lichtes und des Dunkeln,' je nach dem, was wir sein wollen.   Deswegen kann Gregor sagen: Wir Menschen sind 'in gewisser Weise die Väter unserer selbst, die sich selbst, so   wie sie wollen, hervorbringen und aufgrund des eigenen Willens' sich im Sinne der Tugend oder der Schlechtigkeit bilden können.[26]   Gut im Sinne der Tugend wird der Mensch aber, indem er sich an das wirklich Seiende 'bindet' und in diesem Immerseienden bleibt.   Die Bindung an das wirklich Seiende ist das für den Menschen Gute.[27]

---

23   Vgl. De mortuis, ed. G. Heil, GNO IX, 54,10: ἰσόθεον γάρ ἐστι τὸ αὐτεξούσιον.

24   Vgl. das Origenes-Zitat o. S. 313.   J. Daniélou, Aveuglement: L'être et le temps ... 136-138 hat zwar mit Recht auf mehrere einschlägige Parallelstellen bei Gregor hingewiesen, die die Theorie vom Schlechten im Sinne des Bösen als durchgehende Lehre belegen, aber offenbar den stoischen Hintergrund dieser These nicht erkannt.

25   De vita Moysis, GNO VII 1, 59,3 und 59,24.

26   Vgl. ebd. in der Reihenfolge der Zitate, 56,23ff. und 34,11ff.

27   In Eccl. GNO V, 408,2; Ἐμοὶ γάρ, φησί, τὸ προσκολλᾶσθαι τῷ θεῷ ἀγαθόν ἐστι ... Zur προσκόλλησις vgl. 407,15 und 411,1.

Dieses Gute, an das sich der Mensch bindet, ist von allem
sonstigen Seienden grundlegend unterschieden. Gregor hat deswegen
(412,14ff.) dieses Gute selbst allem geschaffenen Sein
gegenübergestellt und die Möglichkeit unserer endlichen Vernunft, zu
diesem Guten 'aufzusteigen', in Zweifel gezogen. Denn alles
Geschaffene, das objektiv gegeben ist, ist dadurch gekennzeichnet, daß
jedes einzelne seine eigene Grenze hat, über die es nicht hinausgehen
kann, solange es ist, was es ist. Die Gregorsche Bestimmung des
menschlichen Seins als eines Wesens, das auf der 'Grenzscheide'
(μεθόριον) steht zwischen Tugend und Schlechtigkeit, widerspricht dem
nicht. Denn indem der Mensch sich selbst zu einem guten oder
schlechten Leben bestimmt, bleibt er doch innerhalb der Grenzen der
menschlichen Natur und wird — dem Wesen nach — weder zu einem Tier
noch zum Engel.[28] Dasselbe gilt auch für den subjektiven Bereich:
Die einzelnen Sinnesvermögen können nur die ihnen je eigenen
Tätigkeiten vollziehen; und auch die intellektuelle Vernunft (καταληπτικὴ
θεωρία) kann nicht außerhalb ihrer selbst treten, sondern bleibt — wie
alles Geschaffene — in sich selbst (ἐν ἑαυτῇ μένει 412,8). Das liegt
nach Gregor darin begründet, daß in allem, was die menschliche
Vernunft erfaßt, der Aspekt der zeitlichen Ausdehnung miterfaßt
wird.[29] Welche Art der Vernunft Gregor bei seiner kritischen Analyse
im Auge hat, wird klar, wenn man auf die Formulierung 412,18-413,5
achtet. Dort wird sie als eine diskursiv erkennende Denkkraft
gekennzeichnet, die, zeitlich bedingt, mit Hilfe der analytischen Methode
vom jeweils Gegebenen zu den Voraussetzungen dieses Gegebenen
aufsteigt. Gregor bezeichnet diese so vorgehende Vernunft als die
'Neugier' und verwendet dabei den Begriff (πολυπραγμοσύνη), der schon

---

28   Vgl. C. Eunom. III 1, GNO II, 43,19; zum Begriff μεθόριος ebd.
     45,2 und bes J. Daniélou, Frontière: L'être et les temps ... 116-
     132. Was die Möglichkeit der Überschreitung der Grenzen in der
     Ordnung der Geister angeht, so scheint sich Gregor (vgl. In Cant.
     or. 15, GNO VI, 446) von Origenes distanziert zu haben.
     Andererseits jedoch scheint es nach C. Eunom. III, 2, GNO II,
     65,1 ff. so zu sein, als bestimme die Prohairesis die jeweilige
     'Natur' — das entspricht genau der origeneischen Lehre. Vgl.
     dazu meinen o.g. Aufsatz.

29   Zur χρονικὴ παράτασις als Signum alles Geschaffenen vgl. auch C.
     Eunom. III,7, GNO II, 225,14 ff.

bei Plotin für das aristotelisch verstandene syllogistische Denken

steht.[30] Gregors Kritik an diesem aristotelischen Begriff des

Denkens läuft darauf hinaus, daß in der Weise der analytischen

Methode zwar alles jeweils Erkannte, aber niemals der Zeitbegriff

selbst beiseite gelassen werden könne,[31] so daß eine 'Ekstase' (ἔξω

ἑαυτὴν στήσειε) im Sinne des Heraustretens aus der Zeitlichkeit, und

damit die einzige Weise, die ἀδιάστατος φύσις erfahren zu können,

unmöglich ist.[32] Die menschliche Natur ist ja durch die Möglichkeit

der Ekstase sowohl von der der endlichen Dinge wie auch der

göttlichen Natur unterschieden.[33] Indem die aristotelisch bestimmte

Vernunfttradition diese Zeitabhängigkeit meist mißachtete, schrieb sie

der menschlichen Vernunft Fähigkeiten zu, die ihr nicht zukommen

können. Deswegen muß nach Gregor auf die zeitliche Bedingtheit und

damit auf die Begrenztheit der menschlichen Vernunft hingewiesen

werden. Da sie selbst begrenzt ist, kann sie auch nur Begrenztes,

Gemessenes, d.h. Endliches erfassen. Das Wesen des unendlichen

---

30 Vgl. dazu meinen Aufsatz Name und Sein. Zu den sprachphiloso-
    phischen Grundlagen in der Schrift Contra Eunomium des Gregor
    von Nyssa: El 'Contra Eunomium I' en la Produccion literaria de
    Gregorio de Nisa (VI Coloquio Internacional sobre Gregorio de
    Nysa) ed. L.F. Mateo-Seco u. J.L. Bastero, Pamplona 1988, 260-
    261. Aus In Cant. or. 11, GNO VI, 334,18 geht hervor, daß sich
    die πολυπραγμοσύνη immer nur — wie in der 7. Oratio des Ecclesi-
    asteskommentars 415,19 — auf das Erfassen der vielfältigen
    Tätigkeiten und Wirkungen des göttlichen Wesens, nicht aber auf
    dieses selbst bezieht. Zu dieser wichtigen Unterscheidung und zur
    diesbezüglichen Kritik an der Arbeit von E. Mühlenberg, Die
    Unendlichkeit Gottes bei Gregor v. Nyssa (1966), vgl. bes. B. Otis,
    Gregory of Nyssa and the Cappadocian conception of time:
    StPatr XIV (1976) 340.

31 Zu παραδραμεῖν (413,2,3) vgl. auch In Cant. or. 6, GNO VI, 183,6;
    or.XII, GNO VI, 357,5. Zum aristotelischen Hintergrund vgl. die
    Anm. 43 meiner in Anm. 30 genannten Abhandlung.

32 Zur Kritik Gregors am traditionellen Ekstase-Begriff und seinem
    eigenen Verständnis vgl. bes. M.-B. von Stritzky, a.a.O. 97 ff.

33 Von der göttlichen Natur heißt es In Cant. or. 5, GNO VI, 158,9:
    οὐδέποτε ἑαυτῆς ἐξισταμένη. Demgegenüber ist es das Proprium
    der menschlichen Natur, über sich hinauszuwachsen; vgl. ebd.
    174,2 ff.; In Inscr. Ps. I,7, GNO V, 43,15 f.; De vita Moys. II,
    GNO VII 1, 139,8. Zum Begriff der Ekstase in diesem Sinne In
    Cant. 309,5 ff.; 156,19.

Göttlichen übersteigt aus diesem Grund die Grenzen der menschlichen Vernunft.[34]

Was die menschliche Seele erlebt, wenn sie auf der Suche nach dem Zeit- und Raumlosen über das hinausgeht, was ihren zeitgebundenen Gedanken zugänglich ist, das hat Gregor in einem eindrucksvollen Bild dargestellt: Wie ein auf einem glatten, steil abfallenden Felsen sitzender Mensch, der mit der Fußspitze das Wasser berührt, keinen Halt für den Fuß und keine Angriffsfläche für die Hand finden kann, so ergeht es auch der sich über ihre Grenzen hinaus vorwagenden Seele. Sie hat nichts — keinen Ort, keine Zeit, kein Maß — was sie als geistigen Stützpunkt zur Erkenntnis der göttlichen Natur benutzen könnte.[35] Die maßlosen Ansprüche der aristotelisch verstandenen diskursiven Vernunft, die so auch den letzten Grund alles Seienden erfassen zu können glaubte, sind aus diesen Gründen nach Gregor zurückzuweisen. Gregors Kritik am Vernunftbegriff der Aristoteliker erscheint so als die früe Konzeption einer kritischen Philosophie im modernen Sinne. Jedenfalls entspricht Gregors Satz am Ende der 7. Oratio (415,22): ἐν δὲ τοῖς ὑπερέκεινα μὴ ἐφιέναι τῇ κτίσει τοὺς ἰδίους ὅρους ἐκβαίνειν, ... ('Im Bereich des Transzendenten es aber nicht der geschaffenen Vernunft zuzulassen, die eigenen Grenzen zu übersteigen')[36] dem Programm einer kritischen Philosophie, wie sie uns schon bei Plotin begegnet[37]. Zugleich muß man sehen, das Gregor durch einem solchen Satz, der schon 411,19 durch die Bemerkung

---

34   Vgl. In Cant. or. 1, GNO II, 29,2: ... τὴν σοφίαν ἐκείνην τὴν ὑπερβαίνουσαν τοὺς ὅρους τῆς ἀνθρωπίνης σοφίας.

35   Vgl. In Eccl. 413,5–414. Zur Argumentation vgl. auch In Cant. or. 12, GNO VI, 357,10 ff. Ein ähnliches Bild verwendet Gregor in De beat. VI, PG 44, 1264B. Vergleichbar für den Bereich der Praxis ist auch das Bild der im Sand Gehenden, die ohne festen Halt nicht vorwärts kommen: De vita Moys. GNO VII 1, 118,13ff.

36   Vgl. auch C. Eun. II 96, GNO II, 254,27: ... τοῖς ἰδίοις ὅροις δι' ἡσυχίας ἐμμένωμεν.

37   Vgl. dazu vom Verf., Metaphysik als Einswerdung. Zu Plotins Begründung einer neuen Metaphysik: Transzendenz. Zu einem Grund-wort der klassischen Metaphysik (Fschr. Klaus Kremer zum 65. Geb.), hg. v. L. Honnefelder/W. Schüßler, Paderborn 1992, 93–114.

vorbereitet worden war: ἀλλ' ἐν τοῖς ἰδίοις ἕκαστον μένον ὅροις τῆς φύσεως ἕως τότε ἔστιν, ἕως ἂν ἐντὸς τῶν ἰδίων ὅρων μένῃ eine ganz bestimmte Position innerhalb der Entwicklung der christlich-neuplatonischen Philosophie einnimmt.   Origenes hatte in dieser Hinsicht eine revolutionäre Neuerung eingeführt durch seine These von der Priorität des Willens vor dem Wesen bzw. der 'Natur'.   Die Art des Wollens wird nicht von irgendwelchen engen Grenzen eines Wesens bestimmt, sondern es ist umgekehrt der Wille, der diese Wesenheit erst festsetzt.   Während diese hier nicht darzulegende Theorie des Origenes im christlichen Denken breit aufgenommen wurde, stieß sie im nichtchristlichen Neuplatonismus auf Ablehnung.   So berichtet z.B. Jamblich von einer bestimmten Lehrmeinung, nach der die menschliche Seele von sämtlichen 'oberen Gattungen' getrennt sei, indem ihr 'eine ihr eigene Grenze ihres Wesens' verliehen wurde.[38]   Nach Jamblich selbst ist das 'Geschlecht' der Götter durch Identität und Invarianz gekennzeichnet, so daß es auf immer gleiche Weise durch 'eine Grenze' (ἑνὶ ὅρῳ) zusammengehalten wird, innerhalb derer es immer 'bleibt' (μένει) und die es 'niemals verläßt' (οὐδέποτε ἐξίσταται).[39]   Und bei Hierokles, dem Neuplatoniker, wird es als die höchste Stufe der Tugend bezeichnet, τοῖς τῆς δημιουργίας ὅροις ἐμμένειν οἷς πάντα κατ' εἶδος διακέκριται.   Wie man sieht, entspricht Gregors Mahnung, daß das Geschaffene die eigenen Grenzen nicht überschreiten solle, ganz den Vorstellungen dieser neuplatonischen Tradition.   Wenn es bei Gregor also öfter, z.B. auch im Ecclesiastes-Kommentar heißt, daß wir gewissermaßen die Väter unserer selbst sind, indem wir uns durch unseren Willen zu dem machen, was wir sind,[40] dann muß derartiges immer unter der Voraussetzung fester, unüberschreitbarer ontologischer Grenzen verstanden werden.[41]   Andererseits jedoch gibt Gregor diesem Neuplatonismus eine ganz eigene Prägung, indem er das grenzenlose

---

38   Vgl. Jamblich, De anima in: Ioannis Stobaios, Eclogae Physicae et Ethicae, Vol. I, ed. C. Wachsmuth, Berlin 1958, 365,22 ff.

39   Jamblich, De mysteriis I,14.

40   In Eccl. or. 6, GNO V, 380,3 ff.   Vgl. auch De v. Moysis GNO VII 1, 34,11ff.; 56,25 ff.

41   Vgl. C. Eun. III, 118, GNO II, 43,19.

Anwachsen und Übersichhinauswachsen der in den Grenzen ihres Wesens
festgelegten Seele als das Charakteristikum einer geschaffenen
geistigen Wesenheit ansieht.[42] Die Vorstellung eines derartigen
Grenzenlosen innerhalb bestimmter Grenzen[43] gewinnt Gregor aber in
der kritischen Auseinandersetzung mit der aristotelischen Lehre vom
'Stehenbleibenmüssen' der Erkenntnis, die dem Unendlichkeitscharakter
der göttlichen Wesenheit nicht gerecht wird.[44] Gerecht wird ihr am
ehesten — gerade weil der Mensch nur eine diskursive, endlichkeits-
bedingte, eines nach dem anderen erfassende Vernunft besitzt — die
Vorstellung eines grenzenlosen Eindringens in diese Welt des Göttlichen,
bzw. der Begriff eines unaufhörlichen 'Aufstiegs'.[45] Auf diese Weise
kann zugleich deutlich werden, daß die menschliche Vernunft aufgrund
dieser Fähigkeit, grenzenlos das vor ihr Liegende zu 'suchen', Abbild
göttlicher Unendlichkeit ist. Allerdings muß dabei beachtet werden,
daß es sich offenkundig um zwei verschiedene Arten des Unendlichen
handelt. Das göttliche unendliche Wesen, das alles Seiende erschaffen
hat, ist nach Gregor das ewig mit sich selbst identische, immer
Gleichbleibende, jeder möglichen Hinzufügung oder Abnahme enthoben,
mit einem Wort: die Fülle aller Wirklichkeit. Deswegen muß diese Art
der Unendlichkeit im Sinne des später sogenannten 'aktuell Unendlichen'
begriffen werden. Das Grenzenlose des menschlichen Strebens nach
dem jeweils Größeren dagegen ist offenkundig eine Form des potentiell
Unendlichen, vergleichbar der Zahlenreihe, der ständig ein weiteres
hinzugefügt werden kann. Nur wenn diese beiden Arten des Unendlichen
unterschieden werden, ist verständlich, daß berechtigterweise von der

---

42 In Cant. or. 6, GNO VI, 174,9.

43 Vgl. dazu auch J. Daniélou, Changement: L'être et le temps ...
   109: 'C'est pourquoi dans l'esprit crée l'infini sera la succession
   infinie d'espaces intérieurs toujours finis, ... '

44 In Cant. or. 6, GNO VI, 180,1: δι'ὧν σαφῶς διδασκόμεθα τὸ
   μήτε τινὶ πέρατι τὸ μεγαλεῖον τῆς θείας ὁρίζεσθαι φύσεως μήτε τι
   γνώσεως μέτρον ὅρον γίνεσθαι τῆς τῶν ζητουμένων κατανοήσεως,
   μεθ' ὃν στῆναι χρή τῆς ἐπὶ τὸ πρόσω φορᾶς τὸν τῶν ὑψηλῶν
   ὀρεγόμενον.

45 Vgl. De v. Moys. 113,3: ... τὸν μέγαν Μωυσέα ἀεὶ μείζω γινόμενον
   μηδαμοῦ ἵστασθαι τῆς ἀνόδου μηδὲ τινα ὅρον ἑαυτῷ ποιεῖσθαι τῆς
   ἐπὶ τὸ ἄνω φορᾶς, ... vgl. ebd. 112,23.

Grenze wie auch vom Unbegrenzten der menschlichen Erkenntnis gesprochen werden kann.[46]

Gregor hat durch diese Konzeption des 'Unbegrenzten' die Verlegenheit der aristotelischen Erkenntnislehre angesichts des göttlichen Wesens vermieden. Das beliebige Stehenbleiben bei einem ersten Prinzip kann der göttlichen Unendlichkeit nicht gerecht werden.[47] Das ist die eine Seite der Kritik. Andererseits aber hat er auch die platonische Lehre von einem schlagartigen, plötzlichen, ganzheitlichen Erfassen im Sinne der ἐπιβολή, d.h. der Intuition abgelehnt. Ausdrücklich wird nämlich das grenzenlose Streben nach dem jeweils Größeren auch mit dem Begriff ὁδεύειν oder διεξοδεύειν (d.h. 'diskursives Erkennen') bezeichnet, der terminologisch den Gegenbegriff zur 'Intuition' darstellt.[48] Auch die Gotteserkenntnis ist also ein sukzessives Erkennen.[49]

Es ist kein Zufall, daß Gregor diese bedeutsame Besinnung auf die Grenzen der Vernunft gerade hier, im Ecclesiasteskommentar, darlegt. Um diese thematische Verflechtung zu durchschauen, muß man sich einerseits das ursprüngliche Thema aller Ecclesiasteskommentare in Erinnerung zurückrufen, andererseits auch beachten, als was Gregor diese 'neugierige' Vernunft der Aristoteliker eigentlich angesehen hat. An einer Stelle des Canticumkommentars bemerkt er, daß er bei dem Nichtzubegreifenden die πολυπραγμοσύνη nicht in Anspruch nehmen will, weil 'durch das φυσιολογεῖσθαι die unzugängliche und unaussprechbare

---

46 So ist bei M.-B. von Stritzky (a.a.O. 65 f.) einerseits von den 'Grenzen der Erkenntnisfähigkeit des Menschen' die Rede, andererseits (90) wird auf die 'Grenzenlosigkeit der Erkenntnis' verwiesen, ohne daß dieser scheinbare Widerspruch reflektiert und aufgelöst würde.

47 Mit Recht spricht E. Mühlenberg, Die Unendlichkeit Gottes bei Gregor von Nyssa, Göttingen 1966, 165 von einer Aufhebung der aristotelischen Logik. Doch auch bereits H. Langerbeck hatte diese Zusammenhänge durchschaut, wie seine Anmerkung zu In Cant. or. 8, GNO VI, 247,11 zeigt.

48 Vgl. vom Verf., Art. 'Intuition', in HWPh Bd. 4, hg. v. J. Ritter u. K. Gründer, Basel/Stuttgart 1976, 524ff.

49 Vgl. In Cant. or. 8, GNO VI, 247,15 ff.

göttliche Natur nicht wahrheitsgemäß erfaßt werden kann'⁵⁰. Daraus
geht hervor, daß die analytische, 'neugierige' Vernunft der Aristoteliker
in Wahrheit die angemessene Weise ist, über Naturdinge zu reden. Sie
ist die der Physik angemesene Weise des Denkens. Es ist schon
richtig, was E. Mühlenberg feststellte: 'ὅρος und πέρας sind "die
Grenze" in physikalischer wie auch in logischer Hinsicht' (a.a.O. 103),
nur muß man auch das Bedingungsverhältnis beider Bereiche erkennen,
um den eigentlichen Punkt der Gregorschen Kritik verstehen zu können.
Das Substantielle dieser Kritik besteht darin, daß die aristotelische
Logik eine allgemeine Lehre von der Struktur des menschlichen Denkens
überhaupt zu sein beansprucht, in Wirklichkeit jedoch nur im Hinblick
auf die Welt der Natur konzipiert ist. Der Ecclesiasteskommentar, die
Physik der christlichen Philosophie, scheint deswegen auch der angemessene Platz zu sein, um bewußt zu machen, daß die Gültigkeit der
Denkweise der aristotelisch verstandenen Vernunft eigentlich auf den
Bereich der sichtbaren Dinge beschränkt bleiben muß und nicht auch
für das 'Jenseitige' beansprucht werden kann. In diesem Sinne ist
auch das 'Schweigen', das in dem Abschnitt 409,8-416,7 thematisiert
wird, nicht als eine geheime, besondere Erkenntnisweise gegenüber dem
göttlichen Sein zu verstehen, sondern als Indiz der Einsicht in die
Begrenztheit der eigenen Vernunft, als Zeichen der Selbstbescheidung
(ἀγαπᾶν) einer Vernunft, die nach Gregor nicht einmal in der Lage ist,
das Wesen der Seele oder die Natur des Körpers zu erkennen oder
Entstehen und Vergehen in der Natur zu erklären. Nach Gregors
durchgehender Lehre — die möglicherweise von der Skepsis nicht
unbeeinflußt ist — hat die 'suchende' d.h. diskursive Vernunft es bisher
nicht vermocht, auch nur eine der geschaffenen Erscheinungen in ihrem
Wesen zu erkennen.⁵¹ In dieser These von der menschlichen
Vernunft eigenen Unmöglichkeit, das Wesen der Dinge zu erkennen, ist

---

50 In Cant. or. 11, GNO VI, 339,16 ff.

51 Vgl. z.B. In Cant. or. 11, GNO VI, 337,16 ff.; De mortuis, GNO
    IX, 44-45; nach C. Eun. II, 115-118, GNO I, 259-260 ist die
    Wesenserkenntnis eines Dinges freilich auch ohne Nutzen. Zur
    Verbindung zwischen Ding- und Selbsterkenntnis vgl. zu In Eccl.
    416,6, auch In Cant. or. 3, GNO VI, 72,12.

die Aristoteleskritik am deutlichsten zu greifen.[52] Gregor – der Locke der antiken Philosophie – nimmt diese These auch am Ende der 7. Oratio des Ecclesiasteskommentars zum Ausgangspunkt seiner abschließenden Überlegungen: Wenn die menschliche Vernunft nicht einmal das Physische in seinem Wesen kennt, wie soll sie dann das Metaphysische erkennen können (416,1 ff.). Aus diesem Grund ist bei der Suche nach dem Wesen Gottes das Schweigen angebracht. So wird die Seele am besten vorbereitet für eine vernunftmäßige Überlegung über die Dinge, 'durch die unser Leben in der Tugend einen Zuwachs erfährt' (416,8). Gregor deutet durch diesen letzten Satz an, daß die letzte Vollendung des menschlichen Lebens nicht nur eine besondere metaphysische Erkenntis, sondern auch das am Schluß von De vita Moysis beschriebene tugendhafte Leben im Sinne der Gottesfreundschaft ist. Von ihm freilich, das sich auf Christus, die 'vollendete Tugend' stützt, gilt genau das, was Gregor als das 'Allerparadoxeste' bezeichnet hat, weil hier Ruhe und Bewegung zusammenfallen. 'Denn der im Aufstieg Begriffene steht auf keinen Fall still und der Stehende macht keinen Aufstieg, hier aber geschieht durch das Innestehen (im Guten) der Aufstieg' (De v. Moys. 118,4 f.).

Auf diese Weise wird in der Oratio 7 des Ecclesiasteskommentars genau das dargestellt, was Gregor in seinem Psalmenkommentar (GNO V, 76,7) einmal programmatisch formuliert hat: Das Gute kommt nur dadurch zustande, daß Ethik und Metaphysik zusammengehen.

---

52 Vgl. J. Daniélou, Grégoire de Nysse et la Philosophie: Gregor von Nyssa und die Philosophie (2. Intern. Koll. über Gregor von Nyssa) hg. von H. Dörrie/M. Altenburger/U. Schramm, Leiden 1976, 3.

14

Some Aspects of Gregory of Nyssa's Moral Theology

in the Homilies on Ecclesiastes

Everett Ferguson

1. Introduction

'The life of virtue' (280,1) or 'training in the virtues' (333,16) is the theme of Gregory of Nyssa's *Homilies on Ecclesiastes.* [1] The subject of the Being of God and certain aspects of his creation requires a moment of silence (Eccl 3:7), 'but there is a moment to speak of the things through which our life increases in virtue' (415,17-416,9; cf. 414,17-19). [2] Thus, of the two parts of religious virtue, the knowledge of God and right conduct [3], the *Homilies on Ecclesiastes* concentrate on the latter.

Virtue is prominent in a large number of Gregory's writings, including *Vita Moysis, In psalmorum inscriptiones, De virginitate, De professione Christiana, De perfectione, De instituto Christiano,* and *Vita Macrinae.* [4] The researcher can very nearly reconstruct

---

1   For the importance of virtue in the Homilies see also 288,14; 292,22; 318,1; 333,19; 354,1; 361,10; 362,14; 365,12; 368,22; 373,12; 374,21; 379,21; 380,12; 385,4; 404,7; 407,1; 416,8; 428,3; 436,14-17.

2   Cf. *V.Moys.* II,110 for a similar listing of questions into which human curiosity is not to inquire.

3   *V.Moys.* II,166. See the discussion in R.E.Heine, Perfection in the Virtuous Life, Cambridge MA, 1975, 115ff.

4   See Evangelos G.Konstantinou, Die Tugendlehre Gregors von Nyssa im Verhältnis zu der antik-philosophischen und jüdisch-christlichen Tradition, Würzburg, 1966, 27-36. I have not seen Wilhem Vollert, Die Lehre Gregors von Nyssa vom Guten und Bösen, Leipzig, 1897.

Gregory's moral theology from the *Homilies on Ecclesiastes*, for
they touch on many of Gregory's characteristic emphases; the full
significance of these ideas in Gregory's thought, however, must be
learned from his other writings. This paper will impose a
systematic presentation on Gregory's comments, which emerge from
the sequence of the biblical text.

2. Theological Tenets

Looking to God

As a result of the Eunomian controversy, Gregory continued,
even in his moral and spiritual treatises, to emphasize the
ultimate unknowability of God. 'The divine is beyond knowledge'
(411,13). No thoughts or ideas about God, 'compared with what is
truly worthy of the subject', can be spoken by human beings
(293,16-294,5).[5] Nevertheless, there is a 'grasp of the transcendent which is gained by analogy' (308,18). This permits an understanding of God as the Good, the source and the goal of virtue.

God as Creator 'is the source both of the soul and of the
body'. Therefore, 'anyone trained in the divine mysteries is
surely aware that the life conformed to the divine nature is
proper and natural to mankind' (284,12-20).

The life of virtue is a life directed toward God. Gregory's
last words in the *Homilies on Ecclesiastes* are these:

> What food and drink are to the body, the means by which
> natural life is preserved, that, for the soul, is to look
> towards the Good; and that truly is a gift of God, to
> gaze upon God ... . For as the fleshly man, he says, gets
> strength by eating and drinking, so the one who looks at
> the good (the true good is he who alone is Good) has the
> gift of God in all his toil — just this, to look upon the
> good for ever, in Jesus Christ our Lord ... .(441,12-442,2)

---

5   See the continuation of the passage through 416,10 (referred
     to above), with which compare *V.Moys.* II,110. For the
     influence of the Eunomian controversy on Gregory's spiritual
     theology, see Heine, chapter III.

As in this passage, Gregory elsewhere defines God as the Good.[6]
The vision of God (or at least the longing to look upon God) has
entered prominently into studies of Gregory's spirituality.[7]   The
inability to experience a direct vision of God in this life and the
limitations on the knowledge of God available to human beings led
Gregory to reformulate what it means to see God: 'the seeing
that consists in not seeing'; 'this truly is the vision of God:
never to be satisfied in the desire to see him'; 'to follow God
wherever he might lead is to behold God.'[8]   With such an
understanding, looking toward God provides direction for the
virtuous life.

Grounded in Christ

The looking to God occurs 'in Christ Jesus our Lord'. 'Every
name and thought of virtue leads back to the Lord of virtues'
(436,17), who is himself 'perfect virtue' (358,9).   'The way back
for the wanderer, and the way of escape from evil, and towards
good' is the Christ, 'who took our weaknesses upon' himself.   He
'speaks to us from our own condition', and 'through these very
weaknesses of our nature shows us the way out of the reach of
evil' (305,14-19).   The Lord's coming in the flesh to dwell among
human beings ('the great mystery of salvation') was in order to
investigate the condition of life on the earth (299,20-300,3; cf.
301,4-6 quoted below) and bring salvation to mankind (299,18-19).
The incarnation was central to Gregory's spiritual theology.   It is

6   *V.Moys.* I,7; II,237; *De an. et res.* (MG 46.93B).
7   W. Völker, Gregor von Nyssa als Mystiker, Wiesbaden, 1955,
     196-218; A. Lieske, Die Theologie der Christusmystik Gregors
     von Nyssa: ZKT 70 (1948) 60-75; J. Daniélou, Platonisme et
     Théologie Mystique, Paris, 1944, 190-199; idem, L'être et le
     temps chez Grégoire de Nysse, Leiden, 1970, 1-17.   Cf. the
     related idea in H.Merki, ΟΜΟΙΩΣΙΣ ΘΕΩ. Von der Platonischen
     Angleichung an Gott zur Gottähnlichkeit bei Gregor von Nyssa,
     Freiburg, 1952, esp. 124-164.   For an analysis of the three
     theophany texts in the *V.Moys.* see my 'Progress in
     Perfection. Gregory of Nyssa's *Vita Moysis*', StPatr 14 (1976)
     307-314; cf. G. Bebis, Gregory of Nyssa's 'De Vita Moysis'. A
     Philosophical and Theological Analysis: GOTR 12 (1967) 369-
     393, esp. 382-392.
8   *V.Moys.* II,163.239.252.

related to each of the theophany texts in *Vita Moysis*,[9] and that work provides the imagery of Christ as the ground or foundation ('rock') of virtue (II,244). Christ leads his people in the way to God and as Commander of the forces of good gives victory over the Adversary and brings peace with God (435,14-436,14).

Free Will

The principal anthropological affirmation of Gregory's moral teaching has to do with free will. As is well known, Gregory was a champion of human freedom, and this was an important foundation of his understanding of virtue.[10] The *Homilies on Ecclesiastes* have a great deal to say about freedom of the will. 'What is not within our control [ἐφ' ἡμῖν] cannot be described as either virtue or vice' (379,21). 'Free choice [προαίρεσις]', Gregory says, 'is wealth' (326,17).

Birth, the very thing over which we might seem to have no control, becomes for Gregory an analogy for the effects of free choice. 'For we become in a way our own parents when through good choice we shape ourselves and bear ourselves and bring ourselves forth to the light ... . Again, we miscarry and produce premature births or mere wind, when the shape of Christ ... has not been formed in us ... . [S]omeone makes himself a child of God through virtue' (380,3-13.[11] The same positive imagery of becoming our own parents through free choice and the negative imagery of a miscarriage or being full of wind occur in connection with free will in *Vita Moysis* (II,1-11).

---

9   See my Progress in Perfection, 312, and A.J. Malherbe and
     E. Ferguson, Gregory of Nyssa. The Life of Moses, New York,
     1978, 15. Cf. Völker, 48-57; Lieske, 49-93.129-168.315-340;
     J. Gaïth, La conception de la liberté chez Grégoire de Nysse,
     Paris, 1953, 148-157.

10   The most extensive study is Gaïth, but see also Heine, 27-61.
     228-240; Konstantinou, 81-95. For the modern theological
     discussion of the relevance of Gregory's thought see E.
     Mühlenberg, Synergism in Gregory of Nyssa: ZNW 68 (1977) 93-
     122.

11   Cf. another use of the birth analogy in 344,21-345,7.

In protecting the nature of God from the charge of causing evil, Gregory in Homily 2 explains that evil results from the abuse of God's gift of freedom: 'The good gift of God, that is free will [αὐτεξούσιον], became a means to sin through the sinful use mankind made of it. For unfettered freedom of the will is good by nature ... but ... man through folly used God's good gifts in the service of evil' (301,20-302,8; cf. 302,18-303,2; 438,14-439,10).[12] The impulses of the soul were created for good, but they can be used for evil. 'Though our power of free will is a good, when it is active for evil it becomes the worst of evils' (428,1-2).

Being and Non-Being

Free will is important for Gregory's whole understanding of the structure of reality.

> So, since evil is regarded as the opposite of good, and absolute virtue is God, evil must be outside God, because its nature is not apprehended· in its being something, but in its not being good ... . Thus evil is regarded as the opposite of good, in the same way as non-being is dis-tinguished from being. So, when in the freedom of our impulse we fell away from the good ... then the unreal nature of evil took substance in those who had fallen away from the good (406,17-407,10).[13]

> An evil resting by itself apart from our free choice does not exist (407,14).

These same ideas, including the illustration of those who close their eyes to the light being responsible for their darkness, are found in Gregory's major discussion of free will in connection with the hardening of Pharaoh's heart in *V.Moys.* II,73-8.

---

12   The same strategy is employed in *V.Moys.* II,73ff.; see Malherbe and Ferguson, 167, n. 93.
13   Cf. *V.Moys.* I,5-7.

For Gregory, 'evil has no substance' (300,22), 'does not exist' (356,9-10), and 'is the deprivation of being' (356,15). Consequently, 'the life of the senses' when 'compared with the true life is unreal and insubstantial' (284,10-11; cf. 289,21-290,1). One purpose of the incarnation was to investigate 'how being became the slave of non-being, how the unreal dominates being' (301,4-6). This view of the substantial unreality of evil and its Neoplatonic background have been often studied.[14]   There are numerous parallels in Gregory's other writings.[15]   Whereas sin is turning to unreality and non-existence, the life of virtue, on the other hand, not only does the good but also participates in that which really is (see the whole passage 406,1-407,17). 'Whatever the thing that is shared in naturally is, what shares in it must conform' (422,14-15).

God as true Being is a 'stable reality' (285,10).   Always the same, he is unchanging good (313,17-18).   This nature of God as absolute Being and absolute Good left the human misuse of free will as the only explanation for evil in the world, but it also provided the basis and the goal for human endeavors in virtue.[16] 'Those who cling to what is unstable do not reach out for what stands for ever' (422,8-9).

Continual Progress

One of the most distinctive emphases in Gregory's moral theology is that perfection in virtue is always to be making progress in virtue.[17]   Gregory gave his classic exposition of this theme of perpetual progress in V.Moys.,[18] but he alludes to it

---

14   E.g., H.F. Cherniss, The Platonism of Gregory of Nyssa, Berkeley 1930, 49-53; D.Balás, ΜΕΤΟΥΣΙΑ ΘΕΟΥ, Rome 1966, 108-120; Völker, 80-91; Heine, 32-39.
15   E.g., V.Moys. II,22-25; In Inscr. Psal. I,8; De virg. 12; De beat. 5.
16   J. Daniélou, L'être et le temps ... , 95-115; cf. Heine, 57.60.78-79 with reference to V.Moys. II,243f.
17   See Progress in Perfection (note 7 above); Heine, 58-59.63-71.97-107; and literature cited in these works, esp. Daniélou, Platonisme ... , 291-307.
18   Especially I,5-10 and II,225-255.   For other references see the notes in Malherbe and Ferguson.

elsewhere, including the *Homilies on Ecclesiastes.* Seeking the Lord is a pursuit of one's entire life: 'For it is not at a fixed moment and an appointed time that it is good to seek the Lord, but never to cease from continual search' (401,2-13).

The two metaphysical bases of continual progress are human mutability and divine infinity.[19] The 'truly good things' belong to the 'one divine and everlasting nature', but sensual things are 'naturally subject to flux and transient', 'unstable' in contrast to 'what stands forever' (422,3-9). These truly good things can be summed up as 'one good thing, the perpetual joy in good things, and that is the child of good deeds' (441,5-6).

Because of the infinite extension of the uncreated Good and the nature of created beings always to be changing, there is no satiety in the enjoyment of spiritual goods.[20] Using Epicurean observations about the kinetic pleasures of food and drink, Gregory describes the cycle of satisfaction and return of appetite in sensual things. In contrast, there is no satiety expected nor fullness found in the search for the true Good (313,8-11). 'Appetite for it and partaking of it are exactly matched, and longing flourishes together with enjoyment, and is not limited by the attainment of what is desired; the more it delights in the Good, the more it flames up with delight; the delight matches the desire' (313,11-15). The work of faith lasts 'in full strength continuously throughout life' (314,8).

---

19   See E. Ferguson, God's Infinity and Man's Mutability. Perpetual Progress according to Gregory of Nyssa: GOTR 18 (1973) 59-78. On the divine infinity see J.E. Hennessy, The Background, Sources, and Meaning of Divine Infinity in St. Gregory of Nyssa (Dissertation, Fordham Univ.), 1963, 273-284; E. Mühlenberg, Die Unendlichkeit Gottes bei Gregor von Nyssa Göttingen, 1966, 147-165. For Gregory's philosophy of change, see J. Daniélou, L'être et le temps ..., 95-115.

20   Cf. *V.Moys.* II,232.235.239 and Heine, 42.76-78; also J.Daniélou, La colombe et la ténèbre dans la mystique byzantine ancienne: ErJb 23 (1954) 400-418.

3.   Psychological Perspectives

Gregory's rejection of satiety already involves a consideration of the psychological perspectives from which he views the life of virtue.   These in turn involve some related practical points for attaining that life.

Soul and Body

Although Ecclesiastes does not offer Gregory opportunity to develop his anthropology,[21] he does define human nature as twofold.   The more familiar way of expressing this dichotomy is to pair soul and body.   The soul is impassible and immortal, but the body is mortal and temporal (284,1-11).   The Creator is the source of both, but the person 'trained in the divine mysteries' has 'escaped from the flesh' and 'glimpsed the higher life' (284,13-19).   There is a twofold manner of life correpsonding to the twofold nature of human beings as soul and body (389,8-10).

Rational and Sensory

In the *Homilies on Ecclesiastes* the dichotomy of human nature is also commonly described in terms of its rational and sensory aspects.   'Our nature is a double one, a combination of mind [νοητῷ] and sense [αἰσθητῷ]'   (419,9), and Gregory makes much of the need for the latter (the flesh) to be submissive to the former (the intellectual) (311,20-312,1).   The purpose of Ecclesiastes was 'to raise the mind above sensation' (280,2-3).   Gregory expresses the goal that 'intelligible things [νοητῶν] might overcome the inclinations of the flesh, so that our nature might not be at war with itself, with the mind choosing some things and the body pulling it towards others, but instead might make the pride of our flesh submissive and obedient to the rational [νοητῷ] part of the soul' (311,17-312,1).   Even in the

---

21   For Gregory's anthropology, in addition to Gaïth and Merki, see A.H. Armstrong, Platonic Elements in St. Gregory of Nyssa's doctrine of Man: DomSt 1 (1948) 113-126; G.B. Ladner, The Philosophical Anthropology of Saint Gregory of Nyssa: DOP 12 (1958) 59-64; and J.P. Cavarnos, St. Gregory of Nyssa on the Origin and Destiny of the Soul, Belmont MA 1956.

first passage noted in the preceding paragraph Gregory shifts to speaking of 'the life of sense-perception' that should be guided by 'knowledge' (284,21-285,1). This manner of speaking does not mean that there is a simple equation of mind with soul and senses with body, but the senses are the point of contact between the rational part of the soul and the body.[22]

Gregory emphasizes the need for the rational faculties to control the non-rational part of human nature. He does not regard the impulses or desires as evil in themselves, but inasmuch as they are the means through which temptation and sin enter human life, they frequently have a negative connotation for him (as in 'the evil array of the passions [παθημάτων]', 383,20-21).[23] He states:

> Every impulse [κίνησις] of the soul was framed for good
> by the One who created our nature, but the mistaken use
> of such impulses produces the drives [ἀφορμάς] towards
> evil ... . Conversely, the power to reject unpleasant
> things, whose name is hate, is an instrument of virtue
> when it is deployed against the enemy, but becomes a
> weapon of sin when it is opposed to the good (427,15-
> 428,6; cf. 303,7-11).

Control of Pleasures

Gregory gives many warnings against the pursuit of pleasure. Although there is a disposition toward the good in the soul (371,20-21), 'the things pursued by humans for the sake of bodily pleasure are pursuit of error and distraction of a soul dragged down from the things above to the things below'. Such things are a damage to rational thought (λογισμοῖς) (372,3-6).[24] Gregory interprets Eccles. 2,2 as meaning 'I set my face against pleasure,

---

22 The comoponents of the soul are described in more Platonic, and more colorful, terms in *V.Moys.* II,96-97.122-123, on which see Heine, 221-227.

23 For the πάθη in Gregory, see Völker, 87-90.117-122; Merki, 93-100; J.Daniélou, 'La colombe', 390-395.

24 Such warnings are, of course, common in Gregory's moral writings. Cf. *V.Moys.* II,60-61.122.271.297-304

being suspicious of its approach' (311,2-4).   He proceeds to
compare pleasure to a wild animal (311,7), a common comparison
with him.[25]   In particular, because of the biblical connotations,
'the passion of pleasure' is identified with a serpent (348,15).
Hence, he gives the advice to kill the head first,[26]   that is to
prevent evil from entering in the first place, because 'the one
who has let in the beginning of passion has admitted the whole
beast into himself' (349,11-350,10).

Gregory advocates limiting physical needs.   'If any one,
yearning for greater possessions, and letting his desire become as
boundless as a sea, has an insatiable greed for the streams of
gain flowing in from every side, let him treat his disease by
looking at the real sea,' which 'does not exceed its boundary ...
but remains at the same volume' (289,3-10).   'Enjoyment cannot
exceed the amount fixed by nature' (289,16).   Whereas spiritual
matters bring continuous enjoyment without satiety, 'there is no
bodily activity which can give lasting pleasure' (312,22).[27]
Therefore, Gregory's advice is for moderation: 'As long as he
lives in the flesh he will care for the physical nature of his own
body just enough to prevent its being deprived of anything'
(326,18-20).[28]

Inducements to Correction

There is implanted in our nature by God 'a great and
powerful weapon for avoiding sin' (315,13-14), the sense of
modesty [αἰδώς] and of shame [αἰσχύνη].   These two emotions,
Gregory says, are closely related, but 'shame is modesty
intensified, and modesty ... is shame moderated' (316,3-4).   Modesty
is often better than fear in turning a person away from sin; and

---

25   Cf. *V.Moys.* 276-277, and Malherbe and Ferguson, 191, n. 390;
     De prof. chr. (GNO VIII,1, 137,17ff).   See Daniélou, Platonisme
     ..., 74-80.
26   The same imagery and advice in *V.Moys.* II,90, 94; cf. *In
     natalem Christi* (PG 46.1133A).
27   See discussion of satiety above.   Cf. *De beat.* 4 (ACW 18,
     126).
28   Cf. Gaïth, 157-168 for 'Liberation by Ascesis' in Gregory.

shame, the stronger emotion, 'which follows criticisms of a fault is enough by iself to correct the sinner' (315,22-316,1).

Confession of sin (ἐξομολόγησις),[29] defined as 'public acknowledgment' (ἐξαγόρευσις), produces the emotion of shame (315,11-12). The public acknowledgment of wrongdoing, then is a means of correction (317,1-4), because of the sense of shame inherent in our nature. 'The person who has branded himself by confessing his secret sins will be given lessons by the memory of his feeling of shame for the rest of his life' (317,10-12). The text of Ecclesiastes contains Solomon's confession of his sins (338,23-329,1).

4.   Means of Moral Progress

Having surveyed Gregory's remarks relevant to the theological and psychological bases for the life of virtue, we may proceed to note some of his observations about some of the means for carrying out the continuous progress toward virtue.

Necessity for Effort

As an ascetic himself and a spiritual guide for other ascetics, Gregory placed considerable emphasis on human effort in the moral life.[30] 'Effort and diligence' are necessary in order to learn wisdom and knowledge (308,9-16; cf. 307,24-308,1), so pain is involved in the pursuit of learning (309,16) (as students of Gregory can attest). Gregory was keenly conscious of the labor involved in giving a morally edifying interpretation of Ecclesiastes (277,3; 278,5-17; 373,2-3). Similarly 'all words are laborious' (Eccl 1,8), because 'those who instruct in virtue first achieve within themselves the things which they teach' (292,222-23). One must make an effort to live virtuously (362,15).

---

29   For penance and exomologesis in Gregory, see Völker, pp. 106-109, who gives other references but not In Ecclesiasten.

30   E.g. V.Moys. II,226, 305; De oratione dominica 2; and the whole of De instituto Christiano.

Help from Angels

To those who make the effort in the life of virtue, divine
assistance is provided. 'The array of angels of the host of
heaven' make up an army under Christ, the heavenly Commander.
Gregory exhorts the human warrior to join forces with the angels
in the fight against the Adversary. With the angels as allies
true peace is achieved (435,1-436,10). The *Vita Moysis* II,45-53
offers a fuller exposition of the angels as helpers in the fight
against the forces of evil.

Scripture Heals

Scripture is part of the divine assistance offered as a
means for moral improvement.[31] The very exposition of
Ecclesiastes, as is true for all of Gregory's exegetically based
works, indicates a belief that instruction in attaining virtue is
to be found in the Scriptures. Gregory was concerned about the
meaning of the titles of the biblical books, the aim of each book,
and the book's service to the church (279,4-20). Moreover, there
are express statements of the healing power conveyed through the
Scripture writer. The Ecclesiast 'heals our life through his
account of his own' (319,11-12).[32] More explicit is the statement
that one may learn how to 'live virtuously by obtaining from the
text [λόγου] some art and method, so to speak, of successful
living' (373,12-13). The Word directs our life to 'what is right'
(374,13-14). Not expressly referring to Scriptures but probably
including them is the reference to 'the heavenly spring, from
which the virtues of the soul germinate and are watered, so that
the grove of good desires may flourish in our souls' (333,19-
334,2).

Gregory often comments on the sequence or order of the
words and events in the Scriptures.[33] He could even find a

---

31   Cf Völker, 111.156-162 on Scripture in Gregory's spirituality.
32   Admittedly 'account' is supplied by the translator, but it is
     a legitimate inference.
33   Cf. *V.Moys.* II,136.148; J. Daniélou, Akolouthia chez Grégoire
     de Nysse: RevSR 27 (1953) 219-249.

lesson in the order of the books in the canon, finding in Genesis and Exodus a connection between birth and death (378,18-23). Although Gregory finds significance in the order in which the account proceeds (307,4-8), his references to sequence in the *Homilies* do not always attribute a spiritual meaning to it (307,17-18).

Examples

Gregory found the examples provided by biblical persons to be demonstrations of his spiritual theology and to be an instruction and encouragement to contemporary aspirants of the virtuous life.[34]   In other writings he takes as examples Abraham[35], Paul[36], and especially Moses[37].   The *Homilies on Ecclesiastes* offer Solomon as an example.   Gregory's method of interpretation permits him to take the 'Ecclesiast' sometimes as Christ (as in 280,8-13; 298,5-13)[38] and sometimes as Solomon, the putative author of Ecclesiastes (305,20).   Since 'we do not learn everything from our own experience' (306,3-4), we learn from the experience of others.   Solomon's experiences with the different forms of pleasure provide the basis for the lessons presented subsequently, especially *Homilies* 2-4.

It is not only persons who provide examples in Gregory's teachings.   The earth itself furnishes a lesson in steadfastness. 'As for those to whom a life directed towards virtue seems burdensome, let their soul be trained by the example of the earth so as to persevere under hardship' (288,13-15).   The occasion for

---

34   The use of personal examples was a common device in the Hellenistic moral literature.   A.J. Malherbe, Moral Exhortation. A Greco-Roman Sourcebook, Philadelphia, 1986, 135-138 and see the index.

35   *Contra Eunomium* 2.85-92 (GNO I,251,15-254,20); *V.Moys.* I,11-14.

36   *De perfectione* (174,24-175,13).

37   *V.Moys.* I,15; II,319.

38   The section continues to list other names or titles of Christ in addition to 'the Ecclesiast'.   This was a favorite exercise by Gregory: the treatise *De perfectione* is built around the names of Christ; cf. *V.Moys.* II,177; Malherbe and Ferguson 180, n. 223.

this surprising conclusion is the text of Ecclesiastes 1,4, 'The
earth stands to eternity', an unchanging state which Gregory
understands as tedious.

5.   Vices and Virtues

The Goal of Life

The Hellenistic philosophical schools were differentiated not
so much by the specific moral advice they gave as by how they
defined the goal or purpose of life.   Gregory gives a
characteristically Christian statement of the goal.[39]   The goal
(σκοπός) of the church is 'godliness' (εὐσέβεια) (279,19).   On this
basis, virtue is 'to turn one's soul to nothing here on earth, but
to have one's effort directed toward what through faith lies in
our hopes before us' (379,11-13; cf. 354,21-22).   The goal or
purpose of life excludes the vices and gives unity to the
individual virtues.

Virtue as the Mean

Gregory sometimes defined virtue in Aristotelian terms as
the mean between extremes.   His wording in the *Homilies on
Ecclesiastes* is 'the middle point between contrasting things'
(375,4-5).   The same description employed in this passage, in
terms of deficiency or excess, and the same illustration of
cowardice and rashness as the extremes in relation to courage,
taken from Aristotle, occur in *V.Moys.* II,288.[40]

Use of Lists and Opposites

A favorite device of Hellenistic moralists was to compile
lists of vices and virtues.[41]   Gregory continued this tradition.   A
long list of vices occurs in describing the evil results of an

---

39   Merki, 108-110, and Konstantinou, 182, define the goal for
      Gregory as to become like God in the state of blessedness.
      Gregory had various ways of formulating the goal: in *V.Moys.*
      II,317 the goal (τέλος) is to be 'called a servant of God'.
40   See Malherbe and Ferguson, 92, n. 403; Konstantinou, 48-52.
      112-118.
41   A.J. Malherbe, Moral Exhortation ..., 32.37.39.42.45-46.73.130.
      136.138-141.159.

immoderate use of wine: 'licentiousness, self-indulgence, injury to youth, deformity to age, dishonour for women, ... death to the understanding, estrangement from virtue' (328,19-329,2).[42]   There continues a list of other effects of wine.   A list of virtues occurs in describing the qualities that a person who gathers riches will not acquire (340,10-12).

The *Homilies on Ecclesiates* show a fondness for arranging lists of opposites.[43]   For instance, the list of miseries in the natural world: ' ... pitiable childhood, dementia in age, unsettled youth, the constant toil of adult life, burdensome marriage, lonely celibacy, the troublesome multitude of children, sterile childlessness, miserliness over wealth, the anguish of poverty' (387,8-13).   A contrast of virtues and vices occurs at 427,6-8: 'Restraint and pleasure, self-control and indulgence, humility and pride, goodwill and perversity, and all the things which are regarded as the opposite of one another' (cf. 402,19-21). Opposites are also used by Gregory in his definitions of words (as 371,3-4) and concepts (355,3-5).

Illustrations

As with any preacher who seeks to communicate with his hearers, Gregory made rich use of illustrations in order to make his points about the moral life.   Even in the *Homilies on Ecclesiastes* the illustrations would be a study in themselves.[44] Gregory draws lessons from athletics (278,5),[45]   carpentry (303,14-304,6), pearl divers (318,10-14), irrigation (319,21-320,4), agriculture (331,1-10); 375,19-376,5; 382,3-9), and shyster lawyers (358,20-359,1).

In view of the language of warfare about the struggle between good and evil, the military imagery is fully developed

---

42   Cf. the list of vices in *V.Moys.* II,25.

43   Cf. *V.Moys.* II,14.

44   T.A. Coggin, The Times of Saint Gregory of Nyssa as reflected in the Letters and the Contra Eunomium, Washington, 1947, draws on the illustrations used in the named works.

45   Cf. *V.Moys.* II,36.   For athletic imagery in the Hellenistic moralists, see Malherbe, index.

(428,19-433,7). The text of Eccles. 2,4 gives occasion for the most elaborately developed illustration in the *Homilies*, the adornment of a house (324,3-326,18).[46] Each part of the house is identified with a virtue, providing one of the longer listings of virtues in the *Homilies*. By far, the most popular discipline drawn on as a source for illutration in the *Homilies* is medicine,[47] a favorite with the Hellenistic moralists and a subject with which Gregory had considerable familiarity.[48]

Particular Sins

Out of the many sins referred to in the *Homilies on Ecclesiastes* certain ones come in for special treatment. In different works Gregory concentrates on different sins, as he singled out envy for special treatment in *V.Moys.* II,256-263. In the *Homilies* at least three subjects get this distinction. Special interest attaches to the subject of slavery (334,4-338,22).[49] Drunkenness comes in for full treatment (327,21-330,11; cf. 347,16ff.). Note may be made too of Gregory's condemnation of usury (343,10-346,14). Furthermore, Gregory designates the love of money, citing I Timothy 6,10, as 'the greatest of [Solomon's] sins' (338,23-339,2; cf. 433,1-3).[50]

Faith and Works

The importance of the incarnation as the divine means of bringing salvation to humanity was noted above. This '*Gospel* must be proclaimed *in the whole world* (Mat 26:13), *every tongue* must confess that *Jesus Christ is Lord, to the glory of God the Father* (Phil 2,11)' (382,12-15). The church is established through the

---

46   The adornment of a house is not one of the more common illustrations in the resources of rhetoricians, but see the briefer use in *V.Moys.* II,71.
47   317,5-9; 319,6-10; 346,17-347,1; 354,13-16; 376,7-9; 384,3-15.
48   See the index in Malherbe, Moral Exhortation, and his 'Medical Imagery in the Pastoral Epistles' in: Paul and the Popular Philosophers, Minneapolis 1989, 121-136; Coggin, 22-25, 137-144. In the *V.Moys.* medical illustrations occur at I,87, 272, 278.
49   See M.M. Bergadà, pp. 193-204.
50   Money was treated by the Hellenistic moralists too as the root of all evil; see Malherbe, *Moral Exhortation* ... p. 109.

gospel message (280,19-20). The gospel must be received in faith:
'There is the same moment for both receiving the saving plant of
faith and pulling up the weeds of unbelief' (382,21-383,2). 'The
one who comes forward in faith finds purification by baptism'
(404,21-22).[51]

'The escape from evil is the beginning of the virtuous life'
(354,1). The divine initiative did not free human beings from
responsibility. 'If you shape your soul in every respect with
good characteristics, if you free yourself from the defilements of
evil, if you wash away from your nature all stain of the filth of
matter, what will you become as you beautify yourself in such
ways? What loveliness will you put on?' (295,9-13). For every
sin there is a corresponding virtue that must be put in its place.
Faith replaces unbelief; justice, what is unjust; humility, pride;
and love, hatred (cf. 383,22-12; 399,9-20).

Gregory links faith and works (or righteous deeds) insepa-
rably together: 'Faith without the works of justice is not enough
to save one from death, nor again is the justice of one's life a
guarantee of salvation if it is on its own, divorced from faith'
(434,3-8; cf. 'work of faith', 314,6).[52]

Love

The one virtue receiving the fullest treatment in the
Homilies on Ecclesiastes is love, the subject of the first half of
the eighth homily. Gregory sets the discussion of love in the
context of the contrast between loving and hating. Love and hate
are related to an 'inner disposition' (ἐνδιάθετος σχέσις) of the
soul, which must be trained to discriminate between good and evil
(417,13; 418,6-8). 'The mistaken disposition of the soul towards
bad things', however, is not really love (421,5-6). Love has a
transforming effect: 'The one who loves the good will also be
good himself, as the goodness which comes to be in him changes

51   See Gregory's sermon *In baptismum Christi; V.Moys.* II,124-
       129.185.277.
52   On justice, or righteousness, cf. *De beatitudinibus* 4 (ACW 18,
       118-120.

the one who receives it into itself' (423,2-4).   Hence, love is
truly the sum of virtue, being directed toward that which is truly
Good, namely God.   'What truly exists is the one and only intrinsically Lovable,' whom scripture commands to love 'with all your
heart'; 'and again the only thing to be hated in truth is the
Inventor of evil, the Enemy of your life' (425,4-10).

6.   Conclusion

        At the beginning and end of his *Vita Moysis* Gregory defined
perfection as always going on towards perfection (I,10; II,306).
His closing words spoke of the goal of the virtuous life and
motives for it:

> This is true perfection: not to avoid a wicked life be-
> cause like slaves we servilely fear punishment, nor to do
> good because we hope for rewards ... .   On the contrary,
> ... we regard falling from God's friendship as the only
> thing dreadful and we consider becoming God's friend the
> only thing worthy of honor and desire.   This, as I have
> said, is the perfection of life. (II,320)

In a similar vein, his *Homilies on Ecclesiastes* declared, 'It is not
one thing to seek, and another to find, but the reward of seeking
is the actual seeking' (400,21-401,2).[53]

---

53   Cf.   *V.Moys.* II,239; *De beatitudinibus* 4 (*ACW* 18, 128); *In
      Canticum* 12 (*GNO* VI,369,24-370,3).

15

Le Omelie di Gregorio di Nissa
e l'interpretazione cristiana antica dell' Ecclesiaste

Sandro Leanza

Oggetto di questa mia relazione è una valutazione delle *Omelie sull'Ecclesiaste*, al fine di individuare e cogliere le analogie e dipendenze del Nisseno dall'esegesi precedente, l'originalità e specificità della sua interpretazione, l'influenza da lui esercitata sulla posteriore esegesi dell'*Ecclesiaste*.

1. La nota caratteristica e distintiva di queste Omelie rispetto a tutti gli altri commenti all'*Ecclesiaste* del periodo patristico — tenendo tuttavia presente che conosciamo pochissimo l'esegesi di Origene — è costituita dal fondamentale impianto teologico e filosofico, prerogativa del resto comune a tutte le opere esegetiche del Nisseno. Della complessa problematica filosofico-teologica agitata in queste *Omelie sull'Ecclesiaste* mi limito a ricordare qui le pagine di carattere ontologico relative alla distinzione e opposizione di realtà sensibile/realtà intellegibile, essere/non essere, bene/male, alla dottrina della cospirazione degli enti ecc.; quelle di carattere antropologico riguardanti la finitezza dell'uomo, il libero arbitrio, la doppia creazione, l'apocatastasi ecc.; quelle di carattere soteriologico, tra cui notevole l'ampia digressione dell'Hom. II, imperniata sull' interpretazione allegorica in chiave soteriologica della parabola evangelica della pecorella perduta; quelle di carattere gnoseologico, tra cui particolarmente rilevante, verso la fine dell'Hom. VII, la lunga e non sempre perspicua digressione sui limiti della percezione sensoriale e della conoscenza umana in genere; infine, le pagine di contenuto più propriamente teologico sull'essenza e natura di Dio, tra le quali sono più particolarmente da segnalare, per il loro carattere

polemico, quelle contro Eunomio (Hom. I e Hom. VIII) sull'incomprensi-
bilità e ineffabilità della natura divina.[1]   Non è possibile, in questa
sede, attardarmi nella discussione di questa complessa problematica,
che richiederebbe ampie trattazioni specifiche per ciascuna delle
tematiche sopra enumerate.[2]   Basti qui aver richiamato l'attenzione
sul carattere marcatamente filosofico, ancor più che teologico,
dell'esegesi del Nisseno, che costituisce la prima e più rilevante
peculiarità delle sue *Omelie sull'Ecclesiaste* rispetto alla restante
esegesi patristica sullo stesso libro biblico.   Tra i commenti del
periodo patristico, quello che più si avvicina sotto questo aspetto
all'opera del Nisseno, senza tuttavia raggiungerne la ricchezza e
profondità di pensiero, è senza dubbio il tardivo *Commentario
all'Ecclesiaste* di Gregorio di Agrigento: ma esso, come ho sottolineato
in un lavoro specifico dedicato a questo autore e come avremo anche
modo di vedere più oltre, deve per l'appunto molto, per il suo
contenuto filosofico e teologico, alle *Omelie sull'Ecclesiaste* del
Nisseno.[3]

Sotto il profilo più strettamente esegetico, le *Omelie
sull'Ecclesiaste* hanno una loro precipua e peculiare fisionomia in virtù
dell'applicazione costante di due principi metodologici che sono
caratteristici dell'ermeneutica del Nisseno: quello dello σκοπός

---

1   Per l'indicazione specifica dei luoghi in cui queste varie tematiche
     ricorrono, rinvio all'*Indice analitico* della mia traduzione (Roma
     1990; *Collana di testi patristici* [= CTP], 86), *sub voces*.

2   Mia sia permesso rinviare, per una sommaria informazione, alle
     note della mia traduzione sopra citata, dove si troverà anche la
     bibliografia specifica relativa alle varie tematiche filosofiche
     affrontate dal Nisseno.   Una illustrazione generale del contenuto
     filosofico-teologico delle Omelie è nella *Prefazione* di A. Siclari a
     Gregorio di Nissa: Omelie sull'Ecclesiaste, trad. di S. Rinaldi,
     Parma 1987.   Vedo ora che anche alcune relazioni di questo
     Convegno affrontano in maniera specifica la trattazione di taluni
     aspetti filosofici e teologici delle *Omelie sull'Ecclesiaste*, anche in
     riferimento alle fonti del pensiero nisseniano e in qualche caso
     con puntuale documentazione, attinta specialmente alla letteratura
     platonica e neoplatonica ma anche a quella patristica, di
     dipendenze e luoghi paralleli.

3   Cfr. S. Leanza, Sul Commentario all'Ecclesiaste di Gregorio di
     Agrigento: *Il Cristianesimo in Sicilia dalle origini a Gregorio
     Magno*, Caltanissetta 1987, 191-220.

e quello dell'ἀκολουθία.   Il principio di ἀκολουθία, che potremmo
tradurre *consequenzialità*, consiste, com'è noto, nella ricerca del
concatenamento rigorosamente logico dei fatti e delle idee nel testo
sacro, non solo nei singoli brani e racconti ma nell'intero libro biblico
considerato nella sua interezza.   L'altro principio, quello dello σκοπός,
consiste nell'individuazione dello scopo specifico di ogni libro biblico.
Entrambi questi principi non sono un'innovazione di Gregorio, ricorrendo
già nella precedente letteratura patristica (Clemente Alessandrino,
Origene, Eusebio) ed essendo anzi addirittura riconducibili alla retorica
e all'ermeneutica classica (Giamblico, Proclo).   Il Daniélou e la
Rondeau hanno tuttavia dimostrato che nessuno prima di Gregorio
aveva utilizzato i due principi di ἀκολουθία e σκοπός congiuntamente,
col rigore, l'organicità e la sistematicità con cui lo fa Gregorio.[4]
Appunto l'impiego congiunto e sistematico di questi due principi
ermeneutici, finalizzato a cogliere, attraverso il rigoroso e
conseguenziale concatenamento delle idee, lo scopo specifico
dell'*Ecclesiaste*, conferisce alle Omelie del Nisseno una solida unità
logica e strutturale, che non ha l'eguali nella rimanente produzione
patristica su questo libro biblico.   Tutta l'argomentazione di Gregorio
infatti, dalla prima all'ultima pagina, si sviluppa in maniera
rigorosamente coerente, per dimostrare l'asserto iniziale, enunciato già
nelle prime battute dell'Hom. I, che "Scopo dell'*Ecclesiaste* è di elevare
l'intelletto al di sopra dei sensi e far sì che l'anima, abbandonando
tutto quello che sembra importante e bello in questo mondo, si rivolga
alle realtà che i sensi non possono percepire e desideri i beni che i
sensi non possono conseguire."[5]   Il richiamo esplicito all'ἀκολουθία è
del resto frequentissimo e rappresenta un vero e proprio *leitmotiv*,[6]
costituendo con ciò stesso un tratto caratteristico di queste Omelie,

---

4   Cfr. Jean Daniélou, Akolouthía chez Grégoire de Nysse: RevSR 27
     (1927) 219-249; *L'être et le temps chez Grégoire de Nysse*,
     Leiden 1970, 18-50. M.J. Rondeau, Exégèse du Psautier et
     anabase spirituelle chez Grégoire de Nysse: *Epektasis. Mélanges J.
     Daniélou*, Paris 1972, 517-531; D'ou vient la technique exégétique
     utilisée par Grégoire de Nysse dans son traité "Sur les titres des
     psaumes'?: *Mélanges d'histoire des religions offerts à H.Ch.
     Puech*, Paris 1974, 263-287.

5   228,2-7 = CTP 86, p.42.

che non ha riscontro negli altri commenti patristici e conferisce al dettato del Nisseno un carattere fortemente unitario. Particolarmente degno di rilievo, a questo proposito, è l'impiego dell'ἀκολουθία nel lungo commento, che abbraccia tre intere Omelie, della pericope di Eccle. 3,1-8: *"Ogni cosa ha il suo tempo e c'è un tempo per ogni cosa sotto il sole... ."* Di questa pericope Gregorio dà, grazie all'ἀκολουθία, un'interpretazione saldamente unitaria in chiave allegorico-psicologica, nella quale riesce a unificare le varie *tempestivitates* enumerate nel testo biblico, sotto il denominatore comune dell'opposizione tra bene e male, tra virtù e vizio, tra Dio e il nemico spirituale, cogliendo talora, con grande perizia, impensabili connessioni anche tra espressioni palesemente e obiettivamente eterogenee.[7]

Segnalo infine, come ultima caratteristica che contraddistingue le Omelie del Nisseno e che non troviamo negli altri commenti antichi all'*Ecclesiaste*, il tema mistico dell'ἐπέκτασις: tema particolarmente caro a Gregorio, e che avrebbe avuto di lì a qualche anno un più ampio e significativo sviluppo nelle *Omelie sul Cantico dei Cantici.* Nelle *Omelie sull'Ecclesiaste* questo motivo appare quale ricerca continua e ininterrotta del vero bene: "quel bene del quale non si aspetta sazietà e non si avverte pienezza, ma del quale aumenta il desiderio quanto più uno ne partecipa e cresce la brama insieme al godimento di esso; quel bene che non finisce con l'appagamento del desiderio, e insieme al desiderio cresce il diletto";[8] quel bene "che una

---

6   Vd. l'indicazione dei numerosi luoghi nell'*Indice analitico* di CTP 86, *s.v.*, p.181.   Segnalo qui specificamente per l'esplicita connessione di σκοπός e ἀκολουθία: Hom. III 317,20f (CTP 86 p.78), "per condurre *conseguentemente* il discorso allo *scopo* che s'era prefisso (*scil.* Salomone)"; Hom. VI 373,3-6 (CTP 86 p.121), "lo scopo di quello che abbiamo indagato all'inizio di questo libro manifesta sopratutto adesso, come mostrerà lo *slivuppo consequenziale del discorso*".

7   Vd. per i particolari la dettagliata illustrazione che ne ho fatto in CTP 86 pp.25-28.

8   Hom. II 313,10-15 (CTP 86 p.75).

volta trovato si continua sempre a cercare... e il cui tempo opportuno di cercarlo consiste nel non cessare mai di cercarlo".[9]

2.   Le peculiarità fin qui rilevate sono di carattere generale e più o meno comuni un po' a tutti gli scritti esegetici del Nisseno.[10]   Sarà interessante valutare adesso l'originalità di Gregorio nell'interpretazione specifica del testo dell'*Ecclesiaste* e vedere che cosa sotto questo aspetto gli derivi invece dall'esegesi precedente o coeva.

Per il periodo precedente, perduta quasi interamente la maggior parte   della   letteratura   esegetica   sull'*Ecclesiaste*,[11]   è   possibile istituire qualche confronto solo con Origene, Dionigi Alessandrino e Gregorio Taumaturgo.   Tra i contemporanei del Nisseno — escludendo del   tutto   Evagrio,   del   quale   possediamo   insignificanti   frammenti catenari,[12] ed altri interpreti dell'*Ecclesiaste* dei quali non ci è rispettive opere.   Le Omelie del Nisseno vengono infatti datate con

9   Hom. VII 400,21-401,8 (CTP 86 pp. 146-147), commento di Eccle. 3,6: *"tempo di cercare e tempo di perdere."*   Gregorio interpreta *"tempo di cercare"* nel senso di "cercare il Signore", e questa ricerca dura tutta la vita (400,10-401,8; 404,19-405,10 = CTP 86 146-147.150.

10   Ho tralasciato di proposito di prendere in considerazione altri motivi tipici dell'esegesi di Gregorio, che pure hanno una notevole applicazione nelle *Omelie sull'Ecclesiaste*, quali il principio del *defectus litterae* e quello dell'ὠφέλεια, perché mi sembrano meno esclusivi del nostro autore, ricorrendo ugualmente e con pari intensità in altri interpreti antichi e sopratutto in Origene. Per essi rinvio comunque alla mia *Prefazione* di CTP 86, pp.19-25.

11   Per un'informazione generale sull'interpretazione dell'*Ecclesiaste* nel Periodo   patristico,   cfr.   S.   Leanza,   *L'Ecclesiaste nell'interpretazione dell' antico cristianesimo*, Messina 1978; L'atteggiamento della più antica esegesi cristiana dinanzi all'epicureismo ed edonismo di Qohelet: *Orpheus* NS 3 (1982) 73-90; L'esegesi patristica di Qohelet, Da Melitone di Sardi alle compilazioni catenarie: Aug. 32 (1992), sub prelo. Vd. pure, ora, la bibliografia approntata da M. Starowieyski e presentata a questo stesso Convegno (pp. 413-448).

12   Di diverso avviso è P. Gehin, che rivendica ad Evagrio, con argomenti a mio avviso inconsistenti, gli scolii catenari del Cod. Paris. Coisl. Gr. 193 e del Cod. Iviron 555.   Cfr. S. Leanza, Pour   une   réédition   des   scolies   à   l'Ecclesiaste   de   Denys d'Alexandrie: *ALEXANDRINA. Mélanges offerts à Cl. Mondésert*, Paris 1987, p.243.

sufficiente certezza agli inizi del 381,[13] mentre il Commentario di Didimo, pur nell'impossibilità di una datazione precisa, è però di certo posteriore a questa data, a motivo della polemica, in esso presente, contro Apollinare di Laodicea, e il Commentario di Girolamo è a sua volta databile con assoluta certezza alla primavera del 389.[14] Esclusa pertanto di necessità la pur remota possibilità di una influenza di questi due commentari sulle Omelie del Nisseno, non resta che concentrare la nostra attenzione sull'opera di Origene, Dionigi Alessandrino e Gregorio Taumaturgo.

Diciamo subito che a tutti e tre questi interpreti Gregorio deve qualcosa. Da Origene — autore di un commento a scolii e di 8 Omelie sull'*Ecclesiaste*, di cui ci sono pervenuti solo frammenti nelle catene[15] — il Nisseno deriva innanzitutto la tipologia iniziale, secondo cui Salomone-Ecclesiaste è tipo di Cristo, e la connessa interpretazione allegorica, fondata anche sul titolo del libro, dell'*Ecclesiaste* come scritto specificamente indirizzato alla Chiesa (ἐκκλησία). Allo stato attuale noi conosciamo questa tipologia origeniana dal *Prologo* del *Commentario al Cantico dei Cantici*, ma certamente Origene la proponeva anche nei perduti scritti esegetici sull'*Ecclesiaste*. Di derivazione chiaramente origeniana (la fonte a noi nota è ancora il *Prologus in Canticum Canticorum*) è pure la concezione dei tre libri salomonici come tre tappe successive del progresso dell'anima nella via della conoscenza, della perfezione e dell'ascesa spirituale, e in particolare la concezione, enunciata dal Nisseno all'inizio della *Omelia sull'Ecclesiaste*, del libro dei *Proverbi* come uno stadio preparatorio alla lettura dell'*Ecclesiaste*. Questo stesso motivo sarà poi ripreso e approfondito da Gregorio, con una certa indipendenza dal modello origeniano, nella I Omelia sul *Cantico dei Cantici*.[16]   E

---

13   Cfr. CTP 86 pp. 15-16.

14   Cfr. per tutto questo CTP 86, p.11.

15   Cfr. S. Leanza, *L'esegesi di Origene al libro dell'Ecclesiaste*, Reggio Calabria 1975.

16   Cfr. Cl. Moreschini, Gregorio di Nissa. *Omelie sul Cantico dei Cantici* (CTP 72), Roma 1988, 6-7.42-45.

derivano ancora da Origene diverse interpretazioni particolari proposte dal Nisseno: innanzitutto e più nota tra tutte, l'interpretazione cristologico-psicologica di Eccle. 2,14 (*"Gli occhi del saggio sono nel suo capo..."*), che identifica gli occhi con l'intelletto e il capo con Cristo, nella quale sono pure di matrice origeniana la polemica, fondata sul principio del *defectus litterae*, contro i seguaci derivano ancora da Origene diverse interpretazioni particolari proposte dal Nisseno: innanzitutto e più nota tra tutte, l'interpretazione cristologico-psicologica di Eccle. 2,14 (*"Gli occhi del saggio sono nel suo capo..."*), che identifica gli occhi con l'intelletto e il capo con Cristo, nella quale sono pure di matrice origeniana la polemica, fondata sul principio del *defectus litterae*, contro i seguaci dell'interpretazione letterale, e la dottrina dell'ἀναλογία tra la sfera dell'anima e quella del corpo;[17] di poi, la lunga interpretazione allegorica, che abbraccia le ultime tre Omelie, della pericope di Eccle. 3,1-8 (*"Ogni cosa ha il suo tempo e c'è un tempo per ogni cosa sotto il sole..."*), la quale è di certo riconducibile nel suo complesso ad Origene, non solo per l'impostazione psicologica tipicamente origeniana di tutta l'interpretazione, ma anche per le numerose analogie riscontrabili tra l'esegesi del Nisseno e quella di altri interpreti solitamente tributari di Origene (Didimo, Dionigi Alessandrino, Girolamo, Olimpiodoro),[18] le quali sono chiaro indizio di una comune matrice origeniana;[19] e ancora, per citare un ultimo esempio, il commento a 2,14-16 sulla presunta identità di sorte tra il saggio e lo stolto, che sulla scorta dello scolio origeniano del Cod. Vat. Gr. 1694 conclude che, a dispetto della comunanza di mali e di beni nella vita presente, la vera differenza consiste nei beni o nei mali che rispettivamente attendono il saggio e lo stolto dopo la morte, nel tempo futuro.[20] In

---

17   Hom. V 356,20-360,16; vd. CTP 86, pp.108sqq. e relativo commento.

18   Coincidenze di volta in volta rilevate nella mia traduzione di CTP 86.

19   Cfr. CTP 86, pp.121-175 e relativo commento, e particolarmente p.125 n.16.

20   Hom. V 360,22-366,2 = CTP 86 pp. 111-115. Per Origene vd. S. Leanza, *L'esegesi di Origene al libro dell'Ecclesiaste*, pp. 11-12.

quest'ultima interpretazione tuttavia, pur nell'evidente dipendenza dal modello origeniano, si coglie anche una significativa innovazione, segno, pui come altrove, della grande personalità del Nisseno. Mentre infatti l'interpretazione di Origene é orientata piuttosto in prospettiva etica e sembra far consistere la differenza tra il saggio e lo stolto soprattutto nella loro diversa ricompensa ultraterrena, Gregorio privilegia una valutazione di tipo intellettuale, più attenta ai valori umani e "storici" dell'individuo, e fa consistere la differenza tra il saggio e lo stolto sopratutto   nella diversa sorte che li attende nel ricordo dei posteri: "Il ricordo del saggio — dice infatti — vive in eterno e si estende nei secoli; il ricordo dello stolto, invece, si spegne insieme con lui. Riguardo a tali uomini infatti anche il profeta dice: *perì il loro ricordo con fragore* (Sal. 9,7), cioè, manifestamente e con tutta evidenza. Dice dunque: *Il ricordo del saggio non dura in eterno allo stesso modo di quello dello stolto* (Eccle. 2,16), giacché la vita del saggio, attraverso il ricordo, si perpetua nei secoli, mentre all'esistenza dello stolto succede l'oblio: tutto il suo operato infatti cade nell'oblio col trascorrere dei giorni. Questo appunto vuol dire con l'espressione: *come il trascorrere dei giorni, tutto è dimenticato* (Eccle. 2,16)."[21]   Ma oltre che nell'interpretazione del testo dell'*Ecclesiaste*, la dipendenza del Nisseno da Origene si avverte qua e là anche nell'interpretazione di altri luoghi biblici, incidentalmente commentati nelle *Omelie sull'Ecclesiaste*. Basti citare l'esempio dell'interpretazione soteriologica della parabola evangelica della pecorella perduta (Mt. 18,12-14; Lc. 15,4-7), che ricorre nell'Hom. II.[22]   Quest'interpretazione è per la verità comune anche ad altri Padri (Ireneo, Metodio di Olimpo),[23] ma è assai significativa la stretta concordanza che è possibile istituire tra la pagina del Nisseno e un brano del *De principiis* origeniano, come appare manifesto dalla seguente sinossi:

---

21   365,13-366,3 = CTP 86, p.115.

22   304,21-305,13 = CTP 86, pp. 66-67.

23   Cfr. in CTP 86, p.66 n.43, la bibliografia sull'argomento.

Greg. Nyss.,	Origene, *De princ.*
Hom.II in Eccle.[24]	II,8,3 iuxta
	Hieron., Ep. 124,6[25]

Venne dunque il Salvatore a cercare	Venit enim Dominus
e salvare ciò che era perduto nella	atque Salvator quaerere
vanità delle cose insussistenti, per	et salvum facere quod
reintegrarlo nel novero delle cose	perierat, ut perditum
esistenti, perché ridiventasse	esse desistat ... Sicut
perfetto il numero delle creature	perditum aliquando non
di Dio, essendo stato ricondotto	fuit perditum, erit
sano e salvo tra ciò che non	tempus quando perditum
perisce ciò che si era perduto.	non erit.

Ma qui è anche da ricordare la singolare coincidenza rilevata da Ronald Heine tra un brano dell'Hom. V di Gregorio e uno scolio catenario di Origene su Mt. 4,4: coincidenza tanto significativa, da far propendere Heine verso l'ipotesi che nella catena evangelica sia stato falsamente attribuito ad Origene, e riportato alquanto liberamente, il testo dell'Hom. V del Nisseno.[26] Io però non sono molto propenso ad accettare questa conclusione del Heine, giacché mi pare che si tratti, tutto sommato e nonostante le significative analogie, di due testi differenti: abbiamo dunque un altro esempio da aggiungere alla documentazione sin qui riportata. Mi pare piuttosto da sottolineare e da condividere in pieno l'idea di fondo che guida il citato contributo dello studioso americano, che cioè Gregorio, al di là delle dipendenze specifiche e particolari riscontrabili in singole interpretazioni, nelle *Omelie sull'Ecclesiaste* ha mutuato da Origene un fondamentale principio ermeneutico di carattere generale, che è quello di spiegare la Scrittura con la Scrittura.[27] Del resto, la fondamen

---

24   305,9-13 = CTP 86, p.67.

25   Ed. Labourt VII, p.102.

26   Cfr. in questo stesso volume, pp. 217-219.

27   La documentazione di Heine è tuttavia attinta esclusivamente all'Hom.V.

tale formazione origeniana del Nisseno si avverte chiaramente in queste Omelie anche sotto il profilo non strettamente esegetico, ma piuttosto filosofico-teologico, per la presenza di dottrine tipicamente origeniane, come ad es.verso la fine dell'Hom. I, congiuntamente, la dottrina della doppia creazione e quella dell'apocatastasi.[28]

Per altro verso bisogna rilevare che talora Gregorio si allontana intenzionalmente dall'esegesi di Origene. Estremamente indicativo in tal senso è, nell'Hom. VII, il caso del commento a Eccle. 3,5 (*"Tempo di abbracciare e tempo di astenersi dall'amplesso"*), nel quale il Nisseno mutua chiaramente dal maestro alessandrino l'interpretazione allegorica che riferisce il testo dell'*Ecclesiaste* all'abbraccio della sapienza, ma ne rifiuta, certo per l'ἀκολουθία che improntâ la sua interpretazione di tutta la pericope, la spiegazione letterale secondo l'ovvia valenza sessuale del testo biblico.[29] Ancor più degno di rilievo, perché coinvolge un problema interpretativo più generale, è il fatto che egli si allontani da Origene nell'interpretazione dei cosidetti "luoghi epicurei", per i quali il padre alessandrino aveva adottato di preferenzala soluzione dell'interpretazione allegorica,[30] e la cui difficoltà Gregorio risolve invece, come vedremo, facendo ricorso alla teoria della prosopopea. E' del resto assai indicativo che, a differenza di quanto fa per le *Omelie sul Cantico dei Cantici*,[31] nelle *Omelie sull'Ecclesiaste* Gregorio non ritenga di doversi giustificare col lettore per aver trattato lo stesso argomento che già aveva trattato Origene: la qual cosa potrebbe essere interpretata come indizio di una maggiore e più risoluta indipendenza dal modello origeniano.

Da Dionigi Alessandrino — autore pur egli di un perduto *Commentario all'Ecclesiaste*, del quale si conservano tuttavia diversi

---

28   Cfr. CTP 86, pp.56-59 (= 294,18-298,3) e relativo commento.

29   Cfr. CTP 86, p. 145 (= 399,5-400,7) e relativo commento.

30   Cfr. S. Leanza: Orpheus NS 3 (1982) 85-86.

31   Cfr. *Hom. in Cant. Cant. Prol.*: "Se anche noi abbiamo voluto affidare allo scritto la nostra fatica, dopo che Origene si era applicato così amorevolmente a questo testo, nessuno ce ne rimproveri: si tenga presente la divina sentenza dell'Apostolo, che dice: *Ciascuno riceverà la propria mercede secondo la propria fatica*" (trad. Moreschini, CTP 72, p.38).

frammenti nelle catene e altrove[32] — Gregorio riprende un'idea fondamentale nella valutazione della figura e dell'operato di Salomone, la quale, come vedremo più oltre, ha conseguenze decisive sulla stessa valutazione e interpretazione complessiva che egli dà dell'*Ecclesiaste*: cioè, che la ricerca del piacere da parte del saggio re, nonché essere fine a se stessa e dettata da cedimento alle passioni, fu una tappa necessaria della sua esperienza umana, protesa alla ricerca della saggezza e del vero bene.[33] Ma Dionigi interpretava anche allegoricamente, come il maestro Origene, i cosiddetti "luoghi epicurei" di *Qohelet*: e su questa strada Gregorio non lo segue più, giacché, come abbiamo accennato più sopra, preferisce risolvere questa difficoltà con la teoria della prosopopea.

Appunto questa teoria della prosopopea, intesa quale soluzione retorica per interpretare gli scomodi passi "epicurei", il Nisseno la deriva da Gregorio Taumaturgo, che l'aveva per primo impiegata nella sua succinta *Metafrasi dell'Ecclesiaste*. Ed è l'ultimo debito del nostro Gregorio nei riguardi dell'essegesi precedente. Bisogna però dire che nella soluzione adottata dal suo predecessore il Nisseno introduce una significativa innovazione. Il Taumaturgo, infatti, aveva immaginato nell'*Ecclesiaste* un dialogo fittizio di Salomone con ipotetici interlocutori edonisti ed epicurei: questo gli permetteva di attribuire a questi ultimi le affermazioni e le idee moralmente e dottrinalmente inaccettabili, e a Salomone, quali risposte alle obiezioni dei suoi interlocutori, le affermazioni contrarie e perfettamente consone all'etica e alla fede cristiana.[34] Spiegazione ingegnosa che, postulando comunque più voci all'interno dell'opera, presenta interessanti analogie con certe moderne teorie pluraliste. Il Nisseno in alcuni luoghi delle sue Omelie riprende fedelmente la spiegazione del

---

32 Cfr. S. Leanza, 'Il *Commentario all'Ecclesiaste* di Dionigi Alessandrino': *Scritti in onore di S. Pugliatti* V, Milano 1978, 399-429; 'Due nuovi frammenti dionisiani sull'Ecclesiaste': *Orpheus NS* 6 (1985) 156-167; 'Pour une réédition...': ALEXANDRINA. Mélanges offerts à Cl. Mondésert, Paris 1987, 243.

33 Scolio su Eccle. 2,1, presso Procopio, *Catena in Ecclesiasten* (CCh.SG 4, p.14; cfr. Hom. II, 309,19-310,6 = CTP 86, pp. 71-72.

34 Cfr. S. Leanza, Orpheus NS 3 (1982) 81-84.

Taumaturgo,[35] che fu del resto abbastanza diffusa anche tra i posteriori interpreti dell'*Ecclesiaste*;[36] altre volte però introduce nella soluzione proposta dal suo predecessore una sua personalissima variazione, che consiste nel supporre che Salomone si ponga da se stesso le obiezioni e quindi le risolva, impersonando in se stesso la duplice figura dell' obiettore e del confutatore: tesi condensata nella felice formula: "L'Ecclesiaste interroga, l'Ecclesiaste risponde."[37]   E ciò non solo al fine di confutare, con tale artifizio retorico, le empie obiezioni degli uomini carnali, ma anche per prevenire e risolvere anzitempo le difficoltà che i futuri lettori avrebbero potuto sollevare.[38]   Come si vede, ancora una volta il nostro esegeta, pur riprendendo idee e soluzioni precedenti, non le recepisce passivamente, ma le rielabora ed atteggia in maniera affatto personale.

3.   Resta da dire dell'influenza esercitata da Gregorio sui posteriori interpreti dell'*Ecclesiaste*.   Per ragioni di brevità e per non dilatare troppo i confini di questa relazione, mi limiterò a prendere in considerazione soltanto due autori della tarda cristianità, nei quali più chiara e distinta si avverte l'eco dell'esegesi del Nisseno: Olimpiodoro e Gregorio di Agrigento.   Per il resto, sarà sufficiente osservare che la fortuna di cui godettero nell'antichità le *Omelie sull'Ecclesiaste* di Gregorio è significativamente testimoniata dall'abbondante utilizzazione, superiore a quella di tutti gli altri commenti sull'*Ecclesiaste*, che ne è stata fatta nelle catene: dalla Catena di Procopio a quella di Policronio, alla Catena Barberiniana, alla cosiddetta Catena dei Tre Padri, al florilegio del Cod. Vat. Gr. 1694: tanto che l'editore delle *Omelie sull'Ecclesiaste*, P. Alexander, ha ritenuto di dover tener presente anche la tradizione catenaria per la costituzione del testo di Gregorio.

---

35   Cfr. ad es. Hom. V, 370,12-371,2 = CTP 86, pp.118-119.

36   Cfr. documentazione in Orpheus NS 3 (1982) 73-90.

37   Cfr. Hom. I, 294,18-295,5; V 360,22-364,6 (= CTP 86, pp.55-56;111-114).

38   Cfr. più ampiamente, per tutto il problema, Orpheus NS 3 (1982) 85-86.

Quanto ad Olimpiodoro, autore nel VI secolo di un *Commentario sull'Ecclesiaste* in parte originale in parte a carattere compilativo, una sorta di Commentario-Catena o Commento catenario, ho già rilevato nelle note alla mia traduzione delle Omelie gregoriane (CTP 86) i numerosi luoghi in cui riecheggia il pensiero e l'esegesi del Nisseno. Ricorderò tuttavia qui alcuni casi più significativi.   Innanzitutto, l'interpretazione allegorica dell'*Ecclesiaste* come libro specificamente indirizzato alla Chiesa (PG 93,480-482), fondata sul titolo stesso del libro e che chiaramente rinvia all'inizio dell'Hom. I del Nisseno (279,4-280,7 = CTP 86, pp.41-42); e ancora l'accento posto sul problema del libero arbitrio, per il quale si veda sopratutto *Comm. in Eccl.* 1,14 (PG 93,492), e, in questo stesso contesto, l'identica interpretazione data dell'ambigua espressione dell'*Ecclesiaste* προαίρεσις πνεύματος, intesa, esattamente come fa Gregorio, nel senso di *libera scelta dello spirito* o *volontà libera di scegliere*, cioè, in ultima analisi, *libero arbitrio* (PG 93,492 e 497).[39]   In alcuni casi la dipendenza di Olimpiodoro da Gregorio è tanto stretta, che solo una lettura comparata dei due testi può darne adeguata dimostrazione.   Tale è il caso del commento a Eccle. 2,3, un passo dal trasparente significato secondo il testo ebraico (*"decisi in cuor mio di dilettare col vino la mia carne,"*) ma che suona davvero incomprensibile nella LXX (tanto da costringere i moderni editori a correggere il testo, per cavarne un senso plausibile): *"Mi volsi a considerare se il mio cuore potesse trascinare la mia carne come il vino."*)   Gregorio interpreta la strana similitudine nel senso che Salomone avrebbe deciso di asservire le passioni della carne all'intelletto, annullandole a quel modo che l'assetato annulla e fa scomparire, tracannandolo avidamente, il vino: *"Mi volsi a considerare se il mio cuore potesse trascinare la mia carne come il vino.   Cioè, come la cura delle realtà intellegibili potesse prevalere sui moti della carne, sì che ...i pensieri della carne fossero obbedienti e sottomessi alla parte razionale dell'anima, venendo trascinato e assorbito l'elemento inferiore da quello che ha maggior dignità, come avviene per quelli che hanno sete: se infatti si accosta il bicchiere alla bocca di un assetato, il vino non rimane nel bicchiere

___

39   Cfr. CTP 86, p.69 n.55.

ma trapassa in colui che beve e scompare, attratto avidamente nel ventre."[40] Spiegazione ingegnosa, per la verità, e che non è certo un caso se ritroviamo identica in Olimpiodoro: *"Mi volsi a considerare se il mio cuore potesse trascinare la mia carne come il vino. La bevanda tracannata da chi beve scompare. Mi volsi dunque a considerare — dice — se ... il mio intelletto potesse essere così forte da distruggere e far scomparire come vino tracannato il desiderio della carne."*[41] Così come non è certo casuale l'identica interpretazione allegorica della successione dei libri *Genesi* ed *Esodo*, intesi rispettivamente come simbolo della nascita e della morte, che tanto Gregorio che Olimpiodoro introducono nel commento di Eccle. 3,2: *"Tempo di nascere e tempo di morire"*:

Greg. Nyss., Hom. VI in Eccle.[42]	Olymp., Comm. in Eccle. 3,2[43]
Molto opportunamente pone all'inizio del discorso questo necessario collegamento, accostando la morte alla nascita: necessariamente infatti la morte segue alla nascita ... Questa stessa verità insegna velatamente, mediante il titolo dei due primi libri sacri, anche Mosè l'amico di Dio, scrivendo l'*Esodo* subito dopo il *Genesi*: in maniera tale che chi pone mente ai due titoli è ammaestrato sul proprio destino dalla stessa successione di questi libri biblici.	Opportunamente l'Eccclesiaste cominciò dalla nascita e dalla morte, ricordandoci questa nostra vita effimera. Per questo anche Mosé, avendo intitolato *Genesi* il primo libro, chiamò subito dopo il secondo *Esodo*, significando simbolicamente il carattere effimero di questa nostra vita.

---

40 Hom. II 311,15-312,5 = CTP 86, p.73.
41 PG 93,493.
42 378,8-24 = CTP 86, p.126.
43 PG 93,508.

E non è neppure casuale l'identica distinzione della realtà in sensibile e intellegibile, introdotta allo stesso punto del commento, cioè nella spiegazione di Eccle. 3,1:

Greg. Nyss.,*Hom. VI in Eccle.*[44]	Olymp., *Comm. in Eccle.* 3,1[45]
Delle realtà esistenti, alcune	Delle realtà esistenti, alcune
sono materiali e sensibili,	sono caduche altre eterne. Quelle
altre intellegibili e	eterne sono anche invisibili e
immateriali... Il presente	si trovano al di sopra del sole.
discorso ci parla delle	Il discorso presente tratta di
realtà terrene, che sono	quelle caduche e che si
sotto il cielo.	trovano sotto il sole.

Una maggiore attenzione merita Gregorio di Agrigento, autore non disprezzabile del VII–VIII secolo, il quale nella sua *Explanatio super Ecclesiasten* instaura un vero e proprio dialogo con il Nisseno, ora per seguirne le idee teologiche e le soluzioni esegetiche, ora per criticarne coraggiosamente spiegazioni e conclusioni che a lui sembrano inaccettabili. Avendo già dedicato a questo autore, come accennavo più sopra,[46] un lavoro particolare, mi permetto di rinviare ad esso per la dettagliata documentazione sia dei luoghi nei quali, talora anche con precisi riscontri verbali, l'Agrigentino dipende dal Padre cappadoce, sia di quelli in cui, invece, polemicamente ne rifiuta e confuta l'interpretazione. Voglio tuttavia ricordare qui almeno alcuni aspetti generali dell'interpretazione dell'Agrigentino, per i quali l'influenza del Nisseno mi sembra particolarmente rilevante e degna di essere evidenziata. Il primo consiste nell'interpretazione complessiva che Gregorio di Agrigento dà dell'*Ecclesiaste*, affermando che scopo di questo libro è insegnarci il disprezzo dei beni terreni, che altro non sono se non vanità, ed esortarci alla ricerca dei veri beni, che sono quelli spirituali;[47] e, parallelamente, che scopo di Salomone nel

---

44   373,21-374,7 = CTP 86, p.122.

45   PG 93,508.

46   Cfr. *supra*, nota 3.

47   Cfr.*Explan. sup. Eccle.* 1,2-3 (PG 98,753 sqq.); 2,4-9 (PG 98,805-809); 2,12 (PG 98,812-813); 2,20-21 (PG 98,829); 3,2 (PG 98,897) ecc.

comporre l'*Ecclesiaste* fu diadditare ai posteri la propria esperienza di
vita quale esempio da non imitare, perché essa potesse servire di
ammaestramento agli uomini nella scelta del vero bene.[48]   Ancora
degna di nota è la particolare forma, tipicamente nisseniana, che
nell'*Explanatio* di Gregorio di Agrigento assume la teoria della
prosopopea: non solo supponendo, come Gregorio Taumaturgo e gli altri
interpreti antichi, un dialogo fittizio di Salomone con ipotetici
interlocutori,[49] ma immaginando più particolarmente, come appunto
Gregorio di Nissa aveva fatto, che Salomone, prevedendo e prevenendo
le future obiezioni, anticipatamente le sollevi e subito dopo le
risolva.[50]   L'influenza del Nisseno si avverte, infine, nella stessa
ricchezza del contenuto filosofico e teologico che caratterizza
l'*Explanatio super Ecclesiasten* di Gregorio di Agrigento.   A questo
proposito è sopratutto da segnalare la stretta dipendenza dal pensiero
nisseniano in uno dei punti dottrinalmente più impegnati del
Commentario dell'Agrigentino, alla dottrina del libero arbitrio.   Il passo
chiave è l'interpretazione di Eccle. 1,13: περισπασμὸν πονηρὸν ἔδωκεν ὁ
θεὸς τοῖς υἱοῖς τῶν ἀνθρώπων, τοῦ περισπᾶσθαι ἐν αὐτῷ, dove Gregorio
intende, esattamente come il Nisseno e fondandosi sui medesimi luoghi
biblici, ἔδωκεν nel senso di *permise*, e attribuisce quindi al libero
arbitrio dell'uomo e non a Dio la responsabilità del male commesso:
"*Cattiva occupazione diede Dio ai figli degli uomini*.   Dice questo non
perché Dio abbia propriamente dato una siffatta occupazione, ma
perché ha permesso loro di fare quello che volessero, a motivo del
loro libero giudizio e della loro libera facoltà di scegliere.   Pertanto
l'espressione ἔδωκεν ὁ θεὸς l'Ecclesiaste l'ha posta senza dubbio in
luogo di συνεχώρησεν, ἀφῆκε (*permise*): come anche Paolo ... dice di
coloro che si sono abbandonati ad ogni nefandezza e cattivo agire:
παρέδωκεν αὐτοὺς ὁ θεὸς ἐν ταῖς ἐπιθυμίαις τῶν καρδίων αὐτῶν (Rom
1,24), e di nuovo: *Poiché non vollero riconoscere Dio*, παρέδωκεν
αὐτοὺς ὁ θεὸς εἰς ἀδόκιμον νοῦν, ποιεῖν τὰ μὴ καθήκοντα (Rom 1,28).

---

48   Cfr.*Explan. sup. Eccle.* 2,4-9 (PG 98,805); 2,20-21 (PG 98,829)
ecc.

49   *Explan. sup. Eccle.* 2,24 (PG 98,833).

50   *Explan. sup. Eccle.* 2,15 (PG 98,820) e 3,21 (PG 98,892-896).

Con la loro libera scelta, essendo pienamente liberi (τῇ σφῶν προαιρέσει, διὰ τὸ αὐτεξουσίους εἶναι) permise loro di fare cose sconvenienti".[51]   E parimenti poco più oltre, intendendo πνεῦμα come sinonimo di ψυχή,[52] spiega l'espressione προαίρεσις πνεύματος come la *libera volontà dell'anima*, che è assolutamente padrona di volgersi tanto al bene quanto al male.[53]   È esattamente la stessa spiegazione già offerta da Gregorio di Nissa nella *II Omelia sull'Ecclesiaste*.[54]

4.   Abbiamo ripetutamente accennato — più sopra a proposito di Dionigi Alesandrino e ultimamente trattando di Gregorio di Agrigento — alla valutazione che Gregorio di Nissa dà della figura storica di Salomone.   Sarà bene spendere qualche parola su questo argomento, anche perché l'interesse del Nisseno per la figura storica di Salomone è stato sovente sottovalutato o addirittura misconosciuto, a motivo dell'interpretazione tipologica che ravvisa in lui il tipo di Cristo.   Tra gli altri uno studioso italiano, il Siclari, ha recentemente fornito un'interpretazione a mio avviso parziale e riduttiva delle *Omelie sull'Ecclesiaste*, dandone una lettura in chiave esclusivamente cristologica, che trascura del tutto l'interesse di Gregorio per la vicenda umana di Salomone.[55]   Mentre a me sembra che le cose stiano esattamente in maniera opposta, e che sia proprio l'interpretazione tipologico-cristologica ad avere, in definitiva, nelle *Omelie sull'Ecclesiaste* minora rilevanza.

La tipologia Ecclesiaste = Cristo è introdotta, com'è noto, da Gregorio verso l'inizio della I Omelia, e si fonda sul facile

---

51   *Explan. sup. Eccle.*   1.13 (PG 98,788-792).

52   ταύτην γὰρ (*scil.* τὴν ψυχήν) πνεῦμα νῦν ὠνόμασε.   Cfr.*Explan. sup. Eccle.* 1,17-18: πνεῦμα γὰρ κἀνταῦθα τὴν ψυχὴν προηγόρευσεν (PG 98,796).

53   PG 98,792.

54   301,3-303,11 = CTP 86, pp.62-64. Per il significato dato dal Nisseno all'espressione προαίρεσις πνεύματος vd. la mia nota in CTP 86, p.69.

55   A. Siclari, *Gregorio di Nissa. Omelie sull'Ecclesiaste* (trad. di S. Rinaldi) Parma 1987, 27-30. Vd. specialmente p. 29, dove si dice che "tutto l'*Ecclesiaste* è letto da Gregorio come una prefigurazione dell'insegnamento di Cristo."

accostamento etimologico di ἐκκλησιαστής ed ἐκκλησία, nonché su un'interpretazione rigorosamente sillogistica degli appellativi e dei titoli dell'Ecclesiaste e di Cristo.   Ma   a dispetto di questa iniziale tipologia, la tematica cristologica ha scarso rilievo nel prosieguo delle Omelie[56] e non può essere neanche lontanamente paragonata all'interpretazione costantemente e ininterrottamente cristologica che lo stesso Gregorio dà nelle   *Omelie sul Cantico dei Cantici*. In realtà, già a partire da metà circa dell'Hom. II,[57] la tipologia cristologica rimane come in ombra, giacché l'autore concentra la sua attenzione sulla figura storica di Salomone[58] e sul valore paradigmatico della sua vicenda umana. A tal proposito, riprendendo, come abbiamo visto, un'idea di Dionigi Alessandrino, Gregorio ritiene che la ricerca del piacere da parte di Salomone, nonché essere fine a se stessa, rientrava nella molteplice esperienza del saggio re, proteso alla ricerca del vero bene e non asservito passionalmente ai sensi.[59] Ma guidato dal concetto dell'ὠφέλεια, il Nisseno va ben oltre la spiegazione di Dionigi, ravvisando nella vicenda di Salomone un valore

---

56   Così anche M. Simonetti, *Lettera e/o allegoria*, Roma 1985, 151 n.167.

57   Da 305,19 in avanti (= CTP 86, pp. 67 sqq.)

58   Cfr. Hom. II 306,11-19 = CTP 86 p.68: "Chi parla è infatti Salomone: quel Salomone che fu il terzo re d'Israele dopo il famoso Saul e dopo David ...   Egli, avendo ricevuto il regno dal padre quando ormai era cresciuta in grandezza la potenza degli Israeliti, fu proclamato re; e non logorò più i sudditi con guerre e battaglie, ma, vivendo in pace con ogni magnificenza, si adoperò non nella conquista di ciò che non aveva, ma nel godimento di ciò di cui abbondava ... ."

59   Cfr. Hom. II 307-314 (CTP 86 pp.68-75), e specialmente 309,21-314,10 (CTP 86 pp.71-72): "Non si diede subito a questa esperienza, né si abbandonò al godimento dei piaceri senza aver prima sperimentato la vita austera e più severa, ma dopo essersi in essa esercitato e aver improntato la sua vita a severità e austerità ..., allora si abbandonò a ciò che appare dilettevole ai sensi, volgendosi ad esso non per moto passionale, ma per indagare se l'esperienza dei sensi così acquisita potesse apportare qualche contributo alla conoscenza del vero bene;" Hom. V 368,9-13 (CTP 86 p.117): "egli non è scivolato nella vita gaudente perché vinto dalla passione, ma è pervenuto ad essa a motivo della sapienza, riuscendo a dominare l'esperienza di tale vita, piuttosto che lasciarsi asservire al suo potere."

esemplare ed educativo per i posteri. A tal riguardo egli prospetta una duplice ipotesi, quella della finzione retorica e quella dellareale esperienza del piacere e dei beni terreni in genere,[60] giustificando in entrambi i casi l'operato di Salomone nella superiore prospettiva dell' ὠφέλεια che ne sarebbe derivata ai posteri. È evidente che la difficoltà maggiore si pone interpretando l'esperienza di Salomone come reale. Ed è infatti a questa eventualità che Gregorio presta più attenzione, concludendo che Salomone l'ha fatto "affinché gli uomini non giudicassero più desiderabili quei beni che sono stati disprezzati da chi, per propria esperienza, ne ha conosciuto la vanità".[61]

Da una visione d'insieme delle *Omelie sull'Ecclesiaste* si ha insomma la netta impressione che, al di là della tipologia cristologica enunciata all'inizio, Gregorio nutra di fatto grande interesse per la figura storica di Salomone, e appaia soprattutto preoccupato di giustificare agli occhi del lettore il suo operato. In ogni caso, egli sembra del tutto dimentico della tipologia cristologica quando, ad esempio, nell' Hom. II dice che "l'Ecclesiaste ... confessa a tutti gli uomini il suo operato: il quale è stato tale che sarebbe più onorevole sconoscerlo e tacerne che parlarne;"[62] o quando nel corso delle Omelie III[63] e IV[64] riprende e biasima in Salomone la smodata ricerca di magnificenza, la cupidigia, l'intemperanza, la superbia e altri analoghi vizi e difetti. Il fatto è che, a differenza del *Cantico dei*

---

60 Cfr. Hom. III 317,19-318,8 (CTP 86 pp.78-79): "Se poi egli abbia fatto realmente queste cose, o se per nostra utilità finga di averle fatte, per condurre conseguentemente il discorso allo scopo che s'era prefisso, questo non posso dirlo con esattezza ... Ma sia che egli a ragion veduta riferisca come avvenute cose non avvenute, e le biasimi come se le avesse sperimentate, affinché noi prima di sperimentarle evitiamo di desiderare quelle cose che egli biasima; o sia anche che deliberatamente si sia abbandonato al godimento di tali piaceri, al fine di esercitare i suoi sensi accuratamente anche mediante la conoscenza di opposte esperienze, questo io lo lascio congetturare a suo piacimento a chi ne ha voglia."

61 Hom. III 319,3-5 (CTP 86 p.79).

62 Hom. III 317,14-19 (CTP 86 p.78).

63 319,11-324,2 (CTP 86 pp.80 sqq.).

64 334,5-338,22 (CTP 86 pp.90 sqq.)

Cantici, l'*Ecclesiaste* non richiedeva necessariamente un'allegoresi continuata, offrendo, col suo noto insegnamento sulla vanità universale, una sufficiente ὠφέλεια anche secondo il senso letterale.[65] Inserendo in questo contesto generale dell'insegnamento sulla vanità la vicenda umana di Salomone, Gregorio può trarne, senza necessità di più richiamare la tipologia cristologica e comunque indipendentemente da essa, una grande ὠφέλεια spirituale, interpretando quella vicenda *iuxta litteram* e traendone quale conclusivo ammaestramento "che gli uomini, apprendendo da chi per esperienza l'ha provato ..., si guardino dall'assalto del male prima di farne esperienza: a quel modo che si attraversano senza danno i luoghi popolati da ladroni e da animali feroci, quando si è prima conosciuto chi già ha corso gli stessi pericoli."[66]   In questa prospettiva non è tanto il tipo di Cristo, come comunemente si ritiene, quanto piuttosto il Salomone storico gaudente e penitente, quello che sperimentò πείρας ἔνεκα i piaceri e ne constatò la vanità, che, in armonia con lo σκοπός dichiarato all'inizio, "ci insegna a non tenere in alcun pregio nessuno dei beni di quaggiù: né la ricchezza, né la gloria, né il dominio, né la gioia le delizie e i banchetti, né alcun'altra delle cose che gli uomini sogliono tenere in pregio: ma a considerare che uno solo è il risultato di tutte queste cose, la vanità, e che non v'è alcun vantaggio al di fuori di essa."[67]

---

65   Cfr. M. Simonetti, *Lettera e/o allegoria,* Roma 1985, 151-152: "In effetti l'*Ecclesiaste,* neutralizzati gli spunti di carattere 'epicureo', ben si prestava a mettere in risalto la vanità del mondo e di tutti i suoi beni ... Gregorio può spiegare il testo dell'*Ecclesiaste* al suo skopòs senza eccessiva allegorizzazione."

66   Hom. IV 346,9-14 (CTP 86 pp.98-99).

67   Hom. IV 352,12-17 (CTP 86 p.103). Estremamente indicativa è la distinzione tra il tipo di Cristo e il Salomone gaudente-penitente esplicitamente introdotta all'inizio dell'Hom. III.   In questo "sdoppiamento" della figura dell'Ecclesiaste è al Salomone storico che viene chiaramente assegnata la funzione di insegnarci, con l'esempio della sua vicenda personale, la vanità di tutti i beni sensibili: "Nella prima omelia abbiamo appreso che colui che raduna tutte le creature e ricerca ciò che era perduto e raccoglie in unità ciò che errava, indaga questa vita terrena (= *tipologia cristologica*)... Nella seconda omelia, invece, abbiamo visto come Salomone accusi la vita dedita ai piaceri e alle passioni, affinché anche noi ci convinciamo a rifiutare tali cose, dal momento che colui che ebbe ogni possibilità di procurarsi ogni

In questo quadro complessivo, mi sembra che assai più che la tipologia cristologica, enunciata all'inizio ma poi scarsamente sfruttata, nelle *Omelie sull'Ecclesiaste* sia predominante un'interpretazione di tipo letterale con impostazione accentuatamente moralleggiante, imperniata su un'attenta meditazione e considerazione della vicenda storica ed umana di Salomone.

---

piacere e godimento e tutte quelle cose che sembrano agli uomini doversi ricercare, ha disprezzato tutto ciò non tenendolo in nessun conto" (314,13-315,7 = CTP 86 p.76). Più sopra ho indicato proprio verso la metà della II Omelia il punto in cui la tipologia cristologica dell'Ecclesiaste comincia a sfumare e a passare in secondo piano.

ENGLISH SUMMARY by S.G. Hall.

1.   Characteristics

In the *Homilies on Ecclesiastes* Gregory deals with fundamental philosophical and theological questions (being/not being; good and evil; freedom of will; etc.) more than all other commentators on *Qohelet*.

Special features:

ἀκολουθία (*consequenzialità*), the search for a rigorously logical concatenation of facts and ideas in the text;

σκοπός, the particular purpose of each biblical book.
Both features have classical and patristic precedent, but the combination is original to Gregory (so Daniélou, Rondeau). This combination gives unity to the exegesis of Ecclesiastes. For σκοπός see esp. 280,2-7.   ἀκολουθία is a *leitmotiv*; it is combined with σκοπός at 317,19-22; 373,3-6. For the effect on sustained exegesis, see especially Eccles. 3,1-8 in Hom. 6-8.

Note also the characteristic theme of ἐπέκτασις at 313,9-15; 400,20-401,2.

2.   Influences on Gregory

From **Origen** Gregory derives the following:

Solomon/Ecclesiast as type of Christ, with Ecclesiastes addressed to the *ecclesia* (279,4-281,2);

3 books of Solomon as a progressive sequence (277,3-278,17);

'eyes in the head' interpreted in terms of the soul and of Christ (356,20-358,10);

various aspects of the exegesis of the antitheses in Hom. 6-8, identified through other writers in the Origenist exegetical tradition.

The good and evil fate as referring to *post mortem* experience (360-367) is in an Origenist scolion, Cod.Vat.Gr. 1694; but Gregory differs in emphasizing historical memory rather than superterrestrial destiny (365,13-366,6).

Seeking the lost in 304,21-305,13 (esp. 305,9-13) is close to Origen, *princ.* II,8,3 (= Jerome *Ep.* 124,6).

The Origenist scolion on Mt 4,4 identified by Heine in a catena is independent of Gregory (*pace* Heine). Above all from Origen comes the principle of interpreting Scripture by Scripture.

Gregory deliberately differs from Origen on Eccles. 3,5, by omitting the literal sexual sense of the clasp/embrace, while adopting the spiritual embrace of Wisdom (397,16-399,20).

Dionysios of Alexandria is followed when the deliberate enjoyment of pleasure (309,8-310,6) refers to the conduct of the historical Solomon.

From **Gregory Thaumaturgos** comes the repeated explanation of the text as a fictitious conversation, *prosopopoea*. But making this conversation the self-interrogation of the Ecclesiast is a feature personal to Gregory of Nyssa (294,18-295,16; 360,22-344,6).

3.   **Influences of Gregory on others**

Olympiodoros has Ecclesiastes addressed to the Church (cf 279-280) and the ambiguous reading of προαίρεσις πνεύματος (307,4-14). On 'swallowing flesh like wine', 311,15-312,5 is close to Olympiodoros, PG 93,493. The allegory of the titles of *Genesis* and *Exodus* (378,16-24) also appears in Olympiodoros. The distinction of sensible from intelligible reality (373,21-374,8) occurs at the same point in Olympiodoros.

Gregory of Agrigentum has many similarities in *Explanatio super Ecclesiasten*: seeking spiritual goods; *prosopopoea*, which is further developed. But he especially repeats Gregory's emphasis on freewill in interpreting προαίρεσις πνεύματος.

4.   **Christological typology**

Against A. Siclari, the christological typology of Hom. 1 plays no large part in the subsequent interpretation. Gregory is more concerned with historical and moral matters: the personal history of Solomon and moral benefits (ὠφέλεια). This is often incompatible with christological interpretation. See 306,11-19; 307-314 esp. 309,21-310,6; 368,9-13. Sometimes the experience of Solomon causes acute difficulties (see 317.9-318,8).

IV STUDIES OF GREGORY AND OF ECCLESIASTES

— 16 —

Verwendung und Bedeutung des Buches *Ecclesiastes* im Werk Gregors von Nyssa außerhalb der *Homiliae in Ecclesiasten*

Hubertus R. Drobner

Der 'Bibelindex zu den Werken Gregors von Nyssa' verzeichnet insgesamt 240 Zitationen des Buches *Ecclesiastes*.[1] Zwar berücksichtigt er lediglich die in den Editionen bereits angegebenen Stellen, man darf aber davon ausgehen, daß damit alle wichtigen wörtlichen und sinngemäßen Zitate erfaßt sind. Davon stehen nur 34 außerhalb der *Homiliae in Ecclesiasten*, wovon noch weitere zehn abzuziehen sind. Bei dreien handelt es sich nämlich um identische Zitate nach verschiedenen Editionen,[2] sechs gehören zum Buch *Ecclesiasticus*.[3] Der Verweis auf Eccl 9,12 in der Edition der *Epistula canonica* bei Migne trifft nicht zu.[4] Das dortige Zitat Μὴ πολὺς ἴσθι πρὸς ἀλλοτρίαν stammt aus Prov 5,20. Von den verbleibenden 24 Stellen beziehen sich zehn auf die Kapitel Eccl 1-3,13, die Thema der *Ecclesiastes*-Homilien sind, 14 auf Eccl 4-11, und zwar in folgender Verteilung:

In Canticum Canticorum	5 (GNO VI 15,3. 22,12. 41,16. 110,4. 132,14-16).
Contra Eunomium	3 (GNO I 76,28. 254,18. 257,24)
De Virginitate	3 (GNO VIII/I, 270,6, 337,2)

---

1   Ed. Hubertus R. Drobner, Paderborn 1988, 54-57.

2   Eccl 1,4 (GNO VIII/I, 270,6 = SC 119, IV,3; 2,14 (GNO S 67,10 = SC 160, II,15,19); 4,10 (GNO VIII I, 337,2 = SC 119, XXIII,3).

3   Sir 3,22 (Si II,111,4); 11,3 (PG 46,556); 24,21 (GNO VIII I, 78,17); 30,11 (PG 46,816); 44 ff. (St 156); 46,17 (Si II, 168,8).

4   PG 45,228 C.

In Pulcheriam	2 (GNO IX, 467,5. 19-21)
De beatitudinibus	2 (PG 44,1277 D. 1280 C)
Adversus Macedonianos	1 (GNO III/I, 102,12)
Adversus Apolinarem	1 (GNO III/I, 214,12)
De beneficentia	1 (GNO IX, 105,21)
In Flacillam	1 (GNO IX, 476,23 f.)
In Hexaemeron	1 (PG 44,92 D)
De opificio hominis	1 (PG 44,152 C)
De oratione dominica	1 (PG 44,1145 C)
De iis qui baptismum differunt	1 PG 46,429 A)
De creatione hominis	1 (GNO S 67,10)

Da, wie gesagt, diese Sammlung nicht auf einer eingehenden und einheitlichen *relecture* aller Werke Gregors beruht, kann aus den Angaben lediglich geschlossen werden, daß das Buch *Ecclesiastes*, abgesehen von seiner monographischen Behandlung in den Homilien, in geringem, aber beständigem Maße zum bibeltheologischen Repertoire Gregors gehörte. Alles weitere kann nur die Einzelanalyse herausarbeiten, die teils nach Inhalt, teils nach den Werken Gregors und teils nach den Bibelzitaten gliedern muß.

A. Anklänge

Den meisten Kirchenvätern, auch Gregor, war bekanntermaßen die Bibel so vertraut, daß sie große Teile davon auswendig kannten und zitierten und unwillkürlich, bzw. zumindest ohne ausdrückliche Kennzeichnung, biblische Worte und Wendungen in ihre Schriften einfließen ließen. Daß dieses Vorgehen im Fall des Buches *Ecclesiastes* außerhalb der *Ecclesiastes*-Homilien nur ein einziges Mal festzustellen ist, darf wohl der insgesamt geringen Zahl der Zitate zugeschrieben werden.

In *De beneficentia* schildert Gregor den in Luxus lebenden Verschwender, der rauschende Feste ausrichtet mit Wein, Schwelgerei, Schauspielern, Musikern und vielem anderen mehr.[5] Die μουσικούς, μουσικάς, erinnern an Eccl 2,8 ᾄδοντας καὶ ᾀδούσας, bleiben aber reine Reminiszenz, ohne als verderbliche Folge des Luxus näher

---

5   GNO IX, 105,18-25.

gedeutet zu werden, wie dies in den vierten *Ecclesiastes*-Homilie geschieht.[6]

Eine interessante Parallele bietet dabei der Hohelied-Kommentar des Origenes, der die Weinknaben und -mädchen als die Mystiker versteht, die den neuen Wein Christi ausschenken, das Mahl also mystisch deutet.[7]

B. Polemik

In seinen dogmatisch-polemischen Traktaten setzt Gregor mehrfach Zitate aus dem Buch *Ecclesiastes* nicht zur theologischen Argumentation, sondern als polemische Waffe ein. Eunomios wirft er vor, seine falsche Theologie könne nicht auf Unkenntnis (ἀμαθία) beruhen (was noch entschuldbar wäre), da er sich sonst in den überflüssigsten Spitzfindigkeiten beschlagen zeige (τὰ περισσὰ σοφιζόμενον), obwohl dies schon die Hl. Schrift verbiete (Eccl 7,16): μὴ σοφίζου περισσά.[8] Gregor folgt in dieser Art der Verwendung des *Ecclesiastes* der Argumentationsweise seines Bruders Basilius gegenüber Eunomios. Dieser hielt ihm vor, er überhebe sich über die Tradition und die Regel der Väter. Er täusche nur Wahrheit vor, um die Menschen zu betrügen. Schon Eccl 1,15 sage: 'Das Krumme wird nicht wieder gerade'; die Kriterien der Wahrheit (der Väter) passen nicht zur Lüge (des Eunomios).[9]

Didymos von Alexandrien erläutert in seinem *Ecclesiastes*-Kommentar Vers 7,16 mit der πανουργία in 2 Kor 4,2. Die Häretiker lebten in dieser Verschlagenheit und verfälschten so das Wort Gottes.[10] Πανουργία ist bei Gregor, wie jetzt aufgrund der Göteborger Konkordanz leicht nachzuprüfen ist, ein recht seltenes Wort.[11] In

---

6   GNO V, 347,4-21.

7   Origenes, Cant.1 (GCS Or 8,94, 24-27).

8   CE I 166 (GNO I, 76,28).

9   CE I 4 (SC 299, 168,86).

10   Didymos, Eccl 215,3-12 (PTA 16,58).

11   Cajus Fabricius/Daniel Ridings, A Concordance to Gregory of Nyssa = SGLG 50 (1989) s.v.

Contra Eunomium bzw. in der *Refutatio confessionis Eunomii* verwendet Gregor es in eben diesem Sinn, um Eunomios, den λογογράφος, der überflüssigen und irreführenden Machenschaften zu zeihen.[12] Eine direkte Verbindung zum *Ecclesiastes* stellt Gregor zwar nicht her, wohn aber zu den Proverbia (8,5), die, nach der Auffassung Gregors ebenfalls von Salomon verfaßt, die Vorbereitung des *Ecclesiastes* darstellen.[13]

In *Adversus Macedonianos* charakterisiert Gregor den Häretiker, der die Gottheit des Sohnes leugnet, noch schärfer in Anlehnung an Eccl 11,5 als 'Knochen im Leib der Schwangeren', nicht einmal als reifen und lebendigen Menschen.[14] Er spricht damit dem Häretiker geradezu seine Existenz ab bzw. sein volles Menschsein. Im Lichte der Bild- und Erlösungstheologie Gregors würde dies bedeuten, daß der Irrtum des Häretikers physische Folgen hat. Da nach Gregor der Mensch auch nach dem Bild des Logos geschaffen ist, würde die Leugnung der Gottheit des Sohnes die Unvollständigkeit des Urbildes bedeuten und konsequenterweise auch die des Abbildes. Oder aber die Sünde der Häresie entstellt das Abbild so sehr, daß es nicht mehr als Mensch zu erkennen ist. Ob diese Schlußfolgerungen allerdings zutreffen, bleibt hypothetisch, denn der Kontext enthält keinerlei Hinweise auf einen Zusammenhang mit der Bildtheologie.

C.   Ecclesiastes 5,1

Zum polemischen Repertoire Gregors im weiteren Sinn gehört das Zitat Eccl 5,1 'äußere kein Wort hastig vor Gott, denn Gott ist im Himmel droben und du auf der Erde unten', das er aber nicht nur in *Contra Eunomium* und *Adversus Apolinarem* einsetzt, sondern das auch eine nicht unwesentliche Rolle in seinen exegetischen Homilien spielt.

Gregor mahnt Eunomios einmal mit diesem Zitat allgemein, nich vorschnell etwas über das Wesen Gottes aussagen zu wollen, da dies für uns Menschen doch unbegreiflich bleibe.[15] Konkreter und

---

13   S.u.S. 375–378.

14   GNO III/I, 102,12.

15   CE II 105 (GNO I, 257,24).

polemischer hat er es kurz zuvor verwandt. Wer (wie Eunomios) sage, man könne durch Erkenntnis (γνῶσις) das göttliche Wesen erkennen, handle eitel (μάταιος — Anklang an Eccl 1,2 u.ö.). Gott ist gegenüber dem Menschen übergroß und dieser verschwindend klein, denn 'Gott ist im Himmel droben und du auf der Erde unten'.[16] Das *Ecclesiastes*-Zitat dient also hier zur polemischen Kritik der Methode des Eunomios und macht ihre Vergeblichkeit schon aufgrund des räumlichen Abstandes deutlich, der zugleich ein wesensmäßiger ist.

In *Adversus Apolinarem* ist es Apolinarios, der den Halbvers 'Gott ist im Himmel droben' zitiert, was Gregor nur wiedergibt.[17] Für den dogmatischen Streitpunkt zwischen Apolinarios und Gregor, ob nun der Mensch, der Gott aufnimmt, lediglich Behältnis Gottes oder aber selbst himmlisch werde, hat der *Ecclesiastes* nur illustrierende Bedeutung, soweit wir das aus dem kurzen Zitat Gregors schließen können. Denn die scharfe Unterscheidung von Eccl 5,1 zwischen Gott im Himmel und dem Menschen auf Erden könnte sehr gut Hauptargument des Apolinarios gewesen sein für die bloße Funktion der Einwohnung des Logos im Menschen Jesus.

Herausragende Bedeutung gewinnt Eccl 5,1 in der zweiten *Oratio dominica* für die spirituelle Theologie Gregors.[18] Er kommentiert den ersten Vers des Vater Unsers 'Vater Unser, der du bist im Himmel' und fühlt sich dadurch an Eccl 5,1 'Gott ist im Himmel droben' sowie Ps 72,28 erinnert 'es ist gut für mich, Gott anzuhangen'. Anhand dieser beiden Bibelstellen entwickelt er kurz seine bekannte Theologie der 'Ομοίωσις Θεῷ. Der Mensch kehrt zu seinem Vater im Himmel zurück durch die Flucht vor den Übeln der Welt, wodurch er Gott ähnlich wird. Bezeichnend ist, wie Gregor dabei die räumlichen Vorstellungen des Himmels überwindet und ihn vielmehr als Zustand oder Lebensweise betrachtet. Denn, fährt er fort, der Mensch, der gerecht, heilig und gut ist wie Gott, gelangt ohne weiteres sofort in

---

16 CE I 94 (GNO I, 254,18).

17 GNO III/I, 214,12.

18 PG 44,1145 C. Vgl. Hubert Merki, ΟΜΟΙΩΣΙΣ ΘΕΩ. Von der platonischen Angleichung an Gott zur Gottähnlichkeit bei Gregor von Nyssa = Par. 7 (1952) 124-127.

den Himmel, da dies keine Frage eines Weges ist. Sondern wer das Gute gewählt hat, besitze das Gute; daher ist man im Himmel, wenn man Gott im Geist ergriffen hat. Diese Schlußfolgerung sieht Gregor in Ps 72,28 'es ist gut für mich, Gott anzuhangen' bestätigt, denn wer zu Gott gehöre, sei mit ihm vereint und also auch an demselben Ort wie er. Diese Loslösung Gregors von räumlichen Vorstellungen hin zur Konzeption von Seinsweisen hatte Jean Daniélou bereits in der Frage der Aufenthalts 'orte' Jesu nach seinem Tode beobachtet;[19] sie wird hier bestätigt.

Der Vergleich mit Origenes, Eusebius, Hieronymus und Olympiodor zeigt auch, daß Gregor mit dieser spirituellen Interpretation eine Sonderposition einnimmt. Bei Origenes sind zwar gewisse Anklänge daran zu finden, wenn er sagt, die Welt, in der wir lebten, sei unten, das den Gerechten verheißene Erbe aber oben im Himmel.[20] In der Philokalie warnt Origenes auch den Weisen, der sein Herz gereinigt hat, damit Christus, die Weisheit, Platz greifen kann, sich stets bewußt zu bleiben, daß die Geschenke Gottes immer den Menschen überragen; sonst verfalle er der ἀσέβεια.[21] Origenes kennt also wohl eine geistliche Deutung von Eccl 5,1 im Zusammenhang des Aufstiegs des Gerechten zu Gott, ein vom Ort losgelöstes Erreichen des Ziels aber nicht. In *De oratione* schließlich interpretiert er Eccl 5,1 lediglich auf den Abstand zwischen Himmlischem und Irdischem hin.[22]

Für Eusebius ist der Abstand zwischen Gott im Himmel droben und dem Menschen auf der Erde unten nur ein weiterer Beweis dessen, daß das Leben *vanitas vanitatum* sei.[23] Im Psalmenkommentar nimmt aber auch er die spirituelle Interpretation auf. Der immense Unterschied zwischen Gott im Himmel und dem Menschen auf Erden

---

19 Vgl. Jean Daniélou, L'état du Christ dans la mort d'après Grégoire de Nysse: HJ 77 (1957) (= Theologie aus dem Geist der Geschichte. Festschrift B. Altaner) 69.

20 Sel 5 in Ps 36 (PG 12,1362 D).

21 Frg Ph I (SC 238, 368-371).

22 Orat 23,4 (GCS Or 2, 352,20-353,1).

23 Ps 51 (PG 55,593)

drücke die Hoffnung des Gerechten aus, einmal zu Gott aufzusteigen.[24] Wir haben also auch hier den grundlegenden Aufstiegsgedanken, der aber nicht weiter ausgeführt wird, schon gar nicht hinsichtlich des Weges oder des Erreichens des Zieles.

Hieronymus und Olympiodor schließlich verbleiben beide auf der kognitiven Ebene wie Gregor in *Contra Eunomius*. Das Begreifen des Menschen sei von der Natur Gottes so weit enfernt wie die Erde vom Himmel.[25] Ein Verstehen der Größe Gottes sei daher für den Menschen völlig unmöglich.[26] Diese kognitive Deutung von Eccl 5,1, greift Gregor nochmals in *De beatitudinibus* auf als Regel zur Interpretation von Schriftworten hinsichtlich der Natur Gottes. Selbst die großen Worte der Schrift seien klein und unzureichend im Vergleich zum Wesen Gottes, das sie nicht erfassen könnten.[27]

D. Mystik, Askese und Spiritualität

1. Die drei Bücher Salomos: Proverbia, Ecclesiastes und Canticum Canticorum

Für Gregor von Nyssa und viele Kirchenväter vor und nach ihm haben die drei atl. Bücher *Proverbia*, *Ecclesiastes* und *Canticum Canticorum* König Salomon zum Verfasser und bilden eine Trilogie mit innerem mystischen und spirituellen Zusammenhang. Bei Gregor stellen sie drei Stufen bzw. drei aufeinander aufbauende Führer des Aufstieges zu Gott dar, wie er sowohl zu Beginn der *Ecclesiastes-* Homilien als auch des Hohelied-Kommentars erläutert.[28] Die *Proverbia* haben also einen geistigen und einen geistlichen Effekt, die insofern zusammenhängen, als ja ohne Verständnis der Schrifttexte ihre geistliche Wirkung nicht eintreten kann. Auf der Basis der durch die *Proverbia* vorbereiteten Erkenntnisfähigkeit und Sehnsucht nach der Tugend zeige das Buch *Ecclesiastes*, daß alles Irdische vergänglich und

---

24 PG 23,612 B.

25 Hieronymus, Eccl V 1 (CChr.SL 72, 291,1-19).

26 Olympiodor, Eccl 5 (PG 93,537 C-540 A).

27 Beat 7 (PG 44,1280 C).

28 Eccl 1 (GNO V, 277,4-278,1); Cant 1 (GNO VI 22, 5-17).

eitel sei und wende so unsere Seele der unsichtbaren, himmlischen Schönheit Gottes zu. So führe der *Ecclesiastes* den, der Vollkommeneres als das Irdische erstrebt, zu den Höhen Gottes. Die Endstufe dieses Aufstiegs wird im Hohenlied erreicht. Nach Motivation und Vorbereitung der Fähigkeit zum Aufstieg durch die *Proverbia* und Hinführung zur Gegenwart des Göttlichen durch Zurücklassung des Irdischen durch den *Ecclesiastes* führe das Hohelied schließlich auf mystische Weise in die inneren Geheimnisse Gottes ein, was erst dadurch möglich ist, daß bereits die Neigung zur Welt überwunden ist.

Aufgrund dieser Theorie überrascht es nicht, daß Gregor auch außerhalb der *Ecclesiastes*-Homilien und insbesondere in seinem Hoheliedkommentar und in *De virginitate* den Prediger mystisch, asketisch und spirituell auslegt, und der Großteil seiner *Ecclesiastes*-Zitate außerhalb der *Ecclesiastes*-Homilien zu dieser Kategorie zählten.

Gregor fügt sich damit in eine lange Auslegungstradition sowohl der griechischen als auch der lateinischen Kirche ein, die *Proverbia*, *Ecclesiastes* und *Canticum* als eine dreistufige Einheit sieht, wenn auch die Interpretationen im einzelnen durchaus differieren.

Die erste Deutung, die wir kennen, ist die Hippolyts, die allerdings nicht bei den großen Kirchenvätern weiterwirkte. Für ihn entsprechen die drei Bücher Salomos den Geheimnissen der Trinität.[29] Lediglich eine anonyme griechische Paraphrase seines Hohenliedkommentars wiederholt diese Erklärung.[30]

Origenes erklärt im Prolog seines Hohenliedkommentares die Funktion der drei Bücher folgendermaßen.[31] Die *Proverbia* lehrten in kurzen, leicht zu verstehenden Vorschriften die Moral, d.h. die rechte Lebensführung. Die *Ecclesiastes* lehre daraufhin die Unterscheidung der natürlichen, irdischen Dinge in nützliche und notwendige und

---

29 Hippolytos, Cant. 1,3-4 (CSCO 264, 23,9-19).

30 Marcel Richard, Une paraphrase grecque résumée du commentaire d'Hippolyte sur le Cantique des Cantiques: Muséon 77 (1964) 137-154 = *Opera Minora* I 18, Turnhout-Leuven 1976; hier I 1-9 (140 f.)

31 GCS Or 8, 76,4-16. 77,30-78,10. 85,12 f.

überflüssige und eitle. Das Hohelied schließlich entzünde die Liebe zum Göttlichen.   *Proverbia, Ecclesiastes* und *Canticum Canticorum* verkörperten also die Dreiheit der *disciplinae moralis, naturalis* und *inspectiva*.   Verglichen mit Gregor scheinen die drei Stufen des Origenes noch vor dessen zu liegen.   Denn während nach Gregor bereits die *Proverbia* die Sehnsucht nach dem Göttlichen entfachen, bleibt dies bei Origenes dem *Canticum* vorbehalten, nachdem das Nichtige von dem für ein geistliches Leben Nützlichen unterschieden wurde.   Denn diese zweite Stufe ist bei beiden gleich.   Für Gregor führt aber diese und die dritte Stufe weiter, nämlich bis zur Begegnung mit Gott und dem mystischen Eindringen in seine Geheimnisse.

Die Dreiteilung des Origenes hat allerdings, mit einzelnen Abwandlungen, den weitaus größeren Nachhall gefunden als die Gregors. Eusebius deutet den Dreischritt auf die Teile eines Schriftkommentars, die immer *moralis, naturalis* und *theologica* sein müßten.[32]

Nach Didymos lehren die *Proverbia* die Ethik, der *Ecclesiastes* die natürlichen Dinge, die wahrnehmbare und sichtbare Schöpfung, und das Hohelied schließlich das Himmlische und Geistige.[33]   Olympiodor teilt sowohl im Prolog seines Proverbien-Kommentars als auch das *Ecclesiastes*-Kommentars so ein: *moralia, naturalia, intelligibilia*; die Proverbien lehrten die rechte Verhaltensweise des Menschen, der Ecclesiast den Sinn der Natur und die Eitelkeit des irdischen Lebens, das Hohelied weise den Weg zum vollkommenen Leben.[34]   Prokop schließlich schreibt den Prolog der *Ecclesiastes*-Homilien Gregors aus,[35] und die *Catena Trium Patrum* (7./8. Jh.) vereint in etwa die Positionen des Origenes und Gregors: In den *Proverbia* übe Salomo den Geist der Menschen für das geistliche Streben vor, indem er durch ethische Philosophie hinführe.   Der Ecclesiast erziehe daraufhin φυσικῶς.[36]

---

32   Eusebius, frg apud Procop (PG 87/2, 1787 D).

33   Didymos, Eccl I 1, 5,31-6,28 (PTA 25,8-14).

34   Olympiodor, frg Prov 1 (PG 93, 469 B);   Eccl pr (477 C).

35   Procopius, Eccl pr (CChr.SG 4, 5,7-6,29 = GNO V, 277,2-280,20).

36   Pr (CChr.SG 11, 3,1-6).

Hieronymus kennt die Dreiteilung Ethik — Physik — Theologie[37], aber auch eine neue Deutung. *Proverbia, Ecclesiastes* und *Canticum* seien gleichsam die Erzieher des Menschen in seinen verschiedenen Lebensaltern.[38] Die *Proverbia* lehrten das Kind, erzögen zur Erfüllung der Aufgaben des Menschen durch Sätze. Der Ecclesiast lehre den reifen Mann, daß er nicht etwa das Irdische für beständig und ewig halte, und das Hohelied vermähle schließlich den Menschen mit dem Bräutigam, Jesus. Hier klingt manches vom Aufstiegsgedanken Gregors an, aber die endgültige Vermählung mit dem Bräutigam scheint bei Hieronymus keine mystische, sondern die des Todes zu sein. Gleichzeitig enthält die Deutung der *Proverbia* den Gedanken der origenischen Tradition, der moralischen Erziehung durch klare Vorschriften, und die *Ecclesiastes*-Interpretation, die bei Origenes und Gregor gleichermaßen vorgebildete Erkenntnis der Vergänglichkeit alles Irdischen. Salonius wird diese Erklärungen des Hieronymus kopieren.[39]

2. ματαιότης

Immer wieder klingt in der geistlichen Auslegung Gregors in verschiedensten Zusammenhängen das Grundthema des *Ecclesiastes* an, die ματαιότης, die Nichtigkeit und Eitelkeit der Welt und des menschlichen Lebens.

Im Hoheliedkommentar erklärt er damit *Cant* 1,2 'deine Brüste übertreffen allen Wein und der Duft deiner Parfüms alle Aromen' und *Cant* 2,7 'Ich habe euch beschworen, Töchter Jerusalems, bei den Kräften und Mächten des Feldes stört nicht die Liebe und weckt sie icht auf, bis sie selbst es will.' Die Braut des Logos ist hier die Kirche (nicht die Seele), an deren Brust die 'noch unmündigen Kinder in Christus' (νήπιοι) trinken. Sie selbst liegt, wie einst Johannes, an der Brust Christi und empfängt von dort das Leben, die Gnade Christi (χάρις), seine Güter (τὰ ἀγαθά) und verborgenen Geheimnisse (τὰ κεκρυμμένα μυστήρια), die sie durch ihre Tradition (ἐκ διαδόσεως)

37 Hieronymus, Eccl I 1 (CChr.SL 72,250,14-251,47).
38 Ebd.
39 Salonius, Eccl (PL 53,993 C-D).

weitergibt.[40]   Gregor führt damit zum Schluß der ersten Hohelied-
Homilie einen Gedanken fort, den er bereits kurz zuvor ausgestaltet
hat.   Die Milch der Kirche sind die göttlichen Lehren, die die νήπιοι
trinken.[41]   Sie sind die unmündigen Kindern angemessene Nahrung.   Da
allerdings die Jugend geneigt ist, in der ματαιότης zu verharren, gilt
es, diese aufgrund der Liebe zu den Brüsten der Kirche abzulegen.[42]

Das Feld in *Cant* 2,7 bedeute nach Mt 13,38 die Welt (Gleichnis
vom Sämann), die nach 1 Kor 7,31 vergeht.   Alles Vergängliche aber
sei nach dem Eccl (1,2 u.ö.) eitel.[43]   Diese Deutung ist dieselbe wie in
der ersten *Ecclesiastes*-Homilie, wo Gregor ebenfalls nach Eccl 1,2 die
materielle Welt als an sich nichtig einstuft.   Ihren Wert beziehe sie
allein aus ihrer Funktion als Führerin zu Gott.[44]

In *De beatitudinibus* deutet Gregor die siebte Seligsprechung
'Selig sind, die Frieden stiften, denn sie werden Söhne Gottes genannt
werden' (Mt 5,9) durch den *Ecclesiastes*.   Um nämlich klar vor Augen
zu stellen, welch große Verheißung es bedeute, 'Söhne Gottes' genannt
zu werden, vergleicht er in Anlehnung an Eccl 1,2 und 5,1 die über-
ragende Größe Gottes mit der ματαιότης des Menschen.[45]

In *De iis qui baptismum differunt* schließlich nimmt Gregor den
Prediger zu einem ganz neuen, eigenen Gedanken auf: wo keine Liebe
sei, da alles ματαιότης ματαιοτήτων.[46]   Man muß diesen Satz wohl
nicht nur auf der zwischenmenschlichen Ebene verstehen, daß Beziehungen unter Menschen erst durch gegenseitige Liebe Bedeutung
gewinnen, sondern durch die Identifikation der Liebe mit Gott.   Dort,
wo Gott nicht ist, ist alles in der Welt eitel.   Das entspricht sowohl

---

40   Cant 1 (GNO VI 40,13-41,13).

41   Ebd. (35,8-10).   Vgl. Hubertus R. Drobner, Die drei Tage zwischen
      Tod und Auferstehung unseres Herrn Jesus Christus.   Eingeleitet,
      übersetzt und kommentiert = PhP 5 (1982) 69.

42   Cant 1 (GNO VI, 41,14-18).

43   Ebd. 4 (132,10-16)

44   GNO V, 283,7-10. 284,18-285,4.

45   Beat 7 (PG 44,1277 D).

46   PG 46,429 A.

der Intention der Aussage des *Ecclesiastes* als auch den übrigen
Interpretationen Gregors.

Selbstverständlich wird das Grundthema des *Ecclesiastes* in
vielfältiger Weise bei den Vätern besprochen. Es zeichnen sich dabei
drei Hauptrichtungen ab:

(1)   Die Qualifizierung nicht-christlicher Lehren als μάταιος. Clemens
        von Alexandrien tut damit kurz die Philosophie Epikurs ab. Wenn
        dieser den Zufall als ein Weltprinzip einführe, dann habe er den
        Ecclesiast nicht verstanden, der doch alles Weltliche als nichtig
        bezeichne.[47]   Eusebius zitiert in seiner *Praeparatio evangelica*
        diese Passage aus den *Stromata* des Clemens[48] und wendet das
        Prinzip schon davor auf die Juden an. Ihre Physiologie sei doch
        nur Eitelkeit der Eitelkeiten.

(2)   Die geistliche Deutung des Origenes.   Die ματαιότης des
        Ecclesiastes meine alles Materielle, Irdische.[49]   Der nach
        Weisheit Strebende bzw. der im christlichen Sinne Weise betrachte
        daher alles Irdische als eitel,[50] und die Freude des Menschen
        über das Irdische, über Ehren und Reichtümer seien falsche
        Freuden.[51]   Der Soldat Gottes müsse vielmehr die Eitelkeit der
        Welt überwinden, indem er nichts tue, was nicht der Sache,
        nämlich dem Aufstieg zu Gott, diene.[52]   Diese spirituelle
        Interpretation findet ebenfalls Widerhall bei Eusebius, in dessen
        Psalmenkommentar: Wer seine Hoffnung auf Gott setze, werde
        nicht zuschanden, alle Sorge um Zeitliches aber sei Eitelkeit.[53]

(3)   Eine sakramentale Erklärung trägt schließlich Cyrill von
        Jerusalem in seinen mystischen Katechesen bei: Bevor der Mensch

---

47 Clemens, str V 14,90,2 (GCS Clem 2³, 385,17-19).

48 Eusebius, praep 13, 13,4 (GCS Eus 8/2, 199,4).

49 Origenes, princ I 7,5 (SC 252,218,160).

50 Cels VII 50 (SC 150,132,17); Cant pr (GCS Or 8, 78,3. 79,14).

51 Num 11,8 (GCS Or 7/2, 92,2 f.).

52 Ebd. 25,3 (236,15).

53 Eusebius, Ps (PG 23,353 C. 596 B).

nicht die χάρις, d.i. die Taufgnade, erlangt habe, sei alles ματαιότης.[54] Die Welt und das Leben des Menschen empfangen also nicht (nur) durch das geistliche Streben des Menschen ihren Sinn, sondern grundlegend durch das Christsein. Nur für den Christen erschließt sich mit Hilfe der Gnade Christi, die in der Taufe empfangen wurde, der Sinn der Welt als Führerin zu Gott.

3. In Canticum Canticorum

Aufgrund des mystischen und spirituellen Zusammenhangs zwischen *Ecclesiastes* und Hohemlied und der generellen geistlichen Auslegung des Predigers durch Gregor ist verständlich, daß er ihn über die bereits behandelten Stellen hinaus gern in seinem Hoheliedkommentar zitiert.

Zu Beginn der ersten Homilie lädt Gregor diejenigen ein, die Auslegung des Hohenliedes zu hören, die nach Paulus den alten Menschen abgelegt und Christus als neues Gewand angezogen haben (Kol 3,9. Ro 13,14). Dieses Gewand sei weiß, wie das Christi bei der Verklärung (Mt 17,2), da die Gläubigen mit ihm verwandelt würden (Phil 3,21). Es ist das weiße Tauf- und Hochzeitskleid, das Gregor asketisch auf die reinen und unbefleckten Gedanken bezieht.[55] Hermann Langerbeck verweist im Apparat der GNO VI auf Eccl 9,8, Claudio Moreschini in der italienischen Übersetzung allerdings nur auf Mt 22,10-13 (Gleichnis vom königlichen Hochzeitsmahl).[56] Daß aber der Zusammenhang mit Eccl 9,8 sehr wohl gegeben ist, erweisen die *Ecclesiastes*-Kommentare und die übrige Auslegungsgeschichte.

Hieronymus versteht das weiße Kleid als das Symbol des Lichtes Christi im paulinischen Sinne, nämlich den neuen Menschen anzuziehen.[57] Für Salonius bedeuten die weißen Kleider die Tugenden und die reinen Taten der Menschen,[58] für Olympiodor das Taufkleid und die

---

54 Cyrillus Hier., myst 4,8 (SC 126,142,10).

55 Cant 1 (GNO VI, 15,3).

56 Claudio Moreschini, Gregorio di Nissa, Omelie sul Cantico dei Cantici. Introduzione, traduzione e note (= CTePa 72), Rom 1988, 37.

57 Hieronymus, Eccl IX 7-8 (CChr.SL 72, 327,189-197).

58 Salonius, Eccl (PL 53,1007 A-B).

tugendhaften Werke. Das Taufkleid könne dabei immer wieder durch die
Tränen der Reue und durch Buße gereinigt werden.[59] Diese Interpretationen der *Ecclesiastes*-Kommentare beruhen auf alexandrinischer
spiritueller Theologie, wie sie vor allem bei Origenes zu finden ist. In
seinem *Exodus*-Kommentar deutet er die weißen Kleider als in der
Taufe gereinigt,[60] im Matthäuskommentar als die Gewänder der
Tugenden, die die Hochzeitskleider für das himmlische Hochzeitsmahl
sind.[61] Cyrill von Jerusalem übernimmt die Gedanken der geistlichen
Weiße des Taufkleides, ergänzt aber, daß sie deswegen weiß seien, weil
der Herr in den Werken dieser Menschen verherrlicht werde.[62] Auch
für die Deutung Gregors darf man daher auf Eccl 9,8 verweisen. Es
überrascht nur, daß Gregor die Relation auf die reinen Gedanken des
Menschen beschränkt, während sonst die Taten im Vordergrund stehen.

Durchaus originell und für spätere Zeiten richtungsweisend ist die
Exegese Gregors zu *Cant* 1,17 'Die Balken unseres Hauses sind Zedern,
unsere Decke sind Zypressen.'[63] Mystisch gehe es dabei um die
Sorgfalt des Menschen in der Abwehr der Versuchungen, die wie Regen
aufs Dach fallen (vgl. Mt 7,25). Die festen Balken des Hauses
bedeuten nämlich die Tugenden, die den Lastern widerstehen. Aber es
gilt, täglich sorgfältig die Stärke der Tugend zu pflegen und zu prüfen,
denn 'das Dach wird herabfallen wegen der Faulheit, und durch die
Muße der Hände wird das Haus das Wasser hereinlassen', wie der
Ecclesiastes (10,18) sagt. Dann trifft geistlich ein, was die *Proverbia*
(27,15) prophezeien: 'Am Tag des Regens treiben die Tropfen den
Menschen aus dem Haus'. Gregor erklärt nicht näher, wie das Haus zu
verstehen sei, aus dem der Mensch aufgrund der Vernachlässigung der
Tugenden am Tag der Versuchung durch die Laster vertrieben werde.
Man muß wohl aus dem Kontext annehmen, daß es das tugendhafte
Leben ist, das er bis dahin geführt hat.

---

59   Olympiodor, Eccl 9 (PG 93, 588 B).

60   Origenes, Ex 11,7 (GCS Or 6,2-15).

61   Origenes, Mt 17,24 (GCS Or 10, 650,22-29).

62   Cyrillus Hier., myst 4,8 (SC 126, 142,7 f.).

63   Cant 4 (GNO VI, 109,13-111,1).

Andere Erklärungen differieren nämlich vor allem in diesem Punkt. Der *Ecclesiastes*-Kommentar des Didymos folgt zunächst ganz Gregors Interpretation.[64] Er geht von Mt 7,24 aus: Wer auf diese Worte Jesu hört, baut ein Haus auf Felsen, in dem auch Balken und Dach gesichert sind. Für ihn, der so als Gerechter seinen Lebenswandel aufrichtet, gilt nicht das Wort der Prov 27,15. Die Balken des Hauses sind die Lehren der εὐσέβεια, worauf als Dach der tugendhafte Lebenswandel ruht. Das Haus sei nach *Cant* 1,17 die Versammlung der Gläubigen. Während also Didymos zunächst ganz der geistlichen Interpretation Gregors folgt, geht er dann zu einer dogmatischen und ekklesiologischen Deutung über, die auch sonst durchgehend weiterwirkt.

Olympiodor gliedert in zwei verschiedene Erklärungen:

(1) Das geistliche Haus der Seele dürfe nicht von der Schlechtigkeit durchtränkt werden, weil der Mensch nachlässig im Guten sei.

(2) Es gelte, das Haus der Kirche gegen die Dämonen zu verteidigen.[65]

Für Hieronuymus bedeutet die Faulheit ebenfalls die Nachlässigkeit in guten Werken, das Haus aber eschatologisch die Heimstatt im Himmel. Es gelte gleichermaßen für jeden Einzelnen wie für die ganze Kirche, die guten Taten nicht zu vernachlässigen, um die ewige Heimat nicht aufs Spiel zu setzen.[66]

4. De virginitate

Der geistliche Sinn des Buches *Ecclesiastes* gilt konsequenterweise in besonderem Maße für den, der die Jungfräulichkeit erstrebt, so daß Gregor in *De virginitate* mehrfach darauf zurückkommt.

Zu Eccl 1,4 'Eine Generation geht und eine andere kommt, aber die Erde besteht in Ewigkeit' bemerkt er, der Jungfräuliche lerne daraus, sich nicht irdischem Besitz zuzuwenden, da er weiß, daß die

---

64 Didymos, Eccl 310,21-311,24 (PTA 24, 140-147).

65 Olympiodor, Eccl 10 (PG 93,604 C-D).

66 Hieronymus, Eccl X 18 (CChr.SL 72, 341,298-342,309).

Erde ihn nur beherberge wie die Generationen vor und nach ihm.[67] In diesem Falle wird als, bei aller grundsätzlichen Vergänglichkeit des Irdischen, die Beständigkeit der Erde im Vergleich zur Kurzlebigkeit des einzelnen Menschen hervorgehoben. Der Mensch ist nur 'Gast auf Erden', alles Irdische ihm nur für so kurze Zeit geliehen, daß sich eine feste Bindung daran nicht lohnt. Olympiodor wird später eine andere Schlußfolgerung aus der relativen Beständigkeit der Welt ziehen: sie bleibe bestehen als Anklägerin der Missetaten, die der Mensch auf ihr vollbracht habe.[68] Damit verbunden sind Vorstellungen des personifizierten Auftretens der Gestirne und Elemente beim jüngsten Gericht, gleichsam ausgestattet mit ewigem Gedächtnis, wie sie z. B. von Athanasius geschildert werden.[69]

Eccl 4,9-10 'besser sind zwei dran als ein einziger; denn ihnen wird guter Lohn zuteil aus ihrer Mühe. Kommen sie nämlich zu Fall, kann der eine dem anderen wieder aufhelfen. Wehe aber dem Einsamen, wenn er fällt, und es ist doch kein zweiter da, ihn aufzurichten!' hat in der Geschichte der Exegese weitere Kreise gezogen. Gregor nimmt sie als Anweisung für den jungen, noch nicht gefestigten Menschen, den Weg der Jungfräulichkeit nicht allein zu beschreiten, sondern sich dazu einen Gefährten zu nehmen.[70] Man ist versucht, darin den Ausdruck persönlicher Erfahrung Gregors zu sehen, der das Ziel der Jungfräulichkeit selbst nicht erreicht hat, während er in seiner nächsten Umgebung, auf dem Familienbesitz Annesi, das Gelingen einer geistlichen Gemeinschaft erlebt und sein Bruder die bedeutendste Ordensregel der Ostkirche verfaßt. Jedenfalls spiegeln sich darin Reflexe der bekannten Schwierigkeiten des Anachoretentums, wenn er von Trugbildern des Traumes und Wahnvorstellungen spricht, die für Offenbarungen der Wahrheit gehalten werden.

---

67 GNO VIII/I, 270, 6.

68 Olympiodor, Eccl 1 (PG 93,481 C).

69 J.B. Bernardin, A Coptic Sermon Attributed to St Athanasius: JThS 38 (1937) 125, f. 105vβ-106rβ.

70 GNO VIII/I, 336,18-337,21.

Wenn auch Eccl 4,9-10 in der uns bekannten Auslegungstradition nicht speziell auf die Jungfräulichkeit bezogen wird, so doch immer auf die Gemeinschaft des christlichen und geistlichen Lebens auf dem Weg zu Gott. Origenes erklärt Lk 10,1 (die Aussendung der Siebzig) mit den Parallelen Mk 6,7 (Aussendung zu zweit) und der langen atl. Tradition, wie man z.B. am *Ecclesiastes* sehe.[71] Ebenso interpretiert Olympiodor: Der Herr sandte auch die Apostel zu zweit aus zur Gemeinschaft im Guten, fügt dann aber eine zweite Deutungsmöglichkeit hinzu: die Gemeinschaft von Leib und Seele.[72] Die übrigen *Ecclesiastes*-Kommentare widerholen mit Nuancen die geistlich-praktische Erklärung:

(1)   Didymos: Man muß Helfer haben, wenn man im Tun guter Werke ausgleitet.[73]

(2)   Ps-Chrysostomus vergleicht mit Mt 18,20 'wo zwei oder drei in meinem Namen beisammen sind, da bin ich mitten unter ihnen'. Die Gemeinschaft lehre die Liebe zueinander, und in den Wechsel-fällen des Lebens sei so Sympathie vorhanden.[74]

(3)   Die *Catena Trium Patrum*: Zwei sind stärker als einer. Sie können sich gegenseitig auf dem Weg zum Guten aufhelfen, wenn sich z.B. ein Praktiker mit einem Theoretiker verbindet.[75]

5. Trost- und Grabreden

Die Nichtigkeit des Lebens, die der Ecclesiast thematisiert, dringt besonders im Augenblick des Todes ins Bewußtsein des Menschen. Gleichzeitig kann aber daraus Trost geschöpft werden, da sie ja im Gegensatz zur Größe Gottes und der ewigen Verheißung steht. So beklagt Gregor in der Trostrede auf den Tod der Kaisertochter Pulcheria nach den Regeln der klassischen Rhetorik die Jugend der Verstorbenen und fragt nach dem unvermeidlichen Warum

---

71   Origenes, Lk frg 158 (GCS Or 9, 290,11 f.).

72   Olympiodor, Eccl 4 (PG 93,529 C-D).

73   Didymos, Eccl 123,23-124,17 (PTA 22,210-215).

74   Ps-Chrys., Eccl IV 9 (CChr.SG 4, 79,39-48).

75   Eccl IV (CChr.SG 11, 33,84-35,119).

des frühen Todes.[76]	Die ebenfalls klassische Antwort der frühen
Vollendung erhält im christlichen Kontext allerdings eine biblische
Begründung.	Viele Stellen der Hl. Schrift schätzen das irdische Leben
gering ein (z.B. Eccl 2,17), vor allem aber ist es Salomo selbst (Eccl
4,2-3 und Sap 4,7-15), der den Verstorbenen vor dem Lebenden glück-
lich preist.	Denn das mühevolle irdische Leben sei im Vergleich zum
ewigen Leben gering einzuschätzen.	Dies gelte selbst für die, die ein
glückliches Erdenleben hatten wie David und Salomo.	Da sie zudem
weise waren, begriffen sie seine Nichtigkeit.

In der Grabrede auf die Kaiserin Flacilla zitiert Gregor das
berühmte Wort Eccl 3,4 'es gibt eine Zeit des Lachens und eine Zeit
des Weinens', das ja eine allgemeine Lebenserfahrung ausdrückt.	Für
Gregor aber ist dies der geistliche Auftrag, seine Seele der jeweiligen
Situation anzupassen.[77]	Viele der uns bekannten *Ecclesiastes*-
Kommentare erläutern Vers 34, kaum aber im Sinne Gregors.	Lediglich
die *Catena Trium Patrum* stellt paraphrasierend fest, das Leben des
Menschen sei eben von Gegensätzen angefüllt[78] und Gregor von
Agrigent schließt aus den notwendigen Wechselfällen des Lebens, die
Weinen und Lachen hervorbringen, daß der Weise sich darauf
vorbereitet, um nicht in Extreme getrieben zu werden.[79]
Wahrscheinlich schreibt er Gregor aus, denn ihre zweite Deutung ist
offensichtlich von Hieronymus übernommen.[80]	Das irdische Leben
nämlich lasse weinen, während das zukünftige Lachen bringe.	Er sieht
seine Interpretation bestätigt durch die zweite Seligpreisung (Lk 6,21)
'selig, die jetzt weinen, denn sie werden lachen.'	Ebenso deutet

---

76	GNO IX 467,5. 19-21.	Vgl. Joachim Soffel, Die Regeln Menanders
	für die Leichenrede in ihrer Tradition dargestellt, herausgegeben,
	übersetzt und kommentiert = BKP 57 (1974) 287 f.

77	GNO IX 476,23 f.

78	Eccl III (CChr.SG 11, 23,19).

79	Gregorius Agrig., Eccl III 5 (PG 98,852A-853B).

80	Hieronymus, Eccl III 4 (CChr.SL 72, 274,50-52).

Dionysios das Weinen als die Zeit des Leidens (mit Christus), die Zeit des Lachens als die Auferstehung mit Christus, was Prokop kopiert.[81]

Salonius und Olympiodor verstehen zwar Weinen und Lachen ebenfalls als Gegensätze der Gegenwart und der Zukunft, aber im Sinne der geistlichen Entwicklung. Dadurch, daß man durch Tränen der Reue sein Leben reinige, könne man in Zukunft lachen (Salonius).[82]   Für Olympiodor gilt die jetzige Trauer den Sünden und dem Untergang von Schülern und Mitbrüdern. Wenn sie in Zukunft Fortschritte im guten und geistlichen Leben machen, wird dies Grund zur Freude sein.[83]

E. Schöpfungstheologie

Ein letzter Kontext der *Ecclesiastes*-Exegese Gregors ist seine Schöpfungstheologie, die vor allem deswegen interessant ist, weil er darin dieselben *Ecclesiastes*-Zitate, die er in den Homilien und anderen seiner Werke spirituell erklärt, gleichsam 'physisch' auf die Beschaffenheit von Welt und Mensch deutet.

Im *Hexaemeron* macht Gregor zu Eccl 1,4 'die Erde besteht für immer' eine im Lichte moderner Physik erstaunliche Aussage: Die vier Elemente aus denen die Welt bestehe, Erde, Feuer, Wasser und Luft, seien so geschaffen, daß sie sich ewig erhielten.[84]   Besser hätte man nach dem antiken Weltbild den Massenerhaltungssatz nicht ausdrücken können, auch wenn Gregor das sicherlich nicht beabsichtigte.   Er verbindet aber sehr wohl eine genaue Beobachtung und Beschreibung der Natur mit der biblischen Botschaft, wie das öfter in seinen Werken zu finden ist.[85]   In *De virginitate* allerdings hatte er denselben Vers auf

---

81   Dionysios Alex., frg (BGL 2,93 f.) = Procop Eccl III 4 (CChr.SG 4, 27,24-28,2).

82   Salonius, Eccl (PL 53,999 C).

83   Olympiodor, Eccl 3 (PG 93,509 C-D).

84   PG 44,92 D.

85   Z.B. s pas (GNO IX, 252,6-16. 259,24-260,6); Beschreibung des menschlichen Körpers und des Wachstums des Getreides; tr sp (GNO IX, 297,11-298,3): Beschreibung der Vollmondnacht.

die Einsicht des Jungfräulichen gedeutet, daß er nur vergänglicher Gast auf der ewig bestehenden Erde sei.[86]

In *De hominis opificio* erklärt Gregor die Struktur des Menschen. Eccl 1,8 'ein Auge wird nicht voll vom Sehen, und ein Ohr wird nicht gefüllt vom Hören' hilft ihm dabei das Phänomen des Zusammenhangs von Gehör, Sprache und Denken zu erklären. Der νοῦς des Menschen teile jedem Organ seine eigene und ausschließliche Funktion zu, so daß das Ohr beständig hört, der Mund nur spricht. Der νοῦς allein koordiniert, so daß man sehr wohl gleichzeitig hören und sprechen kann[87] — auch das eine Naturbeschreibung, die vor moderner Biologie durchaus standhält. Die Diskrepanz dieser biologischen Deutung wird um so deutlicher, wenn man im selben Werk zuvor liest: νοῦς καὶ λόγος θειότης ἔστιν[88] und er in den *Ecclesiastes*-Homilien Eccl 1,8 ebenso deutet: das Wort ist geistliche Führung, weil es Christus selbst ist.[89] Überdies würden Augen und Ohren nicht voll, weil es nichts gebe, was sie füllen könnte. Denn das Auge sehe nur die Oberfläche, nicht das Wesen der Dinge, und kein Wort könne das Ding an sich exakt beschreiben.[90]

Die zweite pseudo-gregorianische Homilie *De creatione hominis* erklärt schließlich den aufrechten Gang des Menschen nach Eccl 2,14: 'Die Augen des Weisen sind in seinem Kopf'. Der Mensch gehe aufrecht, damit er zum Himmel schaue und nicht auf den Bauch, wie das vierfüßige Tier.[91] Wenn auch damit eine gewisse geistliche Deutung der Physiologie des Menschen geschieht, differiert sie doch völlig von Gregors Exegese in der fünften *Ecclesiastes*-Homilie. Dort

---

86 S.o.S. 384.

87 Hom opif 10 (PG 44,152 C). Vgl. Daniel N. DiNardo, Man, Image of God. Sharer in his goodness and reason. The *De Hominis Opificio* of St. Gregory of Nyssa (Lic. Diss. Augustinianum), Rom 1981, 51–65.

88 PG 44,138 B. Vgl. Roger Leys, L'Image de Dieu chez Saint Grégoire de Nysse. Esquisse d'une doctrine = ML.T 49 (1951) 67f.

89 GNO V, 291,15–294,17.

90 Ebd. 294,5–17.

91 GNO S 67,10.

deutet er das Haupt als Christus, in dem die geistlichen Sinne des Menschen verankert seien.[92]

Die letztere Deutung folgt Origenes, der an mehreren Stellen Eccl 2,14 so erklärt: Christus ist das Haupt, das διανοητικόν des Menschen; die Augen sind geistlicher Sinn, die der Weise bei Christus hat, nicht aber der Häretiker.[93] Diese Erklärung übernehmen auch Dionysios von Alexandrien, den seinerseits Prokop kopiert, Didymos, Olympiodor und Gregor von Agrigent, bei den Lateinern Hieronymus und Salonius,[94] wobei der eine oder andere noch eine zweite Deutung oder Nuancen beiträgt. Bei Didymos, Olympiodor, Hieronymus und Salonius ist Christus, das Haupt, nicht der Ort, wo der Weise seine Augen hat, sondern wohin die Augen gerichtet sind. Dionysius, Olympiodor und Gregor von Agrigent führen darüber hinaus je eine zweite Interpretation an, was deutlich zeigt, daß sie verschiedene Exegesen zusammenfassen. Dionysios argumentiert ähnlich wie Gregor, daß die Augen des Verstandes gemeint sein müßten, denn auch ein Schwein habe ja seine Augen im Kopf, allerdings seiner Natur nach auf den Bauch gerichtet. Damit seien die Augen des Menschen zu vergleichen, dessen Verstand nur auf die Lüste gerichtet ist. Für Olympiodor hat nur der die Augen im Kopf, d.h. ist wahrhaft weise, der sich nach oben orientiert, da der Kopf oben, die Füße unten sind. Ähnlich Gregor von Agrigent: die Augen sind die Augen des Geistes derer, die den Willen Gottes tun wollen.

Zwei *Ecclesiastes*-Kommentare weichen von dieser Exegese ab. Die *Catena Trium Patrum* interpretiert den Zusammenhang von Augen und Kopf so, daß der Weise von seinem νοῦς also ἡγεμονικόν bestimmt werde und daher nach oben schaue[95]. Nach Euagrios ist das Haupt

---

92 GNO V, 356,20-360,22.

93 Origenes, Cant pr (GCS Or 8, 65,19); Mt comm ser 132 (GCS Or 11, 268, 23-29); Heracl 20 (SC 67, 96,15-23).

94 Didymos, Eccl 1/1, 48,19-29 (PTA 25, 238-241); Dionysios, frg (BGL 2,91 f.) = Procopius, Eccl II 14 (CChr.SG 4,20,125-21,138); Olympiodor, Eccl 2 (PG 93,500 C-D); Gregorius Agrig., Eccl II 5 (PG 98,817 A-820 A); Hieronymus, Eccl II 14 (CChr.SL 72, 269,257-268); Salonius, Eccl (PL 53,997 B-C).

95 Eccl II (CChr.SG 11, 16,124-132).

des Weisen die Weisheit (eine ausdrückliche Identifikation mit Christus nimmt er aber nicht vor), worin er die Augen der διάνοια hat.[96]

Die Unterschiede in der *Ecclesiastes*-Deutung können nicht mit einer zeitlichen Entwicklung erklärt werden, da in *De hominis opificio* die physische und geistliche Erklärung nebeneinander stehen. Man muß daher wohl in Rechnung stellen, daß Gregor je nach Zusammenhang dieselben Bibelstellen unterschiedlich interpretiert.

F. Ergebnisse

Das Buch *Ecclesiastes* spielt im Werk Gregors von Nyssa außerhalb der *Ecclesiastes*-Homilien nur eine geringe Rolle. Die 24 bekannten Zitate bzw. Anklänge bedeuten im Vergleich zu den bei Gregor bedeutenden atl. Büchern wie Genesis, Exodus, die Psalmen oder Isaias, die um ein Vielfaches mehr zitiert werden, wenig, auch wenn aufgrund eingehender Durchsicht der Schriften Gregors noch manche Stelle entdeckt werden könnte. Das Buch *Ecclesiastes* gehört aber durgehend zum beständigen Bibelrepertoire Gregors in allen Perioden seines Schaffens und in einer Vielzahl von Werken.

Zumeist deutet Gregor den Ecclesiast mystisch, asketisch und spirituell, worin er in vielem der alexandrinischen Tradition, insbesondere Origenes, verpflichtet ist, aber keineswegs nur nachahmender Tradent dieser Tradition. Schon das grundsätzliche Verhältnis von *Proverbia*, *Ecclesiastes* und *Canticum Canticorum* definiert er nach seiner persönlich geformten Theorie des mystischen Aufstiegs zu Gott, das gleiche gilt für die Hohelied-Auslegung etc.

Darüber hinaus verwendet er den Ecclesiasten im Kontext der Schöpfungstheologie, in der geistliche und physische Interpretation nebeneinander stehen, sowie zur formalen Polemik in seinen dogmatischen Traktaten.

---

96   Euagrius in *Catena Barberiana* (487 Labate).

Nur von den mystischen *Ecclesiastes*-Interpretationen Gregors sind Nachwirkungen bekannt, teils in Exzerpten späterer Kommentare, teils in Übernahme der originell gregorianischen Ideen, wobei immer die lückenhafte Überlieferung der Vätertexte in Rechnung zu stellen ist.

Etwas erstaunlich bleibt, daß in Anbetracht der intensiven Beschäftigung mit dem Buch *Ecclesiastes* in den Homilien dieses Buch im weiteren, auch in den späteren Werken, abgesehen von den Hohelied-Homilien, so wenig Einfluß auf die Schriften Gregors gewinnt. Es scheint, als ob Gregor sich zwar einmal intensiv mit dem ersten Teil des *Ecclesiastes* auseinandersetzt, im übrigen aber andere biblische Bücher des Alten und Neuen Testaments für seine Theologie maßgeblicher sind.

17

Die oratio catechetica — ein Zugang zum Gesamtwerk

Gregors von Nyssa[1]

Reinhard Kees

Es gibt verschiedene Möglichkeiten, sich Gregor von Nyssa zu nähern. Der Zugang zum Gesamtwerk ist von entscheidender Bedeutung dafür, wie sich uns sein theologisches Denken in der Gesamtheit darstellt.

Entweder man greift sich ein Thema aus der Vielzahl der von Gregor behandelten Themen heraus und untersucht in verschiedenen Werken die Aussagen zu diesem Thema. Dabei ergeben sich jedoch einige Schwierigkeiten.[2] Es besteht die Gefahr, daß die gefundenen Zitate aus dem Zusammenhang gerissen und ohne Berücksichtigung des Kontextes und der Absicht des ganzen Werkes interpretiert werden. Man muß sich bei dieser Methode besonders kritisch fragen, ob es zulässig ist, die in zeitlich großem Abstand voneinander entstandenen Werke, die unter verschiedenen Bedingungen und mit jeweils verschiedener Absicht verfaßt worden sind, gleichermaßen zur Erarbeitung eines Themas heranzuziehen. Wenn Zitate aus den frühen und den späten Werken ohne Unterschied betrachtet werden, dann wird übersehen, daß

---

1   Im diesem Vortrag gebe ich einige Aspekte meiner kurz vor der Vollendung stehenden Dissertation über die oratio catechetica wieder.

2   Sehr deutlich hat R. Hübner, Die Einheit des Leibes Christi bei Gregor von Nyssa. Untersuchungen zum Ursprung der 'physichen' Erlösungslehre, Leiden 1974 (PP 2) S.27. auf diese Probleme hingewiesen und sie, soweit es möglich war, vermieden.

Gregors Theologie eine sehr wichtige Entwicklung durchlaufen hat.[3]
Eine gründliche Einzeluntersuchung zu einem Thema der Theologie
Gregors kann jedoch auch dazu beitragen, die Entwicklung in einem
Bereich überhaupt erst zu erfassen.[4]   Doch auch dabei gelingt es
nicht immer, die Bedeutung und Stellung des gewählten Themas im
Gesamtgefüge der Theologie und den Einfluß von Veränderungen in einer
Thematik auf andere theologische Bereiche zu erfassen.

Die andere Möglichkeit ist der Zugang über eine eingehende
Analyse eines ausgesuchten Werkes.[5]   Dabei wird das jeweilige Werk
selbstverständlich   unter   Berücksichtigung   der   Absicht,   des
Adressatenkreises und der Enstehungszeit interpretiert.   Auch der
Kontext einer Aussage wird gebührende Beachtung finden.   Doch auch
hier ergeben sich Probleme.   Zum einen spiegelt das ausgesuchte Werk
jeweils nur einen bestimmten Stand in der Entwicklung der Theologie
Gregors wieder.   Zum anderen sind die in dem Werk behandelten Themen
von der Absicht und der Veranlassung des Werkes, jedoch nicht
unbedingt von der Wichtigkeit des Gedankens diktiert worden.   Ihr
Gewicht in dem Gesamtgefüge der Theologie Gregors kann auch so nur
schwer erfaßt werden.

Wer an der Verflochtenheit der theologischen Themen und an der
jeweiligen Bedeutung einzelner Themen innerhalb des Denkens Gregors

---

3   Ein sehr krasses Beispiel, das deutlich zeigt, zu welch abwegigen
    Konsequenzen eine solche Betrachtungsweise des Gesamtwerkes
    führt, ist H.J. Oesterle, Probleme der Anthropologie bei Gregor
    von Nyssa. Zur Interpretation seiner Schrift De hominis opificio:
    Hermes 113 (1985) 101-114.

4   z.B. E. Mühlenberg, Die Unendlichkeit Gottes bei Gregor von Nyssa.
    Gregors Kritik am Gottesbegriff der klassischen Metaphysik,
    Göttingen 1966; bes. S.91ff.

5   Leider gibt es viel zu wenige Monographien, die mit theologischem
    und philologischem Interesse ein Werk Gregors gründlich
    analysieren. Dieses Defizit auszugleichen, ist ein Ziel der Gregor-
    von-Nyssa-Kolloquia, die sich eingehend mit jeweils einem Werk
    oder einer Gruppe von Werken des Nysseners beschäftigen. van
    Winden/van Heck, Colloquii Leidensis Acta (zu de infantibus);
    Spira/Klock, The Easter Sermons; Spira, The biographical Works;
    Mateo-Seco/Bastero, El 'Contra Eunomium I'.

interessiert ist, für den ist m.E. besonders die *or cat* von großen Wert. Sie ist aus drei Gründen besonders dazu geeignet, als Zugang zum Gesamtwerk Gregors zu dienen, von dem ausgehend die anderen Werke erschlossen werden können: 1. wegen ihrer Absicht und Methode, 2. wegen ihrer Struktur und 3. wegen ihrer zeitlichen Entstehung.

1.   Die Katechetische Ausrichtung der *oratio catechetica* und ihre Implikationen

Mit dem ersten Satz der *or cat* zeigt Gregor, mit welchem Ziel er dieses Werk verfaßt hat.[6]   Er möchte zum Wachsen der Kirche beitragen, damit immer mehr Menschen das rettende Wort des Evangeliums hören.[7]   Dazu hält Gregor es nicht nur für notwendig, in theologischen Traktaten Irrlehren zu widerlegen, wie er es in den Werken gegen Eunomius und Apolinarius getan hat,[8] und theologische Probleme tief zu durchdringen und zu entfalten, wie er es in den kleinen trinitätstheologischen[9] und in den großen anthropologischen Werken[10] getan hat.   Die Ergebnisse dieser theologischen Arbeit müssen   auch   so   aufgearbeitet   werden,   daß   sie   für   die Taufunterweisung fruchtbar gemach werden können.   Mit der *or cat* will Gregor dieser Notwendigkeit entsprechen und eine Hilfe zur Katechese, zur Taufunterweisung bieten.[11]

---

6   *or cat* pr. 1, Srawley 1,1 Kapitel- und Abschnittangabe nach Discours catéchétique.   Texte grec, traduction française, introduction et index par L. Méridier (=TDEHC 7), Paris 1908; Seiten- und Zeilenangaben nach The Catechetical Oration of Gregory of Nyssa, ed. J.H. Srawley, Cambridge 1908 (CPT).

7   Dabei geht Gregor davon aus, wie er schon im *antirrh* formuliert hat, daß 'die gute Frucht einer jeden Lehre ...... die Hinzufügung von Geretteten ist.' (*antirrh* GNO III/1 131, 13).   An dieser Frucht ist jede Lehre zu messen.

8   *Eun, ref Eun, antirrh* Abkürzungen der Werke Gregors nach: M. Altenburger/F. Mann, Bibliographie zu Gregor von Nyssa, Leiden 1988.

9   *Eust, graec, Abl.*

10   *op hom, an et res.*

11   Diesem Anliegen entspricht es, daß die *or cat* in der Behandlung der Taufe und des daraus resultierenden christlichen Lebens ihren Abschluß findet.   Sehr deutlich wird der Zusammenhang von Lehre

Er hat dabei zwar immer auch die konkrete Unterweisung und die
Katechumenen in Blick, — sie werden vereinzelt sogar direkt
angesprochen[12] — in erster Linie richtet er sich aber an die
Unterweisenden.   Die *or cat* ist also ein Zwischenglied zwischen
Dogmatik und Katechese — vielleicht unseren Arbeitshilfen für den
katechetischen Unterricht vergleichbar.

Dem Ziel und dem Adressatenkreis entsprechend geht es darum,
die Unterweisenden zur Widerlegung von Einwänden, die gegen die
christliche Lehre erhoben werden, zu befähigen.   Das überzeugendste
Beweismittel ist dabei die Logik, die gedankliche 'Folgerichtigkeit',[13] da
man bei den Hinzukommenden noch nicht mit der Autorität der Schrift
argumentieren kann.   Die Widerlegung von Vorurteilen und Einwänden ist
jedoch kein Selbstzweck.   Die Katechumenen sollen ja nicht bloß-
gestellt, sondern zum Glauben und zur Taufe geführt werden.   Von

---

und Taufe und dem Weg, der bis zur Taufe beschritten werden
muß, in *or cat* 36.1f.

12   Vgl. besonders *or cat* 39–40.   Gerade diese Beobachtung kann zu
der Annahme führen, daß Gregor hier eine Taufansprache zum
letzten Teil seiner *or cat* umgearbeitet hat.

13   Vgl. die Häufung der Begriffe ἀκολουθία bzw. ἀκόλουθον in Argu-
mentationszusammenhängen: *or cat pr.5* Srawley 5,1; *or cat* 5.2
Srawley 21,14 u.ö. zur Bedeutungsvielfalt siehe H. Drobner, Gregor
von Nyssa, Die drei Tage zwischen Tod und Auferstehung unseres
Herrn Jesus Christus.   Eingeleitet, übersetzt und kommentiert von
H.R. Drobner,   Leiden 1982 (PP 5) S.94.   Dieser Begriff hat seine
Bedeutung im Bereich der Logik, der Kosmologie, der Geschichte,
der Trinitätslehre und der Exegese.   Vgl. auch J. Daniélou, L'être
et le temps chez Grégoire de Nysse, Leiden 1970, S.18ff.
Gregor geht bei seiner   Argumentation immer von dem aus, was
auch vom Gesprächspartner   anerkannt ist.   Erkennt der Partner
den gesetzten Ausgangspunkt nicht an, dann geht Gregor in seiner
Argumentationskette noch einen Schritt zurück und stellt einen
noch   allgemeineren   Ausgangspunkt   an   den   Anfang   des
Gesprächsganges.   *or cat pr. 4*, Srawley 3,9ff. Das von beiden
Anerkannte ist die Bedingung, die gegeben sein muß.   In *Eun I* hat
Gregor diese Methode so beschrieben 'Denn wer weiß nicht, daß
jeder gedankliche Schluß seine Ursprünge aus dem Offenbaren und
von jedermann Anerkannten nimmt und dadurch den Glauben an das
Umstrittene herbeiführt?   Und könnte auf andere Weise etwas von
dem Verborgenen ergriffen werden, wenn nicht das Anerkannte uns
zum Verstehen des Unklaren führte?   Wenn aber die Sätze, die als
Ausgang   zur   Klärung   des   Unbekannten   genommen   werden,   den
Vorstellungen der meisten widerstreiten, dann wäre das Unbekannte

dieser positiven Absicht ist die ganze Apologetik der *or cat* bestimmt.[14]

Es geht in der *or cat* nicht nur um einzelne Themen. Gregor ist um Vollständigkeit und Stimmigkeit bemüht. Die Ursachen dazu liegen in der katechetisch-apologetischen Absicht. Maßstab für die Richtigkeit einer theologischen Aussage ist für Gregor die Vernünftigkeit des Gesagten. Indem er erweist, daß die einzelnen Aussagen zueinander passen, daß beispielsweise die verkündigte *Oikonomia* der gelehrten *Theologia* nicht widerspricht, sondern entspricht,[15] wird den Einwänden das Fundament entzogen. So werden aber gleichzeitig systematische Zusammenhänge deutlich. Die Unterrichtenden werden befähigt, die Lehre in ihren inneren Zusammenhängen darzustellen. Sie werden befähigt — wie A. Grillmeier formuliert — 'das Ganze der christlichen Wahrheit von den geistigen Voraussetzungen und Anforderungen ihrer

---

durch sie gar nicht geklärt' (Eun I 219 GNO I 90,11-20; übs. E. Mühlenberg, Unendlichkeit S.99). Diese Methode zwingt Gregor dazu, Einwände wirklich ernst zu nehmen und nach den Hintergründen der Einwände zu fragen. Bei aller gedanklichen Anstrengung ist sich Gregor aber einer entscheidenden Tatsache bewußt: Er kann zwar mit seiner vernünftigen Argumentation erweisen, daß sich die einzelnen Aussagen nicht widersprechen, sondern in einem vernünftigen Verhältnis zueinander stehen. Er kann also mit den Mitteln der vernünftigen Argumentation, wie es der apologetischen Funktion der Theologie entspricht, die 'nicht-Unvernünftigkeit des christlichen Glaubens aufweisen' (B. Studer, Gott und unsere Erlösung im Glauben der Alten Kirche, Düsseldorf 1985, S.24). Die Grundlagen des christlichen Glaubens jedoch kann er mit dieser Methode nicht herleiten. Die jeweilige Richtung der Argumentation und das Ziel, dem der Gesprächspartner am Ende zustimmen soll, sind vorgegeben. Die Hauptaussagen werden von Gregor nicht hergeleitet, sondern gesetzt und dann reflektiert und verteidigt.

14 Die übersetzung von J. Barbel, Gregor von Nyssa. Die Große Katechetische Rede, Oratio catechetica magna. Eingeleitet, übersetzt und kommentiert von J. Barbel, Stuttgart 1971 (BGrL 1) ist m.E. an vielen Stelle, an denen Gregor bewußt positiv von 'Zurechtbringung, Aufrichtung' spricht, zu negativ, so daß diese positive Absicht Gregors nicht deutlich wird. Vgl. *or cat pr.* 2 Srawley 2, 14f u.3,1f mit J. Barbel S.31.

15 Vgl. *or cat* 32,10 Srawley 122,6ff.

Gläubigen und Gemeinden her' darzustellen.[16] Dies macht eine Besonderheit der *or cat* aus. Wir kennen kein anderes Werk Gregors, das sich so um die Gesamtheit und um die Verknüpfung der christlichen Lehre bemüht. Die meisten anderen Werke sind durch einen konkreten Auftrag oder eine theologische Kontroverse veranlaßt. Deshalb beschäftigen sie sich nur mit einigen Themen und haben die Gesamtheit nur mittelbar im Blick.

In der *or cat* dagegen durchdringen sich katechetische, apologetische und systematische Absichten gegenseitig und drängen zur Vollständigkeit, Stimmigkeit aber auch zur Einfachheit und Verstehbarkeit.

Gerade diese letztgenannte Konsequenz der katechetischen Ausrichtung der *or cat* führt dazu, daß sie von vielen Theologen, die sich mit einzelnen Themen Gregors beschäftigen, wenig beachtet wird.[17] Viele Themen, die Gregor in anderen Werken ausführlicher behandelt hat, werden in der *or cat* nur knapp oder nur andeutungsweise behandelt. Der Vollständigkeit der Themen steht die Kürze und Einfachheit der Behandlung gegenüber. Das macht eine Schwäche der *or cat* aus, weil dadurch einige Unklarheiten nicht ausgeräumt werden.

Aus didaktischen Gründen verzichtet Gregor darauf, die Erkenntnis aus der Eunomianischen Kontroverse, daß die Unendlichkeit am ehesten ein Begriff für das Wesen Gottes sein könnte, in der *or cat* zu entfalten.[18] Es ist unter dem Gesichtspunkt der

---

16 A. Grillmeier, Vom Symbolum zur Summa: In ihm und mit ihm. Christologische Forschungen und Perspektiven, Freiburg/Basel/Wien 1978, S.619.

17 Anders ist es bei Werken, die einen größeren Überblick über die Lehrentwicklung in der Alten Kirche geben wollen. z.B. F. Normann, Teilhabe — ein Schlüsselwort der Vätertheologie, Münster 1978 (MBTh 42) S.221. Für ihn empfiehlt es sich, 'mit der Großen Katechetischen Rede ... zu beginnen. Sie hat den Vorzug, daß der Autor durchweg von positiven, christlichen Hauptdogmen handelt.' Vgl. auch B.Studer, Soteriologie. In der Schrift und Patristik, Freiburg 1978 (HDG 3,2a) S.138.

18 Die Lehre von der Unendlichkeit Gottes hätte ohne Schwierigkeiten in den Gedankengang gepaßt. Sie hätte aber dazu geführt, daß die Grundlegung der Theologie für die Unterweisenden und die Unterwiesenen zu kompliziert und sehr befremdend gewesen wäre.

Unterweisung besser, bei dem von allen anerkannten Gedanken der Vollkommenheit zu beginnen. Gregor kann unter Umgehung des Gedanken der Unendlichkeit alle entscheidenden Aussagen — Ausschluß des Gegenteils, von Veränderung, von Mehr oder Minder — aus diesem Begriff schlußfolgern.[19]

Gregor verzichtet auch auf die differenzierte Trinitätstheologie und deren exakte Begriffsbestimmungen, die er in den kleinen trinitarischen Schriften und in den Büchern gegen Eunomius entfaltet hat, und nimmt dabei eine letzte Unklarheit und Undeutlichkeit in Kauf.[20]

Bei der Christologie ist Ähnliches zu bemerken.[21] Gerade das Fehlen der für Gregor typischen Idiomenlehre, die er in den Schriften gegen Eunomius und Apolinarius und in dem kleinen Traktat Ad Theophilum entfaltet hat, ist eine gravierende Schwäche der *or cat*, denn bei der Entfaltung der Soteriologie kann Gregor doch nicht auf seine christologische Grundlage verzichten. Einige wichtige Formulierungen und Gedankengänge kann man dementsprechend nur mit Hilfe anderer Werke erschließen.

---

19 Auch in der Auseinandersetzung mit Eunomius hat Gregor den Gendanken der Unendlichkeit aus dem der Vollkommenheit geschlossen. (Vgl. die Parallelität der Argumentation in *or cat* pr. 4-8 mit *Eun I* 167f). Zu diesen Beobachtungen siehe zuletzt A. Meredith, The Idea of God in Gregory of Nyssa: Studien zu Gregor von Nyssa ... hgg. H. Drobner/Ch. Klock (SVigChr XII) Leiden 1990, S.127ff.

20 Für die Unterweisung reicht es ihm aus, das 'Daß' der Trinität anschaulich herzuleiten, das 'Wie' muß dabei nicht erläutert werden. Dies bleibt ein Geheimnis, *or cat* 3.1 Srawley 15,14f.

21 Gregor lehnt die Frage nach dem 'Wie' der Einigung von Gott und Mensch in Christus in der *or cat* ausdrücklich ab, da sie nur darauf ziele, die Unmöglichkjeit des Berichteten bloßzulegen. Es ist wie bei der Schöpfung wichtig, das 'Daß' zu glauben. Das 'Wie' zu erforschen, ist unangemessen, da es das Denken ohnehin übersteigt (*or cat* 11.1f Srawley 57,6ff). Der hier ausgesprochene Verzicht ist kein genereller, sondern einer, der nur in der *or cat* angebracht erscheint. Mit seiner Idiomenlehre hat Gregor versucht, das 'Wie' der Einigung von Gott und Mensch in Christus genauer zu durchdringen.

Auch verzichtet Gregor ganz und gar auf die Entfaltung seiner in
hex entwickelten Schöpfungslehre. Auch dieser Verzicht wirkt sich
für das Verstehen der Soteriologie hinderlich aus, da die Parallelität zwischen der Lehre von der Simultanschöpfung und der damit
verbundenen Lehre von der Entfaltung des keimhaft Angelegten und
den Aussagen über die Wirkung der Aufstehung Christi erst durch
den Vergleich mit *hex* deutlich wird und eine Verstehenshilfe für die
so wichtigen soteriologischen Formulierungen über die Wirkung der
Auferstehung Christi[22] aus der *or cat* selbst nicht zu entnehmen
ist. Gregor verzichtet auch auf eine eigenständige Entfaltung der
Eschatologie[23] und auf eine ausführliche Darlegung der Ethik.[24]

Der Verzicht auf die ausführliche Entfaltung dieser Themen gibt
der *or cat* im Gesamtwerk Gregors einen weiteren spezifischen
Charakter. Insofern hat J. Barbel recht, wenn er meint, 'So sehr sein
persönliches Denken aber auch hervortritt, man wird die grundsätzliche
Übereinstimmung mit den meisten allgemeinen kirchlichen Überzeugungen
seiner Zeit nicht übersehen. Es sind im ganzen zugleich wesentliche
und allgemein christliche Gedanken, die er bietet.'[25] Gregor stellt also
in der *or cat* aus katechetisch-didaktischen Gründen die

---

22   *or cat 16,9* und *33.3* Srawley 72,6 u. 116.8.

23   Sie wird im Zusammenhang der Anthropologie und Sakramentslehre
angedeutet. Aber auch hier zeigt es sich, daß die Andeutungen
erst auf dem Hintergrund anderer Werke Gregors deutlich werden,
so daß auch dieser Verzicht, die Hauptrichtung der Theologie
Gregors schwächt. Auf eine Ekklesiologie hat Gregor in der *or
cat* ganz verzichtet.

24   Die Grundaussagen sind in *or cat* 40 genannt. Inhaltliche Übereinstimmungen zwischen diesem Kapitel und Gregors Schrift *perf*
geben Anlaß zu der Vermutung, Gregor habe in *perf* die in der *or
cat* nur angedeuteten Gedanken breiter entfaltet. An vielen Stellen
von *perf* wird deutlich, daß dieses Werk die Kontroverse mit
Eunomius z.B. über die Auslegung von Joh. 20,17 voraussetzt. Die
gesamte Tauftheologie, die Verwendung bestimmter Bibelstellen und
vor allem die soteriologische Bedeutung Christi sprechen
entschieden gegen eine Frühdatierung von *perf*.

25   J. Barbel, S.27. Daß in Zusammenhang der Auslassungen in der
or cat auch die Anthropologie genannt werden muß, wie J. Barbel
S.28 meint, ist jedoch nicht einzusehen. Sie ist in der *or cat*
ausführlich, aber eben etwas anders als in *op hom* und *an et res*
dargestellt.

'interpretative' Funktion der Theologie, die — wie B. Studer formuliert — 'also intellectus fidei, als tiefere Erfassung der Glaubensgeheimnisse verstanden werden' kann, zugunsten der 'dogmatischen', von der man ein Urteil darüber erwartet, 'was in der christlichen Lehre als Glaubensnorm für alle zu werten ist, die zur kirchlichen Gemeinschaft gehören wollen,' zurück.[26] Es geht Gregor in der *or cat* also um die grundsätzlichen Aussagen der christlichen Lehre und nicht um tiefe theologische Erörterungen einzelner Themen. Es läßt sich eine Beobachtung auf die *or cat* anwenden, die H. Drobner für die Predigten Gregors mit Hilfe eines Vergleiches deutlich gemacht hat. H. Drobner vergleicht die Predigten mit einem Haus, dessen Fundamente nicht zu sehen sind. Sie seien intellektuell niedriger als die Lehrschriften. Das Denken aber sei dasselbe.[27] Die *or cat* steht vom Niveau her beurteilt zwischen den Predigten und den Lehrschriften.

Es muß zugestanden werden: Die katechetische Ausrichtung der *or cat* steht dem spekulativ-theologischen Interesse Gregors, spezifische Positionen zu einzelnen theologischen Themen zu erarbeiten, entgegen. Aus diesem Grunde ist es verständlich, daß die *or cat* in vielen

---

26 B. Studer, Erlösung S.24; Gregor kann so vorgehen, da er zwischen wichtigen theologischen Aussagen der Kirche und seinen eigenen theologischen überlegungen und Erklärungsversuchen unterscheidet. Diese Erkenntnis Gregors hat H. Drobner, Drei Tage S.102 so formuliert: 'Gregor ist sich bewußt, daß es zwar in den grundsätzlichen Aussage des Glaubens nur eine wahre Lehrmeinung geben kann, ihre Erklärung und Verdeutlichung jedoch eine Vielfalt von Formen annimmt und annehmen muß, von denen die einen manchen einleuchtend und richtig erscheinen, andere wieder anderen.' H. Drobner bezieht sich auf *trid spat* (GNO IX 286,15) wo Gregor im Zusammenhang der Erörterung über das Triduum mortis sagt: 'Denn meine Rede bietet keine feste Antwort, sondern eine Erörterung der Frage und einen Lösungsversuch.' Vgl. auch *op hom* 16 (PG 44,185A), wo Gregor unter einem ähnlichen Vorbehalt die doppelte Schöpfung des Menschen behandelt. Er möchte durch Schließen und durch Bilder nach Möglichkeit als einen Versuch, das Problem zu lösen, eine Antwort geben, die aber kein mit Nachdruck behaupteter Satz ist. In *op hom* 22 (PG 44,204) wird Gregors grundsätzlicher Vorbehalt deutlich. Letztlich werden immer Zweifel bleiben und die Lösung eines Problems immer offen bleiben. 'Ob der Gedanke der Wahrheit des Gesuchten nahekommt, kann nur die Wahrheit selbst wissen.'

27 H. Drobner, Drei Tage S.5.

Publikationen zu Gregor von Nyssa kaum Beachtung findet. Wer nach spezifischen Theologumena Gregors fragt, wird die *or cat* nur beiläufig erwähnen. Wer aber erkennen will, welche Zusammenhänge und Beziehungen es zwischen einzelnen theologischen Aussagen und Themen gibt, welches Gewicht einzelne theologische Grundentscheidungen im Gesamtgefüge der Theologie Gregors haben und wie sich theologische Entscheidungen gegenseitig beinflussen, der wird sich dennoch der *or cat* zuwenden. Gerade dies wird nämlich in der *or cat* trotz des Verzichts auf Ausführlichkeit bei der Entfaltung einzelner Themen aufgrund der Bemühung um Vollständigkeit und Stimmigkeit deutlich, weil Gregor jedem Theologumenon seinen Platz im Duktus der Entfaltung von *Theologia* und *Oikonomia* zugewiesen hat. Wer so fragt, der wird sich die andere Konsequenz der katechetisch-apologetischen Ausrichtung, nämlich die systematisch-theologisch interessante Gliederung und Darstellungsweise der *or cat* zunutze machen und wird an ihr das Gewicht einzelner theologischer Aussagen in anderen Werken Gregors messen.

2.   Die Struktur der *oratio catechetica*: *Theologia* und *Oikonomia*

Auf den ersten Blick hat die *or cat* vier Teile: über Gott, über Schöpfung und Fall, über das Christusgeschehen, über die Sakramente und das Leben der Getauften.[28] Wenn man jedoch fragt, welche größeren Einheiten sich erkennen lassen und wie die Teile aufeinander bezogen sind, dann stellt sich heraus, daß die *or cat* nicht aus vier, sondern aus zwei Teilen besteht, wobei der zweite Teil in drei Abschnitte gegliedert ist. Es ergibt sich die folgende Darstellung des Aufbaus der *or cat*.[29]

---

28   Vgl. J.H.Srawley S.XII.

29   Diese Gliederung entspricht im wesentlichen der, die A. Grillmeier, Symbolum 619 gegeben hat.   A. Grillmeier ist bei der Gliederung der *or cat* aber nicht konsequent. Er unterscheidet die *Theologia* und *Oikonomia*, spricht aber dann von 'einem theologischen Triptychon, da die *Oikonomia* geschieden wird in die Darstellung der historischen Verwirklichung des Heils in Christus und dessen Aneignung in den Sakramenten und im Glauben an den dreieinigen Gott.' Er scheint also in der *Oikonomia* eine Zweigliederung anzunehmen, in der unser Teil 1 und 2 zusammen einen Teil bilden, was dazu führt, daß drei Teile der *or cat* nebeneinanderstehen: ein Teil der *Theologia* und zwei Teile der *Oikonomia*. Doch in der im Anschluß an diese Formulierung gegebenen Gliederung unterteilt

Prolog: Absicht und Methode		*or cat* pr.1-pr.3
I. *THEOLOGIA*		*or cat* pr.4-4.4
	1. Grundlegung der *Theologia*	*or cat* pr.4-pr.8
	2. Trinitätstheologie	*or cat* 1.1-4.4
II. *OIKONOMIA*		*or cat* 5.1-40.8

1. Gottes Heilshandeln in der Schöpfung
Über die Bestimmung des
Menschen zur Teilhabe an Gott
Des Menschen Fall und das Böse
als Veranlassung für Gottes
Heilshandeln in Christus   *or cat* 5.1-8.20

2. Gottes Heilshandeln in Christus
Über die Ermöglichung der Wieder-
herstellung des ursprünglichen
Heils des Menschen   *or cat* 9.1-32.10

3. Gottes Heilshandeln in den Sakramenten
Über die Zueignung des durch
Christus erwirkten Heils   *or cat* 33.1-40.8

Mit diesem Aufbau berücksichtigt Gregor die sich gegen Ende des vierten Jahrhunderts immer stärker abzeichnende Unterscheidung von *Theologia* und *Oikonomia*. Gleichzeitig trägt er aber auch der Erkenntnis Rechnung, daß *Theologia* und *Oikonomia* inhaltlich aufs engste miteinander verflochten sind.

Die Entfaltung der *Oikonomia*, in der es um das biblisch bezeugte Handeln Gottes an der Welt geht, entstammte eher dem kerygmatischen Bereich und hatte sich zunächst in der Bildung von Bekenntnisformeln niedergeschlagen. Die *Theologia*, in der über das innere Verhältnis

---

er wie wir die *Oikonomia* in drei Teile: 1. Schöpfung, 2. Menschwerdung und 3. Aneignung des Heils. Offensichtlich hat er die Unstimmigkeit zwischen dem formulierten Text und der gegebenen Gliederung nicht bemerkt.

Gottes nachgedacht wird, entstammte dagegen eher der theologischen
Reflexion und dem theologischen Streit. Sie hatte sich zunächst in
den Symbolen der Synoden niedergeschlagen. Gregor hat diese 'in der
frühchristlichen Theologie so hart errungene Unterscheidung zwischen
Theologia und Oikonomia' [30] in der or cat klar durchgeführt.

Nachdem in der Forschung festgestellt ist, daß Origenes' de
principiis nicht als systematischer Gesamtentwurf der christlichen
Theologie angesehen werden kann,[31] kommt nun der or cat besondere
Bedeutung zu.

Sie ist nämlich das erste Werk der Theologiegeschichte, in der
die Unterscheidung und zugleich Zusammenstellung und Zuordnung von
Theologia und Oikonomia gefunden werden kann.[32] Deshalb ist gerade

---

[30] A. Grillmeier, Symbolum S.620. Diese Unterscheidung fußt vor
allem auf der Erkenntnis, 'daß das Verhältnis von Einheit und
Dreiheit in Gott rein innergöttlich zu sehen und nicht bloß
"heilsökonomisch" zu lösen war, wie es Schrift und Verkündingung
taten' (A. Grillmeier, Symbolum S.593). Sie führte zum Übergang
von der verkündigten Oikonomia zur reflektierten Theologia.
Vorallem das Symbol von Nicäa beschleunigte und festigte diese
Entwicklung. Indem in Nicäa das 'Verhältnis von Vater und Sohn
rein theologisch' betrachtet wurde, 'und dabei von der Erlösungs-
funktion des Sohnes' abgesehen wurde, war den späteren, an Nicäa
orientierten Theologen die Möglichkeit gegeben, 'zwischen dem Wort
Gottes als Sohn Gottes in seiner ewigen Existenz und dem aus
Maria menschgewordenen Wort in seinem heilsgeschichtlichen Wirken
klar zu unterscheiden' (B. Studer, Soteriologie S.119). Das
Symbol von Nicäa forderte in den Auseinandersetzungen mit den
Arianern und Eunomianern geradezu dazu heraus, die Theologia als
eigenständiges Thema der Theologie losgelöst von der Oikonomia zu
entfalten.

[31] B. Steidle, Neue Untersuchungen zu Origenes' Peri archon: ZNW
40, 1942, 263-242; M. Harl, Structure et cohérence du Peri
Archon: Origeniana. Premier colloque international des études
origeniennes (Monserat 1973). QVetChri 12, Bari 1975, S.11-32.

[32] Vgl. A. Grillmeier, Symbolum S.611ff; vgl. die von M. Baumgarten
in die zehnte Auflage von Überwegs Philosophiegeschichte ein-
gefügte und seither vertretene Beurteilung der or cat als 'die
bedeutendste systematische Leistung nach Origenes' Peri archon'
Überweg-Baumgartner, Grundriss der Geschichte der Philosophie.
T.2. Patristische und scholastische Zeit, 10.Aufl., Berlin 1915,
S.130; bzw. Überweg-Geyer 13.Auflage, Darmstadt 1958, S.84.
Umso verwunderlicher ist es, daß die or cat in dieser Beziehung
so wenig Beachtung gefunden hat, wo doch schon in diesem
Standardwerk der Philosophiegeschichte ihre besondere Bedeutung

in diesem Werk dem Verhältnis von *Theologia* und *Oikonomia* besondere
Aufmerksamkeit zu schenken. Sie werden zwar nacheinander behandelt,
bleiben aber doch aufs engste durch den 'ökonomische(n)' Bezug der
'*Theologia*' und die 'theologische' Tiefe der '*Oikonomia*'³³ miteinander
verknüpft. Wichtigstes Mittel, mit Hilfe dessen Gregor dies immer
wieder verdeutlicht, ist, wie schon erwähnt, die vernünftige
Argumentation, mit der er zeigt, daß es zwischen beiden keine Wider-
sprüche gibt.

Die *Oikonomia* ist — wenn es auch in der Entfaltung nicht gezeigt
wird — die Voraussetzung für die *Theologia*. Die *Theologia* verfährt ja
nicht frei spekulativ, sondern geht von dem biblisch bezeugten
Heilshandeln Gottes aus und fragt nach dessen Grundlage in Gott
selbst. Das wird allein schon in der Tatsache deutlich, daß Gregor
die Gotteslehre als Trinitätslehre entfaltet. Daß 'induktiv aus der
Heilsgeschichte Gewonnene (wird) auch deduktiv vom Gottesbegriff aus'
entwickelt.³⁴ So beschreibt K. Holl das Vorgehen Gregors in der *or
cat.* Von der Gotteslehre kommt Gregor über die Heilsgeschichte zur
Trinitätslehre.³⁵ In *or cat* 39 zeigt sich ganz deutlich, wie sehr die
Soteriologie die Trinitätslehre notwendig macht. Wenn das Heilswerk
Christi nicht in seiner wahren Gottheit verankert ist, ist der Mensch
bei sich selbst geblieben und nicht durch Gott gerettet.

Gregor entwirft nicht nur die *Theologia* von der *Oikonomia* her,
sondern auch umgekehrt. Die *Theologia* wird ausgesprochener Maßen
zum Prüfstein der *Oikonomia*. Die oikonomisch bedingten theologischen
Vorentscheidungen schlagen sich widerum in der Entfaltung der
Soteriologie nieder.³⁶ Durch die Identifizierung von theologischen und

als 'ein System der Theologie', das mit Hilfe der Dialektik die
Glaubensinhalte systematisiere, so stark hervorgehoben worden ist.

33 A. Grillmeier, Symbolum S.596.

34 K.Holl: Amphilochius von Ikonium in seinem Verhältnis zu den
großen Kappadoziern, Tübingen 1904, S.209.

35 ibd.

36 R. Hübner, Einheit S.142f weist im Anschluß an H. Dörrie (Die
platonische Theologie S.24) darauf hin, daß es im vierten Jahr-
hundert sehr verschiedene Erlösungsmodelle gab. Die gravierenden
Unterschiede in der Soteriologie wurden vom 'jeweiligen Gottesbild

oikonomischen Gotteseigenschaften gelingt die deutlichste Verknüpfung. Indem Gregor die metaphysische, klassische Eigenschaft Gottes, die Güte, als Menschenliebe versteht, hat er in ihr den inneren, den 'theologischen' Grund für die *Oikonomia*,[37] und zugleich das Hauptargument für die übereinstimmung von *Theologia* und *Oikonomia*: Das, was Gott in der Schöpfung und im Christusgeschehen getan hat und auch weiterhin im Heiligen Geist durch die Sakramente tut, ist nicht nur nicht unschicklich für ihn, sondern es ist geradezu die eigentliche Äußerung seines Wesens.[38] Besonders deutlich ist dies im zweiten Teil der *Oikonomia*: Gregor zeigt, daß das Christusgeschehen dem Gottesbegriff nicht widerspricht. Im Gegenteil, nur diese Art der Rettung, ist eine, in der gewährleistet ist, daß alle Eigenschaften Gottes gleichermaßen zur Geltung kommen konnten. Nur so entspricht das Handeln Gottes seiner Vollkommenheit. Dem Erweis dieser Erkenntnis widmet Gregor einen sehr gut durchdachten, durchkonstruierten und in sich geschlossenen Teil der *or cat*, die Kapitel 19 bis 24.

Durch die methodische Unterscheidung einerseits und die enge Verbindung von *Theologia* und *Oikonomia* andererseits ist eine Einheit von — wie A. Grillmeier formuliert — 'kosmologischer Schau und geschichtlicher Betrachtung' mitgegeben, bzw. erst ermöglicht, die 'die Größe des frühchristlichen Entwurfes der Glaubenslehre' ausmacht. Weiter formuliert er: 'Nicht weniger als die erste Abzeichnung eines Universalsystems der Weltdeutung ist darin enthalten, eines Systems, das Gott und Welt, Schöpfung und Heilsgeschichte umfaßt. Obwohl Gottes Transzendenz völlig gewahrt wird, ist doch in seinem inneren dreifaltigen Leben der Entwurf der Schöpfung und der Geschichte verankert.'[39] Diese zunächst allgemein formulierten Sätze gelten, wie

---

her ... bestimmt. Deshalb konnte die Frage nach dem Wesen Gottes von der Frage nach der Erlösung nicht getrennt werden.'

37   *or cat 5.3* Sr. 22,8; *or cat 15.2* Sr. 63,8; vgl. auch *sanct pasch* GNO IX 248; *trid spat* GNO IX 282,13; s. H. Drobner, Drei Tage S.90; J.-R. Bouchet, La vision de l'économie du salut selon saint Grégoire de Nysse: RSPhTh 52 (1968) bes. S.634-637.

38   vgl. *or cat 27.6* Sr.105,7; *or cat 36.2* Sr.140,5.

39   A. Grillmeier, Symbolum S.596.

später von A. Grillmeier gezeigt wird,[40] vor allem und erstmalig für Gregors *or cat.*

Nicht nur die bisher behandelte Grobgliederung, sondern auch die Zusammenschau und Ordnung der 'oikonomischen' Themen ist gegenüber anderen Werken in dieser Übersichtlichkeit einmalig. In einem systematisch nach inhaltlichen Gesichtspunkten aufgebauten und gegliederten Gedankengang wird die gesamte Soteriologie entfaltet. So werden Beziehungen zwischen einzelnen Themen deutlich: z.B. der Zusammenhang zwischen den Aussagen über das Christusgeschehen und über die Sakramente, oder die gegenseitige Beeinflussung von Soteriologie, Christologie und Anthropologie. Eine Zusammenschau verschiedener Themen ist zwar in den großen dogmatischen Werken der Eunomianischen und Apolinarischen Kontroversen schon angelegt, weil Gregor dort die jeweils anderen Themen zur Stützung des Umstrittenen heranzieht, jedoch fehlt dort die Übersichtlichkeit und Systematik. Bei einem Vergleich mit den früheren Werken Gregors wird deutlich, daß die immer stärkere Zusammenschau der theologischen Themen nicht ohne Auswirkungen auf die Inhalte selbst geblieben ist.

So ist eine immer stärker werdende Bedeutung des Christusgeschehens in der Soteriologie und Trinitätstheologie zu finden, die zu Konsequenzen in der Anthropologie, z.B. zu einer immer positiveren Bewertung der Leiblichkeit des Menschen führte Andererseits forderte die so veränderte Anthropologie, in der die Erlösungsbedürftigkeit des Menschen, das Angewiesensein auf die Teilhabe an Gott selbst immer deutlicher wurde, ihrerseits eine breitere Entfaltung und tiefere Durchdringung der Soteriologie und Christologie. Es wurde ein immer intensiveres Bedenken des Christusgeschehens notwendig.[41] Das führte zu einer immer stärkeren Bewertung der Auferstehung Christi. Diese

---

40   ibd. 618.

41   In diesen Themen lassen sich Lernprozesse feststellen. Diese im
      einzelnen zu zeigen, und so die Verknüpfung der verschiedenen
      Themen darzustellen, wie sie auch der Theologie der *or cat*
      zugrunde liegen, und damit zugleich die besondere Bedeutung der *or
      cat* im Vergleich zum Gesamtwerk Gregors zu erfassen, ist das
      Ziel eines Teiles meiner Dissertation.

Entwicklung hat sich in der *or cat* niedergeschlagen. Die soteriologische bzw. oikonomische Mitte der *or cat* ist die Auferstehung
Christi.[42]

Es ist deutlich, wie die katechetisch-apologetische Absicht der
or cat die systematisch-theologische Entfaltung inhaltlicher
Zusammenhänge fördert und wie uns dadurch die Möglichkeit gegeben
ist, den Platz und die Wertigkeit der einzelnen theologischen Themen im
Denken Gregors zu entdecken.

3.   **Die zeitliche Stellung der *oratio catechetica* im Gesamtwerk
      Gregors**

Einen Hinweis, der eine absolute Datierung der *or cat* zuläßt,
finden wir weder in der *or cat* noch in irgendeinem anderen Werk
Gregors. Der einzige von Gregor selbst formulierte Anhaltspunkt, der
eine relative Datierung anhand anderer Werke zuläßt,[43] ist eine
Bemerkung in Kapitel 38.[44] Gregor behandelt dort die Bedeutung des
Bekenntnisses zur Trinität für die Taufe und deren Wirksamkeit. Dabei
verweist er auf Werke, in denen er die vorgelegten Fragen in
Auseinandersetzung mit den Gegnern und in Widerlegung ihrer Schriften
nach seinen eigenen Ansichten und mit dem ihm möglichen Eifer
enfaltet hat.[45] Die Werke, die der hier gegebenen Beschreibung am
besten gerecht werden, sind Gregors Bücher gegen Eunomius[46] oder

---

42 Vgl. R. Winling, La résurrection du christ comme principe
    explicativ et comme element structurant dans le *Discours
    catéchétique* de Grégoire de Nysse: StPatr XXII, Leuven 1989,
    S.74-80.

43 Zum Problem von absoluter und relativer Datierung siehe H.
    Drobner, Drei Tage S.190.

44 *or cat* 38.1 Srawley 153,4-9.

45 Gregor verweist hier nicht auf verschiedene Werkgruppen, sondern
    auf Werke, die beide Momente in sich vereinigen. Die großen
    polemisch-apologetischen Werke Gregors sind nie ohne die eigen-
    ständige Reflexion und Entfaltung der eigenen Ansicht, genauso wie
    die Werke, die von keiner konkreten Auseinandersetzung veranlaßt
    sind, nicht ohne apologetische Momente auskommen. Das beste
    Bespiel ist die *or cat* selbst.

46 Das wird von allen, die sich um die Datierung und die damit
    verbundene Interpretation dieser Stelle bemühen, gleichermaßen
    angenommen. J.H. Srawley S.XIV und S.158; L. Méridier S.XIII;

seine kleinen trinitarischen Schriften.[47]   Wichtiger ist die erste Vermutung, da sich *Eun I* und *Eun II* mit großer Wahrscheinlichkeit auf das Jahr 381 datieren lassen.[48]   Demnach kann die *or cat* nicht vor 381 enstanden sein.

Diese relative Datierung nach äußerlichen Hinweisen kann mit Beobachtungen zum entfalteten Inhalt und dem sich daraus ergebenden

---

seine kleinen trinitarischen Schriften.[47]   Wichtiger ist 'Sur les enfants morts prematurement' de Grégoire de Nysse: VigChr 20 (1966) S.181, wo er die Nähe zwischen *infant* und *or cat* aufweist.   J. Barbel S.209 Anm. 341, interpretiert Gregors Hinweis auf die anderen Werke wie J.H. Srawley, ohne jedoch darauf zu verweisen, daß dieser Hinweis zur Datierung wichtig ist. Er datiert die *or cat* in der Einleitung (S.14) ohne Angabe von Gründen in die Jahre 386 oder 387.   In diesem Zusammenhang spricht er von einem nicht erhaltenen Brief an Theophilus mit einer Warnung vor dem Apolinarismus.   Meint er etwa *Theoph.*?

47 G. May, Chronologie S. 61 denkt in diesem Zusammenhang an *Abl, Simpl* und *graec.*   J.H. Srawley, S.XIV Anm.4 und J. Barbel, S.209 Anm.341 verweisen dagegen auf *deit fil*, da *Simpl, Abl* und *Eust* private Adressaten haben und somit hier nicht gemeint sein können.   Ob dieses Argument tatsächlich Beweiskraft hat, muß fraglich bleiben, da wir nicht wissen, in welcher Weise und mit welcher Verbreitung die Schriften Gregors überhaupt publiziert wurden.   Wir wissen nicht, ob die Schriften an private Empfänger weniger in Umlauf waren als die, die keine privaten Addressaten haben. Diese Frage kann für die Datiergung der *or cat* offen bleiben, da wir bei den meisten kleinen trinitarischen Schriften keine konkreten Anhaltspunkte für ihre absolute Datierung finden. Anders ist es im Falle von *deit fil*.   Diese Rede hat Gregor auf der Synode von 383 in Konstantinopel gehalten.   Wenn er also auf diese Rede, die öffentlich vorgetragen worden ist, verweist, hätten wir mit dieser Annahme eine konkrete Hilfe für die Datierung der *or cat*.   Sie könnte nicht früher als 383 enstanden sein.

48 Wenn es als gesichert gelten darf, daß Gregor von Nyssa auf dem Konzil von Konstantinopel Hieronymus und Gregor von Nazianz aus *Eun I* oder *Eun II* vorgetragen hat, dann müssen diese Schriften kurz vor dem Konzil von Konstantinopel 381 enstanden sein.   J.H. Srawley, S.X u.XIV belegt dies mit dem Hinweis auf Hieronymus' *de vir.ill. 128*; ebenso B. Studer, Der geschichtliche Hintergrund des ersten Buches 'Contra Eunomium' Gregors von Nyssa: El 'Contra Eunomium I', Ed. F. Mateo-Seco/L. Bastero.   Pamplona 1988 S.139 u.158 Anm.6.   J. Daniélou, chronologie des oeuvres S.163 weist darauf hin, daß Gregor über diese Schriften mit seinem Bruder Petrus von Sebaste korrespondiert hat (*ep 29* GNO VII/2 8ff).   Dieser ist erst 381 Bischof von Sebaste geworden, was in der Korrespondenz vorausgesetzt wird.   Somit is *Eun I* und *Eun II* mit Sicherheit im Jahr 381 enstanden.

Vergleich mit anderen Werken gefestigt und konkretisiert werden.
Aufgrund der entfalteten Thematik kann beispielsweise Kapitel 27
weitere Argumente für eine relative Datierung der *or cat* liefern. In
or cat 27.3-6 weist Gregor mit zwei Argumenten eine dem Apolinarius
zugeschriebene Position zurück, derzufolge sich Gott vom Himmel her
mit dem Menschen verbunden, d.h. einen himmlischen Leib angenommen
habe.[49] Man findet keine Gründe, die Gregor vom Kontext her zwingen
diese Thematik zu behandeln. Deshalb müssen sie in der Situation der
Unterweisung zur Zeit der Abfassung der *or cat* gesucht werden. Die
hier widerlegte Ansicht des Apolinarius scheint Gregor besonders
gefährlich zu sein. Offensichtlich war die Diskussion um die Lehre des
Apolinarius so lebendig, daß die falschen Vormeinungen auch bei den
Katechumenen vorkamen.

Gregor greift hier auf die Argumente zurück, die er im *antirrh*
entwickelt hat. Es ist wahrscheinlicher, daß er die Häresie des
Apolinarius erst in einem ausführlichen Werk aufgedeckt und widerlegt
hat und dann erst ein Exerpt dieser Argumentation in die *or cat*
eingefügt hat. Die Parallelen und wörtlichen Übereinstimmungen
zwischen dem *antirrh* und der *or cat* bestätigen dies.[50] Für den
antirrh gibt es in der Forschung zwei Termine, die Jahre 386/387 oder
die Jahre um 381/382, d.h. vor 383.[51] Schließt man sich der

---

49 *antirrh* GNO III/1 138 vgl. H. Lietzmann, Apollinaris von Laodicea
    und seine Schule. TU, Tübingen 1904 = Hildesheim/New York
    1970, frgm. 16 u. 17; GNO III/1 143 vgl. frgm. 25; GNO III/1
    146 vgl. frgm. 31; GNO III/1 147 vgl. frgm. 32; GNO III/1 191
    vgl. frgm. 73.

50 Vgl. *or cat* 27.3-6 Srawley 102,11 mit *antirrh* GNO III/1 138f;
    143f; 196; 202.

51 Die späte Datierung vertreten: G. May, Chronologie S.61; E.
    Mühlenberg, Apollinaris von Laodicea, Göttingen, 1969 FKDG 23
    S.90; H. Lietzmann, Apollinaris S.83; jetzt auch R. Winling, La
    resurrection du Christ dans l'*Antirrheticus adversus Apollinarem* de
    Grégoire de Nysse: REAug XXXV 1 (1989) S.16. Die frühere
    Datierung vertreten: J. Lebourlier, À propos de l'état du Christ
    dans la mort: RSPhTh 47 (1963) S.171-180 und J. Daniélou,
    Chronologie des oeuvres S.163. Beide haben den Zusammenhang
    der Datierung vom *antirrh* mit *Theoph* nicht beachtet, sondern
    datieren ganz von inhaltlichen Gesichtspunkten, von der
    Entwicklung der Christologie her. R. Hübner, Einheit 136 Anm.
    166 verweist als wichtiges Gegenargument für die späte Datierung

frühen Datierung des *antirrh* an, so ergibt sich für die Datierung der *or cat* dieselbe Angabe wie nach den Überlegungen zu *Eun*, also nach 381 bzw. 383. Nimmt man dagegen die m.E. wahrscheinlichere spätere Datierung 386 oder 387 für den *antirrh* an, ergeben sich als Entstehungszeit für die *or cat* die Jahre ab 386.

Eine andere inhaltliche Beochbachtung erlaubt es, die Entstehungszeit der *or cat* auch nach hinten hin einzugrenzen. Aufgrund des Fehlens der für Gregors Spätwerk so bedeutenden Lehre vom unendlichen Aufstieg der Seele zum unendlichen Gott, deren theologische Grundlagen in den dogmatischen Werken gelegt worden und daher auch in der *or cat* zu finden sind, die aber in diesen Werken noch nicht entfaltet wird, kann man mit großer Wahrscheinlichkeit davon ausgehen, daß Gregor die großen asketischen Schriften vit *Moys* und *cant* erst nach der *or cat* geschrieben hat. Die *or cat* entstand also nach den großen trinitätstheologischen und christologischen Werken *Eun I, II, III, ref Eun* und *antirrh* — das läßt sich an vielen parallelen Einzelheiten und an wichtigen theologischen Übereinstimmungen im Gegensatz zu den früher entstandenen Werken, z.B. *op hom* und *an et res*, zeigen — und vor den großen asketischen Werken *vit Moys* und *cant*.

In diese Phase der Theologie Gregors gehören vor allem auch die Osterpredigt *trid spat*[52] und die Weihnachtspredigt *diem nat.*[53] Beide Predigten weisen sehr große Parallelen zur *or cat* auf, die diese Datierung der *or cat* ebenfalls stützen.

---

auf die Tatsache, daß Gregor, 'während er gegen Apollinarius schreibt, von der Leugnung der menschlichen Vernunft Christi durch Eunomius, die er dann in der ref. conf. Eun. bekämpft ..., offenbar noch nichts gehört hat, denn er stellt den Apollinarius in diesem Punkt eindeutig als den schlimmeren Häretiker hin.' Er verweist dabei auf *antirrh* GNO III/1 151,7-10 und 205, 21-206,16. Demzufolge muß der *antirrh* seiner Meinung nach zwischen *Eun III* und *ref Eun*, also vor 383 enstanden sein.

52 Nach eingehenden Überlegungen zur Datierung von *Eun III* und *antirrh* folgert H. Drobner, Drei Tage, Exkurs 2 S.190-198, daß als frühestes Datum für *trid spat* Ostern 386 anzusetzen wäre. Die inhaltlichen Parallelen zur *or cat* und diese Datierung bestätigen unsere Datierung der *or cat*. Vgl. ibid. S.190ff und 197.

Für die theologische Wertung der *or cat* ist diese chronologische Einordnung eine sehr wichtige Feststellung.   Sie erhöht den Wert der *or cat*.   Gregor hatte sich, als er die *or cat* verfaßte, zuvor schon mit allen wichtigen Themen der Theologie ausführlich befaßt, mit der Anthropologie,[54] mit der Christologie,[55] mit der Gottes- und Trinitätslehre[56] und mit der Ethik.[57] Besonders in der Eunomianischen und Apolinarischen Kontroverse hatte er seine spezifischen Standpunkte entwickelt, wobei ihm mehr und mehr die Verknüpfung verschiedener theologischer Themen wichtig wurde.   In der *or cat* stellt er die Ergebnisse dieser lebenslangen theologischen Arbeit, gleichsam als ein Exerpt seiner aus der Polemik entwickelten Gedanken, in einem Werk zusammen und bereitet sie für die christliche Taufunterweisung auf.[58] Insofern kann die Anordnung und die Gewichtung der Themen in der *or cat* nicht zufällig sein.   Sie geben im Gegenteil ein authentisches Bild vom Gesamtdenken Gregors in seiner späten Phase.   Auch aus diesem Grund kann die *or cat* einen angemessenen Zugang zum Gesamtwerk Gregors eröffnen.

---

53   J. Daniélou, La chronologie des sermons de Grégoire de Nysse: RevSR 29 (1955) S.365 datiert diese Predigt exakt auf den 25.12.386.   Hinweise auf die Schrift *contra fatum*, die aufgrund eines in ihr erwähnten Erdbebens von Jan. 386 in die Mitte des Jahres zu datieren ist, erlauben eine solche exakte Festlegung. J. Daniélou schreibt, Gregor verspüre eine Notwendigkeit, ein zusammenfassendes Werk über den christlichen Glauben zu verfassen.   Ob sich J. Daniélou mit dieser Äußerung auf *diem nat* oder auf *fat* stützt, ist nicht klar.   Eine Stelle hat er nicht angegeben.   Ein solcher Hinweis wäre aber für die Datierung der *or cat* von größter Wichtigkeit.

54   *hex, op hom, an et res*, dann *mort* und später auch *infant*.

55   *Eun III, ref Eun, Theoph, antirrh.*

56   *graec, Abl, Eusth, diff ess hyp, Eun I, ref Eun.*

57   *virg, prof,* und eventuell *perf* s.oben Anm. 24.

58   Diese Einschätzung teilt auch H. Drobner, Drei Tage S.124 u. 172.

18

Le Livre de l'Ecclésiaste dans l'antiquité chrétienne#

Marek Starowieyski

I.   Introduction

1.   Le livre de l'Ecclésiaste dans l'antiquité chrétienne n'était pas particulèrement populaire.   On ne le citait que rarement, comme on peut s'en rendre compte d'après les quatre volumes de la Biblia Patristica;[1] il n'était pas souvent cité par les écrivains chrétiens et était rarement employé dans la liturgie, car nous ne trouvons que très rarement d'homélies à son sujet.   Mais par ailleurs, les plus anciennes citations de l'Ecclésiaste se trouvent déjà chez les écrivains de la première moitié du IIe s., et les commentaires de ce livre appartiennent aux plus anciens commentaire de la Bible, à savoir aux *Eclogues* de Méliton de Sardes et aux *Hypotyposes* de Clément d'Alexandrie, ce qui montre l'intérêt pour ce livre au tournant des IIe et IIIe siècles.[2]

Il y a quelques raisons qui expliquent cet intérêt.

Le thème existentiel et universel de ce livre — la vanité de tout ce qui existe — a pu trouver dans la société hellénistique une résonnance plus grand, que les autres livres de l'Ancien Testament,

---

J'ai pu préparer ce travail grâce à l'aide de M. Giancarlo Isnardi de Moncalieri (Torino) qui m'a envoyé les photocopies des travaux inaccessibles en Pologne — je voudrais lui exprimer ici mes sentiments d'une vive reconnaissance.

1   *BiPa*, vol. 1, Paris 1975, 210; vol. 2, 1977, 208-210; vol. 3, 213s; vol. 4, 1985, 195; Supplément — Philon, 1982, 90.

2   Cfr notes 15, 17, 24 et 25.

impregnés de la mentalité hébraïque.   Comme nous le verrons, la
plupart des commentaires de ce livre proviennent des milieux alexandrin
et antiochien, deux milieux dans lesquels les cultures païenne, juive et
chrétienne se sont développées parallèlement.   Les pestes, les invasions barbares, la crise économique, sociale et enfin morale du IIe et
IIIe siècles — tel est le climat de ce 'Age of Anxiety', qui correspond
bien au pessimisme du Sage et à ses paroles *vanitas vanitatum et
omnia vanitas.*[3]   Pour les chrétiens, ces paroles étaient encore plus
significatives à cette époque de martyrs[4] et encore plus tard, quand
se développa la vie ascétique et monastique.[5]

Dans les milieux chrétiens et juifs, le livre de l'Ecclésiaste
jouissait d'une grande considération grâce à son auteur.   On
l'attribuait en effet au grand roi Salomon.   Selon un récit juif
transmis partiellement par Jérôme, Salomon l'aurait rédigé à la fin de
sa vie, à l'époque où il avait laissé le royaume et faisait pénitence.[6]
Salomon serait en autre, l'auteur de deux autres livres de l'Ancient
Testament, à savoir du livre des Proverbes et du Cantique des
Cantiques.   Dans le milieu chrétien, deux éminents écrivains, Hippolyte

---

3   Eccl. 1,3.

4   Mais l'Ecclésiaste est cité dans les *Actes des Martyrs* qu'une
     fois, cfr *The Acts of the Christian Martyrs*, éd. H. Musurillo,
     Oxford 1972, 218 (*Les Actes de Montanus et Lucius)*; dans
     l'*Adhortation au martyre* d'Origène il est aussi cité une fois (22).

5   Dans les *Apophtegmes* l'Ecclésiaste est cité 4 fois.   Cfr L.
     Regnault, Les sentences des Pères du désert, 3 recueil et tables,
     Solesmes 1976, 312; dans les *Règles monastiques* — 2 fois (*Règle
     de Ferreol* 3,9 et 24,5s. et *Règle de Paul et Etienne 14,9*; cfr
     V. Desprez, Règles monastiques de l'Occident IVe-VIe siècles,
     Bellefontaine 1980; dans la littérature pacômienne — 31 fois (et
     il y a probablement encore plus de citations); cfr Pachomian
     koinonia, éd. A. Veilleux, vol. 3, Kalamazoo 1982, 255s.   Il faut
     souligner que dans les milieux monastiques on a traduit en copte
     le Commentaire de l'Ecclésiaste de Grégoire de Nysse (cfr nr 14)
     et sont nés les Comméntaires de Evagre Pontique (cfr nr 16) et
     de Nil d'Ancyre (cfr nr 22).

6   Aiunt Hebraei hunc librum Salomonis esse, poenitentiam agentis,
     quod in sapientia divitiisque confisus, per mulieres offenderit
     Deum, *In Ecclesiasten* 1,12, CChr.SL 72,258.   Cfr C.D. Ginsburg,
     Coheleth, London 1861, 27-99; S. Schiffer, Das Buch Kohelet
     nach der Auffassung der Weisen des Talmud und Midrasch und der
     jüdischer Erklärer des Mittelalters, Leipzig 1884.

de Rome (+235) et Origène (+254), on tenté de donner un sens théologique à cette triade. Hippolyte en soulignant l'action de l'Esprit Saint decouvre ici une structure trinitaire: les Proverbes sont liés avec le Père (la Sagesse), l'Ecclésiaste — avec le Fils et son arrivé au monde, le Cantique des Cantiques — avec L'Esprit Saint, la joie et la consolation.[7]   Selon Origène, ces trois livres contiennent toute la 'humana doctrina', à savoir: les Proverbes — l'éthique; 'Ecclésiaste — la science 'naturelle', le Cantiques des Cantiques — la mystique.[8]   Ces trois livres décrivent le progrès de l'âme: le premier est un livre destiné aux debutants spirituels (*incipientes, parvuli*), le second — aux

---

7   I,f. Sapientiam habebat Salomon, non quidem ipse sapientia erat; gratiam invenit a Deo, non autem ipsemet gratia erat; filius erat Davidis, non autem ipsemet Christus erat.   2. Ei gratificatum est a Deo tres libros edicere in mundo, in quibus tribus libris potentiam quamdam demonstrat Spiritus Sancti ductu; quia magisterio gratiae (est) acquisitum verbum, et sapientia cum eo habitante, non expers a Deo fiebat.   3. Tres quasdam divisiones ei adiudicat, quia tres hi libri per voluntatem Spiritus sancti et beati oris (eius) a Spiritu sancto edicti sunt, quia Spiritus Sanctus est qui eloquebatur Trinitatem, ut gratia Patris et Filii et Spiritus Sancti ediceretur.   4. Quia praevie cum sapientia eloquitur Proverbia, per quae admirabilis et inapparens gratia Patris edicitur; et Ecclesiastes e libris (in) quo obtenebratam per verba (illius quae est) ab eo scientiae, nobis ostendit (scillicet) quia Filius erat; tertio una Spiritus Sancti quiddam componit, in cuius laudatione Spiritus sanctus docebat multos.   5. Nunc tres hi unitatis libri facti sunt; tertius autem erat persigillationem Spiritus sancti; quia primo Patrem admirabilem (esse) et opulentiam a sapientia (esse) (est) edictum; (secundo libro) terram congregationem tenebrarum per Filium cognosci et tenebras intelligi mundo (est) edictum; tertius laudatio ad laetificationem Spiritus sancti et ad exsultationem consolationis, et cognitio Dei apparens facta multis.   *Interpretatio Canticis canticorum* I:1-5, CSCO 264/Iber 16, éd. G. Garitte, 1965,23.   Le texte d'Hippolyte n'est conservée que dans la version géorgienne.

8   Salomon ergo tres istas, quas supra diximus generales esse disciplinas, id est moralem, naturalem et inspectivam, distinguere ab invicem ac secernere volens, tribus eas libellis edidit, suo quoque ordine singulis consequenter aptatis.   Primo ergo in Proverbiis moralem docuit locum, succinctis, ut decuit, brevibusque sententiis vitae instituta componens.   Secundum vero quae naturalis appellatur, comprehendit in Ecclesiaste: in quo multa de rebus naturalibus disserens, et inania ac vana ab utilibus necessariisque secernens, reliquendam vanitatem monet, et utilia rectaque sectanda.   Inspectivum quoque locum in hoc libello tradidit, qui habetur in manibus, id est in Cantico canticorum, in

progressants (*proficientes, viri maturae aetatis*), le troisième — aux parfaits (*perfecti, viri consummati*).[9] Nous ne savons pas si cette conception de la triade des livres salomoniques a été inventé par Origène ou s'il l'a repris à la théologie judéo-hellénistique. Probablement ces deux approches des livres de Salomon sont-elles le fruit des réflexions de ces théologiens. En plus, la grande autorité dont jouissait Salomon chez les Juifs a été encore renforcée chez les chrétiens quand, en appliquant la méthode allégorique, ils ont reconnu dans le Salomon-Ecclésiaste la figure du Christe même.[10]

Mais, par ailleurs le livre a également provoqué des controverses tant dans le milieu juif que, après, dans celui des chrétiens à cause de quelques passages qu'on pourrait qualifier d'hédonistes et d'épicuriens, ce qui a conduit à contester sa canonicité. Au IIe s. avant J.Chr. les partisans de Hillel ont affirmé que le livre souillait les mains et qu'il était donc saint, tandis que les adeptes de Schamaï le considératient comme un livre qui ne souillait pas les mains et donc qui n'était pas saint. À Qumran il était probablement considéré comme canonique, car on en a trouvé des exemplaires. Mais encore au IIe s. après J.Chr. dans *Tasepha* on affirme qu'il ne souille pas les mains, car on y trouve la sagesse de Salomon, donc celle d'un roi très sage, mais non une sagesse inspirée. On a traduit l'Ecclésiaste dans le cadre de la Septante, et ainsi il est devenu accessible au monde grec. Philon (+40 après J.Chr.) le cite rarement, mais le

---

quo amorem caelestium divinorumque desiderium incutit animae sub specie sponsae ac sponsi, charitatis et amoris viis perveniendum docens ad consortium Dei. *In Cantica canticorum commentarius*, Prologus, PG 13,74. Le texte d'Origène n'est conservé que dans la version latine de Rufin.

9	Hieronymus, *In Ecclesiasten*, 1,1, CChr.SL 72,250s.

10	Déjà Denys d'Alexandrie a souligné que le titre *Fils de David* qui se donne l'Ecclésiaste (1,1) est le titre de Jésus Christ (cfr Mt 1,1), CCGr 4, 1978, 7. Selon Jérôme: *Secundum intelligentiam spiritalem pacificus et dilectus Dei Patris et Ecclesiastes noster est Christus*, CChr.SL 72,251.

synode de Jamnia (env. 100 après J.Chr.) le considère comme
canonique, bien que, même plus tard, on trouve des rabbins qui le
rejettent.[11]

Les chrétiens, suivant la tradition juive de la Septante, ont
accepté la canonicité de l'Ecclésiaste. Il est vrai qu'on ne trouve
pas de citations de ce libre dans le Nouveau Testament ou, du moins,
leur présence y est assez problématique[12], mais nous les trouvons
déjà chez les écrivains du IIe s.: dans le *Pasteur* d'Hermas (env.
130)[13], chez Justin (+167)[14], chez Clément d'Alexandrie (+env. 212)[15]
et, enfin, chez Tertullien (+220)[16]. Le livre figure aussi sur la liste
des livres de l'Ancien Testament dressée par Méliton de Sardes (fin du
IIe s.), lequel a également composé un recueil d'extraits (ἐκλογαί) de
ce livre.[17]

Malgré le fait que les chrétiens aient accepté la canonicité de
l'Ecclésiaste ainsi que son inspiration qu'ils soulignent, comme nous
l'avons déjà vu chez Hippolyte[18] et nous verrons chez Eusèbe de
Césarée (+339)[19], les discussions autour de ce livre ont recommencé
au IVe et au Ve siècle, particulièrement dans l'école d'Antioche,
fortement attachée dans son exégèse à la *veritas hebraica*. La
controverse a continué au IVe siècle, quand Marcel d'Ancyre (+env.

---

11   M. Filipiak, Księga Koheleta, Poznań 1980, 26-28; AA.VV. Le
      canon de l'Ancien Testament sa formation et sa histoire, Genève
      1984, 15-18, 21, 28s., 51; au sujet de la Septante,   cfr G.
      Dorival/M. Harl/O. Munich, La Bible grec de Septante, Paris 1988;
      sur les citations de Philon, cfr note 1.

12   Cfr M. Filipiak, op.cit. 28; Leanza [v. Abréviations, infra] 5-7.

13   *Mandatum* 7,15, GCS 48,1, 1956, 33,18 (Eccl 12,13).

14.   *Dialogus* 6,2, BAC 166, 1979, 313 (Eccl 12,7).

15   *Stromata* 5,13,90,2, GCS 51, 1965: 385,18 (Eccl 1,2); 1,12,58,1,
      ibidem 37,3-6 (Eccl 1,16-18); 1,12,58,3, ibidem 8-9 (Eccl 7,13).

16   *Adversus Marcionem* 5,4,15, CChr.SL 1,1954, 675 (Eccl 3,17); *De
      virginibus velandis* 1,5, CChr.SL 2,1210 (Eccl 3,17); *De monogamia*
      3,8, CChr.SL 2,1232 (Eccl 3,17); *Apologeticum* 28,3, CChr.SL
      1,140 (Eccl 9,4).

17   Eusebius, HE 4,26,14, SC 31,221; 123,224.15.

18   Cfr note 7.

19   Cfr note suivante.

374) a identifié l'inspiration des livres de la Sainte Ecriture avec la prophétie. Salomon est donc considéré par lui comme prophète et ses trois livres (Proverbes, Ecclésiaste et Cantique des Cantiques) comme des livres prophétiques. Cette opinion est attaqué par Eusèbe de Césarée dans son *Contre Marcellum*; les livres bien qu'ils ne soient pas prophétiques, sont quand même inspirés et canoniques; Salomon n'était pas seulement le plus sage, mais il était aussi comblé de l'Esprit Saint.[20] On trouve des échos de cette discussion encore en IXe siècle chez un exégète syrien, Išodad de Merw.[21]

La discussion se prolongeait dans l'école d'Antioche et dans les écrits de son grand exégète Théodore de Mopsueste (+428), auteur d'un commentaire de l'Ecclésiaste. Les opinions exégétiques de Théodore font encore aujourd'hui l'objet de discussion.[22] Il niait la canonicité de quelques livres de l'Ancien Testament, mais pas de l'Ecclésiaste. De son commentaire de l'Ecclésiaste on a gardé un fragment qui se trouve que dans la version latine des actes du IIe concile de Constantinople (553); concile qui l'a par ailleurs condamné. Comme ce fragment est tiré de son contexte et contient des expressions ambiguës, telles que *'pro doctrina hominum'* et *'ex sua persona'*, il est assez difficile de juger sur une base aussi étroite des opinions de Théodore concernant ces livres. L'opinion de E. Amman, qui

20 *Contra Marcellum*, Prologus, PG 24, 741ss. Eusèbe plusieurs fois cite l'Ecclésiaste, p.e. *Praeparatio evangelica* 11,6, SC 292, 96s.; *Eclogae propheticae* 3,4-5, PG 22,1125-1129, cfr BiPa 1985, vol, 4, 195.

21 CSCO 230/Syr 97, 1963, VIIs, 200; bibliographie nr 40.

22 Sur l'inspiration de l'Écriture Sainte chez Théodore et son exégèse cfr H. Kihn, Theodor von Mopsuestia und Junilius Africanus als Exegeten, Freiburg 1880; L. Pirot, L'oeuvre exégétique de Théodore de Mopsueste, Roma 1913; I.M. Vosté, L'oeuvre exégétique de Théodore de Mopsueste au IIe concile de Constantinople: RB 38 (1929) 282-295; id., De versione Syriaca operum Theodori Mopsuesteni: OCP 8 (1942) 477-481; R. Devreesse, Essai sur Théodore de Mopsueste, Roma 1948 (cfr p. 34s.); E. Amman, DThC 15/1,1946, 245-248; R.A. Greer, Theodore of Mopsuestia, Exegete and Theologian, London 1981; J. Beumer, L'inspiration de la Sainte Écriture, Paris 1972, 31s.

suppose que Théodore attribuait différents types d'inspiration aux différents livres de la Bible est probablement juste.[23]

Toute cette controverse sur la canonicité est née des fragments dans lesquels l'auteur du livre exprime des opinions épicuriennes et hédonistes qui étaient objet de scandale dans les cercles tant juifs que chrétiens, ce que prouve le chapitre 134 de *Diversarum hereseon liber* de Philastrius de Brescia.[24] Il fallait donc leur trouver une explication et, à ce qu'il semble, ce fut là la raison principale qui provoqua des commentaires sur ce livre, particulièrement dans les milieux où ces problèmes etaient discutés, à savoir dans les cercles chrétiens et juifs, voir peut-être chez les païens, c'est à dire à Alexandrie, et, plus tard, à Antioche. Le but primitif des commentaires était donc apologétique, tendance qui disparaît lentement avec le temps. Il y avait aussi, naturellement, un autre raison, le désir de comprendre ce livre qui faisait partie de la Bible.

2.   Je prends le mot 'commentaire' au sens large, entendant par là tout essai d'explication d'un livre de la Sainte Ecriture que ce soit sous forme de commentaire au sens propre ou sous forme d'homélie, de chaîne ou commentaire sous forme d'une chaîne, d'extraits, d'eclogues, etc.

Les plus anciens commentaires du livre de l'Ecclésiaste se prêtent mal à une définition. Les *Eclogues* de la Sainte Ecriture de Méliton de Sardes ne se sont pas conservées et nous ne savons pas,

---

23 His quae pro doctrina hominum scripta sunt, et Salomonia libri connumerandi sunt, id est Proverbia et Ecclesiaste, quae ipse ex sua persona ad aliorum utilitatem composuit, cum prophetiae quidam gratiam non accepissent, prudentiae verso gratiam quae evidenter altera est praeter illam, secundum beati Pauli vocem (1 Cor 12,8-10). *Concilium universale Constantinopolitanum I*, vol.1, éd. J. Straub, Berlin 1971, 66; Mansi 9,2236⁴; PG 66, 697. Selon W. Strothmann, dans la version syriaque du Commentaire de l'Ecclésiaste de Théodore on y trouve une confirmation de cette opinion, Das syrische Fragment ... p. XVIII; bibliographie nr 19. Sur l'opinion de E. Amman, cfr note 22.

24 CChr.SL 9,1957, 298s.; PL 12,1265-1267; Bar Hebraeus, *The Chronography*, éd. E.A. Wallis Budge, 1, Oxford 1932.

si c'étaient des glosses, des scolies ou des extraits.[25]   Les
Hypotyposes de Clément d'Aléxandrie étaient des exposés résumés de
l'Ecriture.   Selon T. Zahn, l'Ecclésiaste était commenté dans un des
trois premiers livres de cette oeuvre.   Parmi les fragments conservés
on   ne   trouve   aucun   fragment   sur   l'Ecclésiaste.[26]   Ces   deux
commentaires sont bien attestés: le fragment de la lettre de Méliton à
Onésime, où l'auteur raconte ses recherches concernant le canon de
l'Ancien Testament, est cité par Eusèbe de Césarée dans son *Histoire
Ecclésiastique*.   Le patriarche Photius dans sa *Bibliothèque* parle des
Hypotyposes, mais il s'occupe de l'aspect dogmatique plutôt que de
l'aspect littéraire de cette oeuvre de Clément.   Ces deux commentaires
sont   habituellement   omis   dans   les   travaux   sur   la   réception   de
l'Ecclésiaste dans la tradition patristique.

Les autres commentaires du IIIᵉ s. ne sont connus que par leurs
titres ou dans de rares fragments, laborieusement rassemblés par les
chercheurs de Messine, sauf la métaphrase de Grégoire le Thamaturge.
Nous ne disposons que de quelques fragments du commentaire d'Hippolyte de Rome (+235).[27]   Comme nous l'avons déjà vu, Origène (+254)
comme Hippolyte a elaboré une classification des livres attribués a
Salomon, reprise par les commentateurs jusqu'au Moyen-Age.[28]   Selon
Jérôme, il a écrit un commentaire sous forme de scolies et l'autre, de
8 homélies qui ne nous est parvenu que fragmentairement.[29]   Malgré le
petit nombre de ces fragments, on peut affirmer — comme l'a montré
S. Leanza que l'exégèse allégorique de l'Ecclésiaste d'Origène a eu un
rôle décisive sur la formation de l'exégèse posterieure de ce livre en
Orient et — à travers le commentaire de Jérôme qui doit beaucoup à
Origène — en Occident jusqu'au Moyen-Age.[30]   Du commentaire du

---

25   Bibliographie nr 1.

26   A. Harnack, Geschichte der altchristlichen Literatur bis Eusebius,
      vol. I,1, Leipzig 1958, 303-308;   cfr Bibliographie nr 2.

27   Bibliographie nr 3.

28   Cfr note 8 et Leanza(Or) [v.Abréviations, infra], passim.

29   Bibliographie nr 4.

30   Cfr Leanza(Or), passim.

troisième écrivain alexandrin, Denys d'Alexandrie (+264) il ne reste pas que des fragments;   mais la publication par A. Labate de la *Catena Hauniensis* — commentaire au forme de chaîne, formée dans la plupart des fragments de Denys, nous permet non seulement de connaître mieux ce commentaire, mais aussi, peut-être, tenter de donner sa reconstruction.[31]

Le premier commentaire, entièrement conservé, provient aussi du milieu alexandrin: c'est la *Métaphrase* du livre de l'Ecclésiaste écrite par un élève d'Origène — Grégoire le Thaumaturge (+env. 270).   C'est plutôt une paraphrase de ce livre qu'un commentaire proprement dit.[32] Jérôme nous signale l'existence d'un commentaire de l'Ecclésiaste de Victorin de Poetovium (+304), qui était encore, lui aussi, sous l'influence de l'école alexandrine; c'est le premier commentaire latin de ce livre, mais malheureusement il ne nous en reste plus qu'un fragment chez Jérôme.[33]

Par Jérôme nous apprenons aussi que Acace de Césarée (+366) a écrit un commentaire du livre de l'Ecclésiaste en 17 livres — ce serait le plus ample commentaire patristique de Qohelet mais il n'en reste aucun fragment.[34]   Jérôme parle aussi du commentaire d'Apollinaire de Laodicée (+390), mais son opinion sur l'oeuvre de son maître reste plutôt négative.[35]

Le commentaire d'Apollinaire ouvre toute une série de commentaires antiochiens de l'Ecclésiaste.   On peut supposer qu'Acace a commenté ce livre dans l'esprit de cette école, bien que Césarée soit restée longtemps sous une forte influence d'Origène.   C'est dans le même esprit nettement antiochien qu'ont été probablement écrits le commentaire entièrement perdu de Diodore de Tarse (+393)[36] — avec

---

31   Bibliographie nr 5.

32   Bibliographie nr 6.

33   Bibliographie nr 7.

34   Bibliographie nr 8.

35   Bibliographie nr 11.

36   Bibliographie nr 13.

lequel peut-être a polemiqué Grégoire de Nysse[37] — et celui de
Théodore de Mopsueste (+428), écrit à la demande de Porphyre, selon
Ebedjesu, ou de Marphoria, selon la Chronique de Séért.[38]   De ce
commentaire il ne nous est probablement resté qu'un fragment grec
inseré dans le commentaire du prophète Michée et déjà mentionné
fragment latin.[39]   La traduction syriaque du commentaire de Théodore
a été retrouvée par H. von Soden à Damas au XXe s. dans un
manuscrit probablement de VI/VIIe siècle.   Elle contient l'introduction
et commentaire jusqu'à Eccl 7,26.   Le texte syriaque sans traduction
a été publiée par W. Strothmann en 1988.[40]   Mar Barhadbešabba
Arbaya, évêque de Halwan au VIe s. nous informe que ce commentaire
n'a pas été brulé par Rabbula, car il n'était pas en ce temps, c'est à
dire au commencement du Ve s. traduit en syriaque.[41]   Selon
W. Strothmann ce commentaire a influencé fortement les nombreux
commentaires syriaques de l'Ecclésiaste: orthodoxes et nestoriens.[42]

Il ne nous serait rien resté des commentaires antiochiens, si
nous ne n'avions pas le Commentaire d'un Ps. Jean Chrysostome, publié
dernièrement par S. Leanza, dont l'exégèse est typiquement
littéraire.[43]   C'est peut-être aussi avec le milieu antiochien qu'est
apparentée l'homélie sur Eccl 1,2 attribuée à S Ephrem (+373), mais
son authenticité est douteuse et de plus nous ne savons pas si elle
provient ou non d'un commentaire de ce livre.[44]   Nous ne pouvons pas
non plus dire grand-chose sur le commentaire de Nil d'Ancyre (IV/VI),

---

37   Bibliographie nr 14; GNO V, Leiden 1986, p.390.

38   Bibliographie nr 19; R. Devreese, op.cit. 34 (cfr note 23).

39   PG 66, 380 (Eccl 11,2).

40   Bibliographie nr 19.

41. PO 4, 381.

42   Cfr Strothmann 216ss.

43   Bibliographie 21.

44   T.J. Lamy suppose qu'Ephrem n'a jamais écrit un commentaire de
     l'Ecclésiaste, même s'il le cite souvent, en commentant p.e. le
     Livre des Proverbes, RB 2 (1893) 9; cfr Bibliographie nr 9.

dont il ne reste que quelques fragments; nous avons quelques exemples de son exégèse dans ses lettres.[45]

Contrairement à certaines opinions, ni Basile le Grand (+379) ni Eustathe d'Antioche (IVᵉ s.) n'ont probablement pas rédigé de commentaire du livre de l'Ecclésiaste. [46]

En IVᵉ s. on trouve encore des commentaires de l'Ecclésiaste chez les Alexandrins. Nous ne pouvons pas savoir, si Athanase (+373) a écrit un seul commentaire à la fois du Cantique des Cantiques et de l'Ecclésiaste ou deux explications separées; l'unique information donnée par Photius est loin d'être claire; de ces commentaires il ne reste rien.[47] Grâce à la découverte des papyrus de Tura nous connaissons le commentaire allégorique de Didyme l'Aveugle (+397), écrit avant l'an 381[48]. C'est de cercles monastiques que provient le commentaire d'Evagre le Pontique (+399) dont il ne reste que quelques fragments grecs, mais peut-être la publication de ce commentaire ou de sa paraphrase en arabe signalée par Géhin, nous apportera-t-elle des éclarcissements.[49] Des mêmes cercles proviennent des fragments coptes du commentaire de Grégoire de Nysse trouvés sous le nom de Shénuté. Grégoire (+394), pendant le carême de 381 a commenté l'Ecclésiaste 1-3,13 en 8 homélies qu'ensuite il a mises par écrit; son exégèse est typiquement allégorique et sous l'influence d'Origène.[50]

Nous ne pouvons pas dire grand'chose du commentaire de Grégoire d'Elvire (IV s.); on ne sait pas, si c'est le fragment d'un commentaire de l'Ecclésiaste ou d'une autre oeuvre.[51] En tout cas, si Grégoire a commenté le livre de l'Ecclésiaste, on peut supposer, qu'il l'a fait dans l'ésprit d'Origène.

---

45   Bibliographie nr 22.

46   Cfr Leanza 27-29.

47   Bibliographie nr 10.

48   Bibliographie nr 15.

49   Bibliographie nr 16.

50   Bibliographie nr 14.

51   Jérôme ne mentionne pas ce commentaire dans la liste des oeuvres de Grégoire dans le *Vir. III.* 105, Firenze 1988, 208.

Le premier commentaire latin conservé est celui de Jérôme
(+419),[52]   C'est aussi son premier commentaire sur un livre de
l'Ancien Testament; il l' écrit en 389. Jérôme y utilise des résultats
de l'exégèse alexandrine (Origène, Didyme), celle d'Antioche (Apollinaire),
des écrivains latins (Victorin de Poetovium) et, enfin, de l'exégèse
juive. Ce commentaire constitue le point de départ des commentaires
latins du Moyen-Age, transmettant à Occident les résultats de l'exégèse grecque. Plusieurs remarques de Jérôme restent valables jusqu'
aujourd'hui. Les excerpta de l'Ecclésiaste dans le *Speculum* d'Augustin
(+430) n'enrichissent pas beaucoup l'histoire de l'exégèse, mais sont
utiles pour la connaissance de l'ancien textes de ce livre.[53]

Les excerpta de Tajon de Saragosse (+683) constituent le
dernier commentaire latin à l'Ecclésiaste de l'époque patristique.[54]
C'est un commentaire composé de fragments tirés des oeuvres de
Grégoire le Grand (+602), un pape très populaire en Espagne
Wisigothique. Il faut ici souligner le fragment du IVᵉ livre des
Dialogues, où le pape explique le titre de l'Ecclésiaste.[55]   Cet

---

52   Cfr Bibliographie nr 18.

53   Cfr Bibliographie nr 20.

54   Cfr Bibliographie nr 34.

55   4.1. Salomonis liber, in quo haec scripta sunt, Ecclesiastes
appellatus est, Ecclesiastes autem proprie concionator dicitur. In
contione vero sententia promitur, per quam tumultuosa turbae
seditio comprimatur, et cum multi diversa sentiat, per contionantis
rationem ad unam sententiam perducuntur. Hic igitur liber idcirco
contionator dicitur, quia Salomon in eo quasi tunultuantis turbae
suscepit sensum, ut ea per inquisitionem dicat, quae fortasse per
temptationem inperita mens sentit. Nam quot sententias quasi per
inquisitionem movit, quasi tot in se personas diversorum suscepit.
2. Sed contionator verax, velut extensa manu, omnium tumultus
sedat eosque ad unam sententiam revocat, cum in eiusdem libri
termino ait: 'Finem loquendi omnes pariter audiamus: Deum time et
mandata eius observa; hoc est enim omnis homo' (12,13). Si
enim in libro eodem per locutionem suam multorum personas non
susceperat, cur ad audiendum loquendi finem secum pariter omnes
admonebat?   Qui igitur in fine libri dicit: 'Omnes pariter
audiamus', ipse sibi testis est, quia in se multorum personas
suscipiens, quasi solus locutus non est. 3. Unde et alia sunt,
quae in libro eodem per inquisitionem moventur, atque alia quae
per rationem satisfaciunt; alia quae ex temptati profert animo
atque adhuc huius mundi delectationibus dediti, alia vero in quibus

intéret pour Qohélet est typique de la part du pape de l'époque de l'invasions des Longobardes en Italie.

---

ea quae rationis sunt disserat atque animum a delectatione compescat. Ibi namque ait: 'Hoc itaque mihi visum est bonum, ut comedat quis et bibat et fruatur laetitia ex labore suo' (5,17). Et longe inferius subiungit: 'Melius est ire ad domum luctus qum ad domum convivii' (7,3). 4. Si enim bonum est manducare et bibere, melius fuisse videbatur ad domum convivii pergere quam ad domum luctus. Ex qua re ostenditur quia illud ex infirmantium persona intulit, hoc vero ex rationis definitione subiunxit. Nam ipsas protinus rationis causas edisserit, et de domo luctus quae sit utilitas ostendit dicens: 'In illa enim finis cunctorum admonetur hominum et vivens cogitat quid futurus sit' (7,3). 5. Rursus illic scriptum est: 'Laetare, iuvenis, in adolescentia tua' (11,9). Et paulo post additur 'Adolescentia enim et voluptas vana sunt' (11,10). Qui dum hoc postmodum vanus esse redarguit, quod prius admonuisse videbatur, patenter indicat quia illa quasi ex desiderio carnali verba intulit, haec vero ex iudicii veritatis subiunxit. 6. Sicut ergo delectationem prius carnalium exprimens, curis postpositis denuntiat bonum esse manducare et bibere, quod tamen postmodum ex iudicii ratione reprehendit, cum esse melius dicit ire ad domum luctus quam ad domum convivii; et sicut laetari debere iuvenem in adolescentia sua quasi ex deliberatione carnalium proponit, et tamen postmodum per definitionem sententiae adolescentiam et voluptatem vana esse redarguit, ita etiam contionator noster velut ex mente infirmantium humanae suspicionis sententiam proponit, dum dicit: 'Unus interitus est hominis et iumentorum, et aequa utriusque conditio. Sicut moritur homo, sic et illa moriuntur. Similiter spirant omnia, et nihil habet homo iumentis amplius' (3,19). 7. Qui tamen ex definitione rationis suam postmodum sententiam profert, dicens: 'Quid habet amplius sapiens stulto, et quid pauper, nisi ut pergat illuc, ubi est vita?' (6,8). Qui igitur dixit: 'Nihil habet iumentis homo amplius', ipse rursum definivit quia habet aliquid sapiens non solum amplius a iumento, sed etiam ab homine stulto, videlicet 'ut pergat illuc, ubi est vita'. Quibus verbis primum indicat quia hic hominum vita non est, quam esse alibi testatur. Habet ergo hoc homo amplius iumentis, quod illa post mortem non vivunt, hic vero tunc vivere inchoat, cum per mortem carnis hanc visibilem vitam consummat. 8. Qui etiam longe interius dixit: 'Quodcumque potest manus tua facere, instanter operare, quia nec opus, nec ratio, nec scientia, nec sapientia erit apud inferos, quo tu properas' (9,10). Quomodo ergo unus interitus est hominis et iumenti, et aequa utriusque conditio, aut quomodo nihil habet homo iumentis amplius, cum iumenta post mortem carnis non vivunt, hominum vero spiritus, pro malis suis operibus post mortem carnis ad inferos deducti, nec in ipsa more moriuntur? Sed in utraque tam dispari sententia demonstratur, quia contionator verax et illud ex temptatione carnali intulit, et hoc postmodum ex spiritali veritate definivit. *Dialogus* 4,4 éd. A. de Vogüé/P. Antin, SC 265, 1980, 26-34.

On a cru qu'un commentaire dialogué de l'Ecclésiaste était l'oeuvre de Salonius, évêque de Génève (Ve s.).[56] D'après les recentes recherches de C. Curti il faut le situer entre le IXe et le XIe siècle. De cette époque provient un court commentaire d'Alcuin (+804).[57]

A la fin de l'époque patristique on remarque en Orient un intérêt croissant pour l'Ecclésiaste. Le commentaire le plus important de cette époque est celui de Grégoire d'Agrigente (VIIe s.).[58] C'est un des meilleurs commentaires du livre de l'Ecclésiaste de l'époque patristique, et il nous montre la culture philosophique, théologique et littéraire de son auteur. Grégoire y donne une synthèse des deux traditions — alexandrine et antiochienne, avec une estimation critique, et même polémique, de ses prédecesseurs. Au commencement il informe qu'il voudrait donner une explication historico-littéraire du livre, mais souvent il en donne aussi d'autres explications. Enfin à la fin de l'époque patristique, Métrophane de Smyrne (IXe s.) a écrit un commentaire de l'Ecclésiaste; ce livre, perdu en grec, est conservé en géorgien, dans la traduction de Jean Cimcimeli (XIIe s.).[59] Certains passages de l'Ecclésiaste ont encore été commentés par Germain, patriarche de Constantinople (+732)[60], ainsi que par Photius (+897) dans ses *Amphilochia*.[61] Enfin, le grand poète, Georges de Pisidie (Ve/VIe s.) a écrit un poème *Sur la vanité du monde*, en s'inspirant de l'Ecclésiaste.[62]

Un intérêt encore plus grand pour l'Ecclésiaste on trouve chez les écrivains syriaques à partir du VIe siècle. Jacques de Saroug (+521) affirme que l'Ecclésiaste n'est pas un livre juif mais chrétien

56 Bibliographie nr 39.
57 Bibliographie nr 38.
58 Bibliographie nr 31.
59 Bibliographie nr 43.
60 Bibliographie nr 36.
61 Bibliographie nr 44.
62 Georges Pisidès, *De vanitate vitae*, PG 92,1581—1599.

et son enseignement a été accepté avec joie par les l'Eglise[63]. Il vient d'être commenté par Narsai (+503)[64].   Daniel de Salaḥ (c.541)[65], chaîne des Jacobites (entre 617 et 657)[66], Hannan d'Adiabène (+610)[67], Jean d'Apamée (avant VIe–VIIe siècle)[68], Elias de Merw (c.660)[69], Jacques d'Edesse (+708)[70], Théodor bar Koni (VIIe s.)[71], Išodad de Merw (c. 850)[72], Sevère le Moine (c. 861)[73], et plus tard par Denys bar Ṣalībī (+1171)[74], Jean de Mossoul (+c.1225)[75] et probablement Barhebraeus (+1286)[76] et Ebedjesus (+1314)[77].   Ces commentaires restent inédits à l'exception de celui de Jean d'Apamée et de Išodad de Merw;   quelques d'entre eux nous connaissons qu'à travers les mentions chez Ebedjesus.   Tous ces oeuvres on été, selon Strothmann, fortement influencés par le commentaire de Théodore de Mopsueste[78].

À la fin de l'époque patristique on voi naître un nouveau genre de commentaires bibliques: les chaînes exégétiques, dont certaines commentent aussi le livre de l'Ecclésiaste. Leur datation est difficile et aproximative.[79] Du VIe s. nous seraient parvenu trois chaînes de

---

63 Strothmann 205; bibliographie nr 25.

64 Bibliographie nr 24.

65 Bibliographie nr 26.

66 Bibliographie nr 29.

67 Bibliographie nr 28.

68 Bibliographie nr 32.

69 Bibliographie nr 33.

70 Bibliographie nr 35.

71 Bibliographie nr 37.

72 Bibliographie nr 40.

73 Bibliographie nr 42.

74 Bibliographie nr 54.

75 Bibliographie nr 55.

76 Bibliographie nr 56.

77 Bibliographie nr 57.

78 Cfr Strothmann 216ss.

79 S. Lucà, CCGr 11, 1983, XXI–XXIV.

ce livre: celle d'Olympiodore d'Aléxandrie[80], celle de Procope de Gaza[81] et la *Catena Barberini*[82]; un peu plus tardives seraient la *Chaîne* de Polychronius[83] et la *Catena Hauniensis*[84], dont nous avons déjà dit un mot; du VIIe ou VIIIe s. provient la *Chaîne des trois*

Pères[85].   Grâce aux recherches de l'école de Messine on connait mieux ces chaînes et on y a retrouvé des fragments des commentaires dont jusqu'à maintenant on ne connaissait que l'existence.   Ils ont montré aussi comment de ces chaînes on peut tirer des informations. Pour donner un exemple: les commentaires d'Origène et de Didyme étaient déjà au VIe s. difficilement accessibles, car à cette époque les catenistes utilisent déjà des excerpta.[86]   Il faut ajouter qu'il existent aussi des chaînes syriaque.[87]

Dans la bibliographie ajoutée à cet article nous avons tâché de donner une liste des commentateurs de l'Ecclésiaste de l'antiquité chrétienne et du Moyen-Age.   Grâce au premiers on pourrait connaître les commentaires d'Evagre et de Métrophanes, améliorer la connais-sance de la tradition du text d'Olympiodore (la traduction géorgienne, selon Tarchnišvili, nous donne, paraît-il, des variantes intéressantes du texte)[88] ou reconstruire l'exégèse antiochienne grâce aux commentaires syriaques, comme on peut en conclure en lisant le commentaire d'Išodad de Merw (+env.850).   Les commentaires médiévaux nous montreront le rôle de ce livre dans la formation de l'ascèse et de la mystique monastique du Moyen-Age.   Malheureusement, on constate que beaucoup de commentaires orientaux et médiévaux demeurent toujours inédits.

---

80   Bibliographie nr 45.

81   Bibliographie nr 46.

82   Bibliographie nr 47.

83   Bibliographie nr 48.

84   Bibliographie nr 49.

85   Bibliographie nr 50.

86   Cfr S Lucà, CChr.SG 11, 1983, XXII.

87   Bibliographie nr 19, 29, 42

88   Cfr Tarchnišvili 234, 323.

3.   Nous pouvons maintenant tirer quelques conclusions de cette énumération des commentaires.

(1)   Par comparaison avec d'autres livres de la Bible, les commentaires du livre de l'Ecclésiaste ne sont pas très nombreux, même si on tient compte des oeuvres perdues.   Les plus anciens proviennent du IIe s.   Les diverses commentaires nous montrent que l'intérêt pour ce livre a beaucoup varié: les périodes de plus grand intérêt sont du IIe au commençement de l'époque byzantine (VIIe–Xe s.) dans l'Orient grec, du VIe au XIIe s. dans l'Orient syrien, et du XIIe s. au XVe s. dans l'Occident.

(2)   De point de vue géographique nous constatons que l'Occident ne s'est pas particulièrement interessé à ce livre avant le Moyen-Age: de l'époque patristique nous ne connaissons que 3 ou 4 titres, et deux commentaires seulement sont conservées.   Au contraire, Qohélet eut un certain succès dans l'Orient grec, particulièrement dans les grands centres culturels, c'est-à-dire à Alexandrie et, un peu plus tard, à Antioche, où les cultures chrétiennes et païennes se côtoyaient.   L'influence du livre fut particuliérement forte à Alexandrie et il fut commenté non seulement par les écrivains alexandrins, mais aussi par des théologiens qui leur étaient lié par eux par la méthode théologique (Grégoire le Thaumaturge, Grégoire de Nysse).   L'Ecclésiaste semble avoir aussi eu un certain succès en milieu antiochien, spécialement dans la littérature syriaque.   Au contraire ce livre dans les autres cercles de l'antiquité chrétienne ne trouve pas grand intérêt: on ne voit que trois traductions des commentaires de l'Ecclésiaste dans la littérature géorgienne, une dans la littérature copte, une dans la littérature arabe et une chez les Arméniens.

(3)   Dans les grandes collections d'homélies patristiques prononcées devant le peuple, par exemple chez Augustin, Césaire d'Arles en Occident ou Jean Chrysostome en Orient on ne trouve pas d'homélies qui intérprètent ce livre.   On peut sans doute en tirer la conclusion que se livre intéressait les intellectuels plutôt que le peuple.

4. Trois auteurs ont éxércé une influence particulière: Origène, Jérôme et Théodore de Mopsueste. Origène a posé les fondements de l'exégèse du livre, tandis que Jérôme non seulement l'a transmise, mais l'a aussi enrichie par ses propres recherches. Il semble que le commentaire de Théodore de Mopsueste a joué dans l'Orient Chrétien un rôle semblable à celui d'Origène dans le monde grec et Jérôme dans le mond latin. Mais tandis qu'il existe une dépendence entre Origène et Jérôme, le commentaire de Théodore semble être indépendant, mais on peut supposer une forte influence de celui de Diodore. La manière dont Origène a classé les livres attribués à Salomon a influencé l'exégèse, tandis que la classifications d'Hippolyte avait eu un moindre succès. Et c'est peut-être, à cause d'Origène que beaucoup des commentateurs de l'Ecclésiaste ont commenté aussi les autres livres attribués à Salomon, ou moins l'un d'entre ces livres[89].

II.   Bibliographie

Abréviations*

Baumstark   A. Baumstark, Geschichte der syrischen Literatur, Bonn 1922 (Berlin 1968).

Beck   H.G. Beck; Kirche und theologische Literatur im byzantinischen Reich, München 1959.

CPG   M. Geerard, Clavis Patrum Graecorum, 1–5, Turnhout 1974–1987.

CPL   E. Dekkers/Ae. Gaar, Clavis Patrum Latinorum, Steenbrugge ²1961.

Deppe   E. Deppe, Koheleth in syrischer Dichtung. Drei Gedichte über das Kohelet-Buch von Afrem, Jakob von Sarug und Johannes von Mossul, Wiesbaden 1975.

Ebedjesus   Ebedjesus, *Catalogus librorum Syrorum*: J.A. Assemani, *Bibliotheca Orientalis*, 3,1, Romae 1725.

---

89 *Proverbes*, *l'Ecclésiaste* et le *Cantique* commentent: Origène, Apollinaire, Diodor de Tarse, Grégoire de Nysse, Taio; *Proverbes* et *l'Ecclésiaste*: Hippolyte, Didyme, Evagre, Olympiodore, Ps. Salonius: *l'Ecclésiaste* et *Cantique*: Athanase, Victorin de Poetovium, Grégoire d'Elvire.

*[Other abbreviations follow S.M. Schwertner, Internationales Abkür-zungsverzeichnis für Theologie und Grenzgebiete, Berlin ²1992.- Editor]

GOF.S   Göttinger Orientforschungen, I Reihe: *Syriaca*, Wiesbaden 1971-

Leanza   S. Leanza, L'Ecclesiaste nell'interpretazione dell'antico cristianesimo, Messina 1978.

Leanza(Or)   S. Leanza, L'esegesi di Origene al libro dell'Ecclesiaste, Reggio Calabria 1975.

Pignon   Laurentii Pignon, Catalogi et Chronica, éd. G. Meerseman, Romae 1936.

Stegmüller   F. Stegmüller, *Repertorium Biblicum Medii Aevi*, I-II, Matriti 1950-1980.

Spicq   C. Spicq, Esquisse d'une histoire de l'exégèse latine du Moyen-Age, Paris 1944.

Strothmann   W. Strothmann, Erkentnisse und Meinungen I: Das Buch Koheleth und seine syrischen Ausleger, GOF.S, 1973, 189-238.

Tarchnišvili M. Tarchnišvili, Geschichte der kirchlichen georgischen Literatur, Città del Vaticano 1955.

1. Generalia

L. Chevallier, H. Rondet

L'idée de 'vanité' dans l'oeuvre de S Augustin: REAug 3 (1957) 221-234.

H. Duesberg

Ecclésiaste. Commentaires sur l'Ecclésiaste: DSp 4, 1960, 47-49.

M. Harl

Les trois livres de Salomon et les trois parties de la philosophie dans les prologues des commentaires sur le Cantique (d'Origène aux chaînes exégétiques grecques): Texte und Textkritik, hrsg. J. Irmscher/F. Paschke/K. Treu, Berlin 1987, 249-269.

Leanza.

Leanza(Or)

S. Leanza

La classificazione dei libri Salomonici e i suoi riflessi sulla questione dei rapporti tra Bibbia e scienze profane da Origene agli scrittori medievali: Aug. 14 (1974) 651-666.

L'esegesi di Origene al libro dell'Ecclesiaste, Reggio Calabria 1975.

Eccl 12,1-7. L'Interpretazione escatologica dei Padri degli esegeti medioevali: Aug. 18 (1978) 191-207 = Leanza 119-148.

L'Ecclesiaste nell'interpretazione dell'antico cristianesimo, Messina 1978.

Sapienziali (libri), Ecclesiaste: DPAC 2, 3087-3091.

L'attegiamento della più antica esegesi cristiana dinanzi all'epicureismo ed edonismo di Qohelet, Orph. NS 3 (1982), 73-90.

I condizionamenti dell'esegesi patristica.   Un caso sintomatico: l'interpretazione di Qohelet: RStB 3 (sous presse).

H. Sieben

Exegesis Patrum, Roma 1981, 38.

Spicq.

Strothmann.

M. Starowieyski

Compte rendu du CChr.SG 4: CoTh 52 (1982) 1,172-174.

2.   **Commentaires patristiques [IIe-IXe s.]**

a.   *Commentaires*

1   **MELITO SARDENSIS** [II s.], CPG 1093a.

'Εκλογαί: Eusebius, *HE* 4,26,14,   SC 31,1952,211; 123,1966, 225; PG 5,1213-1216.

2   **CLEMENS ALEXANDRINUS** [+circa 212], cfr GPG 1380.

In: 'Υποτυπώσεις, Photius, *Bibliotheca* 109, éd. R. Henry, vol. 2, Paris 1960, 79-81.

3   **HIPPOLYTUS ROMANUS** [+circa 235], CPG 1884.

Hieronymus, *De viris illustribus* 61, Firenze 1988, 164.   Cfr Hippolytus, *Interpretatio Cantici Canticorum*, CSCO 264/Iber 16, 1965, 23s.   Ed.: GCS 1, 1897, 179; PG 89,593A-596A. E. Klostermann, Analecta zu Septuaginta, Hexapla und Patristik, Leipzig 1890, 29 [Eccl 2,10;   2,24?]   Cfr Leanza 11s.- A. Labate, Sui due frammenti di Ippolito all'Ecclesiaste, VetChr 23 (1976) 177-187.

4   **ORIGENES** [+256],   CPG 1431; Stegmüller 6169, 6198

Hieronymus, *Epist.* 33,4, éd. J. Labourt, vol. 2, Paris, 1951 41, 42 [excerpta et 8 homélies]; *In Ecclesiasten* 14,13-17, CChr.SL 72, 1959, 288.   Cfr *Libri X in Canticum Canticorum (interprete Rufino), Prologus*, GCS 33, 1925, 75;   PL 13,4. Ed.: Leanza(Or), 10-20;   E. Klostermann, op.cit. 29s.   Cfr Leanza 12-14.- S. Leanza, La classificazione dei libri salomonici e i suoi riflessi sulla questione dei rapporti tra Bibbia e scienze profane da Origene agli scrittori medioevali, Aug. 14 (1974), 651-666.- S. Leanza, L'esegesi di Origene al libro dell'-Ecclesiaste, Reggio Calabria 1975.- S. Leanza, Ancora sull'esegesi origeniana dell'Ecclesiaste: Studi in onore di A. Ardizzoni, 1, Roma 1978, 493-506.- S. Leanza, Sull'autenticità degli scolie origeniani della catena sull'Ecclesiaste di Procopio di Gaza: Origeniana secunda, éd. H. Crouzel/A. Quacquarelli, Roma 1980, 363-369.- S. Leanza, Sulle fonti del Commentario all'Ecclesiaste di Girolamo, ASEs 3 (1986) 173-199.

5 DIONYSIUS ALEXANDRINUS [+264], CPG 1594

Eusebius, *HE* 7,26,3, SC 41, 1955, 211=Hieronymus, *Vir. ill.* 69, Firenze 1988, 176. Ed.: S. Leanza, CChr.SG 4, 1978 (cfr index); W.A. Bienert, Neue Fragmente des Dionysius und Petrus von Alexandrien aus Cod. Vatop. 236: Kl. 5 (1973) 308-313 (authenticité douteuse). A. Labate, *Catena Hauniensis*, CChr.SG 24, 1992. Cfr S. Leanza, Il Commentario sull'Ecclesiaste di Dionigi Alessandrino: Scritti in onore di S. Pugliatti, 5, Mediolani 1978, 397-427.- S. Leanza, Due nuovi frammenti dionisiani sull' Ecclesiaste, Orph. NS 6 (1985) 3-10.- S. Leanza, Pour une réédition des scolies à l'Ecclésiaste de Denys d'Alexandrie: Alexandrina, Mélanges offerts à C. Mondésert, Paris 1987, 239-246.- A. Labate, Il recupero del 'Commentario all'Ecclesiaste' di Dionigi Alessandrino attraverso le catene bizantine (Koinonia 15) 1991.

6 GREGORIUS THAUMATURGUS [+circa 270], CPG 1766

Hieronymus, *Vir. ill.* 65, Firenze 1988, 170: *In Ecclesiasten* 4,13/16, CChr.SL 72, 1959, 288s.; Rufinus, *HE* 7,25; Suidae, Lexicon s.v. Γρηγόριος, éd. A. Adler, 1.1928, 543; PG 10, 981. Ed.: *Metaphrasis in Ecclesiasten*, PG 10, 988-1017.

Versions: *arménienne:* cfr G. Lafontaine, RHE 74 (1979) 636.- *géorgienne:* Ephrem Mcire [+circa 1100], cfr G. Peradze, *OrChr* 35 (1930) 91; Tarchnišvili, 187. Cfr Leanza 17-19.- Leanza(Or), 50.- K.W. Noakes, The Metaphrase of Ecclesiastes of Gregory Thaumaturgos: StPatr 15, Berlin 1984, 196-199.- N. Sagarda, Svatogo Gregoria cudotvorca, episkopa Neokesareiskogo, pereloženie Eklesiasta, Istoričeskoe Čtene 1913, 553-554.

7 VICTORINUS POETOVIONENSIS [+304]

Hieronymus, *Vir. ill.* 74, Firenze 1988, 180; *In Ecclesiasten* 413/16, CChr.SL 72,1959, 289; Cassiodorus, *Divinae institutiones* 5, PL 70,1117A. Cfr Leanza 21s.

8 ACACIUS CAESARIENSIS [+circa 366]

Hieronymus, *Vir. ill.* 98 (17 volumes), Firenze 1988, 202. Cfr Leanza 23s.

9 EPHRAEM [+373]

Ed.: *S Patris nostri Ephraem Syri opera*, 2, Romae 1740, 338-344 [Eccl 1,12]. Traductions: *latine:*ibidem.- *allemande:* S. Euringer, Ephraem, Bd 1, München 1919 (BKV). Authenticité: *pour:* T.S. Lamy, RBib 2 (1893) 9; *contre:* E. Beck, DSp 4, 1960, 791. Cfr A. Dryoff, Zu Ephraem's Rede über 'Alles ist Eitelheit und Geistesplage': Beiträge zur Geschichte des christlichen Altertums und der byzantinischen Literatur, Festgabe A. Ehrhart zum 60. Geburtstag dargebracht, hrsg. A.M. Königer, Bonn 1922, 119-140.- Baumstark 49,8.- Deppe, passim.- Leanza 22.

10 ATHANASIUS ALEXANDRINUS [+373]

Ὑπόμνημα εἰς τὸν Ἐκκλησιαστήν [καὶ εἰς Ἀισματα τῶν ᾀσμάτων]. Photius, *Bibliotheca* 139, éd. R. Henry, vol. 1, Paris 1960, 108: PG 27,1347 [un ou deux commentaires?]. Cfr Leanza 23.

11 **APOLLINARIS LAODICENUS** [+390]

Hieronymus, *In Eccl.*, 4,13-16, CChr.SL 72,1959, 289; 12,5, ibidem, 356. Cfr Leanza 25.

12 **GREGORIUS ILLIBERITANUS** [IV s.], CPL 556b; Stegmüller 2631,2.

Ed.: Fragmenta in Ecclesiasten [3,3; 3,6], CChr.SL 69,1967, 262s. Cfr 428 (authenticité).

13 **DIODORUS TARSENSIS** [+circ 393]

Εἰς τὸν Ἐκκλησιαστήν, Suidae *Lexicon*, s.v. Διόδωρος, éd. A. Adler, 2, 1921, 103; PG 33, 1553. Cfr Leanza 24s.

14 **GREGORIUS NYSSENUS** [+circa 394], CPG 3157

Ed.: W.P. Alexander, Leiden 1962; PG 44, 616-753 L. Vinel, à paraître dans SC. Autres éditions; cfr M. Altenburger/F. Mann, Bibliographie zu Gregor von Nyssa, Leiden 1988, 273.   Version copte: cfr T. Orlandi, Gregorio di Nissa nella letteratura copta: VetChr, 18 (1981) 333-339.   E. Lucchesi, Les homélies sur l'Ecclésiaste de Grégoire de Nysse, CPG (3154 [3157]). Nouveaux feuillets coptes: VigChr 36 (1982), 292s.
Traductions: *arabe:* R. Tuki, Roma 1763.- *française:* F. Vinel, Grégoire de Nysse, Homélies sur l'Ecclésiaste, tr., notes, comm., Paris 1982 (Thèse: Paris/Sorbonne); SC à paraître.- *italiennnes:* A. Siclari/S. Rinaldi, Omelie sull'Ecclesiaste (STCSTA 1), Parma 1987, 47-183.   Cfr OCP 56 (1990) 239s; S. Leanza, Omelie sull' l'Ecclesiate (CTePa 86), Roma 1990, 30-180.- *roumaine:* T. Bodogae, Bucuresti, sous presse.
Cfr Leanza 31-35.- Leanza(Or), 52-55.- R. Bonifazi, L'exegesi di Gregorio Nisseno nelle omelie sull'Ecclesiaste, Perugia 1988 [dissertation, Université de Perouse (Perugia)].- T.J. Dennis, The Relationship between Gregory of Nyssa's attack on Slavery in his Fourth Homily on Ecclesiastes and his Treatise *De hominis opificio*:   StPatr 17/3, Oxford/New York 1982, 1065-1072.- S. Leanza, Omelie sull'Ecclesiaste, Roma 1990 (CTePa 86), Introduzione, 7-35.- Η.Δ. Μουτσούλας, Γρηγόριος ὁ Νύσσης ὡς ἑρμηνευτὴς τῆς Ἁγίας Γραφῆς: Πόνημα εὔγνωμον, τιμητικὸς ἐπὶ τῇ 40ετηρίδι συγγραφικῆς δράσεως καὶ τῇ 35ετηρίδι καθηγεσίας τοῦ Βασιλείου Μ. Βέλλα, ἐπιμελεῖ καθηγήτου Α.Π. Χαστούπη, Ἀθῆναι 1969, 477ss.- A. Siclari, Omelie sull'Ecclesiaste, Parma 1987, Introduzione, 9-44.- F. Vinel, op.cit., II partie.

15 **DIDYMUS ALEXANDRINUS** [+398], CPG 2555

Ed.: *Eccl 1,1-8:* G. Binder/L. Liesenborghs/L. Koenen, Köln 1965.- *Eccl 5-6:* J. Kramer/L. Koenen, Bonn 1970.- *Eccl 8-10:* J. Kramer/E. Krebber, Bonn 1972.- *Eccl 11-12:* L. Liesenborghs, Köln 1965.   Cfr J. Kramer, Einige Bemerkungen zum dritten Band des Ekklesiastes-Kommentars des Didymos, ZPE 7 (1971) 188-192.- S. Leanza, Sul Commentario all'Ecclesiaste di Didimo d'Alessandria: StPatr 17/3, Oxford/New York 1982, 300-316.- S. Leanza, Sulle fonti del Commentario all'Ecclesiaste di Girolamo: ASEs 3 (1986) 173-199.- M. Simonetti, Lettera e allegoria nell' esegesi vetero-testamentario di Didimo: VetChr, 20 (1983) 341-389 (particulièrement 375-385).- D.M. Sanchez, El commentario al

Ecclesiastés de Dídimo Alejandrino. Exégesis y espiritualidad (Studia Teologica Theresianum 9), Roma 1991.

16   EVAGRIUS PONTICUS [+399], CPG 2458(5)

Cfr P. Géhin, Un nouvel inédit d'Evagre le Pontique. Son Commentaire sur l'Ecclésiaste: Byz. 49 (1979) 188-198.- A. Labate, L'Esegesi di Evagrio sull'Ecclesiaste: Studi in Onore A. Ardizzoni, I, Roma 1978, 485-490.- H. Urs von Balthasar, Die Hiera des Evagrius: ZKTh 63 (1939) 181-206 (particulièrement 203s.).   Version arabe: *Ad imitationem Ecclesiaste, Cantici canticorum et Proverbiorum Salomonis*, cfr P. Géhin, art.cit. 195.

17   AMBROSIASTER [IV s.], CPL 185; Stegmüller 1248,1

Ed. *Quaestiones in Vetus et Novum Testamentum* 15, PL 35,2226 (Eccl 7,17);   39, ibidem 2236 (Eccl 9,4).   Cfr G.C. Martini, Le recensioni delle "Questiones veteris et Novi Testamenti" dell' Ambrosiaster: RicRel 1 (1959), 40-62.

18   HIERONYMUS STRIDONENSIS [+419], CPL 583;   Stegmüller 3351 (+vol. IX), cfr 3296, 9315, 11468

Hieronymus, *Epist.* 84,2, éd. J. Labourt, vol. 4, 1954, 126.   Ed.: *Commentarius in Ecclesiasten*, CChr.SL   72, 1959, 248-361; PL 23, 1061-1116.   Cfr Leanza 41-50.- Leanza(Or), 56-68.- F. Cavallera, S. Jérôme. Sa vie, son oeuvre 1, Paris 1922, 136s.- W.W. Cannon, Jerome and Symmachus. Some points in the Vulgate Translation of Koheleth: ZAW 45 (1927) 191-199.- S. Holm-Nielsen, On the Interpretation of Qoheleth in Early Christianity: VT 24 (1974) 168-177.- S. Leanza, Un capitolo sulla fortuna del Commentario all'Ecclesiaste di Girolamo. Il Commentario di Ps. Ruperto di Deutz: CCICr 3 (1985) 357-389.- S. Leanza, Sulle fonti del Commentario all'Ecclesiaste di Girolamo: ASEs 3 (1986) 173-199.- S. Leanza, Tre versioni geronimiane sull'Ecclesiaste: ibid. 4 (1987) 87-108.- S. Leanza, Sul Commentario all'Ecclesiaste di Girolamo. Il problema esegetico: S Jérôme entre l'Occident et l'Orient, éd. Y.M. Duval, Paris 1988, 267-282.

19   THEODORUS MOPSUESTENUS [+428], GPG 3836

Ed. W. Strothmann, Die syrische Fragmente des Ecclesiastes-Kommentars von Theodor von Mopsuestia. Syrischer Text mit vollständigen Wörterverzeichnis, GOF.S 28, 1988.- W. Strothmann, Syrische Katenen aus dem Ecclesiastes-Kommentar des Theodor von Mopsuestia. Syrischer Text mit vollständigen Wörterver-zeichnis,GOF.S 28, 1988.   Cfr Barhadbešabba Arbaya, PO 4,381.- Ebedjesus 19,32.- Strothmann 215-227 (fragments traduits).- Leanza 51s.- W. Strothmann, Der Kohelet-Kommentar des Theodor von Mopsuestia: Religion in Erbe Agyptens (ÄAT 14), 181-196.- J. Voste, De versione syriaca operum Theodori Mopsuesteni: OCP 8 (1942) 477-481.- D.Z. Zaharopoulos, Theodore of Mopsuestia on Bible, New York 1989.

20   AUGUSTINUS HIPPONENSIS(?) [+430],   CPL 272; Stegmüller 1470

Ed.: *Speculum*, PL 34, 924s. (excerpta).   Cfr *De civitate Dei*, 20,3, CChr.SL 48,1955, 701s.

21 PS. IOANNES CHRYSOSTOMUS [V s. ?]

Ed. S. Leanza, CChr.SG 4, 1978, 51-103. Cfr Leanza 53s.-
S. Leanza, ibid., Praefatio, 53-63.

22 NILUS ANCYRANUS [V s.], CPG 6054(4)

Ed.: S. Lucà, Biblica 60 (1979), 237-246; *Epistulae* 2,192, PG
70,300 [Eccl 5,15]; 2,231, ibid. 320 [Eccl 7,4]; 3,178, ibid. 468
[Eccl 5,11]; cfr ibid. 740C; 876 [Eccl 5,11].   Cfr S. Lucà,
L'esegesi di Nilo di Ancira sull'Ecclesiaste: Sileno 3 (1977)
13-39.- S. Lucà, L'esegesi di Nilo sull'Ecclesiaste: Studi in onore
di A. Ardizzoni, 1, Roma 1978.- S. Lucà, Nilo di Ancira sull'
Ecclesiaste. Dieci scolii sconosciuti: Bib. 60 (1979) 237-246.

23 EUCHERIUS [V s.], CPL 489

Ed. Instructiones ad Salonium 1, PL 50, 795 [Eccl 12,5], CSEL
31, 104s.

24 NARASAI [+503]

Cfr Chronique de Séért 9, PO 7, 115; Ebedjesus 53,64; Baumstark
110.

25 IACOBUS SARUGENSIS [+521]

Ed. P. Bedjan, Homiliae selectae Iacobi Sarugensis 3, Paris 1910,
858-875 [Eccl 1,1].   Cfr Baumstark 155,5;   Deppe, passim.
Strothmann 202, 205s.

26 DANIEL DE SALAH [+541]

Fragments dans le commentaire de Sevère, cfr nr 42. Cfr
Baumstark 197; Strothmann 208s.

27 GREGORIUS MAGNUS [+604], cfr TAIO CAESARAUGUSTINUS (nr
34).

28 HANNA ADIABENUS [+610]

Cfr Ebedjesus 59,83; Baumstark 127.

29 CATENA IACOBITARUM [c.617-657]

fragments d'Olympiodore (cfr nr 45) sur l'Eccl 4,17-5,4; 7,8-20;
10,2-7; 11,2.

30 BABAI MAGNUS [+628]

Cfr Baumstark 138.

31 GREGORIUS AGRIGENTINUS [+630?], CPG 7050

Ed.: *In Ecclesiasten libri X*, PG 98, 741-1181.   Cfr Leanza
65-69.- Leanza(Or), 83-90.- G.H. Ettlinger, The Form and the
Method of the Commentary on Ecclesiastes by Gregory of
Agrigentum: StPatr 18/1, Kalamazoo 1985, 317-320.- S. Gennaro,
Influssi di scrittori greci nel Commento sull'Ecclesiaste di
Gregorio di Agrigento: MSLCA 3, Catania 1951, 162-184.- S.
Leanza, Commentario all'Ecclesiaste di Gregorio di Agrigento: Il
cristianesimo in Sicilia dalle Origine a Gregorio Magno,
Caltanissetta 1987, 191-220.- G. Mannelli, Il problema del libero

arbitrio nel Commentario dell'Ecclesiaste di Gregorio di Agrigento: MSLCA 3, 1951, 185-194.

32 IOANNES APAMENSIS [avant VI-VII s.]

Cfr Strothmann 209-214. Ed. W. Strothmann, Koheleth – Kommentar des Joannes von Apamea. Syrischer Text mit volständiges Wörterverzeichnis, GOF.S 30, 1988. Cfr W. Strothmann, Johannes von Apamea, Berlin 1972 (pp. 12, 70).

33 ELIAS DE MERW [+c. 660]

Cfr Ebedjesus 49,148; Baumstark 208.

34 TAIO CAESARAUGUSTANUS [+683], CPL 1269; Stegmüller 7963,3 (+vol. IX)

Ed.: *Excerpta S Gregorii* [c. *Commentarius in Ecclesiasten*], PLS 4, 1754-1772 (A.C. Vega) = EspSagr 56 (1957) 355-372.

35 IACOBUS EDESSENUS [+708]

Fragments dans le commentaire de Sevére nr 42.

36 GERMANUS CONSTANTINOPOLITANUS [+720], CPG 8021

Ed.: PG 101,89-1032 [100-105]; C. Westerink/C. Garton, Buffalo 1979 [Amphilochia 149]

37 THEODORUS BAR KONI [VIII s.?]

Ed.: *Livre des scolies*, Mimre 5,7, CSCO 55/Syr 19, 1910 et 431/Syr 187, 1981, pp. 334-336 et 281-283.

38 ALCUINUS [+804]; Stegmüller 1093 (+vol. VIII), cfr 11468

Ed.: Commentarius in Ecclesiasten, PL 100, 669-722.

39 PS. SALONIUS GENAVENSIS [entre 800-1000 a.],   CPL 499 Stegmüller 7590.

Ed.: *Expositio mystica in Parabolas Salonomis et in Ecclesiasten*, éd, C. Curti, Catania 1964; PL 53,967-1912. Cfr Leanza 56s.- Leanza(Or).- C. Curti, Orph. 11 (1964), 167-184.- C. Curti, Salonio di Ginevra: DPAC 2, Casale 1983, 3070-3073.- V.I.J. Flint, The Author of the Salonii Commentarii in Parabolas Salomonis et in Ecclesiasten: RThAM 37 (1970) 174-186.- J.P. Weiss, Les sources du Commentaire sur l'Ecclésiaste du Pseudo Salonius: StPatr 12, Berlin 1975, 178-183.

40 IŠODAD DE MERW [+c. 850]

Ed.: C. van den Eynde, CSCO 229-230/Syr 96-97, 1963, pp. 197-218, 233-255. Cfr Baumstark, 234.- Strothmann 214.

41 HRABANUS MAURUS ? [+c. 856], Stegmüller 7051,1.

Cfr PL 107,103.

42 SEVERUS MONACHUS [+c. 861]

Contient des fragments de Jacques d'Edesse (nr 35) et de Daniel de Salah (nr 26). Cfr Baumstark 279.- Strothmann 207s.

43 METROPHANES SMYRNENSIS [IX s.]

Ed.: Version géorgienne de Jean Cimcimeli [XII s.] publiée à Tbilisi
en 1920 par Kekelidze; cfr Tarchnišvili, 234, 323.

44   PHOTIUS [+897]

Ed. *Amphilochia*, PG 101;   L.C. Westerink, Photius, *Epistulae et
Amphilochia*, Leipzig (Teubner) 1986.   1,37 = PG 96;   44 = PG
333-340;   61(60) = PG 416s, Westerink 50s.;   62(61) = PG
417=421, Westerink 52-54;   63(62) = PG 421, Westerink 54s.;
64(63) = PG 423-425, Westerink 55-58;   65(64) = PG 425-429,
Westerink 58-61;   66(65) = PG 429-432, Westerink 61-63;   68 =
PG 436, Westerink 65s.;   69 = PG 437-440, Westerink 66-68;   149
= cfr Germanus Constantinopolitanus (nr 36).

b.   *Chaînes exégétiques*

Cfr   R. Devreesse, Chaînes exégétiques grecques, DBS 1, 1928,
1163s.   M. Faulhaber Hohelied-, Proverbien- und Prediger-Katenen,
ThSLG 4, Wien 1902, 139-166.- G. Karo/H. Lietzmann, Catenarum
Graecarum Catalogus, NGWG.PH 3, 1902, 310-312.- A. Labate,
Nuove catene esegetiche sull'Ecclesiaste: Antidoron, Hommage à M.
Géerard, Turnhout 1984, 241-263.- S. Leanza, Le catene esegeti-
che sull'Ecclesiaste: Aug. 17 (1977) 545-552.- S. Lucà, Tentativo
di datare le catene sull'Ecclesiaste ..., CChr.SG   11, 1983, XXI-
XXIV.

45   OLYMPIODORUS [VIe s.],   CPG 7454 [c 103] Stegmüller 6164.

Ed.   Commentarii   in   Ecclesiasten,   PG   93,477-629.   Version
géorgienne de Jean Cincimeli, cfr. Tarchnišvili 234, 323; version
syriaque dans la chaîne des Jacobites (nr 29).

46   PROCOPIUS GAZAEUS [+538],   CPG 7433 [c. 101]

Ed. S. Leanza, Catena in Ecclesiasten, CChr.SG   4, 1978, 5-39.
Cfr Leanza 78.- Leanza(Or), 9-11.- S. Leanza, La catena all'
Ecclesiaste di Procopio di Gaza del Cod. Marc. gr 22 (ff. 67v-
83r): Studia codicologica (TU 124), Berlin 1977, 279-298.- S.
Leanza, CChr.SG 4, 1978, Praefatio, VII-XVII.- S. Leanza, Un
nuovo testimone della catena sull'Ecclesiaste di Procopio di Gaza,
il cod.Vindob.theol.gr. 147: CChr.SG   4 supp. 1983.- S. Leanza,
voir Origène nr 4.

47   CATENA BARBERINIANA [VIe s.],   CPG C 104

Cfr Leanza 77s.- Leanza(Or), 13-20.- A. Labate, La catena sull'
Ecclesiaste de cod. Barberini gr. 388: Aug. 19 (1979) 333-339.

48   POLYCHRONIUS [après VIe s.], CPG C 102

Cfr Leanza 76.- A. Labate, Nuovi codici della Catena sull'
Ecclesiaste di Policronio: Aug. 18 (1978), 551-553.- A. Labate,
Sulla catena all'Ecclesiaste di Policronio: StPatr 18/2 (1990)
21-35.

49 **CATENA HAUNIENSIS** [VIIᵉ s.]; CPG C 105

Ed. A. Labate, CChr.SG 24, 1992. Cfr A. Labate, L'apporto della catena Hauniensis sull'Ecclesiaste per il testo delle versioni greche di Simmaco e della LXX: RBib 35 (1987) 57-61.

50 **CATENA TRIUM PATRUM** [VIIᵉ, VIIIᵉ s.], CPG C 100

Ed. S.Lucà, La Catena dei Tre Padri sull'Ecclesiaste: Studi in honore di A. Ardizzoni, 1, Roma 1978, 557-582.- S.Lucà, Gli scolii sull'Ecclesiaste del Vallicelliano greco Σ 21: Aug. 12 (1979) 287-296. Cfr aussi chaînes syriaques: de Théodore de Mopsueste (nr 19), des Jacobines (nr 29) et du moine Sevère (nr 42).

3. **Commentaires mediévaux**

Cfr Leanza 73s.; H. Duesberg, DSp 4,49-52; Spicq passim.

A. **Orientales**

a. *Byzantins*

51 **NIKETAS SEIDES** [XIIᵉ s.]

Ὑπόθεσις sur l'Ecclésiaste, cfr Beck 617.

52 **MATTHAEUS EPHESENUS** [+après 1340]

Excerpta de l'Ecclésiaste, cfr Beck 789.

b. *Arabes*

EVAGRIUS PONTICUS [cfr nr 16].

GREGORIUS NYSSENUS [cfr nr 14].

c. *Armeniens*

53 **NERSES LAMPRONIANUS** [+1198]

Ed.: M. Herzog, Leipzig 1929.

d. *Géorgiens*

GREGORIUS THAUMATURGUS [cfr nr 6].

METROPHANES SMYRNENSIS [cfr nr 43].

OLYMPIODORUS [cfr nr 44].

e. *Syriaques*

THEODORUS MOPSUESTENUS [cfr nr 19].

Cfr Deppe, passim.- Strothmann, passim.- J. Janisch, Animadversiones criticae in versionem syriacam Peschittonianam in librum Kohelet et Rut, Breslaviae 1871.- A.S. Kamenetzki, Die Peschitta zu Koheleth: ZAW 24 (1904) 181-239.- R. Macina, L'homme à l'école de Dieu. D'Antioche a Nisibe. Profile herméneutique, théologique et kérygmatique du mouvement scoliaste nestorien: POC 32 (1982), 85-124, 262-301.

54 DIONYSIUS BAR ȘALĪBĪ [+1171]

Commentaire pneumatique.   Commentaire pragmatique cfr nr 19.
Ed. W. Strothmann, Koheleth-Kommentar des Dionysius bar Salibi.
Auslegung des Septuaginta-Text, GOF.S 31, 1988. Cfr Baumstark
286.- Strothmann 214s.- V. Vööbus, Neue Funde fur die hand-
schriftliche Überlieferung alttestamentlicher Kommentare des
Dionysius bar Salibi: ZAW 84 (1972) 246-249.

55 IOANNES DE MOSSUL [+c. 1225]

Cfr Baumstark 307.- Deppe, passim.- Strothmann 206s.

56 BARHEBRAEUS [+1286]

Ed. A. Rahlfs, Des Gregorius Abulfaraq genannt Bar Ebhrojo
Anmerkungen zu den salomonischen Schriften, Leipzig 1887.- S.
Katz, Die Scholien zu d. Weisheitsbuche d. Josua bar Sira,
Frankfurt 1892, 892.

57 EBEDJESUS SOBENSIS [+1318]

 Cfr Ebedjesus 198,325.

B. Occidentales

XII⁵ siècle

58 PETRI DAMIANI DISCIPULUS [après 1072]

Ed.: Testimonia de Ecclesiaste 1-5, PL 145,1139-1142.

Cfr Stegmüller 6602,16.

59 GUILLELMUS MERTON, OSAcan [XIIᵉ s.]

Cfr Stegmüller 2969, 2969,5 (+vol. IX).

60 ALBERTUS DE SIEGBURG, OSB [XIIᵉ s.?]

Cfr Stegmüller 1072.

61 ROBERTUS WIGORNIENSIS (Worcester) [XIIᵉ s.]

Cfr Stegmüller 7494.

62 SIGBERTUS GEMBLACENSIS, OSB [+1112]

Ed. A. Boutemy, Latomus 2 (1938) 209-220 (poème).   Cfr
Stegmüller 7361.

63 HILDEBERTUS CENOMANENSIS (Lavardin) [+1133]

Ed. In primum caput Ecclesiasten, PL 171,1271-1276 (poème).
Cfr Stegmüller 3555.

64 GILBERTUS UNIVERSALIS? [1134]

Cfr Stegmüller 2564,2 (+vol. IX).

65 HONORIUS AUGUSTODONENSIS [+1135]

Ed. Quaestiones et responsiones in Ecclesiasten, PL 172, 331-
348. Cfr V.I.J. Flint, The Author of the 'Salonii Commentarii in

Parabolas Salomonis et in Ecclesiasten': RThAM 57 (1970) 174-
186.   Cfr Leanza(Or) 94s.- Spicq 117s.

66 **RUPERTUS TUITIENSIS** (Deutz), OSB [+1135]

Ed. *Commentarius in Ecclesiasten,* PL 168,1195-1306.   Cfr
Leanza(Or) 94.- Hieronymus (nr 17).- Spicq 114-117.- Stegmüller
7560.

67 **HUGO A S.VICTORE**, OSACan [+1141]

Ed. *In Salomonis Ecclesiasten homiliae XIX,* PL 175,112-256.   Cfr
Stegmüller 3812 (+vol. IX); 3812,1; 10614.-   Leanza(Or) 96s..-
Spicq 120-122.

68 **ALULFUS DE TORNACO** [+1141]

Cfr Stegmüller 1202; cfr 6320, Ps. Paterius.

69 **HERVAEUS DE BOURG DIEU (BURGIDOLENSIS)**, OSB [+1150]

Cfr Stegmüller 3259;   cfr 11501.

70 **RUDOLFUS FLAVIACENSIS (FLAIX)**, OSB [c. 1157]

Cfr Stegmüller 7096.

71 **GUAFRIDUS DE CLARAVALLE**, OCist [c. 1170]

Cfr Stegmüller 2413 (+vol. IX).

72 **RICHARDUS A S.VICTORE**, OSACan [+1173]

Ed. *Tractatus de meditandis plagis quae circa finem mundi
eveniunt,* PL 196, 201-212 [Eccl 12,1].   Cfr Stegmüller 7329.-
Leanza(Or) 96.- Spicq 128-132.

73 **ANDREAS A.S.VICTORE**, OSACan [+1175]

Ed. *Expositio historica in Ecclesiasten,* ed. G. Calandra, Palermo
1948.   Cfr Stegmüller 1309.- G. Galarda, op. cit.- Leanza(Or)
97s.- Spicq 130s.

74 **ANSELMUS LAUDINENSIS (LAON)** (?) [+1177]

Ed. *Glossa ordinaria,* PL 113, 1115-1126.   Cfr J. Blic, L'oeuvre
exégétique de Walafrid Strabo et la Glossa ordinaria: RThAM 16
(1949), 5-28.- Leanza(Or) 94.- Spicq 111.- Stegmüller 11803 (vol.
IX).

75 **PETRUS CANTOR** [+1197]

Cfr Stegmüller 6481.- Spicq 134s.

XIII siècle

76 **IACOBUS DE CASSOLIS** [c. 1200]

Cfr Stegmüller 3875.

77 **GUILLELMUS BRITO, OM** [XIII* s.]

Cfr Stegmüller 2837.

78 **PETRUS DE RIGA** [+1209]

Cfr Stegmüller 6825, 2826 (Aurora).

79 **ALEXANDER NECKAM, OSACan** [+1217]

Ed. *De natura rerum*, 1-2, éd. T. Wright, RBMAS 34, 1863, 1-354.
Cfr Stegmüller 1172 (+vol. VIII).

80 **STEPHANUS LANGTON** [+1228]

Cfr Stegmüller 7805 (prologue), 7806, 7807?, 7807,1? 7807,2 =
7814 = Ps. Ioahannes Peckham 4844 (Eccli), 9813.

81 **ODO DE CASTRO RADULFI (GALLUS)** [+1237]

Cfr Stegmüller 6084.

82 **ANTONIUS DE PADUA, OM** [1241]

Opera, Paris 1641, 578-590. Cfr Stegmüller 1404.

83 **GUERRICUS DE S. QUENTINO, OP** [+1245]

Cfr Stegmüller 2669.- Spicq 291.

84 **STEPHANUS DE VENIZEY (ALTISSIODORENSIS), OP** [+après 1248]

Cfr Stegmüller 7957.- Spicq 319.

85 **GUILLELMUS DE ALVERNIA (PARISIENSIS)** [+1249]

Cfr Stegmüller 2802 (+vol. IX), 10198, 11277.- Spicq 322.

86 **GUILLELMUS DE MELITONA, OM** [+1257]

Cfr Stegmüller 2934, 1773 = Bonaventura, 2883 = Guillelmus de
Altona.- Spicq 323.

87 **SIMON HINTON, OP** [c. 1260]

Glossarium totius Veteris Testamenti praeter Psalterium, vol. I.
Cfr Stegmüller 7652, 7694.

88 **GUILLELMUS DE KINGSHAM, OP** [+1262]

Cfr Stegmüller 2901 (+vol. IX).

89 **HUGO DE S. CARO, OP** [+1263]

Ed. *Postillae in Ecclesiasten*, Opera 3, Venetiae 1703, 70-105;
autres éditions Stegmüller vol. III, p. 114. Cfr Stegmüller 7679-
7681 (+vol. IX); 3588 = Ps.Hugo de Billom; 594 = Ps.Hugo
Cistercensis; 5754 = Nicolaus de Gorran (Spicq 326).- Leanza(Or)
98-101.- Spicq 324 (éditions).- Pignon 21, 57, 71.

90 **GUILLELMUS DE ALTONA, OP** [c. 1265]

Cfr Stegmüller 2781 (+vol. IX); 1773 Bonaventura?, 2782, 2783?;
2934 = Guillelmus de Melitona; 7176 = Reginaldus de Alna, 10615.-
Pignon 24,60,71.

91 **BONAVENTURA** [+1274]

Ed. *Expositio in Ecclesiasten*, Opera omnia 6, Quaracchi 1893, 3-
99. Cfr Stegmüller 1773 (+vol. VIII), 5829 = Ps. Nicolaus de
Lyra, 10566; 11301 = Glossa super Bonaventurae Commentarium;

11561 = Anonymus OM, *Tabula alphabetica super Ecclesiasten.-* Leanza(Or) 101-104.- Spicq 293.- C. Vermej, Geschiedenis der exegetische Werken van H.Bonaventura: CFN 2, s'Hertogenbosch 1934, 261-290.

92 **ALBERTUS DE PULTA, OP** [c. 1274]

Cfr Stegmüller 1064,9 (+vol. VIII).

93 **JOHANNES DE ARDENBURGO, OP** [c. 1283]

Cfr Stegmüller 4160.- Pignon 25,62,76.

94 **BERNARDUS DE TRILIA, OP** [+1292]

Cfr Stegmüller 1741.- Pignon 25,61,72.

95 **STEPHANUS BURGUNDUS (DE BISUNTIO), OP** [+1294]

Postillae in Ecclesiasten. Cfr Stegmüller 7702,2.- Pignon 25,61,72.

96 **NICOLAUS DE GORRAN, OP** [1295]

Cfr Stegmüller 5754, 5755, 3681; 3679 = Hugo de S. Caro.- Pignon 26s.- Spicq 326 (douteux).

97 **GUILLELMUS MESSELENUS, OP** [c. 1295]

Cfr Stegmüller 2979.

98 **PETRUS IOHANNES OLIVI, OM** [+1298]

Cfr Stegmüller 6692.- Spicq 346.

XIVe siécle

99 **HERICUS DE ESSEBURN, OP** [XIII/XIVe s.]

Cfr Stegmüller 3164.

100 **GERARDUS DE MINDEN, OP** [XIVe s.]

Cfr Stegmüller 2465.- Pignon 26,61,72.

101 **IOHANNES MARCHESINUS, OM** [c.1300]

Mnemotrectus I. Cfr Stegmüller 4778.

102 **MATTHAEUS DE AQUASPARTA, OM** [+1302]

Brevis expositio libris Ecclesiastae. Cfr Stegmüller 5504.

103 **AEGIDIUS ROMANUS, OESA** [1316]

Cfr Stegmüller 912 (+vol. VIII).

104 **MICHAEL DE FURNO, OP** [+1318]

Cfr Stegmüller 5621.

105 **JACOBUS DE LAUSANNA** [+1322]

Moralitates in Ecclesiasten. Cfr Stegmüller 3915-3918; 8249 = Thomas Waleys.

106 **PAGANUS DE BERGAMO, OP** [c.1323]

Cfr Stegmüller 6249.- Pignon 28,64,74.

107 **PONTIUS CARBONELLI, OM** [c.1336]

Cfr Stegmüller 6985,23.

108 **PETRUS DE BRUNIQUELLO, OESA** [c. 1338]

Cfr Stegmüller 6439.

109 **GUILLELMUS DENCOURT (ENCOURT), OP** [c. 1340]

Cfr Stegmüller 2885 (+vol. IX).

110 **RUPERTUS GALLUS, OCarm** [c. 1341]

Cfr Stegmüller 7387.

111 **PETRUS DE PALUDE, OP** [+ 1342]

Cfr Stegmüller 6762.

112 **IOHANNES BACUNTHORP, OCarm** [+ 1348]

Cfr Stegmüller 4185.

113 **ROBERTUS HOLCOT, OP** [+1349]

Cfr Stegmüller 7414?, 7414,1?, 7414,2 = 4936 Iohannes de S.
Giminiano.- Pignon 33.- Spicq 348.

114 **NICOLAUS DE LYRA, OM** [+1349]

Ed. *Postilla perpetua in Ecclesiasten: Scripturae cursus
completus*, Parisiis 1839, 31-150. Autres éditions des oeuvres de
Nicolas de Lyra; cfr Stegmüller vol. IV, p. 52.

115 **THOMAS WALEYS, OP** [+après 1349]

Cfr Stegmüller 8249, 8249,2-3?, 8260, 2860,1, 2838 = Ps.Thomas
Jorz.- Spicq 348.

116 **ADAMUS DE WODHAM, OM** [+1358]

Cfr Stegmüller Vol. II, p. 14.

117 **IOHANNES WICLIF** [+1364]

Cfr Stegmüller 5073,1.

118 **IOHANNES GORINI [DE S. GEMINIANO]** [+après 1364]

Cfr Stegmüller 4936 (+vol. IX), 7414 = Robertus Holcot?

119 **REGINALDUS DE ALNA, OCist** [c. 1397]

Cfr Stegmüller 7176 (composé en 1396); 2783 = Guillelmus de
Altona.

120 **GUILLELMUS WODFORD, OM** [+1397]

Cfr Stegmüller 3052 (+vol. IX).

XVe siècle

121 MATTHAEUS DE CRACOVIA [+1410]

Cfr Stegmüller 5524

122 HENRICUS DE GOUDA [c. 1425]

Cfr Stegmüller 3177.

123 BARTHOLOMAEUS DE EBORACO, OCist [c. 1430]

Cfr Stegmüller 1580.

124 HEIMISCH DE GANDERSHEIM, OM [+1435]

Cfr Stegmüller 3142,1 (+ vol. IX).

125 NARCISSUS HERZ DE BERCHING [+1442]

Cfr Stegmüller 5659 (+vol. IX).

126 IOHANNES DE WIDENBRUGGE, OESA [c. 1446]

Vaniloquium. Cfr Stegmüller 5124

127 IOHANNES DE BRUYNE, OCarm [+1450]

Cfr Stegmüller 4275?

128 MATTIAS DE SASPÓW [c. 1450]

Cfr Stegmüller 5556 (écrit en 1458).

129 IOHANNES DE CAPOGRAVE, OESA [+1464]

Cfr Stegmüller 4293.

130 GEORGIUS ZINGEL DE SCHLIERSTADT [c. 1470]

Cfr Stegmüller 2452 (+vol. IX).

131 DIONYSIUS CARTUSINUS [+ 1471]

Ed. *Enarratio in Librum Ecclesiastae: Opera omnia,* 7, Montrouil 1898, 209-288. Cfr Stegmüller 2098; Leanza(Or) 105-107.

132 IOHANNES DE BOMALIA, OP [+1477]

Cfr Stegmüller 4256.

133 PETRUS ROSSIUS [+ 1498]

Cfr Stegmüller 6838,17.

XVIe siécle

134 ROBERTUS SHERWOOD [c. 1520]

Cfr Stegmüller 7485 (version de l'Ecclésiaste de l'hebreu, publiée en Anvers 1523).

135 THOMAS DE VIO (CAIETANUS), OP [+1534]

Cfr Stegmüller 8223 (composé en 1534, éditions); A. Colunga, El cardenal Cayetano expositor del Antiguo Testamento: La ciencia tomista 18 (1918) 281-290.

136 **PS. ALBERTUS MAGNUS**

Cfr Stegmüller 1027.

137 **PS. BEDA VENERABILIS**

Cfr Stegmüller 1670, 1671, 10443, 11468.

138 **PS. GREGORIUS MAGNUS**

Cfr Stegmüller 2651.

139 **PS. PETRUS ABELARDUS**

Cfr Stegmüller 6386.

140 **PS. THOMAS AQUINAS**

Cfr Stegmüller 8029 = 1773 = Bonaventura, 8021; P. Castagnol, Il commento all'Ecclesiaste attribuito a S. Tommaso d'Aquino: DT(P) 37 (1934) 278-281.

Commentaires médievaux anonymes en manuscrits.

Stegmüller vol. VI:

141 **8456**

142 **8626** *De tempore et libris Salomonis.*

143 **8657** *Princiupium in Ecclesiasten.*

144 **8672** (XVe s.) *Continentia capitulorum ... Ecclesiastae...*

145 **8724** *Tabula super libros Salomonis.*

146 **8759** (XIVe s.)

147 **9013** (XIIIe s.) Stephanus Langton.

148 **9315** (XVe s.) Ex Hieronymo et Nicolao de Lyra.

149 **9560** *Glossarium.*

150 **9863** *De nominibus Salomonis.*

151 **9886** *Flores librorum Sapientialium.*

152 **10052**

153 **10169** (XIVe s.) *Principium in Ecclesiasten.*

154 **101998** (XIVe s.) cfr 2802 = Guillielmus de Alvernia, 11277.

155 **10198** (XIVe s.) *Additiones in Ecclesiasten.*

Stegmüller, vol. VII:

156 **10202** *Lectura super Eccl. 1-3.*

157 **10217** *Principium in Ecclesiasten.*

158 **10310** (Xe s.) *Quaestiones Ecclesiastae.*

159 **10364** (IXe s.) cfr 1671, 10443, 11468.

160 **10393** (XIIIe s.)

161 **10443** (IX-XIIIᵉ s.)   cfr 1671 Ps.Beda, 10364, 11468.

162 **10512** *Prologus in libros Salomonis.*

163 **10536** *Ecclesiastes secundum Nicolaum de Lyra,* 5866, 5867.

164 **10537** *Dubia circa Ecclesiasten accidentia.*

165 **10605** *Principium in Ecclesiasten.*

166 **10614** *Introitus in Ecclesiasten;* cfr 3812 = Hugo de S.Victore PL 175, 161).

167 **10615** *Principium Ecclesiastae;*   cfr 2781 = Guillelmus de Altona.

168 **10616** (XIIIᵉ s., composé en 1250) *Principium in Ecclesiasten.*

169 **10649** (XIIᵉ s.).

170 **10749.**

171 11277 (XIIIᵉ s.) cfr 2802 = Guillelmus de Alvernia, 10198,1.

172 11301 (XIIIᵉ s.), *Glossa super Bonavenurae Commentarium in Ecclesiasten (1773).*

173 11412 (XIVᵉ s.) *Notabilia super librum Ecclesiastes.*

174 11448 (XIIIᵉ s.) *Principium in Ecclesiasten.*

175 11468 (XIIIᵉ) [Eccl 1,1-7, 12] cfr 1093 = Alcuinus; 1671 = Ps.Beda; 3351 = Hieronymus.

176 11483 (XIIIᵉ s.).

177 11484,1 (XIIIᵉ s.) *Proemium super Ecclesiasten.*

178 11501 (XIIᵉ s.) [Eccl 1-8]; cfr 3259=Hervaemus Burgidolensis.

179 11561 (XIIIᵉ s.) *Tabula alphabetica super Ecclesiasten.*

Anonymus OM; cfr 1773=Bonaventura.

180 11565 (XIVᵉ s.) *Postilla super Ecclesiasten.*

Voir aussi sur les commentaires médievaux inédits: cfr DSp 4, 1960, 50s. et Spicq passim.

Autres textes médievaux latins

181 PREFACES, Stegmüller 460-463

Ed. (D. de Bruyne), Préfaces de la Bible, Namur 1920, 118-122.- *Biblia Sacra iuxta Latinam Vulgatam editionem,* 11, Libri Salomonici, i.e. Proverbia, Ecclesiastes et Canticum Canticorum, Romae 1957, 3-9.

182 SOMMAIRES

Ed. (D. de Bruyne), Sommaires, divisions et ruibriques de la Bible Latine, Namur 1914, 168-170, 408 (manuscrits).

183 DIVISIONS

Ibidem 479.

C. **COMMENTAIRES JUIVES** (d'après les informations de Dr. R.B. Salters, St Andrews)

184 **RABBI SHLOMAH YITZHAKI (RASHI)** [+1105]

Ed. Great Rabbinic Bible; Mikraoth Gedeloth, Venice 1524-1525, en marge.

185 **ABRAHAM IBN EZRA** [+1164]

Stegmüller, vol. VIII, p. 233 (Bibliographie) Ed. ibidem.

186 **RABBI SAMUJEL BEN MEIR (RASHBAM)** [+1174]

Ed. The Commentary of R. Samuel ben Meir (Rashbam) on Qoheleth, éd. S. Taphet and R.B. Salters, Jerusalem/Leiden 1985.

187 **OBADIAH SFORNO** [+1550]

Ed. avec le texte de Qohelet dans Mikraoth Gedeloth.

CPSIA information can be obtained
at www.ICGtesting.com
Printed in the USA
BVOW06*1115070717

488482BV00011B/21/P

9 783110 135862